Sports Law

EDITORIAL ADVISORS

Rachel E. Barkow
Vice Dean and Charles Seligson Professor of Law
Faculty Director, Zimroth Center on the Administration of Criminal Law
New York University School of Law

Erwin Chemerinsky
Dean and Jesse H. Choper Distinguished Professor of Law
University of California, Berkeley School of Law

Richard A. Epstein
Laurence A. Tisch Professor of Law
New York University School of Law
Peter and Kirsten Bedford Senior Fellow
The Hoover Institution
Senior Lecturer in Law
The University of Chicago

Ronald J. Gilson
Charles J. Meyers Professor of Law and Business
Stanford University
Marc and Eva Stern Professor of Law and Business
Columbia Law School

James E. Krier
Earl Warren DeLano Professor of Law Emeritus
The University of Michigan Law School

Tracey L. Meares
Walton Hale Hamilton Professor of Law
Director, The Justice Collaboratory
Yale Law School

Richard K. Neumann, Jr.
Alexander Bickel Professor of Law
Maurice A. Deane School of Law at Hofstra University

Robert H. Sitkoff
Austin Wakeman Scott Professor of Law
John L. Gray Professor of Law
Harvard Law School

David Alan Sklansky
Stanley Morrison Professor of Law
Faculty Co-Director, Stanford Criminal Justice Center
Stanford Law School

Sports Law
Governance and Regulation, 4E

Matthew J. Mitten
Professor of Law and Executive Director
National Sports Law Institute
Marquette University Law School

Timothy Davis
Bess & Walter Williams Professor of Law
Wake Forest University School of Law

Barbara Osborne
Professor, Sport Administration
Department of Exercise and Sport Science
Joint appointment, School of Law
University of North Carolina

N. Jeremi Duru
Professor of Law and Director of the Sport and Society Initiative
Washington College of Law
American University

ASPEN PUBLISHING

Copyright © 2024 Aspen Publishing. All Rights Reserved.

No part of this publication may be reproduced or transmitted in any form or by any means, electronic or mechanical, including photocopy, recording, or utilized by any information storage or retrieval system, without written permission from the publisher. For information about permissions or to request permissions online, visit us at www.AspenPublishing.com.

Cover image credit: iStock.com/Image Source and iStock.com/wdstock

To contact Customer Service, e-mail customer.service@aspenpublishing.com, call 1-800-950-5259, or mail correspondence to:

Aspen Publishing
Attn: Order Department
1 Wall Street
Burlington, MA 01803

Printed in the United States of America.

1 2 3 4 5 6 7 8 9 0

ISBN 979-8-8890-6299-8

Library of Congress Cataloging-in-Publication Data

Library of Congress Cataloging-in-Publication Data application is in process.

About Aspen Publishing

Aspen Publishing is a leading provider of educational content and digital learning solutions to law schools in the U.S. and around the world. Aspen provides best-in-class solutions for legal education through authoritative textbooks, written by renowned authors, and breakthrough products such as Connected eBooks, Connected Quizzing, and PracticePerfect.

The Aspen Casebook Series (famously known among law faculty and students as the "red and black" casebooks) encompasses hundreds of highly regarded textbooks in more than eighty disciplines, from large enrollment courses, such as Torts and Contracts, to emerging electives, such as Sustainability and the Law of Policing. Study aids such as the *Examples & Explanations* and the *Emanuel Law Outlines* series, both highly popular collections, help law students master complex subject matter.

Major products, programs, and initiatives include:

- **Connected eBooks** are enhanced digital textbooks and study aids that come with a suite of online content and learning tools designed to maximize student success. Designed in collaboration with hundreds of faculty and students, the Connected eBook is a significant leap forward in the legal education learning tools available to students.
- **Connected Quizzing** is an easy-to-use formative assessment tool that tests law students' understanding and provides timely feedback to improve learning outcomes. Delivered through CasebookConnect.com, the learning platform already used by students to access their Aspen casebooks, Connected Quizzing is simple to implement and integrates seamlessly with law school course curricula.
- **PracticePerfect** is a visually engaging, interactive study aid to explain commonly encountered legal doctrines through easy-to-understand animated videos, illustrative examples, and numerous practice questions. Developed by a team of experts, PracticePerfect is the ideal study companion for today's law students.
- The **Aspen Learning Library** enables law schools to provide their students with access to the most popular study aids on the market across all of their courses. Available through an annual subscription, the online library consists of study aids in e-book, audio, and video formats with full text search, note-taking, and highlighting capabilities.
- Aspen's **Digital Bookshelf** is an institutional-level online education bookshelf, consolidating everything students and professors need to ensure success. This program ensures that every student has access to affordable course materials from day one.
- **Leading Edge** is a community centered on thinking differently about legal education and putting those thoughts into actionable strategies. At the core of the program is the Leading Edge Conference, an annual gathering of legal education thought leaders looking to pool ideas and identify promising directions of exploration.

*To Rod Smith and Ken Shropshire
for your efforts as founding authors*

Summary of Contents

Contents xi
Preface xxvii
Acknowledgments xxxi

CHAPTER 1: An Introduction to the Study of Sports Law 1

CHAPTER 2: Regulating Interscholastic (High School) and Youth Athletics 15

CHAPTER 3: NCAA Internal Governance of Intercollegiate Athletics and Legal Limits 65

CHAPTER 4: Legal Relationships Between the University and Intercollegiate Athletes 123

CHAPTER 5: Gender Equity Issues in Athletics 161

CHAPTER 6: Racial Equity Issues in Athletics 203

CHAPTER 7: Health, Safety, and Risk Management Issues in Sports 239

CHAPTER 8: Sports Medicine, Concussions, Compensation, and Impairment in Sports 285

CHAPTER 9: Intellectual Property Issues in Sports 311

CHAPTER 10: Coaches' Contracts and Related Issues 347

CHAPTER 11: Professional Sports League Governance and Legal Regulation 373

CHAPTER 12: Professional Sports Labor Law and Labor Relations 411

CHAPTER 13: Representing Players and Teams: The Athlete-Agent Industry 449

CHAPTER 14: Olympic and International Sports Issues 501

Glossary 533
Table of Cases 555
Index 563

Contents

Preface xxvii
Acknowledgments xxxi

Chapter 1: An Introduction to the Study of Sports Law 1

What Is Sports Law? 1
A. The Traditional View: "Sports Law" Does Not Exist 1
B. The Moderate Position: "Sports Law" May Develop into a Field of Law 1
C. "Sports Law": A Separate Field of Law 2

Fundamentals of the Legal System 3

Jurisdiction and the Federal and State Court Systems 4
A. Federal Courts 5
B. State Courts 5
C. Tax and Other Specialized Courts 6

Civil Procedure 6

Using the Case Method to Study Law 8
A. Common Law 8
  1. Precedent 8
  2. How to Brief a Case 9
     Savino v. Robertson 10
     Questions 14

Chapter 2: Regulating Interscholastic (High School) and Youth Athletics 15

Introduction: The Rise of the Regulation of Interscholastic and Youth Athletics at the State, National, and International Levels 15
A. Historical Overview 15
B. Interscholastic and Youth Athletics Regulatory Structure, Governance, and Administrative Processes 16

xi

Judicial Regulation of Interscholastic and Youth Athletics 17

A. State Action 18

Brentwood Academy v. Tennessee Secondary School Athletic Association 19

Questions 22

Notes 22

Tennessee Secondary School Athletic Association v. Brentwood Academy (Brentwood II) 23

Questions 24

B. Eligibility Issues 24

1. Transfer Rules 26

Indiana High School Athletic Association v. Carlberg 27

Notes 29

Problem 2-1 30

2. Outside Competition Rules 30

Questions 31

3. Age Rules 31

Cruz v. Pennsylvania Interscholastic Athletic Association, Inc. 31

Questions 34

Problem 2-2 34

4. No-Pass, No-Play Rules 35

Questions 35

5. Exclusion of Homeschooled Students from Athletic Participation 36

Questions 37

Notes 37

6. Good Conduct Rules 38

Brands v. Sheldon Community School 38

Questions 40

Notes 41

7. Grooming Rules 41

C. First and Fourth Amendment Issues 42

1. Drug Testing 43

Vernonia Sch. Dist. 47J v. Acton 43

Questions 48

Notes 48

2. Freedom of Speech and Association 49

Mahanoy Area Sch. Dist. v. B. L. 49

Notes and Questions 55

3. Freedom of Religion   56
   a. Free Exercise Issues   56
      Questions   57
      Problem 2-3   57
   b. Establishment Clause Issues   58
      Notes and Questions   59
      Problem 2-4   59
D. Review of Game Results   60
   Questions   61
E. Health and Safety Issues in Youth and Interscholastic Sports   61
   Questions   63

Chapter 3: NCAA Internal Governance of Intercollegiate Athletics and Legal Limits   65

Introduction   65

A Brief History: NCAA Governance of Intercollegiate Athletics   65

Questions   69

NCAA Regulatory Authority and Processes   69

A. NCAA: History of Regulation and the Rules Infractions Process   70

B. Institutional Violations of NCAA Rules and Sanctions   71

   University of Southern California Infractions Appeals Committee Report No. 323   72

   Questions   76

   Negotiated Resolution: University of Miami (Florida)   77

   Questions   83

The Penn State University Case   84

   Questions   86

The University of North Carolina Case   87

   Questions   89

C. Individual Responsibility for NCAA Rules Violations and Sanctions   89

   Questions   91

   Problem 3-1   91

Legal Limits on NCAA Regulatory Authority   92

A. Federal and State Civil Rights Law   92

   NCAA v. Smith   92

   Question   94

B. Drug Testing and Privacy   94
   Questions   95
C. Contract and Private Association Laws   95
   Bloom v. NCAA   96
   Questions   99
D. Federal Antitrust Law   100
   1. Introduction   100
   2. Case Law   101
      NCAA v. Board of Regents of the University of Oklahoma   101
      Questions   106
      O'Bannon v. NCAA   110
      Notes and Questions   115
      NCAA v. Alston   116
      Notes and Questions   121

Chapter 4: Legal Relationships Between the University and Intercollegiate Athletes   123

Contractual and NCAA Regulatory Dimensions   123

A. Introduction   123
   1. Contract Formation and Consideration   123
      a. Mutual Assent   123
      b. Consideration and Promissory Estoppel   125
   2. Modification   125
   3. Express and Implied Contracts   126
   4. Performance, Breach, and Remedies   126
      a. Breach   126
      b. Excuses for Nonperformance   127
   5. Damages   127
B. Contractual Aspects of the Athlete and University Relationship   127
   1. Statement of Financial Assistance   128
   2. National Letter of Intent   128
      Questions   130
C. Student-Athlete Financial Aid and Other Benefits   130
   1. NCAA Regulations Governing Contracts and Scholarships   130
      Questions   132
      Note   133

D. Defining the Scope of Institutional Obligations to Student-Athletes   133
   Taylor v. Wake Forest University   133
   Questions   135
   Ross v. Creighton University   135
   Questions   137
   Notes   137
E. NCAA Academic Reform Initiatives   138
   1. NCAA Academic Reform Legislation   139
   2. Academic Progress Rate   140
      Questions   141
F. Limited Scope of Constitutional Protections   142
   1. General Principles: What Is a Property Interest?   142
   2. A Property Interest in Athletic Participation?   144
      Hysaw v. Washburn University of Topeka   144
      Question   146
      Notes   146
G. College Athletes as Employees: Workers' Compensation and Other Implications   147
   1. Workers' Compensation: General Principles   147
   2. College Athletes and Workers' Compensation:
      Waldrep v. Texas Employers Insurance Association   148
      Questions   150
      Notes   150
   3. Student-Athlete Unionization   152
      Questions   154

First Amendment Rights in Intercollegiate Athletics   154
A. Introduction   154
B. The First Amendment and the Media   155
   Questions   157
C. Free Speech   157
D. Religious Liberty Issues   158
   Questions   159
   Problem 4-1   159

Chapter 5: Gender Equity Issues in Athletics   161

Introduction   161
Historical Perspective   161

Gender-Based Exclusion from a Particular Sport   166
Force v. Pierce City R-VI School District   167

Questions   171

Problem 5-1   173

Equal Athletic Participation Opportunities, Benefits, and Treatment   173

A. Accommodation   173

  Cohen v. Brown University   173

  Questions   179

  Problem 5-2   181

B. Equal Benefits and Treatment   182

  Questions   185

Reverse Discrimination Claims and Title IX   185

Neal v. Board of Trustees of the California State Universities   186

Questions   188

Title IX and Sexual Harassment   189

A. Coach-Athlete Sexual Harassment   190

B. Peer Sexual Harassment   191

  Questions   192

Transgender Participation in School-Based Sport   193

Questions   195

Gender-Based Employment Discrimination in Athletics   196

A. Employment Discrimination   196

  Deli v. University of Minnesota   197

  Questions   200

B. Retaliatory Discharge or Punitive Action   200

  Questions   202

Chapter 6: Racial Equity Issues in Athletics   203

Introduction   203

Historical Perspective   203

A. Racial Segregation: Intercollegiate Athletics   204

  1. Formal Rules of Exclusion   204

  2. Informal Rules of Discrimination   205

B. Racial Segregation: Professional Sports 207

C. The Reintegration of Professional and Amateur Sports 208

Race and Racial Equity in Modern Sports 208

A. Coaching and Administrative Opportunities 208

   1. College Sports 208

   2. Professional Sports 210

     Questions 212

B. Intersections 213

   1. Race and Gender 213

   2. Race and Freedom of Expression 214

   3. Race and Socioeconomic Stratification 216

   4. Race and Globalization 218

Case Law 220

A. Academic Racism and Marginalization: NCAA Initial-Eligibility Rules 220

   Questions 222

   Problem 6-1 223

B. Employment Discrimination 224

   ***Jackson v. University of New Haven* 224**

   Questions 230

   Problem 6-2 230

C. Stereotypes: Racially Stereotyped Mascots—Racism or Pride? 231

   1. The NCAA's Approach 232

   2. The Professional Context 233

     Questions 234

     Problem 6-3 235

D. Racially Hostile Environments and Conduct 235

   Problem 6-4 236

   Questions 236

Chapter 7: Health, Safety, and Risk Management Issues in Sports 239

Introduction 239

Liability for Athletics-Related Injuries 240

A. Injury to Athletes 240

   1. Co-Participant Tort Liability 240

Shin v. Ahn 240
Questions 243
Note 243
Problem 7-1 244
2. Co-Participant Criminal Liability 244
People v. Schacker 245
Regina v. McSorley 246
People v. Hall 248
Questions 249
Note 250
Problem 7-2 251

Liability of Educational Institutions (and Organizations) 251

A. High School 251
Kahn v. East Side Union High School District 252
Questions 255
Notes 255

B. Colleges and Universities 258
Orr v. Brigham Young University 260
Questions 261
Notes 262
Problem 7-3 264

C. Injury to Spectators 265
Thurmond v. Prince William Professional Baseball Club, Inc. 267
Questions 269
Notes 269
Problem 7-4 271

Tort Immunities 272

Question 275
Problem 7-5 275
Problem 7-6 276

Validity of Liability Waivers 276

Wagenblast v. Odessa School District No. 105-157-166J 277
Sharon v. City of Newton 279
Notes 281
Questions 282
Problem 7-7 283

Chapter 8: Sports Medicine, Concussions, Compensation, and Impairment in Sports 285

Introduction 285

Sports Medicine Malpractice Liability 285

A. Team Physicians 285

B. Athletic Trainers 288

C. Athlete's Contributory Negligence 288

Injury Compensation for Professional Athletes 289

Pro-Football, Inc. v. Uhlenhake 291

Note 293

DePiano v. Montreal Baseball Club, Ltd. 293

Note 294

Comment: Concussions 295

Participation Rights of Athletes with Physical or Mental Impairments 297

A. Rehabilitation Act of 1973 297

B. Americans with Disabilities Act of 1990 301

  Questions 304

  Notes 304

  Problem 8-1 308

Chapter 9: Intellectual Property Issues in Sports 311

Introduction 311

Trademarks, Logos, and Other Identifying Sports Insignia 312

A. Trademark Infringement and Unfair Competition 313

  1. Name of Sports Team or Event 314

  2. Unauthorized Affixation of Sports Team Mark to Merchandise 315

    National Football League Properties, Inc. v. New Jersey Giants, Inc. 317

    Question 319

    Notes 319

B. Trademark Dilution 320

C. Anticybersquatting Consumer Protection Act of 1999 321

D. Olympic Marks 322

  Problem 9-1 323

Ambush Marketing 324

Problem 9-2 325

Real-Time Game Accounts and Broadcasting Rights 326

A. Historical Background 326

B. Nature and Scope of Copyright Law Protection 327

C. Copyright Infringement of a Sports Broadcast 329

   NFL v. TVRadioNow Corp. 330

   Question 331

   Note 332

D. Misappropriation of Real-Time Game Accounts and Scores 333

   Problem 9-3 334

Athletes' Lanham Act and State Law Privacy, Reputation, and Publicity Rights 334

A. Lanham Act 335

B. State Laws 336

   1. Defamation 336

   2. Right of Privacy 337

   3. Right of Publicity 338

      a. Nature and Scope of the Right of Publicity 339

      b. First Amendment Limitations 341

         Problem 9-4 345

Chapter 10: Coaches' Contracts and Related Issues 347

Introduction 347

Is There a Property Interest in Athletic Employment? 348

   Questions 349

   Problem 10-1 349

A. Termination 350

   1. What Constitutes Termination for "Cause"? 350

      Questions 351

   2. Termination for Rules Violations and Non-Sports-Related Indiscretions 352

      a. Non–Sports-Related Indiscretions 352

      b. Rules Violations 353

      c. Compensation Issues Following Termination 353

d. College Basketball and College Admissions Scandals   354
     Questions   355
     Problem 10-2   356
 3. Termination for Abusive Conduct   356
     Questions   358
     Problem 10-3   358
 4. Free Speech and Retaliation Issues   359
B. Compensation and Other Financial Matters   360
   Question   362
   Questions   364

Termination, Breach, and Liquidated Damages   365
Vanderbilt University v. DiNardo   366
Questions   369
Note   369

Exploring Other Contractual Relationships   369
A. Sponsorship Agreements   370
B. Venue Agreements   370

Chapter 11: Professional Sports League Governance and Legal Regulation   373

Introduction   373

Origin and Evolution of Modern North American Professional Sports Industries   373
A. Evolution of Sports into a Business and Profession   374
B. Unique Features of Professional Team Sports   376
C. The Principal "Players" in the Professional Sports Industries   378
   1. Leagues   378
   2. Clubs or Teams   378
   3. Commissioners   379
   4. Players   379
   5. Players Associations   380
   6. Player Agents   380
   7. Other Industries Integral to Modern Professional Sports   380

Internal League Governance and Commissioner Authority   380
A. Legal Limits on Internal League Governance   381

B. League Commissioner's "Best Interests of the Game" Authority and Legal Limits 383

Charles O. Finley & Co., Inc. v. Kuhn 385

Note 387

Problem 11-1 389

Federal Antitrust Law Limits on League Rules and Governance 389

A. Overview 389

B. Baseball's Antitrust Exemption 391

Flood v. Kuhn 392

Question 393

Note 394

C. Application of Sherman Act §1 395

1. Concerted Action Requirement 395

2. Unreasonable Restraint of Trade 396

   a. Acquisition, Ownership, and Sale of a Franchise 397

   Levin v. NBA 397

   Note 398

   b. Franchise Relocation 399

   c. Restrictions on Intellectual Property Rights Licensing 401

D. Application of Sherman Act §2 405

Problem 11-2 409

Chapter 12: Professional Sports Labor Law and Labor Relations 411

Introduction 411

Contract Law 411

Questions 414

Problem 12-1 414

Labor Law 415

A. Collective Bargaining in the Professional Sports Industries 418

B. Drug Use in Professional Sports 421

Questions 424

Problem 12-2 424

C. Unfair Labor Practices 425

1. League Interference with Players' Rights to Unionize 426

2. League Refusal to Recognize Union as Exclusive Bargaining Representative   426

3. Retaliation Against Union Activists   427

4. Breach of Duty to Bargain in Good Faith or Provide Relevant Information Concerning Mandatory Subjects of Collective Bargaining   429

   Silverman v. Major League Baseball Player Relations Committee, Inc. (Silverman I)   429

   Note   430

5. Discrimination Against Striking Players   432

   Questions   432

D. Union's Duty of Fair Representation   433

E. Labor Arbitration   434

   National & American League Professional Baseball Clubs v. Major League Baseball Players Association   435

   Notes   438

The Intersection of Antitrust and Labor Law   440

Questions   447

Chapter 13: Representing Players and Teams: The Athlete-Agent Industry   449

The Nature of the Athlete-Agent Relationship   450

A. The Agent's Basic Duties   450

B. The Agent's Standard of Care   451

   Zinn v. Parrish   452

   Questions   453

C. Agent Financial Improprieties   453

   Questions   457

   Problem 13-1   458

D. Agent Conflicts of Interest with Athletes   458

   The Detroit Lions, Inc. v. Argovitz   459

   Questions   461

   Note   461

   Problem 13-2   462

Competition for Clients: Conflicts Between Agents   463

A. Introduction   463

B. Consolidation   463

C. Termination 464

NFLPA Standard Representation Agreement 465

D. Disparagement 465

E. What Is Permissible Competition? 466

Questions 467

F. Race and Gender Issues 467

Questions 469

An International Perspective 469

External Regulation and Legislation 470

A. Federal Legislation 471

1. SPARTA 471
2. General Federal Laws 472

Questions 474

B. State Regulation: The UAAA 474

Revised Uniform Athlete Agents Act (2015) 475

Notes 480

Williamson v. Prime Sports Mktg., LLC. 482

Questions 486

Problem 13-3 486

C. Players' Associations 487

1. Authority to Regulate 487

Question 488

2. Regulating the Athlete-Agent Relationship 488

a. Sanctions: Suspensions and Decertification 488

b. Fees/Agent Compensation 489

c. NFLPA Amendments 489

d. MLBPA Amendments 490

e. NBPA Amendments 491

f. Excerpts of Players' Association and NCAA Regulations 492

NFLPA Regulations Governing Contract Advisors 492

Questions 496

NCAA Bylaw Article 12 496

Problem 13-4 498

Ethical Issues 499

Sports Management Network v. Busch 500

Questions 500

Chapter 14: Olympic and International Sports Issues 501

Introduction 501

A. Origin, History, and Objectives of the Olympic and Paralympic Games 502

B. Organization, Governance, and Structure of the Olympic Movement 504

Regulation of Olympic Sports Within the United States 507

Question 511

Limits on the Use of National Law to Regulate Olympic and International Athletic Competition 512

Question 513

Problem 14-1 514

Court of Arbitration for Sport 514

A. Overview 514

B. Disputed Competition Results 517

Yang Tae Young v. International Gymnastics Federation 518

Note 520

Problem 14-2 520

C. Doping Violations and Sanctions 521

1. Strict Liability Standard, Clear Notice Requirements, and Proportionate Sanctions 521

    Question 523

2. Interpretation and Application of the World Anti-Doping Code 523

3. United States Anti-Doping Agency 526

Developing International Issues 528

Notes 530

Glossary 533
Table of Cases 555
Index 563

Preface

FOURTH EDITION

To provide users of our book with the most current and comprehensive sports law and governance text available, we have revised and updated the Fourth Edition to include discussions of the most recent legal and governance developments affecting youth, interscholastic, intercollegiate, Olympic, and professional sports that have occurred since our third edition was published in 2020. The sports industry, at all levels, has experienced significant change in that time period. That change is captured in this text. Among other topics, this edition explores: the impact of recent cases redefining the balance between the free exercise and establishment clause as well as free speech in the high school context; the rapidly changing collegiate sports landscape in light of NCAA constitution and bylaw revisions, name, image and likeness rights, antitrust cases and issues surrounding student-athletes as employees; the first reported judicial opinion interpreting the Revised Uniform Athletes Agent Act; questions about the appropriate breadth of commissioner authority, and the intersection of antitrust law and labor law, in professional sports leagues; the impact of society's racial dynamics on diversity, equity, and inclusion in sports organizations; and transgender athletes' participation in interscholastic and intercollegiate sports as well as related issues in Olympic and international sports. We have updated historical sections of the book as well, to give students a feel for the magnitude of those changes. The Fourth Edition also includes new and refined problems and notes designed to broaden students' understanding and encourage them to wrestle with the kinds of legal and governance problems that are continually arising within the industry. With input from thoughtful users of past editions, we have been able to add new material without unduly expanding the length of the text. As such, the text can still be effectively used in either a two- or three-credit course. We trust you will find this Fourth Edition to be an excellent text for the study of sports law and governance, but if you find there are ways in which we could improve the book, we would love to hear from you. Please feel free to contact any of us at any time with your comments and suggestions: Matt Mitten (matt.mitten@marquette.edu), Tim Davis (davistx@wfu.edu), Barbara Osborne (sportlaw@unc.edu), and Jeremi Duru (duru@wcl.american.edu).

FIRST EDITION

This book, which is adapted from three of the authors' widely used law school text, is designed to introduce undergraduate and graduate students to the various and often differing legal frameworks regulating high school, college, professional, and Olympic sports competition along with important, contemporary topics such as gender and racial equity; health, safety, and risk management; and intellectual property issues in sports. It provides an overview of the significant historical, economic, and sociological issues affecting the development of the laws regulating sports at each level of competition, as well as common sports-related legal issues. The book, which is intended for use as the text in either a two-or three-credit-hour undergraduate or graduate sports law course in sports management or other program, covers a wide variety of contemporary sports law issues of interest to future sports administrators, executives, and business managers, as well as coaches and other sports industry personnel. It has been carefully designed and written to provide undergraduate and graduate professors and students with a comprehensive, multipurpose text that gives a balanced perspective regarding a multitude of legal and regulatory issues that frequently arise in interscholastic, intercollegiate, professional, and Olympic sports industries.

This book begins by providing an introduction to the study of sports law and a brief overview of the U.S. legal system, as well as guidance on how to effectively use the case method to facilitate and enhance learning. In Chapters 2–4, 11–12, and 14, the book covers the internal governance systems for high school, college, professional, and Olympic sports, respectively. These chapters also cover the primary bodies of public law (e.g., private association, constitutional, antitrust, and labor law) that shape, regulate, and constrain each internal governance system. The remaining chapters cover various topics raising legal issues of significance in more than one of the amateur or professional sports industries: coaches' contracts (Chapter 10); gender equity (Chapter 5); racial equity (Chapter 6); health, safety, and risk management (Chapter 7); and intellectual property (Chapter 9).

This text uses the case method, which involves the study of illustrative legal disputes resolved by courts through the litigation process, and establishes a body of legal precedent regulating various aspects of the sports industry. This method of learning is designed to encourage students to engage in critical thinking by identifying the legal issues in each case, the parties' respective arguments, and the court's ruling and rationale for its decision. It stimulates the development of a dialogue between the professor and students (and frequently among students as well). It also facilitates students' understanding of the laws regulating the sports industry. In addition to the illustrative cases (which have been edited substantially), each chapter provides explanatory material, notes, questions, and review problems designed to enable students to understand how basic legal doctrines apply to problems arising in the sports context. Ideally, students can then use this knowledge to identify sports industry legal issues and to understand how they are likely to be resolved.

In addition to helping students develop an understanding of the legal framework regulating high school, college, professional, and Olympic sports and other sports-related legal issues, a sports law course provides several important educational benefits. It exposes students (some of whom may be considering law school) to several different bodies of law and provides them with a general understanding of numerous laws—knowledge that may be useful in future careers other than in the sports industry. In addition, sports law deals with broader issues that merit deeper study and reflection, such as the role of sports in our culture and whether current laws effectively promote appropriate, ethical, and just practices and behavior in the amateur and professional sports industries. We hope that our book encourages thoughtful consideration of these and other important sports-related issues.

Acknowledgments

FOURTH EDITION

Professor Mitten thanks Marquette University Law School and its dean, Joseph D. Kearney, for their continuing support.

Professor Davis thanks Wake Forest University School of Law for its support and Remy Elijah Clodfelter for his research assistance.

Professor Osborne thanks the University of North Carolina Law School for continued research support.

Professor Duru thanks American University's Washington College of Law for its support and Casey Goldenberg for his outstanding research assistance.

FIRST EDITION

Professor Mitten thanks Erica Reib (Marquette Law 2011) for her helpful review of and comments on various draft chapters and Chris Kaminski (Marquette Law 2013) for his assistance in preparing the glossary.

Professor Davis thanks Wake Forest University School of Law for its generous research support and the following Wake Forest students for their research assistance: Justin Bell, Thailer Buari, and Nathan Harrill.

Professor Shropshire wishes to thank students who recently participated in his sports law course at Penn for their helpful comments.

Professor Osborne thanks the University of North Carolina Law School for providing research support and UNC law student Scott Holder for his research assistance.

Professor Smith appreciates the support offered by Dean Rudy Hasl and Associate Dean Eric J. Mitnik.

We also thank the following reviewers, whose insightful comments helped shape this text: Jan Blade, Delaware State University; Sandra Defebaugh, Eastern Michigan University; Gil Fried, University of New Haven; Michael Gentile, Niagara University; Richard Hunter, Seton Hall University; Paul Klein, Duquesne

University; William Nowlan, Lasell College; Marissa Pollick, University of Michigan; Jessie C. Roberson, Ohio University; and Ellen M. Zavian, George Washington University.

Matthew J. Mitten
Timothy Davis
Rodney K. Smith
Kenneth L. Shropshire
Barbara Osborne
N. Jeremi Duru
June 2020

An Introduction to the Study of Sports Law

Should sports law be recognized as an independent substantive area of the law, such as torts, contracts, or employment law? As the following excerpt reveals, scholars have debated this question.

WHAT IS SPORTS LAW?[1]

A. The Traditional View: "Sports Law" Does Not Exist

The traditional view is that sports law represents nothing more than an amalgamation of various substantive areas of the law that are relevant in the sports context. According to this perspective, the term *sports law* is a misnomer, given that sport represents a form of activity and entertainment that is governed by the legal system in its entirety. Adherents to the traditional perspective argue that "sports law simply entails the application of basic legal precepts to a specific industry" that are drawn from other substantive areas of the law. Consequently, no separately identifiable body of law exists that can be characterized as sports law.

B. The Moderate Position: "Sports Law" May Develop into a Field of Law

Other commentators have begun increasingly to question the traditional view that no corpus of law exists that can be characterized as an independent field of law called "sports law. . . . [Some] have staked out what represents a middle ground."

---

[1] This excerpt was originally published at Timothy Davis, 11 Marq. Sports L. Rev. 211 (2001). All citations to authority have been omitted.

Professor Kenneth Shropshire acknowledges that developments, such as state and federal legislation impacting sports (for example, state statutes regulating sports agents, and federal statutes such as Title IX), suggest a "growing sports-only corpus" of law.

Professor Burlette Carter argues that sports law is in the midst of an exciting, yet challenging, transformative process. According to Professor Carter, this process parallels the increased focus by law schools on sports and the growing significance of sports regulation to participants, organizations, and communities. She believes that these developments will better shape the contours of this emerging field of study. This, in turn, will eventually transform sports law from "a course without a corpus" to a widely recognized independent substantive area of law.

C. "Sports Law": A Separate Field of Law

Others argue that sports law currently exists as a field of law. Adherents to this view emphasize the growing body of case and statutory law specific to the sports industry as evidence of the existence of a separately identifiable body of law. Pointing to the increasing body of judicial and legislative law specific to sports, Professor [Simone] Gardiner argues:

> It is true to say that [sports law] is largely an amalgam of interrelated legal disciplines involving such areas as contract, taxation, employment, competition and criminal law but dedicated legislation and case law has developed and will continue to do so. As an area of academic study and extensive practitioner involvement, the time is right to accept that a new legal area has been born — sports law.

Commentators also propose that references to sports law as merely an amalgamation of various other substantive areas of the law ignore an important present-day reality — very few substantive areas of the law fit into separate categories that are divorced from, and independent of, other substantive areas of the law. Doctrinal overlap exists not only within sports law, but within other areas of law as well. According to Professor Carter, "the field of sports law has moved beyond the traditional antitrust and labor law boundaries into sports representation and legal ethics, sports and corporate structure, sports and disability, sports and race, sports and gender, sports and taxation, international issues in sports law, and numerous other permutations."

Proponents of the sports law designation and those sympathetic to the view also argue that reticence to recognize sports law as a specific body of law may reflect attitudes regarding the intellectual seriousness of sports. In this regard, they emphasize the tendency to marginalize the study of sports rather than treat it as any other form of business. The intellectual marginalization of sport has been attributed, in part, to the belief that social relations extant in sports were not deemed proper subjects for reconstruction into legal relationships. Thus, private and public law were considered "inappropriate [mechanisms for] controlling the social norms of sport." The competing and increasingly predominant view, however, casts sports as a significant economic activity suitable, like other big businesses, to regulation, whether it be internal or external.

In the end, whether sports law is recognized as an independent field of law may turn on the perceptions of those who practice, teach, and engage in scholarship related to sports law. Professor Carter asks that we consider the following:

> But what makes a field a field? The answer is that a field becomes a field not because it is inherently so but because in our public legal dealings we shape it as such, defining the concepts and legal norms that will prevail uniquely in that context. It becomes a field because enough people with power on all sides are so affected by it to require some special treatment of it in the law.

Regardless of the position that is adopted regarding the "what is sports law" debate, most would agree that matters arising in the sports law context implicate diverse substantive areas of law. Whether sports law is a separate field of law, a reflection of substantive law related to the sports industry, or some combination, the vast array of substantive legal topics presented in a basic sports law course can sometimes prove surprisingly challenging. To enjoy and ultimately excel in this area, it will be helpful for you to have an introduction to legal basics.

Sports law involves both public and private law. Public law can be broadly described as the law that governs the relationships between the government and individuals, as well as the relationships between individuals that directly affect society. Constitutional law, administrative law, and criminal law are areas of public law that intersect with sports law. Private law governs the relationships between individuals (or corporations); sports law applications include contracts, torts, and the law of private associations. However, you will learn that distinctions in law are rarely clear. Public and private law often intersect in areas such as labor and antitrust. For undergraduate and graduate students interested in working in some capacity in the amateur or professional sports industries, this introduction will help you better understand the legal landscape and will aid you in your work with lawyers, who should be consulted whenever you deal with legal issues.

FUNDAMENTALS OF THE LEGAL SYSTEM

The United States has a federalist government, which means power is shared between the national and state (and local) governments. The basic operating principles for the federal and state governments are embodied in the Constitution. The federal Constitution identifies the fundamental rights of citizens of the United States and delineates limits on the government's ability to interfere with those rights. The federal Constitution applies to all states, and is preeminent; states may grant additional rights, but they may not limit rights that the federal Constitution guarantees. Constitutional cases are based on the interpretation of state constitutions or the federal Constitution. Federal laws that are inconsistent with the U.S. Constitution are invalid—in our legal hierarchy, constitutional provisions are the most significant. That is what is meant when it is said that the U.S. Constitution is the law of the land. State laws that are inconsistent with the state or federal constitutions are also held to be unconstitutional and invalid.

The foundation of the federal government is based upon a balance of power between the executive, legislative, and judicial branches. Each of these branches is a source of law. The executive branch is the President of the United States. The President is ultimately responsible for implementing and enforcing federal laws, through executive orders and through the regulations set forth by the administrative agencies. For example, the U.S. Department of Education promulgates Title IX regulations dealing with gender discrimination under the auspices of administrative legal authority that provides part of the substantive basis of sports law. The President appoints the heads of the federal agencies, who also serve on the President's cabinet.

The legislative branch is responsible for writing, debating, and passing bills. Demonstrating balance of power, bills only become law when the President has signed them. If the President vetoes a bill, Congress has the ability to vote to override the veto.

The role of the judicial branch is to interpret the Constitution or legislation. Balance of power is demonstrated through judicial interpretation of legislation (statutes) or regulations (regulatory materials developed by administrative or regulatory bodies). In these instances, judicial decisions often involve interpreting or determining the applicability and reach of a given regulation or piece of legislation. The judiciary also creates law, known as the common law, through the precedent established in case decisions. The concepts of common law and precedent will be discussed later in this chapter.

State governments are organized similarly. The state constitution embodies the principles upon which the state government operates. Balance of power exists within each state, with the governor of each state representing the executive branch and enforcing the law, state representatives to the legislature who enact the law, and the state (and local) judiciary interprets the law.

There are also local and regulatory decision-making bodies that make law. County governments and school districts, for example, regularly promulgate laws that may provide the grist for a decision in the sports area. High school and collegiate athletic associations may also pass and enforce regulations that provide the basis for decisions in the sports law area.

JURISDICTION AND THE FEDERAL AND STATE COURT SYSTEMS

In the United States, there are two dominant court systems—the federal courts and the state courts. Jurisdiction is the power of the court to hear and determine the outcome of a case. A court establishes this power because of the subject matter of the case or the parties who are involved. Subject matter jurisdiction refers to the particular category of the case, for example, a dispute involving land or the right to use a corporate logo. Personal jurisdiction refers to the court's power over the various parties to the case. Cases in the federal court system or the state courts may involve civil law or criminal law. Disputes between public or private parties are civil law matters which are decided on a preponderance of the evidence standard. Criminal law involves acts that are harmful to society as a whole, so the government represents the people in putting forward a case against a criminal defendant. The government must prove that the defendant committed the crime beyond a reasonable doubt.

Broadly too, particularly in sports law-related cases, parties will seek remedies in "law" or "equity." A remedy at law is primarily one where money damages are sought as a means of compensating the injured party. For example, if a coach feels that he or she is owed an additional salary payment, money will resolve that issue and constitute a remedy at law. However, if a team wanted to retain a coach with special skills or keep him or her from coaching for another team, that would require an equitable remedy, including a court's issuance of an order of specific performance or an injunction. Specific performance would be an order for the coach to continue coaching, and the injunction would bar the coach from coaching another team.

A. Federal Courts

The federal court system is established by Article III of the U.S. Constitution and consists of three levels. At the trial level, the federal courts are divided into 94 districts, with at least one district in each state, the District of Columbia, and Puerto Rico. District courts have original jurisdiction over cases involving federal issues, issues that are based on the U.S. Constitution, federal legislation, regulations, treaties, or cases arising in states that implicate other states and their citizens and residents. Federal judges are nominated by the President, confirmed by the U.S. Senate, and typically serve for life. Decisions of the district court may be appealed to the appropriate circuit court. The federal court of appeals is organized into 12 regional circuits plus a court of appeals for the Federal Circuit. The circuit courts also hear appeals of decisions by the federal administrative agencies. Typically, a panel of three judges hears the arguments on appeal and renders a decision. Parties that are not satisfied may appeal to the Supreme Court, which has discretionary jurisdiction; it selects which cases it will hear. The highest court within the federal judiciary, the Supreme Court consists of nine justices, including the Chief Justice. A Supreme Court decision is final unless there is a constitutional amendment to overturn its decision, Congress alters the Court's decision by changing the law, or the Supreme Court overturns its own decision through a decision in a later case.

B. State Courts

State court systems are established by the state constitution of their respective state. State cases, in turn, involve state issues, issues that are based on state legislation, regulation, and the provisions of that state's constitution. State court systems are also typically three-tiered systems with a trial court, appellate court, and a court of final decision. The names of the appellate level courts vary by state, so a Court of Appeals in one state may be the Supreme Court of another. Because state courts have unique jurisdiction, a party that is not satisfied with the final decision in a state court may not appeal to the federal court. One exception is when there is some conflict between state and federal law such as state constitutional provisions that are inconsistent with federal constitutional law or that deprive citizens and residents of other states of their federal constitutional rights. Judges in the state courts may be elected or appointed, depending upon state law.

C. Tax and Other Specialized Courts

There are other specialized courts and decision makers at the state, federal, and international levels. For example, there are specialized tribunals or courts that decide cases in particular areas of law such as tax. Those specialized tribunals exist at the state and federal levels, and sometimes even at the local and international levels.

While the government legislates, and the judiciary enforces the laws that regulate the sports industry, the majority of regulation occurs within the sports industry. Most sport organizations belong to a league or association that establishes rules for membership and competition. Community recreation and sport programs, as well as some high school athletics associations, are considered state actors (see Chapter 2). However, the National Collegiate Athletic Association (NCAA) (Chapter 3), the U.S. Olympic Committee and national sport governing bodies (Chapter 14), and professional sports leagues (Chapter 11) are all considered private organizations. Generally, courts give tremendous deference to sports organizations to govern their own affairs and create and enforce their own rules. Under the principle of limited judicial review, the courts will intervene in a sport organization's affairs only if the association's rules: (1) violate constitutional rights (when the association is considered a state actor); (2) violate basic notions of fairness or public policy (for private associations); (3) exceed the scope of the association's authority; (4) violates one of the association's own rules; or (5) are applied unreasonably or arbitrarily and capriciously. Generally, the court will not review the merits of a rule, or whether there is a better way for the organization to achieve the same goal.

CIVIL PROCEDURE

The term *procedure* refers to the mechanics of the legal process. Procedure varies between the civil court system and the criminal law system. Although criminal activity occurs within the sport industry, the overwhelming majority of sport law issues fall within the civil law. Civil procedure is the legal method, including rules of practice, which must be strictly adhered to in order to advance through the legal process. This section provides a quick overview of the Federal Rules of Civil Procedure.

The succession of events constituting civil procedure includes complaint, service, answer, discovery, motions, trial, judgment, and appeal. The complaint is the formal legal document that lists the pleadings, or claims, that the plaintiff is bringing forth against the defendant. The purpose of the complaint is to provide notice to the defendant and the court as to the nature of the claims that are asserted. Service is the delivery of a legal document, such as a pleading or complaint, to the adverse party in a legal action. Completion of service requires strict adherence to the rules of the court of that jurisdiction. Upon completion of service, the defendant is subject to the rules of the court in resolving the issue. The defendant must file a formal answer to the complaint; the answer must address all of the allegations in the complaint, whether confirmed or denied, and include any defenses or counterclaims that the defendant will assert. After the answer has been properly filed, the parties may advance to discovery or file motions with the court. The defendant may file a motion to dismiss based on inadequacy of the pleadings. In that case, a court will determine whether the basic outline for a case has successfully been set forth by the plaintiff. If not, a court may dismiss the action.

Assuming the case proceeds, discovery is the process of sharing information between the parties. Interrogatories, written questions for the opposing parties, may be submitted. Similarly, depositions, statements of potential witnesses, may be acquired either orally or in writing. Oral depositions are made under oath, with representatives of both parties present and having the opportunity to cross-examine while the procedure is recorded and/or transcribed. The parties may also request additional information and documents from the opposing party. The purpose of discovery is for all parties to share information to achieve a fair and just resolution.

Either party, or sometimes both parties, may submit a motion for summary judgment. In this situation, the court will apply the law to the facts of the case in the light most favorable to the nonmoving party to determine whether the motion is granted or denied.

Should the case proceed to trial, the parties are required to follow the rules of the court in presenting evidence to support their positions. The trial may be heard by a judge, called a *bench trial*, or by a jury. Civil trials most commonly have six citizens serve on a jury. Throughout the trial, there may be additional motions made by either party. At the end of a bench trial, the judge will render a decision. In a jury trial, the judge will provide the jury with the rules of law upon which they are required to make their decision.

If a party, plaintiff or defendant, loses in a lower court, that party may have a right to appeal. An appeal involves a right by one or both of the parties to contest the legal ruling that was reached at the preceding stage of the litigation process. Generally, appellate courts are quite deferential to the findings of fact made by the trial court because the trial court actually hears the testimony of the witnesses and can evaluate their credibility firsthand. The appellate court does not hear new witnesses or review new evidence—it merely addresses whether there was an error in procedure or in application of the law that adversely affected the outcome of the trial. The appellate court may affirm the lower court decision, overturn the decision of the lower court and render a new decision, or remand the matter back to the lower court with instructions. A party may appeal an appellate court decision. However, the highest court in the process, often called the *Supreme Court*, is unlikely to hear the case unless there are conflicting decisions among the appellate court districts at the state level or among the various circuit courts at the federal level, or unless the case presents a significant legal issue.

USING THE CASE METHOD TO STUDY LAW

The study of law in American law schools is primarily done via the case method, although non-case law and policy-related materials often complement the cases. This book is designed in a manner that takes full advantage of pedagogy based on the study of cases and related materials and problems, which strengthen students' thinking and analytical skills. Going forward, you will read a case or a series of cases on a given topic. For example, in focusing on antitrust law in baseball, the first major or seminal case in the United States was *Federal Baseball Club of Baltimore, Inc. v. National League of Professional Baseball Clubs*, 259 U.S. 200 (1922). By proceeding, often chronologically, through a series of cases, culminating in a study of the latest cases, students learn how law develops. This method also assists students in applying the law and strengthens their capacity to anticipate future legal developments.

A. Common Law

Part of what the case method requires you to do is to bring together the meaning of the cases and to develop the law through the synthesizing of the cases, with each case building on the foundation of prior cases. Through this process, one comes to understand what cases and commentators refer to as the "common law."

1. Precedent

In applying case law, there is little more powerful than a supporting precedent, or a case that provides support for your position. *Precedent* is a holding, or ruling of a court, which establishes authority for the disposition of future similar cases. Ideally, litigants and their attorneys are thrilled to uncover a Supreme Court case addressing exactly the same facts and legal questions that comprise their situation. When they do so, there is often little need to proceed (however, this does not happen often). If one cannot find a Supreme Court decision directly on point, the next best option may be some other highly respected federal or state court with a ruling similar to your matter. Lower courts are to follow the decisions of higher courts within their jurisdiction. In the federal judiciary, district courts must adhere to the decisions of the Court of Appeals for their circuit or distinguish their case from other previously decided cases. Other circuit court or even state court decisions provide influential or persuasive authority. In this search for precedent, lawyers know that cases with slight factual variations can be supportive as well. For example, if you have a case involving an injury to a soccer player and find a case where the facts are similar but the sport is rugby, that case may be strong precedent in your case, unless you can distinguish soccer from rugby in a manner that would persuade a court that the cases should be treated differently as a legal matter.

2. How to Brief a Case

Whether you are reading a case assigned in this text or cases that you find while engaged in a legal research project, briefing each case will help you to better understand the legal issues as well as how the law develops. Every brief should include the following elements: case name and citation, named parties, legal issue(s), key facts, legal rationale, and holding(s).

The case name generally identifies the plaintiff (the person who has filed a lawsuit) and the defendant (the party against whom the lawsuit has been initiated). Typically, the plaintiff's name is on the left and the defendant on the right, although these are sometimes transposed. The numbers and letters after the case name identify the reporter where a written copy of the case decision is published. Historically, law students would have gone to the law library, located the appropriate reporter (the abbreviation in the middle), then found the volume (the first numbers listed) and opened it to the correct page (the numbers after the designated reporter). When using digital legal search engines such as Lexis or Westlaw, you just type in the citation, and the case is delivered right to your computer screen. The name of the court that wrote the decision and the year the case was decided are included in parentheses after the case citation. It is important to note which court (state or federal) and level of court for precedent purposes. It is also helpful to order your cases in chronological order, as well as by jurisdiction, to see how the law develops.

Next, you should identify the plaintiffs and the defendants. All parties are not always included in the case name.

It is often helpful to identify the legal issue, or issues, in the case by posing them in the form of a question. The legal issue is the question of law that the court is deciding. Identifying the legal question is important, as you may find a case that has facts very similar to your own situation, but the court makes a decision on a legal question that is irrelevant to you. This case would not provide strong precedent.

Many students confuse the legal issue with the facts. The key facts include only the information that is necessary for the court to address the legal issue. Some judges will provide extensive background information and paint a lovely backdrop for the case. However, for briefing purposes, it is useful to pare down all of this information to just the facts that come into play in order for the court to make a decision.

The rationale section identifies the various legal theories that the court examines in order to reach a decision. Using an outline format is helpful in this section of the brief. First, identify the legal theory or legislation that the court uses. Next, define that area of law or explain the statute. Finally, show how the court applies the facts of the case to the legal definition. Some cases may address only a single area of the law, while more complex litigation may address a dozen or more legal theories. The key words identified prior to the cases in this text will often help you to identify the key legal theories addressed. If you are reading other cases, you can look at the keynotes (literally identified by a key-shaped symbol) in Westlaw or the headnotes in Lexis. The rationale section of the brief really helps you to identify and digest how the common law develops. It will also assist you in building legal explanations or arguments if you are researching a legal topic. One additional tip—if you are briefing cases for a legal research paper, it is helpful to identify the page number in the case where you found the information in your brief. The page numbers can be found in brackets (for example, [413]) as you are reading the case. This will save you significant time in tracking down your citations for your legal paper.

The final element of the case brief is the holding, or decision of the court. There should be a holding for every legal issue that you have identified. The holding is critically important because it establishes precedent.

The following case provides you with the opportunity to brief a case, as well as learn a little about civil procedure and tort law.

KEY TERMS In reviewing the following materials, note the definition and meaning of the following terms:

- Answer
- Appeal
- Assumption of risk
- Complaint
- Deposition
- Discovery
- Interrogatories
- Negligence
- Recklessness
- Summary judgment

Savino v. Robertson
273 Ill. App. 3d 811 (1995)

JUDGES: Justice McCormick delivered the opinion of the court: Scariano, P.J., and DiVito, J., concur.

[*812] Plaintiff John Savino brought a negligence action against defendant Scott Robertson after plaintiff was struck and injured in the eye by a hockey puck shot by

defendant. The trial court granted defendant's subsequent motion for summary judgment, but allowed [*813] plaintiff to amend the complaint to allege that defendant's conduct was willful and wanton. Upon another motion by defendant, the trial court granted summary judgment in favor of defendant on the amended complaint. On appeal from both orders, plaintiff raises the following issues for our consideration: (1) whether a plaintiff must plead and prove willful and wanton conduct in order to recover for injuries incurred during athletic competition; and (2) whether there was a genuine issue of material fact as to whether defendant's conduct was willful and wanton in injuring plaintiff. We affirm.

Plaintiff and defendant were teammates in an amateur hockey league sponsored by the Northbrook Park District. Plaintiff and defendant also had met in various "pick-up" games prior to playing in the Northbrook league, but they were neither friends nor enemies. On April 20, 1990, plaintiff and defendant were warming up prior to a game. During warm-up, teams skate around and behind their goal on their half of the ice. Plaintiff was on the ice, "to the right of the face-off circle in front of the net." Defendant shot a puck that missed the goal and hit plaintiff near the right eye. Plaintiff lost 80% vision in that eye.

On September 11, 1990, plaintiff filed a one-count complaint against defendant alleging that defendant was negligent and failed to exercise ordinary care in shooting the puck. Specifically, plaintiff alleged that defendant (a) failed to warn plaintiff that he was going to shoot the puck toward plaintiff; (b) failed to wait until a goalie was present before shooting the puck; (c) failed to warn others that he was shooting the puck; (d) failed to follow the custom and practice of the Northbrook Men's Summer League which required the presence of a goalie at the net before shooting; and (e) failed to keep an adequate lookout.

Defendant filed his answer to the complaint and, after interrogatories and discovery depositions were taken, defendant moved for summary judgment. . . . Defendant argued that he was entitled to judgment as a matter of law because plaintiff alleged ordinary negligence. To be entitled to relief for injuries incurred during athletic competition, defendant argued, plaintiff had to plead and prove willful and wanton conduct or conduct done in reckless disregard for the safety of others. The trial court granted defendant's motion for summary judgment and denied plaintiff leave to amend count I of the complaint. Upon reconsideration, the trial court granted plaintiff leave to file an amended complaint to allege a count II based on willful and wanton conduct.

Defendant filed his answer to plaintiff's subsequent amended complaint and the parties engaged in discovery as to count II of that [*814] complaint. Defendant later filed another motion for summary judgment. Defendant argued that, due to plaintiff's admission that his injury was caused by an accident, plaintiff's case presented no genuine issue of material fact with regard to defendant's alleged willful and wanton conduct. Defendant further argued that plaintiff could not show that defendant's action was anything more than an ordinary practice shot normally taken during warm-up sessions.

Plaintiff, on the other hand, argued in his response to defendant's motion that ordinary negligence should be the standard applied to his case rather than willful and wanton conduct, because, since the hockey game had not officially begun, he was not a participant at the time of his injury. Plaintiff attached the affidavit of Thomas Czarnik, a hockey coach at Deerfield High School, to his response. According to Czarnik, it was the custom of amateur hockey leagues to wait until the goalie was present in the net before any practice shots were taken.

Defendant also took Czarnik's deposition. In that deposition, Czarnik described himself as a 15-year acquaintance of plaintiff. . . . Czarnik further stated that he had been a hockey player since childhood and had coached various youth hockey organizations. The Northbrook Hockey League played what was known as "non-check" hockey. Non-check meant non-collision. However, there was still bodily contact in non-check hockey and, in Czarnik's opinion, hockey, regardless of the type, is a contact sport. Czarnik had no knowledge of the rules and usages of the Northbrook Hockey League and had no firsthand knowledge of the incident.

Czarnik also stated that he had seen players in adult hockey leagues take shots at open goals, that is, goals without a goalie present, during the warm-up period and that he had taken shots at open goals. According to Czarnik, the warm-up period was a part of the game of hockey even though the players are not technically playing a game. Czarnik considered plaintiff's injury an accident.

Defendant attached excerpts of Czarnik's deposition in support of his reply to plaintiff's response to the motion for summary judgment. Defendant argued that Czarnik's responses demonstrated that plaintiff could not show, as a matter of law, that defendant's conduct was willful or wanton. Defendant also contended that Czarnik was not a proper expert to render an opinion in this case, given his lack of familiarity with adult hockey leagues and lack of knowledge of the rules and usages of the Northbrook Summer Men's Hockey League. The trial court granted defendant's motion for summary judgment. [*815] Plaintiff now appeals from both orders of the trial court granting summary judgment in favor of defendant.

Our review of the trial court's grant of summary judgment is *de novo*. The granting of summary judgment is proper when the pleadings, depositions, and affidavits show that no genuine issue of material fact exists and the moving party is entitled to judgment as a matter of law. In determining whether summary judgment is proper, the court must construe the evidence in a light most favorable to the non-movant and strongly against the movant.

Plaintiff first argues that he should not have been required to plead willful and wanton conduct in this case because he was not actually "playing" the game of hockey at the time his injury occurred, but rather was participating in the warm-up practice.

The seminal case on this issue is *Nabozny v. Barnhill* (1975), 31 Ill. App. 3d 212. . . . In *Nabozny*, the plaintiff was the goalkeeper for a teenage soccer league and the defendant was a forward from an opposing team. The game's rules prevented players from making contact with the goalkeeper while he is in possession of the ball in the penalty area. During the game, the ball was passed to the plaintiff while he was in the penalty area. The plaintiff fell onto his knee. The defendant, who had been going for the ball, continued to run towards the plaintiff and kicked the plaintiff in the head, causing severe injuries. The trial court directed a verdict in favor of the defendant, holding that as a matter of law the defendant was free from negligence (owed no duty to the plaintiff) and that the plaintiff was contributorily negligent.

In reversing the trial court, the *Nabozny* court held that when athletes engage in organized competition, with a set of rules that guides the conduct and safety of the players, then "a player is charged with a legal duty to every other player on the field to refrain from conduct proscribed by a safety rule." The court then announced the following rule:

> It is our opinion that a player is liable for injury in a tort action if his conduct is such that it is either deliberate, willful, or with a reckless disregard for the safety of the other player so as to cause injury to that player, the same being a question of fact to be decided by a jury.

[*816] Illinois courts have construed *Nabozny* to hold that a plaintiff-participant injured during a contact sport may recover from another player only if the other's conduct was willful or wanton. Plaintiff contends, however, that decisions subsequent to *Nabozny* have misconstrued the court's holding in that case. According to plaintiff, *Nabozny* is to be applied only to conduct during a game because *Nabozny* "involved an injury that occurred during a game and therefore, it implicitly recognizes a distinction with pre-game injuries."

Illinois has enacted a modified comparative fault statute. (*735 ILCS 5/2-1116* (West 1992).) The enactment of this statute, however, has no effect on express assumption of risk, where a plaintiff expressly assumes the dangers and risks created by the activity or a [*817] defendant's negligence, or on primary implied assumption of risk, where a plaintiff knowingly and voluntarily assumes the risks inherent in a particular situation or a defendant's negligence.

In the case at bar, we believe that plaintiff was no less a participant in a team sport merely because he was engaged in "warm-up" activities at the time of his injury. However, assuming *arguendo* that we were to view plaintiff's action using an ordinary negligence standard, we must find that plaintiff knowingly and voluntarily assumed the risks inherent in playing the game of hockey. Plaintiff's own testimony bears out this fact. Plaintiff was an experienced hockey player, playing from the time he was eight years old. He had played in organized adult leagues for approximately 10 years prior to his accident. Plaintiff testified that while it was "customary" for players to wait for a goalie to be present prior to taking practice shots, in his experience he had seen players take shots at open nets. There was no written rule against taking shots at open nets. Plaintiff was also aware, at the time he stepped onto the ice, that there was a risk of being hit with a puck during "warm-ups." Indeed, according to plaintiff, that risk "always" existed. Nonetheless, plaintiff chose not to wear a protective face mask, since it was not required, even though in his estimation 65–70% of his teammates were wearing protective masks during "warm-up" and despite the inherent risk of being hit with a puck, irrespective of the goalie's presence at the net. Based on plaintiff's testimony, we believe that plaintiff voluntarily consented, understood, and accepted the dangers inherent in the sport or due to a co-participant's negligence.

As we have stated, we believe that the distinction plaintiff raises, between the "warm-up" and the actual commencement of the game, to be illusory. Hockey is a contact sport. It is not made less so merely because the participants are "warming up" prior to the commencement of the game. Proof of ordinary negligence will not sustain an action against defendant in this case, merely because plaintiff alleges a violation of a rule. Moreover, the evidence suggests that defendant here did not violate the customs and rules of the league. In addition to plaintiff's testimony, plaintiff's witness Czarnik and teammate Steve Marcordes testified that players may be hit by pucks during "warm-up" and during the game . . . Marcordes, unlike Czarnik, was familiar with the customs and usages of the Northbrook **[*818]** league, so much so that plaintiff testified that he considered Marcordes a "player-coach." Marcordes also testified that it was common for players to take shots at an open net during warm-up.

We find no reason to abandon the well-established precedent of this court, and that of a majority of jurisdictions, that a participant in a contact sport may recover for injury only where the other's conduct is willful or wanton or in reckless disregard to safety. There are a number of reasons justifying the application of this standard to sports-related injury cases. First, the risk of injury accompanies many informal contact sports. Thus, willful and wanton or reckless conduct allows the court to gauge what is and is not permissible conduct under the circumstances. Second, as the court recognized in *Nabozny*, courts must strike a balance between "the free and vigorous participation in sports" and the protection of the individual from reckless or intentional conduct. Third, we believe that the practical effect of applying an ordinary negligence standard would be to open a legal pandora's box, allowing virtually every participant in a contact sport, injured by another during a "warm-up" or practice, to bring an action based on the risks inherent in virtually every contact sport. This is exactly the type of result the courts have sought to avoid. . . . **[*820]** It is undisputed that plaintiff and defendant were teammates in an organized hockey league. There were rules and usages. Reviewing the evidence in a light most favorable to plaintiff, there appears to be no genuine issue of material fact that practice shots were often taken at an open net and such was the custom of the team.

For the foregoing reasons, we affirm both orders of the circuit court granting summary judgment in defendant's favor.

Affirmed.

QUESTIONS

1. How did the court in *Savino* determine whether granting summary judgment is proper?
2. What cases did the court use as precedent in this decision?
3. What legal theories are identified? How are these theories explained?
4. How would you "brief" this case?
5. Provide an example of a future case where this case might serve as a precedent.
6. How was precedent used to determine the outcome of this case?

Regulating Interscholastic (High School) and Youth Athletics

INTRODUCTION: THE RISE OF THE REGULATION OF INTERSCHOLASTIC AND YOUTH ATHLETICS AT THE STATE, NATIONAL, AND INTERNATIONAL LEVELS

A. Historical Overview

In 1851, the state superintendent of schools for Minnesota requested an acre or more of land be "set aside for the physical development of [students]." Mabel Lee, A History of Physical Education and Sports in the U.S.A., 1983, p. 34. A Detroit high school football team existed in 1888, and by 1892, a Detroit high school baseball team traveled to Ann Arbor for an interscholastic game. In late 1895 and early 1896, educators in Wisconsin met to discuss interscholastic athletics and the formation of an association for governance purposes. After the formal organization of the Wisconsin Interscholastic Athletic Association, state athletic associations proliferated throughout the United States, and the National Federation of State High School Associations was formed in 1923.

Participation in interscholastic athletics has grown steadily. The number of high school students participating in interscholastic athletics had increased steadily for 30 years, with a record high of 7,980,886 participants in 2017–2018. Economic challenges likely contributed to the decline of participants in 2018–2019, and the COVID-19 pandemic resulted in a 4 percent decrease in participation through the 2021–2022 school year. It remains to be seen whether slowing growth or declining participation in interscholastic athletics will continue.

Youth athletics continues to proliferate at all levels, with approximately 60 million children (about 56 percent of all youth) playing a variety of sports. A broad array of associations governs youth athletics in the United States, ranging from local park and recreational organizations and YMCAs to national associations such as Little League baseball (http://www.littleleague.org/Little_League_Online.

htm), American Youth Soccer Association (AYSO; *https://ayso.org/about-us/about/*), and Pop Warner football (*http://www.popwarner.com/About_Us/orgchart.htm*). The Amateur Athletic Union (AAU) has also become increasingly involved in youth athletics. See *http://image.aausports.org/codebook/article_I.pdf* (Article I of the Constitution of the AAU). The National Football League (NFL) formed USA Football in an effort to improve coaching in youth football at the interscholastic and non-scholastic levels (see *https://usafootball.com/programs/national-team/coach/* for a discussion of the role of the NFL with youth coaches). Youth athletics in other countries are often overseen by governmental entities (see, e.g., *http://www.sport.gov.tt/* for the national governing body in Trinidad). With concerns rising regarding head and related injuries, as well as other health and safety issues at all levels, governmental bodies are becoming more involved in regulating and exercising increasing oversight in this area.

Increases in participation and the competitiveness in our culture have spawned significant regulation. State and youth associations have also developed increasingly sophisticated and elaborate regulations to govern youth athletics. State and federal legislation will continue to affect interscholastic and youth athletics, with courts playing a role in overseeing the operation of interscholastic and youth athletics.

B. Interscholastic and Youth Athletics Regulatory Structure, Governance, and Administrative Processes

Interscholastic athletics is largely regulated under the rules formulated by public and private high schools that are members of state athletic associations. Youth athletics, in turn, is generally governed by entities that are wholly private (nonpublic) in nature. The presence of public schools in state athletic associations often raises issues of whether the association is public, and hence subject to more judicial scrutiny, or private in nature. Rules governing the playing of the game and participation by boys and girls in interscholastic athletics are adopted by athletic associations at the statewide level. Occasionally, conferences or other groups of schools on a regional basis may adopt rules as well. At the interscholastic level, school boards and local school officials may also adopt rules that will apply to participation in interscholastic athletics. The courts may intervene to deal with disputes, particularly if the governing body or state athletic association is deemed to be public. Some state legislatures have been willing to intervene and enact laws pertaining to some aspects that apply to both interscholastic and youth athletics, particularly health and safety issues.

Actions by youth-governing bodies, state athletic associations, conferences and regional bodies, school districts, school officials, and coaches may be challenged in court. In this chapter, we examine cases that will provide the reader with a sense of how courts (and occasionally legislative bodies) act with regard to interscholastic and youth athletics. If the governing body is determined to be acting in a public capacity, it will be held to higher judicial accountability. Courts, on the other hand, are very deferential to actions taken by private associations, such as nearly all nonscholastic youth athletic associations (e.g., Pop Warner football or Little League baseball), largely permitting them to govern themselves. State-level athletic associations, local school districts, and individual high schools are subject to more oversight, but the courts generally defer to such entities. Courts have long been reluctant to get involved in academic decisions made by those who are directly involved in overseeing or governing schools from the kindergarten through 12th-grade levels. Courts generally consider participation in athletics to be a privilege and not a right and provide those who oversee interscholastic and youth athletics with broad authority or deference. Courts often see schools and those who directly govern the activities of schoolchildren as extensions of the home and parents, and are reluctant to substitute judicial wisdom for that of school officials and parents, even though they are much more willing to get involved in matters involving public institutions.

JUDICIAL REGULATION OF INTERSCHOLASTIC AND YOUTH ATHLETICS

KEY TERMS
- Dictum
- Due process
- Entwinement
- Free speech
- State action

The majority of interscholastic athletics programs operate within public schools, raising the issue of "state action." The rights enumerated in the U.S. Constitution protect against state or governmental action, but not against private action. A government official must recognize a person's federal constitutional rights, but nongovernmental officials or persons acting privately are not required to do so. For example, a court may recognize a right to speak in a public place, but it will not generally extend that right to speak in private contexts. In these materials, we examine whether a state high school athletic association is a state actor for federal constitutional law purposes. Athletic associations are generally considered to be private associations made up of public and private schools in the interscholastic athletics context. Nevertheless, their actions are often so closely related to state or government action that courts must decide whether an athletic association is a state actor for constitutional purposes. If the athletic association is a state or government actor, then it has to act in a manner that respects the constitutional rights of sports participants.

We begin by exploring what is often the threshold question of whether an association or individual is acting on behalf of the state. We also examine several rules and regulations established by state athletics associations, local school districts, or high schools that deal with student-athletes' eligibility to participate in interscholastic sports, including cases challenging mandatory drug testing and asserting claims alleging infringement of free speech, association, and religious rights.

A. State Action

In the early nineteenth century, prior to the Civil War, the Bill of Rights (the first ten amendments to the U.S. Constitution) were held to apply only as against federal action. There were state constitutional provisions that applied at the state level, but the Bill of Rights—including the First Amendment rights of freedom of speech and religion—applied only against the national or federal government. They were not applicable at the state or private level. After the Civil War, which dealt in part with states' rights, the Civil Rights Amendments (Amendments 13 to 15 to the U.S. Constitution) were adopted and ratified. The Fourteenth Amendment, which secured equal protection of law against state action (government action at any level) subsequently came to be read, in a series of cases, that rights included in the first ten amendments (the Bill of Rights) were applicable against state officials or those acting in a governmental capacity at the state or local level. This clause-by-clause or right-by-right determination is referred to as *incorporation*, meaning the incorporation of each of the rights included in the Bill of Rights as against government action at any level. The reason why this is referred to as "state action" is that the Fourteenth Amendment used the language "state action" when it secured the right of equal protection of law to all citizens.

A prerequisite to bringing a claim alleging infringement of a federal constitutional right is that the deprivation of the right occurred as the result of state action. The Fourteenth Amendment to the U.S. Constitution, under which the Bill of Rights has been made applicable to the states, limits enforcement of those rights to cases in which the right has been deprived or limited by a state actor (someone acting on behalf of the state or in some public capacity). If an educational institution or state interscholastic sports association is deemed to be a state actor, it is held to a higher level of judicial accountability than it would be if it were not deemed to be a state actor. State actors are held accountable under the U.S. and state constitutions—private associations generally are not. The *Brentwood I* and *II* cases, discussed *infra*, effectively illustrate this dynamic between state action (the actions of associations that are held to be state actors) and substantive constitutional claims.

The question of whether a state athletic association is a state actor was a troublesome issue for many years, with lower courts reaching differing conclusions on this point. In 2001, in a 5-4 decision in *NCAA v. Tarkanian*, 488 U.S. 179 (1988), the United States Supreme Court held that the National Collegiate Athletic Association (NCAA) is not a state actor. It was not clear, however, whether state interscholastic associations would be considered state actors for purposes of the enforcement of constitutionally protected rights because the decision in the *Tarkanian* case dealt with the NCAA. The issue of whether a state interscholastic athletic association is a state actor was raised before the Supreme Court in *Brentwood v. Tennessee Secondary School Athletic Assn.*, 531 U.S. 288 (2001) (*Brentwood I*).

The *Brentwood I* case raises the question of whether the Tennessee Secondary School Athletic Association (TSSAA) is a state actor. The Court had to resolve this issue before it could examine the claim that the TSSAA had deprived individuals of their constitutional rights of due process and freedom of speech. As you read *Brentwood I*, do not worry about the underlying substantive constitutional issue regarding recruitment and free speech because those issues cannot be addressed until the court determines whether the high school athletics association is a state actor subject to constitutional requirements. State action cases are often quite fact specific, with courts closely examining the facts to determine whether the association is effectively acting as a state or governmental actor. As you read *Brentwood I*, think of the outcome-determinative facts (the facts that influenced the decision). The Court is closely divided, 5-4, in the *Brentwood* and the *Tarkanian* cases. As you read the *Brentwood I* case, think of facts that might cause the Court to decide differently and hold that a state association or other entity is not a state actor subject to actions by individuals or groups seeking enforcement of their constitutional rights.

You will note, as you read the *Brentwood I* case, that five of the nine (a mere majority) justices on the United States Supreme Court agreed that the TSSAA is a state actor. To reach this decision, the five justices in the majority had to distinguish the TSSAA from the NCAA, which the Supreme Court held was not a state or government actor required to provide protection for the constitutional rights of student-athletes and others affected by the NCAA's decisions. As you read the majority and the dissenting opinions, think about whether the court is right. With a change in the makeup of the Court, is it possible that a majority of the Court would agree with the dissenting opinion, which would result in a future decision holding that no state athletic associations are state actors subject to the constraints of the Constitution? Reflect as well on the implications of an association being held to be a state actor in subsequent cases.

Brentwood Academy v. Tennessee Secondary School Athletic Association
531 U.S. 288 (2001)

Justice SOUTER delivered the opinion of the Court.

[Editors' note: We have intentionally retained the discussion of the *Tarkanian* decision in this case, which deals with intercollegiate athletics, believing that "state action" should be considered jointly with high school and intercollegiate sports issues. It is important to remember that interscholastic athletic associations have often been held to be state actors, and therefore subject to constitutional restrictions, while the

NCAA has not been characterized as a state actor. As you read, think about why the NCAA is not a state actor, but state athletic associations often are.]

The issue is whether a statewide association incorporated to regulate interscholastic athletic competition among public and private secondary schools may be regarded as engaging in state action when it enforces a rule against a member school. The association in question here includes most public schools located within the State, acts through their representatives, draws its officers from them, is largely funded by their dues and income received in their stead, and has historically been seen to regulate in lieu of the State Board of Education's exercise of its own authority. We hold that the association's regulatory activity may and should be treated as state action owing to the pervasive entwinement of state school officials in the structure of the association, there being no offsetting reason to see the association's acts in any other way.

I

. . . [I]n *Tarkanian* . . . we found no state action on the part of the NCAA. We could see, on the one hand, that the university had some part in setting the NCAA's rules, and the Supreme Court of Nevada had gone so far as to hold that the NCAA had been delegated the university's traditionally exclusive public authority over personnel. But on the other side, the NCAA's policies were shaped not by the University of Nevada alone, but by several hundred member institutions, most of them having no connection with Nevada, and exhibiting no color of Nevada law. Since it was difficult to see the NCAA, not as a collective membership, but as surrogate for the one State, we held the organization's connection with Nevada too insubstantial to ground a state action claim.

But dictum in *Tarkanian* pointed to a contrary result on facts like ours, with an organization whose member public schools are all within a single State. "The situation would, of course, be different if the [Association's] membership consisted entirely of institutions located within the same State, many of them public institutions created by the same sovereign."

B

Just as we foresaw in *Tarkanian*, the "necessarily fact-bound inquiry," leads to the conclusion of state action here. The nominally private character of the Association is overborne by the pervasive entwinement of public institutions and public officials in its composition and workings, and there is no substantial reason to claim unfairness in applying constitutional standards to it. . . .

[T]o the extent of 84% of its membership, the Association is an organization of public schools represented by their officials acting in their official capacity to provide an integral element of secondary public schooling. There would be no recognizable Association, legal or tangible, without the public school officials, who do not merely control but overwhelmingly perform all but the purely ministerial acts by which the Association exists and functions in practical terms. . . .

To complement the entwinement of public school officials with the Association from the bottom up, the State of Tennessee has provided for entwinement from top down. State Board members are assigned *ex officio* to serve as members of the board of control and legislative council, and the Association's ministerial employees are treated as state employees to the extent of being eligible for membership in the state retirement system. . . .

The entwinement down from the State Board is therefore unmistakable, just as the entwinement up from the member public schools is overwhelming. Entwinement will support a conclusion that an ostensibly private organization ought to be charged with a public character and judged by constitutional standards; entwinement to the degree shown here requires it.

The judgment of the Court of Appeals for the Sixth Circuit is reversed, and the case is remanded for further proceedings consistent with this opinion.

It is so ordered.

Justice THOMAS, with whom The Chief Justice, Justice SCALIA, and Justice KENNEDY join, dissenting.

We have never found state action based upon mere "entwinement." The majority's holding — that the Tennessee Secondary School Athletic Association's (TSSAA) enforcement of its recruiting rule is state action — not only extends state-action doctrine beyond its permissible limits but also encroaches upon the realm of individual freedom that the doctrine was meant to protect. I respectfully dissent.

Commonsense dictates that the TSSAA's actions cannot fairly be attributed to the State, and thus cannot constitute state action. The TSSAA was formed in 1925 as a private corporation to organize interscholastic athletics and to sponsor tournaments among its member schools.

The State of Tennessee did not create the TSSAA. The State does not fund the TSSAA and does not pay its employees. In fact, only 4% of the TSSAA's revenue comes from the dues paid by member schools; the bulk of its operating budget is derived from gate receipts at tournaments it sponsors. The State does not permit the TSSAA to use state-owned facilities for a discounted fee, and it does not exempt the TSSAA from state taxation. No Tennessee law authorizes the State to coordinate interscholastic athletics or empowers another entity to organize interscholastic athletics on behalf of the State. The only state pronouncement acknowledging the TSSAA's existence is a rule providing that the State Board of Education permits public schools to maintain membership in the TSSAA if they so choose.

[T]he State of Tennessee has never had any involvement in the particular action taken by the TSSAA in this case: the enforcement of the TSSAA's recruiting rule prohibiting members from using "undue influence" on students or their parents or guardians "to secure or to retain a student for athletic purposes."

Because I do not believe that the TSSAA's action of enforcing its recruiting rule is fairly attributable to the State of Tennessee, I would affirm [the decision by the lower court holding that the TSSAA is not a state actor].

QUESTIONS

Justice Souter and the majority hold that the TSSAA is a state actor because "[t]he nominally private character of the Association is overborne by the pervasive entwinement of public institutions and public officials in its composition." Do you agree with Justice Souter and the majority, or with Justice Thomas? Why? Can you develop other persuasive arguments not made here? What constitutes sufficient "entwinement" for an association to be held to be a state actor under Justice Souter's test? Does that test clearly articulate a basis on which interscholastic athletic associations can know whether or not they are state actors? Why did the TSSAA aggressively resist being held to be a state actor?

NOTES

The courts in Tennessee continue to rely on the general reasoning in the *Brentwood* case. In *City Press Communs., LLC v. Tenn. Secondary Sch. Ath. Ass'n*, 447 S.W.3d 230 (Tenn. Ct. App. 2014), the court extended the reasoning in the *Brentwood* case in holding that the TSSAA acted as a government agency and therefore was required to produce records under the Tennessee Public Records Act.

Having held in *Brentwood I* that the TSSAA is a state actor, in *Tennessee Secondary School Athletic Assn. v. Brentwood Academy*, 127 S. Ct. 2489 (2007) (*Brentwood II*), the Court considered the merits of the plaintiff high school's federal constitutional law challenges to the TSSAA's anti-recruiting rule on free speech and due process grounds. Brentwood argued that it had a free speech right to send a letter seeking to recruit a potential student to attend and play for Brentwood. The First Amendment of the U.S. Constitution states that "Congress [which has been broadly interpreted to include government generally] shall make no law . . . abridging the freedom of speech. . . ." This provision has been read broadly to protect the freedom of expression in its many forms. Written communications such as letters are protected as a form of speech. In the case, however, the Court declines to find that Brentwood's freedom of speech was abridged.

The Court also examines whether Brentwood was denied due process. The due process clause of the Fourteenth Amendment to the U.S. Constitution provides that no state shall "deprive any person of life, liberty, or property without due process of law." Due process has been interpreted as requiring that a state or government actor afford certain procedures ("due process") before it deprives a person of certain interests: life, liberty, or property. If a person's liberty or property interest is affected by a decision, that party must be afforded fair process, which is generally defined as notice of the fact that his or her interest may be affected or deprived by a decision and a fair hearing prior to that deprivation. In the interscholastic sports context, students and their parents have unsuccessfully asserted that they have a protectable interest or right to participate in interscholastic athletics, which would trigger the due process requirement. However, they have been able, on occasion, to assert that due process is triggered because they have a property interest in the possibility of earning a scholarship.

Tennessee Secondary School Athletic Association v. Brentwood Academy (Brentwood II)
127 S. Ct. 2489 (2007)

Justice STEVENS delivered the opinion of the Court with respect to Parts I, II-B, III, and IV, concluding:

I

[Editors' note: With one judge dissenting, the Court of Appeals held that the TSSAA's anti-recruiting rule is a content-based regulation of speech that is not narrowly tailored to serve its permissible purposes. It also concluded that the TSSAA Board improperly considered *ex parte* evidence during its deliberations, thereby violating Brentwood's due process rights.]

The First Amendment protects Brentwood's right to publish truthful information about the school and its athletic programs. It likewise protects the school's right to try to persuade prospective students and their parents that its excellence in sports is a reason for enrolling. But Brentwood's speech rights are not absolute. . . .

II [Speech]

Brentwood made a voluntary decision to join TSSAA and to abide by its anti-recruiting rule. Just as the government's interest in running an effective workplace can in some circumstances outweigh employee speech rights, so too can an athletic league's interest in enforcing its rules sometimes warrant curtailing the speech of its voluntary participants. . . .

We need no empirical data to credit TSSAA's common-sense conclusion that hard-sell tactics [in a letter] directed at middle school students could lead to exploitation, distort competition between high school teams, and foster an environment in which athletics are prized more highly than academics. . . . [T]he First Amendment does not excuse Brentwood from abiding by the same anti-recruiting rule that governs the conduct of its sister schools. To hold otherwise would undermine the principle, succinctly articulated by the dissenting judge at the Court of Appeals, that "[h]igh school football is a game. Games have rules."

III [Due Process]

The decision to sanction Brentwood for engaging in prohibited recruiting was preceded by an investigation, several meetings, exchanges of correspondence, an adverse written determination from TSSAA's executive director, [and] a hearing before the director and an advisory panel composed of three members of TSSAA's Board of Directors. During the investigation, Brentwood was notified of all the charges against it. At each of the two hearings, Brentwood was represented by counsel and given the opportunity to adduce evidence. No evidence offered by Brentwood was excluded.

Even accepting the questionable holding [of the Sixth Circuit] that TSSAA's closed-door deliberations were unconstitutional, we can safely conclude that any due process violation was harmless beyond a reasonable doubt....

QUESTIONS

1. How did the age of the students targeted for the recruiting mail factor into the Court's decision? Should impressionable young people be shielded from recruiting efforts? Do parents have a role in insulating their children from recruiting efforts? Should students have access to the information contained in such a letter to help them make important decisions in their lives?
2. The court held that Brentwood (the school) had a right or interest in the writing and sending of its letter (speech) and was entitled to due process. It then held that Brentwood had been afforded due process by the TSSAA. Why? This case is a good example of how adequate notice of prohibited conduct and a fair hearing must be offered to satisfy due process requirements.

B. Eligibility Issues

KEY TERMS
- Arbitrary and capricious
- Common law
- Equal protection
- State constitution

The remainder of this chapter deals with substantive issues that have been raised by student-athletes and participants in youth sports and their parents challenging the nature of associational and institutional governance of interscholastic and youth athletics. Eligibility issues arising out of the application and enforcement of transfer, outside competition, good conduct, maximum age, personal appearance and grooming, and home school rules are common. Other cases address mandatory random drug testing and alleged infringement of student-athletes' federal constitutional rights to freedom of expression and religion. Think about the different types of rules and actions typically challenged by young athletes and their parents. Also, consider what the appropriate role of legislative and government administrative bodies should be in protecting young people participating in athletics. As you read these materials, think about the following question: Are courts and legislative and administrative bodies too deferential to state athletic associations, individual educational institutions, and youth organizations involved in governing younger athletes?

The Sport and Development organization refers to evidence that supports the argument that an opportunity to participate in interscholastic and youth athletics may merit legal protection in some form. It notes:

> Sport and physical education is fundamental to the early development of children and youth and the skills learned during play, physical education and sport contribute to the holistic development of young people. Through participation in sport and physical education, young people learn about the importance of key values such as:
>
> - honesty,
> - teamwork,
> - fair play,
> - respect for themselves and others, and
> - adherence to rules.
>
> It also provides a forum for young people to learn how to deal with competition and how to cope with both winning and losing. These learning aspects highlight the impact of physical education and sport on a child's social and moral development in addition to physical skills and abilities. *https://www.sportanddev.org/en/learn-more/sport-education-and-child-and-youth-development*.

Studies have also found that "female and male students who participate in high school team sports through the 12th grade have a school-based identity that correlates to positive academic performance (e.g., an increased 12th-grade GPA and an increased probability of being enrolled in college full time at age 21). This highly positive finding is consistent with prior research evidencing that sports participation, relative to participation in other extracurricular activities such as student government and academic clubs, is "linked to lower likelihood of school dropout and higher rates of college attendance." Matthew J. Mitten and Timothy Davis, *Athlete Eligibility Requirements and Legal Protection of Sports Participation Opportunities*, 8 Va. Sports and Entertainment L.J. 71, 113 (2009).

Consider whether athletic participation is of sufficient importance that it should be protected as a constitutional matter as you read the following materials, which deal with rules established by interscholastic associations and youth organizations. Associations, organizations, and schools promulgating rules governing youth athletics must follow those rules. Occasionally, a court will intervene when a governing body does not follow its own rules. A Mississippi case demonstrates the importance of following rules established by a school or school district. In *Miss. High Sch. Activities Ass'n v. R.T.*, 163 So. 3d 274, 2015 Miss. LEXIS 229 (Miss. 2015), the Mississippi Supreme Court held that once a school decides to create a sports program and establish eligibility rules, it must follow those rules and may be held accountable when it does not do so. The court added that young athletes are among the intended beneficiaries of high school athletic programs and the rules that govern them. Courts will largely defer to sports governing bodies in administering or interpreting their rules, but they may not refuse to follow their own rules.

1. Transfer Rules

High school athletes often challenge transfer rules and regulations adopted by state athletic associations. Transfer rules limit the eligibility of student-athletes to participate immediately in interscholastic competition after they move from one school to another. A common type of transfer rule renders a student-athlete who transfers from one high school to another within the same school district without a corresponding change in his or her parents' residence ineligible to engage in interscholastic competition for a period of time — often as long as an entire school year.

The *Carlberg* case illustrates how courts have resolved a variety of federal and state legal challenges to transfer rules. While reading this case, consider the purposes for which transfer rules are adopted. Reasons typically cited in support of transfer rules include deterring the recruitment of student-athletes (i.e., protecting student-athletes from the pressure and harassment of zealous coaches and fans that might ensue from unregulated recruiting) and affording academics a higher priority than athletics.

In cases involving transfer and other eligibility rules, athletes often argue that the regulation is being applied in an arbitrary and capricious manner, thereby denying them due process of law or violating the law of private associations. In most cases, courts are quite deferential to athletic associations and organizations, in part because judges do not generally believe that it is wise for them to substitute their judgment for that of educators and others who devote their lives to ensuring that interscholastic and youth athletic programs are wisely administered.

In many cases, young athletes claim that they are being denied equal protection. Equal protection claims are based on the Fourteenth Amendment to the U.S. Constitution, which provides that no citizen shall be denied equal protection of the law. As the court notes in *Carlberg*, parties are likely to succeed if they can prove that they have not been treated equally in a case involving a right or if they are members of a class or group that has historically been treated unequally. For example, if the distinction is based on a racial classification (what the courts refer to as a "suspect class"), courts will closely or strictly scrutinize the rule and are likely to find it to be unconstitutional unless it is supported by a compelling interest or reason and is being applied in the least restrictive manner possible. Gender is another class that receives heightened, but not strict, scrutiny (sometimes referred to as "intermediate scrutiny"). For gender-based classifications, the courts seek to determine whether there is an important purpose substantially furthered by the regulation (a less stringent requirement than the compelling interest standard used in race). Gender-based regulations are examined closely, and may be more likely to be judicially upheld than race-based classifications. Courts recognize that associations and regulatory bodies must draw distinctions in making and enforcing general rules that do not raise issues of racial or gender-based discrimination, so such rules need only be supported by a rational reason or basis.

Indiana High School Athletic Association v. Carlberg
694 N.E.2d 222 (Ind. 1997)

SULLIVAN, Justice.

After attending Brebeuf Preparatory School as a freshman (where he swam on the varsity swim team), Jason Carlberg, who lives with his parents near Indianapolis, transferred to Carmel High School for academic reasons. The Indiana High School Athletic Association ("IHSAA") is a voluntary association of public and private high schools that adopts and enforces rules regarding eligibility and similar matters related to interscholastic athletic competition. Applying Rule 19 (the "Transfer Rule"), the IHSAA determined that Carlberg transferred for nonathletic reasons without a change of permanent residence by his parents or guardians. [Editors' note: Under the terms of the rule, he was not permitted to participate on a varsity athletic team for one year.]

After exhausting available administrative remedies, including a hearing before the IHSAA Executive Committee, which denied his appeal, Carlberg alleged, *inter alia*, that application of the Transfer Rule violated his constitutional rights under the due process and equal protection clauses of the Fourteenth Amendment of the U.S. Constitution, and was arbitrary and capricious in violation of Indiana common law. . . .

In its appeal to the Indiana Supreme Court, the IHSAA argued that the Transfer Rule is subject to the rule of limited judicial interference in the affairs of private voluntary membership associations. . . .

[Editors' note: After holding that the IHSAA is a state actor, the court dealt with Carlberg's asserted due process right and found that Carlberg had been given a sufficient hearing. Regarding his equal protection claim, the court held that "[a]bsent a burden upon the exercise of a constitutionally protected right (none is at stake here) or creation of a suspect class (none is alleged here), the general standard of review of state action challenged under the equal protection clause is the rational basis test." It found that the transfer rule's objectives of preserving the integrity of interscholastic athletics, preventing recruiting, and school transfers for athletic reasons are legitimate and concluded that the transfer rule is rationally related to achieving these goals.]

We find resolution of challenges to IHSAA rules and enforcement actions well within the ambit of Indiana common law. Our state constitution specifically recognizes that "knowledge and learning" are "essential to the preservation of a free government" and so mandates a statewide system of free public education. We believe athletics are an integral part of this constitutionally-mandated process of education. . . .

The substantial educational benefits derived from interscholastic athletics, together with the rationale that underlies the determination that IHSAA decisions constitute "state action," help explain why Indiana courts have been so willing to adjudicate disputes between the IHSAA and parties aggrieved by the association's decisions.

The rule in Indiana is that courts exercise limited interference with the internal affairs and rules of a voluntary membership association: a voluntary association may, without direction or interference by the courts, for its government, adopt a constitution, by-laws, rules and regulations which will control as to all questions of discipline, or internal policy and management, and its right to interpret and administer the same is as sacred as the right to make them. . . .

The provisions of the IHSAA Transfer Rule at issue in this case apply to a student who changes schools without a corresponding change of residence by the student's parents. Such a student may participate as a member of a junior varsity or freshman team at his or her new school unless the transfer was either primarily for athletic reasons or as a result of undue influence. However, such a student may not participate in interscholastic athletics as a member of a *varsity* athletic team during the first 365 days after enrollment unless (i) the student meets one of the special criteria set forth in Rule 19-6.1 or (ii) is declared eligible under the IHSAA "Hardship Rule."

Carlberg agrees that he changed schools without a corresponding change of residence by his parents and that none of the special criteria of Rule 19-6.1 nor the Hardship Rule apply. For its part, the IHSAA acknowledges that the transfer was neither for primarily athletic reasons nor as a result of undue influence. Carlberg argues that the IHSAA acted arbitrarily and capriciously when it enforced the Transfer Rule against him where it was undisputed that his transfer was neither primarily for athletic reasons nor as a result of undue influence.

"Arbitrary and capricious" is a narrow standard of review and the reviewing court may not substitute its judgment for the judgment of the IHSAA. The rule or decision will be found to be arbitrary and capricious "only where it is willful and unreasonable, without consideration and in disregard of the facts or circumstances in the case, or without some basis which would lead a reasonable and honest person to the same conclusion."

We do not find the IHSAA decision that Carlberg was ineligible for varsity athletics for 365 days following his transfer to be "willful and unreasonable, without consideration and in disregard of the facts or circumstances in the case, or without some basis which would lead a reasonable and honest person to the same conclusion." First, there is no contention that the IHSAA failed to publicize its interpretation of the rule or failed to apply consistently its interpretation of the rule.

Second, by establishing objective standards for eligibility "governing residence and transfer," including the provision allowing for only limited eligibility upon a transfer not accompanied by a parental change of residence, Rule 19(c) acts as a deterrent to athletically motivated transfers.

Third, the operation of the rule does not sweep too broadly in its proscription. While it is true that some students who change schools neither primarily for athletic reasons nor as a result of undue influence are denied varsity eligibility for one year, conducting a factual inquiry into the motivation for every transfer would impose a considerable burden on both the IHSAA and its member schools. . . .

[Editors' note: Having found that the IHSAA's application of the transfer rule to Carlberg was neither arbitrary nor capricious, the court next considered whether the IHSAA possessed the authority to enforce the transfer rule. The court concluded:

The IHSAA does not derive its authority directly from the legislature but instead from a delegation of authority from member schools. As such, the analysis with respect to the three factors that concern authorizing legislation is conducted best by examining the challenged rule's consistency with the IHSAA's purpose in general and the purpose of the Transfer Rule in particular.

The IHSAA exists "to encourage, regulate, and give direction to wholesome amateur interschool athletic competition between schools who are members." To further this purpose, the IHSAA Articles and By-Laws mandate that it "determine qualifications of individual contestants . . . and provide written communications to establish standards for eligibility." We find authority to take such action, and to delegate that authority to the IHSAA, to be within the powers granted Indiana public school corporations by the legislature. We further find Rule 19-6.2 to fall within the scope of, to be consistent and harmonious with, and not to expand or vary this authority.]

DICKSON, Justice, concurring and dissenting.

I am convinced that the trial court was correct in finding the IHSAA's attempts to apply its Transfer Rule . . . to be arbitrary and capricious and thus improper. . . .

[T]he arbitrariness of the IHSAA's application of its rule becomes apparent in the present case: A rule purporting to limit athletically-motivated transfers and promote education as the primary value of school in fact punishes a student whom the IHSAA found did *not* transfer for an athletic reason and where the uncontradicted evidence points only to academic reasons for the transfer. Common sense instructs that application of the Transfer Rule to limit Jason's opportunities for participation would be blatantly arbitrary and capricious. The trial court was correct in making such a finding. . . .

NOTES

1. Arbitrary and capricious. Courts are disinclined to overrule discretionary decisions made by interscholastic sports associations and youth organizations. The majority opinion in *Carlberg* is illustrative of the deference given—the reluctance to find that the association acted in an arbitrary and capricious manner. The dissenting judge is less willing to defer and would have found the transfer rule, as applied in this case, to be arbitrary and capricious. Should courts be deferential in these cases? As you consider the following cases and materials, think of what kinds of decisions by an association might be considered to be arbitrary and capricious. Remember, because courts are typically quite deferential to associations, the hearing before the association is critical—a student who wishes to transfer must persuade the association to waive their rule or apply it in a manner that permits the transfer or must produce evidence that would cause courts to be concerned with the reasons offered by the association for its prohibition.

2. State constitutional issues. State constitutional provisions may be interpreted as providing the student-athlete with more (but not less) protection than that offered under the federal constitution, in terms of equal protection and other protected rights (e.g., association, education, free exercise, free speech, and privacy). In *Indiana High School Athletic Assn., Inc. v. Avant*, 650 N.E.2d 1164 (Ind. App. 1995), the court acknowledged that the Indiana state constitution provided a higher level of protection to the student-athlete than is afforded under the federal equal protection clause and may provide a basis for judicial relief.

> ### Problem 2-1
>
> Issues related to student-athlete transfers between school districts and schools arise with some frequency. As a member of a committee asked to make recommendations regarding transfer rules what, if any, kinds of rules and guidelines would you recommend the association consider adopting?

2. Outside Competition Rules

Students have challenged outside competition rules—rules that limit competition in a sport outside the interscholastic athletics context. For example, in *Letendre v. Missouri State High School Athletics Assn.*, 86 S.W.3d 63 (Mo. App. 2002), a 15-year-old swimmer, with a goal of swimming competitively and ultimately participating on her high school's swim team, sought to enjoin the Missouri State High School Activities Association (MSHSAA) from enforcing an outside competition rule that prohibited students from competing on both a school and a non-school team in the same sport during the school team's season. The student claimed that the rule violated equal protection for lacking a rational basis because it was "internally inconsistent in that it did not affect those who wished to participate in nonathletic activities both in and outside of school; it did not affect those who participated in one sport in school and another sport outside of school; and it did not apply to athletes who participated in national or Olympic development competitions during a sport season." The court rejected her claim, noting that the association had a rational basis for a general rule that limited students from participating in the same sport at the same time on two different teams.

The court in *Letendre* concluded its opinion with a statement that explains why courts are often disinclined to substitute their judgment for that of an athletic association:

> While we might personally believe that a better rule could be drafted, one that would allow a student athlete who is getting good grades, such as Claire, to compete simultaneously on both her school and non-school swim teams, the law does not permit us to interject our personal beliefs in the name of the Constitution. Claire's constitutional challenges must fail because by-law 235 is rationally related to the MSHSAA's purpose of drafting rules that protect the welfare of the greatest number of high school athletes possible.

Courts have uniformly rejected legal challenges to "outside competition" rules, even if the rule applies only to certain sports and prohibits participation in the same sport outside the time period for interscholastic competition in that sport. To comply with the Amateur Sports Act of 1978's objective of furthering the development of Olympic sports (see Chapter 14, *infra*), however, "outside competition" rules generally provide waivers to enable high school students to try out and qualify for spots on U.S. Olympic teams.

Courts will seek to ensure that the athletic association is following its own rules—if it fails to follow its own rules, the court will generally intervene and require that the rules be followed.

QUESTIONS

Do you agree that high school athletic governing bodies should have broad authority to effectively prohibit students' participation in competitive club sports as a condition of participating in interscholastic athletics? Given the rising importance of competitive youth sports opportunities outside the interscholastic context, should courts and governing bodies be more willing to find ways to facilitate outside competition?

3. Age Rules

KEY TERMS
- Competitive advantage
- Waiver rule

Most governing bodies impose rules that prohibit athletes from engaging in competition at a prescribed age. Age limitations are generally accepted on the ground that governing bodies have a legitimate or reasonable interest in limiting participation by older and often stronger and more physically and mentally mature athletes. Courts do so on the ground that such participation will give the older athlete a competitive advantage. Athletes may seek a waiver of such a rule, but if the governing body refuses to grant the waiver, courts will generally defer to the association in such cases.

The *Cruz* case that follows, however, illustrates an instance in which a court was willing to intervene to permit athletic participation based on federal laws prohibiting disability discrimination. As you read the case, think of the reasons why the court declined to defer to the association.

Cruz v. Pennsylvania Interscholastic Athletic Association, Inc.
157 F. Supp. 2d 485 (E.D. Pa. 2001)

BUCKWALTER, District Judge.

[Editors' note: Luis Cruz was a 19-year-old public school special education student who was educable mentally retarded in his fourth year at Ridley High School, a recipient of federal funding. He had played several sports in his first three years at Ridley High School, including football, wrestling, and track. Because he was a student with a disability, Luis Cruz was educated in accordance with an individualized education program (IEP), pursuant to the federal Individuals with Disabilities Education Act (IDEA). As a "non-graded" student, Luis Cruz was not enrolled in a particular numerical grade. "His window of opportunity to participate in high school instruction and sports at an earlier age was limited and he did not have comparable opportunities as non-special education children, since due to his intellectual limitations he entered elementary school between ages eleven and twelve, rather than at the customary younger age, and then stayed an additional two years over the regular education students."

The defendant was the Pennsylvania Interscholastic Athletic Association, Inc. (P.I.A.A.), a Pennsylvania nonprofit membership corporation composed of most public and many private high schools in Pennsylvania, for a total of approximately 1,350 schools. A purpose of P.I.A.A. is to develop and apply rules regulating interscholastic athletic competition among its members. The P.I.A.A.'s "Age Rule" provided, "A pupil shall be ineligible for interscholastic athletic competition upon attaining the age of nineteen years, with the following exception: If the age of 19 is attained on or after July 1, the pupil shall be eligible, age-wise, to compete through that school year."

A school was required to forfeit a contest for using an ineligible coach or contestant. P.I.A.A. rules permitted students to participate in eight semesters of interscholastic sports; however, Cruz had been permitted to participate in only six semesters. The director of special education services observed that he still needed the remaining two semesters of interscholastic sports activities to interact with peers and adults, familiarize himself with demands and responsibilities, and develop interpersonal skills that would help him maintain employment after high school. Participation in these activities was vital to the development of his self-esteem and self-confidence. Although there was a provision for waiving either the eight-semester or transfer rules, with the key issue usually being "athletic intent," there was no waiver provision for the age rule. This was only the second time that the P.I.A.A. had received a request for a waiver of this rule by a student with an IEP.]

The purposes of [the age rule] are: (1) to protect high school athletes of customary age from the dangers and unfairness of participation with those who are older and thus perhaps physically larger, stronger, and more mature and experienced; (2) to limit the possibility that the team with the over-age student will gain an unfair competitive advantage over opponents; (3) to have available the maximum number of team positions for high school athletes who are of customary age for students in high school; and (4) to maintain uniformity of standards with regard to the age of participants....

[Editors' note: According to Bradley Cashman, the P.I.A.A.'s executive director, the age rule did not provide for any waivers because it would be an overly burdensome task to evaluate competitive advantage in individual cases. An assessment of whether the student would "skew the overall competitiveness of the particular activity," or whether the student would constitute a competitive advantage, would have to be looked at not only sport by sport, but individual by individual. This would be a very difficult, complex, and burdensome assessment involving many variables, including both objective and subjective elements.]

P.I.A.A. estimates that it would have to significantly increase the size of its staff, doubling or tripling it, in order to perform assessments of whether a student would "skew the overall competitiveness of the particular activity" or whether the student would constitute a competitive advantage.

Luis Cruz is not a "star" player in any of his interscholastic sports. Luis Cruz has been included in the football program for an inclusive experience. He is a marginal player and appeared in football games on a very limited basis such as a few kickoffs where the performance apparently was not critical. At the same time, the non-special education students of Ridley High School are attempting to be inclusive. They have rallied around him, as he is a "great team player."

Luis Cruz is not more experienced than other players. In fact, he is less experienced and therefore has played football only on a very limited basis. [H]e is five foot three inches tall and weighs 130 pounds. . . . [His participation therefore presents] no safety threat to others or competitive advantage in the situation presented here. Also, again, there is no "cut" policy on the football squad, so Luis Cruz is not replacing any other student who would otherwise have an opportunity to play.

Luis Cruz has "good basic skills" in wrestling, but there are "a lot of better wrestlers than him." He is not a safety risk factor, but he may have a competitive advantage based on his outstanding dual meet record.

In track, where there is also a no-cut policy, Luis Cruz is not a fast runner, does not displace other students, has no competitive advantage, and represents no safety risk. He runs a minute behind qualifying time in the mile. He has been unable to earn points in dual meets and would only place by default.

[Editors' note: The court ruled that the P.I.A.A. violated the Americans with Disabilities Act (ADA), which is discussed more fully in Chapter 8, for the following reasons.]

It is clear from the findings of fact that Luis Cruz would not fundamentally alter the nature of the competition in football and track and that the modification of the age rule is necessary for him to be able to play in interscholastic competition in those two sports. What is more difficult to assess is whether the modification is reasonable. Initially, that involves a determination as to whether the age rule is essential to the P.I.A.A. sports program. . . .

It now seems clear that a rule is essential to a program unless it can be shown that the waiver of it would not fundamentally alter the nature of the program.

This determination must be made on an individual basis. The court has looked at the specific facts applicable to Luis Cruz in reaching its conclusion stated earlier in this opinion. In doing so in this case, it is clear that Luis Cruz playing on the football team and track team would not fundamentally alter the nature of P.I.A.A. interscholastic competition.

P.I.A.A. argues that requiring it to develop a waiver system which would assess whether an over-age student would have a competitive advantage over opponents in a given sport would be unreasonable, as it would require complex fact-finding as well as extremely difficult judgments about leadership skills, motivational abilities, physical maturity, benefits of experience, quickness, agility, strength, and sport-specific abilities which are extremely difficult to measure. . . .

In light of the other waivers which the P.I.A.A., through district committees, routinely considers, namely transfer and 8 term waivers (some of which require the determination of athletic intent), and in view of the apparent ability of the P.I.A.A. to make what must be very difficult decisions in those waiver cases, I do not believe that an age waiver rule would put an undue burden on the P.I.A.A. The statistics to date suggest that there may not be many occasions for the age waiver to be requested. . . .

[Editors' note: The court issued the following order: "(1) Defendant is restrained and prohibited from application and enforcement of its by-law as to age ineligibility with respect to Luis Cruz, unless done so pursuant to a waiver rule which provides for an individual evaluation of him. (2) Thus, as to any interscholastic sports in which Luis Cruz wishes to participate, the defendant must entertain an application for waiver of its by-laws as to age ineligibility rules pursuant to procedures that it establishes. (3) Failure to adopt such waiver procedures in a timely manner as to Luis Cruz will result under this opinion in his being eligible to participate in interscholastic football and track for the 2001–2002 school year."]

QUESTIONS

1. What is the rationale for a minimum or maximum age for participation in a sport? Will older, more experienced, players necessarily have a competitive advantage? Do older players subject younger players to an increased likelihood of being injured or harmed? Should a general rule furthering such interests keep an athlete from participating if he or she does not constitute a competitive advantage or does not increase the threat of injury to other athletes?
2. Why did the association refuse to adopt a waiver provision as a part of its age limitation? Is the court's requirement that the association adopt and act on such a waiver appropriate, or is the court exceeding its authority? Should courts mandate the drafting of certain rules by a legislative body or association?

Problem 2-2

A young girl who is 13 years old has been promoted to the 12th grade because of high academic performance. She is 5'5" tall and weighs 123 pounds. She wants to participate in varsity lacrosse. Her parents are supportive and join in their daughter's belief that participation in athletics provides a student with character-building opportunities. The association has a rule that provides that students must be 14 to participate in sports that involve physical contact. The coach and the team do not want the girl to participate, fearing that she will cause them to be less aggressive in their play. As principal, you are going to meet with the young girl and her parents. What will you say as a legal and practical matter?

4. No-Pass, No-Play Rules

Eligibility rules commonly referred to as "no-pass, no-play" rules were initially promulgated in the early 1980s as state legislatures, athletic associations, and individual institutions sought to strike an appropriate balance between participation in academics and athletics. No-pass, no-play rules are designed to condition participation in extracurricular activities, including sports, on students achieving a certain academic performance. The first no-pass, no-play statute, which was enacted in Texas, provided:

> A student, other than a mentally retarded student, enrolled in a school district in this state shall be suspended from participation in any extracurricular activity sponsored or sanctioned by the school district during the grade reporting period after a grade reporting period in which the student received a grade lower than the equivalent of 70 on a scale of 100 in any academic class.

No-pass, no-play rules have been controversial as a policy matter, and questions have been raised regarding whether they achieve their ultimate objective — better academic performance. Opponents of the rules argue that they may increase the number of students who simply drop out of school because the one thing that keeps them there — participation in athletics — has been taken away. Such rules, however, are generally held to be legally acceptable unless they are being applied inappropriately.

Students deemed ineligible to participate in interscholastic sports have challenged the legality of no-pass, no-play rules on equal protection and due process grounds. Starting from the premise that participation in extracurricular activities is neither a fundamental right nor an infringement on the rights of a suspect or protected class, courts have applied a rational basis test in addressing equal protection challenges. The application of such a standard almost invariably leads them to conclude that no-pass, no-play rules are rationally related to their intended goals because they are designed to further academic objectives. Similarly, courts have rejected due process challenges to no-pass, no-play rules because a student's interest in participating in extracurricular activities is not a protected property or liberty interest.

QUESTIONS

1. Since no-pass, no-play rules are generally upheld by courts, the critical issue is whether an association should adopt such a rule and what its terms should be. These policy issues are raised at the state legislative, associational, and institutional levels. An educational institution, for example, may create more (but not less) stringent standards. As a member of a school board, would you favor increasing the required GPA from the 2.0 required by the state athletic association to a 2.25 within your school district?

2. Would it make a difference to you if your school district did a study and discovered that athletes with a 2.25 average are 25 percent more likely to graduate from high school than athletes who maintain the minimal 2.0 average?

5. Exclusion of Homeschooled Students from Athletic Participation

In two important cases, courts have addressed the issue of the eligibility of homeschooled students to participate in extracurricular sporting activities. In *Jones v. West Virginia State Board of Education*, 622 S.E.2d 289 (W.Va. 2005), plaintiffs sought to have their 11-year-old child, whom they homeschooled, try out for the Mannington Middle School wrestling team. The West Virginia Secondary School Activities Commission (WVSSAC) denied their request on the ground that only full-time students were permitted to participate in interscholastic athletics. Plaintiffs filed a complaint seeking declaratory, equitable, and injunctive relief. The trial court found in favor of plaintiffs and entered the injunction.

On appeal, the West Virginia Supreme Court addressed three issues: (1) Did the WVSSAC breach a statutory duty by not allowing homeschoolers to participate in interscholastic athletics? (2) Did the WVSSAC violate the West Virginia equal protection rights of homeschooled children by prohibiting them from participating in interscholastic athletics? (3) Did the WVSSAC breach its duty to promulgate reasonable rules and regulations by implementing a total ban on allowing homeschooled children to participate in interscholastic athletics?

The court held in favor of the WVSSAC on all three issues. With respect to the alleged breach of a statutory duty, the court held that the plain language of the relevant statute imposed an obligation on the school superintendent to provide assistance and resources to the person providing the homeschool instruction (here, the student's mother). The statute, however, did not require that resources, including interscholastic athletics, be provided to the homeschooled student himself.

The court also held that the WVSSAC did not violate plaintiffs' equal protection rights. In reaching this conclusion, the court first found that participation in interscholastic athletics is neither a fundamental nor a constitutional right under the West Virginia constitution. Consequently, any classification affecting participation in interscholastic athletics will be upheld as long as it is rationally related to a legitimate state interest. Among the several grounds offered by defendant as providing a rational basis for excluding homeschooled children, the court focused on two as offering sufficient justification: "(a) promoting academics over athletics, and (b) protecting the economic interests of the county school systems." With respect to the former, the court examined the grade requirements for participating in extracurricular activities. It found that homeschooled children are graded on different standards than public school children and that converting such grades would impose a burden on the school district. Moreover, the different grading standards would impede the ability of school officials to maintain the academic standards required for participation in interscholastic sports. The court noted that a parent could withdraw an underperforming student from the public school system and homeschool him or her to retain the student-athlete's eligibility.

As it relates to protecting the economic interests of the county school system, the court emphasized that money is apportioned to schools based on attendance in class. According to the court, requiring counties to spend limited funds to support athletic participation of homeschooled students (from whom no funds are allocated) would create a financial burden. Finally, the court held that the WVSSAC did not breach its duty to promulgate reasonable rules and regulations. Even though homeschooled students are totally banned from interscholastic athletics participation, the court held it is not arbitrary and capricious because it is rationally related to the two legitimate state purposes discussed above.

In *Reid v. Kenowa Hills Public Schools*, 680 N.W.2d (Mich. Ct. App. 2004), the court similarly resolved a homeschooled student's challenge to a rule of the Michigan High School Athletic Association (MHSAA) providing that only students enrolled in school for at least 20 hours may participate in extracurricular sports.

QUESTIONS

1. Given the growth of the homeschool movement in the United States, it is likely that this issue will be raised in both judicial and legislative arenas. Should courts require schools to permit homeschooled athletes to participate in interscholastic athletics? As a matter of policy, should homeschooled students be permitted by governing bodies to participate in athletic competition?
2. What reasons favor such a policy, and what reasons can be raised in opposition to it? Would your answer change at all if a homeschooled child desired to participate in tennis or golf, compared to one who wanted to participate in football?

NOTES

Approximately 30 states now have laws permitting homeschooled students to participate in interscholastic sports. These rules have been dubbed "Tim Tebow" laws, after Tim Tebow, who had been homeschooled, gained notoriety on the football field at the collegiate and professional levels. See *https://www.nytimes.com/2012/02/09/sports/virginia-home-schoolers-make-a-play-to-join-high-school-teams.html*.

Not surprisingly, success on the part of homeschooled students has been primarily legislative in nature, not through litigation. Given the growth of the homeschool movement in the United States, and its power in the lobbying and legislative senses, it is likely that legislative success at the state level will continue.

6. Good Conduct Rules

KEY TERMS
- Eighth Amendment (cruel and unusual punishment)
- Hearsay
- Liberty interest
- Procedural due process
- Property interest
- Substantive due process
- Temporary restraining order

Individual high schools and governing bodies generally have broad authority to discipline and impose sanctions (such as the loss of their athletic eligibility or limitations on their ability to participate) on young athletes who engage in conduct that is considered inappropriate. Good conduct rules vary, but they all prohibit a range of activities, which can include the consumption and use of drugs, tobacco, and alcohol; violations of the law; and conduct that violates community norms of appropriate behavior. Student-athletes who are punished for violating good conduct rules have asserted various legal challenges with limited success. Courts afford considerable, albeit not complete, deference to schools and governing bodies to use good conduct rules to regulate participant behavior. While courts have been very deferential as to rules regulating conduct at the school, questions have been raised regarding the nature and scope of their authority to promulgate rules governing off-campus behavior and the extent to which the association or school has legitimate interests in regulating such conduct. We have previously introduced procedural due process and related issues, but this case examines such issues in greater depth.

Brands v. Sheldon Community School
671 F. Supp. 627 (N.D. Iowa 1987)

[Editors' note: The student, a member of his school's wrestling team, amassed a nearly perfect record in four years of competition and is a defending state champion, attracting the attention of the media and college coaches. After hearing from students and others regarding allegations that the student had been involved with others in sexual intercourse with a 16-year-old student at a party in his home, the principal concluded that the student had been involved in actions detrimental to the best interests of the school district and had "committed a breach of discipline by engaging in conduct which interfered with the maintenance of school discipline and by engaging in behavior which was antagonistic to the rights of (name redacted) to attain her education." As a result of this determination, the principal declared the student to be ineligible to participate in the sectional, district, and state wrestling tournaments. The parents appealed to the superintendent, who granted the parents' request for a closed hearing before the school board. The board heard from the student and others and deliberated for several hours. At the close of those deliberations, the board made extensive findings of fact in upholding the disciplinary action taken in the case. The student sought a temporary restraining order and a preliminary injunction permitting him to participate in the state wrestling tournament. The trial court granted a temporary restraining order. The school district appealed.

The court first rejected plaintiff's Fourteenth Amendment equal protection claim because he had not "alleged that he was treated differently because of his race, ethnicity, gender, or any other suspect classification, and his interests in wrestling or receiving a college scholarship are not among the small set of rights fundamental enough to warrant separate protection under the equal protection clause." Likewise, the Eighth Amendment claim was rejected because school discipline generally does not constitute cruel and unusual punishment, with the court recognizing that the Eighth Amendment primarily deals with severe criminal punishment.]

Procedural Due Process

The majority of the plaintiff's complaints . . . are most relevant to his right to procedural due process. To consider those complaints, however, the Court must first find that the plaintiff is being deprived of liberty or property by the defendant. If not, no procedural protections were "due" to the plaintiff under the Constitution.

The Supreme Court has consistently held that the existence of a protected liberty or property interest does not depend upon the seriousness of the loss the plaintiff would suffer as a result of the government's action.

A clear majority of courts addressing this question in the context of interscholastic or intercollegiate athletics has found that athletes have no legitimate entitlement to participate. One court has stated that "a student's interest in participating in a single year of inter-scholastic athletics amounts to a mere expectation rather than a constitutionally protected claim of entitlement."

[Another] court recognized a property interest where . . . the plaintiff's "continued status as a member of the . . . football team during his last year was very important to [his] development educationally and economically in the future." . . . When scholarships are awarded at the discretion of a college coach, and such discretion has not yet been exercised, no property interest in the receipt of a scholarship can exist, and the plaintiff cannot invoke his expectation that he would earn a scholarship at the state tournament in order to claim a property interest in wrestling there.

If any property interest of the plaintiff is involved in this case, it is a property right created by the defendant's own Disciplinary Policy and Administrative Rules. When a government must follow mandatory laws or regulations which limit its discretion to make a decision in any way or for any reason, those laws or regulations can create a property right which is deprived if those regulations are not followed. However, the plaintiff was not deprived of this right because [the school followed its rules].

Even if this Court were to recognize a protected interest in participation, the Court is satisfied that the plaintiff received all process due to him. The plaintiff and his mother were notified of the charges against him and were told of opportunities for appeal.... The plaintiff was given an opportunity to explain his side of the story to the principal prior to the suspension.... He was given a five- to six-hour evidentiary hearing within ten days of the initial suspension, which was also early enough to permit the Board to reverse the administration's decision before the plaintiff would be precluded from participating in the state tournament....

As long as a decision rests upon "some evidence," due process may have been satisfied. Hearsay which has a "rational probative force" can constitute substantial evidence, which is a higher standard than "some evidence."

In this case, there appears to be little or no evidence in the hearing record directly contradicting the Board's hearsay-based finding that the plaintiff "as well as three other male youths engaged in multiple acts of sexual intercourse with a sixteen-year-old female student of the Sheldon Community School District...."

Substantive Due Process

The plaintiff can show that his right to substantive due process was denied if the Board's decision was arbitrary or capricious; or if it violated one of the substantive due process rights such as the right to privacy, which cannot be deprived no matter how much procedural protection is used.

The Court is persuaded that the Board's decision was not arbitrary or capricious. The Board's objectives were legitimate....

The Board's findings indicate that it was not merely trying to impose its moral standard upon the plaintiff; the Board found that his acts injured another student and disrupted the school. These are legitimate school board concerns. Moreover, the school has not regulated the plaintiff as a student; by revoking his eligibility without suspending or expelling him, it has regulated him as a representative of the school, and has chosen a sanction which limits his ability to represent the school without limiting his basic rights as a student. For these reasons, the Court finds that whatever right the plaintiff has to sexual privacy ... was not violated in this case, and the last possible ground for finding a likelihood that his substantive due process rights were violated is rejected.

QUESTIONS

1. Does a school district or a youth organization have a legitimate interest in regulating student-athlete behavior outside school or the playing field? What kinds of rules, if any, should be promulgated to regulate student-athlete and youth behavior outside school or competition?
2. Consistent with *Brands*, courts generally find that student-athletes do not possess a property interest in athletic participation that requires procedural due process. Notwithstanding the general rule that no such interest exists, *Brands* recognizes that student-athletes have a liberty interest in not being treated arbitrarily or capriciously.

NOTES

1. Due process challenges. One area in which due process issues often arise involve actions by disciplinary bodies to take away championships. For example, lawyers have challenged Little League International's decision to take away Jackie Robinson West's Little League 2014 United States championship on procedural, not substantive, grounds. The plaintiffs in that case do not deny that they had ineligible players on the roster. Rather, they questioned the procedures and timing of Little League International's decision.

2. A less deferential approach. In *Scott v. Oklahoma Secondary School Activities Association*, 313 P.3d 891 (Okla. 2013), the court found that the Oklahoma Secondary School Activities Association (OSSAA) had acted in an arbitrary and capricious manner in sanctioning a student-athlete without clearly indicating which rules the student-athlete had violated, particularly where those sanctions involved monetary penalties. The majority in *Scott* argued for a less deferential judicial view than has prevailed in the past:

> Competition in sports is more than a mere passing enjoyment for students. Particularly in rural areas, athletic teams are the glue which holds the community together. The college and post-college careers of student athletes often have their genesis at the secondary school level, and for some provide the only path to higher education. The OSSAA wields too much control over their future to be allowed to act in an arbitrary and capricious manner in applying its rules. It must be reasonable, it must be conscientious, and it must be fair. From now on, we trust, it will be.

It will be interesting to see whether this far less deferential approach will be followed by other jurisdictions. The Oklahoma Supreme Court's recognition of the importance of athletics to communities and student-athletes is also worthy of note and may be a step in the direction of recognizing that participation in sports is more than a mere privilege that is subject to judicial deference to association and institutional decisions that implicate student-athletes and coaches. Courts and legislative bodies may become less deferential to governing bodies. They have been very deferential under a participation in sports as a privilege model (the historic approach). Under a heightened sensitivity to participation in sports as more than a mere privilege evidenced in *Scott*, courts and legislative bodies may become more willing to intervene. Should they?

7. Grooming Rules

Courts have dealt with several cases involving grooming rules. Most cases involving the validity of personal appearance and grooming rules arose during the turbulent period of time from 1965 to 1975 in the United States. These cases often raise claims based on the constitutional right of expression, which is grounded in the First Amendment. In *Tinker v. Des Moines Independent Community Sch. Dist.*, 393 U.S. 503 (1969), a public school dress code prohibited students from wearing black armbands. Finding that the prohibition violated the students' First Amendment rights, the Supreme Court concluded:

> The school officials banned and sought to punish petitioners for a silent, passive expression of opinion, unaccompanied by any disorder or disturbance on the part of petitioners. There is here no evidence whatever of petitioners' interference, actual or nascent, with the schools' work or of collision with the rights of other students to be secure and to be let alone. Accordingly, this case does not concern speech or action that intrudes upon the work of the schools or the rights of other students.

Appearance and grooming rules have been challenged on the ground that they are arbitrary and capricious. In *Davenport v. Randolph County Bd. of Educ.*, 730 F.2d 1395 (11th Cir. 1984), two student-athletes challenged a grooming policy requiring that they be clean shaven, contending that the policy was unconstitutional because it was arbitrary and unreasonable to require 14- and 15-year-old adolescents to shave in order to participate in high school athletics. The court noted that in the high school environment, there is "a per se rule that [grooming regulations] are constitutionally valid," on the ground that grooming regulations are a reasonable means of furthering a school board's undeniable interest in teaching hygiene, instilling discipline, asserting authority, and compelling uniformity. The court acknowledged, however, that if the plaintiffs had provided evidence of a medical condition that made shaving harmful, they might not be subject to the rule.

Courts generally defer to schools regarding appropriate grooming rules. However, some courts have been less deferential. See, e.g., *Holsapple v. Woods*, 500 F.2d 49 (7th Cir. 1974) (a student's right to wear hair at any length or in any desired manner is an ingredient of personal freedom protected by the U.S. Constitution); *Gorman v. St. Raphael's Academy*, 2002 WL 31455570 (R.I. Super. Ct.) (academy's regulation of the hair of male students is arbitrary and capricious because it bears no rational relation to the legitimate mission statement of the school, nor does it in any way inhibit or enhance the learning process or order and discipline of the school). On the other hand, for a recent court decision refusing to defer in a hair-length case on the basis of gender discrimination, see *Hayden v. Greensburg Community School Corp.*, 743 F.3d 569 (7th Cir. 2014), in which the court noted: "The [plaintiffs] are entitled to judgment on their Title IX claim for the same reasons we have already discussed with respect to the equal protection claim. . . . The hair-length policy is applied only to the boys team, with no evidence concerning the content of any comparable grooming standards applied to the girls team." There was a strong dissent in the *Hayden* case that would have deferred to the school. Should courts be deferential in grooming cases? Should hair-length or related cases be subject to gender discrimination claims?

C. First and Fourth Amendment Issues

The cases in the prior sections often raised constitutional questions: procedural due process (adequate notice and a fair hearing are required when a liberty or property interest is implicated); substantive due process (infringement of a privacy or personal autonomy right or acting in an arbitrary and capricious manner); and denial of equal protection of the law (singling out an individual or identifiable group for differential treatment). Additional constitutional claims also arise out of alleged violation of First Amendment privacy, freedom of speech, and religion rights, and Fourth Amendment protections against unreasonable searches and seizures.

1. Drug Testing

KEY TERMS
- Clearly erroneous
- Privacy interest
- Search and seizure
- Suspicionless
- Warrant

Like society at large, drug use pervades all levels of athletic competition, including competition among high school athletes. The National Federation of State High School Associations does not require that high schools develop a drug-testing program for athletes. Nevertheless, some high school districts throughout the country have implemented random drug-testing programs that require students to consent to testing as a condition of being eligible to participate in interscholastic athletics. These policies vary by individual school district, with testing done for illegal recreational drugs, such as marijuana, and performance-enhancing drugs, such as anabolic steroids, the use of which is a growing problem among high school athletes.

Prior to 1995, lower federal courts were split on whether drug testing of high school athletes by public schools violates the Fourth or Fourteenth Amendment, as unreasonable searches or violations of due process, respectively.

In the following case, the United States Supreme Court considered whether suspicionless random drug testing of high school athletes is constitutional.

Vernonia Sch. Dist. 47J v. Acton
515 U.S. 646 (1995)

Justice SCALIA delivered the opinion of the Court.

[Editors' note: The Student Athlete Drug Policy adopted by School District 47J in the town of Vernonia, Oregon, authorized random urinalysis drug testing of students who participated in the district's school athletics programs. Drugs had not been a major problem in Vernonia schools. In the mid- to late-1980s, however, teachers and administrators observed a sharp increase in drug use. Students began to speak out about their attraction to the drug culture, and to boast that there was nothing the school could do about it. Along with more drugs came more disciplinary problems.

Student athletes were among the leaders of the drug culture. This caused the district's administrators particular concern since they believed that drug use increased the risk of sports-related injury. Expert testimony at the trial confirmed the deleterious effects of drugs on motivation, memory, judgment, reaction, coordination, and performance. The high school football and wrestling coach witnessed a severe sternum injury suffered by a wrestler, and various omissions of safety procedures and misexecutions by football players, all attributable in his belief to the effects of drug use.

Initially, the district responded to the drug problem by offering special classes, speakers, and presentations designed to deter drug use. However, the drug problem persisted. Ultimately, the district adopted a Student Athlete Drug Policy (Policy) at a meeting, which parents in attendance gave their unanimous approval.

The school board approved the Policy for implementation in the fall of 1989. Its expressed purpose was to prevent student athletes from using drugs, to protect their health and safety, and to provide drug users with assistance programs.

The Policy applied to all students participating in interscholastic athletics. Students wishing to play sports were required to sign a form consenting to the testing and obtain the written consent of their parents. Athletes were tested at the beginning of the season for their sport. In addition, once each week of the season, the names of the athletes were placed in a "pool" from which a student, with the supervision of two adults, blindly drew the names of 10 percent of the athletes for random testing. Those selected are notified and tested that same day, if possible. Students to be tested entered an empty locker room accompanied by an adult monitor of the same sex and provided a urine sample. After the sample was produced, it was given to the monitor, who checked it for temperature and tampering and then transferred it to a vial.

The samples were sent to an independent laboratory, which routinely tested them for amphetamines, cocaine, and marijuana. Other drugs, such as lysergic acid diethylamide (LSD), could be screened at the request of the district, but the identity of a particular student did not determine which drugs will be tested. The laboratory's procedures were 99.94 percent accurate. If a sample tested positive, a second test was administered as soon as possible to confirm the result. If the second test was negative, no further action was taken. If the second test was positive, the athlete's parents were notified, and the school principal convened a meeting with the student and his parents, at which the student was given the option of (1) participating for six weeks in an assistance program that included weekly urinalysis, or (2) suffering suspension from athletics for the remainder of the then current season and the next athletic season. The student was then retested prior to the start of the next athletic season for which he or she was eligible. The Policy stated that a second offense resulted in automatic imposition of option (2); a third offense resulted in suspension for the remainder of the then current season and the next two athletic seasons.

In the fall of 1991, respondent James Acton, then a seventh grader, signed up to play football at one of the district's grade schools. He was denied participation, however, because he and his parents refused to sign the testing consent forms. The

Actons filed suit, seeking declaratory and injunctive relief from enforcement of the Policy on the grounds that it violated the Fourth and Fourteenth Amendments to the United States Constitution and Article I, §9, of the Oregon Constitution.]

II

In [a prior case,] we held that state-compelled collection and testing of urine, such as that required by the Policy, constitutes a "search" subject to the demands of the Fourth Amendment.

As the text of the Fourth Amendment indicates, the ultimate measure of the constitutionality of a governmental search is "reasonableness." [W]hether a particular search meets the reasonableness standard "'is judged by balancing its intrusion on the individual's Fourth Amendment interests against its promotion of legitimate governmental interests.'" Where a search is undertaken by law enforcement officials to discover evidence of criminal wrongdoing, this Court has said that reasonableness generally requires the obtaining of a judicial warrant. Warrants cannot be issued, of course, without the showing of probable cause required by the Warrant Clause. But a warrant is not required to establish the reasonableness of *all* government searches; and when a warrant is not required (and the Warrant Clause therefore not applicable), probable cause is not invariably required either. A search unsupported by probable cause can be constitutional, we have said, "when special needs, beyond the normal need for law enforcement, make the warrant and probable-cause requirement impracticable."

We have found such "special needs" to exist in the public school context. There, the warrant requirement "would unduly interfere with the maintenance of the swift and informal disciplinary procedures [that are] needed," and "strict adherence to the requirement that searches be based upon probable cause" would undercut "the substantial need of teachers and administrators for freedom to maintain order in the schools." The school search we approved in [a prior case], while not based on probable cause, *was* based on individualized *suspicion* of wrongdoing. As we explicitly acknowledged, however, "'the Fourth Amendment imposes no irreducible requirement of such suspicion.'" We have upheld suspicionless searches and seizures to conduct drug testing [in some other contexts].

III

The first factor to be considered is the nature of the privacy interest upon which the search at issue intrudes. . . . Central, in our view, to the present case is the fact that the subjects of the Policy are (1) children, who (2) have been committed to the temporary custody of the State as schoolmaster. . . .

Fourth Amendment rights . . . are different in public schools than elsewhere; the "reasonableness" inquiry cannot disregard the schools' custodial and tutelary responsibility for children. For their own good and that of their classmates, public school children are routinely required to submit to various physical examinations, and to be vaccinated against various diseases. . . . Particularly with regard to medical examinations and procedures, therefore, "students within the school environment have a lesser expectation of privacy than members of the population generally."

Legitimate privacy expectations are even less with regard to student athletes. School sports are not for the bashful. They require "suiting up" before each practice or event, and showering and changing afterwards. Public school locker rooms, the usual sites for these activities, are not notable for the privacy they afford.

There is an additional respect in which school athletes have a reduced expectation of privacy. By choosing to "go out for the team," they voluntarily subject themselves to a degree of regulation even higher than that imposed on students generally. In Vernonia's public schools, they must submit to a preseason physical exam, they must acquire adequate insurance coverage or sign an insurance waiver, maintain a minimum grade point average, and comply with any "rules of conduct, dress, training hours and related matters as may be established for each sport by the head coach and athletic director with the principal's approval." [S]tudents who voluntarily participate in school athletics have reason to expect intrusions upon normal rights and privileges, including privacy.

IV

Having considered the scope of the legitimate expectation of privacy at issue here, we turn next to the character of the intrusion that is complained of. . . . Under the District's Policy, male students produce samples at a urinal along a wall. They remain fully clothed and are only observed from behind, if at all. Female students produce samples in an enclosed stall, with a female monitor standing outside listening only for sounds of tampering. These conditions are nearly identical to those typically encountered in public restrooms, which men, women, and especially schoolchildren use daily. Under such conditions, the privacy interests compromised by the process of obtaining the urine sample are in our view negligible.

The other privacy-invasive aspect of urinalysis is, of course, the information it discloses concerning the state of the subject's body, and the materials he has ingested. In this regard it is significant that the tests at issue here look only for drugs, and not for whether the student is, for example, epileptic, pregnant, or diabetic. Moreover, the drugs for which the samples are screened are standard, and do not vary according to the identity of the student. And finally, the results of the tests are disclosed only to a limited class of school personnel who have a need to know; and they are not turned over to law enforcement authorities or used for any internal disciplinary function.

V

Finally, we turn to consider the nature and immediacy of the governmental concern at issue here, and the efficacy of this means for meeting it. . . .

That the nature of the concern is important — indeed, perhaps compelling — can hardly be doubted. Deterring drug use by our Nation's schoolchildren is at least as important as enhancing efficient enforcement of the Nation's laws against the importation of drugs, or deterring drug use by engineers and trainmen [two prior cases in which drug testing was found to be constitutional]. School years are the time when the physical, psychological, and addictive effects of drugs are most severe. . . . And of course the effects of a drug-infested school are visited not just upon the users, but upon the entire student body and faculty, as the educational process is disrupted. . . . Finally, it must not be lost sight of that this program is directed more narrowly to drug use by school athletes, where the risk of immediate physical harm to the drug user or those with whom he is playing his sport is particularly high. Apart from psychological effects, which include impairment of judgment, slow reaction time, and a lessening of the perception of pain, the particular drugs screened by the District's Policy have been demonstrated to pose substantial physical risks to athletes. . . .

We are not inclined to question — indeed, we could not possibly find clearly erroneous — the District Court's conclusion that "a large segment of the student body, particularly those involved in interscholastic athletics, was in a state of rebellion," that "[d]isciplinary actions had reached 'epidemic proportions,'" and that "the rebellion was being fueled by alcohol and drug abuse as well as by the student's misperceptions about the drug culture." . . .

VI

Taking into account all the factors we have considered above — the decreased expectation of privacy, the relative unobtrusiveness of the search, and the severity of the need met by the search — we conclude Vernonia's Policy is reasonable and hence constitutional.

We caution against the assumption that suspicionless drug testing will readily pass constitutional muster in other contexts. The most significant element in this case is the first we discussed: that the Policy was undertaken in furtherance of the government's responsibilities, under a public school system, as guardian and tutor of children entrusted to its care. . . .

Justice O'CONNOR, with whom Justice STEVENS and Justice SOUTER join, dissenting.

The population of our Nation's public schools, grades 7 through 12, numbers around 18 million. By the reasoning of today's decision, the millions of these students who participate in interscholastic sports, an overwhelming majority of whom have given school officials no reason whatsoever to suspect they use drugs at school, are open to an intrusive bodily search. . . . I find unreasonable the school's choice of student athletes as the class to subject to suspicionless testing — a choice that appears to have been driven more by a belief in what would pass constitutional muster (indicating that the original program was targeted at students involved in any extracurricular activity) than by a belief in what was required to meet the District's principal disciplinary concern. . . . [I]t seems quite obvious that the true driving force behind the District's adoption of its drug testing program was the need to combat the rise in drug-related disorder and disruption in its classrooms and around campus. I mean no criticism of the strength of that interest. On the contrary, where the record demonstrates the existence of such a problem, that interest seems self-evidently compelling. . . . And the record in this case surely demonstrates there was a drug-related discipline problem in Vernonia of "'epidemic proportions.'" The evidence of a drug-related sports injury problem at Vernonia, by contrast, was considerably weaker. . . .

Having reviewed the record here, I cannot avoid the conclusion that the District's suspicionless policy of testing all student athletes sweeps too broadly, and too imprecisely, to be reasonable under the Fourth Amendment.

QUESTIONS

1. Why does the *Acton* majority uphold suspicionless testing of high school athletes for recreational drug use?
2. Would suspicion-based drug testing accomplish high school administrators' legitimate objectives equally well without intruding on students' privacy rights? Should student-athletes be singled out?
3. School districts may not be required to have drug testing policies in place for students, athletes, or others. However, they may be permitted to do so under the circumstances outlined in the *Acton* case. As a policy matter, would you support such a policy? What kinds of facts might persuade you that such a policy is necessary? How would you fix the drug testing policy presented in *Acton* based on the decision in the case?

NOTES

1. **Acton extended.** In *Board of Education of Indep. Sch. Dist. No. 92 of Pottawatomie County v. Earls*, 536 U.S. 822 (2002), the Supreme Court upheld the constitutionality of mandatory suspicionless drug testing of all students participating in high school extracurricular activities. The only consequence of a positive test for illegal drugs was to limit the student's privilege of participating in extracurricular activities; it did not result in the imposition of any other discipline or have any academic consequences. If the suspicionless search resulted in discipline in the form of suspension or expulsion from school, do you think the Court would have found in favor of the students?

2. **State constitutions.** Although the Court approves mandatory drug testing for students desiring to participate in extracurricular activities under the Fourth Amendment of the U.S. Constitution, such policies may still face challenges under state constitutional provisions. In *York v. Wahkiakum*, 178 P.3d 995 (Wash. 2008), the Washington Supreme Court considered the constitutionality of a school district's blanket suspicionless random drug testing program for student-athletes. Although the court acknowledged that the district's drug testing policy did not violate the Fourth Amendment of the U.S. Constitution, it concluded that the Washington state constitution provided a higher level of protection. It held that the district's drug testing policy violated a provision of the state

constitution that provides, "No person shall be disturbed in his private affairs, or his home invaded, without authority of law." Other state courts have refused to interpret their state constitutions more broadly and have upheld suspicionless searches.

2. Freedom of Speech and Association

KEY TERMS
- Freedom of speech
- *In loco parentis*
- Retaliation

Previously, in discussing grooming rules, we introduced the concept of freedom of expression. In those cases, we noted that the courts often defer to athletic associations and schools even though First Amendment rights are implicated. In the following materials, we explore this concept in greater depth.

The First Amendment of the United States Constitution, together with many similar provisions in state constitutions, protects against government limitations of the right to speak (freedom of expression), to assemble (freedom to associate), and to share information through print and other media (freedom of the press). In the following case, the Supreme Court considers whether a student's free speech rights were violated when she was disciplined by the school for using vulgar language and gestures in a Snapchat post criticizing the school and the school's cheerleading team.

MAHANOY AREA SCH. DIST. v. B. L.
141 S. CT. 2038 (2021)

Justice BREYER delivered the opinion of the Court.

A public high school student used, and transmitted to her Snapchat friends, vulgar language and gestures criticizing both the school and the school's cheerleading team. The student's speech took place outside of school hours and away from the school's campus. In response, the school suspended the student for a year from the cheerleading team. We must decide whether the Court of Appeals for the Third Circuit correctly held that the school's decision violated the First Amendment. Although we do not agree with the reasoning of the Third Circuit panel's majority, we do agree with its conclusion that the school's disciplinary action violated the First Amendment.

B. L. (who, together with her parents, is a respondent in this case) was a student at Mahanoy Area High School, a public school in Mahanoy City, Pennsylvania. At the end of her freshman year, B. L. tried out for a position on the school's varsity cheerleading squad and for right fielder on a private softball team. She did not make the varsity cheerleading team or get her preferred softball position, but she was offered a spot on the cheerleading squad's junior varsity team. B. L. did not accept the coach's decision with good grace, particularly because the squad coaches had placed an entering freshman on the varsity team.

That weekend, B. L. and a friend visited the Cocoa Hut, a local convenience store. There, B. L. used her smartphone to post two photos on Snapchat, a social media application that allows users to post photos and videos that disappear after a set period of time. B. L. posted the images to her Snapchat "story," a feature of the application that allows any person in the user's "friend" group (B. L. had about 250 "friends") to view the images for a 24 hour period.

The first image B. L. posted showed B. L. and a friend with middle fingers raised; it bore the caption: "Fuck school fuck softball fuck cheer fuck everything." The second image was blank but for a caption, which read: "Love how me and [another student] get told we need a year of jv before we make varsity but tha[t] doesn't matter to anyone else?" The caption also contained an upside-down smiley-face emoji.

B. L.'s Snapchat "friends" included other Mahanoy Area High School students, some of whom also belonged to the cheerleading squad. At least one of them, using a separate cellphone, took pictures of B. L.'s posts and shared them with other members of the cheerleading squad. One of the students who received these photos showed them to her mother (who was a cheerleading squad coach), and the images spread. That week, several cheerleaders and other students approached the cheerleading coaches "visibly upset" about B. L.'s posts. Questions about the posts persisted during an Algebra class taught by one of the two coaches.

After discussing the matter with the school principal, the coaches decided that because the posts used profanity in connection with a school extracurricular activity, they violated team and school rules. As a result, the coaches suspended B. L. from the junior varsity cheerleading squad for the upcoming year. B. L.'s subsequent apologies did not move school officials. The school's athletic director, principal, superintendent, and school board, all affirmed B. L.'s suspension from the team. In response, B. L., together with her parents, filed this lawsuit in Federal District Court.

B

The District Court found in B. L.'s favor. It first granted a temporary restraining order and a preliminary injunction ordering the school to reinstate B. L. to the cheerleading team. In granting B. L.'s subsequent motion for summary judgment, the District Court found that B. L.'s Snapchats had not caused substantial disruption at the school. Consequently, the District Court declared that B. L.'s punishment violated the First Amendment, and it awarded B. L. nominal damages and attorneys' fees and ordered the school to expunge her disciplinary record.

On appeal, a panel of the Third Circuit affirmed the District Court's conclusion. In so doing, the majority noted that this Court had previously held in *Tinker* that a public high school could not constitutionally prohibit a peaceful student political demonstration consisting of "pure speech" on school property during the school day. 393 U. S., at 505-506. In reaching its conclusion in *Tinker*, this Court emphasized that there was no evidence the student protest would "substantially interfere with the work of the school or impinge upon the rights of other students." But the Court also said that: "[C]onduct by [a] student, in class or out of it, which for any reason — whether it stems from time, place, or type of behavior — materially disrupts classwork or involves substantial disorder or invasion of the rights of others is . . . not immunized by the constitutional guarantee of freedom of speech."

Many courts have taken this statement as setting a standard — a standard that allows schools considerable freedom on campus to discipline students for conduct that the First Amendment might otherwise protect. But here, the panel majority held that this additional freedom did "not apply to off-campus speech," which it defined as "speech that is outside school-owned, -operated, or -supervised channels and that is not reasonably interpreted as bearing the school's imprimatur." Because B. L.'s speech took place off campus, the panel concluded that the *Tinker* standard did not apply and the school consequently could not discipline B. L. for engaging in a form of pure speech.

A concurring member of the panel agreed with the majority's result but wrote that the school had not sufficiently justified disciplining B. L. because, whether the *Tinker* standard did or did not apply, B. L.'s speech was not substantially disruptive.

C

The school district filed a petition for certiorari in this Court, asking us to decide "[w]hether [*Tinker*], which holds that public school officials may regulate speech that would materially and substantially disrupt the work and discipline of the school, applies to student speech that occurs off campus." We granted the petition.

II

We have made clear that students do not "shed their constitutional rights to freedom of speech or expression," even "at the school house gate." . . . But we have also made clear that courts must apply the First Amendment "in light of the special characteristics of the school environment." *Hazelwood School Dist. v. Kuhlmeier*, 484 U. S. 260 (1988). One such characteristic, which we have stressed, is the fact that schools at times stand in loco parentis, i.e., in the place of parents. See *Bethel School Dist. No. 403 v. Fraser*, 478 U. S. 675 (1986).

This Court has previously outlined three specific categories of student speech that schools may regulate in certain circumstances: (1) "indecent," "lewd," or "vulgar" speech uttered during a school assembly on school grounds (2) speech, uttered during a class trip, that promotes "illegal drug use," and (3) speech that others may reasonably perceive as "bear[ing] the imprimatur of the school," such as that appearing in a school-sponsored newspaper.

Finally, in *Tinker*, we said schools have a special interest in regulating speech that "materially disrupts classwork or involves substantial disorder or invasion of the rights of others." These special characteristics call for special leeway when schools regulate speech that occurs under its supervision.

Unlike the Third Circuit, we do not believe the special characteristics that give schools additional license to regulate student speech always disappear when a school regulates speech that takes place off campus. The school's regulatory interests remain significant in some off-campus circumstances. The parties' briefs, and those of amici, list several types of off-campus behavior that may call for school regulation. These include serious or severe bullying or harassment targeting particular individuals; threats aimed at teachers or other students; the failure to follow rules concerning lessons, the writing of papers, the use of computers, or participation in other online school activities; and breaches of school security devices, including material maintained within school computers.

Even B. L. herself and the amici supporting her would redefine the Third Circuit's off-campus/on-campus distinction, treating as on campus: all times when the school is responsible for the student; the school's immediate surroundings; travel en route to and from the school; all speech taking place over school laptops or on a school's website; speech taking place during remote learning; activities taken for school credit; and communications to school e-mail accounts or phones. And it may be that speech related to extracurricular activities, such as team sports, would also receive special treatment under B. L.'s proposed rule.

We are uncertain as to the length or content of any such list of appropriate exceptions or carveouts to the Third Circuit majority's rule. That rule, basically, if not entirely, would deny the off-campus applicability of *Tinker*'s highly general statement about the nature of a school's special interests. Particularly given the advent of computer-based learning, we hesitate to determine precisely which of many school-related off-campus activities belong on such a list. Neither do we now know how such a list might vary, depending upon a student's age, the nature of the school's off-campus activity, or the impact upon the school itself. Thus, we do not now set forth a broad, highly general First Amendment rule stating just what counts as "off campus" speech and whether or how ordinary First Amendment standards must give way off campus to a school's special need to prevent, e.g., substantial disruption of learning-related activities or the protection of those who make up a school community.

We can, however, mention three features of off-campus speech that often, even if not always, distinguish schools' efforts to regulate that speech from their efforts to regulate on-campus speech. Those features diminish the strength of the unique educational characteristics that might call for special First Amendment leeway.

First, a school, in relation to off-campus speech, will rarely stand in loco parentis. The doctrine of in loco parentis treats school administrators as standing in the place of students' parents under circumstances where the children's actual parents cannot protect, guide, and discipline them. Geographically speaking, off-campus speech will normally fall within the zone of parental, rather than school-related, responsibility.

Second, from the student speaker's perspective, regulations of off-campus speech, when coupled with regulations of on-campus speech, include all the speech a student utters during the full 24-hour day. That means courts must be more skeptical of a school's efforts to regulate off-campus speech, for doing so may mean the student cannot engage in that kind of speech at all. When it comes to political or religious speech that occurs outside school or a school program or activity, the school will have a heavy burden to justify intervention.

Third, the school itself has an interest in protecting a student's unpopular expression, especially when the expression takes place off campus. America's public schools are the nurseries of democracy. Our representative democracy only works if we protect the "marketplace of ideas." This free exchange facilitates an informed public opinion, which, when transmitted to lawmakers, helps produce laws that reflect the People's will. That protection must include the protection of unpopular ideas, for popular ideas have less need for protection. Thus, schools have a strong interest in ensuring that future generations understand the workings in practice of the well-known aphorism, "I disapprove of what you say, but I will defend to the death your right to say it." (Although this quote is often attributed to Voltaire, it was likely coined by an English writer, Evelyn Beatrice Hall.)

. . . Taken together, these three features of much off-campus speech mean that the leeway the First Amendment grants to schools in light of their special characteristics is diminished. We leave for future cases to decide where, when, and how these features mean the speaker's off-campus location will make the critical difference. This case can, however, provide one example.

III

Consider B. L.'s speech. Putting aside the vulgar language, the listener would hear criticism, of the team, the team's coaches, and the school — in a word or two, criticism of the rules of a community of which B. L. forms a part. This criticism did not involve features that would place it outside the First Amendment's ordinary protection. B. L.'s posts, while crude, did not amount to fighting words. And while B. L. used vulgarity, her speech was not obscene as this Court has understood that term. To the contrary, B. L. uttered the kind of pure speech to which, were she an adult, the First Amendment would provide strong protection. (First Amendment protects "even hurtful speech on public issues to ensure that we do not stifle public debate". . . . The inappropriate . . . character of a statement is irrelevant to the question whether it deals with a matter of public concern").

Consider too when, where, and how B. L. spoke. Her posts appeared outside of school hours from a location outside the school. She did not identify the school in her posts or target any member of the school community with vulgar or abusive language. B. L. also transmitted her speech through a personal cellphone, to an audience consisting of her private circle of Snapchat friends. These features of her speech, while risking transmission to the school itself, nonetheless . . . diminish the school's interest in punishing B. L.'s utterance.

But what about the school's interest, here primarily an interest in prohibiting students from using vulgar language to criticize a school team or its coaches — at least when that criticism might well be transmitted to other students, team members, coaches, and faculty? We can break that general interest into three parts.

First, we consider the school's interest in teaching good manners and consequently in punishing the use of vulgar language aimed at part of the school community. . . .

B. L. spoke under circumstances where the school did not stand in loco parentis. And there is no reason to believe B. L.'s parents had delegated to school officials their own control of B. L.'s behavior at the Cocoa Hut. Moreover, the vulgarity in B. L.'s posts encompassed a message, an expression of B. L.'s irritation with, and criticism of, the school and cheerleading communities. Further, the school has presented no evidence of any general effort to prevent students from using vulgarity outside the classroom. Together, these facts convince us that the school's interest in teaching good manners is not sufficient, in this case, to overcome B. L.'s interest in free expression.

Second, the school argues that it was trying to prevent disruption, if not within the classroom, then within the bounds of a school-sponsored extracurricular activity. But we can find no evidence in the record of the sort of "substantial disruption" of a school activity or a threatened harm to the rights of others that might justify the school's action. Rather, the record shows that discussion of the matter took, at most, 5 to 10 minutes of an Algebra class "for just a couple of days" and that some members of the cheerleading team were "upset" about the content of B. L.'s Snapchats. But when one of B. L.'s coaches was asked directly if she had "any reason to think that this particular incident would disrupt class or school activities other than the fact that kids kept asking . . . about it," she responded simply, "No." As we said in *Tinker*, "for the State in the person of school officials to justify prohibition of a particular expression of opinion, it must be able to show that its action was caused by something more than a mere desire to avoid the discomfort and unpleasantness that always accompany an unpopular viewpoint." The alleged disturbance here does not meet *Tinker*'s demanding standard.

Third, the school presented some evidence that expresses (at least indirectly) a concern for team morale. One of the coaches testified that the school decided to suspend B. L., not because of any specific negative impact upon a particular member of the school community, but "based on the fact that there was negativity put out there that could impact students in the school." There is little else, however, that suggests any serious decline in team morale — to the point where it could create a substantial interference in, or disruption of, the school's efforts to maintain team cohesion. As we have previously said, simple "undifferentiated fear or apprehension . . . is not enough to overcome the right to freedom of expression."

It might be tempting to dismiss B. L.'s words as unworthy of the robust First Amendment protections discussed herein. But sometimes it is necessary to protect the superfluous in order to preserve the necessary. . . . "We cannot lose sight of the fact that, in what otherwise might seem a trifling and annoying instance of individual distasteful abuse of a privilege, these fundamental societal values are truly implicated." *Cohen*, 403 U. S., at 25.

• • • • • • • • •

Although we do not agree with the reasoning of the Third Circuit's panel majority, for the reasons expressed above, resembling those of the panel's concurring opinion, we nonetheless agree that the school violated B. L.'s First Amendment rights. The judgment of the Third Circuit is therefore affirmed.

It is so ordered.

In a concurring opinion, Justice Alito deviated from the majority by taking a stronger stance on the limitations of school authority to discipline off-campus speech; if students are neither on campus nor participating in a school activity, the school should not limit their speech. Justice Thomas completely disagreed in his dissent. According to Thomas, the *Tinker* precedent gives schools the authority to regulate speech that is connected to the management or successful operation of the school. As speech that degrades the school program and staff "in front of" other students, the school is justified in disciplining that behavior. The dissent emphasizes the location where the speech is made is not as important as who the speech impacts. In this vein, Justice Thomas scolds the Court for not addressing whether social media communication is on-campus speech if the message is received on campus.

NOTES AND QUESTIONS

1. Matters of public concern. The First Amendment generally protects speech that is a *matter of public concern*, while speech that is of a personal nature is not protected. In what ways was B. L.'s Snapchat post a matter of public concern?

2. Student's Free Speech Rights Not Infringed. In *Wildman v. Marshalltown Sch. Dist.*, 249 F.3d 768 (8th Cir. 2001), a basketball player wrote a letter to her teammates complaining about the coaches' roster choices (Wildman did not make the varsity team) and asked for the team's support to "do something about this." The coaches were informed of the letter by parents of girls on the team and met with the athletic director and the school principal to discuss how to manage the matter. The coaches then met with Wildman, told her the letter was disrespectful, and demanded she apologize to her teammates. Wildman refused to apologize and sat out the remainder of the season. She filed a lawsuit claiming the school violated the Free Speech Clause by conditioning her continued participation on writing a letter of apology to her teammates. The Eighth Circuit affirmed the district court's dismissal of Wildman's case by granting summary judgment to the school. Consider whether the *Wildman* case could or should be decided differently given the precedent established in *Mahanoy*.

3. National Anthem Protests. The national anthem protests inspired by Colin Kaepernick in 2016 have been imitated by high school athletes across the country. Community backlash (often through social media) can be harsh, and school administrators are in the difficult position of choosing to support students' free speech rights versus sanctioning the players based on the *Tinker* disruption standard. Some schools have exercised the "teachable moment" approach to discuss the free exchange of ideas embodied in the First Amendment. Others have banned student-athletes from kneeling during the anthem and suspended them for their protest. If you were the general counsel for the school district, what would you recommend to school administrators? Is a one-rule-fits-all approach legally defensible or does the administration have to consider the totality of the circumstances to avoid legal liability based on *Acton, supra*?

3. Freedom of Religion

The First Amendment of the U.S. Constitution and similar amendments in many state constitutions mandate that government or state actors "make no laws respecting an establishment of religion" or "prohibiting the free exercise [of religion]." Laws respecting an establishment of religion are prohibited because government should not establish or prefer one religion over another. Free exercise, in turn, recognizes that the right of individuals to freely exercise their religious conscience is a right that should be protected against state action. Free exercise and establishment issues may arise in the context of interscholastic sports under either federal or state constitutions. For example, religious students may argue that being scheduled to participate in athletics on a religious holiday or day of worship recognized in their religious faith violates their right to freely exercise their religion. Athletic associations and others, in turn, may argue that scheduling athletic events to accommodate religious concerns does not violate a student's right to freely exercise her religion because the student does not have to participate. Associations also argue that accommodating a religious student, by changing their schedule, may constitute an establishment of religion—a preference for one religion over another. The wearing of yarmulkes, crosses, or other religious symbols in competition has also raised free exercise issues and establishment issues. Students argue that their faith requires that they wear the symbol, but associations argue that the wearing of such religious symbols may increase the likelihood of injury or may give the appearance that the association or institution is endorsing that religious exercise. Another way in which religious liberty issues often arise is when students desire to pray in a public context.

a. Free Exercise Issues

In *Menora v. Illinois High School Ass'n*, 683 F.2d 152 (5th Cir. 1980), the court upheld a rule that forbade student-athletes from wearing hats or other headwear (with the sole exception of a headband no wider than two inches) while playing basketball against a claim that this rule infringed on the religious freedom of Orthodox Jews who sought to wear yarmulkes during play. Despite dealing with a serious free exercise claim, the court accepted the association's assertion that the rule preserved the safety of players by ensuring that a player would not trip over a yarmulke that had fallen from a player's head.

In *Walsh v. Louisiana High School Athletic Association*, 616 F.2d 152 (5th Cir. 1980), the court upheld a transfer rule against a claim that it burdened a student's free exercise of religion rights. The parents sought to have their children educated in Lutheran schools, as a matter of faith, and argued that the transfer rule prohibiting their children from participating for a period of time in interscholastic athletics infringed their free exercise rights. The court found that the burden on free exercise was minimal and held that it did not constitute a legally cognizable infringement because the transfer provision was religiously neutral, generally applicable, and did not distinguish between private and parochial schools.

Prior to *Employment Division v. Smith*, 494 U.S. 872 (1990), in which Justice Scalia, writing for a majority of the Supreme Court, rejected the strict scrutiny (compelling interest) test that the Court had previously used to deal with religious liberty cases and held that neutral laws of general applicability—laws that do not intentionally discriminate against religion or religious exercise—are not subject to free exercise limitations under the free exercise clause of the First Amendment of the U.S. Constitution. It should be noted, however, that statutory or regulatory accommodations of religious exercise are permissible. Athletic associations may create rules that accommodate the free exercise of religion. It is clear, for example, that associations may permit school transfers on religious grounds. Indeed, that is one of the lessons of *Employment Division v. Smith*—such matters are largely left to the democratic or regulatory process at the state and federal levels. Furthermore, a student may argue for a religious accommodation or exemption under a state constitutional right of free exercise provision, which may be interpreted to provide broader rights than similar provisions under the U.S. Constitution.

More than 20 states have reacted negatively to Justice Scalia's weakening of the free exercise test and have passed state statutes that are designed to ensure that religious exercise receives a higher level of protection or scrutiny. In those states, or in states in which the state constitution is interpreted to provide more protection for religious exercise, it is more likely that free exercise of religion on the part of students will be protected.

QUESTIONS

1. The First Amendment offers no protection to parents, student-athletes, or coaches unless they can establish they are actually being discriminated against on religious grounds or can persuade a regulatory or legislative body to provide them with an accommodation. Do you agree with the judicial precedent making it very difficult to successfully assert the infringement of a religious liberty right in this context?
2. Given that a plaintiff has to establish that he or she has actually been discriminated against on religious grounds to prevail in a free exercise case, what kind of proof might be presented to establish such a claim?
3. It is very difficult to prove religious discrimination because people seldom acknowledge that they have discriminated. Should the burden be on the plaintiff to prove discrimination?

Problem 2-3

A coach at a high school removed a student-athlete from his team for insubordination because the student had asked her teammates to join with her after the game in a prayer. Every member of the team attended, and the girl

> prayed for the team and also prayed that "coach will be blessed to be able to do a better job of coaching us as a team." The student and her parents are meeting with you, as the school superintendent, and have asked you to reinstate her on the team. What would you do?

b. Establishment Clause Issues

The Establishment Clause prohibits state actors from engaging in activities that have the effect of establishing a religion or endorsing a religion. One issue that regularly arises is the question of whether prayers may be offered prior to, or as a part of, interscholastic athletic events sponsored by public schools. The recent Supreme Court decision in *Kennedy v. Bremerton Sch. Dist.*, 142 S. Ct. 2407 (2022) held that a public high school football coach who displayed a "quiet, private prayer" in the middle of the field after the football game had concluded was engaged in private speech. The act as described by the Court was not a violation of the Establishment Clause as the postgame period was a time when coaches were free to attend briefly to personal matters and students were engaged in other activities; therefore, the Court found that prayers were not offered while Kennedy was acting within the scope of his duties as a coach.

The *Kennedy v. Bremerton Sch. Dist.* decision is significant, as the majority discarded the use of the *Lemon* test in determining whether there is a violation of the Establishment Clause, instead favoring the "reference to historical practices and understandings" approach used by the Court in *Town of Greece v. Galloway*, 572 U.S. 565 (2014). While the majority opinion stressed that the circumstances in this case did not involve a coach leading the team in prayer, the dissenting opinion by Justice Sotomayor provided photographic evidence that the coach was not only leading his team, but also the opposing team, in a large group prayer at midfield immediately after the game. The majority's definition of the coach's act as a "quiet private prayer" and the elimination of the Lemon test may indicate a broadening of free speech and free exercise rights and a limitation on the Establishment Clause.

Previously, in *Santa Fe Independent Sch. Dist. v. Doe*, 530 U.S. 290 (2000), the Supreme Court held that a high school's policy permitting student-led prayer at football games was unconstitutional. Writing for the majority, Justice Stevens held that pregame prayers delivered "on school property, at school-sponsored events, over the school's public address system, by a speaker representing the student body, under the supervision of school faculty, and pursuant to a school policy that explicitly and implicitly encourages public prayer" are public speech and therefore prohibited. Justice Stevens and the majority applied an objective test and found that students in the district "will unquestionably perceive the inevitable pregame prayer as stamped with her school's seal of approval." Chief Justice Rehnquist, joined by Justices Scalia and Thomas, believed the Court was acting prematurely because the policy had not been put into practice. The dissenters were not convinced that speech (a prayer) under the policy would necessarily violate the Establishment

Clause because the speaker would be a private individual (not a public official), and the prayer, therefore, would be private rather than school-sponsored speech. It is unclear whether or how the recent decision in *Kennedy v. Bremerton Sch. Dist.* impacts the clear direction provided by the Court in *Sante Fe*.

NOTES AND QUESTIONS

1. The majority in the *Santa Fe* case indicated that religious activities may still occur in the interscholastic athletics context if a public school's or state high school's athletics association (determined to be a state actor) is not viewed as sponsoring or endorsing the religious activity. What activities might be appropriate? If the captain of a public high school team led his team in prayer without the participation or knowledge of the coach, would that be permissible? What if an athlete were injured and his teammates spontaneously knelt in prayer around him? If a school's mascot is the crusaders or the saints, should the school be prohibited from using that name on establishment grounds?

2. Cases involving prayer by high school student-athletes and coaches often raise free speech, free exercise, and establishment clause issues. Students often argue, for example, that they have a (free exercise and speech) right to pray. When students make such an argument, however, the offering of such prayers often raise establishment clause issues because the prayers appear to be endorsed, preferred, or supported by public schools or officials. How should the tension between the student's free exercise and expression rights be balanced with a public school's need to avoid establishing a religion?

    In *Matthews v. Kountze Independent Sch. Dist.*, 2017 Tex. App. LEXIS 9165, the Texas Court of Appeals held that high school cheerleaders who displayed religious messages on run-through banners at football games were exercising private speech rights. Although the cheerleaders were part of a school-sponsored organization and the run-through banners were prominently displayed on the football field just before the start of the game, the court held the banners were not school-sponsored speech that violated the Establishment Clause. Are these cases consistent with *Bremerton* or *Santa Fe*, and can they be reconciled based on these precedents?

Problem 2-4

A coach at a public high school has been bringing players together regularly for a prayer before practice and competition. Does the coach's act violate the Establishment Clause? Given that it is likely that the coach's action violates the Establishment Clause, are there other possible ways in which religious interests of coaches and players can or should be accommodated or recognized in the public interscholastic context? For example, could the coach have the students pause for a moment of silence?

D. Review of Game Results

With the increasing use of instant replay to confirm or overrule on-the-field decisions by referees, judicial reconsideration of on-the-field decisions by referees where instant replay is not in use may become more common. While it is likely that courts will continue to be deferential to state athletic associations and governing bodies in their handling of such incidents, cases of this sort raise interesting legal and moral issues, as evidenced by a recent case in Oklahoma. With 64 seconds remaining in the Oklahoma playoff game in November 2014, Douglass High School took a 25–20 lead over Locust Grove. The receiver for Douglass High caught a short pass and ran more than 50 yards to the end zone. Video depicted a Douglass coach running excitedly along the sideline, appearing to unintentionally bump one of the referees. The referee threw a flag and invalidated the touchdown. Under association rules, however, the violation is minor, calling for a 5-yard penalty to be assessed on the extra-point attempt or the ensuing kickoff. Locust Grove went on to win the game.

The Oklahoma Secondary School Activities Association later apologized to Douglass High, labeling the referees' mistake "inexcusable." Nevertheless, the association found that state and national bylaws do not permit protesting the outcome of a game because of an official's error on the field. Oklahoma City public school officials disagreed and sought judicial relief to have some of, or all the game replayed. Questions of racism were also raised by fans from Douglass High, an inner-city school with a team made up predominantly of players of color.

Judge Bernard M. Jones II, serving on the District Court in Oklahoma City, initially issued a temporary restraining order prohibiting Locust Grove from playing its scheduled semifinal playoff game. The Oklahoma City school district supported Douglass High, arguing that fairness justified overruling a correctable mistake. Brandon Carey, general counsel for Oklahoma City public schools, argued that the Douglass case was unique because the district was not questioning the judgment of the referee; rather, it was seeking relief in an instance in which the referee made a mistake based on his misunderstanding of the penalty prescribed by the rule. Judge Jones ultimately denied the district's request to have all, or part of, an Oklahoma high school football playoff game replayed after a critical mistake by the referees negated a late touchdown. Judge Jones noted that he was aware of no precedent allowing a court to order the replay of a high school football game, and he expressed concern that there was no way to ensure that a replay would be fair to both teams because the conditions of the disputed contest could not be replicated. The judge expressed concern that a "slippery slope of solving athletic contests in court instead of on campus will inevitably usher in a new era of robed referees and meritless litigation due to disagreement with or disdain for decisions of gaming officials." Judge Jones added that the referees' error "could be considered by many as a tragedy," but deferred to the association given that both teams agreed to be bound by the rules of the state high school activities association. School officials declined to appeal the decision. See Cliff Brunt, Oklahoma Judge Says Disputed High School Game Won't Be Replayed, Associated Press, https://www.kansas.com/sports/article4422819.html.

QUESTIONS

1. Does fairness dictate that the game be replayed?
2. If the court intervened, does the case involve a slippery slope that would lead to inappropriate litigation and judicial oversight of referees' decisions or is the district right in asserting that this is a unique case that warrants judicial intervention? Can you conceive of an instance in which the court should intervene? If the referee acted out of racial bias, as some have argued, should his erroneous call be overruled by the association, the court, or Locust Grove? How would one prove racial bias?
3. Did the high school association make the right decision?
4. Should Locust Grove have agreed to replay the game or permit Douglass High to play in the state championship, in the interest of teaching the athletes a lesson in good sportsmanship? If you represented Locust Grove or its school district, what would you do? How would you communicate your decision to the athletes and the student body as a whole?

E. Health and Safety Issues in Youth and Interscholastic Sports

Unlike state high school athletic associations, most youth governing bodies are not state actors and do not have to provide constitutional protections to their participants. The exception would be youth recreational bodies that are public in nature. Therefore, courts generally are even more deferential to the decisions of private governing bodies, like Pop Warner, USA Football, AYSO, and the AAU, than they are to public governing bodies, like many high school athletic associations. Nevertheless, courts and legislative bodies do oversee some activities of youth athletic governing bodies. In particular, they get involved in health and safety issues. Indeed, courts have long held private entities responsible for torts or personal injuries that they caused through negligence or otherwise. Sports personal injury law is discussed in detail in Chapters 7 and 8.

As more attention has been directed to health and safety issues — particularly serious head injuries at all levels — it is not surprising that governing entities, courts, and legislative bodies are exercising more authority in those areas in an effort to limit or prevent injuries. This is particularly true in the case of youth sports, where the participants are not as physically developed. The governing bodies regularly take action to protect the health and safety needs of their participants, in the form of playing and related rules. For example, in an effort to limit head injuries and to ensure that participants and their parents that youth football is safe, USA Football has initiated an expansive program entitled "Heads-up Football," which is designed to protect against injuries of all kinds through safety rules and training for coaches. In creating and implementing those rules and training, USA Football and the NFL have teamed with the Centers for Disease Control (CDC). See *http://usafootball.com/coach*.

Head injury cases are proliferating at all levels. There are serious concerns regarding head injuries on the part of younger athletes in particular because studies have confirmed that such injuries have a greater impact on younger brains. There are also concerns that younger people are more impressionable and less able to decide whether they should decline to play for health and safety reasons. It is not surprising, therefore, that schools and governing bodies are facing litigation involving injuries to young participants. In *Limones v. Sch. Dist.*, 161 So. 3d 384 (Fla. 2015), the Florida Supreme Court reiterated that schools have a common law duty to adequately supervise student-athletes. The court noted that the school's duties "regarding athletic activities include: 1. Providing adequate instruction, 2. Supplying appropriate equipment, 3. Reasonably selecting or matching athletes, 4. Properly supervising the event, and 5. Utilizing appropriate post injury efforts to protect against aggravation." With the increased knowledge regarding health and safety issues, it is likely that this common law duty will be enforced with greater stringency. But see *Mehr v. FIFA*, 2015 WL 4366044 (N.D. Cal.) (dismissing negligence claims against worldwide, national, and state soccer governing bodies because "[p]laintiffs have alleged no basis for imputing to any defendant a legal duty to reduce the risks inherent in the sport of soccer, or to implement any of the 'Consensus Statement' guidelines or concussion management protocols, and have alleged no facts showing that any defendant took any action that increased the risks beyond those inherent in the sport").

In an Illinois case filed in 2015, *Bukal v. Illinois High School Association*, plaintiffs are seeking to change concussion policies along with improved management and handling of head injuries. This lawsuit seeks to require medical doctors to be on the sidelines of high school sporting events, and to force the governing body, the Illinois High School Association (IHSA), to cover the costs of medical examinations for high school football players back to 2002. Although the IHSA denies that the new implementations are a response to the lawsuit, they have adopted a "Play Smart. Play Hard" initiative, which establishes a council to review current procedures and concussion management best practices. The IHSA argues, as other governing bodies surely would as well, that requiring doctors on staff would create a "have-have not" situation in which less affluent schools would be substantially burdened in an economic sense, which would lead to the dissolution of their football programs. This Illinois lawsuit illustrates that attorneys might invoke similar strategies in other states as well as help a national push for stronger safety procedures and protocols.

In the fall of 2015, Florida became the first state to require high school athletes to complete a course on concussions before they are allowed to compete in interscholastic sports. Coaches have been required to take similar online courses, which are free, for five years. Under the new rule, once a player completes the course, his or her parent or parents are required to sign a compliance form on behalf of their child. Participants receive a certificate of completion that remains on file with their coach. The Florida High School Athletic Association (FHSAA) will randomly check to confirm that certificates have been filed for every player on a team. If coaches fail to provide a certificate for every player on their team, the coach will be suspended until every team member completes the course. The rule applies to both noncontact and contact sports.

Legislative bodies are also involved in this area. In 2011, Wisconsin passed an act related to "concussions and other head injuries sustained in youth athletic activities," and the Pennsylvania legislature passed the Safety in Youth Sports Act. In July 2014, the California legislature passed more specific legislation, the Cooley Bill, to protect youth football players by restricting contact practices. That bill restricts schools and coaches to two contact football practices per week in California. It also provides that no contact practice may exceed 90 minutes in length and limits the head impact sustained by middle and high school age participants in an effort to ensure that the incidence of injuries is lessened and players do not return from head injuries too quickly. In January 2015, California passed an additional statute requiring schools that offer athletic programs to remove any athlete suspected of sustaining a concussion for the rest of that day's activities and mandating that the athlete be examined by a licensed health care provider in order to return to play. If a participant has been determined to have sustained a concussion, he or she will be subject to a concussion protocol consisting of a seven-day period of monitoring and testing under the guidance of the licensed health care provider. Participants are also required to submit a head injury form at the beginning of each season as a baseline. Other states and youth organizations may adopt similar statutes or rules as litigation and media attention continue to increase in response to schools and governing bodies that fail to take precautions against foreseeable injuries, and as efforts like those in California have the effect of raising the standard of care.

In 1997, Congress passed the Volunteer Protection Act to ensure that volunteers would be protected against liability in certain cases, in an effort to ensure that people would continue to volunteer to coach and work in youth athletics. Acts like this evidence the tension that is present in this area. On the one hand, there is a desire to protect young participants from injury. On the other hand, there is a recognition that subjecting volunteers (coaches and other personnel) to liability will make it more difficult to provide opportunities for young people to participate in athletics. How those tensions are balanced will have a major impact on youth sports and have to be managed as decisions are made by governing organizations, courts, and legislative bodies.

QUESTIONS

If you were serving as a member of a board of directors of a governing organization, would you recommend adding new health and safety rules and protocols? Do such rules increase the standard of care and make it more likely that the organization and its members will be held to a higher duty of care (i.e., do such actions potentially increase liability)? Do such rules increase the costs for members and participants? If costs increase, is it possible or likely that opportunities to participate may decrease? Do you think the Florida rule requiring the taking of a course by participants was adopted, in part, to protect the school district? Does it protect the school district?

NCAA Internal Governance of Intercollegiate Athletics and Legal Limits

INTRODUCTION

This chapter examines the governing authority of the National Collegiate Athletic Association (NCAA) and federal and state law limitations thereon. This chapter begins with a brief overview of the NCAA's general history and its internal governance system, particularly its rules enforcement processes. It then addresses how various federal and state laws, including federal antitrust and civil rights statutes as well as state contract and private associations law, affect the NCAA's regulatory authority.

A BRIEF HISTORY: NCAA GOVERNANCE OF INTERCOLLEGIATE ATHLETICS

The NCAA includes almost 1,100 colleges and universities organized into three divisions based on the nature of their intercollegiate athletic programs. Division I (D-I) offers full athletic scholarships to many of its athletes and is the highest level of competition in most sports; Division II (D-II) also offers athletic scholarships and competes at an intermediate competitive level; and Division III (D-III) does not offer athletic scholarships and is the lowest and most student-centered competitive level. The discussion in this chapter focuses on NCAA Division I. With the passage of so-called autonomy legislation in 2015, five power conferences were given autonomy within the NCAA governance in the form of additional legislative authority, effectively creating another decision-making tier.

There are other associations engaged in the regulation of intercollegiate athletics. The National Association of Intercollegiate Athletics (NAIA) includes approximately 250 colleges and universities and conducts numerous national championships. It also offers programs designed to enhance the experience of student-athletes, including their Champions of Character program that encourages schools to take actions designed to develop character traits among student-athletes. The National Christian College Athletic Association (NCCAA) was incorporated to provide an association for Christ-centered collegiate institutions that are committed to athletic competition as an integral component of education, evangelism, and encouragement. The United States Collegiate Athletic Association (USCAA), another smaller national organization, was organized for the purpose of holding national championships in a number of sports for very small schools. The National Junior College Athletic Association (NJCAA) is made up of more than 500 junior and community colleges throughout 24 regions in the United States that sponsor men's and women's intercollegiate athletic teams, which compete for national championships in three divisions, based on levels of competitiveness. These collegiate athletic associations have rules and standards by which its member schools are governed and through which student-athletes' participation is regulated, but the focus of this chapter is on the NCAA. Although the rules and governance structures differ among the various national associations that govern intercollegiate athletics, much of what you will learn by examining how the NCAA is legally regulated is relevant to all of these governing bodies.

Students, with some faculty oversight, initially were the major force in running intercollegiate athletics. With the deaths of 18 intercollegiate football players in 1905, President Theodore Roosevelt invited university officials to participate in a White House Conference to review football rules. These efforts to reform football led to the formation of a Rules Committee and the formation of the Intercollegiate Athletic Association, which in 1910 was renamed the NCAA.

Interest in intercollegiate sports and attendant increases in commercialization led the highly respected Carnegie Foundation for the Advancement of Education to issue, in 1929, a significant report regarding intercollegiate athletics, which concluded:

> [A] change of values is needed in a field that is sodden with the commercial and the material and the vested interests that these forces have created. Commercialism in college athletics must be diminished and college sport must rise to a point where it is esteemed primarily and sincerely for the opportunities it affords to mature youth.

After the Depression and World War II, with a dramatic increase in access to higher education on the part of all segments of society, largely through government support for returning military personnel to cover the costs of attending college, public interest in intercollegiate athletics expanded significantly. Commercial pressures intensified with the advent of television, the presence of radio in the vast majority of homes in the United States, and the broadcasting of major sporting events. These factors, coupled with a series of gambling scandals and recruiting excesses, caused the NCAA to promulgate additional rules, resulting in an expansion of its governance authority. In 1948, the NCAA enacted the "Sanity Code," which was designed to "alleviate the proliferation of exploitive practices in the recruitment of student-athletes." To enforce the rules in the Sanity Code, the NCAA created the Constitutional Compliance Committee. Neither the Sanity Code with its rules nor the Constitutional Compliance Committee with its enforcement responsibility was particularly successful because the only possible sanction was expulsion, which was so severe that enforcement of the rules was ineffectual.

Two other developments in the 1950s contributed to the transformation of the NCAA into a major regulatory body: (1) Walter Byers became executive director of the NCAA and personally contributed to strengthening the NCAA and its enforcement division; and (2) the NCAA negotiated its first contract to televise intercollegiate football, valued in excess of $1 million, opening the door to increasingly lucrative future television contracts.

In the coming decades, the NCAA gained broader enforcement power but found itself caught between two critiques. On the one hand, it was criticized for responding inadequately to the increased commercialization of intercollegiate athletics, with all its attendant excesses. On the other hand, it was criticized for unfairly exercising its regulatory authority.

In difficult economic times for higher education in the 1980s, presidents increasingly found themselves caught between the pressures applied by influential members of boards of trustees and graduates, who often demanded winning athletic programs, and faculty, who feared the rising commercialization of athletics and its impact on academic values and their institutions' budgets. In the mid-1980s, the presidents became increasingly involved in the governance of intercollegiate athletics through the NCAA, taking some of the power away from athletics directors and faculty representatives who had previously largely controlled governance of intercollegiate athletics.

In 1984, in *NCAA v. Board of Regents of the University of Oklahoma*, 468 U.S. 85 (1984), the U.S. Supreme Court held that the NCAA television plan for D-I football violated federal antitrust law. This decision ultimately gave birth to the Bowl Championship Series (BCS).

In 1989, the Knight Commission, with support in the form of a $2 million grant from the Knight-Ridder newspaper chain, recommended a series of significant reforms that included more presidential involvement and control. The Knight Commission has also become a major force in offering reform recommendations on a periodic basis. The presidents, with guidance from groups like the Knight Commission, began to become increasingly concerned with cost containment and ensuring that academic values continue to be central to the governance of intercollegiate athletics. However, the pressure to produce income largely through the revenue-producing sports of football and men's basketball (and at some institutions, other sports produce revenue as well) has made it difficult to ensure academic values. Nevertheless, the presidents and others have been successful in implementing some reforms that are helping to increase graduation rates of college athletes participating in the major revenue-producing sports. (See the discussion of academic reform initiatives in Chapter 4.)

Since 2010, college athletics has changed significantly. Financial assistance for college athletes has increased, a commercially successful playoff structure for

NCAA FBS football was created outside the governance structure of the NCAA, academic standards for college athlete eligibility have increased with a corresponding increase in graduation rates, and more attention has been focused on college athletes' mental and physical health and safety. The NCAA's Committee on Infractions and the Infractions Appeals Committee have also significantly increased sanctions for violations of NCAA rules by members at the D-I level.

On January 20, 2022, the NCAA membership across Divisions I, II, and III voted to adopt a new association constitution and governance structure. The preamble of the constitution states the basic purpose of the NCAA is "to support and promote healthy and safe intercollegiate athletics, including national championships, as an integral part of the education program and the student-athlete as an integral part of the student body" (Division I Manual, 2022-2023, Constitution Preamble, p.1). Article 1 identifies the core principles for the association and its members:

- The primacy of the academic experience;
- The collegiate student-athlete model, which does not permit pay for play;
- Integrity and sportsmanship, which promotes the ideals of higher education and human development including respect, fairness, civility, honesty, responsibility, academic integrity, and ethical conduct;
- Protecting, supporting, and enhancing the physical and mental health and safety of student-athletes;
- Reinforcing the responsibility of the members to monitor and control the athletics program and ensure rule compliance;
- A commitment to diversity, equity, and inclusion to create environments that promote an atmosphere of respect for and sensitivity to the dignity of every person;
- Conducting programs free of gender bias in athletics activities, hiring, leadership, and advancement;
- Establishing divisional recruiting standards to promote informed decisions and balance the interests of student-athletes, their educational institution, and intercollegiate athletics overall.

Article 2 describes the organization and responsibilities of the association and provides a streamlined association-wide governance structure. Association-wide oversight is provided by the Board of Governors, which consists of nine voting members who serve two-year terms: four representatives from Division I, including "at least one member institution president or chancellor and one conference commissioner"; one member *each* from the Division II and Division III Presidents Council; two "independent" members who may not be paid by any member institutions; and one recently graduated NCAA student-athlete. Ex-officio members of the board include the NCAA president, the chairs of each of the three divisions' councils, the president of an Historically Black College and University (HBCU) selected by the divisional representatives among the voting members, and one recently graduated NCAA student-athlete from each of the two divisions not represented by the voting student-athlete board member.

The duties and responsibilities of the Board of Governors include approving and overseeing the association budget, hiring and supervising the association president, and approving contracts related to media rights and revenue production. The board is also responsible for adopting and implementing legal strategy, risk mitigation, and government relations for the association. When issues affect the association as a whole, the board holds the authority to convene a joint meeting of the presidential and legislative bodies for all divisions. Similarly, if a constitutional amendment is required, or if a division has enacted legislation that may violate the association's constitution, the board holds the authority to call for a vote of the entire membership. (Division I Manual, Constitution, Article 2 Organization, pp.3-4.)

Questions regarding the NCAA and its values persist, as academic and commercial (i.e., revenue-related) tensions create new crises on a regular basis. Recent scandals have included an FBI investigation and the successful conviction of ten defendants, including an Adidas executive, five NCAA assistant basketball coaches, and others who facilitated bribery of top high school basketball players to attend Adidas-sponsored institutions. Another FBI bribery investigation discovered a conspiracy where assistant coaches across a variety of sports were paid to add non-athletes to their rosters to gain preferential admissions. In 2021, the NCAA suspended its rules prohibiting college athletes from earning compensation for the use of their name, image, and likeness (NIL) and subsequent "collectives"—outside entities created to provide NIL opportunities for college athletes have proliferated. The drive to generate greater revenues through television contracts to pay for the increasing costs of D-I athletics programs has spurred major athletics programs to shift conferences resulting in the potential demise of the PAC-12 conference (at the time of publication).

QUESTIONS

1. If calls for reform, which are common in the media, are not grounded in a sense of the historical development of the regulatory rubric governing intercollegiate athletics, are they likely to be successful?
2. Is it possible for highly commercialized athletics programs to also align with academic values and college athlete well-being?

NCAA REGULATORY AUTHORITY AND PROCESSES

KEY TERMS

- Committee on Infractions (COI)
- Infractions Appeals Committee (IAC)
- Lack of institutional control
- Order to show cause
- Unethical conduct

A. NCAA: History of Regulation and the Rules Infractions Process

The NCAA is an association of colleges and universities that develops rules and regulations for the governance of intercollegiate athletics among those member institutions. Those rules and regulations are the product of legislation that is generally developed and proposed by member institutions and committees within the NCAA, which are made up of representatives from member institutions. Full-time employees of the NCAA assist in executing and enforcing those rules.

In 1954, to ensure fairness and a level playing field in intercollegiate athletics, the NCAA formed the Committee on Infractions (COI) to interpret NCAA rules and impose penalties on member institutions for rules violations. Concerns were frequently raised regarding the allegedly unfair manner in which the COI imposed sanctions against member institutions and others, such as coaches, for NCAA rules violations. For example, in the late 1970s, Jerry Tarkanian asserted that the NCAA and its COI violated his federal due process rights by finding him guilty of NCAA rules violations and effectively requiring his termination as coach of the University of Nevada, Las Vegas (UNLV) men's basketball team, despite a UNLV internal investigation finding that he had not violated any NCAA rules. In a 1988 landmark decision, *NCAA v. Tarkanian*, 488 U.S. 179 (1988), the U.S. Supreme Court held that the NCAA is not a state actor, freeing it from having to comply with federal constitutional requirements such as providing due process in its rules enforcement proceedings. In other words, the NCAA does not have to provide constitutionally mandated procedural due process safeguards in its investigative or rules enforcement process to its member institutions and others defending themselves in proceedings before the COI. (*Tarkanian* is discussed in Chapter 2 in comparison to the *Brentwood Academy I* case, in which the Supreme Court ruled that a state high school athletic association is a state actor and subject to federal constitutional limitations.)

After *Tarkanian*, NCAA member institutions continued to be concerned about the need for greater procedural due process in NCAA rules enforcement proceedings. A Special Committee to Review the National Collegiate Athletic Association Enforcement and Infractions Process (Review Committee) was formed to evaluate the NCAA's rules enforcement process. In 1991, the Review Committee issued a report that included a series of recommended reforms designed to ensure that the NCAA operated in a more timely, fair, and consistent manner. For both political and fairness reasons, the NCAA voluntarily adopted most of these recommendations, which provide institutions and others indirectly subject to the NCAA's regulatory authority (e.g., coaches) with enhanced procedural due process protections. In 1993, the NCAA created the Infractions Appeals Committee (IAC), whose function is to review the COI's findings and sanctions, which was one of the Review Committee's recommendations. Working collectively, the COI, IAC, Management Council, conferences, and member institutions and their personnel play the critical role in fulfilling the mission of the NCAA enforcement program, which is summarized in Bylaw 19 in the 2022–2023 *NCAA Manual*. Bylaw 19.01.1 sets forth the mission of the infractions program:

> It is the mission of the NCAA infractions program to uphold integrity and fair play among the NCAA membership, and to prescribe appropriate and fair penalties if violations occur. One of the fundamental principles of the infractions program is to ensure that those institutions and student-athletes abiding by the NCAA constitution and bylaws are not disadvantaged by their commitment to compliance. The program is committed to the fairness of procedures and the timely resolution of infractions cases. The ability to investigate allegations and penalize infractions is critical to the common interests of the Association's membership and the preservation of its enduring values.

Bylaw 19.01.2, in turn, provides that "The infractions program shall hold institutions, coaches, administrators, and student-athletes who violate the NCAA constitution and bylaws accountable for their conduct, both at the individual and institutional levels." *Id.* at page 337.

The NCAA adopted major reforms of the enforcement and penalty structure in 2018 by increasing the levels of violations to four rather than two, and then in 2022 by adopting just three levels of violations. A series of helpful figures and graphic summaries of the infractions penalty structure and guidelines, including a very helpful summary of the recently adopted four-level penalty structure, can be found in Bylaws 19.01.1 (Level I Violation: Severe Breach of Conduct), 19.01.2 (Level II Violation: Significant Breach of Conduct), and 19.01.3 (Level III Violation: Breach of Conduct). Figure 19-1 in the NCAA Manual provides a summary of penalty guidelines. See 2022–2023 NCAA Manual.

The following excerpts from reported decisions of the IAC are illustrative of procedural and substantive issues that often arise in the NCAA rules enforcement process. Given the nature of these cases, it is clear that institutions need to develop educational, monitoring, and compliance programs for athletic department personnel, coaches, college athletes, and others who deal with the detailed rules and regulations that govern intercollegiate athletics. These cases were decided under the former two-level enforcement system (i.e., major and secondary (i.e., minor) infractions). As you read the cases, think about how they might be decided differently under the three-level enforcement structure.

B. Institutional Violations of NCAA Rules and Sanctions

In the enforcement process, the COI and the IAC have the authority to impose penalties on NCAA member institutions for rules violations by institutional personnel (e.g., athletics administrators, coaches, boosters) and college athletes. Two important issues that arise in the infractions process are whether the conduct and activities of the institution demonstrate a lack of institutional control or a failure to monitor compliance with NCAA rules.

The following decisions and discussion provide illustrative examples of a university's lack of institutional control or failure to monitor its athletic programs that resulted in violations of NCAA extra benefits, amateurism, ethical conduct, and/or academic integrity rules.

University of Southern California Infractions Appeals Committee Report No. 323
May 26, 2011

[Editors' note: The COI found that the University of Southern California (USC) had acted in a manner evidencing a lack of institutional control relating to impermissible inducements, extra benefits, and exceeding staff limits. In a separate proceeding, the COI also found that a coach had engaged in unethical conduct. According to the COI's report, "The general campus environment surrounding the violations troubled the committee." The COI indicated that the university failed to heed clear warning signs, did not have proper controls in place to monitor rules compliance, failed to regulate access to locker rooms and practice facilities, and in some instances failed to be proactive in investigating concerns.

Between 2004 and 2005, a former star (elite) football student-athlete and his family members formed a partnership with two individuals to create a sports agency. After that agreement was entered into, the student-athlete and his family asked for and received substantial financial assistance from the partners of the agency. The receipt of those benefits rendered the student-athlete ineligible to play in intercollegiate athletics. Early in 2006, one of the agency partners contacted an assistant football coach asking for assistance in convincing the student-athlete to adhere to his agreement with the agency. The assistant coach, however, failed to notify university compliance staff of this potential violation and thereafter provided false and misleading information to the NCAA's enforcement staff, which ultimately resulted in the COI finding that the coach had violated ethical conduct rules. The former football student-athlete and his family and friends received benefits from another sports marketing agency during 2005-2006. The former football student-athlete, who went on to play professional football, refused to cooperate fully with the NCAA's investigation.

The case also included multiple impermissible inducements from a sports agent or representative to a former star (elite) basketball student-athlete and his family and friends. The former head men's basketball coach, the assistant men's basketball coach, an institutional compliance staff member, a faculty athletics representative, and the athletics director all knew that this representative had previously committed two separate NCAA violations. Nevertheless, they did not take steps to monitor the relationship between the player and the representative.

The COI concluded that the football program violated coaching staff limit rules by hiring a consultant who analyzed video footage, attended practices, and discussed his observations with the coach. The COI also found that a former tennis student-athlete used an athletics department long-distance access code to make 123 unauthorized international telephone calls valued at over $7,000.

The COI acknowledged the difficulty that attends investigating matters involving violation of amateurism rules. In determining the penalties to be imposed, the COI considered the university's self-imposed penalties but felt that they were inadequate given the gravity of the violations.

The penalties imposed by the COI included four years of probation, public reprimand and censure, a two-year postseason ban for football, a one-year postseason ban for men's basketball, vacation of regular and postseason wins for all three involved sports, scholarship reductions for football and men's basketball, recruiting restrictions for men's basketball, a $5,000 penalty, forfeiture of $206,200 in revenue from the 2008 NCAA Division I Men's Basketball Championship, and limitations for the access granted to boosters and university personnel to team charters, practices, locker rooms, and so forth. The COI also mandated that the university dissociate itself from three boosters, including former football and men's basketball student-athletes.

On appeal, the university raised the following issues: reduction of the penalties on the ground that they "are not supported by the facts and are excessive" and that some of the COI's findings of violations "are contrary to the evidence, based upon facts that do not constitute a violation and compromised by a procedural error."]

Findings of Violations

The institution argues the following with respect to findings of violations:

- *The finding of unethical conduct is "contrary to the evidence, based on incompetent evidence and compromised procedural error. . . ."*

While this argument was included in the institution's appeal, [it lacks standing] to appeal that finding since it was made against the institution's former football coach and not the institution itself.

- *The [COI] "erred in concluding that the [sports marketers] were representatives of USC's athletic interests. . . ."*

The institution specifically takes issue with the [COI's] findings that [the sports marketers] "became representatives of USC's athletics interests by hiring three USC student-athletes" and that "summer positions were created exclusively for USC student-athletes." The [COI] "weighed conflicting evidence" and ultimately concluded that the internship at least initially was created exclusively for student-athletes of the institution. [Citations to record omitted throughout.]

We are persuaded that there is sufficient evidence to support the [COI's] conclusions regarding these issues and find no basis on which to reverse the pertinent findings.

- *The [COI's] finding of lack of institutional control "should be set aside because some of the facts found by the committee did not constitute a violation of NCAA rules, and the committee failed to consider a number of factors."*

One of the institution's principal arguments regarding this point is that the [COI] based its finding of lack of institutional control on a "heightened duty" to monitor elite student-athletes, and that "NCAA bylaws do not set forth any 'heightened duty' standard, nor do they differentiate between 'elite' athletes and other student-athletes." However, we do not see the COI's statements as establishing a new or different standard not permitted by the applicable bylaws. Rather, we note the COI's explanation that "high profile athletes at a high profile program are at greater risk and need to be more vigilantly monitored," and its corollary conclusion that at this institution the "resources committed to compliance were inadequate. . . ."

[W]e find no basis on which to reverse the COI's finding of lack of institutional control. More particularly, but without limitation, there was evidence sufficient to permit the COI to determine that the institution had devoted inadequate resources to its compliance program, especially when the institution had devoted inadequate resources to its compliance program especially when the institution learned that problems with the compliance program were developing.

Penalties

The institution argues that penalties imposed by the COI were excessive and to that extent constituted an abuse of discretion. More specifically, the institution argues that (a) the COI "has imposed significantly lesser sanctions in major infractions cases based on similar violations"; (b) "abused its discretion in imposing a two-year post-season ban and drastic scholarship reductions in football for violations in this case"; and (c) "the scholarship reductions are excessive, particularly when considering their unintended impact."

The committee (IAC) stated in the Alabama State case as follows:

> An abuse of discretion in the imposition of a penalty occurs if the penalty: (1) was not based on a correct legal standard or was based on a misapprehension of the underlying substantive legal principles; (2) was based on a clearly erroneous factual finding; (3) failed to consider and weigh material factors; (4) was based on a clear error of judgment, such that the imposition was arbitrary, capricious, or irrational; or (5) was based in significant part on one or more irrelevant or improper factors. . . .

Guided by that standard, we find no abuse of discretion in the imposition of either the two-year postseason ban or the grants-in-aid reduction. We note in particular the COI's recognition that this was the institution's sixth major infractions case involving football, and that the institution had last been before the COI in June 2001, fewer than four years before the violations which occurred in this case. Thus, the institution was a "repeat-violator" under Bylaw 19.5.2.3 and therefore at risk for enhanced penalties set forth in Bylaw 19.2.5.2.3.2. As the COI stated in response to the institution's appeal:

> Although the COI ultimately chose not to impose any of the enhanced penalties, it noted that "stiff sanctions are warranted in light of the serious violations found by the subcommittee and the fact that the institution is a "repeat violator." Those stiff penalties are particularly warranted because the school failed to take to heart the lessons it should have learned in 2001.

Thus, we believe that the penalties imposed make clear to the institutions the message which the COI intended to convey:

> Similar strong penalties will be meted out to institutions that do [not] take the problem of sports agents and their runners seriously. It is not enough for the institutions simply to educate student athletes about the dangers of unscrupulous agents. Schools must have appropriate staff and procedures in place to combat this significant problem. An institution that does not foster a climate of compliance on its campus should expect serious consequences.

In reaching this decision, [the IAC] closely considered both the institution and the COI's substantial arguments regarding the application to this case of prior decisions of both the COI and [IAC]. Indeed, we have recognized since the University of Mississippi (May 1, 1995) case that a "factor of particular significance in considering an appeal of penalties is the review and analysis of the penalty or penalties imposed when compared with the penalty or penalties imposed in other cases with similar characteristics. However, we also stated in the 2002 University of Alabama case that "the COI must have latitude in tailoring remedies to the particular circumstances involved in each case and that the universe of relevant cases is not static, but evolving." Given this latitude afforded the COI, there is no basis on which to conclude that the COI departed from prior decisions, much less to any impermissible extent.

The institution placed particular reliance on the COI's decision in the 1996 Florida State case, arguing that the case "illustrates how the COI historically has penalized universities for amateurism violations." While the institution's observations regarding the case may be correct, we also make clear that the principle of guidance from prior decisions is not an unyielding directive. It is instead a matter of considered judgment to be applied along with all other factors which this committee has recognized should guide the COI and IAC. One very important factor in the application of that principle, and in determining the extent to which a prior decision should guide a present decision, is change in the matters to which the decisions of the COI and IAC are directed. The COI should not be strictly bound to a decision made fifteen years earlier, when the circumstances of intercollegiate athletics were qualitatively different than those which presently obtain. This, of course, does not mean that prior decisions provide no restraint on or guidance to the COI and IAC, or that insignificant changes in the environment in which NCAA member institutions operate can justify ignoring those prior decisions. It means only that the guidance provided by prior decisions is, and always has been, a matter of judgment. In this case, we cannot say that the COI improperly exercised that judgment.

QUESTIONS

1. The USC case involved violations of amateurism rules regulating college athletes' relationships with agents or representatives (boosters). Is the amateurism principle consistent with the operation of highly commercialized intercollegiate athletics in major revenue-producing sports (generally football and men's basketball) at schools like USC? The NCAA permits institutions to pay college athletes a cash stipend in addition to tuition, room and board, fees, and books to cover the full cost of attendance at the university. Does the adoption of such legislation constitute recognition on the part of the NCAA that college athletes should be "paid more"? Is the possibility of graduation (along with payment of the full cost of attendance) sufficient compensation for college athletes in revenue-producing sports, or should they receive additional cash payments?

2. The NCAA and conferences require that institutions demonstrate that they are exercising adequate institutional control over their athletics programs. What did USC do (or fail to do) that constituted a lack of institutional control? What can be done to ensure that there is sufficient institutional control?

3. In the concluding paragraphs of its opinion, the IAC discusses the role of precedent (i.e., prior decisions) regarding penalties. How much reliance may an athletic administrator place on previous decisions of the IAC and COI? What is the impact of this lack of certainty on the operation of athletics programs? Does this indicate that the NCAA is now committed to imposing more stringent sanctions? If so, what is its objective in doing so?

4. Bylaw 4, on page 9 of the 2022-2023 *NCAA Manual*, provides that an institution is responsible for actions taken by boosters, donors, or other individuals associated with the athletics program. USC was held responsible for the actions of certain "representatives"—individuals associated with the athletic department. In 2002, the IAC upheld strong sanctions against the University of Alabama (which like USC was a repeat violator) for the actions of certain individuals in using inducements (money) to try to recruit athletes to the university. In the Southern Methodist University (SMU) case, involving a repeat offender and decided in 1987, the NCAA imposed what has been referred to as the "death penalty" for SMU's football program, shutting it down for two years, which effectively decimated the program for many years. The COI and the IAC declined to impose the death penalty in the USC or Alabama cases, even though in each one, the university was a repeat offender involved in major infractions. Why do you think the NCAA declined to impose the death penalty in these cases? When should it consider the imposition of the death penalty?

5. While the IAC indicates that it is not adopting a new standard for institutional duty to monitor higher profile student-athletes, it appears that institutions with higher profile student-athletes are being held to a standard that requires closer scrutiny of their activities and relationships. If so, what steps should USC and other institutions with higher profile student-athletes take to ensure compliance with NCAA rules?

Negotiated Resolution: University of Miami (Florida)
February 24, 2023

The University of Miami (Florida) (Miami); head women's basketball coach (head coach); and NCAA enforcement staff agree with the violations and penalties detailed below. The parties also agree that this case should be resolved as Level II–Mitigated for the institution and for the head coach.

In May 2022, the enforcement staff learned of a representative of the institution's athletics interests and prominent Miami-area businessman's (booster) possible involvement with multiple transfer prospective student-athletes, including two four-year women's basketball prospective student-athletes (prospects) who were nationally recognized social media influencers. As a result, the enforcement staff requested that the institution produce all communications, among other records, between institutional staff members and the booster. During the production of those records, the institution identified communication between the head coach and booster regarding the prospects.

Around the same time, the enforcement staff identified a photo on the booster's Twitter account from April 13 that included the booster, booster's son, prospects and prospects' parents. The institution and enforcement staff began a collaborative investigation, which resulted in the following information. . . .

The institution began recruiting the prospects after they entered the NCAA transfer portal in March 2022. Based on her limited knowledge of the prospects at that time, the head coach was initially uncertain if they would be a good fit in her program and wanted to ensure that basketball was their priority. After learning more about them from coaches at their previous institution and speaking with them, it became clear that their motivation for transferring was to join a winning program that could help them reach the NCAA tournament.

The prospects' father had businesses in the Miami/Fort Lauderdale, Florida, area, and the family planned a visit to Florida shortly before Easter. Because they would be in the area, the prospects were also interested in coordinating an official visit to the institution. The head coach had limited availability for the visit due to preexisting personal commitments; however, she agreed the staff should accommodate the prospects' request and arranged an abbreviated official visit beginning April 15.

In April 2022, the head coach met the booster and his sons for the first time at a university event for institutional administrators and staff, donors and prospective donors to welcome the new director of athletics and head football coach. The head coach received a late invitation to this event after the director of athletics realized that neither she nor the men's basketball head coach had been invited. The head coach reported that, at the time of the event, she believed it was a university celebration for the new director of athletics and head football coach. Although the event may have been for donors and prospective donors, the head coach said that was not her understanding or frame of reference and said she did not know the booster was a representative of the institution's athletics interests. However, she was aware that he was a prominent Miami-area businessman involved in name, image and likeness (NIL) activities with Miami student-athletes, describing him during her interview as "an NIL guy."

At the event, the booster and his two sons approached the head coach and talked about the prospects' upcoming official visit to Miami. The booster and his sons also talked about the prospects' social media presence and the possibility of engaging them in a business venture. The head coach did not initiate the interaction or meeting and did not initiate any discussions at the event about the prospects. The investigation did not determine how the booster and his sons knew the institution was recruiting the prospects.

On April 12, 2022, following the university event, the head coach called the booster to learn more about him and his work. The head coach reported that, at the time, she believed it would not be a "bad thing" if the prospects got to know the booster due to their mutual interests in social media and related business activities. When the head coach began texting with the booster, the head coach was unaware that the booster had already been in contact with the prospects' agent about arranging a meeting with them the next time they were in the area. The following day, the booster forwarded the head coach a message he had received from the prospects' agent in which the agent said: "Hi [booster], yes lots of moving parts with visits, travel and family. The [prospects] are enthusiastic about the prospects of one day working together. Given their schedules we are going to hold off on a meeting for now and will look to follow up in the next few weeks." In forwarding the message to the head coach, the booster added, "Usually not a great sign but let's see." The head coach responded: "Well damn. I'll make sure the [prospects] know who you are." The booster responded that it was "important," he was "here to help" and he wanted "women's [basketball] to be huge for UM [Miami]."

Separately, the head coach asked the assistant coach to contact the prospects and explain that the booster was a legitimate businessperson. As a result of the assistant coach's call, the prospects agreed to meet with the booster. The head coach then sent a text message to the booster to confirm the prospects would "love to talk to him" and asked when he would be available. The booster asked the head coach to connect the family with him so he could invite the prospects and their parents to dinner at his home the following evening, and the head coach responded, "wow will do thank you goodnight." The booster then worked with the prospects' agent to make the meeting arrangements.

The prospects arrived in the Miami area a few days prior to the start of their official visit with family, using their own funds for their flight, accommodations and other expenses. On the morning of April 13, 2022, the head coach provided the booster profiles of the prospects, which the women's basketball staff had created for institutional staff members in preparation for their official visit. Later that evening, two days prior to the beginning of their official visit, the prospects and their parents met with the booster and his son at the booster's home in Miami. The booster provided the family a tour of his home and a chef-prepared dinner. During the meeting, the booster promoted the institution when he talked with the family about his children's experiences at the institution, including his sons' prior participation on the baseball team, and his admiration for the institution and the city of Miami. The head coach was not aware that this dinner had occurred until she saw the picture the booster sent her after the dinner took place, which was the same picture he had posted on social media.

The prospects completed their abbreviated official visit to the institution April 15 and, after completing an official visit to a different institution, notified the head coach of their commitment to attend the institution. The prospects reported that the dinner with the booster did not have an impact on their decision to commit to or enroll at the institution.

The head coach reported that she was not aware the booster was a representative of the institution's athletics interests when she facilitated an introduction between the booster and the prospects because she had never met the booster prior to April 2022, and he had not donated to the women's basketball program directly. The head coach also said in her interview that she believed at that time she could make introductions and share factual information with third parties involved in NIL. She agreed in her interview that, after receiving subsequent guidance, the booster was a representative and her communications with the booster about the prospects were impermissible.

Still, the head coach failed to ask questions regarding the permissibility of her involvement in connecting the prospects with the booster. Specifically, she did not communicate with compliance after the university event or leading up to or during her communications with the booster to clarify whether her actions would be consistent with NCAA rules. After the booster asked the head coach to connect him to the prospects, the head coach reported feeling uncomfortable with the situation. This discomfort should have prompted the head coach to seek guidance from compliance about her interactions with the booster. The head coach's involvement to connect the family and the booster resulted in an impermissible recruiting contact and recruiting inducement.

I. Parties' Agreements

A. Agreed-upon findings of fact, violations of NCAA legislation and violation levels.

1. *[NCAA Division I Manual Bylaws 13.1.2.1, 13.2.1, 13.10.1.1, and 13.10.1.4 (2021–2022)]*

The institution, head coach and enforcement staff agree that between April 7 through 13, 2022, the head coach and an assistant women's basketball coach facilitated an impermissible contact between a booster and two prospects and their parents.

Additionally, the head coach violated NCAA publicity legislation when she commented about the prospects to the booster and provided him information about their official visit. . . .

2. [NCAA Division I Manual Bylaw 11.1.1.1 (2021–2022)]

The institution, head coach and enforcement staff agree that in April 2022, the head coach is presumed responsible for the violations detailed in Agreed-Upon Finding of Fact No. 1 and did not rebut the presumption of responsibility. Specifically, the head coach did not demonstrate that she promoted an atmosphere for compliance due to her knowledge of and personal involvement in the violations detailed in Agreed-Upon Finding of Fact No. 1. Further, the head coach failed to consult with compliance to ensure that she and her staff complied with NCAA legislation and failed to identify potential NCAA violations regarding the women's basketball program's involvement of the booster in the recruitment of the four-year women's basketball prospective student-athletes.

B. Agreed-upon aggravating and mitigating factors.

Pursuant to NCAA Bylaw 19.5.12.1.3-(e), the parties agree that the aggravating and mitigating factors identified below are applicable. The parties assessed the factors by weight and number and agree that this case should be properly resolved as Level II–Mitigated for the institution and the head coach.

In reaching a mitigated classification for the institution, the parties agreed that significant weight should be given to the mitigating factors in Bylaws 19.9.4-(b) and 19.9.4-(c) because the institution accepted its responsibility for the violation, imposed appropriate and meaningful corrective actions and agreed to and met expedient deadlines for document production and interviews. Also, while there are two Level II violations in this case, one is a derivative of the underlying violation. Therefore, the parties agreed not to give the Bylaw 19.9.3-(g) "multiple Level II violations" aggravating factor substantial weight. The parties agreed that the same analysis applied for the head coach concerning Bylaws 19.9.4-(b) and 19.9.4-(c).

The parties further agreed that 19.9.3-(b) "a history of Level I, II or major violations" carried less-than-standard weight because the violations in the institution's most recent infractions case did not concern the women's basketball program.

[Eds. The Negotiated Resolution then lists the aggravating and mitigating factors for the institution and the involved head coach.]

. . .

II. Parties' Agreed-upon Penalties

All penalties agreed upon in this case are independent and supplemental to any action that has been or may be taken by the NCAA Division I Committee on Academics through its assessment of postseason ineligibility, historical penalties or other penalties.

In addition to the core penalties detailed below, the institution implemented a series of corrective actions designed to demonstrate accountability for the violations and its commitment to ongoing rules education and monitoring efforts relating to the case. Those actions are detailed in the Appendix.

Pursuant to Bylaw 19.5.12.1.3-(e), the parties agree to the following penalties:

Core Penalties for Level II–Mitigated Violations (Bylaw 19.9.5)

1. Probation: One year of probation from February 24, 2023 through February 23, 2024.
2. Financial penalty: The institution shall pay $5,000 plus 1% of the women's basketball budget to the NCAA.
3. Recruiting restrictions (applied during the 2022-23 year):
   a. A 7% reduction from the permissible number of official visits in women's basketball.
   b. A reduction of nine recruiting-person days from the permissible number of recruiting-person days in women's basketball.
   c. The institution shall prohibit recruiting communications by all women's basketball staff members for three weeks beginning with the opening date of the transfer portal (March 13 through April 2, 2023).

Core Penalties for Level II – Mitigated Violations (Bylaw 19.9.5)

4. Head coach restriction: The head coach violated head coach responsibility legislation when she did not demonstrate that she promoted an atmosphere for compliance due to her knowledge of and personal involvement in the violations detailed in Agreed-Upon Finding of Fact No. 1. Bylaw 19.9.5.5 and the Figure 19-1 penalty guidelines contemplate head coach suspensions to address head coach responsibility violations. In anticipation of this penalty, Miami and the head coach agreed to a 10% suspension and applied the penalty to the first three contests of the 2022-23 women's basketball regular season. Specifically, the head coach was not permitted to be present in the facility where the contests were played, and no contact or communication with women's basketball coaching staff members or student-athletes occurred during the three contests. The prohibition included all coaching activities for the period of time that began at 12:01 a.m. on the day of the contest and ended at 11:59 p.m. that day. During that period, the head coach did not participate in any coaching activities, including, but not limited to, team travel, practice, video study, recruiting and team meetings. The results of those contests from which the head coach is suspended shall not count toward the head coach's career coaching record.

Additional Penalties for Level II–Mitigated Violations (Bylaw 19.9.7)

5. Public reprimand and censure through the release of the negotiated resolution agreement.

6. During the period of probation, the institution shall:
   a. Continue to develop and implement a comprehensive educational program on NCAA legislation to instruct coaches, the faculty athletics representative, all athletics department personnel and all institutional staff members with responsibility for recruiting legislation.
   b. Submit a preliminary report to the office of the Committees on Infractions by April 15, 2023 setting forth a schedule for establishing this compliance and educational program.
   c. File with the office of the Committees on Infractions annual compliance reports indicating the progress made with this program by December 15, 2023. Particular emphasis shall be placed on rules education and monitoring related to NCAA NIL activities, boosters and publicity legislation.
   d. Inform prospects in the women's basketball program in writing that the institution is on probation for one year and detail the violations committed. If a prospect takes an official paid visit, the information regarding violations, penalties and terms of probation must be provided in advance of the visit. Otherwise, the information must be provided before a prospect signs a National Letter of Intent.
   e. Publicize specific and understandable information concerning the nature of the infractions by providing, at a minimum, a statement to include the types of violations and the affected sport programs and a direct, conspicuous link to the public infractions decision located on the athletics department's main webpage "landing page" and in the media guides for the women's basketball program. The institution's statement must: (i) clearly describe the infractions; (ii) include the length of the probationary period associated with the case; and (iii) give members of the general public a clear indication of what happened in the case to allow the public (particularly prospects and their families) to make informed, knowledgeable decisions. A statement that refers only to the probationary period with nothing more is not sufficient.

7. Following the receipt of the final compliance report and prior to the conclusion of probation, the institution's president shall provide a letter to the Committee on Infractions affirming that the institution's current athletics policies and practices conform to all requirements of NCAA regulations.

. . .

VIII. Division I Committee on Infractions Approval

Pursuant to NCAA Bylaw 19.5.12, the panel approves the parties' negotiated resolution agreement. The panel's review of this agreement is limited. Panels may only reject a negotiated resolution agreement if the agreement is not in the best interests of the Association or if the agreed-upon penalties are manifestly unreasonable. *See* Bylaw 19.5.12.2. In this case, the panel determines the agreed-upon facts, violations, aggravating and mitigating factors, and classifications are appropriate for this process. Further, the parties classified this case as Level II-Mitigated for Miami and the head women's basketball coach's violations. The agreed-upon penalties align with the ranges identified for core penalties for Level II-Mitigated cases in Figure 19-1 and Bylaw 19.9.5 and the additional penalties available under Bylaw 19.9.7. Pursuant to Bylaw 19.5.12.4, this negotiated resolution has no precedential value.

The COI advises Miami, and the head women's basketball coach that they should take every precaution to ensure that they observe the terms of the penalties. The COI will monitor the institution while it is on probation to ensure compliance with the penalties and terms of probation and may extend the probationary period, among other action, if the institution does not comply or commits additional violations. Likewise, any action by the institution, and/or the head women's basketball coach contrary and to the terms of any of the penalties or any additional violations shall be considered grounds for prescribing more severe penalties and/or may result in additional allegations and violations. . . .

QUESTIONS

1. In response to public criticism for the NCAA's perceived failure to appropriately punish the actions of the booster by dissociation, the Division I COI provided additional explanation and an admonition in a preamble for the Miami Negotiated Resolution confirmation:

> Based on the specific facts developed during the investigation and the timing of the submission of the case to the Division I Committee on Infractions, the panel accepts the parties' submission. The investigation did not develop any facts directly linking activities around name, image and likeness to the prospects' recruitment to or decision to enroll at the University of Miami. During its review, however, the panel was troubled by the limited nature and severity of institutional penalties agreed-upon by Miami and the enforcement staff—namely, the absence of a disassociation of the involved booster. Further, this case was processed prior to the adoption of NCAA Bylaw 19.7.3, which went into effect on January 1, 2023, and presumes that a violation occurred in cases involving name, image and likeness offers, agreements and/or activities. Based on legislation in effect at the time of submission, the panel cannot presume that activities around name, image and likeness resulted in NCAA violations.
>
> Although the parties asserted that a disassociation penalty would be inappropriate based on an impermissible meal and an impermissible contact, today's new NIL-related environment represents a new day. Boosters are involved with prospects and student-athletes in ways the NCAA membership has never seen or encountered. In that way, addressing impermissible booster conduct is critical, and the disassociation penalty presents an effective penalty available to the COI.
>
> Considering the facts and circumstances in this case, however, the panel did not determine that the absence of a disassociation rendered the penalties manifestly unreasonable or the agreement to be against the best interests of the Association. Pursuant to Bylaw 19.10.6, this approved agreement has no precedential value. The COI will strongly consider disassociation penalties in future cases involving NIL-adjacent conduct.

Given that NCAA infractions decisions (and negotiated resolutions) have no precedential value, what is the value of the COI statement? If Bylaw 19.7.3 had been in effect at the time of the impermissible contact, would the penalties be different?

2. Division I Bylaw 19.7.3 states:

> In cases involving name, image and likeness offers, agreements and/or activities in which related communications and conduct are subject to NCAA regulation, the infractions process (including interpretive requests) shall presume a violation occurred if circumstantial information suggests that one or more parties engaged in impermissible conduct. The enforcement staff may make a formal allegation based on the presumption. The hearing panel shall conclude a violation occurred unless the institution or involved individual clearly demonstrates with credible and sufficient information that all communications and conduct surrounding the name, image and likeness activity complied with NCAA legislation. *(Adopted: 10/26/22 effective 1/1/23)*

The NCAA enforcement staff generally has the burden of proving an institution has committed a rules violation. Should NIL cases be treated differently? What are the pros and cons of this approach?

THE PENN STATE UNIVERSITY CASE

On November 17, 2011, NCAA President Emmert wrote a letter to Penn State President Rodney Erickson in which he stated, in pertinent part:

> As we have discussed, on November 5, 2011, the NCAA first learned about allegations of sexual abuse of young boys occurring in the athletic facilities of Pennsylvania State University, perpetrated by a former assistant head football coach. Further, at the same time the NCAA learned that these alleged acts occurred over two decades and that individuals with present or former coaching responsibilities may have been aware of this behavior. The recount of these tragic events in the Grand Jury Report is deeply troubling, and if true, individuals who were in a position to monitor and act upon learning of potential abuses appear to have been acting starkly contrary to the values of higher education, as well as the NCAA. I am writing to notify you that the NCAA will examine Penn State's exercise of institutional control over its intercollegiate athletics program, as well as the actions, and inactions, of relevant responsible personnel. . . .

President Emmert then stated the NCAA constitutional and bylaw provisions requiring institutional control, monitoring, and ethical conduct and asked for Penn State's response to the following questions:

1. How has Penn State and/or its employees complied with the Articles of the NCAA Constitution and bylaws implicated in this case?
2. How has Penn State exercised institutional control over the issues identified in and related to the Grand Jury Report? Were there procedures in

place that were or were not followed? What are the institution's expectations and policies to address conduct that has been alleged in this matter upon discovery by any party?
3. Have each of the alleged persons to have been involved or have notice of the issues identified in and related [to this matter] behaved consistent with principles and requirements governing ethical conduct and honesty? If so, how? If not, how?
4. What policies and procedures does Penn State have in place to monitor, prevent, and detect the issues identified in [this case,] or to take disciplinary or corrective action if such behaviors are found?" . . .

Penn State responded by hiring the law firm of Judge Louis Freeh, a former FBI director, to investigate the matter. In compiling that report, Freeh's law firm and those working with them interviewed 430 university employees and other individuals and reviewed over 3.5 million e-mails and documents. The Freeh report concluded, "Our most saddening finding is the total disregard [by Penn State officials] for the safety and welfare of [the abuse] victims."

Rather than engaging in further investigation or hearings, President Emmert and the leadership of the NCAA stated that the Freeh report chronicled "an unprecedented failure of institutional integrity leading to a culture in which a football program was held in higher esteem than the values of the institution, the values of the NCAA, the values of higher education, and most disturbingly the values of human decency." It also pressured the university to enter into a consent decree pursuant to the findings of the Freeh report, which imposed a $60 million sanction on the university (a sum equal to the average gross annual revenue generated by the football program). That penalty was to be placed in an endowment to support national programs designed to prevent child sexual abuse. The sanctions also included a four-year postseason ban from college football and included a vacating of all the team's wins from 1998 through 2011, which were to be reflected in the record of its legendary coach Joe Paterno. Other penalties included a reduction in scholarships. In addition, Penn State was placed on probation and required to enter into an Athletics Integrity Agreement, which mandated the appointment of an independent Athletics Integrity Monitor who would provide regular reports to the NCAA. Former U.S. Senator George Mitchell was appointed to serve as the first monitor.

In an effort to avoid potentially stronger sanctions to their football program, including the possibility of the death penalty, and in an effort to demonstrate their commitment to the values shared with other NCAA members, Penn State cooperated with the NCAA and quickly agreed to the consent decree. From the outset, concerns were raised regarding the propriety of the consent decree and the authority of the NCAA to sanction Penn State for actions related to the child abuse scandal. President Emmert responded to such criticism by stating, "We cannot look to NCAA history to determine how to handle circumstances so disturbing, shocking, and disappointing. . . . As the individuals charged with governing college sports, we have a responsibility to act. These events should serve as a call to every single school and athletics department to take an honest look at its campus environment and eradicate the 'sports are king' mindset that can so dramatically cloud the judgment of educators."

Some scholars expressed concerns regarding whether the NCAA overstepped its authority and failed to comply with its own rules in disciplining Penn State. See, e.g., Matthew J. Mitten, *The NCAA's Unprecedented Disciplinary Action Against Pennsylvania State University: Its Coercive Means Don't Justify the Laudable Ends, But Is There a Legal Remedy?*, 41 Pepp. L. Rev. 321 (2014). Lawsuits were filed on behalf of Coach Paterno, who had died of cancer during the aftermath of the consent decree. Monitoring reports from Senator Mitchell found that Penn State had moved effectively to deal with the underlying cultural problems that had contributed to the university's cover-up or failure to disclose matters related to the child abuse accusations. Armed with those findings—and, no doubt, in response to continuing criticism—the NCAA began the process of lifting the sanctions, beginning with the scholarship limitations and then moving to the postseason ban, in part due to a recognition that such limits harmed college athletes who bore no responsibility for Penn State's handling of the matter.

In an apparent response to the Penn State consent decree, the Commonwealth of Pennsylvania enacted the Institution of Higher Education Monetary Penalty Endowment Act, mandating that the fine assessed against Penn State be paid to the treasury of Pennsylvania. A suit was filed by the Commonwealth under the Act to require the NCAA to comply with this requirement. A series of embarrassing e-mails written by NCAA personnel were released late in the fall of 2014, as the Commonwealth of Pennsylvania's case was proceeding to trial. On January 16, 2015, as part of a settlement in the lawsuit brought by Pennsylvania, the NCAA entered into a new consent decree with Penn State University that reinstated the wins vacated in the prior consent decree and stipulated the following *(http://www.ncaa.org/about/resources/media-center/news/ncaa-reaches-proposed-settlement-corman-lawsuit)*:

- Penn State agree[d] to commit a total of $60 million to activities and programs for the prevention of child sexual abuse and the treatment of victims of child sexual abuse.
- Penn State acknowledge[d] the NCAA's legitimate and good-faith interest and concern regarding the [child sex abuse] matter.
- Penn State and the NCAA would enter into a new Athletics Integrity Agreement (with the concurrence of the Big Ten) that includes best practices with which the university [was] committed to comply and that provides for the university to continue to retain the services of Sen. George Mitchell and his firm to support the university's activities under the Athletics Integrity Agreement and in the areas of compliance, ethics, and integrity.

QUESTIONS

1. It has been argued that the NCAA did not have any authority to intervene in a case involving sexual abuse of young boys by a former coach. Proponents of this position argue that it should have been left to the legal system, which

found the coach guilty of multiple counts. Opponents of the action also argue that the NCAA acted improvidently when it did not follow its own hearing and investigative processes, instead choosing to simply rely on the Freeh report, which had been commissioned by Penn State. Do you agree? Was it wise for the NCAA to act promptly? Why do you think it did so? Should the NCAA have intervened? What repercussions would the NCAA potentially have suffered if they failed to intervene in this high-profile case? Can it be argued that Penn State did, in fact, seek to receive some competitive advantage (or at least avoid a major disadvantage) by covering up the child abuse scandal?
2. The sanctions in this case were "unprecedented." Do you think they were excessive? It has been reported that the NCAA leadership seriously considered the suspension of the football program (the death penalty). Should they have invoked the death penalty?
3. The USC and Penn State cases appear to be evidence that the NCAA is taking a much stronger role in sanctioning infractions occurring at institutions with commercially successful and well-known football and athletic programs. Why is it doing this?

The Penn State and USC cases involved major coaches, who were also penalized by removal from their coaching positions. In the Penn State case, other university personnel, including the athletics director and president, were removed from their positions by the university. The following section examines the sanctioning of coaches and other personnel in more detail.

THE UNIVERSITY OF NORTH CAROLINA CASE

On March 12, 2012, the COI determined that the University of North Carolina, Chapel Hill (UNC) was responsible for multiple violations, including academic fraud, involving a former coach and a former tutor, who had been involved in working with college athletes. Both were found to have engaged in unethical conduct, including failure to cooperate. The university was also penalized with a one-year postseason ban, reduction of 15 football scholarships, vacating of records, and three years of probation. After that decision was rendered, new and extremely serious allegations of academic fraud involving thousands of students, many of whom were college athletes, over an 18-year period began to surface, due initially to revelations disclosed to the media. In response to those reports, in June 2014, the NCAA released a statement indicating that it had reopened its investigation of UNC. One year later, the NCAA issued a notice of allegations to the University of North Carolina, noting, "It is important to remember the following information about the NCAA members' rules on academic misconduct:

- "An NCAA member school is responsible for determining if violations of its academic standards occurred.

- "Schools are responsible for the quality of the degree programs offered for all students, including college athletes. Generally, academic issues are managed first and foremost by the faculty member in the classroom, second by that faculty member's department head, next by their dean, then the provost, and finally the president or chancellor. NCAA rules do not address course curriculum, rigor, or content.
- "Ultimately, member schools must determine if the courses for which they are giving credit and the degrees they are awarding meet the academic standards of the school and its overall mission.
- "While schools are in the best position to determine compliance with academic standards on campus, the enforcement staff will consider if other infractions occurred.
- "These might include violations of progress toward degree requirements, extra benefit rules or ethical conduct obligations. Any alleged violation of NCAA rules would be investigated and decided through the formal infractions process." See *NCAA Sends Notice of Allegations to University of North Carolina*, http://www.ncaa.org/about/resources/media-center/news/ncaa-sends-notice-allegations-university-north-carolina.

The university hired an independent investigator who found that thousands of students received credit for fraudulent or fake classes. He also found that counselors had directed college athletes into the classes in an effort to keep them eligible. The university fired four employees and disciplined five others. Deeply embarrassed by the academic improprieties, UNC proceeded to institute over 70 policy changes on campus to assure the integrity of its academic programs. See *Actions and Initiatives: Moving Forward Together* at https://carolinacommitment.unc.edu/actions-and-initiatives/. On August 14, 2015, UNC disclosed additional violations in women's basketball and men's soccer and submitted its report to the NCAA enforcement staff. The new violations in women's basketball involved the providing of improper assistance by a tutor, whereas the soccer violations involved recruiting violations.

In April of 2016, the NCAA issued an amended notice of allegations (NOA) and on August 3, 2016, the University of North Carolina replied with a strong, 73-page response that argued:

> The Amended Notice of Allegations refer to core academic issues of course structure, content, and administrative oversight that are beyond the scope of authority granted to the NCAA by its members. Such matters concern fundamental issues of institutional and academic integrity, not athletics compliance, and the University has addressed them with its accreditor. They are not the proper subject of an NCAA enforcement option. See Julian Council, *UNC Responds Strongly to the NCAA's Revised Notice of Allegations*, http://www.tarheelblog.com/2016/8/3/12361714/unc-ncaa-allegations-notice-of-allegations-response.

The Committee on Infractions issued its decision on October 12, 2017, essentially agreeing with the university that this was an academic scandal outside the purview of the NCAA and finding only a failure to cooperate by the former AFAM chair and a department administrator. The COI issued a show cause order for that department chair who had resigned in 2011. See *University of North Carolina at Chapel Hill Public Infractions Decision*, Oct. 13, 2017, *https://www.ncaa.org/sites/default/files/Oct2017_University-of-North-Carolina-at-Chapel-Hill_InfractionsDecision_20171013.pdf*.

QUESTIONS

1. Should the NCAA get involved in academic matters of this sort? Why might institutions oppose such legislation? Is this a matter of college athlete welfare? Does this sort of activity create a competitive advantage or disrupt a level playing field?
2. Bylaw 14.02.1, adopted April 28, 2016, states: "All institutional staff members and college athletes are expected to act with integrity and honesty in all academic matters. Post-enrollment academic misconduct includes any violation or breach of an institutional policy regarding academic honesty or integrity (e.g., academic offense, academic honor code violation, plagiarism, academic fraud)." Does this bylaw strike the right balance between academic independence at the institutional level and maintaining academic integrity in intercollegiate athletics, as well as a level playing field, on a national level? Does an athletics department have the ability to monitor institutional academic honesty or integrity?

C. Individual Responsibility for NCAA Rules Violations and Sanctions

In addition to penalties assessed against institutions for lack of institutional control and other infractions, institutions, conferences, and ultimately the COI can fashion penalties to deal with NCAA rule violations by coaches and other personnel. Bylaw 10.1 addresses "unethical conduct" on the part of a student-athlete or staff member (coach, professor, tutor, student manager, etc.). It generally notes that failure to cooperate in an investigation, involvement in academic fraud, providing extra benefits, dishonesty, and inappropriate interaction with an agent constitute possible examples of unethical conduct. Under Bylaw 11.1.1, a head coach is presumed to be responsible for the actions of all institutional staff members who report to the coach, directly or indirectly. A head coach is required to promote an atmosphere of compliance within his or her program and must monitor the activities of all institutional staff members involved with the program who report, directly or indirectly, to the coach.

On July 14, 2023, the NCAA issued its public infractions decision for violations in the University of Tennessee football program. From September 2018 through November 2020, a dozen members of the football staff committed more than 200 individual infractions of recruiting rules and direct payments to prospective student-athletes and their families resulting in impermissible inducements and benefits worth approximately $60,000. The Division I Committee on Infractions approved a negotiated resolution agreement identifying 22 collective Level I violations including four ethical conduct violations, head coach responsibility, and failure to monitor the football program. Noting exemplary cooperation from the university including self-reporting, fully investigating, notifying the NCAA enforcement staff of the need for additional investigation and self-imposing significant corrective actions, penalties included five years of probation; reduction in football scholarships, official visits, unofficial visits, recruiting communications, and evaluation days during probation; show cause orders for the former employees: head coach, director of recruiting, assistant director of recruiting, and former assistant coach; vacating records for 23 games in which ineligible players participated; dissociation of a booster; and additional self-imposed penalties prohibiting purchasing of football postseason broadcast advertising, and annual mandatory compliance seminars and program reviews. While NCAA penalty guidelines require postseason bans for Level I standard cases, the new NCAA constitution states that penalties imposed should not punish programs or student-athletes who were not involved in the infractions. Instead, the COI panel prescribed an enhanced financial penalty based on the financial impact postseason bans would have had on the program: $8 million attributed to the 2023 and 2024 postseason play, $5,000 plus 3 percent of the football program budget as a legislated fine, and an additional fine related to participation in the 2020 Gator Bowl game by ineligible players. See University of Tennessee, Knoxville Public Infractions Decision at *https://ncaaorg.s3.amazonaws.com/infractions/decisions/Jul2023D1INF_TenneseePublicReport.pdf*. What objectives are furthered by imposing a ban on postseason competition for repeated and/or serious violations of NCAA rules. Are financial penalties a better option? What unintended consequences might this sanction have?

A significant question arises as to whether the NCAA should follow the lead of professional leagues and punish athletes for off-the-field conduct. During the fall of 2015, issues arose regarding the penalization of college athletes for off-the-field behavior. The University of Georgia, for example, worked with the NCAA and held its star running back out of four games (or 30 percent of the season) for accepting more than $3,000 in cash from multiple individuals for autographed memorabilia and other items over a two-year period. In another case that garnered wide national attention, a former Heisman Trophy winner and star football player at Florida State University was suspended by his football coach for only *one-half* of a game for a series of major off-the-field activities, including theft and a very serious continuing allegation of sexual assault. The student-athlete also played baseball at Florida State and had previously been suspended for three games by his baseball coach for the same offenses. Should coaches be given wide latitude in deciding whether to suspend a player? Should that be left to the Faculty Athletics Committee, as is done at some institutions? What kinds of pressures exist in such a case? Should the NCAA get involved in such matters, given that it may be difficult for institutions to act against their own interest by sitting a valuable player? If the NCAA gets involved, what should the nature of that involvement be?

Recent cases make it very clear that universities must closely monitor their coaches and athletic programs, and head coaches must closely monitor the activities of their assistant coaches, under a liberal standard presuming that head coaches know what their assistants are doing. In 2016, the NCAA accused Rick Pitino, then men's basketball coach at the University of Louisville, of failing to monitor a staff member. This scandal involved an assistant coach who was paying escorts to have sex with recruits. Pitino claimed no knowledge of the situation. That same defense did not save Pitino's job when, a year later, an FBI investigation uncovered bribes paid by Adidas to Brian Bowen's father to influence the recruit to attend Louisville. Pitino, in turn, sued the university for unlawful termination and Adidas for knowingly and recklessly causing him emotional distress. Both lawsuits were settled in 2019, with Louisville agreeing to note that Pitino had resigned in his personnel file in exchange for Pitino dropping his lawsuit. The terms of the Adidas settlement were confidential.

QUESTIONS

1. Is this move to hold coaches accountable for rules compliance by limiting or ending their careers appropriate? Should head coaches be held responsible for the acts of assistant coaches? If so, under what standard (actual knowledge, constructive knowledge, or a presumption of knowledge)? Should coaches also be held responsible by their institutions for low graduation rates of their college athletes?

2. Should athletics directors and university presidents be held responsible for the operation of their athletic departments, as well as the conduct of coaches and other personnel?

    Orders to show cause are used as a means of disciplining coaches (and other personnel associated with an institution's athletics program) for NCAA rules violations by preventing employment as a coach at another NCAA member university during a prescribed period of time. Is this an effective way to prevent coaches from ignoring NCAA rules?

Problem 3-1

As a director of compliance at a major D-I university, the athletic director has asked you to prepare a short memorandum indicating what lessons you have learned from the cases discussed in these materials. In particular, she wonders what you would recommend to avoid the institutional control problems that resulted in severe penalties to USC and the unethical conduct in coaching violations that led to coaches being given orders to show cause that resulted in their being prevented from coaching at the D-I level in the future. What should the university do to minimize the likelihood that it and its coaches will be subject to severe NCAA penalties?

LEGAL LIMITS ON NCAA REGULATORY AUTHORITY

As previously discussed, in *NCAA v. Tarkanian*, the Supreme Court ruled that the NCAA is a private association rather than a state actor; therefore, it is not subject to the legal requirements of the U.S. Constitution. However, the NCAA must comply with its contractual obligations to its member institutions and their intercollegiate athletes who are third-party beneficiaries of this contractual relationship, according to *Bloom v. NCAA, infra*. In addition, the NCAA's rules, agreements, and decisions must comply with applicable federal and state civil rights laws, as well as the law of private associations and antitrust law.

A. Federal and State Civil Rights Law

Virtually all public and private universities receive some federal funds and therefore must comply with federal civil right statutes such as Title IX and the Rehabilitation Act of 1972. As the following case illustrates, this does not necessarily mean that the NCAA is subject to these federal laws.

KEY TERMS
- Civil Rights Restoration Act
- Deference
- Performance-enhancing drugs

NCAA v. Smith
525 U.S. 459 (1999)

GINSBURG, Justice.

This case concerns the amenability of the National Collegiate Athletic Association (NCAA or Association) to a private action under Title IX of the Education Amendments of 1972. . . . Title IX proscribes sex discrimination in "any education program or activity receiving Federal financial assistance."

Renee M. Smith sued the NCAA under Title IX alleging that the Association discriminated against her on the basis of her sex by denying her permission to play intercollegiate volleyball at federally assisted institutions. . . . Dues payments from recipients of federal funds, we hold, do not suffice to render the dues recipient subject to Title IX. . . .

I

[Editors' note: Smith received her bachelor's degree from one institution in two and a half years and attended graduate school at another institution, where she sought to participate in intercollegiate volleyball. She was not permitted to do so, under an NCAA rule that permitted students to use their athletic eligibility at the institution where they received their undergraduate degree if they were pursuing a graduate degree at the same institution. The same rule, however, did not permit students to participate in intercollegiate athletics at other institutions where they might be pursuing their graduate education. Smith sought a waiver of the rule, as permitted under the rule, but the NCAA refused to grant it. Smith challenged the application of this rule to her on the ground that the NCAA granted more waivers to male than female athletes and, therefore, violated Title IX, which limits discrimination based on gender.]

The NCAA moved to dismiss Smith's Title IX claim on the ground that the complaint failed to allege that the NCAA is a recipient of federal financial assistance. In opposition, Smith argued that the NCAA governs the federally funded intercollegiate athletics programs of its members, that these programs are educational, and that the NCAA benefited economically from its members' receipt of federal funds. . . .

II

Under the Civil Rights Restoration Act of 1987 (CRRA), 102 Stat. 28, 20 U.S.C. §1687, a "program or activity" includes "all of the operations of . . . a college, university, or other postsecondary institution, or a public system of higher education . . . any part of which is extended Federal financial assistance." . . . Thus, if any part of the NCAA received federal assistance, all NCAA operations would be subject to Title IX.

We have twice before considered when an entity qualifies as a recipient of federal financial assistance. In *Grove City College v. Bell*, we held that a college receives federal financial assistance when it enrolls students who receive federal funds earmarked for educational expenses. Finding "no hint" that Title IX distinguishes "between direct institutional assistance and aid received by a school through its students," we concluded that Title IX "encompass[es] *all* forms of federal aid to education, direct or indirect."

Entities that receive federal assistance, whether directly or through an intermediary, are recipients within the meaning of Title IX; entities that only benefit economically from federal assistance are not.

Unlike the earmarked student aid in *Grove City*, there is no allegation that NCAA members paid their dues with federal funds earmarked for that purpose. At most, the Association's receipt of dues demonstrates that it indirectly benefits from the federal assistance afforded its members. This showing, without more, is insufficient to trigger Title IX coverage. . . .

III

Smith, joined by the United States as *amicus curiae*, presses two alternative theories for bringing the NCAA under the prescriptions of Title IX. First, she asserts that the NCAA directly and indirectly receives federal financial assistance through the

National Youth Sports Program [that the] NCAA administers. Second, Smith argues that when a recipient cedes controlling authority over a federally funded program to another entity, the controlling entity is covered by Title IX regardless whether it is itself a recipient. . . .

We do not decide in the first instance issues not decided below. . . .

For the reasons stated, we conclude that the Court of Appeals erroneously held that dues payments from recipients of federal funds suffice to subject the NCAA to suit under Title IX. Accordingly, we vacate the judgment of the Third Circuit and remand the case for further proceedings consistent with this opinion.

QUESTION

Should the NCAA be subject to Title IX, in a broader sense, and should dues payments from recipients of federal funds suffice to subject the NCAA to a suit under Title IX?

B. Drug Testing and Privacy

As a condition of participating in intercollegiate athletics, athletes are required to provide written consent to random drug testing for substances prohibited by the NCAA during NCAA championship competitions and out-of-season testing programs. The NCAA's list of banned substances includes performance-enhancing drugs such as anabolic steroids, stimulants (e.g., cocaine and amphetamines), and certain illegal recreational drugs such as marijuana and heroin. See NCAA, *NCAA Drug Testing Program 2021-22*, https://ncaaorg.s3.amazonaws.com/ssi/substance/2021-22/2021-22SSI_DrugTestingProgram.pdf. In effect, a student-athlete's compliance with the NCAA's drug testing program, which has been alleged to violate his or her civil rights protected by state law, is a condition of eligibility to compete in intercollegiate athletics. In *Brennan v. Board of Trustees for University of Louisiana Systems*, 691 So. 2d 324 (La. App. 1997), the court was deferential in upholding the NCAA's drug-testing program against a claim that the privacy right of the student-athlete should be protected. The *Brennan* court rejected the plaintiff's indirect challenge to the NCAA's drug-testing program, even though it includes recreational and not just performance-enhancing drug use.

The sanction generally imposed on a student-athlete who tests positive for a banned substance is ineligibility to participate in any intercollegiate sports for one year and loss of one season of eligibility. (Athletes ineligible to participate in Olympic or international sports competition for violating the World Anti-Doping Code also are ineligible to participate in NCAA intercollegiate sports during the period of their suspension.) The student-athlete, in conjunction with his or her institution, has the right to appeal the finding of a positive drug test to the NCAA's Committee on Competitive Safeguards and Medical Aspects of Sports.

That committee may reduce the penalty based on the student-athlete's relative degree of fault for a doping violation. After a hearing, the committee may reduce the length of the student-athlete's suspension to one-half of the season of competition in the particular sport or determine that no suspension is appropriate based on extenuating circumstances.

In January 2015, the Committee on Competitive Safeguards and Medical Aspects of Sports (CSMAS) recommended extensive changes to the NCAA's drug-testing policies including more testing for performance-enhancing substances, based on research showing that their usage drops significantly when college athletes believe they have at least a 30 percent chance of getting caught. In 2023, the CSMAS recommended removing cannabis from the list of banned drugs in favor of a harm reduction philosophy that would be similar to the approach taken for alcohol with the intent to address harmful use behaviors at an institutional level.

QUESTIONS

Does the NCAA have a valid justification for testing adult athletes for the usage of recreational drugs that are not performance enhancing? Should the NCAA recognize the student-athlete's right of privacy and restrict its drug testing accordingly? If so, how should it do so?

C. Contract and Private Association Laws

Courts generally are deferential to the NCAA regarding its interpretation and enforcement of its own rules and regulations, particularly its student-athlete eligibility rules. As you read the following case, consider whether such judicial deference is warranted in this context and results in a fair and principled resolution of the issues. Note also that even though the NCAA bylaws at issue in *Bloom* have been rendered moot because of developments related to NIL, see discussion *infra*, the case continues to illustrate the deference courts have historically afforded the NCAA in enforcing its bylaws and the standard adopted to determine whether judicial intervention is warranted to circumscribe the NCAA's actions.

KEY TERMS
- Arbitrary and capricious
- Confidentiality
- Declaratory and injunctive relief
- Good faith and fair dealing
- Restitution rule
- Standing
- Subpoena
- Third-party beneficiary

Bloom v. NCAA
93 P.3d 621 (Colo. App. 2004)

DAILEY, J.

I. Background

Bloom, a high school football and track star, was recruited to play football at CU [the University of Colorado]. Before enrolling there, however, he competed in Olympic and professional World Cup skiing events, becoming the World Cup champion in freestyle moguls. During the Olympics, Bloom appeared on MTV, and thereafter was offered various paid entertainment opportunities, including a chance to host a show on Nickelodeon. Bloom also agreed to endorse commercially certain ski equipment, and he contracted to model clothing for Tommy Hilfiger.

Bloom became concerned that his endorsements and entertainment activities might interfere with his eligibility to compete in intercollegiate football. On Bloom's behalf, CU first requested waivers of NCAA rules restricting student-athlete endorsement and media activities and, then, a favorable interpretation of the NCAA rule restricting media activities.

The NCAA denied CU's requests, and Bloom discontinued his endorsement, modeling, and media activities to play football for CU during the 2002 fall season. However, Bloom instituted this action against the NCAA for declaratory and injunctive relief, asserting that his endorsement, modeling, and media activities were necessary to support his professional skiing career, something which the NCAA rules permitted.

Bloom requested that the NCAA restrictions be declared inapplicable, and that the NCAA and CU be enjoined from applying them, to activities originating prior to his enrollment at CU or wholly unrelated to his prowess as a football player.

IV. Standing

[Editors' note: The court first addressed the NCAA's assertion that Bloom lacked standing to pursue either his contract claims or his arbitrary and capricious argument.]

Courts are reluctant to intervene, except on the most limited grounds, in the internal affairs of voluntary associations. . . . Even then, it would appear that a plaintiff must ordinarily allege an invasion of some type of civil or property right to have standing.

Here, Bloom is not a member of the NCAA, and he does not have a constitutional right to engage in amateur intercollegiate athletics at CU. Nor does he assert any property interest in playing football for CU.

However, to the extent Bloom's claim of arbitrary and capricious action asserts a violation of the duty of good faith and fair dealing that is implied in the contractual relationship between the NCAA and its members, his position as a third-party beneficiary of that contractual relationship affords him standing to pursue this claim.

In sum, we conclude that Bloom has third-party beneficiary standing to pursue what in essence are two claims for violation of his contractual rights.

V. Probability of Success

[In asserting that he is entitled to injunctive relief,] Bloom contends that the trial court erred in assessing the probability of success on his contract claims. We disagree.

A. Interpretation of NCAA Bylaws

In interpreting a contract, we seek to give effect to the intent and the reasonable expectations of the parties. . . . To determine the intent and expectations of the parties, we view the contract in its entirety, not in isolated portions . . . and we give words and phrases their plain meaning according to common usage.

Bloom relies on NCAA Bylaw 12.1.2, which states that "[a] professional athlete in one sport may represent a member institution in a different sport." He asserts that, because a professional is one who "gets paid" for a sport, a student-athlete is entitled to earn whatever income is customary for his or her professional sport, which, in the case of professional skiers, primarily comes from endorsements and paid media opportunities.

We recognize that, like many others involved in individual professional sports such as golf, tennis, and boxing, professional skiers obtain much of their income from sponsors. We note, however, that none of the NCAA's bylaws mentions, much less explicitly establishes, a right to receive "customary income" for a sport.

Unlike other NCAA bylaws, the endorsements and media appearance bylaws do not contain any sport-specific qualifiers. In our view, when read together, the NCAA bylaws express a clear and unambiguous intent to prohibit student-athletes from engaging in endorsements and paid media appearances. . . .

The clear import of the bylaws is that, although student-athletes have the right to be professional athletes, they do not have the right to simultaneously engage in endorsement or paid media activity and maintain their eligibility to participate in amateur competition. And we may not disregard the clear meaning of the bylaws simply because they may disproportionately affect those who participate in individual professional sports. . . .

Thus, even if the bylaws were viewed as ambiguous, the record supports the trial court's conclusion that the bylaws would ultimately be interpreted in accordance with the NCAA's and its member institutions' construction of those bylaws.

B. Application of Bylaws to Bloom

The U.S. Supreme Court has recognized the NCAA as "the guardian of an important American tradition, namely, amateurism in intercollegiate athletics."

Under that tradition, "college sports provided an important opportunity for teaching people about character, motivation, endurance, loyalty, and the attainment of one's personal best — all qualities of great value in citizens. In this sense, competitive athletics were viewed as an extracurricular activity, justified by the university as part of its ideal objective of educating the whole person."

The NCAA's "Principle of Amateurism" states:

> Student-athletes shall be amateurs in an intercollegiate sport, and their participation should be motivated primarily by education and by the physical, mental and social benefits to be derived. Student participation in intercollegiate athletics is an avocation, and student-athletes should be protected from exploitation by professional and commercial enterprises.

The NCAA's purpose, in this regard, is not only "to maintain intercollegiate athletics as an integral part of the educational program," but also to "retain a clear line of demarcation between intercollegiate athletics and professional sports."

Similar concerns underlie the NCAA's prohibition on paid entertainment activity. Paid entertainment activity may impinge upon the amateur ideal if the opportunity were obtained or advanced because of the student's athletic ability or prestige, even though that activity may further the education of student-athletes such as Bloom, a communications major.

In this case, Bloom presented evidence that some of his acting opportunities arose not as a result of his athletic ability but because of his good looks and on-camera presence. However, the record contains evidence that Bloom's agent and the Tommy Hilfiger company marketed Bloom as a talented multi-sport athlete, and a representative from a talent agency intimated that Bloom's reputation as an athlete would be advantageous in obtaining auditions for various entertainment opportunities. . . .

Under these circumstances, we perceive no abuse of the trial court's discretion in failing to fault the NCAA for refusing to waive its rules, as requested by CU, to permit Bloom "to pursue any television and film opportunities while he is a student-athlete at CU."

Bloom also asserts that the NCAA is arbitrary in its application of the endorsement and media bylaws. He notes that, while the NCAA would bar him from accepting commercial endorsements, it will allow colleges to commercially endorse athletic equipment by having students wear the equipment, with identifying logos and insignias, while engaged in intercollegiate competition. But the trial court determined, and we agree, that this application of the bylaws has a rational basis in economic necessity: financial benefits inure not to any single student-athlete but to member schools and thus to all student-athletes, including those who participate in programs that generate no revenue.

Bloom further argues that the NCAA is arbitrary in the way it applies its bylaws among individual students. Bloom presented evidence that, in one instance, a student-athlete was permitted to make an unpaid, minor appearance in a single film. But the NCAA could rationally conclude that this situation was different: Bloom did not seek permission to make an unpaid appearance in one specific instance; he wanted to take advantage of any number of television and film opportunities, and he wanted to be paid. . . .

> Bloom has thus failed to demonstrate any inconsistency in application which would lead us to conclude that the NCAA was arbitrarily applying its rules.
>
> Finally, we are not convinced that the NCAA treated Bloom unfairly in the manner in which it denied the requests to waive or interpret its rules. . . .
>
> For these reasons, we agree with the trial court that Bloom failed to demonstrate a reasonable probability of success on the merits.

QUESTIONS

1. Why did the court hold that the NCAA's application of its endorsement and media bylaws was not arbitrary and capricious? As is true of other private associations, courts afford considerable deference to the NCAA in enforcing its rules and regulations. Notwithstanding the policy of judicial deference, courts will intervene into the affairs of private associations when the association has acted in violation of its own rules, regulations, and policies.

2. In *NCAA v. Lasege*, 53 S.W.3d 77 (Ky. 2001), the Supreme Court of Kentucky ruled in favor of the NCAA, which had prohibited Muhammad Lasege, a University of Louisville basketball player, from participating in intercollegiate sports. Prior to his matriculation at Louisville, Lasege played basketball in Russia under a professional contract and engaged in other conduct that the NCAA found to be in violation of its amateurism rules. Ruling on the athlete's claim that the NCAA acted arbitrarily and capriciously when it declared him ineligible, the Kentucky Supreme Court held that:

   > [A] ruling is arbitrary and capricious only where it is "clearly erroneous, and by 'clearly erroneous' we mean unsupported by substantial evidence." Here, the NCAA's ruling has strong evidentiary support—Lasege unquestionably signed contracts to play professional basketball and unquestionably accepted benefits.

   The *Lasege* court also validated the NCAA rule that permits the organization to seek restitution from its member institutions as a result of rules violations such as those that Louisville committed when it allowed Lasege to play. The Indiana Supreme Court noted the tensions that arise in restitution cases:

   > Undeniably, the Restitution Rule imposes hardship on a school that, in compliance with an order of a court which is later vacated, fields an ineligible player. On the other hand, use of an ineligible player imposes a hardship on other teams that must compete against the teams fielding ineligible players. While schools will contend that [it] is unfair when they have to forfeit victories earned with an ineligible player on the field because they complied with a court order, competing schools will reply that it is unfair when they have to compete against a team with an ineligible student athlete because a local trial judge prohibited the school or the IHSAA from following the eligibility rules.

   Courts have upheld the restitution rule. Do you agree with the courts?

D. Federal Antitrust Law

1. Introduction

The primary objective of federal antitrust law is to preserve a competitive economic marketplace that results in the efficient production of desirable products and services (e.g., entertainment such as college sports) at the lowest possible prices, which benefits consumers (e.g., college sports fans). It also protects the individual economic rights of the NCAA's educational institutions, coaches, student-athletes, and others. Federal antitrust litigation against the NCAA challenging allegedly anticompetitive conduct generally has been brought under §1 of the Sherman Act (15 U.S.C. §1), which provides that "[e]very contract, combination . . . or conspiracy in restraint of trade or commerce" is illegal. The NCAA also is subject to §2 of the Sherman Act (15 U.S.C. §2), which prohibits monopolization or attempts to monopolize trade or commerce, although litigation asserting §2 claims against the NCAA historically has been unsuccessful. See, e.g., *Association of Intercollegiate Athletics for Women v. NCAA*, 735 F.2d 577 (D.C. Cir. 1984) (rejecting allegation that the NCAA unlawfully used its monopoly regulatory power over men's intercollegiate sports to facilitate its entry into the regulation of women's intercollegiate sports and to force the Association of Intercollegiate Athletics for Women, a competing national governing body, out of existence).

Sherman Act §1 provides an important limit on the collective internal governance of intercollegiate athletics by NCAA member schools and conferences on a national or divisional level. The NCAA has no blanket exemption from the federal antitrust laws merely because it is a nonprofit organization whose member colleges and universities are educational institutions. In *Hennessey v. NCAA*, 564 F.2d 1136 (5th Cir. 1977), the Fifth Circuit observed that "[w]hile the participating athletics [*sic*] may be amateurs, intercollegiate athletics in its management is clearly business, and big business at that." *Id.* at 1150. The court concluded, "While organized as a non-profit organization, the NCAA and its member institutions are, when presenting amateur athletics to a ticket-paying, television-buying public, engaged in a business venture of far greater magnitude than the vast majority of 'profit-making' enterprises." *Id.* at 1149, n.14.

The collective adoption and enforcement of NCAA and divisional rules by its member universities, as well as other agreements concerning the production, marketing, and governance of intercollegiate athletics, constitutes concerted action for purposes of §1 of the Sherman Act. Because virtually all of these rules and agreements are potentially subject to antitrust challenge, college sports administrators need to have a basic understanding of this complex area of law and how federal courts have applied it to college sports, particularly in recent years.

At the outset, keep in mind that NCAA intercollegiate athletics are based on a philosophical *amateur/education model*, although Division I FBS football as well as men's and women's basketball have evolved into a *commercial/education* model because of their widespread popularity and commercial success. Similar to efforts to apply federal labor and state workers' compensation laws to change the historical legal relationship between a university and its student-athletes (discussed in

Chapter 4), the plaintiffs in the following antitrust cases effectively are seeking to establish a *commercial/professional model* for at least those college sports. As you read these materials, consider whose economic interests have been furthered by judicial application of §1 to output market restraints (e.g., NCAA limits on a particular sport's number of televised games (*Bd of Regents*)) and input market restraints (e.g., NCAA rules capping coaches' salaries (*Law*) or limiting the value of athletic scholarships (*O'Bannon*) or other educational benefits (*Alston*)) as well as whether and how courts' decisions have furthered the interests of college sports fans.

2. Case Law

KEY TERMS
- Anticompetitive effects
- Horizontal restraint (e.g., price-fixing, output limitations)
- Illegal per se rule
- Input market
- Output market
- Procompetitive justification
- "Quick look" rule of reason
- Rule of reason

The following 1984 Supreme Court decision illustrates that despite §1's broad statutory language, only NCAA rules or agreements that unreasonably restrain trade violate federal antitrust law.

NCAA v. Board of Regents of the University of Oklahoma
468 U.S. 85 (1984)

Justice STEVENS delivered the opinion of the Court.

The University of Oklahoma and the University of Georgia contend that the National Collegiate Athletic Association has unreasonably restrained trade [in violation of §1 of the Sherman Act] in the televising of college football games. . . .

With the exception of football, the NCAA has not undertaken any regulation of the televising of athletic events. . . .

[Editors' note: In separate agreements, the NCAA granted the American Broadcasting Company (ABC) and the Columbia Broadcasting System (CBS) each the right to telecast 14 regular-season football games in accordance with certain "ground rules." Each network agreed to pay a specified "minimum aggregate compensation to the participating NCAA member institutions" during the four-year period in an amount that totaled $131,750,000. The plan also contained "appearance requirements" and "appearance limitations" that pertained to each of the two-year periods that the plan was in effect. The basic requirement imposed on each of the two networks was that it must schedule appearances for at least 82 different member institutions during each two-year period. Under the appearance limitations, no member institution was eligible to appear on television more than a total of six times and more than four times nationally, with the appearances to be divided equally between the two carrying networks. The number of exposures specified in the contracts also set an absolute maximum on the number of games that could be broadcast. It limited the total amount of televised intercollegiate football and the number of games that any one team could televise. No NCAA member university was permitted to make any sale of television rights except in accordance with the basic plan.

Some years ago, five major conferences, together with major football-playing independent institutions, organized the College Football Association (CFA). The original purpose of the CFA was to promote the interests of major football-playing schools within the NCAA structure. The Universities of Oklahoma and Georgia, respondents in this case, were members of the CFA. Beginning in 1979, CFA members began to advocate that colleges with major football programs should have a greater voice in the formulation of football television policy than they had in the NCAA. They developed an independent television plan and entered into a 1981 contract with the National Broadcasting Company (NBC) that would have permitted a greater number of its members' games to be televised, and would have increased the overall football television revenues realized by CFA members. In response, the NCAA publicly announced that it would take disciplinary action against any CFA member that complied with the CFA-NBC contract, which would apply to other sports as well as football. Although respondents obtained a preliminary injunction against the NCAA's threatened disciplinary action, most CFA members were reluctant to enter into the proposed contract with NBC and the agreement was never consummated.]

II

There can be no doubt that the challenged practices of the NCAA constitute a "restraint of trade" in the sense that they limit members' freedom to negotiate and enter into their own television contracts. . . . In that sense, however, every contract is a restraint of trade, and as we have repeatedly recognized, the Sherman Act was intended to prohibit only unreasonable restraints of trade.

It is also undeniable that these practices share characteristics of restraints we have previously held unreasonable. The NCAA is an association of schools which compete against each other to attract television revenues, not to mention fans and athletes. As the District Court found, the policies of the NCAA with respect to television rights are ultimately controlled by the vote of member institutions. By participating in an association which prevents member institutions from competing against each other on the basis of price or kind of television rights that can be offered to broadcasters, the NCAA member institutions have created a horizontal restraint — an agreement among competitors on the way in which they will compete with one another. A restraint of this type has often been held to be unreasonable as a matter of law. Because it places a ceiling on the number of games member institutions may televise, the horizontal agreement places an artificial limit on the quantity of televised football that is available to broadcasters and consumers. . . .

Horizontal price fixing and output limitation are ordinarily condemned as a matter of law under an "illegal per se" approach because the probability that these practices are anticompetitive is so high; a per se rule is applied when "the practice facially appears to be one that would always or almost always tend to restrict competition and decrease output." In such circumstances a restraint is presumed unreasonable without inquiry into the particular market context in which it is found. Nevertheless, we have decided that it would be inappropriate to apply a per se rule to this case. This decision is not based on a lack of judicial experience with this type of arrangement, on the fact that the NCAA is organized as a nonprofit entity, or on our respect for the NCAA's historic role in the preservation and encouragement of intercollegiate amateur athletics. Rather, what is critical is that this case involves an industry in which horizontal restraints on competition are essential if the product is to be available at all.

As Judge Bork has noted: "[S]ome activities can only be carried out jointly. Perhaps the leading example is league sports. When a league of professional lacrosse teams is formed, it would be pointless to declare their cooperation illegal on the ground that there are no other professional lacrosse teams." R. Bork, *The Antitrust Paradox* 278 (1978). What the NCAA and its member institutions market in this case is competition itself — contests between competing institutions. Of course, this would be completely ineffective if there were no rules on which the competitors agreed to create and define the competition to be marketed. A myriad of rules affecting such matters as the size of the field, the number of players on a team, and the extent to which physical violence is to be encouraged or proscribed, all must be agreed upon, and all restrain the manner in which institutions compete. Moreover, the NCAA seeks to market a particular brand of football — college football. The identification of this "product" with an academic tradition differentiates college football from and makes it more popular than professional sports to which it might otherwise be comparable, such as, for example, minor league baseball. In order to preserve the character and quality of the "product," athletes must not be paid, must be required to attend class, and the like. And the integrity of the "product" cannot be preserved except by mutual agreement; if an institution adopted such restrictions unilaterally, its effectiveness as a competitor on the playing field might soon be destroyed. Thus, the NCAA plays a vital role in enabling college football to preserve its character, and as a result enables a product to be marketed which might otherwise be unavailable. In performing this role, its actions widen consumer choice — not only the choices available to sports fans but also those available to athletes — and hence can be viewed as procompetitive. . . .

III

Because it restrains price and output, the NCAA's television plan has a significant potential for anticompetitive effects. The findings of the District Court indicate that this potential has been realized. The District Court found that if member institutions were free to sell television rights, many more games would be shown on television, and that the NCAA's output restriction has the effect of raising the price the networks pay for television rights. Moreover, the court found that by fixing a price for television rights to all games, the NCAA creates a price structure that is unresponsive to viewer demand and unrelated to the prices that would prevail in a competitive market. And, of course, since as a practical matter all member institutions need NCAA approval, members have no real choice but to adhere to the NCAA's television controls. . . .

[The] NCAA television plan on its face constitutes a restraint upon the operation of a free market, and the findings of the District Court establish that it has operated to raise prices and reduce output. Under the Rule of Reason, these hallmarks of anti-competitive behavior place upon petitioner a heavy burden of establishing an affirmative defense which competitively justifies this apparent deviation from the operations of a free market. We turn now to the NCAA's proffered justifications. . . .

V

Throughout the history of its regulation of intercollegiate football telecasts, the NCAA has indicated its concern with protecting live attendance. This concern, it should be noted, is not with protecting live attendance at games which are shown on television; that type of interest is not at issue in this case. Rather, the concern is that fan interest in a televised game may adversely affect ticket sales for games that will not appear on television. . . . Under the current plan, games are shown on television during all hours that college football games are played. The plan simply does not protect live attendance by ensuring that games will not be shown on television at the same time as live events.

There is, however, a more fundamental reason for rejecting this defense. The NCAA's argument that its television plan is necessary to protect live attendance is not based on a desire to maintain the integrity of college football as a distinct and attractive product, but rather on a fear that the product will not prove sufficiently attractive to draw live attendance when faced with competition from televised games. At bottom the NCAA's position is that ticket sales for most college games are unable to compete in a free market. The television plan protects ticket sales by limiting output — just as any monopolist increases revenues by reducing output. By seeking to insulate live ticket sales from the full spectrum of competition because of its assumption that the product itself is insufficiently attractive to consumers, petitioner forwards a justification that is inconsistent with the basic policy of the Sherman Act. "[T]he Rule of Reason does not support a defense based on the assumption that competition itself is unreasonable."

VI

Petitioner argues that the interest in maintaining a competitive balance among amateur athletic teams is legitimate and important and that it justifies the regulations challenged in this case. We agree with the first part of the argument but not the second.

Our decision not to apply a per se rule to this case rests in large part on our recognition that a certain degree of cooperation is necessary if the type of competition that petitioner and its member institutions seek to market is to be preserved.

It is reasonable to assume that most of the regulatory controls of the NCAA are justifiable means of fostering competition among amateur athletic teams and therefore procompetitive because they enhance public interest in intercollegiate athletics. The specific restraints on football telecasts that are challenged in this case do not, however, fit into the same mold as do rules defining the conditions of the contest, the eligibility of participants, or the manner in which members of a joint enterprise shall share the responsibilities and the benefits of the total venture.

The NCAA does not claim that its television plan has equalized or is intended to equalize competition within any one league. The plan is nationwide in scope and there is no single league or tournament in which all college football teams compete. There is no evidence of any intent to equalize the strength of teams in Division I-A with those in Division II or Division III, and not even a colorable basis for giving colleges that have no football program at all a voice in the management of the revenues generated by the football programs at other schools.

The interest in maintaining a competitive balance that is asserted by the NCAA as a justification for regulating all television of intercollegiate football is not related to any neutral standard or to any readily identifiable group of competitors.

The television plan is not even arguably tailored to serve such an interest. It does not regulate the amount of money that any college may spend on its football program, nor the way in which the colleges may use the revenues that are generated by their football programs, whether derived from the sale of television rights, the sale of tickets, or the sale of concessions or program advertising. The plan simply imposes a restriction on one source of revenue that is more important to some colleges than to others. There is no evidence that this restriction produces any greater measure of equality throughout the NCAA than would a restriction on alumni donations, tuition rates, or any other revenue-producing activity. At the same time, as the District Court found, the NCAA imposes a variety of other restrictions designed to preserve amateurism which are much better tailored to the goal of competitive balance than is the television plan, and which are "clearly sufficient" to preserve competitive balance to the extent it is within the NCAA's power to do so. And much more than speculation supported the District Court's findings on this score. No other NCAA sport employs a similar plan, and in particular the court found that in the most closely analogous sport, college basketball, competitive balance has been maintained without resort to a restrictive television plan.

Perhaps the most important reason for rejecting the argument that the interest in competitive balance is served by the television plan is the District Court's unambiguous and well-supported finding that many more games would be televised in a free market than under the NCAA plan. . . .

VII

The NCAA plays a critical role in the maintenance of a revered tradition of amateurism in college sports. There can be no question but that it needs ample latitude to play that role, or that the preservation of the student-athlete in higher education adds richness and diversity to intercollegiate athletics and is entirely consistent with the goals of the Sherman Act. But consistent with the Sherman Act, the role of the NCAA must be to preserve a tradition that might otherwise die; rules that restrict output are hardly consistent with this role. Today we hold only that the record supports the District Court's conclusion that by curtailing output and blunting the ability of member institutions to respond to consumer preference, the NCAA has restricted rather than enhanced the place of intercollegiate athletics in the Nation's life. Accordingly, the judgment of the Court of Appeals is Affirmed.

Justice WHITE, with whom Justice REHNQUIST joins, dissenting.

Although some of the NCAA's activities, viewed in isolation, bear a resemblance to those undertaken by professional sports leagues and associations, the Court errs in treating intercollegiate athletics under the NCAA's control as a purely commercial venture in which colleges and universities participate solely, or even primarily, in the pursuit of profits. Accordingly, I dissent. . . .

The NCAA, in short, "exist[s] primarily to enhance the contribution made by amateur athletic competition to the process of higher education as distinguished from realizing maximum return on it as an entertainment commodity." *Association for Intercollegiate Athletics for Women v. NCAA*, 558 F. Supp. 487, 494 (DC 1983), *aff'd*, 236 U.S. App. D.C. 311, 735 F.2d 577 (1984). In pursuing this goal, the organization and its members seek to provide a public good — a viable system of amateur athletics — that most likely could not be provided in a perfectly competitive market. See *Hennessey v. NCAA*, 564 F.2d 1136, 1153 (CA5 1977). "Without regulation, the desire of member institutions to remain athletically competitive would lead them to engage in activities that deny amateurism to the public. No single institution could confidently enforce its own standards since it could not trust its competitors to do the same." Note, *Antitrust and Nonprofit Entities*, 94 Harv. L. Rev. 802, 817–818 (1981). The history of intercollegiate athletics prior to the advent of the NCAA provides ample support for this conclusion. By mitigating what appears to be a clear failure of the free market to serve the ends and goals of higher education, the NCAA ensures the continued availability of a unique and valuable product, the very existence of which might well be threatened by unbridled competition in the economic sphere. . . .

. . . I believe that the lower courts "erred by subjugating the NCAA's educational goals (and, incidentally, those which Oklahoma and Georgia insist must be maintained in any event) to the purely competitive commercialism of [an] 'every school for itself' approach to television contract bargaining." . . .

QUESTIONS

1. The Supreme Court's majority characterizes the NCAA's restrictions on televised college football games as commercial activity subject to Sherman Act scrutiny. They conclude that NCAA members "compete against each other to attract television revenues, not to mention fans and athletes," and are economic competitors. By contrast, in his dissent, Justice White, who played college football at University of Colorado and finished second in the 1937 Heisman

Trophy balloting, asserts that the majority erroneously characterizes intercollegiate athletics "as a purely commercial venture in which . . . universities participate solely, or even primarily, in the pursuit of profits."

Tom McMillen, a former All-American college basketball player at the University of Maryland (and also a congressman from 1987–1993), argues that *Board of Regents* was wrongly decided because "the NCAA's loss of monopoly broadcast power [has led] to an escalating competition for money among schools." McMillen supports Justice White's dissent, arguing that "the NCAA monopoly 'fosters the goal of amateurism by spreading revenues among various schools and reducing the financial incentives towards professionalism.'" Tom McMillen, *"Whizzer" White Had It Right When It Came to TV Money*, NCAA News, May 27, 2002, at 4. Given the twenty-first-century realities and multibillion dollar commercialization of college sports as well as professionalization effort, do you agree with the *Board of Regents* majority or dissent (and McMillen)?

2. To determine whether an agreement unreasonably restrains trade, courts historically have applied either per se or rule of reason analysis. The objective of either standard is "to form a judgment about the [net] competitive significance of the restraint," although the respective application of these tests is quite different. Restraints deemed to be predominantly anticompetitive, as a matter of law or fact, are found to be unreasonable and thus illegal under the antitrust laws. Under the per se rule, certain restraints are conclusively presumed to be illegal as a matter of law because of their significant adverse effects on competition and lack of redeeming procompetitive virtues. Under the rule of reason, the anticompetitive effects of the challenged restraint are balanced against its procompetitive effects on a case-by-case basis, considering the specific facts introduced into evidence by the parties, to determine its net competitive effects.

   Although the Supreme Court notes that agreements among industry competitors (e.g., Burger King, McDonald's, and Wendy's fast-food restaurants) to fix prices and limit output generally are illegal per se, why does it analyze the legality of the NCAA's television plan (an output restriction raising the price networks paid for college football television rights) under the rule of reason? What procompetitive objectives generally justify NCAA rules and regulations? Why did the *Board of Regents* majority conclude that none of them justify the NCAA's anticompetitive television plan?

   The federal antitrust laws are intended to ensure that consumers receive the benefits of a competitive marketplace. Have college football fans benefited from judicial invalidation of the NCAA's exclusive college football television plan? How much impact has the decision in the *Board of Regents* case had on the commercialization of college football from 1984 to the present?

• • • • • • • •

Although *Board of Regents* held that antitrust law prohibits the NCAA from exclusively selling or limiting the total number of televised college football games (or fixing the price of broadcasting rights), this case did not rule that groups of NCAA universities cannot jointly license television or other media rights to college football games. Today, college football television contracts generally are negotiated and entered into by athletic conferences on behalf of their member universities, which has generated the recent expansion of the B1G, SEC, and Big Twelve conferences to 14 or more member universities. Because no individual conference historically had a sufficiently large enough share of the college football broadcasting market to adversely affect competition in it, conference members' joint licensing of their football broadcasting rights generally did not create significant antitrust concerns. However, as some Division I FBS athletic conferences grow in size and national scope with resulting adverse economic effects on other athletic conferences and universities, potential Sherman Act §1 issues may arise.

The *Board of Regents* case considered the validity of NCAA rules that restrain the intercollegiate athletics output market (e.g., a limit on the total number of televised college football games), whose adverse effects on consumer welfare are readily apparent. Next, we consider the validity of NCAA rules limiting competition among universities in the input market for the resources necessary to produce intercollegiate sports such as the services of coaches and college athletes.

In *Law v. NCAA*, 134 F.3d 1010 (10th Cir. 1998), a federal appellate court ruled that fixed maximum salaries for Division I "restricted-earnings" basketball coaches established by an NCAA bylaw (the REC Rule) violated §1. Characterizing coaching services as a necessary input to produce intercollegiate athletic competition, the court analyzed the legality of this restraint under the rule of reason, the standard that *Board of Regents* applied to NCAA restraints on the output market.

The *Law* court described the rule of reason standard for evaluating the net competitive effects of a challenged collective restraint of trade as follows:

> Courts have imposed a consistent structure on rule of reason analysis by casting it in terms of shifting burdens of proof. Under this approach, [1] the plaintiff bears the initial burden of showing that an agreement had a substantially adverse effect on competition. If the plaintiff meets this burden, [2] the burden shifts to the defendant to come forward with evidence of the procompetitive virtues of the alleged wrongful conduct. If the defendant is able to demonstrate procompetitive effects, [3] the plaintiff then must prove that the challenged conduct is not reasonably necessary to achieve the legitimate objectives or that those objectives can be achieved in a substantially less restrictive manner.

Id. at 1019.

Applying the "quick look" rule of reason because the NCAA did not satisfy its burden of proof under step 2 above, the court ruled that capping the salaries of restricted-earnings coaches below the level that free market competition previously had established is horizontal price-fixing, with clear anticompetitive effects that were not justified by any countervailing procompetitive benefits. It concluded that "[t]he NCAA's cost containment justification is illegitimate because . . . [r]educing costs for member institutions, without more, does not justify the anti-competitive effects of fixing the price of [coaches' salaries]." *Id.* at 1023. The court found "no evidence that limits on restricted-earning coaches' salaries would be successful in reducing deficits, let alone that such reductions were necessary to save college basketball" from being destroyed by overspending. While recognizing that the NCAA's need to ensure competitive balance in intercollegiate athletics is a valid procompetitive justification, the court determined that the NCAA had not proved that "the salary restrictions enhance competition, level an uneven playing field, or reduce coaching inequities" among its member schools. *Id.* at 1023. It observed that this restriction "does not equalize the overall amount of money Division I schools are permitted to spend on their basketball programs," *Id.* at 1024, and there is "no reason to think that the money saved by a school on the salary of a restricted-earnings coach will not be put into another aspect of the school's basketball program, such as equipment or even another coach's salary, thereby increasing inequity in that area." *Id.* at 1023.

The coaches whose economic interests were adversely affected by the REC Rule (including those coaching sports other than basketball) ultimately won a jury verdict of $22.3 million, which, with mandatory tripling of damages under the Sherman Act, resulted in a total award of $66.9 million from the NCAA. The NCAA ultimately agreed to pay $54.5 million to settle this lawsuit, and the court awarded approximately $20 million in attorneys' fees and costs to plaintiffs' attorneys. See *Law v. NCAA*, 108 F. Supp. 2d 1193 (D. Kan. 2000) (approving revised settlement plan as fair, reasonable, and adequate).

In *Board of Regents*, the Supreme Court recognized that NCAA schools compete against each other to attract student-athletes to their intercollegiate athletic programs. Although uniform eligibility rules both define and limit the permissible nature and scope of economic competition among NCAA members for student-athletes' services, lower courts historically characterized all NCAA student-athlete eligibility rules as noncommercial activity not subject to antitrust scrutiny. See, e.g., *Smith v. NCAA*, 139 F.3d 180, 185-86 (3d Cir. 1998) ("[E]ligibility rules are not related to the NCAA's commercial or business activities. Rather than intending to provide the NCAA with a commercial advantage, the eligibility rules primarily seek to ensure fair competition in intercollegiate athletics."). Without any detailed legal or factual analysis, intercollegiate athlete eligibility rules were presumed necessary to preserve amateurism, academic values, and/or competitive balance in intercollegiate athletics, notwithstanding scholarly commentary that these rules should be characterized as commercial activity with their respective net competitive effects individually analyzed under the rule of reason.

In *Agnew v. NCAA*, 683 F.3d 328, 339 (7th Cir. 2012), the Seventh Circuit considered "whether and when the Sherman Act applies to the NCAA and its member schools in relation to their interaction with student-athletes." Based on *Board of Regents*, the court stated that certain forms of NCAA regulation such as student-athlete eligibility rules are "presumptively procompetitive" and should be judicially characterized as reasonable restraints "'in the twinkling of an eye' . . . at the motion-to-dismiss stage" of a §1 claim. *Id.* at 341. The court explained: "Beyond the obvious fact that the Supreme Court explicitly mentioned eligibility rules as a type that 'fit[s] into the same mold' as other procompetitive rules, they are clearly necessary to preserve amateurism and the student-athlete in college football. Indeed, they define what it means to be an amateur or a student-athlete and are therefore essential to the very existence of the product of college football." *Id.* at 343. On the other hand, the Seventh Circuit distinguished eligibility rules from NCAA maximum limits on the number of scholarships a university may award for a particular sport and their (then-existing) one-year duration, which it found to have adverse commercial effects on student-athletes that must be justified under the rule-of-reason scrutiny. It noted that these rules do not "help preserve the existence of the student-athlete . . . since they actually limit the number of athletes awarded financial aid and the amount of financial aid that can be awarded." *Id.* at 345.

In contrast to *Smith, Agnew*, and other cases holding that NCAA student-athlete eligibility rules are valid as a matter of law, the following case holds that an NCAA eligibility rule that precluded its member universities from offering college athletes a full cost-of-attendance scholarship is a commercial restraint that violates the full rule of reason. However, it generally upholds the NCAA rules requiring college athletes to be amateurs, which prohibit their receipt of "cash payments untethered to their education expenses" because "not paying student-athletes is *precisely what makes them amateurs.*"

O'Bannon v. NCAA
803 F.3d 1049 (9th Cir. 2015), *cert. denied*, 137 S. Ct. 277 (2016)

Bybee, Circuit Judge:

. . . For more than a century, the National Collegiate Athletic Association (NCAA) has prescribed rules governing the eligibility of athletes at its more than 1,000 member colleges and universities. Those rules prohibit student-athletes from being paid for the use of their names, images, and likenesses (NILs). The question presented in this momentous case is whether the NCAA's rules are subject to the antitrust laws and, if so, whether they are an unlawful restraint of trade.

After a bench trial and in a thorough opinion, the district court concluded that the NCAA's compensation rules were an unlawful restraint of trade. It then enjoined the NCAA from prohibiting its member schools from giving scholarships up to the full cost of attendance at their respective schools and up to $5,000 per year in deferred compensation, to be held in trust for student-athletes until after they leave college. As far as we are aware, the district court's decision is the first by any federal court to hold that any aspect of the NCAA's amateurism rules violate the antitrust laws, let alone to mandate by injunction that the NCAA change its practices.

We conclude that the district court's decision was largely correct. Although we agree with the Supreme Court and our sister circuits that many of the NCAA's amateurism rules are likely to be procompetitive, we hold that those rules are not exempt from antitrust scrutiny; rather, they must be analyzed under the Rule of Reason. Applying the Rule of Reason, we conclude that the district court correctly identified one proper alternative to the current NCAA compensation rules — *i.e.*, allowing

NCAA members to give scholarships up to the full cost of attendance — but that the district court's other remedy, allowing students to be paid cash compensation of up to $5,000 per year, was erroneous. We therefore affirm in part and reverse in part. . . .

III

A. *Board of Regents* Did Not Declare the NCAA's Amateurism Rules "Valid as a Matter of Law"

We consider, first, the NCAA's claim that, under *Board of Regents*, all NCAA amateurism rules are "valid as a matter of law." . . .

[T]he NCAA contends that any Section 1 challenge to its amateurism rules must fail as a matter of law because the *Board of Regents* Court held that those rules are presumptively valid. We disagree.

The *Board of Regents* Court certainly discussed the NCAA's amateurism rules at great length, but it did not do so in order to pass upon the rules' merits, given that they were not before the Court. Rather, the Court discussed the amateurism rules for a different and particular purpose: to explain why NCAA rules should be analyzed under the Rule of Reason, rather than held to be illegal per se. . . .

What is more, even if the language in *Board of Regents* addressing amateurism were *not* dicta, it would not support the tremendous weight that the NCAA seeks to place upon it. The Court's opinion supports the proposition that the preservation of amateurism is a legitimate procompetitive purpose for the NCAA to pursue, but the NCAA is not asking us to find merely that its amateurism rules are procompetitive; rather, it asks us to hold that those rules are essentially exempt from antitrust scrutiny. Nothing in *Board of Regents* supports such an exemption. To say that the NCAA's amateurism rules are procompetitive, as *Board of Regents* did, is not to say that they are automatically lawful; a restraint that serves a procompetitive purpose can still be invalid under the Rule of Reason if a substantially less restrictive rule would further the same objectives equally well. See *Bd. of Regents*, 468 U.S. at 101 n. 23 ("While as the guardian of an important American tradition, the NCAA's motives must be accorded a respectful presumption of validity, it is nevertheless well settled that good motives will not validate an otherwise anticompetitive practice."). . . .

In sum, we accept *Board of Regents*' guidance as informative with respect to the procompetitive purposes served by the NCAA's amateurism rules, but we will go no further than that. The amateurism rules' validity must be proved, not presumed.

B. The Compensation Rules Regulate "Commercial Activity"

The NCAA next argues that we cannot reach the merits of the plaintiffs' Sherman Act claim because the compensation rules are not subject to the Sherman Act at all. The NCAA points out that Section 1 of the Sherman Act applies only to "restraint[s] of trade or commerce," 15 U.S.C. §1, and claims that its compensation rules are mere "eligibility rules" that do not regulate any "commercial activity."

This argument is not credible. Although restraints that have no effect on commerce are indeed exempt from Section 1, the modern legal understanding of "commerce" is broad, "including almost every activity from which the actor anticipates economic gain." Phillip Areeda & Herbert Hovenkamp, *Antitrust Law: An Analysis of Antitrust Principles and Their Application*, ¶ 260b (4th ed. 2013). That definition surely encompasses the transaction in which an athletic recruit exchanges his labor and NIL rights for a scholarship at a Division I school because it is undeniable that both parties to that exchange anticipate economic gain from it. . . .

IV

Like the district court, we follow the three-step framework of the Rule of Reason: "[1] The plaintiff bears the initial burden of showing that the restraint produces significant anticompetitive effects within a relevant market. [2] If the plaintiff meets this burden, the defendant must come forward with evidence of the restraint's procompetitive effects. [3] The plaintiff must then show that any legitimate objectives can be achieved in a substantially less restrictive manner."

A. Significant Anticompetitive Effects Within a Relevant Market

[T]he district court made the following factual findings: (1) that a cognizable "college education market" exists, wherein colleges compete for the services of athletic recruits by offering them scholarships and various amenities, such as coaching and facilities; (2) that if the NCAA's compensation rules did not exist, member schools would compete to offer recruits compensation for their NILs; and (3) that the compensation rules therefore have a significant anticompetitive effect on the college education market, in that they fix an aspect of the "price" that recruits pay to attend college (or, alternatively, an aspect of the price that schools pay to secure recruits' services). These findings have substantial support in the record. . . .

B. Procompetitive Effects

[T]he NCAA offered the district court four procompetitive justifications for the compensation rules: (1) promoting amateurism, (2) promoting competitive balance among NCAA schools, (3) integrating student-athletes with their schools' academic community, and (4) increasing output in the college education market. The district court accepted the first and third and rejected the other two. . . .

[The] district court found, and the record supports that there is a concrete procompetitive effect in the NCAA's commitment to amateurism: namely, that the amateur nature of collegiate sports increases their appeal to consumers. We therefore conclude that the NCAA's compensation rules serve the two procompetitive purposes identified by the district court: integrating academics with athletics, and "preserving the popularity of the NCAA's product by promoting its current understanding of amateurism." *O'Bannon*, 7 F.Supp.3d at 1005.17. . . .

C. Substantially Less Restrictive Alternatives

The third step in the Rule of Reason analysis is whether there are substantially less restrictive alternatives to the NCAA's current rules. We bear in mind that — to be viable under the Rule of Reason — an alternative must be "virtually as effective" in serving the procompetitive purposes of the NCAA's current rules, and "without significantly increased cost." . . .

The district court identified two substantially less restrictive alternatives: (1) allowing NCAA member schools to give student-athletes grants-in-aid that cover the full cost of attendance; and (2) allowing member schools to pay student-athletes small amounts of deferred cash compensation for use of their NILs.18 *O'Bannon*, 7 F.Supp.3d at 1005–07. We hold that the district court did not clearly err in finding that raising the grant-in-aid cap would be a substantially less restrictive alternative, but that it clearly erred when it found that allowing students to be paid compensation for their NILs is virtually as effective as the NCAA's current amateur-status rule.

1. Capping the permissible amount of scholarships at the cost of attendance

. . . All of the evidence before the district court indicated that raising the grant-in-aid cap to the cost of attendance would have virtually no impact on amateurism: Dr. Mark Emmert, the president of the NCAA, testified at trial that giving student-athletes scholarships up to their full costs of attendance would not violate the NCAA's principles of amateurism because all the money given to students would be going to cover their "legitimate costs" to attend school. Other NCAA witnesses agreed with that assessment. *Id.* at 983. Nothing in the record, moreover, suggested that consumers of college sports would become less interested in those sports if athletes' scholarships covered their full cost of attendance, or that an increase in the grant-in-aid cap would impede the integration of student-athletes into their academic communities. . . .

A compensation cap set at student-athletes' full cost of attendance is a substantially less restrictive alternative means of accomplishing the NCAA's legitimate procompetitive purposes. And there is no evidence that this cap will significantly increase costs; indeed, the NCAA already permits schools to fund student-athletes' full cost of attendance. The district court's determination that the existing compensation rules violate Section 1 of the Sherman Act was correct and its injunction requiring the NCAA to permit schools to provide compensation up to the full cost of attendance was proper.

2. Allowing students to receive cash compensation for their NILs

In our judgment, however, the district court clearly erred in finding it a viable alternative to allow students to receive NIL cash payments untethered to their education expenses. . . .

We cannot agree that a rule permitting schools to pay students pure cash compensation and a rule forbidding them from paying NIL compensation are both *equally* effective in promoting amateurism and preserving consumer demand. Both we and the district court agree that the NCAA's amateurism rule has procompetitive benefits. But in finding that paying students cash compensation would promote amateurism as effectively as not paying them, the district court ignored that not paying student-athletes is *precisely what makes them amateurs.*

Having found that amateurism is integral to the NCAA's market, the district court cannot plausibly conclude that being a poorly-paid professional collegiate athlete is "virtually as effective" for that market as being as amateur. Or, to borrow the Supreme Court's analogy, the market for college football is distinct from other sports markets and must be "differentiate[d]" from professional sports lest it become "minor league [football]." *Bd. of Regents*, 468 U.S. at 102. . . .

The difference between offering student-athletes education-related compensation and offering them cash sums untethered to educational expenses is not minor; it is a quantum leap. Once that line is crossed, we see no basis for returning to a rule of amateurism and no defined stopping point; we have little doubt that plaintiffs will continue to challenge the arbitrary limit imposed by the district court until they have captured the full value of their NIL. At that point the NCAA will have surrendered its amateurism principles entirely and transitioned from its "particular brand of football" to minor league status. *Bd. of Regents*, 468 U.S. at 101–02. . . . We thus vacate that portion of the district court's decision and the portion of its injunction requiring the NCAA to allow its member schools to pay this deferred compensation.

V

We vacate the district court's judgment and permanent injunction insofar as they require the NCAA to allow its member schools to pay student-athletes up to $5,000 per year in deferred compensation. We otherwise affirm. . . .

THOMAS, Chief Judge, concurring in part and dissenting in part:

I largely agree with all but one of the majority's conclusions. I respectfully disagree with the majority's conclusion that the district court clearly erred in ordering the NCAA to permit up to $5,000 in deferred compensation above student-athletes' full cost of attendance.

. . . There was sufficient evidence in the record to support the award. The district court's conclusion that the proposed alternative restraint satisfied the Rule of Reason was based on testimony from at least four experts — including three experts presented by the NCAA — that providing student-athletes with small amounts of compensation above their cost of attendance most likely would not have a significant impact on consumer interest in college sports. *O'Bannon*, 7 F.Supp.3d at 976–77, 983–84, 1000–01. It was also based on the fact that FBS football players are currently permitted to accept Pell grants in excess of their cost of attendance, and the fact that Division I tennis recruits are permitted to earn up to $10,000 per year in prize money from athletic events before they enroll in college. *Id.* at 974, 1000. The majority characterizes the weight of this evidence as "threadbare." I respectfully disagree.

The NCAA's own expert witness, Neal Pilson, testified that the level of deferred compensation would have an effect on consumer demand for college athletics, but that paying student-athletes $5,000 per year in trust most likely would not have a significant impact on such demand. He also testified that any negative impact that paying student-athletes might have on consumer demand could be partially mitigated by placing the compensation in a trust fund to be paid out after graduation. . . .

The majority also dismisses the testimony given by expert witness Dr. Daniel Rascher demonstrating that consumer interest in major league baseball and the Olympics increased after baseball players' salaries rose and professional athletes were allowed to compete in the Olympics. * * * Rascher also testified that consumer demand in sports such as tennis and rugby increased after the sports' governing boards permitted athletes to receive payment. *O'Bannon,* 7 F.Supp.3d at 977. . . .

The district court accepted the testimony of multiple experts that small amounts of compensation would not affect consumer demand, and then used the lowest amount suggested by one of the NCAA's experts. The district court was within its right to do so.

NOTES AND QUESTIONS

Analysis and Aftermath of O'Bannon. The Ninth Circuit three-judge panel agrees that not permitting student-athletes to receive a full cost-of-attendance scholarship is an antitrust violation, but the majority and dissent sharply disagree regarding the district court's determination that an additional $5,000 annual stipend will not preclude the NCAA's legitimate procompetitive purposes from being achieved. Is preserving "amateurism" as defined by NCAA student-athlete eligibility rules necessary for Division I FBS football and basketball to maintain their enormous popularity that generates multi-billion-dollar revenues annually? From the perspective of the fans, what distinguishes college sports (e.g., Division I FBS football and basketball) from their corresponding professional sports (e.g., NFL football and NBA basketball)?

After the *O'Bannon* district court decision, the NCAA redefined and increased the value of an athletic scholarship to permit student-athletes to receive an economic benefit equal to the full cost of attendance at his or her university, which is consistent with the Ninth Circuit majority's ruling. See discussion of this NCAA legislation in Section C of this chapter, *supra.* On February 3, 2017, the NCAA agreed to pay $208.7 million to settle the damages part of the lawsuit filed by former student-athletes who claimed that capping the economic value of their scholarships to the costs of tuition, room, board, books, and fees violated federal antitrust law.

In re NCAA Athletic Grant-In-Aid Cap Antitrust Litigation, 375 F. Supp. 3d 1058 (N.D. Cal. 2019), the federal district court (the *O'Bannon* trial judge) held that NCAA rules prohibiting university-provided compensation and benefits related to education above the value of a full cost-of-attendance scholarship for the services of Division I men's and women's and FBS football players is horizontal price-fixing by its member universities. It found no "procompetitive justification for caps on education-related benefits . . . inherently limited by their actual cost and that can be provided in kind, not in cash" and enjoined the NCAA from prohibiting universities from providing tangible items related to the pursuit of academic studies (e.g., computers, musical instruments, science equipment), expenses for study abroad, and post-eligibility paid internships and scholarships to complete degrees at other institutions. The court permitted the NCAA to limit the value of academic and graduation awards and incentives provided "in cash or a cash-equivalent to a level that the record shows is not [consumer] demand-reducing [for college sports] or inconsistent with NCAA amateurism." Because the NCAA currently permits student-athletes to receive cash-equivalent Visa cards valued at $5,600 for high levels of team performance in Division I basketball and FBS football (which expert testimony established had not reduced consumer demand for these sports), the court enjoined the NCAA from limiting the annual value of university-provided academic and graduation awards and incentives to less than this amount (i.e., $5,600).

Both sides appealed the district court's decision. The student-athletes asserted the district court should have enjoined all of the NCAA's challenged compensation limits, including those "untethered to education." The NCAA argued that the district court improperly invalidated and enjoined its reasonable rules on education-related compensation and benefits. The Ninth Circuit affirmed and held that "the district court struck the right balance in crafting a remedy that both prevents anticompetitive harm to Student-Athletes while serving the procompetitive purpose of preserving the popularity of college sports." 958 F.3d 1239 (9th Cir. 2020).

In its consideration of the appeal of this case (which was re-titled below), the Supreme Court explained how antitrust law limits the internal governance of intercollegiate sports by the NCAA's member educational institutions and athletic conferences in the twenty-first century, the first time it addressed college sports antitrust issues since its 1984 *Board of Regents* decision.

NCAA v. Alston
141 S.Ct. 2141 (2021)

Justice GORSUCH.

[Editors' note: The district court's order enjoined only NCAA rules limiting education-related compensation or benefits that conferences and schools may provide to student-athletes playing Division I football and basketball. It did not prohibit NCAA member schools from agreeing not to provide college athletes with compensation and benefits unrelated to education. The court's injunction permitted cash awards for academic achievement to be limited so long as those limits are no lower than the cash awards allowed for athletic achievement (currently $5,980 annually), while permitting the NCAA and its members to propose a definition of compensation or benefits "related to education." The court's injunction applied only to NCAA and multi-conference agreements, thereby allowing individual conferences to impose tighter restrictions on the provision of education-related compensation or benefits by their respective member schools. The Supreme Court limited its review only to the NCAA rules that were enjoined.]

II

A

In the NCAA's view, the courts should have given its restrictions at most an "abbreviated deferential review," before approving them. . . .

As the NCAA observes, this Court has suggested that sometimes we can determine the competitive effects of a challenged restraint in the "'twinkling of an eye.'" That is true, though, only for restraints at opposite ends of the competitive spectrum. For those sorts of restraints — rather than restraints in the great in-between — a quick look is sufficient for approval or condemnation. . . .

The NCAA *accepts* that its members collectively enjoy monopsony power in the market for student-athlete services, such that its restraints can (and in fact do) harm competition. [T]he district court found (and the NCAA does not here contest) that student-athletes have nowhere else to sell their labor. Even if the NCAA is a joint venture, then, it is hardly of the sort that would warrant quick-look approval for all its myriad rules and restrictions.

Nor does the NCAA's status as a particular type of venture categorically exempt its restraints from ordinary rule of reason review. We do not doubt that some degree of coordination between competitors within sports leagues can be procompetitive. Without some agreement among rivals — on things like how many players may be on the field or the time allotted for play — the very competitions that consumers value would not be possible. Accordingly, even a sports league with market power might see some agreements among its members win antitrust approval in the "'twinkling of an eye.'"

But this insight does not always apply. That *some* restraints are necessary to create or maintain a league sport does not mean *all* "aspects of elaborate interleague cooperation are." While a quick look will often be enough to approve the restraints "necessary to produce a game," a fuller review may be appropriate for others. See, *e.g., Chicago Professional Sports Ltd. Partnership v. National Basketball Assn.*, 95 F.3d 593, 600 (CA7 1996) ("Just as the ability of McDonald's franchises to coordinate the release of a new hamburger does not imply their ability to agree on wages for counter workers, so the ability of sports teams to agree on a TV contract need not imply an ability to set wages for players").

The NCAA's rules fixing wages for student-athletes fall on the far side of this line. Nobody questions that Division I basketball and FBS football can proceed (and have proceeded) without the education-related compensation restrictions the district court enjoined; the games go on. Instead, the parties dispute whether and to what extent those restrictions in the NCAA's labor market yield benefits in its consumer market that can be attained using substantially less restrictive means. That dispute presents complex questions requiring more than a blink to answer.

B

Even if background antitrust principles counsel in favor of the rule of reason, the NCAA replies that a particular precedent ties our hands. The NCAA directs our attention to *Board of Regents*, where this Court considered the league's rules restricting the ability of its member schools to televise football games. On the NCAA's reading, that decision expressly approved its limits on student-athlete compensation — and this approval forecloses any meaningful review of those limits today. . . .

Most particularly, the NCAA highlights this passage:

> "The NCAA plays a critical role in the maintenance of a revered tradition of amateurism in college sports. There can be no question but that it needs ample latitude to play that role, or that the preservation of the student-athlete in higher education adds richness and diversity to intercollegiate athletics and is entirely consistent with the goals of the Sherman Act." . . .

Board of Regents may suggest that courts should take care when assessing the NCAA's restraints on student-athlete compensation, sensitive to their procompetitive possibilities. But these remarks do not suggest that courts must reflexively reject *all* challenges to the NCAA's compensation restrictions. Student-athlete compensation rules were not even at issue in *Board of Regents*. And the Court made clear it was only assuming the reasonableness of the NCAA's restrictions: "It is reasonable to *assume* that most of the regulatory controls of the NCAA are justifiable means of fostering competition among amateur athletic teams and are therefore procompetitive. . . ." Accordingly, the Court simply did not have occasion to declare — nor did it declare — the NCAA's compensation restrictions procompetitive both in 1984 and forevermore.

Our confidence on this score is fortified by still another factor. Whether an antitrust violation exists necessarily depends on a careful analysis of market realities. If those market realities change, so may the legal analysis.

When it comes to college sports, there can be little doubt that the market realities have changed significantly since 1984. Since then, the NCAA has dramatically increased the amounts and kinds of benefits schools may provide to student-athletes. . . . Nor is that all that has changed. In 1985, Division I football and basketball raised approximately $922 million and $41 million respectively. By 2016, NCAA Division I schools raised more than $13.5 billion. *Ibid.* From 1982 to 1984, CBS paid $16 million per year to televise the March Madness Division I men's basketball tournament. In 2016, those annual television rights brought in closer to $1.1 billion.

Given the sensitivity of antitrust analysis to market realities — and how much has changed in this market — we think it would be particularly unwise to treat an aside in *Board of Regents* as more than that. . . .

C

The NCAA submits that a rule of reason analysis is inappropriate for still another reason — because the NCAA and its member schools are not "commercial enterprises" and instead oversee intercollegiate athletics "as an integral part of the undergraduate experience." . . .

To the extent it means to propose a sort of judicially ordained immunity from the terms of the Sherman Act for its restraints of trade — that we should overlook its restrictions because they happen to fall at the intersection of higher education, sports, and money — we cannot agree. This Court has regularly refused materially identical requests from litigants seeking special dispensation from the Sherman Act on the ground that their restraints of trade serve uniquely important social objectives beyond enhancing competition. . . .

The "orderly way" to temper that Act's policy of competition is "by legislation and not by court decision." The NCAA is free to argue that "because of the special characteristics of [its] particular industry," it should be exempt from the usual operation of the antitrust laws — but that appeal is "properly addressed to Congress." . . .

III

A

[Under the rule of reason], "the plaintiff has the initial burden to prove that the challenged restraint has a substantial anticompetitive effect." Should the plaintiff carry that burden, the burden then "shifts to the defendant to show a procompetitive rationale for the restraint." If the defendant can make that showing, "the burden shifts back to the plaintiff to demonstrate that the procompetitive efficiencies could be reasonably achieved through less anticompetitive means." . . .

. . . As its first step, the district court required the student-athletes to show that "the challenged restraints produce significant anticompetitive effects in the relevant market." [B]ased on a voluminous record, the district court held that the student-athletes had shown the NCAA enjoys the power to set wages in the market for student-athletes' labor — and that the NCAA has exercised that power in ways that have produced significant anticompetitive effects. Perhaps even more notably, the NCAA "did not meaningfully dispute" this conclusion.

[T]hen, the district court proceeded to the second step, asking whether the NCAA could muster a procompetitive rationale for its restraints. . . . [[T]he court found the NCAA failed "to establish that the challenged compensation rules . . . have any direct connection to consumer demand."

While finding the NCAA had failed to establish that its rules collectively sustain consumer demand, the court did find that "some" of those rules "may" have procompetitive effects "to the extent" they prohibit compensation "unrelated to education, akin to salaries seen in professional sports leagues." The court then proceeded to what corresponds to the third step of the framework, where it required the student-athletes "to show that there are substantially less restrictive alternative rules that would achieve the same procompetitive effect as the challenged set of rules." And there, of course, the district court held that the student-athletes partially succeeded — they were able to show that the NCAA could achieve the procompetitive benefits it had established with substantially less restrictive restraints on education-related benefits. . . .

C

Finally, the NCAA attacks as "indefensible" the lower courts' holding that substantially less restrictive alternatives exist capable of delivering the same procompetitive benefits as its current rules. The NCAA claims, too, that the district court's injunction threatens to "micromanage" its business.

Once more, we broadly agree with the legal principles the NCAA invokes. As we have discussed, antitrust courts must give wide berth to business judgments before finding liability. Similar considerations apply when it comes to the remedy. Judges must be sensitive to the possibility that the "continuing supervision of a highly detailed decree" could wind up impairing rather than enhancing competition. Judges must be wary, too, of the temptation to specify "the proper price, quantity, and other terms of dealing" — cognizant that they are neither economic nor industry experts. Judges must be open to reconsideration and modification of decrees in light of changing market realities, for "what we see may vary over time." . . .

Once again, though, we think the district court honored these principles. The court enjoined only restraints on education-related benefits — such as those limiting scholarships for graduate school, payments for tutoring, and the like. The court did so, moreover, only after finding that relaxing these restrictions would not blur the distinction between college and professional sports and thus impair demand — and only after finding that this course represented a significantly (not marginally) less restrictive means of achieving the same procompetitive benefits as the NCAA's current rules. . . .

Some will think the district court did not go far enough. By permitting colleges and universities to offer enhanced education-related benefits, its decision may encourage scholastic achievement and allow student-athletes a measure of compensation more consistent with the value they bring to their schools. Still, some will see this as a poor substitute for fuller relief. At the same time, others will think the district court went too far by undervaluing the social benefits associated with amateur athletics. For our part, though, we can only agree with the Ninth Circuit: "'The national debate about amateurism in college sports is important. But our task as appellate judges is not to resolve it. Nor could we. Our task is simply to review the district court judgment through the appropriate lens of antitrust law.'" That review persuades us the district court acted within the law's bounds.

The judgment is *Affirmed*.

Justice KAVANAUGH, concurring.

. . . The Court's decision marks an important and overdue course correction, and I join the Court's excellent opinion in full.

But this case involves only a narrow subset of the NCAA's compensation rules — namely, the rules restricting the *education-related* benefits that student athletes may receive, such as post-eligibility scholarships at graduate or vocational schools. The rest of the NCAA's compensation rules are not at issue here and therefore remain on the books. Those remaining compensation rules generally restrict student athletes from receiving compensation or benefits from their colleges for playing sports. And those rules have also historically restricted student athletes from receiving money from endorsement deals and the like.

I add this concurring opinion to underscore that the NCAA's remaining compensation rules also raise serious questions under the antitrust laws. . . .

Everyone agrees that the NCAA can require student athletes to be enrolled students in good standing. But the NCAA's business model of using unpaid student athletes to generate billions of dollars in revenue for the colleges raises serious questions under the antitrust laws. In particular, it is highly questionable whether the NCAA and its member colleges can justify not paying student athletes a fair share of the revenues on the circular theory that the defining characteristic of college sports is that the colleges do not pay student athletes. And if that asserted justification is unavailing, it is not clear how the NCAA can legally defend its remaining compensation rules.

If it turns out that some or all of the NCAA's remaining compensation rules violate the antitrust laws, some difficult policy and practical questions would undoubtedly ensue. Among them: How would paying greater compensation to student athletes affect non-revenue-raising sports? Could student athletes in some sports but not others receive compensation? How would any compensation regime comply with Title IX? If paying student athletes requires something like a salary cap in some sports in order to preserve competitive balance, how would that cap be administered? And given that there are now about 180,000 Division I student athletes, what is a financially sustainable way of fairly compensating some or all of those student athletes?

Of course, those difficult questions could be resolved in ways other than litigation. Legislation would be one option. Or colleges and student athletes could potentially engage in collective bargaining (or seek some other negotiated agreement) to provide student athletes a fairer share of the revenues that they generate for their colleges, akin to how professional football and basketball players have negotiated for a share of league revenues. Regardless of how those issues ultimately would be resolved, however, the NCAA's current compensation regime raises serious questions under the antitrust laws. . . .

NOTES AND QUESTIONS

1. Analysis and Effects of *Alston*. Which specific NCAA rules were judicially invalidated by *Alston*? Justice Kavanaugh's concurring opinion casts doubt on the continuing validity of *O'Bannon*'s holding that NCAA rules may prohibit its member schools from offering intercollegiate athletes "cash sums untethered to educational expenses." Based on the *Alston* majority opinion, do NCAA rules limiting the value of an athletic scholarship to the full cost of attendance at each member university violate §1? Note that the answer probably depends on whether maintaining "amateurism" is a valid procompetitive justification for this limit on competition for intercollegiate athletes' playing services.

During the 2021–22 academic year, the University of Mississippi became the first NCAA university to pay its intercollegiate athletes $5,980 annual stipends for meeting its minimum standards to maintain their academic eligibility and being on a team roster. Rather than paying annual cash stipends, Iowa State University has chosen to defer paying its intercollegiate athletes any cash awards until they graduate. Approximately 50 NCAA universities currently pay academic stipends to their respective intercollegiate athletes.

2. Post-*Alston* Antitrust Validity of NCAA and Divisional Rules Under "Quick Look" Rule of Reason. *Alston* acknowledges that "even a sports league with market power might see some agreements among its members win antitrust approval in the 'twinkling of an eye,'" observing that "a quick look will often be enough to approve the restraints 'necessary to approve a game.'" This suggests that NCAA rules of the game for each sport such as the number of players on a team, characteristics of the playing field, and approved or prohibited equipment for an intercollegiate sport should be judicially presumed to be procompetitive lawful restraints. What about student-athlete academic eligibility requirements? Student-athlete health and safety requirements such as NCAA divisional drug testing policies and sanctions for violations? NCAA Division I sanctions imposed on a coach for violating an applicable state NIL law or the Division I interim NIL policy prohibiting the offering of an NIL rights deal to recruit a student-athlete to the university?

3. Possible Congressional Intervention. Given the complexity and uncertainty associated with antitrust challenges to student-athlete amateurism and other eligibility rules, the NCAA could seek a congressional exemption from antitrust law that would permit its member institutions to spend the substantial revenues generated from intercollegiate athletics on increased educational support for all student-athletes. A 2015 study, *The Economic Value of College Majors*, by Georgetown University's Center on Education and the Workforce, concluded that the average difference between the lifetime wages of college and high school graduates is $1 million. See *https://cew.georgetown.edu/wp-content/uploads/Exec-Summary-web-B.pdf*. If you were a member of Congress, in exchange for exempting student-athlete eligibility rules from antitrust challenge, what assurances or conditions would you require from NCAA member schools and conferences to ensure that commercialized intercollegiate athletics are primarily an educational endeavor and that student-athletes receive valuable educational benefits for their playing services? See generally Matthew J. Mitten & Stephen F. Ross, *A Regulatory Solution to Better Promote the Educational Values and Economic Sustainability of Intercollegiate Athletics*, 92 Ore. L. Rev. 837, 876-877 (2014) ("A federal regulatory commission [sh]ould have the necessary authority to establish rules that effectively prevent intercollegiate athletics from crossing the line between a commercial/education model and a commercial/professional model for intercollegiate sport, enhance the academic integrity of intercollegiate athletics, promote more competitive balance in intercollegiate sports competition, and require university athletic departments to operate with fiscal responsibility. The 'carrot' of antitrust immunity would provide the NCAA, athletic conferences, and their member institutions with a significant incentive to adopt and comply with its rules to achieve these objectives[.]").

Legal Relationships Between the University and Intercollegiate Athletes

CONTRACTUAL AND NCAA REGULATORY DIMENSIONS

A. Introduction

An examination of the contractual nature of the relationship between intercollegiate athletes and their colleges and universities is an appropriate starting point for studying the various dimensions of this relationship. To facilitate your understanding, we begin with a discussion of basic contract law principles.

KEY TERMS
- Breach
- Consideration
- Contract
- Damages
- Express contract
- Implied contract
- Modification
- Mutual assent
- Offer
- Promise
- Promissory estoppel

1. Contract Formation and Consideration

a. Mutual Assent

The law of contracts deals with promises and the legal effect of the promises that individuals or groups of individuals make to each other. A key concept in the body of law known as contracts is a *promise*, which involves a person making a commitment to do or not to do something in the future. Another important concept is *contract*, which is defined as "a promise or a set of promises for the breach of which the law gives a remedy, or the performance of which the law in some way recognizes as a duty." Restatement (Second) of Contracts §1. In other words, a "contract is simply an agreement, oral or written, that can be enforced in court." Katherine Currier & Thomas E. Eimermann, *Introduction to Paralegal Studies* 171 (4th ed. 2010).

Consider the following scenario. If a professor and student agree that the student will serve as a research assistant during the summer term at $10 per hour, they have entered into a contract. The professor promised to pay the student $10 per hour, and the student, in turn, promised to serve as the professor's research assistant. To reiterate, an enforceable contract resulted from their communication.

Often, one party to a contract is referred to as the *promisor* and the other as the *promisee*. The promisee is the party who seeks to enforce the promise. The promisor is the party who has allegedly refused to honor the promise. Thus, if the professor alleged that no contract existed, the professor would be the promisor and the student would be the promisee.

For an exchange of promises to create an enforceable contract, there must be (1) an agreement (mutual assent), which generally arises when one or more persons make an offer to one or more other persons who accept the offer, and (2) consideration to support the promise. *Consideration* refers to something of legal value that is exchanged between the parties.

An *offer* is defined as a promise to do or not to do something conditioned on the other party promising to do something in return or actually doing what the offer requested. For a promise to give rise to an offer, it must specifically express an intention to enter into a contract if the other party accepts the offer. An *acceptance* is the expression of intent to enter into a contract on the terms set forth in the offer. An acceptance is effective only if communicated to the offeror by the person or persons to whom the offer was directed.

The offeror is said to be the *master* of the offer, in that the offeror can specify the manner the offer can be accepted. Thus, if the offer specifies that it can only be accepted by performance, then the parties have entered into a unilateral contract. For example, suppose an offeror promises to give a teenager $20 if the teenager climbs a flagpole within five minutes. The offeror has created an offer for a unilateral contract. A unilateral contract will arise if the offeree, the teenager, climbs the flagpole within the five minutes required by the offer.

More commonly, however, the offer expressly or impliedly permits an acceptance by an exchange of promises. In the case of the research assistant, the professor made an offer to hire and pay the student at a certain rate in return for the student's promise to serve as a research assistant. The student's affirmative response constituted an acceptance of the offer and the two, the offer and the acceptance, combined to satisfy the mutual assent requirement of an enforceable contract. Assuming that consideration is present, the parties have entered into a bilateral contract, which arises pursuant to an exchange of promises.

Suppose that instead of accepting the professor's offer to work for $10 per hour, the student responded to the offer by stating, "I will not work for $10 but will work for you for $12 per hour." In this instance, no contract arises. The student has made a counteroffer that terminates the original offer made by the professor. In its place is a new offer made by the student, in which the student offers to work in exchange for $12 per hour. If the professor says, "I accept," a contract has arisen pursuant to the terms of the student's counteroffer.

b. Consideration and Promissory Estoppel

Consideration is defined as follows: "A performance or return promise is bargained for if it is sought by the promisor in return for making his promise and is given by the promisee in exchange for that promise." *Restatement (Second) of Contracts* §71. In our scenario, the professor made the offer to the student seeking to induce the student to promise to perform as a research assistant. At the same time, the student made the promise to perform in response to and seeking the promise from the professor to pay $10 per hour. Therefore, they exchanged or promised to exchange something of value that each sought from the other.

A promise may give rise to a legal obligation even though there is no consideration to support the promise. The concept of *promissory estoppel* provides for the enforceability of a promise based on the justifiable reliance of the promisee on that promise. Therefore, if a person makes a promise with reason to know that the promisee is likely to rely on that promise, and the promisee does justifiably rely (changes their position), the promise is binding based on the promisee's reliance. Assume that the professor promised the student an unpaid summer research position. After the professor made the promise, the student received an offer for a paid internship with a company. In reliance on the professor's promise of an unpaid internship, the student rejected the offer of the firm. Subsequently, the professor reneged on the promise. The student could have a claim against the professor for promissory estoppel.

2. Modification

Parties often seek to change the terms of their agreement. When this occurs, they may seek to modify their contract. As was true of the original contract to which the parties agreed, a *modification* requires mutual assent (agreement to change the terms) and consideration. A lack of consideration will render the attempted modification unenforceable if the promisee's performance is no different than what it originally promised to do. The preexisting duty rule provides that "a promise to perform a pre-existing obligation is not sufficient consideration in exchange for a promise by the other party." *Restatement (Second) of Contracts* §73. In our scenario, assume the professor originally agreed to pay and the student agreed to work for $10 per hour. The professor subsequently promised to pay the student $12 per hour. If the student is to perform the same services as originally agreed, the modification is ineffective due to a lack of consideration, and the professor's promise would be unenforceable if the professor later were to refuse to pay the student the increased amount. On the other hand, if the professor promised to pay the student $12 per hour because the nature of the services the student was to perform had changed, then the modified contract would be enforceable. The student's duties under the modified agreement would be different from the duties that the student originally agreed to undertake.

3. Express and Implied Contracts

A distinction is sometimes made between an express contract and an implied contract. An *express contract* is simply one where the mutual assent arises from the words exchanged between the parties to the contract. An *implied contract* is one where the mutual assent arises from their conduct. Even though this distinction is sometimes made, it has no real legal significance. Returning to our scenario, assume that the professor and the student generally discuss but never expressly agree that the student will provide services at $10 per hour. Assume also that the student provides and the professor accepts the student's research services. They will have entered into an implied contract. If $10 per hour is the generally recognized rate for research assistant services at their university, the professor will more than likely be required to pay $10 per hour.

Even if mutual assent and consideration are present, circumstances may nevertheless bar the enforcement of the contract. Contract law recognizes defenses that will render a contract unenforceable. These defenses include misrepresentation (fraud), undue influence, duress, mistake, illegality, the statute of frauds (i.e., the agreement was not memorialized in a writing or record as required by law), and lack of capacity of one or both parties (i.e., at least one of the parties to the contract was mentally incompetent or a minor).

4. Performance, Breach, and Remedies

a. Breach

In our scenario, assume that the professor and student have entered into an enforceable contract. The student, who was to be paid on a weekly basis, works for three weeks, but the professor unjustifiably refuses to make any of the three payments due to the student. The professor has breached the contract. A breach occurs when there is an unexcused nonperformance of a legal duty. Because a court would likely find that the professor's breach was a material breach, not only would the student be able to sue for damages (the payments due), the student would also be entitled to discontinue performing obligations under the contract.

A party may also commit a breach by anticipatory repudiation, which occurs when a party, before the time when its performance is due, unequivocally expresses an unwillingness or inability to perform the agreed-upon obligations. Assume that two weeks before the student is to begin to work for the professor, the student decides to work at a law firm for the summer and so informs the professor. The student has anticipatorily repudiated the contract and unless the repudiation is properly retracted, the professor may sue the student for breach. In addition, the professor's obligation to pay the student is discharged.

b. Excuses for Nonperformance

A party's breach of contract may be excused. The impossibility doctrine excuses a party's nonperformance where performance has become objectively impossible due to no fault of the promisor, and the promisor has not assumed the risk of performing even if performance were to become impossible. Illness is considered a form of impossibility. Thus, if the student is incapacitated, such as being unable to perform because of illness, the student's nonperformance will be excused, and the expected performance obligation will be discharged. A party's nonperformance will also be excused when its performance becomes impracticable or by frustration of purpose (where the underlying purpose of the contract is so defeated as to be worthless).

5. Damages

Where a party's nonperformance is unjustified, the other party is entitled to a remedy for breach. Contract damages seek to compensate the injured party for the actual loss from breach. The preferred remedy in American law is monetary relief. Requiring the breaching party to perform as promised, specific performance, is considered an extraordinary form of relief and only will be awarded under limited circumstances.

Returning to our scenario, assume that the student works, but the professor pays only part of the agreed-upon salary. The student would be entitled to damages, most likely measured by the difference between the promised payment and what was actually paid. If the professor promised to pay the student a total of $800 but paid only $600, the student would be entitled to recover $200 as damages.

Assume that the student unjustifiably refuses to work for the professor. Because this is a personal services/employment contract, the professor cannot seek specific performance, which would involve going to court and requesting that the court order the student to work for the professor. The professor would, however, be entitled to monetary damages measured by the difference between what the professor promised to pay the student and the additional cost, if any, that the professor would be required to pay to hire another student to perform the services of the breaching student.

In the above scenario, the nonbreaching party was awarded its expectation damages. We note, without discussion, that damages may also be measured based on protecting the nonbreaching party's reliance and restitution interests.

B. Contractual Aspects of the Athlete and University Relationship

KEY TERMS
- National Letter of Intent
- One academic year in residence
- Statement of Financial Assistance

The contractual relationships between scholarship athletes and their institutions arise principally out of the Statement of Financial Assistance and the National

Letter of Intent (NLI). These documents largely define the nature of the obligations that athletes owe to their colleges or universities and the obligations that these educational institutions owe to their scholarship athletes.

1. Statement of Financial Assistance

College athletes who obtain athletic scholarships sign form documents commonly referred to as a Statement of Financial Assistance. Pursuant to a Statement of Financial Assistance, a college agrees to extend financial aid to student-athletes to the extent of "the total cost of tuition and fees, room and board, books and supplies, transportation and other expenses related to attendance at the institution." NCAA, 2022–23 NCAA Division I Manual, Bylaw 15.02.2 (hereinafter NCAA Manual). The purpose of the financial aid award is to assist and enable college athletes to pursue a program of study and to participate in the educational process of the institution. In exchange for the university's commitment, an athlete promises to attend a particular college and to compete in intercollegiate athletics. An athlete's right to continue to receive financial assistance is contingent on the athlete remaining academically eligible to participate in the institution's athletic program. Athletes also promise to comply with the rules and regulations of their institutions, athletic conferences (e.g., Southeastern Conference (SEC)), and their athletic association (e.g., National Collegiate Athletic Association (NCAA)). Athletes also promise to adhere to athletic department and team policies.

2. National Letter of Intent

The other key document that defines the scholarship athlete and university relationship is the National Letter of Intent (NLI). The purposes of the NLI include reducing and limiting recruiting pressure on student-athletes. See National Letter of Intent, *About the National Letter of Intent (NLI)*, http://www.nationalletter.org/about-TheNli/index.html.

    Several implications flow from a prospective scholarship athlete signing an NLI. By signing an NLI, a prospective athlete agrees for a minimum period of one year to attend the institution named in the NLI (hereinafter referred to as "named institution"). Thereafter, other institutions must cease all recruiting contacts with the athlete. Conversely, the named institution may freely contact the athlete. The NLI is not effective unless the athlete has received a promise in writing from the named institution to provide financial aid for an entire academic year. Assuming the athlete complies with NCAA financial aid eligibility requirements and is admitted to the named institution, the athlete is entitled to a scholarship for a minimum of one full academic year from the named institution. An athlete who fails to attend the named institution will be penalized by having to serve one academic year in residence at and losing one year of athletic eligibility to compete in all sports at the new institution in which the athlete enrolls. Finally, an athlete's one-year commitment remains effective even if the coach for whom the athlete anticipated he or she would play leaves the named institution.

All NLI provisions are available at *http://www.nationalletter.org/nliProvisions/index.html*. The following is a sampling of key provisions of the NLI.

THE NATIONAL LETTER OF INTENT

2. Financial Aid Requirement. At the time I sign this NLI, I must receive a written offer of athletics financial aid for the entire academic year from the institution named in this document. The offer must list the terms, conditions and amount of the athletics aid award. . . . In order for this NLI to be valid, my parent/legal guardian and I must sign the NLI and I must also sign the offer of athletics aid . . . prior to submission to the institution named in this document, and any other stated conditions must also be met. If the conditions stated on the financial aid offer are not met, this NLI shall be declared null and void. . . .

7. Letter Becomes Null and Void. This NLI shall be declared null and void if any of the following occur:

> **a. Admissions Requirement.** This NLI shall be declared null and void if the institution named in this document notifies me in writing that I have been denied admission or, by the opening day of classes in the fall . . . , has failed to provide me with written notice of admission, provided I have submitted a complete admission application. . . .
>
> If I am eligible for admission, but the institution named in this document defers my admission to a subsequent term, the NLI will be declared null and void; however, this NLI remains binding if I defer my admission.
>
> **b. Eligibility Requirements.** This NLI shall be declared null and void if, by the opening day of classes in the fall . . . , I have not met NCAA initial eligibility requirements; NCAA, conference or institution's requirements for athletics financial aid; or two-year college transfer requirements. . . . (1) This NLI shall be rendered null and void if I become a nonqualifier per the NCAA Eligibility Center. This NLI remains valid if I am a partial qualifier per NCAA Division II rules unless I do not meet the institution's policies for receipt of athletics aid. . . .
>
> **e. Recruiting Rules Violation.** If eligibility reinstatement by the NCAA student-athlete reinstatement staff is necessary due to NCAA and/or conference recruiting rules violations, the institution must notify me that I have an option to have the NLI declared null and void due to the rules violation. It is my decision to have the NLI remain valid or to have the NLI declared null and void, permitting me to be recruited and not be subject to NLI penalties.

11. Coaching Changes. I understand I have signed this NLI with the institution and not for a particular sport or coach. If a coach leaves the institution or the sports program (e.g., not retained, resigns), I remain bound by the provisions of this NLI. I understand it is not uncommon for a coach to leave his or her coaching position.

QUESTIONS

1. Identify a requirement that must be satisfied before the NLI commits a scholarship athlete to a particular institution.
2. Identify a circumstance under which an athlete would no longer be bound to an institution by the NLI.
3. You are a scholarship athlete whose decision to sign with a particular institution is influenced by your desire to play for a certain coach. After you sign an NLI and before you arrive on campus, the coach leaves to work at another institution. Can you immediately follow the coach to the new institution? What are the consequences of your doing so?
4. What principle that underlies the NLI program is reinforced by having athletes commit to an educational institution rather than to a coach? What are the pros and cons of this approach?

C. Student-Athlete Financial Aid and Other Benefits

1. NCAA Regulations Governing Contracts and Scholarships

In determining the terms of the athletic scholarship between a university and its student-athletes, it is important also to consider applicable NCAA regulations. NCAA Bylaw Article 15, which governs institutional financial aid to athletes, is particularly significant. From an association-wide perspective, Article 15 regulates how many scholarships an institution is allowed to give to athletes in a particular sport. For example, a football team is permitted to give more scholarships than a baseball team. (See NCAA Manual, Bylaw 15.5.)

Article 15 also speaks to the specifics of the financial aid that institutions award to athletes. Pursuant to NCAA legislation adopted in 1973, institutions were restricted to only awarding athletes one-year renewable athletic scholarships. Effective August 2012, NCAA amended legislation permits institutions to award multiyear scholarships. (NCAA Manual, Bylaws 15.01.5 and 15.02.8.) Because the legislation is permissive, institutions have the discretion to award athletic scholarships from one to a maximum of five years.

Three of the five autonomy conferences have adopted conference-specific legislation pursuant to which their institutions will offer multiyear scholarships. The Big Ten led the way when it announced in October 2014 that its institutions would offer multiyear scholarships in all sports. The Big Ten policy also permits its institutions, consistent with NCAA financial aid rules effective in 2012, to award athletic aid to an athlete who returns to the school to complete his or her degree if his or her education was interrupted for a legitimate reason. See NCAA Manual, Bylaw 15.01.5.2; Steve Berkowitz & Daniel Uthman, *Big Ten guarantees graduate opportunity for its athletes*, USA Today, Oct. 8, 2014, *https://www.usatoday.com/story/sports/college/2014/10/08/big-ten-graduation-opportunity-guarantee/16945187/*. The Big 12 and Pac-12 subsequently adopted similar policies.

NCAA regulations also strictly limit the circumstances under which an institution can cancel or reduce the amount of the athletic scholarship during the term of the scholarship. Suppose an athlete has been awarded a one-year athletic scholarship. If the athlete suffers an injury playing sports or practicing during that year, the athlete's scholarship cannot be canceled. On the other hand, the scholarship can be canceled if the athlete becomes ineligible to participate in intercollegiate athletics, voluntarily withdraws from athletic participation, or engages in serious misconduct warranting substantial disciplinary action.

At the NCAA's 2015 Convention, autonomy schools adopted legislation seeking to protect the integrity of multiyear scholarships. The 2015 legislation prevents colleges and universities from reducing, canceling, or not renewing athletic financial aid, including multiyear scholarships, for athletic-related reasons, including injury or illness. NCAA Manual, Bylaw 15.3.5.2. Student-athletes are entitled to a hearing if their financial aid is reduced or canceled during the term of the award or is not renewed at the end of the term. *Id.* at Bylaw 15.3.2.3. This scholarship legislation is mandatory for autonomy schools but permissive for non-autonomy schools. See *id.* at Bylaws 15.02.5 and 15.5.3.2.1.

NCAA legislation has also redefined an athletic scholarship to encompass not only tuition, room, board, books, and fees, but also the incidental costs of attending college, such as transportation and miscellaneous personal expenses. The gap between how the NCAA traditionally defined an athletic scholarship and the true cost of attendance has been estimated at between $2,000 and $5,000 annually per student. The additional cost to colleges and universities of awarding true-cost-of-attendance scholarships has been estimated to range from $1 to $2.5 million per institution. The full cost-of-attendance legislation is mandatory for autonomy schools but is permissive for non-autonomy schools. See *id.* at Bylaws 15.02.5 and 15.5.3.2.1.

Effective October 2018, the NCAA implemented new rules regarding athlete transfers to other schools. Under pre-June 2018 bylaws, athletes had to obtain the permission of their coaches before contacting other schools to discuss the possibility of transferring. Similarly, institutions wishing to recruit athletes interested in transferring had to seek the permission of athletes' schools. Now, athletes are permitted to initiate the transfer process and seek a scholarship at a different school by notifying their coaches of their desire to transfer. Within two business days of such notification, coaches must enter the athletes' names in an NCAA-managed database (known as the transfer portal) to indicate these athletes may be recruited by another college or university. Other schools may thereafter recruit the athletes. Notwithstanding the new rule, athletic conferences are permitted to impose more restrictive transfer policies for intra-conference transfers. NCAA Manual, Bylaw 13.1.1.3.1. For an overview of transfer policies and procedures, see NCAA, *NCAA*

Guide for Four-Year Transfers, NCAA.org, http://fs.ncaa.org/Docs/eligibility_center/Transfer/FourYearGuide.pdf.

Student-athletes, who seek to transfer a second time and be immediately eligible for intercollegiate competition at the school to which the athletes transferred, must seek (through their institutions) a transfer waiver from an NCAA committee. Citing concerns that multiple transfers by an athlete could negatively impact an athlete's progress toward a degree, in January 2023, the NCAA adopted more stringent waiver requirements. Waivers will only be granted for extenuating circumstances, including mental health. *DI Board statement regarding transfer waiver*, NCAA.org, Sept. 12, 2023, https://www.ncaa.org/news/2023/9/12/media-center-di-board-statement-regarding-transfer-waivers.aspx. The NCAA's denial in 2023 of waiver petitions of athletes, including those who transferred to the University of North Carolina and Florida State University, generated considerable controversy. Nicole Auerbach & Chris Vannini, *NCAA says violent threats were directed at committee members following waiver decisions*, The Athletic, Sept. 12, 2023, https://theathletic.com/4857113/2023/09/12/ncaa-threats-committee-members-transfers/.

QUESTIONS

1. Prior to 2012, what was the duration of a scholarship athlete's contract with his or her college? Beginning in 2012, may a university award an athlete a two-year athletic scholarship? May it award a three-year athletic scholarship? A four-year athletic scholarship?
2. Assume that an institution grants an athlete a one-year athletic scholarship. In the middle of the athlete's sports season, the athlete's coach becomes dissatisfied with the athlete's athletic performance. At this point, may the coach cancel or reduce the amount of the athlete's scholarship because the athlete's performance has not met the coach's expectations?
3. What limitations, if any, are imposed on the discretion that institutions have to refuse to renew an athlete's scholarship?
4. An athlete, who received a four-year athletic scholarship, suffered an athletic-related injury at the beginning of her third-year. The injury rendered the athlete incapable of playing the sport for which she was recruited or any other sport. May the university terminate the athlete's scholarship prior to the beginning of her fourth year?
5. Prior to 2015, what was the gap between the amount an athlete received from an athletic scholarship and the full cost of attendance? What is the estimated cost to universities to provide full cost-of-attendance scholarships?
6. Beginning in 2015, are all universities required to provide full cost-of-attendance scholarships to athletes?
7. Assume that an NFL draft-eligible athlete was a projected first-round draft pick entering his final season. During his last season, he suffers a severe injury causing him to go undrafted. Could he have done anything to protect his future earnings if he attended an autonomy school?

> **NOTE**

For additional discussions of the contractual aspects of the athlete/university relationship, see the following: Debra D. Burke & Angela J. Grube, *The NCAA Letter of Intent: A Voidable Agreement for Minors?*, 81 Miss. L.J. 265 (2011); Ray Yasser, *The Case for Reviving the Four-Year Deal*, 86 Tul. L. Rev. 987 (2012).

D. Defining the Scope of Institutional Obligations to Student-Athletes

> **KEY TERMS**
> - Breach of contract
> - Duty of good faith
> - Educational malpractice
> - Reasonable academic progress

Litigation has ensued over the scope of the respective obligations that arise out of the student-athlete and university relationship. Colleges maintain that the primary contractual obligation they owe to their athletes is the provision of financial aid. Nevertheless, athletes have filed lawsuits urging courts to impose obligations on institutions that are not specifically articulated in the principal contract documents (i.e., Statement of Financial Aid and the NLI). Much of this litigation involves student-athletes' efforts to broaden the scope of the obligations their institutions owe to them. The following cases reveal, however, that courts have been very reluctant to expand the rights of athletes or to impose obligations on institutions beyond those duties expressly spelled out in the contract documents. *Taylor* addresses the fundamental obligations that result from the contractual relationship between scholarship athletes and their institutions. *Ross* focuses on the extent to which terms, other than those expressly delineated in the contract, should be incorporated into the athlete/university contract in order to promote the academic interests of college athletes.

Taylor v. Wake Forest University
191 S.E.2d 379 (N.C. App. 1972)

CAMPBELL, Judge.

[Editors' note: Gregg Taylor, a student-athlete at Wake Forest University, and his father alleged that the university wrongfully terminated the athlete's football scholarship after he refused to participate in football because of his poor academic performance. Taylor's grade point average (GPA) for the first semester of his freshman year was 1.0 on a 4.0 scale. As a result of this poor academic showing, Taylor refused, and in fact was ineligible, to play football during the spring term of his freshman year. Taylor's second semester GPA improved to 1.9, which restored his academic eligibility to participate (at that time, Wake Forest required a 1.35 GPA after freshman year). He refused, however, to play football during his sophomore year. Following a hearing before the university's Faculty Athletic Committee, Wake Forest terminated Taylor's scholarship after his sophomore year because of his failure to participate in the football program. Taylor, who ultimately received a degree from Wake Forest, sought to recover expenses that he incurred in completing his junior and senior years at the university.]

Plaintiffs contend that . . . a jury should determine whether Gregg Taylor acted reasonably and in good faith in refusing to participate in the football program at Wake Forest when such participation interfered with reasonable academic progress.

The plaintiffs' position depends upon a construction of the contractual agreement between plaintiffs and Wake Forest. . . . [T]he position of the plaintiffs is that it was orally agreed between plaintiffs and the representative of Wake Forest that:

> [I]n the achievement and athletic involvement, participation in athletic activities could be limited or eliminated to the extent necessary to assure reasonable academic progress.

And plaintiffs were to be the judge as to what "reasonable academic progress" constituted.

We do not agree with the position taken by plaintiffs. The scholarship application filed by Gregg Taylor provided:

> I agree to maintain eligibility for intercollegiate athletics under both Conference and Institutional rules. Training rules for intercollegiate athletics are considered rules of the Institution, and I agree to abide by them.

Both Gregg Taylor and his father knew that the application was for "Football Grant-In-Aid or A Scholarship," and that the scholarship was "awarded for academic and athletic achievement." It would be a strained construction of the contract that would enable the plaintiffs to determine the "reasonable academic progress" of Gregg Taylor. Gregg Taylor, in consideration of the scholarship award, agreed to maintain his athletic eligibility and this meant both physically and scholastically. As long as his grade average equaled or exceeded the requirements of Wake Forest, he was maintaining his scholastic eligibility for athletics. Participation in and attendance at practice were required to maintain his physical eligibility. When he refused to do so in the absence of any injury or excuse other than to devote more time to studies, he was not complying with his contractual obligations.

The record disclosed that Wake Forest fully complied with its agreement and that Gregg Taylor failed to do so. . . . [S]ummary judgment was proper.

> **QUESTIONS**

In *Taylor*, the court identified two requirements necessary for athletes to maintain their athletic eligibility. What are they? Do you view one as being more important than the other, or are they of equal importance?

Ross v. Creighton University
957 F.2d 410 (7th Cir. 1992)

RIPPLE, Circuit Judge.

[Editors' note: In the spring of 1978, Kevin Ross, a high school senior from an academically disadvantaged background, accepted an athletic scholarship to attend Creighton University and to play on its varsity basketball team. When he enrolled, Ross's academic level was far below that of the average Creighton student. Ross scored in the bottom-fifth percentile of college-bound seniors taking the American College Test, while the average freshman admitted to Creighton with him scored in the upper 27 percent.

During Ross's attendance at Creighton from 1978 until 1982, he maintained a D average and acquired 96 of the 128 credits he needed to graduate. Many of Ross's credits were in courses such as Marksmanship and Theory of Basketball, which did not count toward a university degree. Ross alleged that Creighton's Athletic Department advised him to take these courses and employed a secretary to read his assignments and prepare and type his papers. Ross also asserted that Creighton failed to abide by its promise to provide him with sufficient and competent tutoring. When he left Creighton, Ross had the overall language skills of a fourth grader and the reading skills of a seventh grader.

Ross filed a lawsuit asserting several claims, including a tort-based educational malpractice claim and a breach of contract claim. The district court granted the university's motion to dismiss all of Ross's claims and he appealed the decision. (See Chapter 7 for an overview of tort law principles.)

With respect to the educational malpractice claim, Ross asserted that Creighton owed a duty to educate him and breached its duty when it failed to do so. The appellate court agreed with the district court's dismissal of Ross's educational malpractice claim. The court identified several policy reasons, drawn from cases involving nonathlete students, for rejecting Ross's educational malpractice claim: (1) the lack of a satisfactory standard of care by which to evaluate educators since theories of education differ; (2) the inherent uncertainties about the cause and nature of damages because several factors (e.g., the student's attitude, motivation, temperament, past experience, and home environment) converge to affect the student's learning experience, which in turn makes it very difficult to establish that the teacher's conduct proximately caused a student's learning deficiency; (3) recognizing such a claim would create a flood of litigation, the sheer volume of which could overburden schools; and (4) an educational malpractice action would embroil the courts into overseeing the day-to-day operations of schools, which could implicate a university's academic freedom and autonomy.

Turning to Ross's breach of contract claims, the court stated he alleged that "Creighton agreed, in exchange for Mr. Ross's promise to play on its basketball team, to allow him an opportunity to participate, in a meaningful way, in the academic program of the University despite his deficient academic background." Ross alleged that Creighton breached its contract with him by failing to (1) "provide adequate and competent tutoring services," (2) "require [Ross] to attend tutoring sessions," and (3) afford Ross "a reasonable opportunity to take full advantage of tutoring services."]

The Contract Claims

There is no question, we believe, that Illinois would adhere to the great weight of authority and bar any attempt to repackage an educational malpractice claim as a contract claim. As several courts have noted, the policy concerns that preclude a cause of action for educational malpractice apply with equal force to bar a breach of contract claim attacking the general quality of an education. . . .

To state a claim for breach of contract, the plaintiff must do more than simply allege that the education was not good enough. Instead, he must point to an identifiable contractual promise that the defendant failed to honor. Thus, as was suggested in *Paladino*, if the defendant took tuition money and then provided no education, or alternately, promised a set number of hours of instruction and then failed to deliver, a breach of contract action may be available. *Paladino*, 454 N.Y.S.2d at 873. . . .

We read Mr. Ross' complaint to allege more than a failure of the University to provide him with an education of a certain quality. Rather, he alleges that the University knew that he was not qualified academically to participate in its curriculum. Nevertheless, it made a specific promise that he would be able to participate in a meaningful way in that program because it would provide certain specific services to him. Finally, he alleges that the University breached its promise by reneging on its commitment to provide those services and, consequently, effectively cutting him off from any participation in and benefit from the University's academic program. To adjudicate such a claim, the court would not be required to determine whether Creighton had breached its contract with Mr. Ross by providing deficient academic services. Rather, its inquiry would be limited to whether the University had provided any real access to its academic curriculum at all.

Accordingly, we must disagree respectfully with our colleague in the district court as to whether the contract counts of the complaint can be dismissed at the pleadings stage. . . . [W]e believe that the district court can adjudicate Mr. Ross' specific and narrow claim that he was barred from *any* participation in and benefit from the University's academic program without second-guessing the professional judgment of the University faculty on academic matters. . . .

Accordingly, the judgment of the district court is affirmed in part and reversed and remanded in part for proceedings consistent with this opinion. . . .

[Editors' note: Ross eventually settled his lawsuit for $30,000.]

QUESTIONS

1. In *Ross*, what reasons did the court articulate for refusing to recognize an educational malpractice claim? The reasons articulated by the court were drawn from cases not involving college athletes. Was the court justified in relying on these reasons? Are athletes' relationships with their universities distinguishable from nonathlete-students' relationship with their universities? See Timothy Davis & N. Jeremi Duru, Understanding Sports Law 49–56 (2022) (discussing the contours of the college athlete and university contractual relationship).
2. Although the court rejected Ross's breach-of-contract claim to the extent it merely restated a tort claim for educational malpractice, what is the narrow exception to the general rule of no liability that the court recognized?
3. What standard did the court adopt in *Taylor* for determining if a student-athlete is making reasonable academic progress? Do you agree with the standard?

NOTES

1. Jackson v. Drake University. Another leading case, *Jackson v. Drake University*, 778 F. Supp. 1490 (S.D. Iowa 1991), reveals the reluctance of courts to imply terms into the agreement as a means of expanding the obligations that a university owes to athletes. In *Jackson*, a basketball player alleged that the coaching staff of Drake University's men's basketball team engaged in improper conduct, such as failing to provide independent tutoring and adequate counseling and requiring him to turn in plagiarized work, which undermined the athlete's ability to play basketball and to succeed academically. According to Jackson, the coaching staff's conduct amounted to a breach of contract because "the express contract between him and Drake implicitly granted him the right to an educational opportunity and the right to play basketball for a Division I school." *Id.* at 1493. The court held that "the financial aid agreements do not implicitly contain a right to play basketball." *Id.* The court also refused to impose an obligation on Drake to provide Jackson with an educational opportunity.

In a case arising out of the University of North Carolina at Chapel Hill's academic scandal, the court ruled that the NCAA assumed neither a duty of reasonable care to safeguard athletes' educational opportunity nor a fiduciary duty to protect athletes' access to educational opportunities. *McCants v. NCAA*, 201 F.Supp.3d 732 (M.D. N.C. 2016); see also *McAdoo v. Univ. of North Carolina at Chapel Hill*, 736 S.E.2d 811, 822–23 (N.C. Ct. App 2013) (ruling that plaintiff's alleged loss of future income as an NFL player caused by the university's determination that a college athlete was ineligible to play football his senior year was too speculative to afford the player standing to assert a contract-based claim).

2. Discontinuation of Sports. Student-athletes also have been unsuccessful in their attempts to imply into their agreements limitations on an institution's discretion to discontinue a particular sport. See e.g., *Equity in Athletics, Inc. v. Dep't of*

Educ., 675 F. Supp. 2d 660 (W.D. Va. 2009) (finding the discontinuance of seven men's sports and three women's sports in an effort to bring an athletic program into compliance with Title IX did not impinge on the substantive and procedural due process rights of the student-athletes). The question presented in these cases implicates the broader topic of whether student-athletes possess a property interest in participating in intercollegiate athletics, which is discussed *infra*. See also *George v. George Washington Univ.*, 2022 WL 1719002 (D. D.C. May 27, 2022) (rejecting athlete's argument that the university breached implicit understanding between him and his coach that the men's rowing team would not be demoted from varsity to club status).

3. Rights Arising from Oral Promises. In *Fortay v. University of Miami*, 1994 WL 62319 (D. N.J. Feb. 17, 1994), an intercollegiate athlete maintained that his contract with the University of Miami (UM) impliedly obligated the university to provide the guidance necessary to allow him to develop his football talents. The athlete asserted that oral promises by then-outgoing head coach Jimmy Johnson, his successor coach, and other UM officials supported a breach of contract claim. The district court ruled that Fortay alleged facts sufficient to support a breach of an oral contract claim. It ruled, however, that the Letter of Intent and other contract documents did not give rise to the alleged implied obligations. Accord *Lesser v. Neosho County Community Coll.*, 741 F. Supp. 854, 865 (D. Kan. 1990) (refusing to imply a promise that plaintiff would have a position on a baseball team). Thus, courts have been reluctant to impose liability on institutions for oral promises allegedly made to athletes. See e.g., *Searles v. Trustees of St. Joseph's College*, 695 A.2d 1206 (Me. 1997) (refusing to enforce alleged oral promise to athlete that university would pay his medical bills if he continued to play on the school's basketball team). See also *Eppley v. Univ. of Delaware*, 2015 WL 156754 (D. Del. Jan. 12, 2015) (dismissing plaintiff's negligent misrepresentation claim against the university that allegedly resulted from coach's promise to guarantee athlete a scholarship for four years); *Giuliani v. Duke University*, 2010 WL 1292321 (M.D. N.C. Mar. 30, 2010) (holding that neither a coach's oral statements nor the provisions of the university's policy manuals were enforceable as binding contracts).

For commentary regarding these issues, see Barbara Osborne, *The Myth of the Exploited Student-Athlete*, J. Intercollegiate Sport, 7(2), 143–52 (2014); Mary Grace Miller, *The NCAA and the Student Athlete: Reform Is on the Horizon*, 46 U. Rich. L. Rev. 1141 (2021); Timothy Davis, *Absence of Good Faith: Defining a University's Educational Obligation to Student-Athletes*, 28 Hous. L. Rev. 743, 783 (1991).

E. NCAA Academic Reform Initiatives

KEY TERMS
- Academic Progress Rate (APR)
- Clustering
- Initial eligibility standards
- Jock majors
- Satisfactory progress

1. NCAA Academic Reform Legislation

How likely is it that a Kevin Ross-type scenario would occur today? NCAA rules seek, in part, to reduce the likelihood that an intercollegiate athlete will leave college after three or four years with the learning deficiencies of Kevin Ross. These rules include initial eligibility standards (which are discussed in Chapter 6, *infra*) and the NCAA's Academic Performance Program, which consists of the Academic Progress Rate and satisfactory progress rules. With respect to the latter, NCAA rules require that, as a condition to eligibility for participation, student-athletes take a curriculum that allows them to make progress toward obtaining a degree. Particularly pertinent NCAA bylaws in this regard include 14.4.3.1, "Fulfillment of Credit-Hour Requirements," and 14.4.3.2, "Fulfillment of Percentage of Degree Requirements." Over time, the NCAA heightened certain of these requirements. For a discussion of the NCAA's academic standards see generally Timothy Davis, *Assessing the Racial Implications of NCAA Academic Measures*, 29 William & Mary J. Race, Gender & Social Justice 1, 26 (2022); Kevin Brown & Antonio Williams, *A Critical Race Theory Perspective on "Pay for Play,"* 29 J. Legal Aspects Sport, 30 (2019).

The above-described bylaws and other "satisfactory progress rules" were a part of Division I academic reforms enacted by the NCAA between 2002 and 2004. Another component of the NCAA's reform efforts were the significant revisions made to its initial eligibility rules; NCAA revised eligibility rules deemphasize standardized test scores (i.e., the SAT and ACT), place greater emphasis on high school grades, and increase the number of core course requirements. (The history of and changes to initial eligibility requirements are detailed in Chapter 6.)

In 2012, the NCAA adopted heightened Division I initial eligibility standards that became effective August 1, 2016. Substantial changes were made to the core course requirements such as when core courses must be completed and the required GPA that athletes must achieve in those courses. In order to compete in intercollegiate athletics, students enrolling on August 1, 2016, and thereafter were required to: (1) earn at least a 2.3 GPA in core courses; (2) meet an increased sliding-scale standard (for example, an SAT score of 820 requires a 2.5 high school course GPA); and (3) successfully complete 10 of the 16 total required core courses before the start of their seventh semester in high school (7 out of the 10 courses must be successfully completed in English, math, and science). The modifications also articulated the academic requirements for academic redshirts. As discussed in Chapter 6, *infra*, in 2023, the NCAA elected to remove the standardized test requirement component from its initial eligibility standards. *See* Meghan Durham, *NCAA Division I Council modernizes rules for coaching limits*, NCAA (Jan. 11, 2023), https://www.ncaa.com/news/ncaa/article/2023-01-11/ncaa-division-i-council-modernizes-rules-coaching-limits. For a detailed discussion of the forgoing academic requirements, see 2022–23 NCAA Manual, Bylaw 14; NCAA, *2016 NCAA Division I Initial-Eligibility Academic Requirements*, http://www.ncaa.org/sites/default/files/High_School_IE_Standards.pdf (2016); Amy Wimmer, *New eligibility standards now in place for freshmen*, NCAA.org, Sept. 16, 2016, http://www.ncaa.org/about/resources/

media-center/news/new-eligibility-standards-now-place-freshmen" http://www.ncaa.org/about/resources/media-center/news/new-eligibility-standards-now-place-freshmen.

Some academics and college administrators lauded the revisions as likely to achieve their goal of improving graduation rates. Others, however, warned that the revised rules may have a negative impact on academic achievement. Some are concerned that more athletes will be steered toward "jock majors"—fields of study that allow college athletes to "maneuver through the maze of academic requirements and remain eligible to compete." Welch Suggs, *Jock Majors*, Chron. Higher Educ. A33 (Jan. 17, 2003). As expressed by one commentator, "[T]he march toward tougher standards and, the NCAA hopes, higher graduation rates begs a crucial question, however: What do numbers matter if players are being sent into academic programs that won't give them a meaningful education or marketable skills?" *Id.* at A34. The clustering of players in particular majors is not a new phenomenon. For a discussion of clustering and its impact, see Timothy Davis, *The Racial Caste System in College and Professional Sports*, 9 Tex. A&M L. Rev. 599, 630–37 (2022); Amanda L. Paule-Kobe, *Identifying Athlete's Majors and Career Aspirations: The Next Step in Clustering Research*, 1 J. Athlete Development and Experience 1 (Mar. 2019); Justin Ferguson, *Most Popular Academic Majors for 2015 Power 5 Conference Football Players*, Aug. 6, 2015, https://bleacherreport.com/articles/2521779-most-popular-academic-majors-for-2015-power-5-conference-football-players.

2. Academic Progress Rate

In May 2004, the NCAA adopted legislation that instituted a metric known as the Academic Progress Rate (APR). It was designed to give a real-time "snapshot" into the academic progress of individual teams at member institutions. In commenting on this reform, then-NCAA president Myles Brand stated, "For the first time, the NCAA will have the ability to hold institutions and teams accountable for the academic progress of their student athletes." Welch Suggs, *NCAA Weighs New Penalties for Academic Laggards*, Chron. Higher Educ., April 23, 2004, A42 (discussing NCAA's incentives/disincentives program).

To calculate an institution's APR, the NCAA examines each scholarship-receiving athlete on an intercollegiate team at a member institution and determines whether the player has remained academically eligible to participate in intercollegiate athletics and whether the student has chosen to remain enrolled at the school. Teams are awarded one point for meeting each of these standards during a given semester, resulting in each athlete earning the school a possible maximum of two points per semester and four points per year if the institution uses a two-semester calendar; alternatively, schools that use a quarter system can be awarded a maximum of eight total points per athlete. After determining each athlete's individual score, each team gets a final APR score; 1,000 is the maximum APR a team can earn. The NCAA initially established a four-year minimum of 900 for an institution to avoid being penalized. The failure of a team to reach the minimum APR exposes a college to the assessment of penalties including scholarship and recruiting restrictions and a team's loss of eligibility for postseason competition.

For additional discussion of how the Academic Progress Rate works, see Michelle B. Hosick, *Academic Success Stories Transcend Improved APRs*, NCAA News, June 9, 2010; Michelle B. Hosick, *Division I Beginning Major APR Assessment*, NCAA News, June 9, 2010.

In 2011, the NCAA Board of Directors enacted enhanced academic performance measures. One change, which took effect in 2012–13, increased the APR benchmark to 930 (which the NCAA states corresponds to a 50 percent graduation rate). The potential impact of the changes to the APR penalty structure were realized in dramatic fashion when the NCAA declared that because of a low four-year APR, the University of Connecticut men's basketball team, which in 2011 was the NCAA national champion, would be ineligible to participate in postseason play during the 2012–13 season. Connecticut appealed the penalty arguing that its men's basketball team's APR for 2010–11 and the first semester of 2011 were perfect. Its appeal was rejected.

Overall APR numbers released over the past several years indicate positive trends. NCAA officials attribute improved athlete academic performance, as measured by the APR, to several policy adjustments, including (1) more stringent progress-toward-degree requirements, (2) a rule allowing intercollegiate athletes who fit a certain academic profile to transfer, (3) increased core course requirements for incoming athletes, and (4) a requirement that transfer athletes earn an eligibility point in order to receive financial aid at the school to which they are transferring.

The following summarizes the trajectory of APR scores:

> Data demonstrate that average four-year APRs have risen since the metric's introduction. For the four-year period ending 2014–15, the average APR was 979 for all Division I men's and women's sports. This compares to an average APR of 984 for the four-year period ending 2020–21. The APRs for men's basketball teams were 958 and 965 for the periods ending 2011–12 and 2020–21, respectively. For Division I FBS football, the average APRs were 958 in 2011–12 and 968 in 2020–21. The four-year average APRs for HBCUs also improved from 912 in 2009–10, peaking at 970 in 2019–20, and declining to 955 for the 2020–21 period (citations omitted).

Davis, *supra*, 29 William & Mary J. Race, Gender & Social Justice at 26 (discussing the history and racial implications of the NCAA Academic Performance Program, and *Manassa v. NCAA*, No. 1:20-cv-3172 (S.D. Ind. filed Dec. 10, 2020), in which athletes at historically black colleges and universities allege the APR is racially discriminatory).

QUESTIONS

1. Which institutional body or bodies determines whether a student-athlete is making progress toward a degree?
2. Which institutional body or bodies determine if an athlete is academically eligible to participate in intercollegiate athletic competition?

3. Can you think of majors at your undergraduate institution in which a disproportionate number of athletes are enrolled? What makes these majors appealing to athletes? Would you consider them "jock majors"?
4. Under the current guidelines, student-athletes are required to make progress toward a degree. Should there be additional limitations as to what degrees athletes may pursue? Why or why not?
5. Do you think that the penalties for failing to meet the APR requirements will improve the quality of education for athletes? Or will it simply funnel more athletes into "jock majors"?
6. Why might football and men's basketball continue to post low multiyear D-I APRs in spite of the increased APR requirements?

F. Limited Scope of Constitutional Protections

KEY TERMS
- Contract rationale
- Economic rationale
- Fourteenth Amendment
- Procedural due process
- Promissory estoppel
- Property interest or right
- Scholarship rationale
- Substantive due process

1. General Principles: What Is a Property Interest?

Under the U.S. Constitution, before a person is deprived of life, liberty, or property by "state action," procedural due process—adequate notice and a fair hearing—must be given. Substantive due process also provides a party with a means of determining whether a constitutionally protected substantive right has in fact been infringed. In such cases, (1) the plaintiff must establish the requisite "state action"; (2) the party must be a person; and (3) an interest in life, liberty, or property must be threatened or infringed. Then, the court must determine whether these property interests were violated without either procedural or substantive due process. The state action requirement (which is satisfied by a public university's conduct) is addressed at length in Chapter 2. In the case of student-athletes, coaches, or other personnel, the requirement that the party be a person is easily met. The major issue remaining generally is whether a property or liberty interest has been implicated.

The question of whether a student-athlete possesses a property or liberty interest most often arises where athletes, seeking to retain their athletic eligibility, challenge either NCAA or institutional eligibility determinations that terminate an athlete's ability to continue to engage in intercollegiate competition. In asserting these challenges, athletes claim that the Fourteenth Amendment protects against deprivation of property without due process.

One commentator states that student-athletes have most often advanced four theories in arguing that they possess a constitutionally protected property interest in sports eligibility. The four theories are the following:

- **Economic Rationale:** student-athletes possess a property interest in training for lucrative careers as professional athletes.
- **Educational Rationale:** an athlete's athletic participation is a substantial part of the educational experience.
- **Scholarship Rationale:** the loss of an athletic scholarship deprives an athlete of benefits—athletic, educational, and financial—that result from being awarded a scholarship in exchange for athletic participation.
- **Contractual Rationale:** the athlete and university scholarship constitutes a contract that confers benefits (e.g., right to participate in intercollegiate athletics) that cannot be deprived without due process.

Brian L. Porto, Note, *Balancing Due Process and Academic Integrity in Intercollegiate Athletics: The Scholarship Athlete's Limited Property Interest in Eligibility*, 62 Ind. L.J. 1151, 1158–59 (1987).

A leading case that rejected the economic rationale is *Colorado Seminary v. NCAA*, 417 F. Supp. 885 (D. Colo. 1976), *aff'd*, 580 F.2d 320 (10th Cir. 1978), wherein the court rejected plaintiffs' argument that a constitutionally protected property interest in athletic participation stems from the vital role college athletics play in providing a training ground for a career in professional sports. Notes one commentator, "Because so few former college athletes ever sign a professional contract, college athletes' economic interests in professional sports opportunities are speculative and not of constitutional dimensions." Porto, *supra*, at 1158.

Although a clear majority of courts have ruled that student-athletes possess no constitutionally protected interest in athletic competition, a few courts have found that an athlete's future economic interests were not too speculative. In *Behagen v. Int'l Conference of Faculty Representatives*, 346 F. Supp. 602 (D. Minn. 1972), the court took "judicial notice of the fact that, to many, the chance to display their athletic prowess in college stadiums and arenas throughout the country is worth more in economic terms than the chance to get a college education." *Id.* at 604. This is a minority judicial position.

Courts also have largely rejected the contract rationale as a basis for establishing a property interest in intercollegiate athletics participation. Arguing in support of the contractual rationale, one commentator writes, "The scholarship agreement is the sort of 'mutually explicit understanding,' . . . which supports a claim of entitlement to participate in intercollegiate athletics." Porto, *supra*, at 1168–69.

The case that follows examines whether a scholarship athlete possesses a property interest in athletic participation. In reviewing the case, consider the rationales on which athletes rely in asserting the existence of a property interest.

2. A Property Interest in Athletic Participation?

Hysaw v. Washburn University of Topeka
690 F. Supp. 940 (D. Kan. 1987)

SAFFELS, Judge.

[Editors' note: This civil rights and breach of contract action arose out of allegations by several black football players that they were treated in a racially discriminatory manner by the university's coaching staff and administrations. The players, all of whom were awarded football scholarships for the 1986–1987 school year, alleged that promises of full scholarships had not been carried out; many also felt that their white teammates were favored by the coaching staff. Each player signed a financial aid agreement with Washburn. The written agreements did not promise that the plaintiffs would be allowed to play football for Washburn. A series of events transpired that culminated in the players boycotting team practices and the administration removing them from the football team. All of the players involved received the financial aid allocations promised them for the 1986–87 school year.

In their lawsuit, the players alleged that their removal from the team violated constitutional rights, including their free speech, liberty, and property rights in violation of 42 U.S.C. §1983, violated 42 U.S.C. §1981, and breached their contracts with Washburn University. The university requested summary judgment on all of the plaintiffs' claims.]

... A. Property Rights

Plaintiffs . . . argue they held a property interest in contractual rights to play football for Washburn, and argue that by breaching their scholarship contracts the defendants have deprived them of a property right without due process.

Property rights "are created and their dimensions are defined by existing rules or understandings that stem from an independent source such as state law." [*Board of Regents v. Roth*, 408 U.S. 564, at 577 (1972).] Only after a protectable property interest has been established do we then determine whether due process was afforded.

Plaintiffs claim defendants deprived them of their contractual rights under the scholarship agreements to play football for Washburn University. However, plaintiffs have only established a property right in the scholarship funds. No deprivation of those funds took place. Plaintiffs had no other protectable property interest. "To have a property interest in a benefit, a person clearly must have more than an abstract need or desire for it. He must have more than a unilateral expectation of it. He must, instead, have a legitimate claim of entitlement to it." *Roth*, 408 U.S. at 577. Plaintiffs concede that the only source for their alleged property interest is their scholarship agreements. The court has determined that the only interests created by those agreements are interests in receiving scholarship funds. Any other terms plaintiffs attempt to read into those agreements are, without supporting evidence, no more than "unilateral expectations." The court will therefore grant defendants' summary judgment motion on this claim.

B. Liberty Interests

Plaintiffs Battle and Chapman next argue that defendants infringed upon their liberty interests in pursuing a college football career. This claim arises out of those plaintiffs' efforts to be recruited by the nearby Emporia State University football team after they were dismissed from the Washburn team. . . .

A due process claim is made out only if the liberty interest allegedly violated is protectable under the Constitution. Again we look to an independent source of law to determine whether plaintiffs held a legitimate interest in the right to pursue a college football career. Only if this right is a protected liberty right under state law have plaintiffs made out a Section 1983 violation.

The plaintiffs concede that no right to pursue a college football career exists under well-established Tenth Circuit law. . . . [D]amage to an individual's reputation by a state official is not enough to establish a due process violation. Something more must be shown; a tangible interest must be established. . . .

The court finds no tangible interest here. *Roth* held that defamatory comments made by a government employer which cast a cloud over an employee's future employment prospects could constitute a deprivation of liberty. Plaintiffs now ask this court to extend the holding in *Roth* to the present situation; in effect, they are asking the court to equate government employment with a football scholarship. The court is unwilling to take such a giant leap. While no constitutional right to a government job exists, the Supreme Court has noted that qualification for a government job is a "privileg[e] of first-class citizenship." *Anti-Fascist Committee v. McGrath*, 341 U.S. 123, 183, 95 L. Ed. 817, 71 S. Ct. 624 (1950) (J. Douglas, concurring). Plaintiffs have offered no reason why a right to pursue a collegiate athletic career should be afforded the same status, and the court likewise sees no reason to do so. . . .

III. Breach of Contract

The law in Kansas is well-established that when a written contract exists and its language is clear and unambiguous, the language controls. . . . Plaintiffs argue they were promised that they would be allowed to play football during the 1986–87 season. Yet the written scholarship contracts they signed make no indication of such promises. In fact, the only promises in those written contracts were that the players would receive money. Plaintiffs provide no other evidence, other than "understandings" and "expectations," that they were promised a position on the 1986 team. . . . Plaintiffs concede that they received all disbursements on time. Defendants therefore met all their obligations under the contracts. . . .

QUESTION

In *Hysaw*, the court concluded that plaintiffs only established a property right in the scholarship funds. What would have to be present in order for a plaintiff to establish a property right to play football?

NOTES

1. The absence of a property interest. The majority of courts continue to adhere to the principle articulated in *Hysaw* as illustrated by *Hart v. NCAA*, 550 S.E.2d 709 (W. Va. 2001). Hart, a fifth-year senior on the Appalachian State University wrestling team, sought to compete in a lower weight class than that in which he had previously competed. An NCAA regulation prevented wrestlers from competing in a weight class that differed from the class in which they had competed prior to a certain date. After the NCAA rejected plaintiff's request for a waiver of the regulation, he eventually filed a lawsuit asserting a denial of an opportunity to fulfill his scholarship contract and to compete in intercollegiate competition. The West Virginia Supreme Court ruled that "participation in interscholastic athletics . . . does not rise to the level of a constitutionally protected 'property' or 'liberty' interest. . . ." *Id.* at 86. See also *NCAA v. Yeo*, 171 S.W.3d 863, 869 (Tex. 2005) (rejecting an athlete's claim that she possessed a property or liberty interest under the Texas constitution because of her unique "reputation as a world-class athlete in home country of Singapore"); but see *Hall v. Univ. of Minnesota*, 530 F. Supp. 104, 108 (D. Minn. 1982) (concluding because what was at stake for the athlete was his ability to obtain a no-cut contract with the NBA, "[t]he plaintiff would suffer a substantial loss if his career objectives were impaired"); see also Davis & Duru, *supra* at 62-69 (discussing the constitutional rights of intercollegiate athletes).

2. Rules violations. Athletes have asserted claims alleging deprivation of a constitutionally protected property interest when universities revoke or refuse to renew athletes' scholarships because the athletes violated rules. *Hysaw* recognizes that a scholarship athlete has a property right in the financial value of an existing athletic scholarship which may be revoked by a public university for misconduct if appropriate procedural due process (i.e., fair notice and a hearing) is provided. See *Radwan v. Manuel*, 55 F. 4th 101, 128 (4th Cir. 2022) (holding athletes possess a property interest in their scholarships for a term of the scholarship that can only be terminated for cause); see also *Conard v. University of Washington*, 834 P.2d 17, 22 (Wash. 1992) (stating that "[u]nless a legitimate claim of entitlement to the renewal of plaintiffs' scholarships was created by the terms of the contract, by a mutually explicit understanding, or by substantive procedural restrictions on the part of the decisionmaker, plaintiffs have no constitutional due process protections).

In *Webb v. Washington State Univ.*, 475 P.3d 1051 (Wash. Ct. App. 2020), a scholarship football player was dismissed from the team following his arrest for shoplifting even though he was never charged with a crime. The head football coach claimed the arrest violated football team rules including those prohibiting stealing or doing anything to hurt the team. The University's Athletic Award Appeal Committee upheld the coach's dismissal. During the appeal hearing, the athlete testified on his behalf. He was then asked to leave before the Committee heard the testimony of three witnesses including the head of football operations. The Committee affirmed the coach's dismissal of the athlete, who was not provided with a written decision by the Committee.

The trial court's dismissal of the athlete's procedural due process claim was reversed by the Washington Court of Appeals. Ruling that the athlete possessed a property interest in his multiyear scholarship, the court concluded that the hearing violated the athlete's procedural due process rights. It then provided guidance on the type of proceeding that would protect an athlete's rights. It stated that an athlete has a right to: "(1) receive a written copy of any information on which the nonrenewal recommendation is based, (2) present and rebut evidence, (3) have the hearing conducted by an objective decision maker, (4) be represented by counsel, (5) have a record made of the hearing for review purposes, and (6) receive a written decision from the hearing board setting forth its determination of contested facts and the basis for its decision." The court also refused to permit the defendant members of the Committee to avail themselves of qualified immunity as a defense.

G. College Athletes as Employees: Workers' Compensation and other Implications

KEY TERMS
- Catastrophic injury insurance program
- Contract of hire
- National Labor Relations Act (NLRA)
- National Labor Relations Board (NLRB)
- Right to control
- Unions
- Workers' compensation

1. Workers' Compensation: General Principles

Workers' compensation laws, which are governed by state law, provide a simple and inexpensive method for workers to obtain compensation and medical expenses for work-related injuries or diseases. The theory of these laws is that industries should bear the burden of industrial accidents as a component of the cost of production. Under workers' compensation legislation, benefits are available to injured workers regardless of an employer's common law tort or other statutory liability. These laws, however, preclude employee tort actions against employers, and limit the amount of damages that can be recovered. Thus, employees waive tort claims against their employers in exchange for a simplified, but limited, recovery under workers' compensation laws.

Generally, a person injured while performing services for compensation is considered an employee if two elements are present: (1) an express or implied contract to hire, and (2) employee status. A contract to hire binds an employer to pay compensation to an employee who performs services, sets forth the place to perform such services and work to be performed, and sets the compensation for the performance of the work. Assuming the existence of a contract to hire, the inquiry shifts to whether the contract gives rise to an employer-employee relationship.

Courts often adopt one of the following standards to determine an employment relationship: (1) the right to control the details of the work test, or (2) the relative nature of the work test. The right to control test examines whether the employer possessed the right to control the manner, means, and details of the worker's performance. Factors that demonstrate the requisite right of control include the terms of the employment agreement, the actual exercise of control, the method of payment, the furnishing of equipment, and the right to terminate the worker. An alternative standard used by some courts is the relative nature of the work test. Pursuant to this test, "employees are those who as a matter of economic reality are dependent upon the business to which they render service." Leo L. Lam, Comment, *Designer Duty: Extending Liability to Manufacturing for Violation of Labor Standards in Garment Industry Sweatshops*, 141 U. Pa. L. Rev. 623, 651 (1992). This test is likely to be satisfied where a worker performs tasks integral to the employer's regular business and does not provide an independent business or professional service vis-à-vis the employer. The principal consideration under the nature of the work test is the relationship between the services provided and the regular business of the alleged employer.

2. College Athletes and Workers' Compensation: *Waldrep v. Texas Employers Insurance Association*

Most states do not expressly include or exclude scholarship athletes from coverage under their respective workers' compensation statutes, nor do they provide a system of compensation for injured intercollegiate athletes. Thus, courts must determine whether or not scholarship athletes are covered "employees."

Some early cases held that an injured intercollegiate athletes could recover workers' compensation benefits if they held university jobs unrelated to athletics. See, e.g., *Van Horn v. Indus. Accident Comm'n*, 33 Cal. Rptr. 169 (Cal. Ct. App. 1963). After the *Van Horn* case, California amended its workers' compensation statute to expressly exclude college athletes from its coverage. Other states that expressly exclude college athletes from the definition of an employee for workers' compensation purposes include Hawaii, New York, Oregon, and Vermont. In contrast, Nebraska has established an administrative system for providing medical and disability benefits to injured university athletes. See, e.g., Neb. Rev. Stat. §85-106.05 (2019).

Courts now generally hold that athletes who suffer injuries while participating in intercollegiate athletics are not entitled to workers' compensation benefits. See e.g., *Rensing v. Indiana State Univ. Bd. of Trustees*, 444 N.E.2d 1170 (Ind. 1983) (holding that student-athletes are not entitled to workers' compensation benefits).

A leading case in this regard is *Waldrep v. Texas Employers Insurance Association*, 21 S.W.3d. 692 (Tex. Ct. App. 2000). In 1972, Kent Waldrep agreed to play football for Texas Christian University (TCU). In exchange, TCU agreed to provide financial aid "to the extent of room, board, tuition, fees and $10.00 per month for incidentals. . . ." *Id.* at 696. In October 1974, while playing football for TCU against the University of Alabama, Waldrep sustained a severe injury to his spinal cord and was paralyzed below the neck. In 1991, Waldrep filed a workers' compensation claim for his injury. The Texas Workers' Compensation Commission awarded workers' compensation benefits to Waldrep. On an appeal of the commission's finding, a jury ruled in favor of TCU. Waldrep appealed this adverse result.

The Texas Court of Appeals framed the issue before it as "whether, for workers' compensation law purposes, a recipient of a scholarship or financial aid from a university" is an employee. In upholding the jury's judgment in favor of TCU, the appellate court considered: whether a contract of hire existed between Waldrep and TCU, and whether Waldrep was an employee for workers' compensation purposes under the right to control test.

Concluding there was evidence to support the jury's finding that no contract of hire arose, the court stated:

> It is undisputed that before Waldrep signed the Letter of Intent and Financial Aid Agreement, both he and TCU understood that his recruitment and future football career at TCU would be governed by and subject to the rules of the NCAA. . . . The record indicates that the NCAA's policies and rules in effect at that time exhibited a concerted effort to ensure that each school governed by these rules made certain that student-athletes were not employees. Indeed, the rules declared that the fundamental policy of the NCAA was "'to maintain intercollegiate athletics as an integral part of the educational program and the athlete as an integral part of the student body, and, by so doing, retain a clear line of demarcation between college athletics and professional sports.'" Following its policy, the evidence reflects that the NCAA rules made the principle of amateurism foremost and established several requirements to ensure that the student-athlete would not be considered a professional. . . .

Id. at 699–700. The court also pointed to evidence (e.g., TCU never having placed Waldrep on its payroll) establishing that neither Waldrep nor TCU treated the financial aid Waldrep received as "pay" or "income."

With respect to the right of control, Waldrep argued that because the TCU football coaches exercised dominion over his college life, he was an employee. Rejecting Waldrep's argument, the court concluded:

> The record reflects that TCU *exercised* direction and control over all of the athletes in its football program, including non-scholarship players, while they were participating in the *football program*. Waldrep admitted that his high school coaches exercised the

same type of control over his participation in sports as the coaches at TCU. Waldrep further testified that he did everything that the coaches told him to do because he wanted to, because he loved the game, and because he wanted to be the best, not because he had to. The evidence is clear that TCU did not have the right to direct or control all of Waldrep's activities during his tenure at the school. The NCAA rules protected Waldrep's financial-aid award even if his physical condition prevented him from playing football for any reason. . . . Moreover, TCU could not simply cancel Waldrep's grant-in-aid based on his "athletic ability or his contribution to [the] team's success," or even, in certain circumstances, if he quit. *Id.*

The fact that the athletic department at TCU established practice and meeting times to be observed by those playing football does not establish that TCU had the *right* to direct and control all aspects of the players' activities while enrolled in the university. Waldrep's acceptance of financial aid from TCU did not subject him to any extraordinary degree of control over his academic activities.

Waldrep clearly presented evidence that TCU *exercised* direction or control over some of his activities while a student at the university. Perhaps the jury might have found this sufficient to prove that TCU had the *right* to direct the means or details of Waldrep's activities, but the jury declined to do so. . . .

Id. at 702.

QUESTIONS

For employees, what are the advantages and disadvantages of workers' compensation? According to the *Waldrep* court, what was the essence of Waldrep's and TCU's understanding regarding the nature of their relationship? What action might the Texas legislature have taken if the court had ruled in favor of Waldrep?

NOTES

1. Control. The *Waldrep* court concluded that even though the university "*exercised* direction and control over all of the athletes in its football program" (emphasis in original), TCU did not have the "right to direct or control all of Waldrep's activities during his tenure at the school." Moreover, Waldrep's participation in football "did not subject him to any extraordinary degree of control over his academic activities." Do you agree with the court's conclusion? Which factor seems most influential in the court's assessment that the requisite right to control for workers' compensation purposes is absent? In responding, consider the following comments taken from *University of Colorado v. Derdeyn*, 863 P.2d 929 (Colo. 1993), a drug-testing case that hinged in part on whether college athletes have a lessened expectation of privacy:

> CU's athletic director testified in relevant part that the NCAA sets limits on financial aid awards, playing seasons, squad size, and years of eligibility; that the NCAA requires that CU maintain records of each athlete's academic performance; that

the "athletes that eat at training tables are football and men's basketball and the other athletes eat in the dorms or at their off-campus residences"; that some coaches within their discretion impose curfews; that athletes are required to show up for practice; that athletes are "advised . . . on what they should take for classes"; that "we have a required study hall in the morning and in the evening"; and that it is "fair to say that the athletes are fairly well regulated." A student athlete testified in relevant part that "Yes," "if you are an NCAA athlete, you have to keep a certain grade average," and "Yes," "if your grades drop below that average, then you are not eligible for competition."

Id. at 940–41. For helpful commentary, see Richard T. Karcher, *Big-Time College Athletes' Status as Employees*, 33 ABA J. Lab. & Emp. L. 31 (2017); Robert A. McCormick & Amy Christian McCormick, *Myth of the Student-Athlete: The College Athlete as Employee*, 81 Wash. L. Rev. 71 (2006); see also Davis & Duru, *supra*, at 402–03.

2. Minimum wage for student-athletes? Scholarship athletes have unsuccessfully argued that they are employees and as such are entitled, pursuant to the federal Fair Labor Standards Act (FLSA), to receive a minimum wage salary for playing intercollegiate athletics on behalf of their colleges and universities. In *Berger v. NCAA*, 843 F.3d 285 (7th Cir. 2016), the Seventh Circuit held that "student-athletes are not employees and are not entitled to a minimum wage under the FLSA." *Id.* at 293. It also concluded that the former athletes' relationships to the NCAA were too tenuous for the athletes to be considered NCAA employees.

In *Dawson v. NCAA*, 932 F.3d 905 (9th Cir. 2019), the Ninth Circuit similarly upheld the lower court's dismissal of a complaint by ex-USC linebacker, Lamar Dawson, alleging that the NCAA and Pac-12 violated the FLSA and the California Labor Code by not paying college football players minimum wage or overtime pay. The court held that revenue generated by student-athletes in revenue sports did not automatically give rise to employee status. *Id.* at 910. The court also held that "under California law, athletes are generally deemed not to be employees of their schools." *Id.* at 913.

A federal district court reached a different result in *Johnson v. NCAA*, 556 F. Supp. 3d 491 (E.D. Pa. 2021). There, college athletes class sued their respective NCAA Division I colleges and universities and the NCAA alleging student-athletes who engage in intercollegiate athletic competition are employees of their universities and the failure of their institutions to pay them violated the FLSA and certain state minimum wage laws. After rejecting several defenses raised by defendants and finding that the plaintiffs' complaint should not be dismissed, the court reasoned in part:

> "[C]onstru[ing] the complaint in the light most favorable to the plaintiff," . . . we find that the Complaint plausibly alleges that NCAA D1 interscholastic athletics are not conducted primarily for the benefit of the student athletes who participate in them, but for the monetary benefit of the NCAA and the colleges and universities that those student athletes attend. We further find that the Complaint plausibly alleges that the NCAA D1 interscholastic athletics are not part of the educational

opportunities provided to the student athletes by the colleges and universities that they attend but, rather, interfere with the student athletes' abilities to participate in and get the maximum benefit from the academic opportunities offered by their colleges and universities.

Id. at 506. See Davis & Duru, *supra*, at 59–61.

3. Loss-in-value insurance. The NCAA has established a program that enables qualified "exceptional" intercollegiate athletes to obtain a preapproved loan to purchase disability insurance. This policy is designed to protect talented athletes against the loss of expected future earnings should they suffer a disabling injury or illness while in college. NCAA, *Loss-in-Value Insurance Information*, https://www.ncaa.org/sports/2015/12/18/loss-of-value-insurance-information.aspx.

3. Student-Athlete Unionization

In *Northwestern University and College Athletes Players Association (CAPA)*, Case 13-RC-121359 (National Labor Relations Board Region 13, March 26, 2014), a regional office of the National Labor Relations Board (NLRB) found that scholarship football players at Northwestern University, who had not exhausted their athletic eligibility, were employees as defined by the National Labor Relations Act (NLRA), and therefore could decide whether to be represented for collective bargaining purposes (i.e., unionize). In reaching the result, the regional director deemed the grant-in-aid received by scholarship athletes as compensation. The ruling also focused on the control that Northwestern exercises over its scholarship football players.

The decision stated that coaches and universities exercise extensive control over almost every aspect of the scholarship players' lives, including: (1) the preseason and in-season training regimes that dictate players' activities; (2) monitoring players' behavior and adherence to NCAA and team rules, which includes the power of coaches to discipline players for violations; (3) control over players' private lives that manifest either in restrictions or requiring players to obtain permission from coaches on matters ranging from players' making living arrangements, applying for outside employment, making posts on social media, using drugs and alcohol, and traveling off campus; and (4) making academic decisions. The ruling's characterization of student athletes as employees was antithetical to the NCAA's conceptualization of amateurism.

Northwestern appealed the ruling to the NLRB. Approximately a year after Northwestern University's appeal was filed, the five-member NLRB unanimously dismissed the football players' petition that they be recognized as employees for collective bargaining purposes. *Northwestern University and College Athletes Players Association (CAPA)*, Petitioner, 362 NLRB No. 167 (Aug. 17, 2015). According to the Board, "because of the nature of sports leagues (namely the control exercised by the leagues over the individual teams) and the composition and structure of [Football Bowl Subdivision] football (in which the overwhelming majority of competitors are public colleges and universities over which the Board cannot assert jurisdiction), it would not promote stability in labor relations to assert jurisdiction in this case." *Id.* at 3. After noting that Northwestern is the only private school in the Big Ten, the Board explained because many of Northwestern's competitors are public institutions, the Board would not possess the authority to assert jurisdiction over them. Thus, the Board's resolution of a labor issue involving one university and its player could have leaguewide ramifications for teams, most of which would be outside the Board's jurisdiction. "Consequently, 'it would be difficult to imagine any degree of stability in labor relations' if we were to assert jurisdiction in this single-team case." *Id.* at 5 (citing *The North American Soccer League*, Case 2–RC–17740 (June 30, 1978)). The Board also strongly suggested that exercising jurisdiction could upset competitive balance. *Id.* at 4–5. The Board limited its decision to the Northwestern University football players, stating that it need not address "whether it might assert jurisdiction in another case involving grant-in-aid scholarship football players (or other types of scholarship athletes). . . ." *Id.* at 1.

It is important to note that the Board did not rule on whether college athletes are employees. In this regard, the Board stated that it reached its decision without deciding "whether the scholarship players are employees." *Id.* at 6.

In September 2021, the NLRB's general counsel sent a memo to the board's regional offices expressing her opinion that college athletes who attend private colleges and universities fall within the National Labor Relations Act's definition of employees and as such should be classified as employees under federal labor law. NLRB, *NLRB General Counsel Jennifer Abruzzo Issues Memo on Employee Status of Players at Academic Institutions*, News & Publications (Sept. 29, 2021), *https:// www.nlrb.gov/news-outreach/news-story/nlrb-general-counsel-jennifer-abruzzo-issues-memo-on-employee-status-of*. The memo emphasized the considerable control that institutions exercise over their intercollegiate athletes and the revenue generated by athletes' services.

In February 2022, the National College Players Association (NCPA) filed unfair labor practice (ULP) charges against the University of Southern California (a private university) and UCLA (a public university) as well as the Pac-12 Conference and the NCAA, which alleges they are misclassifying college football players and men's and women's basketball players as student-athletes rather than "employees" (which they allegedly are because of the joint control exercised over them, including by rules restricting their communications with the media). On December 15, 2022, the NLRB regional office found that the plaintiffs should be permitted to move forward with their claim for adjudication on the merits. NLRB general counsel, NLRB General Counsel, Jennifer Abruzzo, remarked:

> [T]he [conclusion that the] unfair labor practice complaints "have merit is based on a determination that USC, the Pac-12 Conference, and the NCAA, as joint employers, have maintained unlawful rules and unlawfully misclassified scholarship basketball and football players as mere "student-athletes" rather than employees entitled to protections under our law.

"This kind of misclassification deprives these players of their statutory right to organize and to join together to improve their working/playing conditions if they wish to do so," she added. "Our aim is to ensure that these players can fully and freely exercise their rights."

NLRB Opens door for union for college athletes, CNN.com, Dec. 15, 2022, https://www.cnn.com/2022/12/15/business/nlrb-unfair-labor-practice-athletes-usc-pac-12-ncaa/index.html.

In the most recent development, 15 players on the Dartmouth men's basketball team have taken steps toward unionization. "The New England-based local 560 chapter of the Service Employees International Union (SEIU) filed a petition [with the NLRB] seeking an election to become the representative of the players. . . ." Dana O'Neil, *Dartmouth men's basketball players file NLRB petition to unionize*, The Athletic, Sept. 14, 2023, https://theathletic.com/4862946/2023/09/14/dartmouth-basketball-players-union/.

QUESTIONS

What might have been the likely practical and political consequences of a board ruling in favor of Northwestern's football players? Would such a decision have transformed the relationship between students and their universities? If so, how? For insightful commentary, see Roberto L. Corrada, *The Northwestern University Football Case: A Dissent*, 11 Harv. J. Sports & Ent. L. 15 (2020) (providing a critical analysis of the NLRB's determination); Marc Edelman, *The Future of College Athlete Players Unions: Lesson Learned from Northwestern University and Potential Next Steps in the College Athletes' Rights Movement*, 38 Cardozo L. Rev. 1627 (2017); Karcher, *supra*.

FIRST AMENDMENT RIGHTS IN INTERCOLLEGIATE ATHLETICS

A. Introduction

In addition to contract and other private causes of action, those associated with intercollegiate athletics may be able to assert constitutional rights in the intercollegiate context. Equal protection or equality rights as set forth in the Fourteenth Amendment to the U.S. Constitution and in state constitutional provisions, for example, are discussed in Chapter 5 (gender equity) and Chapter 6 (racial equity). Courts will only reach (decide) constitutional issues when a case cannot be decided on a private, non-constitutional ground, such as a contract right.

As was the case in the interscholastic area (see Chapter 2), student-athletes, coaches, and others may raise issues regarding alleged violations of their rights under the First Amendment of the U.S. Constitution by state actors. In the

Tarkanian case, discussed in Chapter 2, the Supreme Court held that the NCAA is not a state actor. The NCAA, therefore, is not obligated to afford coaches, students, and others their constitutional rights, including their First Amendment rights. Nevertheless, state universities and colleges may be obligated to do so. Lawsuits seeking to protect alleged infringement of such rights arise in a number of contexts.

In deciding those cases, courts consider the maturity of the athletes involved in determining whether rights have been infringed. High school or younger students are often treated differently than more mature college students. Secondary schools often act in an *in loco parentis* (in the place of the parent) capacity. High schools are, therefore, often afforded greater power to regulate the speech and expression of their students than is afforded to colleges and universities. As you read the following materials, reflect on how First Amendment and other constitutional standards may be different at the intercollegiate and interscholastic or high school levels.

First Amendment rights have been raised with respect to athletic department officials' and athletes' interaction with the media, as well as alleged violations of an athlete's freedom of religion by a public university. The materials in this section are only intended to be illustrative of the kinds of issues and analyses that arise and are not intended to be exhaustive in their treatment of the First Amendment area.

KEY TERMS
- Actual malice (knowing falsity, reckless disregard for the truth)
- Defamation
- Establishment clause
- Freedom of expression
- Free exercise clause
- Free speech
- In loco parentis
- Invasion of privacy
- Public figure
- Retaliation
- Truth as a defense

B. The First Amendment and the Media

Athletic administrators, coaches, and college athletes often have conflicts with the broadcast and print media. With the public attention and commercialization of sports, it is not surprising that the media has extended its coverage into matters that might have been deemed, in other contexts, to be private in nature. For example, criminal accusations or other comments in the media that deal with the private lives of college athletes and coaches may be given broad coverage in the media, particularly in the case of high-profile coaches, college athletes, and administrators. High-profile administrators, coaches, and athletes receive less protection against incursions by the media into their private lives than most individuals do, under defamation law and the right of privacy, because they have been held to be public figures. If a high-profile administrator, coach, or athlete decides to pursue recovery for alleged defamatory falsehoods against the media, he or she must prove that the media acted with "actual malice," "knowing falsity," or "reckless disregard for the truth" in publishing a falsehood (truth is a defense in such cases) as required under applicable First Amendment case law. Such proof is not easy to muster, and it is clearly difficult for a high-profile athletic figure to recover if he or she is deemed to be a public figure. See e.g., *Talley v. Time, Inc.*, 923 F.3d 878 (10th Cir. 2019) (because he could not establish defendant engaged in actual malice, the court dismissed the lawsuit of a booster who alleged he was libeled in a *Sports Illustrated* article regarding the alleged practice of paying players in violation of NCAA bylaws); *Turner v. Wells*, 879 F.3d 1254 (11th Cir. 2018) (offensive line coach's inability to establish actual malice by defendant warranted dismissal of his defamation suit).

The landmark Supreme Court case *Curtis Publishing Co. v. Butts*, 388 U.S. 130 (1967), arose from the accusations in a newspaper accusing Wally Butts, the athletic director at the University of Georgia, of attempting to "fix" a 1962 football game between the Universities of Georgia and Alabama. In a libel action filed in federal court, Butts sought $5 million compensatory and $5 million punitive damages. The jury returned a verdict for $60,000 in general damages and for $3 million in punitive damages. The trial court reduced the total to $460,000. In a strongly divided set of opinions, the Court held that the *New York Times* actual malice (knowing falsity or reckless disregard for the truth on the part of the media, in this case the Curtis Publishing Company) standard applied in the case of someone in the position of Athletic Director Butts.

Even though the public-figure status invoked in the *Butts* case makes it very difficult for someone in the position of Butts to prevail in a defamation action, the *Butts* case provides a means by which a party might prevail—by proving that the media acted with reckless disregard, with full knowledge of the harm that is likely to result from the publication. In fact, Butts ultimately prevailed on just such a ground.

In *Bilney v. The Evening Star Newspaper Co.*, 406 A.2d 652 (Md. App. 1979), six members of the University of Maryland's men's basketball team sued two newspapers alleging invasions of privacy and intentional infliction of emotional distress. In finding that the athletes were public figures, the court stated as follows:

> The gravamen of their complaint, both in terms of the invasion of privacy and intentional infliction of mental distress counts, was that [the defendants] willfully, wrongfully, and maliciously invaded [and obtained the plaintiffs'] confidential University records and published private and privileged facts about their private lives.
>
> [The student-athletes] achieved the status of public figures solely by virtue of their membership on the University basketball team. Their possible exclusion from the team whether for academic or any other reason was therefore a matter of legitimate public interest. Had they quit the team or withdrawn from the University, the public would be entitled to ask and to speculate as to the reasons for such action. That the threat of exclusion was academically based does not lessen the legitimacy of

the public interest. Appellants were not in the same posture as other students, whose scholastic standing, in its entirety, was purely of private concern; when their standing reached the point of affecting their eligibility to play basketball for the University, the privacy of that status became somewhat attenuated. Publication of that eligibility-threatening status was not unreasonable and did not trample upon community mores. Having sought and basked in the limelight, by virtue of their membership on the team, appellants will not be heard to complain when the light focuses on their potentially imminent withdrawal from the team. We thus [hold] that, upon the undisputed evidence in this case, the publications in question did not constitute a tortious invasion of privacy.

Id. at 660.

QUESTIONS

1. Should coaches in revenue-producing sports be treated as public figures for defamation and privacy purposes, thereby permitting the media with broad latitude to write or broadcast about them? Should college athletes in those sports be treated as public figures as well?
2. Do you agree with the decision in *Bilney*? Should presidents and other administrators at a university be considered public figures?

C. Free Speech

As adults, are the college athletes' free speech rights entitled to more or less protection than high school students, whose rights were discussed by *Mahanoy Area Sch. Dist. v. B. L.*, 141 S. Ct. 2038 (2021), *supra,* in Chapter 2? See generally *Pinard v. Clatskanine School District 6J*, 446 F.3d 964, 978 (9th Cir. 2006) ("[I]f the plaintiffs can show that their protected speech was a 'substantial or motivating factor' in the defendant's decision to suspend them from the team permanently, and the defendants fail to show that they 'would have taken the same action even in the absence' of that speech, then the defendants violated plaintiffs' First Amendment rights."). In *Radwan v. Manuel*, 55 F. 4th 101 (2d Cir. 2022), an athlete was removed from a soccer team and lost her athletic scholarship after she made an obscene hand gesture at the end of a televised championship game. The court held that "[i]n light of the absence of a decision by the Supreme Court or this Court on the application of the First Amendment to vulgar speech (or expression) by a university student while representing the university at a school-sponsored event, as well as the lack of any consensus among other courts on this issue, we conclude that the defendants are entitled to qualified immunity").

In *Ridpath v. Board of Governors Marshall University*, 447 F.3d 292 (4th Cir. 2006), a compliance officer at Marshall University became aware of a number of violations of NCAA rules, including the school's practice of providing athletes with jobs at "above-market" wages. After bringing this information to the attention of university officials, the compliance officer alleged he was prevented from assisting in the investigation, blamed for the violations, and subjected to "corrective action" resulting in a transfer to another position on campus that significantly diminished his ability to obtain future employment in his chosen occupation of athletic compliance. The Sixth Circuit ruled that a public university employer "contravenes a public employee's First Amendment rights when it discharges or refuses to rehire the employee or when it makes decisions relating to the promotion, transfer, recall and hiring in the exercise of that employee's free speech rights." *Id.* at 316. The court held that the plaintiff had sufficiently alleged that he was speaking as a private citizen and not as a public employee, and that his interest in exercising his First Amendment rights was not outweighed by the university's interest in his speech because the school was unable to show how the plaintiff's remarks had interfered with its legitimate operations. Thus, the court found that the plaintiff had properly alleged First Amendment claims for retaliation and chilling of his free speech rights. See Chris Hanna et al., *College Athletics Whistle-Blower Protection*, 27 J. Legal Aspect Sport 209 (2017) (advocating for enhanced protection for athletic personnel who report possible NCAA violations); see also Frank D. LoMonte & Virginia Hamrick, *Running the Full-Court Press: How College Athletic Departments Unlawfully Restrict Athletes' Right to Speak to the New Media*, 99 Neb. L. Rev. 86 (2020).

D. Religious Liberty Issues

As noted previously, religious liberty issues often arise in the interscholastic athletics context. Religious liberty issues are discussed in greater length in Chapter 2, which deals with interscholastic athletics. Similar issues arise at the intercollegiate level.

Some of the areas where it can be anticipated that religious liberties will be implicated in the intercollegiate athletic context include the following: (1) recognition of religious activity on the part of athletes, coaches, and athletic personnel; (2) accommodating the religious interests of competitors (e.g., coaches and conferences have been known to be sensitive to the religious interests of athletes and have rescheduled events and have relieved athletes of practice and other obligations so that they could exercise their religious conscience); and (3) accommodating religious educational institutions (e.g., Brigham Young University refuses to participate in athletic events on Sundays, the Sabbath for members of the Church of Jesus Christ of Latter-day Saints, which has resulted in its being placed in brackets in the NCAA men's basketball tournament that will permit adherence to its Sabbath).

Courts have been reluctant to recognize rights of religious conscience by requiring institutions or associations to accommodate the religious conscience of administrators, coaches, and college athletes. Nevertheless, although the NCAA, conferences, and coaches have often been willing to permit such accommodations, this is not always the case. The courts have indicated, however, a willingness to intervene to avoid discrimination against certain religious groups. It should be noted that proving religious discrimination is very difficult—few individuals admit to such discrimination. Erin B Edwards, *College Athletics, Coercion, and the Establishment Clause: The Case of Clemson Football*, 106 Va. L. Rev. 1533 (2020).

QUESTIONS

1. Even though it is not subject to the constraints of the federal constitution because it is not a state actor (see *NCAA v. Tarkanian* in Chapter 1), the NCAA has exempted brief religious observances by athletes, including pausing to pray or express religious gratitude in the end zone after scoring a touchdown, from its general rule that prohibits players from celebrating or drawing attention to themselves on the football field. Some interscholastic associations have refused to exempt such activities from rules against celebration. Do you agree with this exemption? Does it prefer religion over other interests of athletes?
2. Athletes at the intercollegiate level are generally older and more mature than high school or interscholastic athletes. Does this distinction as to levels of maturity provide a legitimate basis for permitting more religion or religious exercise on the part of intercollegiate athletes than on the part of interscholastic athletes? In responding, recall the discussion of religious liberty issues in the interscholastic sports context in Chapter 2(c)(3).
3. State constitutional or legislative (statutory) issues may arise regarding religious liberty and other rights. Remember, even if federal constitutional law does not require that the religious conscience of student-athletes be recognized, state constitutional law may do so.

Problem 4-1

You are the athletic director at a major state (public) university, and a Muslim student-athlete has asked to meet with you to discuss a dispute he has with his coach. The coach insists that athletes maintain a rigorous diet, which includes eating certain meals each day. The Muslim student wishes to follow his religious conscience and fast on certain days and avoid eating some of the meals prescribed by the coach. He also eats a more vegetarian diet than the high-protein fare established by the coach. Before the meeting, you call the coach, and he says that although he respects the athlete for his religious conviction, it is imperative that he eat with the team for health purposes and to maintain team morale. He is fearful that yielding to this athlete's religious beliefs would simply open a Pandora's box, permitting athletes to contrive all kinds of reasons for getting out of his strict dietary regimen. The coach also indicated that the diet was devised in conjunction with his trainer and is believed to maximize performance on the part of athletes. What do you say to the athlete and coach?

Gender Equity Issues in Athletics

INTRODUCTION

In this chapter, we explore issues related to gender equity in athletics. A brief history is followed by sections focusing on the development of the law in this area over the past four decades. Gender discrimination issues were first raised through equal protection claims, with additional regulation for school-based sports programs coming from Title IX of the Educational Amendments of 1972, 20 U.S.C. §1681, and the various regulations, policy interpretations, and other documents issued by the Office of Civil Rights (OCR) of the U.S. Department of Education (DOE). Increasing athletics participation opportunities for girls and women has introduced other gender-based legal issues, such as sexual harassment and pregnancy discrimination, to the world of sports. Although much of the focus on gender equity in athletics has centered on female participants, gender discrimination issues also exist for women who wish to work in sports, including as administrators, coaches, officials, and journalists.

HISTORICAL PERSPECTIVE

In the United States, progress toward gender equality in athletics has occurred, but it has been slow in coming. An invidious myth that women are not competitive and therefore not interested in sports has been perpetuated throughout American culture. Although Native American women participated in a variety of sports and competitive activities, European social customs and religious beliefs precluded female settlers in the United States from participating in athletics. The first girls' interscholastic athletic activity—gymnastics—was introduced at the Latin School for girls in Salem, Massachusetts in 1821, but women's participation in competitive athletics remained virtually invisible throughout the nineteenth century.

It was not until after passage of the Nineteenth Amendment in 1919 that some of the cultural opposition to the involvement of women in athletics began to dissipate. In 1920, female swimmers became the first American women to be accorded full Olympic status. As the United States became more industrialized and increasing numbers of women entered the workforce, industrial league athletics programs became popular. Professional athletics opportunities for women developed in golf, tennis, and in barnstorming teams in basketball. During World War II, the All-American Girls Professional Baseball League was established. While some progress was made in creating opportunities for females to compete in sports, the cultural shift after World War II, which dictated that athletics participation was not appropriate for "ladies," stagnated these efforts. However, visionaries such as the Iowa Girls' High School Athletic Union established a statewide program in 1954 that placed girls on equal footing with boys in high school athletics.

In the late 1960s and early 1970s, women finally made significant strides in terms of their participation in competitive intercollegiate athletic events. In 1966, the first intercollegiate women's basketball tournament was played in Pennsylvania, and the Commission on Intercollegiate Athletics for Women (CIAW) was established in 1967. The CIAW was formed for the purpose of increasing participation by women in competitive sports, which led to the first women's national championship competition in 1969, in the sport of gymnastics. In 1971, the first national intercollegiate athletics association to govern women's sports, the Association for Intercollegiate Athletics for Women (AIAW), was formed, replacing the CIAW and offering seven national championships for women (it was not until 1982 that the NCAA began offering national championships for women in all three of its divisions).

The 1970s proved to be a historic decade in terms of increased participation by women in athletics in the United States. Title IX of the Education Amendments of 1972 was enacted by Congress to eliminate discrimination based on sex in educational programs or activities and was signed into law by President Richard M. Nixon on June 23, 1972. The legislation did not specifically mention athletics, but it did require the promulgation of regulations to achieve gender equity in educational opportunities.

The regulations, 34 C.F.R. §106.41, which became effective on July 21, 1975, provided significant momentum for increased participation for women in organized athletics at the interscholastic and intercollegiate levels. The regulations defined equal opportunity in athletics in two parts: equal accommodation and equal treatment. *Equal accommodation* measured whether the participation opportunities by selection of sports and levels of competitions reflected the interests and abilities of both sexes. *Equal treatment* examined whether male and female participants had similar access to a list of program components including provision of equipment and supplies, locker rooms, practice and competitive facilities, medical and training facilities and services, housing and dining facilities and services, and travel and per diem allowances; scheduling of games and practice times; access to coaching and academic tutoring as well as compensation for coaches and tutors; and publicity. 34 C.F.R. §106.41(c). Expectations for compliance were incremental, with elementary schools given one year, middle and high schools given two years, and colleges and universities given three years to adjust their programs.

Political opponents immediately rallied in an effort to limit the scope of Title IX as applied to intercollegiate athletics with seven bills or resolutions unsuccessfully proposed between 1974 and 1977. The first was proposed by Senator John Tower of Texas, who attempted to exempt revenue-producing sports from Title IX regulation, as well as funds received from donations to athletics programs. The Tower Amendment was rejected in committee. 120 Cong. Rec. 15,322-15,323 (1974). Senator Jesse Helms of North Carolina was also opposed to Title IX, first attempting to disapprove of the regulations in their entirety, 121 Cong. Rec. 17,300 (1975), then introducing S. 2146 to prohibit the application of the regulations to athletics, "Prohibition of Sex Discrimination, 1975," Hearings Before the Senate Subcommittee on Education of the Committee on Labor and Public Welfare on S. 2106, 94th Cong., 1st Sess., Sept. 16-18, 1975, and finally reintroducing S. 2146 as S. 535 in 1977. All attempts failed in committee. Interestingly, Senator James McClure of Idaho tried to distinguish athletics programs from educational programs or activities by proposing an amendment that would limit Title IX requirements to "the curriculum or graduation requirements of the institutions." 122 Cong. Rec. 28136 (1976). In the House, Representative James O'Hara of Michigan twice attempted to propose bills that would have allowed schools to use money earned from a revenue-producing sport only on that sport, or first on that sport, regardless of gender inequities in the athletics program. 121 Cong. Rec. 21,685 (1975).

Meanwhile, a revolution was occurring on the courts and on the fields and tracks at schools across the country. By 1978, the number of female high school student-athletes grew from 300,000 to more than 2 million. Women's participation in intercollegiate athletics doubled from 32,000 participants in 1971 to more than 64,000 participants in 1977. Hundreds of complaints of gender discrimination were filed with the U.S. Department of Health, Education, and Welfare (HEW), while schools lamented that they were unsure about Title IX requirements for compliance. In response, HEW issued a policy interpretation in 1979 regarding the application of Title IX to athletics. 44 Fed. Reg. 71,413 et seq. The policy interpretation provided additional information regarding items to be measured to determine compliance with the regulations. Schools were particularly concerned with proving that they were effectively accommodating the interests and abilities of both male and female students.

The policy interpretation introduced a three-part test, allowing schools to choose any one of the following three ways to prove that they were providing equal participation opportunities:

(1) Whether intercollegiate level participation opportunities for male and female students are provided in numbers substantially proportionate to their respective enrollments; or
(2) Where the members of one sex have been and are underrepresented among intercollegiate athletes, whether the institution can show a history and continuing practice of program expansion which is demonstrably responsive to the developing interest and abilities of the members of that sex; or
(3) Where the members of one sex are underrepresented among intercollegiate athletes, and the institution cannot show a continuing practice of program

expansion such as that cited above, whether it can be demonstrated that the interests and abilities of the members of that sex have been fully and effectively accommodated by the present program.

Although the three-part test has become what many people characterize as Title IX, for compliance purposes, it is only one of several provisions that measure the effective accommodation requirement. Overall compliance with Title IX as applied to athletics is measured by looking at all required program component areas and comparing the men's program as a whole to the women's program as a whole to determine whether any disparities are substantial enough to be discriminatory.

Title IX is meant to be self-enforcing, meaning that schools are supposed to voluntarily comply with the law. The administrative process of Title IX enforcement is set forth in §88.71 of the Title IX regulation. Anyone who believes a school is not complying may file a complaint, and the OCR may also initiate periodic compliance reviews of colleges and universities. The Department has 90 days to investigate and inform the institution (and the complainant, if applicable) of its findings. If the investigation indicates that an institution is complying, the Department states this, and the case is closed.

For those institutions that are not in compliance, the Department outlines the violations found and provides an additional 90 days to resolve violations by obtaining a voluntary compliance agreement from the institution. According to the regulations, schools that are not in compliance may lose their federal funding. 45 C.F.R. §§80.8–80.11 and 45 C.F.R. Part 81. However, no school has ever met that fate. Instead, the OCR works with the institution to create a plan that will correct the violation, with a specific timetable for reaching interim goals as well as full compliance. When agreement is reached, the Department notifies the institution that its plan is acceptable. The Department is then obligated to review periodically the implementation of the plan.

People who believe they are being discriminated against on the basis of sex are not required to file a complaint with the OCR and exhaust administrative options before filing a lawsuit. In *Cannon v. University of Chicago*, 441 U.S. 677 (1979), the Supreme Court held that although the legislation did not expressly empower an individual to bring a Title IX lawsuit, there was an implied private right to do so.

Responsibilities for enforcing Title IX shifted to the DOE's OCR in 1980, when the HEW was reorganized. One of the OCR's first official acts was to issue an interim investigators manual dealing with Title IX and athletics. In 1982, the OCR also issued *Guidance for Writing Title IX Intercollegiate Athletics Letters of Findings*. In spite of these enforcement guides, Title IX was not vigorously enforced during the 1980s. Then, in *Grove City College v. Bell*, 465 U.S. 555 (1984), the Supreme Court held that Title IX applied only to programs that benefited directly from federal funds. By mandating a program-specific tie to federal funding, the *Grove City* decision seriously limited the OCR's jurisdiction over university athletic programs, few of which receive federal funding. The Supreme Court had accomplished in one decision what politicians had been unable to do since the 1975 Regulations—eliminate athletics from Title IX requirements. Congress made its displeasure known by passing the Civil Rights Restoration Act, despite a veto effort. *See* 20 U.S.C. §1687 (1988). This act mandates an institution-wide approach: All programs and activities sponsored by educational institutions that receive federal funds, including their athletics departments, are bound by the requirements of Title IX.

Typically, Title IX complainants (usually female student-athletes) were not involved in OCR investigations, and resolution of complaints may or may not have included provisions that would make the complainant whole. Litigants were limited to equitable relief until 1992, when the Supreme Court unanimously held in *Franklin v. Gwinnett County Public Schools*, 503 U.S. 60 (1992), that prevailing plaintiffs can recover monetary damages and attorneys' fees for intentional violations of Title IX. The *Gwinnett* decision, coupled with increased enforcement activity on the part of the OCR, contributed to a significant rise in the number of Title IX athletics cases. In 1992, the National Collegiate Athletic Association (NCAA) completed a gender equity study, which increased awareness of these issues and encouraged institutions to take appropriate action. Gender equity was also included as a component in the athletics certification process the NCAA instituted during the 1990s.

In 1994, Congress passed the Equity in Athletics Disclosure Act (EADA), 20 U.S.C. §1092(g), which requires all federally funded institutions of higher education to disclose information regarding their athletics programs. The first annual reporting date was October 1, 1996. EADA reports provide a source of information that has increased public awareness and constitutes a better evidentiary basis for quantifying gender inequities under the Title IX regulations.

In the early 2000s, Title IX was once again targeted politically, this time in the campaign promises of President George W. Bush to eliminate affirmative action and racial quotas. In 2002, the Secretary of Education, Rod Paige, created the Commission on Opportunity in Athletics to investigate whether Title IX was fair to both boys and girls. A total of 15 men and women, primarily representing the interests of major NCAA Division I (D-I) athletics programs, were assembled to hear testimony through four Town Hall meetings across the United States. The commission then filed a final report on February 28, 2003, with several recommendations. Unhappy with what they perceived as a politically tainted process, two commissioners filed a Minority Report voicing their concerns. Secretary Paige accepted both reports and publicly declared that the DOE would not act on any recommendation that did not have unanimous support.

However, on March 25, 2005, the DOE issued modified guidelines for determining compliance with the third prong of the OCR's three-part test. Under these guidelines, educational institutions could establish whether the athletic interests and abilities of the underrepresented gender have been effectively accommodated simply by administering an Internet or e-mail survey. Nonresponse was allowed to be interpreted as a lack of interest—a significant research flaw that was recognized by the NCAA. The association urged the DOE to honor its prior commitments to strongly enforce the standards of long-standing Title IX athletics policies while also discouraging its own members from relying on an e-mail survey as the sole measure of women's interest in athletics. NCAA News Release, June 22, 2005. In July 2005, the powerful Senate Appropriations Committee in turn called on the DOE to rescind the guideline. The DOE, under President Bush, did not relent, but in April 2010, under President Barack Obama, the policy was finally withdrawn.

Private litigation and government enforcement activity under Title IX have resulted in increased athletic participation opportunities for women and increased equity in funding and resources. However, it is generally conceded that the goal of gender equity in athletics has not been fully achieved. Women continue to be underrepresented in intercollegiate athletics—approximately 44 percent of athletics participants are women (see *http://www.ncaa.org/about/resources/media-center/news/number-ncaa-college-athletes-reaches-all-time-high*)—and female participation in interscholastic athletics is only 42 percent of all participants, although disparities vary tremendously state by state (see *https://www.nfhs.org/media/1020412/2018-19_participation_survey.pdf*). At all levels, female athletes still do not have access to equivalent athletic facilities, equipment, and other resources.

The following materials and problems present the legal, practical, and policy aspects of gender equity issues in connection with intercollegiate and interscholastic athletics. Title IX litigation regarding intercollegiate athletics has often focused on gender equity in terms of athletic participation opportunities, whereas the emphasis in interscholastic athletics litigation has focused on providing girls with access to equal sports facilities and other benefits of athletic participation. Nevertheless, all aspects of Title IX are fully applicable to all levels of interscholastic and intercollegiate sports, as well as high school and university intramural and recreational athletic programs.

GENDER-BASED EXCLUSION FROM A PARTICULAR SPORT

The first sports-related gender equity cases were brought by female students in the 1970s and 1980s seeking the opportunity to play an interscholastic sport traditionally offered only for males. Historically, boys have had a wider variety of sports to participate in than girls, particularly in contact sports. Even if there was no girls' team, athletic governing body or school district rules often prohibited girls from playing on boys' teams regardless of their ability level. The following case illustrates that courts generally held that such exclusion is illegal sex discrimination.

KEY TERMS
- Equal protection
- Intermediate scrutiny

Force v. Pierce City R-VI School District
570 F. Supp. 1020 (W.D. Mo. 1983)

ROBERTS, District Judge.

[Editors' note: Nichole Force, a 13-year-old female student enrolled in the eighth grade at Pierce City Junior High School in Missouri, sought an injunction that would have allowed her to compete for a place on the school's eighth-grade football team. She had already been involved to a considerable extent in athletics (swimming, diving, organized softball, organized basketball, and elementary school football) and had grown up with two brothers who excelled at football and who encouraged and helped her in her own athletic endeavors.

Pierce City Junior High School is a public school facility made up of the seventh, eighth, and ninth grades that sponsored an interscholastic athletics program. Boys could participate in football during the fall, basketball during the winter, and track during the spring. The corresponding sports for girls were volleyball, basketball, and track.

The boys' athletics coach for the school said he would let Nichole participate if school administration officials approved. However, school board members expressed concern over the potential precedent involved in granting her request (e.g., the possibility that boys would wish to participate on the girls' volleyball team and that high school girls might wish to play on the high school football team), the potential safety risk to a female competing in a contact sport with males, the administrative difficulties that might ensue (arrangements for locker room facilities, etc.), and that, at least as some board members understood it, the applicable provisions of Title IX and its regulations or Section 1.6 of the Missouri State High School Activities Association (MSHSAA) rules might be violated by permitting coeducational participation in a contact sport. The board voted unanimously to deny the request. While "they all agreed" Nichole would be a good football player and would have no problems playing, they also said that if she were permitted to play, the same allowance would have to be made for all other girls as well.

Nichole contended that this refusal to allow her an opportunity to play football was based solely on the fact that she was a female rather than a male and that this sex-based determination violated her right to the equal protection of the laws under the Fourteenth Amendment and 42 U.S.C. §1983.]

II. Discussion

The record makes clear, and I find, that defendants' refusal to grant plaintiff's request is the product of a gender-based classification. Stated simply, only males are permitted to compete for a place on the Pierce City Junior High School eighth grade football team. Since Nichole is a female, that opportunity is denied to her.

The principles which must govern in this situation are summarized in the opening passages of Section II of the Supreme Court's recent decision in *Mississippi*

University for Women v. Hogan, 458 U.S., 102 S.Ct. 3331, 73 L.Ed.2d 1090 (1982). I can do no better than to quote those passages here:

> Because the challenged policy expressly discriminates among applicants on the basis of gender, it is subject to scrutiny under the Equal Protection Clause of the Fourteenth Amendment. Our decisions also establish that the party seeking to uphold a statute that classifies individuals on the basis of their gender must carry the burden of showing an "exceedingly persuasive justification" for the classification. The burden is met only by showing at least that the classification serves "important governmental objectives and that the discriminatory means employed" are "substantially related to the achievement of those objectives."
>
> Although the test for determining the validity of a gender based classification is straightforward, it must be applied free of fixed notions concerning the roles and abilities of males and females. Care must be taken in ascertaining whether . . . the objective itself reflects archaic and stereotypic notions. Thus if the . . . objective is to exclude or "protect" members of one gender because they are presumed to suffer from an inherent handicap or to be innately inferior, the objective itself is illegitimate.
>
> If the State's objective is legitimate and important, we next determine whether the requisite direct, substantial relationship between objective and means is present. The purpose of requiring that close relationship is to assure that the validity of the classification is determined through reasoned analysis rather than through the mechanical application of traditional, often inaccurate, assumptions about the proper roles of men and women. . . .

Defendants do not quarrel with the fact that the present case must be governed by these principles; indeed they candidly acknowledge that fact. They argue, rather, that in the circumstances shown here a gender-based classification fully satisfies those principles. To that end, they identify four "important governmental objectives" which are said to be at stake: (a) maximization of equal athletic educational opportunities for all students, regardless of gender; (b) maintenance of athletic educational programs which are as safe for participants as possible; (c) compliance with Title IX of the Educational Amendments of 1972 and the regulations thereunder; and (d), compliance with the constitution and by-laws of MSHSAA. According to defendants, there is a "substantial relationship" between each of these objectives and a gender based classification which would prevent any female from competing with males for a place on the Pierce City Junior High School eighth grade football team.

Defendants' suggestion with respect to the necessity of compliance with Title IX can, I think, be dealt with in relatively short order. There is in fact nothing whatsoever in Title IX, or in its implementing regulations (34 C.F.R. §106.41(b)), which would mandate the action defendants have taken here. To the contrary, Title IX's regulations leave each school free to choose whether co-educational participation in a contact sport will be permitted. Allowing Nichole Force to compete with males for a place on the Pierce City Junior High School eighth grade football team would no more violate those regulations than would refusing her that opportunity. Title IX simply takes a neutral stand on the subject.

Nor in my judgment can defendants' point regarding compliance with MSHSAA rules withstand scrutiny. A school can hardly validate an otherwise unconstitutional act (assuming for the moment that there is one here) by noting that it has agreed with other schools to commit that act. There can be no doubt, of course, that MSHSAA performs a valuable and needed service for the schools and citizens of this state. But its rules cannot transcend constitutional requirements, and a member school's adherence to those rules cannot make constitutional that which is not.

I accordingly reject defendants' "objectives" (c) and (d) as providing any sort of appropriate predicate for the action taken here. Defendants' first two points, however, have more meat to their bones, and are deserving of more detailed treatment. Each will be examined separately below.

A. Maximizing Participation in Athletics

One might wonder, at first blush, how denying all females the right to participate in a sport — which is the case here, since Pierce City eighth grade girls are not allowed to compete for a place on the only football team which might be available to them — will result in maximizing the participation of both sexes in athletics. And the short answer is that it probably does not. Defendants' argument in this regard, however, is sufficiently sophisticated to merit more than first blush treatment.

That argument proceeds on three interrelated theories. Defendants suggest, first, that males (as a class) will outperform females (as a class) in most athletic endeavors, given male size, speed, and greater ratio of lean body mass. That being so, the argument proceeds, the best way in which to encourage and maximize female participation in athletics is by providing separate male and female teams, where males compete only against males and females only against females, since otherwise males will dominate the competition and ultimately discourage female participation. Pursuant to this idea, defendants have established separate interscholastic athletic programs for the two sexes in the Pierce City secondary schools, with the fall season sport being football for males and volleyball for females. But if (second) Nichole Force is permitted to compete for a place on the football team, then other girls must be accorded the same privilege, and boys must be allowed to compete for positions on the volleyball team. When (third) that happens, the girls will lose their best athletes, the boys will come to dominate volleyball, and overall female participation will ultimately wither.

Based upon the expert testimony presented in this case, I am willing to accept the proposition that the average male, even at age 13, will to some extent outperform the average female of that age in most athletic events, although the matter may be open to some dispute. And I note, without being called upon to decide the issue, that a number of courts have held that the establishment of separate male/female teams in a sport is a constitutionally permissible way of dealing with the problem of potential male athletic dominance. . . . Beyond these two points, however, I am unable to accept defendants' argument.

The principal difficulty with the remaining portions of that argument, it seems to me, is that the various hypotheses used to bind it together are just that — hypotheses, and nothing more. There is, for example, no factual indication that the girls' eighth grade volleyball team will be blighted by the defection of its best players to the football field, if Nichole Force is allowed to play football. . . . [Even if this were the case,] the governmental interest in redressing past discrimination against women in athletics is sufficient to justify a regulation which excludes boys from participating on girls' teams, even though girls are allowed to compete on boys' teams. . . .

Each sport has its own relatively unique blend of requirements in terms of skills and necessary physical attributes, and each person, male or female, will for a variety of reasons probably find one or another sport more enjoyable and rewarding than others. In point of fact, volleyball is *not* football; and baseball is *not* hockey; and swimming is *not* tennis. Accordingly, if the idea is to "maximize educational athletic opportunities for all students, regardless of gender," it makes no sense, absent some substantial reason, to deny all persons of one sex the opportunity to test their skills at a particular sport. Of course there may be certain exceptional instances in which there is a "substantial reason" for such an exclusion, as for example where peculiar safety and equipment requirements demand it [boxing was used as an example] . . . or perhaps where excluding males is necessary to redress past inequality and to foster female participation. But those instances would, I think, be relatively rare, and would need to be factually established. And that is precisely where defendants' present argument fails, as far as the instant case is concerned.

I do not question the idea that maximizing the participation of both sexes in interscholastic athletic events is a worthy, and important, governmental objective. Nor do I question the sincerity of defendants' efforts in that regard. In the circumstances of this case, however, I must and do hold that the gender based classification used by defendants does not bear a sufficiently "substantial" relationship to that objective to withstand a constitutional challenge.

B. Safety

Neither do I question the fact that the "maintenance of athletic educational programs which are as safe for participants as possible" is an "important governmental objective." [However], the "safety" factor which defendants would utilize to prevent any female from playing eighth grade football — including those who could play safely — is not applied to males at all, even to those who could not play safely. All this tends to suggest the very sort of well-meaning but overly "paternalistic" attitude about females which the Supreme Court has viewed with such concern. . . . [T]here is an insufficient relationship between defendants' announced goal of "safety" and a rule which automatically excludes all eighth grade females from competing with eighth grade males for a place on a football team. That holding, I note, is consistent with the result reached by virtually every other court which has considered this same sort of "safety" argument in connection with male/female competition in contact sports. . . .

Conclusion

Nichole Force obviously has no legal entitlement to a starting position on the Pierce City Junior High School eighth grade football team, since the extent to which she plays must be governed solely by her abilities, as judged by those who coach her. But she seeks no such entitlement here.

Instead she seeks simply a chance, like her male counterparts, to display those abilities. She asks, in short, only the right to try.

I do not suggest there is any such thing as a constitutional "right to try." But the idea that one should be allowed to try — to succeed or to fail as one's abilities and fortunes may dictate, but in the process at least to profit by those things which are learned in the trying — is a concept deeply engrained in our way of thinking; and it should indeed require a "substantial" justification to deny that privilege to someone simply because she is a female rather than a male. I find no such justification here.

[Editors' note: The court enjoined defendants from refusing to allow Nichole Force to compete for membership on the Pierce City Junior High School eighth-grade interscholastic football team on the same basis that males are allowed to compete.]

QUESTIONS

1. What is the standard of review for a gender-based discrimination claim under equal protection?
2. In *Williams v. School District of Bethlehem, PA*, 998 F.2d 168 (3d. Cir. 1993), a boy asserted his right to participate on the girl's field hockey team. In a decision that dealt with Title IX (whether field hockey is a contact sport that would justify his exclusion) and constitutional issues, including a challenge under the state equal rights amendment, the court remanded the case for the trial court to determine whether there were physical differences between girls and boys that would justify excluding the boy. The appellate court directed the trial court to examine whether "boys are more likely to dominate the school's athletic program if admitted to the girls' teams."

   In *Force*, what justification did the court offer regarding a regulation that would exclude boys from participating on girls' teams, even though girls would be permitted to participate on boys' teams? Do you agree with the court's reasoning?
3. Both the Equal Protection Clause and Title IX's regulations permit "separate but equal" athletic teams in the same sport for both sexes. When there are "separate but equal" teams, in assessing equality one court noted, "There may be differences depending upon the effects of such neutral factors as the level of student interest and geographic locations. Accordingly, the standard should be one of comparability, not absolute equality." *Hoover v. Meiklejohn*, 430 F. Supp. 164, 170 (D. Colo. 1977).

NOTES

1. Contact sports exemption. Why didn't Nichole Force assert a Title IX claim that she was being discriminated against by being prohibited from an activity (playing football) because of her sex? Title IX regulations §106.41(b) states:

A recipient may operate or sponsor separate teams for members of each sex where selection for such teams is based upon competitive skill or the activity involved is a contact sport. However, where a recipient operates or sponsors a team in a particular sport for members of one sex but operates or sponsors no such team for members of the other sex, and athletic opportunities for members of that sex have previously been limited, members of the excluded sex must be allowed to try-out for the team offered unless the sport involved is a contact sport. For the purposes of this part, contact sports include boxing, wrestling, rugby, ice hockey, football, basketball and other sports the purpose or major activity of which involves bodily contact.

In *Mercer v. Duke University*, 190 F.3d 643 (4th Cir. 1999), a case involving a challenge by a woman seeking to participate in intercollegiate football, the appellate court held:

> Because appellant has alleged that Duke allowed her to try out for its football team (and actually made her a member of the team), then discriminated against her and ultimately excluded her from participation in the sport on the basis of her sex, we conclude that she has stated a claim under the applicable regulation, and therefore under Title IX. We take to heart appellees' cautionary observation that, in so holding, we thereby become "the first Court in United States history to recognize such a cause of action." . . . Where, as here, however, the university invites women into what appellees characterize as the "traditionally all-male bastion of collegiate football," we are convinced that this reading of the regulation is the only one permissible under law.

Mercer stands for the proposition that once a woman has been permitted to participate in a contact sport like football, she cannot be removed from the team for reasons clearly unrelated to her ability as a player (Mercer was an accomplished kicker). On remand, Mercer was awarded $1 in compensatory damages and $2 million in punitive damages. On appeal, the punitive damage award was vacated. Nevertheless, Mercer was awarded approximately $350,000 in attorney fees.

Should women be permitted to participate in male contact sports? Private universities such as Duke are not state actors subject to federal equal protection claims, although state gender discrimination laws may apply. Title IX applies to any institution that receives any federal funding, regardless of whether the institution is public or private. Is there any justification for refusing to permit girls from participating in contact sports, particularly if they have the talent necessary to make the team?

2. Equal protection differences for race vs. gender. Consider the similarities and differences between racial and gender equity issues in sport. The equal protection clause of the Fourteenth Amendment requires application of strict scrutiny in the racial context (racial distinctions can be drawn only when supported by a compelling state interest applied in the least restrictive manner). In the gender equity context, an intermediate equal protection standard is all that is required (the government interest must be substantial but not necessarily compelling, and the fit between the interest and the gender distinction has to be narrowly tailored but does not have to be the least restrictive means to the government's end). This makes it possible to distinguish on gender grounds in a manner that would be impermissible in the racial context. Ironically, the more permissive discrimination standard in the gender area has clearly been instrumental in increasing opportunities in athletics for women, while the more restrictive standard in the racial context has made it more difficult for the government to effectively address racial inequities in sports.

Problem 5-1

A 14-year-old girl wants to try out for the boys' wrestling team and is not interested in participating in any other sports. She is an exceptionally talented athlete who has regularly lifted weights for the past two years and is in excellent physical condition. Although she has no prior experience in wrestling, her dream is to one day earn a gold medal as a member of the U.S. Olympic women's wrestling team. No other girls at her high school are interested in wrestling. The team's coach has refused to allow "a girl to try out for a man's sport." If you were her parent, would you be willing to file a lawsuit on her behalf to challenge this decision? If you were the school's principal, how, if at all, would you counsel the coach?

EQUAL ATHLETIC PARTICIPATION OPPORTUNITIES, BENEFITS, AND TREATMENT

Although equal protection claims may also be asserted, Title IX is currently the law most frequently utilized to remedy gender discrimination in interscholastic and intercollegiate athletics. Despite numerous challenges, Title IX, its regulations, policy interpretations, and other guidance materials have been validated by every court that has tried these issues. The following case established the judicial framework that has been followed by every other court in assessing whether a college athletics program provides equal participation opportunities.

A. Accommodation

KEY TERMS
- Effective accommodation
- Substantial proportionality
- Three-part test

Cohen v. Brown University
101 F.3d 155 (1st Cir. 1996), cert. denied, 520 U.S. 1186 (1997)

BOWNES, Senior Circuit Judge.

This is a class action lawsuit charging Brown University, its president, and its athletics director (collectively "Brown") with discrimination against women in the operation of its intercollegiate athletics program, in violation of Title IX. . . .

This suit was initiated in response to the demotion in May 1991 of Brown's women's gymnastics and volleyball teams from university-funded varsity status to donor-funded varsity status. Contemporaneously, Brown demoted two men's teams, water polo and golf, from university-funded to donor-funded varsity status. As a consequence of these demotions, all four teams lost, not only their university funding, but most of the support and privileges that accompany university-funded varsity status at Brown. . . .

Brown operates a two-tiered intercollegiate athletics program with respect to funding: although Brown provides the financial resources required to maintain its university-funded varsity teams, donor-funded varsity athletes must themselves raise the funds necessary to support their teams through private donations. The district court noted that the four demoted teams were eligible for NCAA competition, provided that they were able to raise the funds necessary to maintain a sufficient level of competitiveness, and provided that they continued to comply with NCAA requirements. The court found, however, that it is difficult for donor-funded varsity athletes to maintain a level of competitiveness commensurate with their abilities and that these athletes operate at a competitive disadvantage in comparison to university-funded varsity athletes. . . .

Brown's decision to demote the women's volleyball and gymnastics teams and the men's water polo and golf teams from university-funded varsity status was apparently made in response to a university-wide cost-cutting directive. . . .

Plaintiffs alleged that, at the time of the demotions, the men students at Brown already enjoyed the benefits of a disproportionately large share of both the university resources allocated to athletics and the intercollegiate participation opportunities afforded to student athletes. Thus, plaintiffs contended, what appeared to be the even-handed demotions of two men's and two women's teams, in fact, perpetuated Brown's discriminatory treatment of women in the administration of its intercollegiate athletics program. . . .

The district court . . . summarized the history of athletics at Brown, finding . . . that, while nearly all of the men's varsity teams were established before 1927, virtually all of the women's varsity teams were created between 1971 and 1977, after Brown's merger with Pembroke College. The only women's varsity team created after this period was winter track, in 1982.

In the course of the trial on the merits, the district court found that, in 1993–94, there were 897 students participating in intercollegiate varsity athletics, of which 61.87% (555) were men and 38.13% (342) were women. During the same period, Brown's undergraduate enrollment comprised 5,722 students, of which 48.86% (2,796) were men and 51.14% (2,926) were women. The district court found that, in 1993–94, Brown's intercollegiate athletics program consisted of 32 teams, 16 men's teams and 16 women's teams. Of the university-funded teams, 12 were men's teams and 13 were women's teams; of the donor-funded teams, three were women's teams and four were men's teams. At the time of trial, Brown offered 479 university-funded varsity positions for men, as compared to 312 for women; and 76 donor-funded varsity positions for men, as compared to

30 for women. In 1993–94, then, Brown's varsity program — including both university- and donor-funded sports — afforded over 200 more positions for men than for women. Accordingly, the district court found that Brown maintained a 13.01% disparity between female participation in intercollegiate athletics and female student enrollment. . . .

In computing these figures, the district court counted as participants in intercollegiate athletics for purposes of Title IX analysis those athletes who were members of varsity teams for the majority of the last complete season. . . .

The district court found from extensive testimony that the donor-funded women's gymnastics, women's fencing and women's ski teams, as well as at least one women's club team, the water polo team, had demonstrated the interest and ability to compete at the top varsity level and would benefit from university funding.

The district court did *not* find that full and effective accommodation of the athletics interests and abilities of Brown's female students would disadvantage Brown's male students.

II

Title IX . . . specifies that its prohibition against gender discrimination shall not "be interpreted to require any educational institution to grant preferential or disparate treatment to the members of one sex on account of an imbalance which may exist" between the total number or percentage of persons of that sex participating in any federally supported program or activity, and "the total number or percentage of persons of that sex in any community, State, section, or other area." 20 U.S.C.A. §1681(b) (West 1990). Subsection (b) also provides, however, that it "shall not be construed to prevent the consideration in any . . . proceeding under this chapter of statistical evidence tending to show that such an imbalance exists with respect to the participation in, or receipt of the benefits of, any such program or activity by the members of one sex."

Applying §1681(b), the prior panel held that Title IX "does not mandate strict numerical equality between the gender balance of a college's athletic program and the gender balance of its student body." The panel explained that, while evidence of a gender-based disparity in an institution's athletics program is relevant to a determination of noncompliance, "a court assessing Title IX compliance may not find a violation solely because there is a disparity between the gender composition of an educational institution's student constituency, on the one hand, and its athletic programs, on the other hand. . . ."

[A 1978 OCR] Policy Interpretation establishes a three-part test, a two-part test, and factors to be considered in determining compliance under 34 C.F.R. §106.41(c)(1) [which provides a non-exhaustive list of ten factors to be considered in determining whether equal athletics are available to both genders]. At issue in this appeal is the proper interpretation of the first of these, the so-called three-part test, which inquires as follows:

(1) Whether intercollegiate level participation opportunities for male and female students are provided in numbers substantially proportionate to their respective enrollments; or

(2) Where the members of one sex have been and are underrepresented among intercollegiate athletes, whether the institution can show a history and continuing practice of program expansion which is demonstrably responsive to the developing interests and abilities of the members of that sex; or
(3) Where the members of one sex are underrepresented among intercollegiate athletes, and the institution cannot show a continuing practice of program expansion such as that cited above, whether it can be demonstrated that the interests and abilities of the members of that sex have been fully and effectively accommodated by the present program.

44 Fed. Reg. at 71, 418.

The district court held that, "because Brown maintains a 13.01% disparity between female participation in intercollegiate athletics and female student enrollment, it cannot gain the protection of prong one." Nor did Brown satisfy prong two. While acknowledging that Brown "has an impressive history of program expansion," the district court found that Brown failed to demonstrate that it has "maintained a continuing practice of intercollegiate program expansion for women, the under-represented sex." . . . [T]he fact that Brown has eliminated or demoted several men's teams does not amount to a continuing practice of program expansion for women. As to prong three, the district court found that Brown had not "fully and effectively accommodated the interest and ability of the under-represented sex" to the extent necessary to provide equal opportunity in the selection of sports and levels of competition available to members of both sexes. . . .

IV

A

Title IX is not an affirmative action statute; it is an anti-discrimination statute, modeled explicitly after another anti-discrimination statute, Title VI. No aspect of the Title IX regime at issue in this case — inclusive of the statute, the relevant regulation, and the pertinent agency documents — mandates gender-based preferences or quotas, or specific timetables for implementing numerical goals.

Like other anti-discrimination statutory schemes, the Title IX regime permits affirmative action. In addition, Title IX, like other anti-discrimination schemes, permits an inference that a significant gender-based statistical disparity may indicate the existence of discrimination. Consistent with the school desegregation cases, the question of substantial proportionality under the Policy Interpretation's three-part test is merely the starting point for analysis, rather than the conclusion; a rebuttable presumption, rather than an inflexible requirement. In short, the substantial proportionality test is but one aspect of the inquiry into whether an institution's athletics program complies with Title IX. . . .

From the mere fact that a remedy flowing from a judicial determination of discrimination is gender-conscious, it does not follow that the remedy constitutes "affirmative action." Nor does a "reverse discrimination" claim arise every time an anti-discrimination statute is enforced. While some gender-conscious relief may adversely impact one gender — a fact that has not been demonstrated in this case — that alone would not make the relief "affirmative action" or the consequence of that relief "reverse discrimination." To the contrary, race- and gender-conscious remedies are both appropriate and constitutionally permissible under a federal anti-discrimination regime, although such remedial measures are still subject to equal protection review. . . .

Brown has contended throughout this litigation that the significant disparity in athletics opportunities for men and women at Brown is the result of a gender-based differential in the level of interest in sports and that the district court's application of the three-part test requires universities to provide athletics opportunities for women to an extent that exceeds their relative interests and abilities in sports. . . .

We view Brown's argument that women are less interested than men in participating in intercollegiate athletics, as well as its conclusion that institutions should be required to accommodate the interests and abilities of its female students only to the extent that it accommodates the interests and abilities of its male students, with great suspicion. To assert that Title IX permits institutions to provide fewer athletics participation opportunities for women than for men, based upon the premise that women are less interested in sports than are men, is (among other things) to ignore the fact that Title IX was enacted in order to remedy discrimination that results from stereotyped notions of women's interests and abilities.

Interest and ability rarely develop in a vacuum; they evolve as a function of opportunity and experience. The Policy Interpretation recognizes that women's lower rate of participation in athletics reflects women's historical lack of opportunities to participate in sports. . . . [T]here exists the danger that, rather than providing a true measure of women's interest in sports, statistical evidence purporting to reflect women's interest instead provides only a measure of the very discrimination that is and has been the basis for women's lack of opportunity to participate in sports. Prong three requires some kind of evidence of interest in athletics, and the Title IX framework permits the use of statistical evidence in assessing the level of interest in sports. Nevertheless, to allow a numbers-based lack-of-interest defense to become the instrument of further discrimination against the under-represented gender would pervert the remedial purpose of Title IX. We conclude that, even if it can be empirically demonstrated that, at a particular time, women have less interest in sports than do men, such evidence, standing alone, cannot justify providing fewer athletics opportunities for women than for men. Furthermore, such evidence is completely irrelevant where, as here, viable and successful women's varsity teams have been demoted or eliminated.

Finally, the tremendous growth in women's participation in sports since Title IX was enacted disproves Brown's argument that women are less interested in sports for reasons unrelated to lack of opportunity. . . .

Brown's relative interests approach is not a reasonable interpretation of the three-part test. This approach contravenes the purpose of the statute and the regulation because it does not permit an institution or a district court to remedy a gender-based disparity in athletics participation opportunities. Instead, this approach freezes that disparity by law, thereby disadvantaging further the under-represented gender. Had Congress intended to entrench, rather than change, the status quo — with its historical emphasis on men's participation opportunities to the detriment of women's opportunities — it need not have gone to all the trouble of enacting Title IX.

VII

Brown may achieve compliance with Title IX in a number of ways: It may eliminate its athletic program altogether, it may elevate or create the requisite number of women's positions, it may demote or eliminate the requisite number of men's positions, or it may implement a combination of these remedies. I leave it entirely to Brown's discretion to decide how it will balance its program to provide equal opportunities for its men and women athletes. I recognize the financial constraints Brown faces; however, its own priorities will necessarily determine the path to compliance it elects to take. . . .

Brown's proposed compliance plan stated its goal as follows: The plan has one goal: to make the gender ratio among University-funded teams at Brown substantially proportionate to the gender ratio of the undergraduate student body. To do so, the University must disregard the expressed athletic interests of one gender while providing advantages for others. The plan focuses only on University-funded sports, ignoring the long history of successful donor-funded student teams. . . .

Brown states that it "seeks to address the issue of proportionality while minimizing additional undue stress on already strained physical and fiscal resources."

The general provisions of the plan may be summarized as follows: (i) Maximum squad sizes for men's teams will be set and enforced. (ii) Head coaches of all teams must field squads that meet minimum size requirements. (iii) No additional discretionary funds will be used for athletics. (iv) Four new women's junior varsity teams — basketball, lacrosse, soccer, and tennis — will be university-funded. (v) Brown will make explicit a de facto junior varsity team for women's field hockey.

The plan sets forth nine steps for its implementation, and concludes that "if the Court determines that this plan is not sufficient to reach proportionality, phase two will be the elimination of one or more men's teams."

The district court found Brown's plan to be "fatally flawed" for two reasons. First, despite the fact that 76 men and 30 women participated on donor-funded varsity teams, Brown's proposed plan disregarded donor-funded varsity teams. Second, Brown's plan "artificially boosts women's varsity numbers by adding junior varsity positions on four women's teams." As to the propriety of Brown's proposal to come into compliance by the addition of junior varsity positions, the district court held:

> Positions on distinct junior varsity squads do not qualify as "intercollegiate competition" opportunities under the Policy Interpretation and should not be included in defendants' plan. . . . "[I]ntercollegiate" teams are those that "regularly participate in varsity competition." See 44 Fed. Reg. at 71,413 n.l. Junior varsity squads, by definition, do not meet this criterion. Counting new women's junior varsity positions as equivalent to men's full varsity positions flagrantly

violates the spirit and letter of Title IX; in no sense is an institution providing equal opportunity if it affords varsity positions to men but junior varsity positions to women.

The district court found that these two flaws in the proposed plan were sufficient to show that Brown had "not made a good faith effort to comply with this Court's mandate." . . .

The district court ordered Brown to "elevate and maintain women's gymnastics, women's water polo, women's skiing, and women's fencing to university-funded varsity status. . . ."

We agree with the district court that Brown's proposed plan fell short of a good faith effort to meet the requirements of Title IX as explicated by this court in *Cohen II* and as applied by the district court on remand. . . .

It is clear, nevertheless, that Brown's proposal to cut men's teams is a permissible means of effectuating compliance with the statute. . . . [A]lthough the district court's remedy is within the statutory margins and constitutional, we think that the district court was wrong to reject out-of-hand Brown's alternative plan to reduce the number of men's varsity teams. After all, the district court itself stated that one of the compliance options available to Brown under Title IX is to "demote or eliminate the requisite number of men's positions." Our respect for academic freedom and reluctance to interject ourselves into the conduct of university affairs counsels that we give universities as much freedom as possible in conducting their operations consonant with constitutional and statutory limits.

Brown therefore should be afforded the opportunity to submit another plan for compliance with Title IX. . . . Accordingly, we remand the case to the district court so that Brown can submit a further plan for its consideration. In all other respects the judgment of the district court is affirmed. . . .

VIII

Affirmed in part, reversed in part, and remanded for further proceedings. . . .

QUESTIONS

1. As noted in *Cohen* and subsequent cases, a school can prove compliance with the participation opportunities requirement under Title IX by independently showing that they meet the requirements of any one prong of the three-part test. How did the *Cohen* court apply the substantial proportionality test?
2. There have been efforts to exclude intercollegiate football from this equation (i.e., only male sports other than football would count for purposes of the proportionality analysis). What are the advantages or disadvantages of this approach? Does this approach eliminate sex discrimination or perpetuate inequities?

3. In order to prove compliance with Title IX's effective accommodation requirement, a school may establish that it has a history and continuing practice of adding sports for the underrepresented gender, which is usually female student-athletes. Why did Brown University fail to prove compliance on this ground? The issue of a history of continuous expansion has been examined in subsequent cases. In those cases, and among commentators, it is understood that the expansion needs to be continual and, where possible, done according to a formal policy or plan. See *Boucher v. Syracuse University*, 164 F.3d 113 (2d Cir. 1999), discussing the second part of the three-part test.

4. Opponents of Title IX have consistently complained that women are not as interested in sports as men. This argument has been uniformly rejected by the courts. Is this a valid defense under the third prong of the three-part test?

5. Acrobatics and Tumbling (a derivative of competitive cheer) is recognized by the NCAA as an emerging sport for women. Several interscholastic athletics governing bodies have already recognized cheer as a sport, offering state championships. Proponents of competitive cheer as a sport argue that females should not be limited to participating in traditional male sports and that including cheer as a sport would offer more competitive opportunities for females. Opponents emphasize that "adding" cheer would not actually increase opportunities because females currently participate in the activity even though it is not a varsity sport; it would merely allow schools to count cheerleaders as athletes for Title IX compliance purposes. They also posit that promoting cheerleading as a varsity sport promotes a stereotype of appropriate roles for females that is demeaning. What do you perceive as the pros and cons of sanctioning competitive cheer as a varsity sport? See *Biediger v. Quinnipiac University*, 667 F.3d 910 (2d Cir. 2012), for a judicial ruling that cheerleading, at least as it was conducted at Quinnipiac University, was not a varsity sport for Title IX participation purposes.

6. Many school districts still struggle to provide equitable participation opportunities. Chicago School District 29, through a settlement agreement with OCR on July 1, 2015 (see *http://www2.ed.gov/documents/press-releases/chicago-public-schools-agreement.pdf*) is required to add teams or additional levels of competition in at least 12 high schools in the 2015–16 school year and continue to add new opportunities annually until the district can demonstrate full compliance with at least one prong of the three-part test.

7. In 2018, Eastern Michigan University cut four sports (two men's and two women's) for cost savings. Two female student-athletes representing a class of current and future participants of the women's tennis and softball teams filed a Title IX lawsuit for failure to provide effective accommodation under the three-part test. The case settled in January 2020: EMU agreed to continue to support the reinstated women's tennis team but was not required to revive women's varsity softball. Instead, EMU is adding a new women's lacrosse team, promised an additional $2 million for women's sports over the next three years, and must pay $125,000 to the two named plaintiffs along with their attorney's fees. Why was EMU allowed to drop women's softball? Given the precedent in the *Brown* case, why would schools continue to try to drop women's teams?

Problem 5-2

You are the athletic director at a mid-level D-I university with a very successful men's basketball team that generates net revenues of approximately $2.5 million. The basketball coach is paid $1.5 million per year — a substantial portion of which comes from privately raised funds. The men's basketball coach has also insisted that to remain competitive in recruiting athletes, he needs the use of a private jet and improved practice and training facilities for his team. With the hiring of a new coach at a nationally competitive salary ($500,000, plus some incentives), the men's football program has been improving, and that has had a positive economic impact. Three years ago, the men's football team was operating at a loss of over $1 million per year, but it is now losing only $300,000 per year. The women's basketball team produces revenue, but it operates at a net loss of over $250,000 per year. Other men's and women's athletics programs generate very little revenue. The net result is that the athletic program is being run at a deficit of approximately $1 million per year. The president of the university has been pressured by state legislators and is required by mandate from the university's board of trustees to operate the university's athletic program with a balanced budget. The president has communicated this mandate to you, as the athletics director, and has made it clear that the athletics budget needs to be balanced within two years.

Currently, 61 percent of the students at the university are women and 39 percent are men. Participation figures in intercollegiate athletics are almost reversed, with 63 percent male and 37 percent female participation in intercollegiate athletics. The football team has 110 participants, including a number of walk-ons. The school is considering adding women's swimming or women's softball, and its athletics conference recognizes both sports. The university has pool facilities that can easily be converted to use for a women's swimming team, but there is only limited interscholastic competition in swimming in the general geographical area of the university. There is interscholastic competition in softball in the area, but there are no facilities at the university. Building new facilities would involve substantial costs, and the cost of operating the softball team would be slightly higher per student-athlete than operating a swimming program. An interest survey indicates somewhat more interest in participating in softball than swimming on the part of women attending the university.

There has been some talk of dropping the men's track team, which would help some in terms of proportionality, but concerns have been raised in the community that doing so would eliminate a disproportionate number of athletes of color. Men's baseball might also be cut, but it is quite popular with the chairperson of the university's board of trustees, whose son plays on the team.

From time to time, some of the coaches of the women's teams have complained that they are paid less than their male counterparts, their teams

> receive less academic support (e.g., the men's basketball team takes two tutors with them on trips that exceed two days, but no other teams are permitted to bring tutors on trips), their practice and training facilities are not as good as those used by the men, and they are not given the same amount of support in terms of fund-raising and media coverage.
>
> What steps would you take to address these problems? What additional facts would you want to know? What practical problems may arise as you deal with the gender equity and related issues raised in this problem?

B. Equal Benefits and Treatment

The majority of Title IX cases have focused on equal participation opportunities, but a significant number of cases have also examined the requirements for equal benefits and treatment of student-athletes. *McCormick v. School District of Mamoroneck*, 370 F.3d 275 (2d Cir. 2004), illustrates judicial application of OCR regulations to determine whether an educational institution has afforded female athletes equivalent treatment and benefits as compared to male athletes. The plaintiffs in *McCormick* were two girls who claimed that their school districts violated Title IX by scheduling girls' high school soccer in the spring and boys' high school soccer in the fall. Because the New York regional and state championships in soccer were scheduled at the end of the fall season, the plaintiffs claimed that the district deprived girls, but not boys, of the opportunity to compete in their sports championships. Girls' soccer was the only sport offered at the defendant school districts that was scheduled out of the state championship competition season. Because of conflicts with other opportunities to play soccer during the spring, plaintiffs decided not to play on their high school soccer teams. Plaintiffs alleged that the school districts did not provide equal opportunities to girls and boys in the scheduling of games and practice time.

The court established the following road map for compliance with Title IX:

1. Is there disparity in a program component (e.g., scheduling of games) that negatively affects one sex? "[A] disparity is a difference, on the basis of sex, in benefits, treatment, services, or opportunities that has a negative impact on athletes of one sex when compared with benefits, treatment, services, or opportunities available to athletes of the other sex." *Id.* at 293.
2. Is the disparity substantial enough to deprive members of that sex of equality of opportunity? *Id.*
3. Is the disparity disadvantaging one sex in a component of a school's athletics program offset by a comparable advantage to that sex in another component of the athletics program? Compliance is determined on a program-wide rather than sport-specific basis. For example, "a school that provides better equipment to the men's basketball team than to the women's basketball

team would be in compliance with Title IX if it provided comparably better equipment to the women's soccer team than to the men's soccer team. . . ." *Id.* At 293–94.
4. Can the school establish that the "differences in kind, quality, or availability were the result of nondiscriminatory factors"? *Id.* At 292.

Applying the foregoing standards, the court found that the scheduling of girls' soccer in the spring created a disparity—"boys can strive to compete in the Regional and State Championships in soccer and girls cannot." *Id.* at 294.

The court next found that (1) the disparity was significant enough to deny girls equality of athletic opportunity in that scheduling soccer out of championship season placed a ceiling on "the possible achievement of the female soccer players that they cannot break through no matter how hard they strive," and (2) the disparity sent a message that girls on the soccer teams were "not expected to succeed" and their school did not value their athletic abilities as much as those of boys. Moreover, the disadvantage in scheduling of girls' soccer had not been offset by any advantage to girls in another area.

The court also rejected defendants' alleged nondiscriminatory justifications that moving girls' soccer to the fall would be financially and administratively burdensome. It noted that the "fact that money needs to be spent to comply with Title IX is obviously not a defense to the statute." *Id.* 297. The court also stated: "There is no reason that the boys' soccer teams should be entitled to the fields, coaches, and officials in the fall simply because they were in the fall first." Noting that all students must make choices, the court rejected defendants' argument that moving soccer to the fall would hurt girls because it would require them to choose between soccer and other sports. It also suggested the defendants make adjustments such as alternating the season during which boys and girls would play soccer if field space was limited.

In another case involving equivalent benefits, *Daniels v. School Board of Brevard County, Florida (Daniels I)*, 985 F. Supp. 1458 (M.D. Fla. 1997), members of a high school girls' softball team and their parents sued a school board alleging disparities between the girls' softball team and the boys' baseball programs. Disparities in benefits identified by the court included the following: (1) the boys' baseball field had an electronic scoreboard, and the girls' field had no scoreboard (sending a message that girls' softball was not as valuable as boys' baseball); (2) the boys' baseball team had a batting cage, and the girls' softball team did not; (3) the bleachers on the girls' softball field were of lesser quality and seated fewer spectators than those on the boys' field; and (4) disparities (to the disadvantage of girls) existed with respect to signage, bathroom facilities, concession stands, press box, announcer's booth, field maintenance, and lighting.

The court concluded:

[T]he cumulative effect of the inequalities in the two athletic programs is so significant as to give Plaintiffs a substantial likelihood of success on the merits of the Title IX and Florida Act claims. The Defendant has chosen to favor the boys' baseball team with a lighted playing field, a scoreboard, a batting cage, superior bleachers, signs publicizing the team, bathroom facilities, and a concession stand/press box/announcer's booth, but has not seen fit to provide the girls softball team with any of these things. This disparity implicates several of the considerations listed in 34 C.F.R. §106.41. See §106.41(2) ("provision of equipment and supplies"), (3) ("[s]cheduling of games and practice times"), (7) ("[p]rovision of . . . practice and competitive facilities"), (8) ("[p]rovision of . . . training facilities"), and (10) ("[p]ublicity").

The Defendant seeks to avoid liability on the basis that it provides equal funding for the boys' and girls' programs. According to the Defendant, each team has a separate booster club which engages in separate fund-raising activities. The Defendant suggests that it cannot be held responsible if the fund-raising activities of one booster club are more successful than those of another. The Court rejects this argument. It is the Defendant's responsibility to ensure equal athletic opportunities, in accordance with Title IX. This funding system is one to which Defendant has acquiesced; Defendant is responsible for the consequences of that approach.

Id. at 1462. The Court determined that plaintiffs were entitled to a preliminary injunction to remedy these gender inequities. Since public funds were at stake, however, the Court afforded defendant an opportunity to submit a plan addressing how it proposes to remedy them.

In a subsequent case, *Daniels v. School Board of Brevard County, Florida (Daniels II)*, 995 F. Supp. 1394 (M.D. Fla. 1997), the court assessed the compliance plan submitted by the defendant. The school board proposed not to spend any funds to remedy the inequities identified in *Daniels I* because of "financial limitations and tight budgetary constraints under which the School Board is forced to operate. Any monies spent on athletics must obviously be taken from another area of operations which is already lacking in funds." *Id.* at 1395.

The court rejected the board's proposed remedial measures, which largely involved taking away boys' advantages rather than enhancing components of the girls' softball program.

In giving the School Board the opportunity to submit a plan, the Court had hoped for constructive input, such as a long-range fiscal plan to remedy the inequities identified in the Court's prior Order. Unfortunately, the Board's plan leaves much to be desired; it creates the impression that the Board is not as sensitive as it should be regarding the necessity of compliance with Title IX. The Court is inclined to agree with Plaintiffs that many of the Board's proposals seem more retaliatory than constructive. The Board's approach essentially imposes "separate disadvantage," punishing both the girls and the boys, rather than improving the girls' team to the level the boys' team has enjoyed for years. The Court is sensitive to the financial constraints imposed upon public educational institutions in this day and age; that is yet another reason the Court gave the Board an opportunity to submit a remedial plan, rather than simply entering an injunction decreeing the expenditure of funds by a date certain. However, the fact remains that Plaintiffs have presented substantial evidence that the School Board has violated, and continues to violate, an Act of Congress mandating gender equality in public education.

Id. at 1397.

QUESTIONS

1. What is the specific harm that plaintiffs suffered in *McCormick* as a result of being treated unequally? In *Daniels I*?
2. Although compliance with Title IX requires a comparison of boys' and girls' sports on a program-wide basis, *McCormick* and *Daniels I* demonstrate that disparate treatment of male and female teams for the same sport may be significant enough to violate this law. What constitutes an illegal disparity for purposes of Title IX? Other cases in which female athletes have prevailed in unequal treatment claims at the high school or college level include *Communities for Equity v. Michigan High School Athletic Assn.*, 178 F. Supp. 2d 805 (W.D. Mich. 2001); *Landow v. School Bd. of Brevard County*, 132 F. Supp. 2d 958 (M.D. Fla. 2000);*Ollier v. Sweetwater Union High School District*, 768 F.3d 843 (2014); and *Parker v. Franklin County Community School Corporation*, 667 F.3d 910 (2012).
3. The women's softball coach at Midland College, Texas, filed a Title IX lawsuit claiming discrimination against the women's team for inferior facilities and academic support. The court dismissed the claim for lack of subject matter jurisdiction because Ramos did not have standing to bring claims on behalf of the softball players who were able to file claims themselves. *Ramos v. Midland Coll.*, 2017 WL 10841724 (W.D. Tex. June 29, 2017). What other options does Ramos have to complain about inequities if the college will not act? Is it likely that the players will file a lawsuit?
4. Like effective accommodation cases, courts are reluctant to order a school to take specific action to remedy gender-based unequal treatment that violates Title IX. Rather, courts allow schools the flexibility to formulate their own compliance plan within certain parameters. In this regard, do courts afford schools too much deference? Why did the court in *Daniels II* reject the proposed remedial measures suggested by the school board? What type of changes did the court hope that the board would enact? However, in *Portz v. St. Cloud St. Univ.*, 2019 WL 3492457 (D. Minn. Aug. 1, 2019), the court issued a permanent injunction to force SCSU to eliminate inferior locker room conditions and replace women's equipment on the same schedule as men's, among other deficiencies. Is an injunction a more effective remedy?

REVERSE DISCRIMINATION CLAIMS AND TITLE IX

Although Title IX has been instrumental in increasing opportunities for girls' sports participation, a persistent and invidious criticism of Title IX is that it hurts men's sports. Courts have uniformly held that cutting men's sports in an effort to achieve substantial proportionality in athletic participation opportunities does not violate Title IX or male athletes' equal protection rights. See, e.g., *Miami Univ. Wrestling Club v. Miami Univ.*, 302 F.3d 608 (6th Cir. 2002); *Chalenor v. University of N. D.*, 291 F.3d 1042 (8th Cir. 2002); *Kelly v. Board of Trustees*, 35 F.3d 265 (7th Cir. 1994);

Equity in Athletics, Inc. v. Dept. of Educ., 675 F. Supp. 2d 660 (W.D. Va. 2009). While budget reductions and limitations may challenge athletics administrators' creativity in managing broad-based athletics programs, choices must be made in a way that provides equal opportunity. Ideally, schools would remedy past discrimination by increasing opportunities for women. However, Title IX allows schools to choose the type of athletics program they offer. See Jocelyn Samuels and Kristen Galles, *In Defense of Title IX: Why Current Policies Are Required to Ensure Equality of Opportunity*, 14 Marq. Sports L. Rev. 11, 31 (2003).

The *Neal* case, which follows, involves a gender reverse-discrimination lawsuit in which male college athletes allege that the discontinuance of their sport violates Title IX and their federal equal protection rights. It illustrates the reasoning and analysis courts often employ in rejecting the claims of male student-athletes.

Neal v. Board of Trustees of the California State Universities
198 F.3d 763 (9th Cir. 1999)

HALL, Circuit Judge:

[This] suit alleged that the decision of California State University, Bakersfield ("CSUB") to reduce the number of spots on its men's wrestling team, undertaken as part of a university-wide program to achieve "substantial proportionality" between each gender's participation in varsity sports and its composition in the campus's student body, violated Title IX and the Equal Protection Clause of the United States Constitution. . . .

Defendant/Appellant CSUB is a large public university where female students outnumbered male students by roughly 64% to 36% in 1996. The composition of CSUB's varsity athletic rosters, however, was quite different. In the 1992–93 academic year, male students took 61% of the university's spots on athletic rosters and received 68% of CSUB's available athletic scholarship money.

[Editors' note: This imbalance prompted a Title IX lawsuit by the California chapter of the National Organization for Women (NOW). A consent decree arising from a settlement of the lawsuit mandated, among other things, that each California State campus have a proportion of female athletes that was within five percentage points of the proportion of female undergraduate students at that school. Because of budgetary constraints, CSUB adopted squad-size targets, which would encourage the expansion of the women's teams while limiting the size of the men's teams. To comply with the consent decree, CSUB opted for smaller men's teams across the board, rejecting the alternative of eliminating some men's teams entirely. As part of this across-the-board reduction, the size of the men's wrestling team was capped at 27. Despite protests by the wrestling coach and team captain, the smaller CSUB wrestling team performed exceptionally well, winning the Pac-10 Conference title and finishing third in the nation in 1996. In 1996–97, the men's wrestling roster was capped at 25, and 4 of these spots went unused. Nevertheless, in response to the rumored elimination of the men's wrestling team, on January 10, 1997, the team filed this lawsuit. The district court granted a preliminary injunction to prevent CSUB from reducing the size of the wrestling team.]

Appellees . . . suggest that gender-conscious remedies are appropriate only when necessary to ensure that schools provide opportunities to males and females in proportion to their relative levels of interest in sports participation. By contrast, Appellants contend that schools may make gender-conscious decisions about sports-funding levels to correct for an imbalance between the composition of the undergraduate student body and the composition of the undergraduate student athletic participants pool. This disagreement has real significance: Men's expressed interest in participating in varsity sports is apparently higher than women's at the present time — although the "interest gap" continues to narrow — so permitting gender-conscious remedies until the proportions of students and athletes are roughly proportional gives universities more remedial freedom than permitting remedies only until expressed interest and varsity roster spots correspond. . . .

In other words, Appellees' interpretation of Title IX would have allowed universities to do little or nothing to equalize men's and women's opportunities if they could point to data showing that women were less interested in sports. But a central aspect of Title IX's purpose was to *encourage* women to participate in sports. The increased number of roster spots and scholarships reserved for women would gradually increase demand among women for those roster spots and scholarships.[4]

Title IX is a dynamic statute, not a static one. It envisions continuing progress toward the goal of equal opportunity for all athletes and recognizes that, where society has conditioned women to expect less than their fair share of the athletic opportunities, women's interest in participating in sports will not rise to a par with men's overnight. The percentage of college athletes who are women rose from 15% in 1972 to 37% in 1998, and Title IX is at least partially responsible for this trend of increased participation by women. . . . Title IX has altered women's preferences, making them more interested in sports, and more likely to become student athletes. . . .

Adopting Appellees' interest-based test for Title IX compliance would hinder, and quite possibly reverse, the steady increases in women's participation and interest in sports that have followed Title IX's enactment.

A number of courts of appeals have addressed another potentially dispositive issue in this appeal — namely, whether Title IX permits a university to diminish athletic opportunities available to men so as to bring them into line with the lower athletic opportunities available to women. Every court, in construing the Policy Interpretation and the text of Title IX, has held that a university may bring itself into Title IX compliance by increasing athletic opportunities for the underrepresented gender (women in this case) *or* by decreasing athletic opportunities for the overrepresented gender (men in this case). . . . An extensive survey of Title IX's legislative history and the regulations

---

[4]That is, the creation of additional athletic spots for women would prompt universities to recruit more female athletes, in the long run shifting women's demand curve for sports participation. As more women participated, social norms discouraging women's participation in sports presumably would be further eroded, prompting additional increases in women's participation levels. . . .

promulgated to apply its provisions to college athletics concluded that boosters of male sports argued vociferously before Congress that the proposed regulations would require schools to shift resources from men's programs to women's programs, but that Congress nevertheless sided "with women's advocates" by deciding not to repeal the HEW's athletics-related Title IX regulations. Congress thus appears to have believed that Title IX would result in funding reductions to male athletic programs. If a university wishes to comply with Title IX by leveling down programs instead of ratcheting them up, as Appellant has done here, Title IX is not offended. . . .

Finally, the district court below rejected the interpretation of Title IX advocated by the OCR and Appellants on the ground that such a reading of the statute might violate the Constitution. . . .

[T]he Seventh Circuit has held that "the remedial scheme established by Title IX and the applicable regulation and policy interpretation are clearly substantially related to" the objective of prohibiting "educational institutions from discriminating on the basis of sex. . . ." The district court's final basis for rejecting the OCR's interpretation of Title IX was therefore erroneous. . . .

We REVERSE, and VACATE the preliminary injunction.

QUESTIONS

1. In *Neal*, why does the Ninth Circuit reject plaintiffs' claim that capping rosters for men's sports or eliminating men's teams violates Title IX? Based on statistical data, it appears that most schools are adding women's sports without cutting men's sports and that men's sports participation has continued to increase (not decrease) at a slightly higher proportion as women's sports participation grows. While some men's program have been cut, women's sports have been cut from college programs as well. Limited budgets are not the reason for cutting men's teams, as the wealthiest programs are the ones that are cutting men's sports. Donna Lopiano, *It's Time for Straight Talk About Title IX*, Sports Bus. J., April 30—May 6, 2001, at 33.

2. *Title IX at 50: A Report by the National Coalition for Women and Girls in Education* was published by the National Women's Law Center on June 7, 2022 as the nation prepared for the fiftieth anniversary of Title IX on June 23, 2022:

> Despite the progress made since 1972, girls and women still receive more than one million fewer opportunities than boys and men to play sports in high school and college. And when they do have a chance to play sports, women and girls often receive worse facilities, uniforms, and equipment; inexperienced coaches; and less support and publicity from their schools—all of which send the message that they are "less than" their male peers. Furthermore, many LGBTQI+ students are discouraged or even actively prevented from playing school sports. NCWGE urges the federal government to promote gender equity in athletics by reviewing and refreshing its Title IX athletics guidance, increasing compliance reviews at schools, expanding data collection on athletics, protecting the rights of LGBTQI+ student athletes, and much more.

What are the primary barriers preventing equity in high school and college athletics programs? Is 50 years long enough for equity to be achieved?

TITLE IX AND SEXUAL HARASSMENT

Title IX prohibits all forms of sex discrimination in educational programs and activities at schools that receive federal funding. Sexual harassment is a form of discrimination based on sex and is therefore prohibited under Title IX. In 1997, the OCR issued its first *Sexual Harassment Guidance: Harassment of Students by School Employees, Other Students, or Third Parties*, 62 Fed. Reg. 12,034 et seq., to inform school officials of their obligations under Title IX to protect students from sexual harassment. In *Gebser v. Lago Vista Independent School District*, 524 U.S. 274 (1998), the Supreme Court established that acts of teacher-student sexual harassment were actionable under Title IX and the following year held that schools may also be liable for peer harassment. See *Davis v. Monroe County Board of Education*, 526 U.S. 629 (1999).

Title IX regulations enacted in 2020 define sexual harassment as:

"Sexual harassment means conduct on the basis of sex that satisfies one or more of the following:

(1) An employee of the recipient conditioning the provision of an aid, benefit, or service of the recipient on an individual's participation in unwelcome sexual conduct;
(2) Unwelcome conduct determined by a reasonable person to be so severe, pervasive, and objectively offensive that it effectively denies a person equal access to the recipient's education program or activity; or
(3) "Sexual assault" as defined in 20 U.S.C. 1092(f)(6)(A)(v), "dating violence" as defined in 34 U.S.C. 12291(a)(10), "domestic violence" as defined in 34 U.S.C. 12291(a)(8), or "stalking" as defined in 34 U.S.C. 12291(a)(30)."

34 C.F.R. §106.30 (a).

According to the Supreme Court in *Davis*, the plaintiff must prove the following to establish a Title IX sexual harassment claim: that the plaintiff is a member of a protected group; that they were subjected to unwelcome sexual harassment; that the harassment was based on sex; that the conduct was severe and pervasive enough to create an abusive educational environment; and that the institution knew of the conduct and intentionally failed to take proper action. *Davis*, 526 U.S. at 634–35 (1999). In *Bostic v. Smyrna Sch. Dist.*, 418 F.3d 355 (2d Cir. 2005), the court acknowledged that a teacher's harassment of a student falls within the ambit of Title IX but ultimately refused to hold the school liable because there was no proof that the school had actual knowledge of a sexual relationship between a 15-year-old student and her track coach.

The Supreme Court in *Gebser* and *Davis* did not address the issue of whether a school could raise an affirmative defense by having an effective sexual harassment policy, but schools must adopt and publish grievance procedures to address sexual discrimination. Schools are expected to send a notice of policies and procedures to students, parents (for elementary and secondary students), and employees that includes where complaints may be filed. Once policies and procedures are established, it is expected that the school will actually adhere to the procedures when complaints are made alleging harassment. This would include an adequate, reliable, and impartial investigation of the complaint, including the opportunity to present witnesses and other evidence, conducted within a designated, prompt time frame. Notice of the outcome of the complaint must be given to the parties involved with assurances provided that the school will take corrective measures to eliminate current harassment and similar instances of harassment in the future. In *Ericson v. Syracuse Univ.*, 35 F. Supp. 2d 326 (S.D. N.Y. 1999), a complaint was filed by former members of the women's tennis team alleging that their former coach sexually harassed them. The athletes claimed that some university administrators who investigated the charges had actual knowledge of the harassment but conspired to conduct a sham investigation. The court held that there was sufficient evidence to state a claim against the university under Title IX.

A. Coach-Athlete Sexual Harassment

Although the liability of the institution is the same whether the harasser is a teacher or a coach and the victim is a student-athlete or a non-student-athlete, there are unique circumstances in the athletics context that merit close attention. The number of female athletes has increased dramatically over the past 50 years, but the number of female coaches has decreased. In 1972, 90 percent of the coaches of collegiate women's teams were women, but in 2022, women represented 42 percent of head coaches of women's teams and only 4.6 percent of head coaches of men's teams in NCAA Division I. (See *https://www.tidesport.org/_files/ugd/c01324_d0d17cf9f4c7469fbe410704a056db35.pdf*). This is even worse in youth sports, with women representing only 26 percent of the 6.5 million adult volunteers nationwide (see *https://www.aspeninstitute.org/wp-content/uploads/2022/11/national-coach-survey-report-preliminary-analysis.pdf*). This increases the ratio of men coaching female athletes and also increases the opportunity and possibility of sexual harassment. Male coach/female athlete is not the only context in which sexual harassment occurs, but it is significantly greater than any other combination. Other factors have also been identified as creating special opportunities for sexual harassment: (1) the coach–student-athlete relationship, which is marked by the immense authority and power coaches exercise over student-athletes and the one-on-one contact coaches have with student-athletes; (2) the physical nature of sports, in which coaches often apply a hands-on approach to instructing athletes and frequent physical contact between coaches and athletes for celebratory purposes; and (3) focus on the athlete's body, around which daily discussions between coach and student-athlete revolve. Nancy Hogshead-Maker and Sheldon E. Steinbach, *Intercollegiate Athletics'*

Unique Environment for Sexual Harassment Claims: Balancing the Realities of Athletics with Preventing Potential Claims, 13 Marq. Sports L. Rev. 173 (2003). Recent scandals also illuminate the tragic reality of sexual misconduct by team physicians and athletic trainers in both school and club sport settings.

To combat sexual abuse in youth sport, Congress enacted the Protecting Young Victims from Sexual Abuse and Safe Sport Authorization Act of 2017 (Public Law No: 115-126, Feb. 14, 2018) to protect youth and Olympic athletes from sex abuse and to designate the United States Center for SafeSport as the independent authority to develop training, practices, policies, and procedures to prevent abuse. SafeSport's mission is to "make athlete well-being the centerpiece of our nation's sports culture through abuse prevention, education, and accountability." U.S. Center for SAFESPORT, available at *https://uscenterforsafesport.org/wp-content/uploads/2022/05/StratPlanPublic22_050522_v2.3.pdf*. The USOPC and NGBs are required to adhere to the Minor Athlete Abuse Prevention Policies, while other youth sport organizations may utilize these policies, training and education services, and additional resources. The Center provides a confidential online reporting system, investigates complaints, issues decisions, and assigns sanctions. Since July 1, 2023, SafeSport has issued 829 lifetime bans. SafeSport provides a centralized disciplinary database as a resource for keeping the public informed about individuals who have been issued temporary restrictions or sanctions in violation of the SafeSport Code at *https://uscenterforsafesport.org/response-and-resolution/centralized-disciplinary-database8*.

B. Peer Sexual Harassment

Almost 85 percent of female athletes report having experienced sexually harassing behaviors, and complaints of peer harassment are increasing dramatically. At the University of Pittsburgh, a female swimmer filed a lawsuit seeking reinstatement to the university swim team. She claimed that she was discriminated against because she was released as a result of her complaints of harassment against a swimmer on the men's team. A former placekicker on the University of Colorado football team publicly alleged that she was sexually harassed by her teammates, who treated her "like a piece of meat" and called her "names that are unrepeatable." The student-athlete indicated that she reported the incidents to the coach several times during the season, but the harassment persisted. She ultimately transferred to the University of New Mexico. See *Female Place-Kicker Alleges Harassment at University of Colorado*, Aug. 22, 2003, *http://sports.espn.go.com/espn/wire?id=1601161*. A school is liable for peer or third-party harassment if an official with apparent authority knew or reasonably should have known of the harassment and failed to reasonably respond.

Accusations of sexual assault and rape involving intercollegiate student-athletes at dozens of schools have made the headlines, embarrassing the athletics departments and the institutions. Sexual assault or rape is a severe form of sexual harassment and may be sufficient to establish a hostile environment actionable under Title IX. See *Vance v. Spencer County Pub. Sch. Dist.*, 231 F.3d 253 (6th Cir.

2000); *Brzonkala v. Virginia Polytechnic Institute*, 132 F.3d 949, 959 (4th Cir. 1997). Colleges and universities have also been named as defendants in lawsuits when student-athletes have raped other students, both on and off campus. In *Williams v. Board of Regents of the University System of Georgia*, 477 F.3d 1282 (11th Cir. 2007), a female student was allegedly gang-raped by three male student-athletes in an on-campus dormitory. The plaintiff argued that the university was liable under Title IX because the coach, athletics director, and university president were all aware that the student-athlete who attacked the plaintiff had a history of sexual assaults before he was recruited and admitted to the university. The Eleventh Circuit held that given the past history of the recruited student-athlete, the institution had "before the fact notice" and should have made efforts to prevent future harassment from occurring.

In *Simpson v. University of Colorado*, 500 F.3d 1170 (10th Cir. 2007), plaintiffs alleged they were sexually assaulted at an off-campus party by football players and recruits. According to plaintiffs, the University of Colorado (CU) had an official policy that paired recruits with "female ambassadors" to ensure that the recruits would be shown a good time. In determining the viability of plaintiffs' Title IX claim, the court framed the central issue as whether a risk existed that a sexual assault might occur during a recruiting visit. The court found evidence sufficient to establish such a risk, including the head football coach's general knowledge of the serious risk of sexual assault during recruiting visits, the coach's specific knowledge that assaults had occurred during recruiting visits at CU, the coach's maintenance of an unsupervised player-host program notwithstanding this knowledge, the inadequacy of steps taken by CU to reduce the risk of sexual assaults during recruiting visits, and conduct by the head coach in resisting recruiting reforms.

In settlement of plaintiffs' claims, CU agreed to pay the victims a total of $2.5 million. The settlement terms also required CU to hire an external Title IX monitor who will focus on the university's sexual harassment and gender discrimination issues, and to add staff to its victims' assistance center. See Allison Sherry, *$2.85 Million CU Settles Case Stemming from Recruit Scandal*, Denver Post, Dec. 6, 2007, at A01.

QUESTIONS

1. How can universities prevent student-athletes from committing sexual assault or rape? Does the revenue-producing and spectator-driven nature of D-I athletics place significant pressure on legal counsel, athletic directors, and/or coaches to cover up misconduct by student-athletes who participate in sports such as football and basketball?
2. In the *Williams* and *Simpson* cases, none of the defendants were convicted of criminal sexual assault or rape charges, yet the universities were held liable under Title IX. Explain the legal liability standard.
3. The Title IX sexual harassment regulations reinforce that the procedural rights of complainants and respondents in Title IX investigations and hearings on campus must have "strong, clear procedural rights in a predictable, transparent

grievance process designed to reach reliable outcomes." The school bears the burden of proof with the respondent presumed innocent. Schools can choose whether to use a preponderance of the evidence standard or a clear and convincing evidence standard. What are the advantages and disadvantages of using preponderance of the evidence versus clear and convincing evidence as the standard for an institutional disciplinary hearing?

4. It is important to note that individual school officials (such as coaches or athletics administrators) can also be held personally liable for acts of harassment under §1983 for violating a student's civil rights in addition to a school's liability under Title IX. Timothy Davis and Keith E. Smith, *Eradicating Student-Athlete Sexual Assault of Women: Section 1983 and Personal Liability Following* Fitzgerald v. Barnstable, 2009 Mich. St. L. Rev. 629.

TRANSGENDER PARTICIPATION IN SCHOOL-BASED SPORT

Sociology, psychology, biology, and physiology all indicate that human beings exist more on a continuum than in the binary classification of men and women that society and the law have constructed. Discriminatory treatment of individuals based on characteristics related to sex, such as sexual orientation, gender identity, and physiological disorders of sex development, is an area of evolving legal issues, including those that impact sport.

Access to sport participation opportunities is particularly challenging for transgender athletes. In 1975, Richard Raskin underwent gender reassignment surgery and became Renee Richards. Upon winning a tennis tournament in California, Richards was outed as transgender. The U.S. Open responded by implementing a chromosome test to determine sex, thereby preventing Richards from competing. Richards filed a lawsuit against the United States Tennis Association (USTA) seeking an injunction allowing her to "qualify and/or participate in the United States Open Tennis Tournament, as a woman in the Women's Division." *Richards v. U.S. Tennis Assn.*, 93 Misc. 2d 713, 714 (1977). Richards challenged the use of the Barr body test to determine sex, claiming violations of the Fourteenth Amendment and New York State Human Rights Law. The court agreed that the USTA instituted the Barr body test specifically to prevent Richards from competing. While the USTA contended the test was needed for fairness and to keep out imposters, the court sided with the medical evidence that showed Richards's "muscle development, weight, height and physique fit within the female norm." *Id.* at 721. In granting the preliminary injunction allowing Richards to play, the court allowed Richards to become the first transgender woman to play professional sport in the United States. She lost in the first round of the U.S. Open to Virginia Wade.

On November 30, 2010, the Ladies Professional Golfers Association changed its "female at birth" requirement to allow transgender membership in response to a federal lawsuit filed by a transgender woman in a California case. *Lawless v. LPGA et al.*, Case No. 4:10CV04599 (N.D. Cal. 2010).

At the high school level, state laws and state high school athletics associations dictate whether athletes may participate based on sex at birth or current gender identity. The Transgender Law and Policy Institute encourages all states to allow K–12 transgender youth to participate in their affirmed gender. While the majority of state high school athletics associations historically had an inclusive policy that allowed K–12 transgender youth to participate in their affirmed gender, the issue of transgender athlete participation has become highly politicized since 2020. Idaho was the first state to bar transgender girls from participating in girls and women's sports, enacting the Fairness in Women's Sports Act on March 27, 2020. Twenty more states have since enacted legislation banning transgender girls from participating in sport at the high school and sometimes college level, and ten more states have legislation proposed. However, in *Hecox v. Little*, 479 F. Supp. 3d 930 (August 17, 2020), the Idaho District Court enjoined the State of Idaho from enforcing the statute prohibiting transgender female athletes from participating in women's sports as the plaintiffs were likely to succeed on the merits that the law violates the Equal Protection Clause of the Fourteenth Amendment (pp. 985, 987). On the other hand, in *B.P.J. v. West Virginia State Bd. of Educ.*, 2023 WL 111875 (S.D. W. Va.), after initially granting a preliminary injunction against implementation of West Virginia's Save Women's Sports Bill, the court held that it did not violate the Equal Protection Clause or Title IX and dissolved the injunction.

As educational institutions that receive federal funding are subject to Title IX, the Office for Civil Rights for the U.S. Department of Education provides resources for LGBTQI+ students that state:

> The mission of the U.S. Department of Education's Office for Civil Rights (OCR) is to ensure equal access to education and to promote educational excellence through vigorous enforcement of civil rights in our nations' schools. To serve this mission, OCR enforces civil rights laws to protect all students from unlawful discrimination and harassment based on race, color, national origin, sex, disability, and age. This includes students who are lesbian, gay, bisexual, transgender, queer, questioning, asexual, intersex, nonbinary, or identify their sexual orientation or gender identity in other ways (LGBTQI+).
>
> Bullying, harassment, exclusion from school activities, and other forms of discrimination can interfere with LGBTQI+ students' access to a safe and inclusive school environment. Federal law, however, requires schools to ensure that LGBTQI+ students and other students have equal access to all aspects of a school's programs and activities.

Resources for LGBTQI+ Students, *https://www2.ed.gov/about/offices/list/ocr/lgbt.html*.

In 2005, Keelin Godsey was one of the first openly transgender student-athletes to compete in an NCAA Championship. Godsey, who identifies as male, won two national championships in the Division III Women's hammer throw and earned All-American status in shot put, weight throw, discus throw, and hammer throw. Godsey went on to compete at the 2008 U.S. Olympic Trials, finishing eighth in the hammer throw; he placed fifth in the women's hammer throw at the U.S. Olympic Trials in 2012. Godsey then retired from competition to begin medical transition. Cyd Zeigler, *Trans Hammer Thrower Keelin Godsey Narrowly Misses U.S. Olympic Team*, Outsports, June 21, 2012.

At its January 19, 2022 meeting, the NCAA Board of Governors approved an updated transgender student-athlete participation policy governing college sports. *Transgender Student-Athlete Participation Policy* at *https://www.ncaa.org/sports/2022/1/27/transgender-participation-policy.aspx*. The updated NCAA policy calls for transgender student-athlete participation for each sport to be determined by the national governing body of that sport, subject to review and recommendation by the NCAA Committee on Competitive Safeguards and Medical Aspects of Sports to the NCAA Board of Governors. If there is no NGB policy for a sport, the international federation policy would be followed. If there is no international federation policy, previously established IOC policy criteria would be followed. The NCAA policy went into effect with the 2022 winter championships. Transgender student-athletes were required to document sport-specific testosterone levels beginning four weeks before their sport's championship selections in the winter and spring of 2022. In the 2022–23 academic year, transgender student-athletes documented testosterone levels at the beginning of their season and a second documentation six months after the first. Transgender student-athletes will also document testosterone levels four weeks before championship selections. Full implementation of the NCAA policy will begin with the 2023–24 academic year.

QUESTIONS

1. Competitive advantage is often raised as a concern for MTF transgender participants. Should there be more concern for MTF competitors than for FTM competitors who are also transitioning using hormone treatments? For an article exploring the issue of whether transgender athletes have a competitive advantage, see Steven Petro, *Do Transgender Athletes Have an Unfair Advantage at the Olympics?*, *https://www.washingtonpost.com/lifestyle/style/do-transgender-athletes-have-an-unfair-advantage-at-the-olympics/2016/08/05/08169676-5b50-11e6-9aee-8075993d73a2_story.html*.

2. Four female high school athletes filed a lawsuit alleging that the Connecticut Interscholastic Athletic Conference's non-discrimination policy allowing transgender students to compete in the sex category they identify with violates Title IX because the participation of transgender females in girls' high school athletic events results in "fewer opportunities for victory, public recognition, athletic scholarships, and future employment" for students born female. Plaintiffs requested damages and two injunctions, one to enjoin future enforcement of the policy and one to alter the records of certain prior CIAC-sponsored girls' track events to remove the records achieved by two transgender athletes. The district court dismissed the claims stating they were moot, and the plaintiffs lacked standing, which was affirmed by a Second Circuit panel. *Soule v.*

Connecticut Ass'n of Sch., Inc., 57 F.4th 43 (2d Cir. 2022). One of the plaintiffs has now twice beaten the two transgender athletes she wanted banned—after stating in her complaint that it was unfair and impossible to beat them.

3. In *Johnston v. Univ. of Pittsburgh of the Com. Sys. of Higher Educ.*, 97 F. Supp. 3d 657 (W.D. Pa. 2015), the court held that the university's policy of requiring students to use sex-segregated bathroom and locker room facilities based on students' natal or birth sex, rather than their gender identity, does not violate Title IX's prohibition of sex discrimination. What legitimate purpose is served by forcing a self-identified student to use facilities for the opposite sex?

GENDER-BASED EMPLOYMENT DISCRIMINATION IN ATHLETICS

A. Employment Discrimination

KEY TERMS
- Equal Pay Act
- Title VII
- Title IX

There are more women currently employed in administrative and coaching positions in intercollegiate athletics than ever before. However, only 22.3 percent of athletics directors are women, which is dramatically lower than the 90 percent representation in the 1970s, when most colleges and universities had separate men's and women's athletics departments. There are no female administrators at all in 11.3 percent of college athletics programs. Less than half (43.4 percent) of women's athletics teams have a female head coach, even though the majority (56.8 percent) of paid assistant coaches of women's teams are women. The gender barrier for female coaches is also apparent, as less than 3 percent of men's teams are coached by a female head coach. Sports medicine and sports information lag woefully behind, with only 32.4 percent of women employed as head athletics trainers. Athletics communications appears to mirror the professional sports media, as only 12.1 percent of sports information directors are women. See *http://www.tidesport.org/college-sport.html*.

Fuhr v. School Dist. of Hazel Park, 364 F.3d 753 (6th Cir. 2004), illustrates the sports cultural bias against hiring female coaches. Geraldine Fuhr had significant experience as the girls' varsity basketball coach at Hazel Park High School for ten years and concurrently as the assistant boys' varsity basketball coach for eight years. Fuhr applied for the boys' varsity coach position, and only one other candidate, a male teacher who had been coaching the boys' freshman basketball team for the past two years, also applied. Both candidates were interviewed, and the superintendent of schools informed the search committee that several members of the school board did not want Fuhr as the boys' coach and that they had to honor their wishes. The president of the school board announced that he "was very concerned about a female being the head boys' basketball coach in Hazel Park." *Id.* at 757. Barnett, the other candidate, was hired, and Fuhr sued the school district for sex discrimination under Title VII and the Elliot-Larsen Act, a Michigan civil rights act that prohibits gender discrimination. A jury held in Fuhr's favor, awarding her $455,000 in damages. Subsequently, the district court ordered Hazel Park to hire Fuhr as the boys' varsity basketball coach. Hazel Park appealed, but the Sixth Circuit affirmed, finding that Hazel Park had intentionally discriminated against Fuhr on the basis of sex by not hiring her as the head boys' basketball coach.

In addition to barriers in employing women in college athletics programs, a gender gap also exists in salaries, with female coaches earning on average only 62 percent of what male coaches make. Barbara Osborne and Marilyn V. Yarbrough. *Pay Equity for Coaches and Athletic Administrators: An Element of Title IX?*, 34 U. Mich. J.L. Reform 231 (2001). In the mid-1990s, two cases were decided that marked important victories for plaintiffs alleging gender-based employment discrimination in intercollegiate athletics. In *Tyler v. Howard Univ.*, No. 91-CA11239 (D.C. June 28, 1993), a women's basketball coach claimed that the disparity between her salary and that of the men's basketball coach and the difference in their office facilities violated Title IX, the Equal Pay Act, and state law. The Howard men's basketball coach was paid $34,500 more annually than Tyler and had a spacious office, while Tyler's office was in a storage room. The jury awarded Tyler $2.34 million in damages, although the judge eventually reduced the award to $250,000. This case marked the first time a plaintiff had received a jury award based on such allegations. Similarly, in *Pitts v. Oklahoma State Univ.*, No. CIV-93-1341-A (W.D. Okla. 1994), another jury awarded damages of $36,000 to a women's college golf coach because her salary was $28,000 a year less than the men's golf coach. She alleged that this disparity violated Title IX and other laws.

The following case illustrates the various alleged causes of action and potential remedies for gender-based wage discrimination by educational institutions against those seeking to ensure compliance with Title IX in the context of athletics.

Deli v. University of Minnesota
863 F. Supp. 958 (D. Minn. 1994)

MAGNUSON, District Judge.

Background

Plaintiff Katalin Deli is the former head coach of the University of Minnesota (University) women's gymnastics team. In June 1992, the University terminated her employment. Ms. Deli challenged this dismissal through the University grievance procedure. After review, the University upheld the termination, finding there existed just cause for her termination. . . .

Deli filed the present action against the University, alleging the University improperly paid her less than head coaches of several men's athletic teams. Deli contends that this pay differential, allegedly based on the gender of the athletes she coached, constituted prohibited discrimination on the basis of sex, in violation of Title VII of the Civil Rights Act, 42 U.S.C. §2000e; the Equal Pay Act, 29 U.S.C. §206(d); and Title IX. . . .

Plaintiff contends the Defendant discriminated in the compensation it paid her on the basis of the gender of the athletes she coached. Significantly, Plaintiff does not claim that the University discriminated against her on the basis of Plaintiff's gender, i.e., she does not claim that the University's motivation for paying her less money than the coaches of men's sports was the fact that Plaintiff was a woman and the coaches of men's sports were men. Plaintiff also does not challenge in this action the circumstances, justification or legality of her discharge from employment by the University. . . .

I. Title VII Claim

Title VII prohibits employers from "discriminating against any individual with respect to his compensation . . . *because of such individual's* race, color, religion, sex or national origin. . . ." 42 U.S.C. §2000e-2(a)(1) (1981). [Emphasis added.] The clear terms of the statute prohibit discrimination in compensation based on the sex of the recipient. The statute does not proscribe salary discrimination based on the sex of other persons over whom the employee has supervision or oversight responsibilities. Even assuming, arguendo, that the University did discriminate in payment of salaries on the basis of the gender of the athletes the Plaintiff coached, such discrimination is not within the scope of Title VII, which prohibits discrimination based on the claimant employee's gender. . . .

II. Equal Pay Act Claims

A. "Factor Other than Sex" Exception

Plaintiff Deli also claims the Defendant violated the Equal Pay Act because it paid Plaintiff less than the coaches of men's athletics teams, thus discriminating against her on the basis of the gender of the athletes she supervised. Again assuming arguendo that the Defendant did discriminate in the payment of salary based on the gender of athletes supervised, such action would not support this Plaintiff's claim for violation of the Equal Pay Act.

The Equal Pay Act (EPA) prohibits an employer from discriminating between employees on the basis of sex by paying wages to employees . . . at a rate less than the rate at which [the employer] pays wages to employees of the opposite sex . . . for equal work on jobs the performance of which requires equal skill, effort, and responsibility, and which are performed under similar working conditions, except where such payment is made pursuant to . . . (iv) a differential based on any other factor other than sex. 26 U.S.C. §206(d)(1). . . . After review of the admittedly less-than-clear language of the statute and its history, this Court concurs with the reasoning of the Seventh Circuit — the EPA prohibits discrimination based on the gender of the claimant only and does not reach compensation differentials based on the gender of student athletes coached by a claimant. . . .

B. Position Not Substantially Equal

Even if Plaintiff had alleged discrimination in salary based on her own gender, her claim could not withstand summary judgment. . . . [T]he Ninth Circuit recently held that a women's basketball coach who was paid less than a men's basketball coach at the same university failed to show that she would likely prevail on her claims for violation of the Equal Pay Act or Title IX. *Stanley v. University of Southern California*, 13 F.3d 1313 (9th Cir. 1994). The Ninth Circuit affirmed that, consistent with the Equal Pay Act, an employer may pay different salaries to coaches of different genders if the coaching positions are not substantially equal in terms of skill, effort, responsibility, and working conditions. . . . In order to state an Equal Pay Act claim, a Plaintiff must show her position was substantially equal to that of the comparator positions with respect to each of the foregoing attributes.

The comparators Deli has chosen in this suit are the coaches of the men's football, hockey and basketball teams. Defendant has presented evidence to show that all three of those teams are larger than the women's gymnastics team. The University also proffers evidence that the head coaches in those sports supervise more employees than Deli supervised. Further, Defendant has provided evidence to show that the three teams enjoy significantly greater spectator attendance and generate substantially more revenue for the University than the women's gymnastics team. Finally, the University has alleged and provided evidence to support its contention that the coaches of the three men's athletic teams have greater responsibility for public and media relations than Deli had as the coach of the women's gymnastics team. The foregoing evidence alone, if undisputed, is enough to show the Plaintiff's job and that of the head coaches of men's basketball, football and hockey are not "substantially equal" in terms of responsibility and working conditions. . . . Deli offers no evidence to refute the foregoing. . . .

III. Title IX Claims

Plaintiff's Title IX claims fail on the merits. . . . According to the OCR Policy Interpretation, differential compensation of coaches violates Title IX "only where compensation or assignment policies or practices deny male and female athletes coaching of equivalent quality, nature or availability" 44 Fed. Reg. at 71416. . . . The Investigator's Manual confirms that the crux of the inquiry is whether differentials in coaches' compensation result in denial of equal athletic opportunity for athletes. "The intent of [the regulation implementing Title VII] is for equal athletic opportunity to be provided to participants, not coaches." OCR Title IX Investigator's Manual (1990) at 58.

Plaintiff does not assert in her Complaint or elsewhere that the athletes she supervised received lesser quality coaching as a result of the difference between Plaintiff's salary and salaries paid to coaches of the men's football, hockey and basketball

> teams.... Because Plaintiff does not claim or provide any evidence to suggest that due to her receipt of a lower salary than that received by coaches of some men's athletic teams, Plaintiff's coaching services were inferior in "quality, nature or availability" to those provided to the men's teams, she has failed to make out a prima facie claim for violation of Title IX. The Defendant is entitled to summary judgment on Plaintiff's Title IX claims....

QUESTIONS

1. Why did *Deli* reject plaintiff's Equal Pay Act (EPA) and Title IX claims? What would a plaintiff have to plead and prove to establish successful claims under each of these federal statutes?

    After the *Stanley* decision relied on by the *Deli* court, the Equal Employment Opportunity Commission (EEOC) revised its guidelines to clarify how the EPA should be applied in such cases. The guidelines require that an educational institution provide a non-gender-based reason for paying a male coach more than a female coach. Men and women involved in coaching are to be evaluated based on their duties, not their sports. Should the EEOC adopt further guidelines to address what many female coaches refer to as the "chicken and egg" problem—that is, if they were paid more and given more resources to market their programs, would they be able to overcome social inequities that have developed over a long period of time and develop programs that would be as successful as men's programs? A pertinent Title IX regulation states:

    > A recipient shall not make or enforce any policy or practice which, on the basis of sex: (a) Makes distinctions in rates of pay or other compensation; (b) Results in the payment of wages to employees of one sex at a rate less than that paid to employees of the opposite sex for equal work on jobs the performance of which requires equal skill, effort, and responsibility, and which are performed under similar working conditions.

    34 C.F.R. §106.54 (2003).

2. Female athletes often state that they prefer male coaches, and most male athletes state that they prefer male coaches. Is this a justification for hiring a male coach over a female coach? Why or why not? What can or should be done to increase the number of women working in sports?

B. Retaliatory Discharge or Punitive Action

Men and women have asserted that they have been discharged in retaliation for complaining about gender disparities in institutions' athletic programs. Fresno

State University has been involved in litigation related to gender discrimination for much of the past decade. First, Diane Milutinovich, an athletics administrator, was dismissed from her position after she complained about inequities in the men's and women's athletics programs. Then the women's volleyball coach, Lindy Vivas, and women's basketball coach, Stacy Johnson-Klein, were fired after questioning administrators and complaining about inequities in facilities, staffing, and employment between the men's and women's athletics programs. Fresno State settled with Milutinovich for $3.5 million. Juries in separate trials found that the university intentionally discriminated against the coaches and awarded $5.85 million to Vivas and $19.1 million to Johnson-Klein.

A threshold issue is whether there is an implied private right of action under Title IX for retaliation on behalf of employees of educational institutions who raise concerns regarding compliance with the substantive provisions of Title IX. In *Jackson v. Birmingham Board of Education*, 125 S. Ct. 1497 (2005), in a 5–4 decision, the Supreme Court resolved a split in the circuits when it held that Title IX's private right of action encompasses retaliation against an employee who complains about gender-based discrimination. The court explained:

> Title IX prohibits sex discrimination by recipients of federal education funding. The statute provides that "[n]o person in the United States shall, on the basis of sex, be excluded from participation in, be denied the benefits of, or be subjected to discrimination under any education program or activity receiving Federal financial assistance." 20 U.S.C. §1681(a). More than 25 years ago, in *Cannon v. University of Chicago*, 441 U.S. 677, 690–693 (1979), we held that Title IX implies a private right of action to enforce its prohibition on intentional sex discrimination. In subsequent cases, we have defined the contours of that right of action. In *Franklin v. Gwinnett County Public Schools*, 503 U.S. 60 (1992), we held that it authorizes private parties to seek monetary damages for intentional violations of Title IX. We have also held that the private right of action encompasses intentional sex discrimination in the form of a recipient's deliberate indifference to a teacher's sexual harassment of a student, *Gebser v. Lago Vista Independent School Dist.*, 524 U.S. 274, 290–291 (1998), or to sexual harassment of a student by another student, *Davis v. Monroe County Bd. of Ed.*, 526 U.S. 629, 642 (1999).
>
> In all of these cases, we relied on the text of Title IX, which, subject to a list of narrow exceptions not at issue here, broadly prohibits a funding recipient from subjecting any person to "discrimination" "on the basis of sex." 20 U.S.C. §1681. Retaliation against a person because that person has complained of sex discrimination is another form of intentional sex discrimination encompassed by Title IX's private cause of action. Retaliation is, by definition, an intentional act. It is a form of "discrimination" because the complainant is being subjected to differential treatment. [Citations omitted.] Moreover, retaliation is discrimination "on the basis of sex" because it is an intentional response to the nature of the complaint: an allegation of sex discrimination. We conclude that when a funding recipient retaliates against a person *because* he complains of sex discrimination, this constitutes intentional "discrimination" "on the basis of sex," in violation of Title IX. *Jackson v. Birmingham Board of Education*, 125 S. Ct. 1497 (2005).

QUESTIONS

1. Why is retaliation a viable cause of action under Title IX if it is not included in the Title IX regulations?

• • • • • • • • • •

As more girls participate in sports and more women seek degrees and careers in the sports industry, gender discrimination will remain a critical legal issue. Because sports are still generally considered a male domain in the United States, gender equity in the sports arena has lagged behind cultural norms in education and in business. Awareness and education are key components in preventing discrimination, while enforcement and litigation serve to correct injustices and punish those who perpetuate discrimination.

Racial Equity Issues in Athletics

INTRODUCTION

This chapter focuses on racial inequity, an increasingly complex issue in sports. Notwithstanding its prevalence, the role of race in sports is often overlooked until a particular event brings it into focus. The event may be a derisive comment made by a television personality in reference to an athlete of color, an instance of one athlete racially abusing another during a game, or an allegation that a head coaching aspirant was denied an employment opportunity because of race. The event could also be one that marks progress toward racial equity, such as a person of color becoming majority owner of a professional sports franchise. Events seemingly unrelated to sports may also inspire discussion of race in sports. Following the election of President Barack Obama as the first African-American President in United States history, for instance, commentators wondered if his achievement might portend a substantial increase in access to administrative positions in sports for people of color.

The goal of this chapter is to introduce some of the issues that arise when examining race in the sports context. It attempts to achieve this goal through commentary and leading cases that address race-related issues. The chapter begins with historical perspectives regarding the role of race in American sport.

HISTORICAL PERSPECTIVE

During the early years of collegiate and professional sports, a period extending from after the Civil War to the late 1800s and early 1900s, African-Americans participated in organized sports at the amateur and professional levels, including boxing, horse racing, baseball, and cycling. The opportunity to participate during this period was not accompanied by equitable treatment. African-Americans were both exploited for their athletic ability and subjected to the indignities that flowed from racial discrimination. They routinely suffered racial epithets and discriminatory acts (e.g., physical attacks) from fans, opposing players, and even their own teammates.

The early years of inclusion in amateur and professional sports, albeit limited, were followed by a period during which formal and informal rules excluded blacks from organized professional and collegiate sports. One scholar cites two reasons for the segregation of sports:

> The most obvious [reason] was simply the desire of whites not to associate with African-Americans. . . . Associated with this desire for separation was . . . the other broad explanation: a view that African-Americans were inferior. This view, of course, finds its roots in slavery and provided a common excuse for separation of the races.

Kenneth L. Shropshire, *In Black and White: Race and Sports in America*, 31 (1996). This period of segregation was followed by what some have coined the reintegration of sports, which is discussed in this chapter.

The following discussion illustrates the web of formal and informal rules that historically prevented African-American athletes from playing for white southern colleges and universities and severely limited their ability to play for northern colleges and universities. In reading these materials, be mindful that similar rules were used to enforce segregation in professional sports in America.

A. Racial Segregation: Intercollegiate Athletics[1]

1. Formal Rules of Exclusion

During the late nineteenth and early twentieth centuries, legally countenanced segregation affected virtually every aspect of social behavior and interaction in the United States, including sports. In college sports, a series of rules and customs limited black participation to historically black colleges and a few predominantly white colleges.

In the South, prohibitions against blacks attending white colleges and universities effectively excluded the black athlete from playing for predominantly white southern institutions. Moreover, Jim Crow laws enacted to prohibit whites and blacks from social interaction extended to bar direct sporting competition between them. For example, a Texas Penal Code provision, enacted in 1933, prohibited any "boxing, sparring, or wrestling contest or exhibition between any person of the Caucasian or 'White' race and one of the African or 'Negro' race. . . ." Likewise, a 1932 Atlanta city ordinance prohibited amateur baseball clubs of different races from playing within two blocks of each other.

More broadly written statutes prohibited any form of athletic competition between whites and African-Americans. Legislative Act 579 is illustrative. Enacted by the Louisiana legislature in 1956, the statute prohibited interracial

---

[1]This section is adapted from Timothy Davis, *The Myth of the Superspade: The Persistence of Racism in Intercollegiate Athletics*, 22 Fordham Urban L.J. 615 (1995).

sports participation. Although similar legislation was defeated in Mississippi, Mississippi state institutions adopted what has been referred to as unwritten but ironclad segregation policy. That such a policy was adopted with respect to sport may be explained by the fact that Mississippi led former states of the Confederacy in enacting laws and policies to ensure what was effectively apartheid.

One commentator observed, "What was left for blacks generally was participation of black against black and the formation of Negro leagues. At a less organized level, it meant acceptance of the Jim Crow laws which called for separate (but almost never equal) playgrounds, public parks, swimming pools, and other recreational facilities." John A. Lucas & Ronald A. Smith, Saga of American Sport 275 (1978). Under such a regime, the idea of competition in the South between white and black collegians was out of the question.

2. Informal Rules of Discrimination

During that time, blacks played sports for a limited number of northern colleges and universities such as Harvard, Amherst, and Oberlin. Informal rules reinforced by social strictures, however, were nearly as effective as legislation in limiting the opportunities available to black athletes to compete at predominantly white institutions outside the South.

These informal limitations appeared in various guises. In some instances, they manifested as a virtual prohibition of African-Americans from becoming student-athletes. For instance, few black students competed in sports for Catholic universities, because most such institutions excluded African-American students during this period. Often, informal Jim Crow rules prohibited blacks from playing sports for the schools that did admit black students.

African-American students' experience at the University of Kansas is illustrative. No formal Jim Crow laws were passed in the state of Kansas. Nevertheless, the official policy of the university attempted to minimize the presence of black students in order to remove them from the mainstream of the school's social and extracurricular activities. One historian notes, "Blacks were denied practically every right except that of attending classes." Raymond Wolters, The New Negro on Campus: Black College Rebellions of the 1920s 316 (1975). The university's denial of African-American students' rights to participate in most extracurricular activities included the right to participate on the university's athletic teams. The head of athletics at Kansas in the 1930s insisted, "[N]o colored man will ever have a chance as long as [I am here]." Loren Miller, *The Unrest Among College Students*, 34 Crisis 187 (1927). The situation at University of Kansas illustrates the lack of opportunity for black students to compete for Northern universities, which often paralleled those institutions' attitudes and policies toward black students in general.

The environment encountered by black students and student-athletes at the University of Kansas was not unique. Certain athletic conferences, such as the Missouri Athletic Conference (with the exception of Nebraska), systematically excluded black athletes pursuant to so-called gentlemen's agreements that prohibited blacks from participating in league contests. These gentlemen's agreements constituted a series of written rules or tacit understandings precluding black participation in organized sports.

The reach and impact of these gentlemen's agreements extended beyond the walls of the institutions that relied on them to exclude black athletes. They severely affected the few black athletes who were participating for Northern universities. Prior to World War II, most Northern teams with blacks on their rosters either did not schedule games against Southern teams or would leave their African-American players at home when the team traveled south. It has also been suggested that a promise to withdraw voluntarily from games against Southern schools was an element of the consideration that some Northern institutions extracted from their black athletes.

Illustrations abound of Northern schools forcing black players to sit out games against Southern teams. For instance, in 1916, Paul Robeson, a member of Rutgers University's football team, was barred from the field of play when Washington and Lee College threatened not to play if he was allowed to participate. Such racially exclusionary practices resulted in black colleges providing the only significant opportunities for the black athlete to compete in college athletics prior to the 1930s.

Northern institutions adopted other exclusionary informal rules as well. Informal quotas typically restricted the slots open to black athletes to no more than one or two players on a team. In addition to numerical quotas, Northern colleges imposed another requirement that limited the number of black student-athletes allowed to compete on their teams. Many of these institutions imposed a "superspade" requirement. In other words, the typical African-American student-athlete playing for a predominantly white college prior to the 1930s tended to be an exceptionally talented starter.

Black student-athletes competing for the few predominantly white colleges willing to admit them were not spared the indignities of racism at their home institutions. They were routinely excluded from the mainstream of campus social, academic, and athletic life. Black student-athletes were typically not permitted to reside in campus housing or otherwise engage in campus social life. They encountered demeaning comments from coaches, teammates, and other members of the university community, as well as the populace of the local communities in which those colleges were located. This sense of isolation was heightened by an absence of other black students, as well as black faculty, coaches, or administrators.

By the end of World War II, virtually every major collegiate program outside the South had opened its doors to permit at least one African-American player to compete for it. Southern colleges and universities resisted this fundamental change in college sports and continued after World War II to exclude African-American student-athletes. The integration of college sports at predominantly white colleges in the South did not occur until the latter part of the 1960s, during which time the numbers of African-American student-athletes competing for these institutions mushroomed. For example, whereas African-Americans represented 22 percent of all collegiate basketball student-athletes in the South in 1970, by 1985 this figure had increased to 61 percent. For discussions of the integration of intercollegiate sports, see Timothy Davis, *The Myth of the Superspade: The Persistence of Racism in Intercollegiate Athletics*, 22 Fordham Urban L.J. 633–37 (1995); Timothy Davis, *Race and Sports in America: An Historical Overview*, 7 Va. Sports & Enter. L.J. 291 (2008); and Forest J. Berghorn, *Racial Participation and Integration in Men's and Women's Intercollegiate Basketball: Continuity and Change, 1958–1985*, 5 Sociology Sport J. 107, 111 (1988).

B. Racial Segregation: Professional Sports

Prior to World War II, the experiences of racial and ethnic minorities in professional sports largely paralleled those of their amateur counterparts. Baseball provides an excellent illustration of the experiences of African-Americans in professional sports during that period. It is estimated that approximately 24 blacks played organized professional baseball during the 1880s. By the 1890s, however, segregation of professional baseball emerged pursuant to a gentleman's agreement that resulted in the total exclusion of black and dark-skinned Latino players from Major League Baseball (MLB). Seeking alternative venues in which to play baseball, blacks and dark skinned Latinos played in the Negro Leagues and Latin America, and barnstormed against white players. (Opportunities for interracial play in a barnstorming capacity were reduced beginning in the 1920s, when MLB's first commissioner, Judge Kenesaw Landis, prohibited major league all-star teams from competing against the Negro Leagues teams.) Fair-skinned Latinos were permitted to play in MLB during its segregated era. Those who played, however, were subjected to images that depicted them as "lazy, passive, and inferior" and other forms of discrimination that continued into the post–World War II era. In addition, Latinos during that time systematically received lower-paying contracts than their white counterparts.

In dealing with segregated sports leagues, black athletes acted as African-Americans did with respect to other segregated institutions (e.g., cultural and educational); they found opportunity in parallel leagues. Baseball's Negro Leagues provide one of the better examples of an alternative developed to provide opportunities despite the exclusion of blacks from major sports leagues.

The term "Negro Leagues" generally has been used somewhat casually to refer to teams that played in the United States between 1880 and 1955. Alfred D. Mathewson, *Major League Baseball's Monopoly Power and the Negro Leagues*, 35 Am. Bus. L.J. 291, 292 (1998). These consisted primarily of black professional baseball players and black owners. *Id.* Although formal leagues existed, "particularly the Negro American and National Leagues," most Negro League teams were unaffiliated with a formal league and operated independently. *Id.* Most of these teams traveled throughout the United States barnstorming, and "[f]requently, the games were significant social events in Black communities. Even those teams that were members of formal leagues barnstormed before, during, and after joining leagues. The Kansas City Monarchs, who introduced night baseball in 1930, and the Indianapolis Clowns were two of the most successful barnstorming teams." *Id.* at 293.

C. The Reintegration of Professional and Amateur Sports

Baseball remained segregated until Jackie Robinson joined the Brooklyn Dodgers in 1947. The formal desegregation of baseball would not occur, however, until 1959, when the Boston Red Sox, the last major league baseball team to field an all-white roster, promoted Pumpsie Green to the major leagues. The National Football League (NFL) had been integrated from the year of its founding in 1920 until 1934, when a gentlemen's agreement between NFL owners, seeking to remake the league, banned the signing of black players. Daniel Coyle, *Invisible Men*, Sports Illustrated, Dec. 15, 2003, 124. The NFL was reintegrated in 1946 when Kenny Washington joined the Los Angeles Rams. Like football, basketball had less of an exclusionary history than baseball. African-Americans competed against whites in professional basketball up until World War I. In 1950, a year after the National Basketball Association (NBA) was formed, Chuck Cooper was drafted by the Boston Celtics. In 1966, basketball also provided the first African-American head coach in a major professional sports league when Bill Russell became head coach of the Celtics. See Kenneth L. Shropshire, *In Black and White: Race and Sports in America*, 29–31 (1996).

A confluence of social, political, and economic variables resulted in the integration of professional sports and broader American society. Significant among these variables are: (1) expectations for desegregation created by the "democratic idealism spawned by World War II;" (2) opportunities created by a shortage of players because of World War II's decimation of the talent pool of white athletes; (3) political activism by blacks and their white allies demanding the desegregation of professional sports; (4) Supreme Court desegregation decisions; and (5) enactment of federal civil rights legislation. Additional factors converged to provide incentives for colleges and universities to recruit African-American student-athletes, including political decisions, such as congressional passage of the G.I. Bill (which increased the presence of African-Americans on college campuses) and the increased professionalism of college sports following World War II. Historian Adolph Grundman posits that colleges' recruitment of African-Americans served a dual purpose: it helped these schools strengthen their athletic programs, while at the same time it promoted the advancement of race relations.

RACE AND RACIAL EQUITY IN MODERN SPORTS

A. Coaching and Administrative Opportunities

1. College Sports

As discussed above, racial segregation dominated collegiate athletics for the bulk of the twentieth century. Segregationist philosophies began to lift during the final third of the century and opportunities for athletes of color at primarily white institutions expanded to the point at which 50 percent or more of major collegiate football programs' rosters were composed of African-Americans. Opportunities for African-American coaches, however, remained limited. The Southeastern Conference (SEC) was particularly stubborn. The SEC comprises schools in the heart of the American South (e.g., the University of Alabama, the University of Georgia, the University of Mississippi, etc.), the region of the country in which racial oppression has historically been the most pervasive and severe. At the turn of the millennium, no SEC school had ever employed an African-American as head football coach or athletic director, the two athletic department positions generally considered to hold the greatest power. In December 2003, Sylvester Croom broke that barrier when he became head coach of Mississippi State University's football team. When hired, however, he became only the fifth active African-American head football coach among the then 117 schools that made up the NCAA's Division I-A (now Football Bowl Subdivision (FBS)). By 2008, despite the fanfare surrounding Croom's hire, little had changed nationally with respect to racial disproportionality in collegiate football coaching. As such, the Black Coaches Association, an advocacy organization for African-American collegiate coaches, called on the NCAA to initiate a college version of the NFL's Rooney Rule, which requires that each NFL team looking for a head coach interview at least one candidate of color before filling the position (the Rooney Rule is discussed in greater detail in section B, *infra*). Although the NCAA refused to implement a Rooney Rule analog, state legislators from around the country expressed interest in requiring their state universities to interview at least one candidate of color when making hires in their athletic departments, and one state, Oregon, passed legislation to that effect. In July 2009, Oregon passed a law requiring its seven public universities to interview at least one candidate of color before hiring a head coach or athletic director. In 2015 Oregon passed an additional law requiring that the state's Higher Education Coordinating Commission more closely monitor the universities' compliance with the interview protocols. For further detail on the grassroots movement that propelled the Oregon legislation, see Michael McCann, The Oxford Handbook of American Sports Law (Oxford University Press, 2017), specifically Chapter 27: The Rooney Rule's Reach: How the NFL's Equal Opportunity Initiative for Coaches Inspired Local Government Reform.

In the aftermath of George Floyd's murder in 2020, the West Coast Conference (WCC), a Division I conference of universities, which includes Brigham Young, Gonzaga, and Loyola Marymount, followed the state of Oregon's lead in trying to expand equitable opportunity. It passed the "Russell Rule," named after NBA Hall of Famer and civil rights icon Bill Russell (who played basketball at the WCC's University of San Francisco), which requires every WCC school to interview at least one person of color or one woman when hiring an athletic director, senior administrator (e.g., assistant or associate athletic director), head coach, or full-time assistant coach. The initiative has already produced substantial diversity gains. During the 2021–22 hiring cycle, seven of the 15 head coaches hired, 49 of the 93 assistant coaches hired, and 16 of the 18 senior administrators hired were a person of color or a woman. Jesse Washington, *The "Russell Rule" promotes a wider group of candidates for college coaching jobs*, Andscape.com (Jan. 26, 2023), *https://andscape.com/features/the-russell-rule-promotes-a-wider-group-of-candidates-for-college-coaching-jobs/*.

While the State of Oregon and the WCC are relative bright spots, coaching and administrative opportunities for people of color in college sports generally present a rather bleak picture. For the 2021–22 season, the racial demographics of combined head coaching positions in all Division I men's sports were as follows: Whites, 84.1 percent; African-Americans, 9.9 percent; Latinos, 1.8 percent; and Asian Americans, 0.7 percent. Similar numbers are present in all Division I head coaching positions for women's sports: Whites, 80.6 percent; African-Americans, 10.2 percent; Latinos, 2.2 percent; and Asian Americans, 1.6 percent. The trend follows for Division II and III head coaching positions, where Whites hold 85.2 percent and 89.0 percent of men's teams' positions and 84.5 percent and 88.1 percent of women's teams' positions, respectively. People of color are underrepresented in athletic director positions as well. During the 2021–22 season, 78.6 percent of athletic directors were white, 14.3 percent were African-American, 2.7 percent were Latinx, and 0.6 percent were Asian. See Richard Lapchick, *The 2022 Racial and Gender Report Card: College Sport*, ESPN.com, Mar. 22, 2023.

For annually updated numbers and links to various reports addressing racial matters in sport, visit the "Racial and Gender Report Card" published annually by DeVos Sport Business Management at *https://www.tidesport.org/racial-gender-report-card*.

2. Professional Sports

People of color are beginning to make inroads in coaching and senior-level administrative positions in U.S. professional sports, but progress is uneven. Consider the NBA and the NFL, both of which have player populations that are disproportionately black. In 2022, half of the 30 head coaches in the NBA were black, and eight of them had been hired in the previous 12 months, signaling a dramatic upward trajectory of equitable opportunity. Tim Reynolds, *Half of NBA's Franchises Now Have Black Coaches*, Associated Press, June 2, 2022, *https://www.nba.com/news/half-of-nba-teams-now-lead-by-black-coaches*. In contrast, the 32-team NFL began the 2021 season with three black head coaches, and by mid-January, 2022, after two were fired, the league was left with only one. Moreover, on February 1, 2022, one of the two fired head coaches, Brian Flores, formerly of the Miami Dolphins, filed an explosive class action lawsuit against the NFL and all of its teams accusing them of discriminating against coaches of color in their hiring practices and denying them equal opportunity and pay compared with their white counterparts. Ira Boudway, *Brian Flores, the Coach Who Called Out the NFL*, Bloomberg.com, Dec. 14, 2022, *https://www.bloomberg.com/news/articles/2022-12-14/brian-flores-the-coach-who-called-out-the-nfl-bloomberg-50-2022#xj4y7vzkg*.

Two decades earlier the NFL faced the threat of an employment discrimination lawsuit when civil rights lawyers Johnnie Cochran and Cyrus Mehri challenged the league's abysmal head coach diversity numbers. The parties, however, avoided litigation and together crafted a diverse slate interviewing process designed to foster greater opportunities for coaches of color to ascend to the head coach positions. The process, known as the Rooney Rule, required that at least one person of color be interviewed as a candidate for all head coaching vacancies. Shortly thereafter, the NFL extended the rule to the general manager position. See N. Jeremi Duru, Advancing the Ball: Race, Reformation, and the Quest for Equal Coaching Opportunity in the NFL 86 (Oxford University Press, 2011).

For several years following its adoption, the Rooney Rule was quite successful in increasing the numbers of NFL head coaches and general managers of color. During the 12 years before the Rooney Rule's enactment (1990–2002), the NFL featured four head coaches of color and one general manager of color, whereas during the 12 years after enactment (2003–15), the NFL featured 16 head coaches of color and eight general managers of color. Just as notably, those head coaches and general managers of color had generally been successful. During the 12 years before the Rooney Rule's enactment, only one head coach or general manager of color had led a club to the Super Bowl, whereas during the 12 years after enactment, 10 head coaches and general managers of color led their clubs to the Super Bowl, two of whom did so twice. See N. Jeremi Duru, *The Rooney Rule's Reach: How the NFL's Equal Opportunity Initiative for Coaches Sponsored Local Government Reform*, Oxford Handbook on Sports Law (Oxford University Press 2018).

The diversity gains, however, began tapering considerably in 2012, and by 2018 the number of head coaches of color in the league was plummeting, as clubs increasingly engaged in sham Rooney Rule interviews (interviewing candidates of color but not seriously considering them). In 2020 and 2021, the NFL revamped the Rooney Rule to require that clubs interview at least two candidates of color (rather than just one) for all head coaching positions, and all offensive, defensive, and special teams coordinator positions.

None of the NFL's Rooney Rule reforms, however, targeted the sham interview problem, and the problem grew, ultimately forming the core of Flores's suit. Flores detailed in his complaint, for instance, his experience interviewing for the New York Giants' head coaching job in January of 2022, a job that would ultimately go to then-Buffalo Bills offensive coordinator Brian Daboll, who is white. Three days before Flores's interview with the Giants, New England Patriots Head Coach Bill Belichick (a longtime mentor to Flores) sent Flores a text congratulating him on receiving the Giants' job. Upon realizing his mistake, Belichick followed up with a text reading: "Sorry—I [messed] this up. I double checked and . . . I think they are naming Brian Daboll. I'm sorry about that." Mark Maske & Nicki Jhabvala, *Former Dolphins Coach Brian Flores Sues NFL and Its Teams, Alleging Racial Discrimination*, The Washington Post, Feb. 1, 2022, https://www.washingtonpost.com/sports/2022/02/01/brian-flores-lawsuit-nfl-discrimination/. Flores nonetheless sat for the interview. After the interview, which ostensibly satisfied the Rooney Rule, the Giants hired Daboll. In April 2022, Steve Wilks, former Arizona Cardinals head coach, and Ray Horton, an NFL assistant who had interviewed for the Tennessee Titans' head-coaching job in 2016, both joined Flores's lawsuit, complaining of similar experiences. The NFL moved for all of the claims to be arbitrated, but in March 2023, United States District Judge Valerie Caproni issued a determination that the majority of Flores's claims would remain in federal court while Wilks's and Horton's claims would proceed through arbitration. All of the claims are currently pending.

Other professional sports leagues in the United States fall on the spectrum between the NBA and the NFL with respect to head-coaching diversity; none are as diverse as the NBA, but none are facing active employment discrimination litigation. With respect to other high-level administrative positions (e.g., general manager, CEO, and president), people of color continue to be substantially underrepresented across the American sporting landscape. This is the case even in the NBA where, despite 50 percent of the league's head coaches being of color in 2022, only 7 percent of the league's CEOs or presidents were of color. See Richard Lapchick, *The 2022 Racial and Gender Report Card: National Basketball Association* 5, 52, Aug. 10, 2022.

While high-level administrative positions in American sports clubs are extremely nondiverse, they are markedly more diverse than club ownership ranks. For years, Michael Jordan was the only African-American with a majority ownership stake in a major American professional sports club, but in 2023 Jordan sold his stake in the NBA's Charlotte Hornets leaving no African-American majority owners in professional sports clubs and just a few majority owners of color in American sports.

QUESTIONS

1. Explanations offered for the dearth of African-American college head football coaches include interference by influential white alumni and fans that hinders the hiring of African-American head football coaches and the refusal of athletic administrators to admit that a problem exists in hiring procedures. In the collegiate ranks, but also in the NFL, some have argued that African-American head football coaches are simply held to a higher standard. At the NFL's 2019 Quarterback Coaching Summit, which was designed to assist aspiring African-American football coaches, NFL Executive Vice President of Football Operations Troy Vincent matter-of-factly stated, "We can sell a non-winning white coach, but we struggle to sell a winning black coach." Jim Trotter, *Quarterback Coaching Summit Spotlights Minority Coaches*, ESPN.com, June 25, 2019, http://www.nfl.com/news/story/0ap3000001034559/article/quarterback-coaching-summit-spotlights-minority-coaches. Do you agree or disagree with any of the foregoing reasons? Are there other reasons for the underrepresentation of people of color in coaching and management positions in college and professional sports? Professor Kenneth Shropshire, in his seminal book on race and sports, *In Black and White: Race and Sports in America*, argues that the inability of African-Americans to break into leadership is attributable in large part to negative stereotypes. He contends that these stereotypes, in conjunction with the "good old boy" system of hiring, result in lower numbers of blacks in authority positions in sports. Do you agree?

2. Stacking involves the assignment of certain individuals to specific athletic positions based on race or ethnicity rather than ability. The clearest illustration of this phenomenon is the quarterback position in football, which was long off-limits to African-Americans. Dave Meggyesy of the Sports Business Journal explained in a 2002 article that rather than allow African-Americans to compete at "thinking" positions such as quarterback, they were often "stacked" at positions like running back and wide receiver. He noted, though, that between 1992 and 2002, the number of African-American NFL quarterbacks had nearly tripled, to nearly 21 percent of all NFL quarterbacks, and suggested that stacking might be a thing of the past. See David Meggyesy, *Let Players Decide Who Coaches Will Be*, Sports Bus. J., Oct. 21–27, 2002. In the two decades since, the number of African-American NFL quarterbacks has further increased, and as of 2022, they constituted 29 percent of all NFL quarterbacks. African-American players, however, constitute roughly 60 percent of all NFL players, so African-American quarterbacks remain drastically underrepresented. Why does such stacking continue? Might it signal the continued resonance of old stereotypes that African-Americans are not well-suited to playing a cerebral position like quarterback? Does stacking exist in other professional and amateur sports? If so, in which sports and for which positions?

B. Intersections

1. Race and Gender

The racial demographics of women who participate in college sports exemplifies the intersection of race and gender. In 2021–22, African-American women accounted for approximately 39.9 percent of Division I women basketball players and 21.8 percent of Division I outdoor track athletes. The profile of women of color participating in Division I athletics overall during the 2021–22 season was as follows: African-Americans comprised 11.7 percent, Latinas 5.7 percent, Asians 2.4 percent, and Native Americans 0.4 percent. Females of two or more races comprised 6.4 percent. Richard Lapchick, *The 2021 Racial and Gender Report Card: College Sport*, Mar. 22, 2023.

The data suggest that women of color are not participating in the increased athletic opportunities created by sports such as rowing, golf, lacrosse, and soccer, which many institutions added to comply with Title IX. Consequently, women of color appear not to be in a position to derive the same level of benefits from Title IX as white women. Law professors Deborah Brake and Verna Williams explain:

> For the African-American females who decide to pursue athletics, racism and patriarchy in the culture of sport present additional barriers to their continued participation. Consider, for example, that black females frequently are steered into particular sports or positions within sports. Black females are more prevalent in basketball or track . . . [and] the persistence of stereotypes about black women's proper place in sport constrains the athletic opportunities deemed appropriate for them.

Deborah L. Brake & Verna L. Williams, *The Heart of the Game: Putting Race and Educational Equity at the Center of Title IX*, 7 Va. Sports & Ent. L.J. 199, 210–11 (2008). See Alfred D. Mathewson, *Remediating Discrimination Against African-American Female Athletes at the Intersection of Title IX and Title VI*, 2 Wake Forest J L. & Pol'y 295 (2012); Lauren Smith, *Black Female Participation Languishes Outside Basketball and Track*, Chron. of Higher Educ. (June 29, 2007).

These barriers to African-American participation in certain sports have prompted litigation. For instance, in 2018, Nadirah McRae, a female African-American high school field hockey and lacrosse player, filed a federal class action lawsuit against the Philadelphia School District. In the suit, McRae accused the school district of derailing African-American girls' athletic ambitions by refusing to let predominantly African-American schools play field hockey and lacrosse against predominantly white schools. The lawsuit, which asserts Title VI and Title IX claims, alleges that in an effort to reserve field hockey and lacrosse "for its magnet schools and more privileged high schools, which are not predominately lower-income and African-American," the school district essentially created a Negro League, restricting predominantly African-American schools to games against other such schools and robbing "the [African-American] girls of opportunities to improve their skills and to be seen by college scouts and recruiters." *McRae v Sch. Reform Comm'n et al.*, 2018 WL 4283056 (E.D Pa.). The case was subsequently settled.

2. Race and Freedom of Expression

Are athletes and coaches of color expected to behave in a way that dilutes their racial identity? Consider that some African-Americans have complained that white coaches and players are afforded much greater latitude to express themselves than their African-American counterparts. According to this view, African-American athletes and coaches run the risk of incurring costly sanctions if they speak out on racially or politically sensitive issues.

No athlete in recent American history has more notably expressed his views on racial matters than former San Francisco 49ers quarterback Colin Kaepernick. In 2016, Kaepernick began kneeling during the pre-game playing of the national anthem to protest inequities in the American criminal justice system. He was widely criticized and endured death threats for the remainder of the season. Kaeperick's protest polarized the NFL, the United States, and many other parts of the world and became a lightning rod issue. Once Kaepernick's contract with the 49ers expired, he was unable to secure a new contract, despite being in his prime, being a well-regarded quarterback, and having just a few years earlier led his team to the Super Bowl. Kaepernick suspected collusion on the part of the league and its franchises, and in October 2017 filed a grievance under the NFL's Collective Bargaining Agreement. As the arbitrator handling the case was preparing to rule, the parties settled. Consequently, it is difficult to know how the arbitrator, or a reviewing court of appeal, would have analyzed the case. And because many athletes of color fear that taking controversial stands with respect to race will damage or end their careers, there is little case law at the intersection of race and freedom of expression in collegiate and professional sports. Former University of Arkansas at Fayetteville (UAF) Head Basketball Coach Nolan Richardson and former NBA player Craig Hodges, however, both suffered adverse employment actions after making public statements regarding racial inequity and both brought federal lawsuits. Neither suit was successful.

Richardson, an African-American, was head coach at UAF from 1985 until he was fired in March 2002. Richardson claimed that "he was fired because of his race and because he spoke out on [racial] matters of public concern. . . ." *Richardson v. Sugg*, 325 F. Supp. 2d 922 (E.D. Ark. 2004). UAF denied the allegations and asserted that Richardson was fired because of statements he made indicating he had lost interest in the job, such as "[i]f they go ahead and pay me my money, they can take the job tomorrow." *Id.* at 937.

In assessing Richardson's First Amendment claim, the court explained that:

> To prove a violation of her or his First Amendment rights, a public employee must demonstrate that the speech in which he is engaged is protected speech. To establish this, he must show that the speech can be "fairly characterized as constituting a matter of public concern," and not a matter of private interest. Speech is a "matter of public interest or concern" when it touches upon "any matter of political, social or other concern to the community." Opposition to racial discrimination *is* a "matter of inherently public concern." (internal footnotes omitted).

Id. at 941–42.

Applying the foregoing standard, the court rejected Richardson's claim. Richardson appealed, and the Eighth Circuit affirmed the district court's decision.

Free speech considerations lie at the core of the issues raised in *Hodges v. National Basketball Association*, 1998 WL 26183 (N.D. Ill. 1998), as well. There, Hodges alleged that the NBA conspired to keep him out of basketball because he was "an outspoken African-American activist" who commented on political issues, particularly those involving the African-American community. *Id.* at *1. As framed by the court, Hodges asserted that "racial discrimination is at the root of the conspiracy, a conclusion supported by the fact that white players with backgrounds similar to his are free to express themselves politically without suffering any retaliation." *Id.* The court did not have an opportunity to address the merits of Hodges's claims. His suit was dismissed because it was not filed within the applicable two-year statute of limitations period.

Public racial protests in sport, while rare during Richardson's and Hodges's time, and only slightly less so when Kaepernick took his knee, have become far more commonplace since. The catalyzing event was George Floyd's 2020 death from asphyxiation as a Minneapolis police officer kneeled on his neck for over nine minutes. Floyd's murder, which was at the time the most recent instance in a long string of African-Americans killed by police officers, seemed to represent an inflection point, and scores of professional and collegiate athletes grew vocal in calling for societal reform. Because the COVID-19 pandemic had forced sports across the country to shut down, athletes expressed their views over social media and through video posts. For instance, a group of high-profile NFL players, including Patrick Mahomes, Saquon Barkley, and Odell Beckham, Jr., created a video decrying police brutality, demanding that "Black Lives Matter," and challenging NFL Commissioner Roger Goodell to make a statement on the issue. Goodell did so, stating in a response video: "We, the National Football League, believe Black Lives Matter."

Goodell went on to acknowledge that the NFL was wrong in not addressing police brutality over the previous several years and in seeking to stop players' peaceful Kaepernick-inspired on-field protests designed to bring attention to systemic racial discrimination. Among other efforts to quash protests, the NFL had in 2018 enacted a rule requiring players to stand during the playing of the national anthem if they remain on the field; otherwise, the rule required that they stay in the locker room during the anthem or their team would be fined. The National Football League Players Association (NFLPA) responded by filing a non-injury grievance on behalf of all players against the NFL, arguing that the unilaterally imposed anthem rule is "inconsistent with the collective bargaining agreement and infringes on player rights." Chris Chavez, *NFLPA Files Grievance Over NFL's New National Anthem Policy*, Sports Illustrated, July 10, 2018, https://www.si.com/nfl/2018/07/10/nflpa-grievance-nfl-national-anthem-policy. The NFL initially fought the NFLPA on the matter but ultimately relented and has ceased to enforce the rule since.

Like the NFL, the U.S. Soccer Federation (USSF) previously had a rule requiring that players stand during the national anthem. In 2020, however, Megan Rapinoe of the U.S. Women's National Soccer Team challenged the rule by kneeling as Kaepernick had, and after some controversy the USSF repealed the rule. Athletes in other leagues—such as Major League Soccer and the National Women's Soccer League—have also engaged in protest, kneeling during the anthem and wearing Black Lives Matter t-shirts. If particular club owners or entire leagues or sports governing bodies initiate rules to stamp out protests, and if they do not relent as the NFL and USSF ultimately did, might the First Amendment be a tool to which protesting players can turn? Does the *Richardson v. Sugg* case shed any light on this question? What if the dynamic is reversed; that is, if a team seeks in unison to protest systemic racial discrimination and one player refuses to join? Consider *Hening v. Adair*, 644 F. Supp.3d 303 (W.D. Va. 2022). In that case, a former Virginia Tech women's soccer player, Kiersten Hening, filed a federal lawsuit against the team's coach, Charles Adair, whom she claimed accused her of "doing her own thing" when she refused to kneel before a game with her teammates and then subjected her to abuse and retaliation. Hening sought a ruling that would require Adair to "undergo First Amendment training" and that would also award her compensatory and punitive damages. The case settled in January 2023 for $100,000, but with no requirement that Adair undergo any sort of training.

3. Race and Socioeconomic Stratification

Many commentators have drawn attention to one example of the intersection of race and socioeconomic stratification in arguing that African-American student-athletes, who are disproportionately overrepresented in revenue-producing collegiate sports, specifically football and basketball, are exploited and thus disadvantaged economically and academically. See, e.g., Frank J. Vandall & Tallulah Lanier, *Black Youths Lost, White Fortunes Found: Sports Betting and the Commodification and Criminalization of Black Collegiate Athletes*, 2021 U. Ill. L. Rev. 1821, 1830; Goldburn P. Maynard Jr., *They're Watching You: How the NCAA Infringes on the Freedom of Families*, 2018 Wis. L. Rev. Forward 1, 10 (2018).

Recall the discussion in Chapter 3 regarding recent legal developments in many states permitting collegiate student-athletes to utilize their name, image, and likeness (NIL) for profit and the NCAA's suspension of its rules against such use. Some have opposed these developments as antithetical to the collegiate athletics mission, and debate currently rages as to whether NIL rights are too expansive and should be cordoned. At the same time, as also detailed in Chapter 3, student-athletes are pushing for employee status and remuneration under the National Labor Relations Act and the Fair Labor Standards Act. These efforts, too, have been opposed. In that African-American student-athletes are disproportionately overrepresented in collegiate revenue-producing sports, is this battle over student-athletes having access to some of that revenue essentially a civil rights battle?

Another phenomenon at the intersection of race and socioeconomic stratification regards access to high school athletics. High schools that serve students from wealthy households often offer more extensive athletic opportunities than those that serve students from under-resourced households. Given that African-American and Latinx students hail disproportionately from under-resourced households, their athletic options are disproportionately limited. In 2018, four New York City high school students argued that this was the case in their city. These students, as part of a class action with help from New York Lawyers for the Public Interest, sued the city for violating its human rights laws through "its unequal handling of the Public School Athletics League." More specifically, the plaintiffs alleged that "[t]he city's human rights laws prohibit depriving any public accommodation to a class of citizens, based on race," and that "[t]he Department of Education is in violation of [those laws] by discriminating against black and Latino students because they provide more sports teams and a greater variety of sports to students of other races." Ben Chapman, *Advocates and Students Sue City over School Sports Discrimination*, N.Y. Daily News, June 21, 2018. To support their allegation, the plaintiffs noted that:

- The city's Department of Education spends 17% more on sports for white and Asian students than for African-American and Latinx students;
- Over 17,000 African-American and Latinx students attend high schools offering no sports at all; and
- For those African-American and Latinx students who do have sports offered at their high schools, they have on average 10 fewer sports available to them than do white students. See *id*.

In 2021, the parties settled, with the city committing to "group certain nearby high schools so they can share . . . sports teams [and to] create 200 new sports teams by spring 2024." Alex Zimmerman, *Settlement to Give Black and Latino Students More Access to NYC High School Sports Teams*, NewYorkChalkbeat.com, Nov. 17, 2021, https://ny.chalkbeat.org/2021/11/17/22788370/psal-lawsuit-sports-inequity-settlement.

4. Race and Globalization

As is true for many industries, American sport has been impacted by globalization. Illustrations include the worldwide televising of American professional sports, playing American professional sports in overseas venues, international sales of licensed merchandise, programs created to increase the global popularity of American professional sports leagues, and the increasing numbers of foreign athletes who play in American professional sports leagues. The dramatic increase in the recruitment of Latin American players by MLB teams raises the issue of the unsavory side of globalization. Commentators allege that MLB teams systematically afford Latin American baseball prospects less favorable treatment than American baseball prospects. See, e.g., Jorge Castillo, *Why Haven't MLB and Players Agreed on an International Draft? Money, Mistrust, and More*, L.A. Times.com, July 8, 2022, https://www.latimes.com/sports/story/2022-07-08/mlb-international-draft; Angela White, Comment, *Curtailing MLB's Recruiting Abuses of Latin American Talent*, 2 Mich. St. Int'l L. Rev. 699 (2017). A small proportion of Latin American prospects become MLB stars. The vast majority wash out of baseball before making it to the major leagues, or even the minor leagues, and "[u]nlike players in the U.S., Latin American players are not encouraged to have a backup plan." Instead, pseudo-agents, known as *buscónes*, who work loosely with MLB teams to identify young talent, often "encourage these children to forgo a formal education to focus on baseball full-time." White, *supra*, at 718. Angela White argues in her article, *Curtailing MLB's Recruiting Abuses of Latin American Talent*, that this system, "which is essentially unstructured and unregulated," must be reformed. *Id.*

Another race-related issue on the international stage is athletes being subject to racist behavior while playing. This phenomenon is most prevalent at European soccer matches where racist signs and chants have been commonplace for decades. In April 2019, UEFA (Union of European Football Associations) president Aleksander Ceferin acknowledged the magnitude of the problem: "It's 2019. How can that happen? I'm ashamed that here in Europe not a weekend goes by without a discriminatory act taking place in a football stadium, amateur level or professional level. I'm ashamed to see extremist movements use our sport as a vehicle for their messages of hate and intolerance." While FIFA and UEFA protocol empower referees to stop matches if spectators racially abuse players, referees rarely do so. Liam Twomey, *UEFA President "Ashamed" at Number of Racist Incidents in European Football*, ESPN.com, Apr. 2, 2019, https://www.espn.com/soccer/uefa-champions-league/story/3814751/uefa-president-ashamed-at-number-of-racist-incidents-in-european-football. In the absence of European soccer governing bodies and their referees taking aggressive action to stamp out racial abuse of players at games, might the European Union step in to protect the players? Although the EU "has no direct authority over sport," legal scholar Michael Ryan argues that Article 13 of the Treaty of Amsterdam "could be interpreted to permit the EU to enact measures to combat spectator racism" and could therefore empower the European Union to address the issue through law. See Michael W. Ryan, *The European Union and Fan Racism in European Soccer Stadiums: The Time Has Come for Action*, 20 Fla. J. Int'l L. 245 (2009).

Currently, however, soccer players of color in Europe are left largely unprotected and to their own devices. While some athletes have understandably walked off of the field in protest, others have taken to social media to challenge the racist behavior. For instance, after being serenaded with monkey noises and having bananas thrown at them and other players of color in Spain's First Division, La Liga, during the 2013–14 season, Neymar and Dani Alves, both from Brazil and at the time playing for FC Barcelona, planned a social media counterattack. They decided that when a banana was next thrown at one of them during a game, he would peel it and eat it on the field in view of the cameras, and Alves did just that on April 27, 2014. Immediately thereafter, Neymar posted a picture on social media sites of him eating a banana, with the note, "We are all monkeys." Before long other athletes, celebrities, and dignitaries around the world—including Brazil's President—posted similar messages in solidarity with the targeted players. In addition to raising awareness of racial abuse in soccer, the social media campaign ensured that authorities pursued the perpetrator, and he was ultimately arrested on charges "related to racist provocation." James Rush, *Revealed: How Barcelona Players PLANNED Banana-Eating Riposte in Advance—As Fruit-Throwing Fan Is Arrested*, Daily Mail, Apr. 30, 2014. Racist abuse from fans, however, has continued, particularly in La Liga. For instance, Real Madrid striker Vinicius "Vini" Jr. (from Brazil) has been frequently abused since he joined Real Madrid in 2018 and was racially abused no fewer than eight times during the 2022–23 season. After one particularly vile verbal attack, Vini began a shouting match with the perpetrators and followed up with Instagram posts, including the following: "This wasn't the first time, or the second, or the third. . . . Racism is normal in La Liga. The competition thinks it's normal, the federation does too, and opponents encourage it." Vini's posts prompted authorities in Spain to prosecute three of the perpetrators and, like the activism of Neymar and Dani Alves several years earlier, sparked international conversation. Most notably, Brazil's President implored FIFA and La Liga to "take measures so we don't allow racism and fascism to take over." Mauricio Savarese, *Brazil's President, Players Support Vinicius Junior, Criticize Racism in Spanish League*, AP, May 21, 2023, *https://apnews.com/article/brazil-lula-vinicius-racism-spain-23c422fd5b422eabfb7545ce107a3dd8*. Sadly, history provides no reason to believe that racist fan abuse in La Liga or elsewhere in European soccer will recede.

Yet another issue that demonstrates the confluence of race and internationality involves some leagues' player age eligibility rules. For instance, both the NBA and WNBA have eligibility rules permitting non-U.S. citizens to enter the leagues at a younger age than U.S. citizens. Given that the NBA's and WNBA's domestic player pools are largely black and that their international player pools are largely non-black, consider whether these age eligibility rules might be viewed as racially discriminatory. For further exploration of this argument, see N. Jeremi Duru, *This Field Is Our Field: Foreign Players, Domestic Leagues, and the Unlawful Racial Manipulation of American Sport*, 84 Tul. L. Rev. 613 (2010).

CASE LAW

KEY TERMS
- Disparate impact
- Disparate treatment
- Initial eligibility rules
- Prima facie case

The cases and summaries that follow address four (among many) contexts in which race has emerged as an issue in sports: (1) the development and promulgation of NCAA initial-eligibility rules; (2) employment discrimination claims asserted by coaches of color; (3) the use by American sports teams of Native American mascots, names, and symbols; and (4) racially hostile environments. Collectively, these cases provide a glimpse into the complexity of the race-related legal issues that arise in sports.

A. Academic Racism and Marginalization: NCAA Initial-Eligibility Rules

The topic of manipulating eligibility rules to bring about higher-level academic performance can cause stakeholders a great deal of trepidation. Initial-eligibility rules are designed to improve the academic level of achievement of those playing intercollegiate sports. This is done by establishing eligibility rules requiring higher grade point averages (GPAs) and standardized test scores. Over the years, these escalating standards have served to increase graduation rates, but not without controversy.

In 1983, NCAA initial-eligibility rules, known as Proposition 48, were enacted to take effect in 1986. Proposition 48's minimum standards required that a student-athlete achieve a minimum GPA of 2.0 in at least 11 designated high school courses (core courses). In addition, it required a minimum combined score of 700 on the SAT or 15 on the ACT. In 1992, the NCAA enacted Proposition 16, which increased the number of core courses in which a student must have a minimum GPA and created an eligibility formula that put a greater emphasis on test scores, which, on net, heightened the eligibility threshold. Critics assailed the requirements of both Proposition 16 and Proposition 48 as racially biased. They argued that heightened standards would reduce many African-American student-athletes' access to college, standardized tests are culturally biased against African-Americans, and standardized tests fail to take into account the unique circumstances of student-athletes. Proponents of stricter initial-eligibility rules argued that such requirements would help to restore academic integrity to colleges and universities that had been undermined by scandals arising within intercollegiate athletics and represented a means of ensuring that student-athletes have a reasonable chance of obtaining a meaningful degree. Informative discussions of the debate surrounding the enactment of NCAA initial-eligibility rules can be found in Timothy Davis, *The Myth of the Superspade: The Persistence of Racism in Intercollegiate Athletics*, 22 Fordham Urban L.J. 615 (1995) and Kenneth L. Shropshire, *Colorblind Propositions: Race, the SAT, and the NCAA*, 8 Stan. L. & Pol'y Rev. 141 (1997).

Not surprisingly, courts have been called on to enter the debate. In 1997, student-athletes of color sued the NCAA, claiming that Proposition 16 violated regulations promulgated under Title VI of the 1964 Civil Rights Act because of its disparate impact on African-American athletes. The district court concluded that Proposition 16 did in fact have a disparate impact on African-American athletes in violation of the regulations and permanently enjoined the enforcement of Proposition 16. It did so even though it accepted the NCAA's stated justification that Proposition 16 was a way to raise all student-athletes' graduation rates. *Cureton v. NCAA*, 37 F. Supp. 2d 687 (E.D. Pa. 1999).

On appeal, however, the Third Circuit reversed that decision. *Cureton v. NCAA*, 198 F.3d 107 (3d Cir. 1999). The appellate court concluded that the regulations in question applied only to specific programs or activities using federal funds, not to the whole entity. Because the NCAA program allegedly receiving direct funding was not at issue, the regulations could become applicable only if the NCAA had controlling authority over some relevant program receiving federal funding, such as a member school's athletic scholarship program. The court concluded that the NCAA did not exercise controlling authority over member institutions' ultimate decisions about student-athletes' eligibility to participate in athletics, and thus it was not subject to the regulations. For discussions of *Cureton v. NCAA* and the controversy surrounding the standardized test component of the NCAA's initial-eligibility rules, see Diane Heckman, *Tracking Challenges to NCAA's Academic Eligibility Requirements Based on Race and Disability*, 222 Ed. L. Rep. 1 (2007); Eli D. Oates, *Cureton v. NCAA: The Recognition of Proposition 16's Misplaced Use of Standardized Tests in the Context of Collegiate Athletics as a Barrier to Educational Opportunity for Minorities*, 35 Wake Forest L. Rev. 445 (2000); and Kenneth L. Shropshire, *Colorblind Propositions: Race, the SAT, and the NCAA*, 8 Stan. L. & Pol'y Rev. 141 (1997).

Another example is *Pryor v. NCAA*, 288 F.3d 548 (3d Cir. 2002). In that case, the plaintiffs, black student-athletes, alleged that "[t]he NCAA purportedly tried to improve graduation rates among black student athletes by adopting Proposition 16, a facially neutral rule that establishes scholarship and athletic eligibility criteria for incoming student athletes. As a result of these criteria, Plaintiffs allege, Proposition 16 has caused increased numbers of black student athletes to lose eligibility for receiving athletic scholarships and for participating in intercollegiate athletics during their freshmen year. Plaintiffs further alleged that defendant knew of these effects and intended them. And thus, Plaintiffs suggest that the NCAA actually adopted Proposition 16 to 'screen out' more black student athletes from ever receiving athletic scholarships in the first place, with the asserted goal of increased graduation rates serving as a mere 'pretext.' . . ." The *Pryor* court ruled that the issue of purposeful discrimination under Title VI of the Civil Rights Act of 1964 and 42 U.S.C. §1981 should be explored further and remanded the case to the lower court.

What are your thoughts? Is there any reason that the NCAA would seek to reduce the number of black student-athletes eligible to compete?

In November 2002, the NCAA passed legislation that radically altered its initial-eligibility rules. This legislation became effective with the class of student-athletes who matriculated in 2005. The revised initial-eligibility standards eliminate the cutoff score for the standardized test component of the initial eligibility requirements. For example, under the alteration, a student with a 3.0, or solid B average, needed to score 620 on the SAT to be eligible for competition and financial aid during his or her first year. The minimum SAT score ranged from 400 (for students with a GPA of 3.55 or more) to 1010 (for students with a 2.0 GPA). The scoring range on the SAT is 400 to 1600. The number of core courses increased from 13 to 14 for student-athletes who matriculated in 2005. This number increased to 16 for students who entered college in 2008. Late NCAA president Myles Brand explained that "the goal in developing the most recent eligibility models was to maximize graduation rates while minimizing disparate impact. . . ." *Athlete Graduation Rates Continue to Climb*, NCAA News, Sept. 1, 2003, at 1, 11. In 2012, the NCAA passed legislation imposing even stricter initial eligibility rules, which apply to students who entered college after August 1, 2016. However, in response to testing inconveniences spurred by the COVID-19 pandemic in 2020, the NCAA waived the minimum standardized test score requirement for incoming freshmen athletes. In 2023, the NCAA elected to remove the requirement altogether. See Meghan Durham, *NCAA Division I Council Modernizes Rules for Coaching Limits*, NCAA, Jan. 11, 2023, https://www.ncaa.com/news/ncaa/article/2023-01-11/ncaa-division-i-council-modernizes-rules-coaching-limits.

Although racial disparities in the Graduation Success Rates (GSR) for NCAA athletes have narrowed over the years, the November 2022 GSR release revealed that they persist. The Division I GSR for African-American athletes was 81 percent while the GSR for Division I white athletes was 94 percent. The GSR gap for African-American and white female Division I athletes is notably smaller, with African-American females achieving a GSR of 90 percent and white females achieving a GSR of 97 percent. NCAA Research, *Trends in NCAA Division I Graduation Rates*, NCAA 14, 15, Nov. 22, 2022.

QUESTIONS

1. What are the implications of the NCAA's change in its initial-eligibility rules? What impact will it have on the ability of colleges and universities to enroll student-athletes and provide them with scholarships? Do the revised standards

enhance the importance of the academic standards adopted by each institution for the admission of student-athletes? Can the increased NCAA graduation rate be considered a success when the graduation rate for African-Americans is substantially lower than the overall rate?

2. In 2014, following alleged academic improprieties in the University of North Carolina's athletic program, an independent report revealed that thousands of UNC students took fraudulent "paper classes," that nearly 50 percent of those students were athletes, and that a disproportionate number of the athletes were African-American. Kenneth L. Wainstein et al., *Investigation of Irregular Classes in the Department of African and Afro-American Studies at the University of North Carolina at Chapel Hill*, 33-36, 125 (2014). After the report's release, several former UNC student-athletes sued the university, arguing that coaches and athletic administrators directed them to take these classes to pad their grade point averages and keep them eligible to represent the school athletically. The suits settled in 2017, so the court did not reach the merits. Similar allegations have been made against other NCAA schools. If the complaining student-athletes were in fact directed to take fraudulent courses, what might the NCAA do to prevent such grade manipulation by member institutions?

Problem 6-1

The NCAA is considering a number of proposals designed ostensibly to increase graduation rates of basketball players at the Division I level. The National Association for Coaching Equity and Development has asked for your advice regarding a couple of the proposals. One proposal is designed to improve graduation rates by creating disincentives for NCAA programs with lower graduation rates. The proposal in question would provide for a reduction of two scholarships for programs with graduation rates that fall below 75 percent and four scholarships for programs with graduation rates below 60 percent. A number of coaches fear that the proposals will harm their programs because they take players from weaker high schools, many of which are poorly funded inner-city schools in which a large percentage of the students are of color. The coaches believe that it is more difficult to maintain the higher graduation standards with student-athletes from these underresourced schools. As such, they believe the proposal is questionable on racial equity grounds. A second proposal calls for incentives in the form of additional scholarships for schools with graduation rates above 80 percent (one new scholarship at 80 percent, two at 90 percent, and three at 100 percent). Once again, many of the coaches believe this requirement may benefit universities that recruit heavily from wealthier school districts, which include fewer students of color. A few coaches in the association disagree and support the graduation incentives and disincentives as necessary to increase the number of athletes of color graduating from universities. Are there legal or ethical problems with the proposals as outlined?

> What response should the National Association for Coaching Equity and Development offer to such proposals at the legislative level within the NCAA? Consider the following materials.

B. Employment Discrimination

As discussed previously, race has been identified as a factor that limits access to coaching and administrative positions and promotion opportunities for people of color in college and professional sports. In the few instances in which coaches of color have alleged racial discrimination in hiring and promotion in sports, they have resorted to Title VII of the Civil Rights Act of 1964 and Section 1981 of the Civil Rights Act of 1866. Title VII prohibits discrimination in employment. Under Title VII, a plaintiff is likely to assert claims premised on disparate treatment (which focuses on intentional racial discrimination) or disparate impact (which focuses on the use of facially neutral employment practices) that unjustifiably discriminate against members of a protected group. Section 1981 is broader in scope in that it applies to the making, performance, and enforcement of all contracts, not just employment contracts. Section 1981 proscribes intentional discrimination.

Jackson v. University of New Haven provides a detailed examination of the proof that plaintiffs must establish in order to prevail in Title VII and Section 1981 actions. *Jackson* also reveals that the proof required to establish a cognizable Title VII or Section 1981 claim limits the effectiveness of these antidiscrimination statutes for those seeking redress for alleged racial discrimination.

Jackson v. University of New Haven
228 F. Supp. 2d 156 (D. Conn. 2002)

DRONEY, District Judge.

I. Introduction

[Editors' note: James C. Jackson (Jackson) brought a lawsuit alleging that the University of New Haven (UNH) and its athletic director, Deborah Chin, discriminated against him in hiring in violation of federal antidiscrimination laws. The court granted defendants' motion for summary judgment.]

II. Facts

In February 1999, the head football coach at the University of New Haven ("UNH") left to take a position with the Cleveland Browns of the National Football League. This dispute arises out of the ensuing search for a new head coach at UNH.

Beginning in early February of 1999, UNH posted the head coach position both internally and with the "NCAA market," an online professional publication for university and college athletics. The postings for the head coaching position listed the following requirements:

> A bachelor's degree is required, master's degree preferred. *Successful collegiate coaching experience required*. Experience in recruiting, game coaching and knowledge of NCAA rules and regulations is essential.

Further, the duties were listed as follows:

> Implement and manage all aspects of a national caliber Division II football program in accordance with NCAA and university regulations. Areas of responsibility include, but are not limited to coaching, recruiting qualified student athletes, budget management, scheduling, hiring and supervising coaching staff, academically monitoring student-athletes, and promotions and fund-raising.

After receiving 36 applications, UNH's Search Committee, which had been established to select a new head coach, decided to interview six applicants — all of whom had college coaching experience and are Caucasian. Jackson, an African-American, was not among the six applicants interviewed. Jackson had no college experience, but had been a professional minor league football coach, earned several "coach of the year" honors as such a coach, and was inducted into the minor league football hall of fame. The defendants assert that they decided not to interview Jackson because he lacked the requisite collegiate coaching experience. From the six applicants interviewed, the Search Committee ultimately selected Darren Rizzi, who had been an assistant coach at UNH for four years, to fill the position of head coach.

At the heart of this dispute lies the "collegiate coaching experience" requirement. The parties are in agreement that the posted job qualifications included that requirement and that all of the applicants selected for interviews possessed such experience. However, the parties differ markedly in their characterizations of that prior experience requirement. The defendants maintain that prior NCAA coaching experience was essential to ensure the selection of a candidate sufficiently well-versed in NCAA rules and regulations to both pass the NCAA's annual tests on such regulations and manage the UNH football team successfully. Jackson, however, asserts that the requirement of previous collegiate coaching experience was not necessary to ensure familiarity with NCAA rules and regulations and that it served to exclude otherwise qualified minority applicants, such as himself.

Jackson asserts that the requirement that applicants have prior college coaching experience amounts to discrimination in violation of 42 U.S.C. §1981, 42 U.S.C. §2000d (Title VI), and 42 U.S.C. §2000e-5 (Title VII). Jackson asserts all three of these statutory causes of action against defendant UNH. However, only the §1981 claim is asserted against defendant Chin.

Jackson appears to base his complaint on both the "disparate treatment" and "disparate impact" theories of recovery in that he alleges both that the challenged qualification had a discriminatory effect upon African-Americans (disparate impact) and that the defendants intentionally discriminated against him based on his race (disparate treatment). . . .

IV. Analysis

A. Disparate Treatment Claim

As mentioned, Jackson alleges that he has been discriminated against in violation of 42 U.S.C. §§1981, 2000d (Title VI), and 2000e-5 (Title VII). To the extent that he claims that he has been discriminated against intentionally, the U.S. Supreme Court has developed a "burden shifting framework" for claims brought under Title VII alleging "disparate treatment." *McDonnell Douglas Corp. v. Green*, 411 U.S. 792, 802, 93 S.Ct. 1817, 36L.Ed.2d 668 (1973). Courts have subsequently applied the same burden-shifting framework articulated in *McDonnell Douglas* to disparate treatment claims arising under 42 U.S.C. §§1981 and 2000d (Title VI). . . . Thus, because the test is the same under each of the three statutes, this Court will apply the same *McDonnell Douglas* burden-shifting framework to the plaintiff's disparate treatment claim.

Under the burden-shifting framework of *McDonnell Douglas*, a plaintiff alleging disparate treatment based on race and national origin must first establish a prima facie case of discrimination. 411 U.S. at 802, 93 S.Ct. 1817. The burden then shifts to the defendant to offer a legitimate, nondiscriminatory rationale for its actions. See *James v. New York Racing Ass'n*, 233 F.3d 149, 154 (2d Cir.2000). Finally, if the defendant does offer a non-discriminatory reason for its decision, the burden again shifts to the plaintiff to show that the defendant's stated reason is a mere pretext for discrimination. See Id. (citing *St. Mary's Honor Ctr. v. Hicks*, 509 U.S. 502, 506–10, 113 S.Ct. 2742, 125 L.Ed.2d 407 (1993)). In some circumstances, . . . after the plaintiff offers evidence to show that the defendant's asserted non-discriminatory reason for the hiring is pretextual, the evidence that established the prima facie case will be sufficient to survive a summary judgment motion. . . . Here, the burden-shifting framework does not reach this stage because Jackson has failed to establish a prima facie case.

To establish a prima facie case of discrimination, a plaintiff must show (1) membership in a protected class, (2) qualification for the employment, (3) an adverse employment decision, and (4) circumstances that give rise to an inference of discrimination. *McDonnell Douglas*, 411 U.S. at 802, 93 S.Ct. 1817. . . . Courts have acknowledged this framework is "not inflexible," but that "in establishing a prima facie case the plaintiff must show that [he] applied for an available position for which [he] was qualified, but was rejected under circumstances that give rise to an inference of discrimination." *Brown v. Coach Stores, Inc.*, 163 F.3d 706, 710 (2d Cir. 1998) (citing *Texas Dep't of Cmty. Affairs v. Burdine*, 450 U.S. 248, 253, 101 S.Ct. 1089, 67 L.Ed.2d 207 (1981)) (internal quotation marks omitted).

The parties do not dispute that Jackson is a member of a protected class. Nor do they dispute that the defendants' decision to hire Rizzi instead of Jackson was adverse to him. However, the parties disagree as to whether Jackson meets the second prong of *McDonnell Douglas:* qualification for the position. In their Motion for Summary Judgment, the defendants assert that Jackson was not qualified because he failed to meet an express condition of the employment, that he did not have prior NCAA coaching experience. Although he maintains that he is qualified, Jackson does not dispute that prior collegiate coaching was an expressly listed qualification for the UNH head coach position, nor does he contend that he had any prior experience coaching in college. However, Jackson's subjective determination that he is qualified for the position is not enough to carry his burden of making out a prima facie case.

Consistent with this understanding, courts have afforded employers considerable latitude in selecting employment qualifications. For example, in *Schaffner v. Glencoe Park Dist.*, 256 F.3d 616 (7th Cir. 2001) the Seventh Circuit considered the "qualification prong" of the *McDonnell Douglas* burden-shifting framework in the context of an ADEA claim. 256 F.3d at 620. There the plaintiff was denied a promotion to the position of "program manager" for park recreational programs — a position that listed as one of its requirements one of several types of bachelor's degrees. The court held that the plaintiff failed to meet the qualification prong of the *McDonnell Douglas* test because she did not possess any of the specified degrees, and was therefore not qualified for the position. . . .

[D]eference must be given the defendants in selecting college coaching experience as a qualification for the position of head coach. Nor is it appropriate for this Court to mandate that the defendants equate Jackson's experience in coaching minor league football with college coaching experience. . . .

There are, however, limits to an employer's latitude in selecting hiring criteria. For example, in *Howley v. Town of Stratford*, 217 F.3d 141 (2d Cir. 2000) the Second Circuit rejected the defendant's argument that the plaintiff, a female firefighter, was "ineligible" for a promotion to assistant-chief because she did not have the required four years of line-officer experience. 217 F.3d at 151. The Court acknowledged that the town was "entitled to set its own criteria" for the position but held that because the Town had "relaxed" that standard for two male firefighters, the plaintiff's lack of experience should not have resulted in summary judgment for the defendant. *Id.* at 151–52.

Here, there is no claim, and Jackson has put forth no evidence, that the defendants failed to apply the prior college coaching experience requirement uniformly to African-Americans and others. Absent any such showing, the defendants are entitled to the deference in selecting hiring criteria recognized in *Thornley*. Moreover, the prior college coaching experience requirement at issue here appears reasonable on its face. There is an obvious and significant nexus between the defendants' need to select a head coach well-versed in NCAA regulations and the requirement that candidates have actual experience in college coaching. Thus, Jackson has failed to make out a prima facie case of disparate treatment in that he has failed to demonstrate that he was qualified for the position of head coach. As Jackson has failed to meet his burden, this Court grants summary judgment as to his disparate treatment claim brought pursuant to 42 U.S.C. §§1981, 2000d (Title VI), and 2000e-5 (Title VII).

B. Disparate Impact

Unlike disparate treatment, in asserting a claim of disparate impact under Title VII a plaintiff need not allege that the discrimination was intentional. *Griggs v. Duke Power Co.*, 401 U.S. 424, 430-32, 91 S.Ct. 849, 28 L.Ed.2d 158 (1971) ("[G]ood intent or absence of discriminatory intent does not redeem employment procedures or testing mechanisms that operate as 'built in head winds'"). It is enough that a facially-neutral policy, such as the prior college coaching experience requirement at issue here, be shown to have an adverse impact on a protected group....

However, unlike disparate treatment, the disparate impact theory of recovery is available only for claims brought pursuant to Title VII, and not for claims under 42 U.S.C. §1981 or §2000(d) (Title VI). The U.S. Supreme Court has held that these latter provisions can only be violated by intentional discrimination and that they therefore cannot support a "disparate impact" claim. See *Alexander v. Sandoval*, 532 U.S. 275, 280-85, 121 S.Ct. 1511, 149 L.Ed.2d 517 (2001) (holding that §2000d (Title VI) proscribes only intentional discrimination and therefore does not support a disparate impact theory of recovery) (citing *Regents of Univ. of Cal. v. Bakke*, 438 U.S. 265, 98 S.Ct. 2733, 57 L.Ed.2d 750 (1978)).... Thus, to the extent that Jackson alleges a disparate impact theory of recovery, his claim is cognizable only under Title VII.

Disparate impact cases, like disparate treatment cases, are governed by a "burden-shifting" framework. The Second Circuit reviewed the disparate impact burden-shifting framework in *NAACP, Inc. v. Town of East Haven*, 70 F.3d 219, 225 (2d Cir.1995):

> "[A] plaintiff may establish a prima facie case of disparate impact by showing that use of the test causes the selection of applicants . . . in a racial pattern that significantly differs from that of the pool of applicants." Such a showing can be established through the use of statistical evidence which discloses a disparity so great that it cannot reasonably be attributed to chance. To establish a prima facie case, the statistical disparity must be sufficiently substantial to raise an inference of causation. After a prima facie case is established, the employer has the burden of coming forward with evidence to show that the test has "'a manifest relationship to the employment in question.'" If the employer can make such a showing, the plaintiff may nonetheless prevail if he can suggest alternative tests or selection methods that would meet the employer's legitimate needs while reducing the racially disparate impact of the employer's practices. [Citations omitted.]

Id. at 225.... As the Court noted in *East Haven*, this framework was statutorily enacted by the Civil Rights Act of 1991. *Id.* at 225 fn. 6. See also 42 U.S.C. §2000e-2(k).

Here, as in the disparate treatment context, Jackson has failed to meet his burden of setting forth a prima facie case of disparate treatment. In making out a prima facie case for disparate impact under Title VII, the plaintiff bears the burden of demonstrating that a specific policy or practice of the defendant has had a disproportionately negative impact on the plaintiff's protected class. 42 U.S.C.

Section 2000e-2(k)(1)(A) . . . ; *Griggs*, 401 U.S. at 432, 91 S.Ct. 849. "To make this showing, a plaintiff must (1) identify a policy or practice, (2) demonstrate that a disparity exists, and (3) establish a causal relationship between the two." *Robinson*, 267 F.3d at 160 (citing 42 U.S.C. §2000e-2(k)(1)(A)(I)). Here, Jackson alleges that the defendants' facially neutral hiring criteria (requiring prior college coaching experience), had a discriminatory impact on African-Americans. Specifically, Jackson asserts that because African-Americans have historically been under-represented in the ranks of NCAA coaches, this requirement disproportionately excludes African-Americans from consideration.

Statistics are often an important component of a disparate impact claim. See *Robinson*, 267 F.3d at 160 ("[S]tatistical proof almost always occupies center stage in a prima facie showing of a disparate impact claim"). . . .

The defendants here attack the sufficiency of the plaintiff's statistics. They argue that the plaintiff has not offered any statistical evidence to indicate a causal link between UNH's prior college coaching experience requirement and its negative impact on African-Americans. However, Jackson does offer statistics suggesting a causal link between the prior experience requirement and its impact on African-Americans, by comparing the pool of applicants to those who were ultimately selected for interviews. Jackson notes that, of the 14 applicants whose race was identified, only 10% of the Caucasians (1 out of 10) did not have college coaching experience, but 50% of the African-American candidates (2 out of 4) did not have college coaching experience. Further, Jackson noted that all six of the applicants selected for interviews were Caucasian. However, this statistical evidence fails to establish a sufficient causal link between the defendants' employment criterion and its impact on African-Americans. The Second Circuit has recognized that exceedingly small sample sizes often result in statistically unreliable evidence. *Lowe v. Commack Union Free Sch. Dist.*, 886 F.2d 1364, 1371–72 (2d Cir. 1989) (holding that the fact that two out of three candidates under age 40 received favorable ratings while only 16 out of 34 candidates over age 40 received such ratings did not support a disparate impact claim in part because of "the unreliability of such a small statistical sample") (superseded by statute on other grounds). The Second Circuit has also indicated that a plaintiff's statistics must meet a certain threshold level of substantiality. . . . Here, the relevant sample size is only 14 (of the 36 applicants, the race of only 14 has been identified), which is too small to yield a statistically significant result. . . . In this case, the plaintiff has failed to provide a sufficiently substantial disparity to survive summary judgment, because the sample is too small.

In addition to the statistics discussed above, the plaintiff has presented an article from the *Sports Business Journal*, which purportedly demonstrates the disparity of college football coaches that are African-American. However, this article — without more — does not present the type of substantial statistical evidence contemplated by the Second Circuit in *Smith*. It is only two pages long, and most of it is an opinion piece rather than a scientific statistical analysis. . . . [T]he essence of a disparate impact analysis is a *comparison*. In *Carter v. Ball*, 33 F.3d 450 (4th Cir. 1994) . . . , the court emphasized that "[i]n a case of discrimination in hiring or promoting, the relevant comparison is between the percentage of minority employees and the percentage of potential minority applicants in the qualified labor pool. . . . The mere absence of minority employees in upper-level positions does not suffice to prove a *prima facie* case of discrimination without a comparison to the relevant labor pool." *Id.* . . .

Finally, also in support of his disparate impact claim, the plaintiff asserts that the use of the prior college coaching experience requirement has yielded discriminatory results when applied to other athletic programs at UNH. The plaintiff contends that only one out of 23 coaches hired since 1993, when the plaintiff asserts the prior college coaching experience requirement was adopted for most head coaching positions at UNH, has been African-American. However, even if true, the Supreme Court held in *Wards Cove* that "[t]he percentage of nonwhite workers found in other positions in the employer's labor force is irrelevant to the question of a prima facie statistical case of disparate impact." 490 U.S. at 653, 109 S.Ct. 2115. Thus, the plaintiff has failed to meet his burden of establishing a prima facie case of disparate impact, and this Court also grants summary judgment as to that claim.

For the forgoing reasons, the defendant's Motion for Summary Judgment . . . is GRANTED and the case is DISMISSED.

QUESTIONS

1. The plaintiff based his complaint on "disparate treatment" and "disparate impact" grounds. What is the difference between these arguments as a factual and a legal matter?
2. How much latitude should a university be given in setting coaching experience and related requirements as a prerequisite for consideration in the hiring process? If you were representing a university involved in such a search, what would you recommend as a legal and practical matter?

Problem 6-2

Midwestern State University, a Football Bowl Subdivision (FBS) power that had fallen on hard times, advertised for a new head football coach. The ad indicated that previous football coaching experience was required. Several applicants applied, including Coach Ross, the head football coach at another college, who was also a friend and former colleague of Midwestern's athletic director, Shoemaker. Ross, who had over 15 years of collegiate coaching experience, including eight years as a head coach, applied after being persuaded by Shoemaker to do so. Ross and Shoemaker are both white.

A search committee, chaired by Shoemaker, reviewed numerous applications and invited two applicants for on-campus interviews. One applicant was Ross. The other was an African-American, Coach Pegues, who had played college and professional football. Pegues coached at an FBS institution for four years, where he served first as running back coach and then

> as wide receiver coach. From there, Pegues moved to the NFL, where he coached for seven years for two teams. He served as quarterback coach for the first team for two years. For the past five years, Pegues has served as offensive coordinator for a different NFL team.
>
> During the on-campus interviews, Ross and Pegues met with various constituencies, including football student-athletes, the search committee, a faculty committee, and athletic department personnel. Both received favorable responses from the groups with whom they met. However, the faculty, athletes, and athletic department personnel stated that they preferred Pegues. During the search committee's deliberations, Shoemaker stated: "Perhaps I shouldn't say this, but I have to be honest. I feel uneasy with Pegues. How do we know if he'll be outspoken like those athletes back in 2020 who were vocal about 'Black Lives Matter'? I'm also concerned with how the major donors to our football program will react to him. We wouldn't want to lose a major source of financial support by hiring this guy. It wouldn't be worth it." After vigorous debate, the search committee concluded that both candidates were qualified to serve as head football coach. The committee understood, however, that it served in an advisory capacity and the final decision rested with the athletic director, Shoemaker.
>
> Shoemaker extended an offer to Ross, who declined. Shoemaker decided not to extend an offer to Pegues. In explaining why he did not, Shoemaker stated, "Pegues is highly qualified, and I wish him well. I simply don't think he is a good fit for our program."
>
> Pegues has come to your office seeking advice on whether he should pursue an action for employment discrimination on account of race. How would you advise him?

C. Stereotypes: Racially Stereotyped Mascots — Racism or Pride?

American sports teams have been using Native American names and mascots for over a century, beginning with baseball's Boston Braves in 1912. Thousands of professional, collegiate, and high school sports teams have done the same since. Whether such use is appropriate, however, engenders intense debate. The United States governing body for Lacrosse, a game invented by Native Americans, is the one sports governing body that has taken a definitive stance on the matter. In 2019, US Lacrosse released a statement reading: "While some people contend these mascots are harmless and are even respectful of indigenous communities, the reality is that they represent the continued dehumanization of Native peoples." The statement went on to announce that US Lacrosse would ban the use of "offensive or stereotypical mascots and logos at events that US Lacrosse controls." Paul Ohanian, *US Lacrosse Position Statement on Native American Mascots*, US Lacrosse, Feb. 7, 2019, https://www.uslacrosse.org/blog/us-lacrosse-position-statement-on-native-american-mascots. Lacrosse aside, the use of Native American names and mascots is an unresolved hot-button issue across collegiate and professional sport.

1. The NCAA's Approach

The NCAA has taken an approach that seeks to satisfy both those who believe the use of Native American names and mascots honors Native Americans and those who believe that such use is disparaging. Although the NCAA does not prohibit the use of Native American names and mascots generally, it "prohibits NCAA colleges and universities from displaying hostile and abusive racial/ethnic/national origin mascots, nicknames or imagery at any of the 88 NCAA championships." Gary T. Brown, *Policy Applies Core Principles to Mascot Issue*, 42 NCAA News, Aug. 15, 2005, at 1, 19. Because hosting and participating in NCAA championships is the ultimate goal for collegiate athletic programs, this policy strongly disincentivizes schools from using such names and mascots. If, however, a school can show that its use of a Native American name or mascot is not "hostile and abusive," the NCAA permits its use. Generally, for a school to make such a showing, it must satisfy the NCAA that the namesake tribe has "formally approved of the use of the mascot, name, and imagery." *NCAA Executive Committee Approves Native American Mascot Appeals Process*, http://fs.ncaa.org/Docs/PressArchive/2005/Announcements/NCAA%2BExecutive%2BCommittee%2BApproves%2BNative%2BAmerican%2BMascot%2BAppeals%2BProcess.html.

Through this process, several institutions, including Florida State University, Central Michigan University, and the University of Utah, have established to the satisfaction of the NCAA's Executive Committee that their use of a Native American name, mascot, or symbol honors, rather than disparages, Native Americans. Other institutions have been unable to satisfy the NCAA's requirement because they did not have formal approval from the namesake tribe. For instance, when the University of North Dakota (UND) sought an exception to the NCAA's rule in 2005, arguing that its team name, the "Fighting Sioux," was not "hostile and offensive," two Sioux tribes opposed the school's use of the name, and the school's effort failed. Rebecca Aronauer, *Tribes' Views on Mascot Names Hold Sway with NCAA*, Chron. Higher Educ., Oct. 15, 2005. Several years of litigation ensued, but UND ultimately conceded and changed its teams' name to the Fighting Hawks.

Many other universities, pursuant to grassroots pressure or under no pressure at all, have decided over the years to abandon their Native American names and mascots, and, in 2019, Maine became the first U.S. state to ban the use of Native American names and mascots in all of its public educational institutions. At the time of this writing, 20 other state legislatures have either passed or introduced legislation to do the same. Scott Neuman, *As Schools Face Calls to Drop Native American Mascots, Some Could Lose State Money*, NPR.org, April 19, 2023, https://www.npr.org/2023/04/19/1170590167/native-american-school-mascots-new-york-ban.

2. The Professional Context

None of America's major professional sports leagues have moved to ban or limit the use of Native American names and mascots. Consequently, the effort to eliminate Native American names and mascots has taken place on a club-by-club basis. The most notorious such battle in American sports history involved the NFL club known as the Washington Redskins from 1933 through 2020. For decades, the club fought off multiple lawsuits and clung to its name (a dictionary defined racial slur), its mascot (a Native American man with a headdress), and its fight song ("Hail to the Redskins, Hail Victory, Braves on the Warpath . . ."). The suits took an interesting approach. Plaintiffs did not challenge the club's right to use the name and images. Rather, they challenged the club's right to trademark the term "Redskins" under the theory that losing trademark protection would dilute the worth of the name and prompt the club to turn to a different name with which the club could make more money. In 1992, Suzan Harjo and six other plaintiffs petitioned the U.S. Patent and Trademark Office's Trademark Trial and Appeal Board (TTAB) to cancel the six federal trademark registrations held by the club, which does business under the name Pro Football, Inc. (Pro-Football). Plaintiffs argued that use of the word "redskin(s)" is "scandalous," "may . . . disparage" Native Americans, and may cast Native Americans into "contempt, or disrepute" in violation of section 2(a) of the Lanham Trademark Act of 1946. In 1999, the board canceled the registrations, finding that the marks "may disparage" Native Americans or "bring them into contempt or disrepute." *Harjo v. Pro-Football, Inc.*, 50 U.S.P.Q.2d 1705, 1749 (Trademark Tr. & App. Bd. 1999).

On appeal, the United States District Court for the District of Columbia reversed the TTAB on two grounds: (1) the TTAB's finding of disparagement was not substantiated; and (2) the plaintiffs' claims were barred under the doctrine of laches, which prohibits plaintiffs from unreasonable delay in bringing a claim. The United States Court of Appeals for the D.C. Circuit then affirmed the district court's ruling that laches barred the claim, but did not reach the question of disparagement. *Pro-Football, Inc. v. Harjo*, 565 F.3d 880 (D.C. Cir. 2009). While the *Harjo* case was pending, Amanda Blackhorse and several fellow plaintiffs—who could prove as a legal matter that they did not engage in unreasonable delay and therefore faced no laches doctrine obstacle—filed a petition to cancel the club's trademarks, just as the *Harjo* plaintiffs had. As it did in *Harjo*, the TTAB in *Blackhorse* canceled the trademark registrations, but unlike in *Harjo*, the district court on appeal in *Blackhorse* affirmed the trademark cancellations. The court determined that "the findings of fact in Blackhorse were more thorough than the findings of fact in Harjo" and that "the term 'redskin' . . . was offensive and [a term] that 'may disparage' a substantial composite of Native Americans." *Pro-Football, Inc. v. Blackhorse*, 112 F. Supp. 3d 439, 486, 488 (E.D. Va. 2015), *vacated*, 709 F. App'x 182 (4th Cir. 2018).

Pro Football appealed, and with the laches defense irrelevant, the *Blackhorse* plaintiffs and their supporters were optimistic. While the appeal was pending, however, the United States Supreme Court decided a separate but similar case, *Matal v. Tam*, 137 S.Ct. 1744 (2017), which essentially rendered the *Blackhorse* case moot. The *Tam* case involved a musical band that sought to trademark its name—The Slants—but was rejected, as the term "slant" was deemed potentially to disparage Asians. The Supreme Court determined that the trademark should be allowed, declaring that the Lanham Act provision disallowing terms or phrases that "may disparage" persons of a particular background from receiving federal trademark protection is a First Amendment free speech violation. *Matal v. Tam*, 137 S.Ct. 1744, 1765 (2017). The *Blackhorse* plaintiffs, whose claim relied on that very Lanham Act provision, shortly thereafter abandoned their lawsuit, giving Pro Football Inc. the victory.

In the midst of the legal saga, then-Redskins' owner Dan Snyder explained that he is a "lifelong Redskins fan" who loves "the tradition" of the club and insisted "we'll never change the name. . . . It's that simple. NEVER—you can use caps."

Snyder, however, would be forced to eat his words, as public pressure ultimately prevailed where legal action had failed. The police killing of George Floyd and other African-Americans in early 2020 (discussed earlier in this chapter) ignited a national conversation about race and racial subjugation, prompting those who oppose Native American team names and mascots to demand change. In July 2020, under intense pressure from both activists and sponsors, the club announced it would change its name. It played the 2020 and 2021 seasons as the "Washington Football Team" before adopting the name "Commanders" in advance of the 2022 season. Jabari Young, *Washington Football Team Officially Renamed Washington Commanders, Ending a Search That Took More Than One Year*, CNBC.com, Feb. 2, 2022, https://www.cnbc.com/2022/02/02/washington-football-team-officially-renamed-washington-commanders.html.

QUESTIONS

1. Should it matter that an entity using a Native American name or symbol seeks to do so with dignity? If so, what if members of the general U.S. population, or of the Native American population, or of the particular namesake tribe's population, disagree on whether the use is dignified?

2. Consider the University of Notre Dame's use of the "Fighting Irish" name and leprechaun mascot. Does it raise the same issues as a school's use of a Native American name and mascot? A 2021 Quality Logo Products survey found that Notre Dame's Fighting Irish leprechaun, which was adopted by a former school president who was Irish, is the nation's fourth most offensive college football team mascot, behind only San Diego State's Aztec Warrior, Florida State's Osceola and Renegade, and the University of Hawaii's Vili the Warrior. Although "The Fighting Irish" originated as a derogatory term for Irish Catholic students in the early 1900s, Notre Dame has vociferously defended its team name and mascot: "[T[here is no comparison between [our] nickname and mascot and the Indian and warrior names [and] mascots used by other institutions such as the NFL team formerly known as the Redskins. None of these institutions were founded or named by Native Americans who sought

to highlight their heritage by using names and symbols associated with their people. Our symbols stand as celebratory representations of a genuine Irish heritage at Notre Dame, a heritage that we regard with respect, loyalty and affection." Jeremy Layton, Natalie O'Neill & Georgett Roberts, *Notre Dame Leprechaun Considered Offensive, According to Survey* available at *https://nypost.com/2021/08/25/notre-dame-leprechaun-considered-offensive-according-to-survey/*. Do you find Notre Dame's statement compelling? Why or why not?

3. In 2023, George Washington University changed the name of its athletics teams from the "Colonials" to the "Revolutionaries." It did so out of concern that using the name "Colonials" suggested support of colonization, the process by which a group of people takes over the land of others, often subjugating the original inhabitants. Victoria Hernandez, *George Washington University Changes Mascot Name to Revolutionaries*, USAToday.com, May 24, 2023, *https://www.usatoday.com/story/sports/2023/05/24/george-washington-university-changes-mascot-name-to-revolutionaries/70253218007/*. In that the name "Colonials" does not reference or disparage any particular racial or ethnic group, is the concern and consequent name change an overreaction?

Problem 6-3

In 2019, Donor gave $10 million to University. In 2023, Donor pledged another $50 million to University to construct a new state-of-the-art hockey facility for the school. Well into the construction of the facility, controversy erupted concerning whether University should change its nickname, the "Warring Cherokee," and its logo, a majestic Indian head that was designed three years ago by a highly regarded Native American artist. University has one of the nation's top athletic programs. It is also one of the country's leading schools in Native American studies and graduates an estimated 20 percent of the Native American doctors in the United States. The controversy arose when a group of white and Native American students and nonstudents protested the nickname and logo. The controversy was only heightened after Donor entered the fray. Donor threatened to halt construction if the school did not retain the name and logo. As legal counsel for University, how would you advise University to proceed? Are there ethical issues to consider?

D. Racially Hostile Environments and Conduct

The history of sports is replete with examples of racially hostile environments emanating from acts perpetrated by teammates, coaches, and opposing players toward athletes of color. However, as Professor Phoebe Williams explains in her seminal article on the topic—*Performing in Racially Hostile Environments*—fans can also create racially hostile environments. Consider the following problem.

Problem 6-4

A highly paid and very talented African-American NFL running back, Jerome Crawford, had a reputation for being outspoken on what he believed were racial inequities within American society. This resulted in conflicts between Crawford and his teammates as well as team management. During an away game, Crawford was subjected to verbal abuse from fans. Although most of the fans' statements were not racially based, a few were. The latter included threats, such as "we will kill you," and a dummy in blackface hanging from a noose wearing Crawford's jersey number. Crawford reacted by directing an obscene gesture toward the fans. Because of his response, Crawford was fined $10,000 by the NFL for lack of professionalism. Crawford refused to play until the league and individual teams implemented measures to protect African-American players and other players of color from racially motivated abuse by fans. You are general counsel for the team on which Crawford plays. What advice should you give team management as to how it should respond to Crawford's refusal to perform? Once you have settled on an answer, move on to the following materials.

When examining fan-based racial animus, it is important to consider what leagues and teams can and should reasonably expect from athletes on the receiving end of overtly racial statements and conduct. According to Professor Williams, the prevailing attitude is that it becomes the obligation of the athlete as a professional not to lose control. Consequently, professionalism shifts responsibility "for providing an environment free of racial harassment from the employer to the athlete player." Phoebe Williams, *Performing in Racially Hostile Environments*, 6 Marq. Sports L.J. 287, 311 (1996). Consider whether this is a reasonable burden for racially abused professional athletes to bear. Consider the following questions as well.

QUESTIONS

1. Should team owners and league administrators hold fans accountable for racial abuse stemming from activity during a game but expressed through social media outlets such as Instagram rather than in the game venue? In 2012, during the early days of social media, the Washington Capitals' Joel Ward, one of the NHL's few black players, scored a Game 7 playoff overtime goal to propel the Capitals past the Boston Bruins and into the Eastern Conference Semifinals. A "racist tweetstorm" followed in which Ward was menacingly threatened and derided by Bruins fans. The next day Ted Leonsis, the Capitals' owner, issued the following statement:

Shame on these folks who decided to take to their keyboards and show their ignorance and their racism and hate. What these people have said and done is unforgivable. I hope they are now publicly identified and pay a huge price for their beliefs. There should be zero tolerance for this kind of hate mongering.

If those who tweeted the racial abuse are publicly identified, should part of the "huge price" Ted Leonsis calls for include league-enforced discipline, such as a prohibition on attending future NHL games? This is precisely what the English Premier League—England's top-flight soccer league—has instituted. Under league-wide rules, individuals who are discovered to have racially abused league players online (or in a stadium) will be banned from all Premier League matches. Paul MacInnes, *Racist Abusers to Be Banned from all Premier League Grounds*, Guardian.com, Aug. 10, 2021, *https://www.theguardian.com/football/2021/aug/10/racial-abusers-to-be-banned-from-all-premier-league-grounds*. Should American professional sports leagues follow the English Premier League's lead? Would they face legal obstacles in doing so?

2. What if fans' abuse of players does not include overtly racist statements or conduct? Consider a 2019 incident in which Shane Keisel, a white Utah Jazz basketball fan sitting close to the court at a game in Utah's home arena, reportedly told the Oklahoma City Thunder's Russell Westbrook, who is African-American, to "get down on [his] knees like [he] used to." Westbrook interpreted the comment as racially motivated (in suggesting African-American subservience) and threatened violence upon Keisel and his wife. Keisel acknowledged heckling Westbrook but denied any racial intent. Within days, the NBA fined Westbrook $25,000 for threatening violence, and the Jazz permanently banned Keisel from its home arena. Keisel responded to the ban by suing the Jazz and Westbrook for $100 million. Jeff Zillgitt, *Utah Jazz Fan Banned from Arena Sues Team, Russell Westbrook for $100 million*, USAToday.com, Dec. 17, 2019, *https://www.usatoday.com/story/sports/nba/jazz/2019/12/17/banned-fan-shane-keisel-sues-utah-jazz-russell-westbrook/2677631001/*. Westbrook's threat was certainly inexcusable, but was his anger reasonable? Even if so, might such fan harassment—whether or not clearly racially motivated—be justified as a tool calculated to throw off a player's game? Should leagues and sports regulatory bodies view racial taunts differently than despicable non-racial comments made about a player or a player's family member?

3. Racial abuse of athletes is not limited to the professional, or even collegiate, context. Some examples of high school competitions in various parts of the country that have recently been marred by racist taunts and behavior follow:

- During a 2023 basketball game between two rival Texas high schools, students from one school shouted the N-word at an opposing player of color. In addition, many in the student section, composed of white students, dressed in do-rags and fake face tattoos for their self-proclaimed "Thug Night" theme.
- In the fall of 2022, two Sacramento high schools forfeited their football seasons after players from one school posted a mock slave auction on TikTok and players from another created a Snapchat group named "Kill the Blacks."

- Also in Sacramento, "ape sounds" were made towards an African-American high school soccer player in the spring of 2022.
- In 2021, students at a San Diego high school flung tortillas at basketball players from the opposing school, which was predominately Latinx.

Priya Sridhar, *California Bill Aimed at Stopping Racism in High School Sports*, NBC San Diego, Apr. 21, 2023; Olivia Land, *Texas High School Basketball Fans Accused of Racist Taunts, Offensive Clothing at Games*, New York Post, Jan. 26, 2023. Should the racial abuse of high school athletes be treated differently than such abuse of adult athletes?

4. How about the racial abuse of elementary school-age athletes? In 2018, *The Guardian* published an article on the plight of Juniors FC, a soccer team based in Boise, Idaho, composed of eight- and nine-year-old players, most of whom are of color. The team's coach explained that his players have endured being called "niggers" and "wetbacks" and have taken the field while adults have said things such as "here come the future convicts" and "watch out for your wallets." Tim Froh, *Anonymous Letters and Threats: How Racism Came to Stalk US Youth Soccer*, Guardian, Feb. 15, 2018. How should youth sports governing bodies address such conduct?

In light of the difficulty involved in eliminating racially abusive fan behavior, differentiating racially abusive behavior from non-racial abuse designed to distract or anger a player, and addressing the issue at different levels of sports, perhaps a more subdued form of fan support is in order across all of sports. In golf, fans are generally expected to behave in a courteous and reserved manner while viewing matches and supporting their favorite golfers. When you next view a football, basketball, soccer, or hockey game, consider whether shifting to a "golf etiquette" model would be desirable, and if so, whether it would be feasible.

Health, Safety, and Risk Management Issues in Sports

INTRODUCTION

This chapter illustrates health and safety issues, and the corresponding need for careful risk management, which arise in sports-related contexts. Initially, we explore how common law tort principles allocate the risks of injury and establish liability rules for injuries occurring while individuals observe or participate in sporting events. The materials demonstrate judicial recognition that the unique characteristics and features of athletic competition may require modification of general tort principles to further various policy objectives. Also, courts have uniquely applied criminal law principles to determine what injury-causing conduct constitutes criminally culpable behavior between participants in sporting events. The chapter also examines the liability of high schools and colleges to athletes participating in sports activities. It concludes with a discussion of sovereign and qualified immunity defenses that may shield public high schools and colleges from liability for injuries incurred by their athletes. We begin, however, with an overview of basic tort principles.

A *tort* is a wrong, a careless or intentional act that causes harm to another. It is a private, civil law concept that comes from societal expectations of appropriate interpersonal actions and behavior. Negligence is an unintentional tort that occurs when a person fails to behave in a way that protects others from unreasonable harm. This is determined by examining four elements: duty, breach, causation, and damage. *Duty* is established by the relationship between the parties, which indicates the obligatory conduct one party owes to another. *Breach* is the failure to act as a reasonable person would in the same or similar circumstance. *Causation* occurs when the natural and unbroken sequence of events foreseeably produces an event without which the harm would not have occurred. Finally, *damage* is the actual harm or injury directly related to the breach or act that was sustained and should be compensated for in order to make things right. *Intentional torts* are those civil wrongs that result in harm to another by an act knowingly committed. Intent does not have to be malicious but merely indicates that the tortfeasor wanted to commit an act with an understanding of the consequences that would likely result from it. *Reckless behavior* falls somewhere between the carelessness of negligence and the deliberateness of an intentional act. Note the way courts in the following cases identify and define these tort principles.

LIABILITY FOR ATHLETICS-RELATED INJURIES

A. Injury to Athletes

1. Co-Participant Tort Liability

KEY TERMS
- Assumption of risk
- Inherent risk
- Intentional tort
- Negligence: duty, breach, causation, damage
- Reckless conduct

Injuries frequently occur during all levels of athletic competition and are an inherent risk of participating in sports, which participants generally assume and must bear the resulting costs. Inherent risks include all of the ordinary harms that a sport participant would reasonably expect to occur while engaged in athletic activities. In some instances, a fellow participant or another party may be liable for an injury caused by tortious conduct during a sports event. The following case considers the appropriate legal standard for co-participant tort liability.

Shin v. Ahn
165 P.3d 581 (Cal. 2007)

CORRIGAN, J.

In *Knight v. Jewett* (1992) 3 Cal.4th 296, 11 Cal.Rptr.2d 2, 834 P.2d 696 (*Knight*), we considered the duty of care that should govern the liability of sports participants. We recognized that careless conduct by co-participants is an inherent risk in many sports, and that holding participants liable for resulting injuries would discourage vigorous competition. Accordingly, those involved in a sporting activity do not have a duty to reduce the risk of harm that is inherent in the sport itself. They do, however, have a duty not to increase that inherent risk. Thus, sports participants have a limited duty of care to their co-participants, breached only if they intentionally injure them or "engage[ ] in conduct that is so reckless as to be totally outside the range of the ordinary activity involved in the sport." This application of the *primary assumption of risk doctrine* recognizes that by choosing to participate, individuals assume that level of risk inherent in the sport.

This case represents the next generation of our *Knight* jurisprudence. *Knight* involved touch football. We expressly left open the question whether the primary assumption of risk doctrine should apply to noncontact sports, such as golf. We address that question here. We hold that the primary assumption of risk doctrine does apply to golf and that being struck by a carelessly hit ball is an inherent risk of the sport. As we explain, whether defendant breached the limited duty of care he owed other golfers by engaging in conduct that was "so reckless as to be totally outside the range of the ordinary activity involved in [golf]" depends on resolution of disputed material facts. Thus, defendant's summary judgment motion was properly denied. . . .

Plaintiff and defendant were playing golf with Jeffrey Frost at the Rancho Park Golf Course in Los Angeles. Defendant, the first of the threesome to complete the 12th hole, went to the 13th tee box. Plaintiff and Frost then finished putting and followed him. Frost took the cart path to the 13th tee box, which placed him perpendicular to, or slightly behind, defendant and to his right. Plaintiff took a shortcut, which placed him in front of defendant and to his left. Plaintiff stopped there to get a bottle of water out of his golf bag and to check his cell phone for messages. He did so even though he knew (1) that he was in front of the tee box, (2) that defendant was preparing to tee off, and (3) that he should stand behind a player who was teeing off. Defendant inadvertently "pulled" his tee shot to the left, hitting plaintiff in the temple. When struck, plaintiff was 25 to 35 feet from defendant, at a 40- to 45-degree angle from the intended path of the ball. Plaintiff claims his injuries were "disabling, serious, and permanent. . . ."

A majority of this court has since extended *Knight's* application of the primary assumption of risk doctrine to other sports. . . .

[*Cheong v. Antablin*, 946 P.2d 817 (Cal. 1997),] involved skiing. One skier sued another for injuries he suffered when the other skier turned and unintentionally ran into him. We concluded that, "under the applicable common law principles, a skier owes a duty to fellow skiers not to injure them intentionally or to act recklessly, but a skier may not sue another for simple negligence. . . ."

[*Avila v. Citrus Community College Dist.*, 131 P.3d 383 (Cal. 2006)] involved intercollegiate baseball. A pitcher on the Rio Hondo Community College team (Rio Hondo) hit a batter on the Citrus Community College team (Citrus). The next inning the Citrus pitcher allegedly retaliated by hitting a Rio Hondo batter with a "beanball." The Rio Hondo player sued the Citrus Community College District for negligence. We held the suit was barred by the primary assumption of risk doctrine. It is against the rules of baseball to intentionally throw at a batter. Nevertheless, "being intentionally thrown at is a fundamental part and inherent risk of the sport of baseball. It is not the function of tort law to police such conduct."

The lesson to be drawn from *Knight* and its progeny, as well as the weight of authority in sister states, is that the primary assumption of risk doctrine should be applied to golf. Thus, we hold that golfers have a limited duty of care to other players, breached only if they intentionally injure them or engage in conduct that is "so reckless as to be totally outside the range of the ordinary activity involved in the sport."

The Court of Appeal relied too heavily on one of golf's rules of etiquette involving safety. Golf's first rule of etiquette provides that "[p]layers should ensure that no one is standing close by or in a position to be hit by the club, the ball or any stones, pebbles, twigs or the like when they make a *stroke* or practice swing." (USGA, The Rules of Golf, *supra*, §1, Etiquette, p. 1.)

Rules of etiquette govern socially acceptable behavior. The sanction for a violation of a rule of etiquette is social disapproval, not legal liability. This is true, generally, of the violation of the rules of a game. "The cases have recognized that, [in sports like football or baseball], even when a participant's conduct violates a rule of the game and may subject the violator to internal sanctions prescribed by the sport itself, imposition of legal liability for such conduct might well alter fundamentally the nature of the sport by deterring participants from vigorously engaging in activity that falls close to, but on the permissible side of, a prescribed rule." . . .

Here, summary judgment was properly denied because there are material questions of fact to be adjudicated.

In determining whether defendant acted recklessly, the trier of fact will have to consider both the nature of the game and the totality of circumstances surrounding the shot. In making a golf shot, the player focuses on the ball, unlike other sports in which a player's focus is divided between the ball and other players. That is not to say that a golfer may ignore other players before making a shot. Ordinarily, a golfer should not make a shot without checking to see whether others are reasonably likely to be struck. Once having addressed the ball, a golfer is not required to break his or her concentration by checking the field again. Nor must a golfer conduct a headcount of the other players in the group before making a shot.

Many factors will bear on whether a golfer's conduct was reasonable, negligent, or reckless. Relevant circumstances may include the golfer's skill level; whether topographical undulations, trees, or other impediments obscure his view; what steps he took to determine whether anyone was within range; and the distance and angle between a plaintiff and defendant.

Here plaintiff testified at his deposition that he and defendant made eye contact "as I was cutting up the hill." He did not make clear, however, how far he had proceeded up the hill, how far away he was from the defendant, or whether he was stationary when the eye contact occurred. At his deposition, defendant said he looked to see if the area "directly ahead" of him was clear. It is not apparent just how broad or limited that area was. This record is simply too sparse to support a finding, as a matter of law, that defendant did, or did not, act recklessly. This will be a question the jury will ultimately resolve based on a more complete examination of the facts. We do not suggest that cases like this can never be resolved on summary judgment, only that this record is insufficient to do so.

The judgment of the Court of Appeal is affirmed. The case is remanded with directions that litigation should continue under the primary assumption of risk doctrine.

QUESTIONS

As a matter of policy, should the liability standard for co-participant injuries occurring in amateur sports be the same as for professional sports? In determining the appropriate standard, should any distinction be drawn among adult recreational or intramural sports, intercollegiate athletics, high school sports, and youth sandlot games? Why or why not?

NOTE

The prevailing standard for co-participant liability. An overwhelming majority of courts hold that whether a co-participant is liable to another for an injury during athletic competition is assessed according to an intentional or reckless conduct standard. Additionally, most courts also find that injuries resulting from a co-participant's violation of the rules of a sport typically will not alone result in the breach of one's legal duty owed to fellow participants because rules violations are inherent and anticipated aspects of sports contests. The intentional/reckless standard of care is premised on the recognition that injuries are an inherent part of sports participation and a desire to avoid chilling vigorous competition in sporting events. Courts have expressed concern that imposing legal liability based on a mere failure to use reasonable care (i.e., negligent conduct) while participating in a sport will lead to a flood of litigation. In *Pfenning v. Lineman*, 947 N.E.2d 392 (Ind. 2011), however, the court adopted a variation of the limited duty rule (discussed in detail later in this chapter). The court stated that rather than focusing on the existence or nonexistence of a duty, emphasis should be placed on whether the duty was breached. It held that negligence claims against a co-participant will not result in liability if the conduct is within the ordinary range of that of participants in the sport. Having adopted this standard, the court stated that "as to the golfer's hitting an errant drive which resulted in plaintiff's injury, such conduct is clearly within the range of ordinary behavior of golfers and thus is reasonable as a matter of law and does not establish the element of breach required for a negligence action." *Id.* at 404. See generally, Timothy Davis & N. Jeremi Duru, *Understanding Sports Law* 310-18 (2022) (discussing the standards adopted by courts to govern co-participant liability).

In determining the legal standard for co-participant liability, a few courts continue to draw a distinction between different sports based on the inherent risks of physical contact among participants or with the sport's playing equipment or other instrumentalities. However, as illustrated by *Shin*, the trend is toward the abandonment of the contact versus noncontact sport distinction and toward a focus on whether the risk of injury is inherent to the sporting activity. See *Nixon v. Clay*, 449 P.3d 11, 18 (Utah 2019) (rejecting the contact versus noncontact sport distinction in favor of an inherent risk standard); but see *Ludman v. Davenport Assumption Sch.*, 895 N.W.2d 902 (Iowa 2017) (continuing to recognize the contact-sport exception).

> **Problem 7-1**
>
> Consider whether any of the following conduct should give rise to tort liability:
>
> (a) During his warm-up between innings, a high school pitcher deliberately throws at an opposing team's player and hits him in the ribs while the batter is in the batter's circle attempting to time the pitcher's pitches.
> (b) A professional boxer throws a third below-the-belt punch in a match, is disqualified by the referee, and seriously injures his opponent.
> (c) A National Hockey League (NHL) player strikes an opposing player on the head with his fist during a fight and renders him unconscious.
> (d) A college hockey player breaks an opponent's nose during a fight and is given a three-game suspension for violating league rules prohibiting any fighting.

2. Co-Participant Criminal Liability

KEY TERMS
- Assault
- Assumption of risk
- Felony reckless manslaughter
- Manslaughter

As was discussed in the tort cases involving co-participant liability, American society values free and vigorous participation in athletics activities. Some people lament that competitive contact sports are becoming too violent, while others believe that high levels of aggression enhance the entertainment value of sports. Still others believe that severe acts of violence in the athletics arena should be punished in the same way that those acts would be treated in society—using the criminal law system.

Criminal law protects the health, safety, and welfare of society. All crimes have two components, a voluntary, conscious act, known as *actus reas*, and an evil intention, known as *mens rea*. The criminal code defines what action and corresponding mentality constitute a crime in that jurisdiction. A relatively minor affront to society is generally a misdemeanor, and the guilty party may be assessed a fine or a jail sentence of less than one year. More serious offenses are known as felonies and may result in larger fines and longer periods of incarceration. A prosecutor represents the people/society in the case and has the burden of proving that the defendant is guilty beyond a reasonable doubt.

In an early case, *People v. Fitzsimmons*, 34 N.Y.S. 1102, 1109 (1895), the court instructed the jury as follows in a case involving the prosecution of a professional boxer for a blow that killed his opponent during a sparring exhibition:

The public has an interest in the personal safety of its citizens, and is injured where the safety of any individual is threatened, whether by himself or another. A game which involves a physical struggle may be a commendable and manly sport, or it may be an illegal contest. This depends upon whether it is a game which endangers life. . . .

[I]f the rules of the game and the practices of the game are reasonable, are consented to by all engaged, are not likely to induce serious injury, or to end life, if then, as a result of the game, an accident happens, it is excusable homicide.

No rules or practice of any game whatever can make that lawful which is unlawful by the law of the land, and the law of the land says you shall not do that which is likely to cause the death of another.

The jury acquitted the defendant of manslaughter.

The following cases provide a modern view of criminal liability for injuries that occur during competitive or recreational sports. Note how each court defines both the action of the defendant, as well as the accompanying mental state.

People v. Schacker
670 N.Y.S.2d 308 (N.Y. Dist. Ct. 1998)

Donohue, Judge.

[Editors' note: During a hockey game, a player, Robert Schacker, struck another player in the back of his neck after a play was over and the whistle had been blown. The struck player's head hit the crossbar of the net, and he suffered a concussion. A brain scan and other testing revealed that the struck player's injuries were minor.

The defendant, Schacker, who was charged with assault, pled not guilty. The court stated that for the defendant to be convicted, the prosecution had to prove that "the defendant possessed the conscious intent to cause physical injury to the complainant." The court added, "The fact that the act occurred in the course of a sporting event is a defense that tends to deny that the requisite intent was present."]

Persons engaged in athletic competition are generally held to have legally assumed the risk of injuries which are known, apparent, and reasonably foreseeable consequences of participation. Hockey players assume the risk of injury by voluntarily participating in a hockey game at an ice rink.

This tort rule states a policy "intended to facilitate free and vigorous participation in athletic activities." *Benitez v. New York City Board of Education*, 73 N.Y.S.2d 650, 657, 543 N.Y.S.2d 29, 541 N.E.2d 29. This policy would be severely undermined if the usual criminal standards were applied to athletic competition, especially ice hockey. If cross checking, tripping, and punching were criminal acts, the game of hockey could not continue in its present form.

The complainant does not assume the risk of reckless or intentional conduct. However, it must be recognized that athletic competition includes intentional conduct that has the appearance of criminal acts. In fact, in many sporting events, physical injuries are caused by contact with other players. However, the players are "legally deemed to have accepted personal responsibility for" the risks inherent in the nature of sport. This includes intentional acts which result in personal injury. Thus, in order to allege a criminal act which occurred in a hockey game, the factual portion of the information must allege acts that show that the intent was to inflict physical injury which was unrelated to the athletic competition. Although play may have terminated, the information herein does not show that the physical contact had no connection with the competition. Furthermore, the injuries must be so severe as to be unacceptable in normal competition, requiring a change in the nature of the game. That type of injury is not present in this case. Firstly, the physical injury resulted from hitting the net, not from direct contact with the defendant. Secondly, the hospital records do not indicate severe trauma to the complainant.

The idea that a hockey player should be prosecuted runs afoul of the policy to encourage free and fierce competition in athletic events. The People argued at the hearing that this was a non-checking hockey league. While the rules of the league may prohibit certain conduct, thereby reducing the potential injuries, nevertheless, the participant continues to assume the risk of a strenuous and competitive athletic endeavor. The normal conduct in a hockey game cannot be the standard for criminal activity under the Penal Law, nor can the Penal Law be imposed on a hockey game without running afoul of the policy of encouraging athletic competition.

For the foregoing reasons, the interest of justice requires a dismissal of this charge pursuant to CPL 170.40.

Regina v. McSorley
2000 B.C. Prov. Ct. 0116 (Crim. Div. 2000)

KITCHEN, Judge.

[Editors' note: The Vancouver Canucks and the Boston Bruins were both struggling to make the playoffs. Early during the game's first period, Marty McSorley and Donald Brashear engaged in a fight, consisting mainly of clutching and grappling while blows were exchanged. Brashear was much more successful at this than McSorley, delivering several heavy lefts to the side and top of McSorley's head, but with surprisingly little effect. The fight ended with Brashear apparently delivering a heavy body blow and wrenching McSorley to the ice surface. McSorley did react to this; it is clear he was in considerable pain at this time. He promptly came to his feet after the linesmen intervened and skated off to the penalty box, showing no adverse effects from the encounter. Brashear, for his part, skated past the Boston bench "dusting off" his hands, suggesting he had made short work of McSorley. This was obviously intended to upset the Boston players.

At the midpoint of the first period, McSorley again attempted to fight with Brashear. McSorley approached Brashear from behind and cross-checked him to the ice. As Brashear was coming to his feet, helmet off, McSorley used his glove to swat Brashear about the head several times. Brashear failed to respond to this and attempted to skate away. The referee gave McSorley three penalties for this — back-to-back two-minute minors for cross-checking and roughing and a ten-minute major for inciting. Shortly afterward, Brashear himself was penalized for interfering with the Boston goalie during play.

From the Brashear penalty in the middle of the first period until the middle of the third period, the game had settled down, and play between the two teams had evened out. During the third period, Brashear was making a play to come from the corner to the front of the Boston net. A Bruin slashed Brashear to prevent this and was given a penalty. During the stoppage in play, Brashear returned to the Vancouver bench, performing what witnesses described as a Hulk Hogan pose for the benefit of the Boston bench. Once again this was an obvious attempt to antagonize the opposing players, and it was effective. Boston complained to the referee, but no action was taken; it was determined that the Boston players had been mocking him at the same time.

With 20 seconds left in the game, which the Canucks were certain to win, McSorley was sent on to the ice by the Bruins coach to regain Boston pride by challenging Brashear to fight again. McSorley unsuccessfully tried to do so. With only 3 seconds left to play, McSorley, while skating up from behind him, struck Brashear in the head with his stick, bringing it around with his hands together on a horizontal plane like a baseball bat swing. As he was struck on the side of the head, Brashear's helmet was lifted out of position and his shoulder shrugged upward, an apparent reflex reaction to the blow of the stick. The blow was of significant force and caused Brashear to fall to the ice and strike his head. As he collapsed to the ice, he had a grand mal seizure before recovering consciousness. Brashear suffered a grade three concussion and could not take part in physical activity for another month. See *https://www.youtube.com/watch?v=-gQ4_qDwSng* to view the incident giving rise to Marty McSorley's prosecution.]

[T]here is an unwritten code of conduct agreed to by the players and the officials. This amalgam of written rules and the unwritten code leads to composite rules, such as the following. It is a legitimate game strategy to slash another player, but if done with sufficient force, and if the referee sees it, then the offender's team plays one player short for two minutes. It is a legitimate game strategy to fight another consenting player, but the offenders are kept off the ice for a period of time determined by the referee. . . .

So the rules of the NHL game of hockey consist of the written rules in the rulebook, a co-existing unwritten code of conduct impliedly agreed to by the players and officials, and guidelines laid down by the officials from game to game. It is within this somewhat indefinite framework that players must play the game. . . .

It is the position of the Crown that this body of evidence permits only two possibilities — that McSorley deliberately struck Brashear to the head without Brashear's consent, or that he recklessly struck him to the head, not necessarily aiming for the head directly. Recklessness in this case may be likened to willful blindness — ignoring a known risk. . . .

If the blow to the head was intentional, it is common ground that it was an assault. Brashear himself said in evidence that he did not consent to being struck in that manner. The other witnesses agreed that stick blows to the head were not permitted in either the written rules, or the unwritten code . . . players in the NHL would not accept a blow such as that as part of the game. . . .

If the slash was intended for the shoulder, delivered with the intention of starting a fight, my conclusion would be that it was within the common practices and norms of the game. . . .

I conclude that the following occurred.

McSorley had fought Brashear and he had been briefly hurt. He was nevertheless prepared to fight him again, but Brashear frustrated his attempts to do so. Brashear taunted the Boston players and was seen to be responsible for taking the Boston goalie out of the game. This was all fairly routine for McSorley. He was credible when he said he was prepared to let things wind down at the end of the game.

Then Laperriere effectively directed him to get Brashear with about twenty seconds left. This was really too little time to fight but he felt himself pressured to do something. He found himself gliding in from centre ice toward Brashear, sizing him up for possible ways to confront him. Brashear crossed directly in front of him, presenting an easy target. Brashear was the focus of all of McSorley's and Boston's frustrations. McSorley had to do something; he might still be able to start a fight. In the words of McSorley, "It has to be an instantaneous reaction." He had an impulse to strike him in the head. His mindset, always tuned to aggression, permitted that. He slashed for the head. A child, swinging as at a Tee ball, would not miss. A housekeeper swinging a carpetbeater would not miss. An NHL player would never, ever miss. Brashear was struck as intended.

Mr. McSorley, I must find you guilty as charged.

People v. Hall
999 P.2d 207 (Col. 2000)

BENDER, Justice.

We hold that Nathan Hall must stand trial for the crime of reckless manslaughter. While skiing on Vail mountain, Hall flew off of a knoll and collided with Allen Cobb, who was traversing the slope below Hall. Cobb sustained traumatic brain injuries and died as a result of the collision. The People charged Hall with felony reckless manslaughter. . . .

The charge of reckless manslaughter requires that a person "recklessly cause the death of another person." For his conduct to be reckless, the actor must have consciously disregarded a substantial and unjustifiable risk that death could result from his actions. We hold that, for the purpose of determining whether a person acted recklessly, a particular result does not have to be more likely than not to occur for the risk to be substantial and unjustifiable. A risk must be assessed by reviewing the particular facts of the individual case and weighing the likelihood of harm and the degree of harm that would result if it occurs. Whether an actor consciously disregarded such a risk may be inferred from circumstances such as the actor's knowledge and experience, or from what a similarly situated reasonable person would have understood about the risk under the particular circumstances.

We hold that under the particular circumstances of this case, whether Hall committed the crime of reckless manslaughter must be determined by the trier of fact. Viewed in the light most favorable to the prosecution, Hall's conduct — skiing straight down a steep and bumpy slope, back on his skis, arms out to his sides, off-balance, being thrown from mogul to mogul, out of control for a considerable distance and period of time, and at such a high speed that the force of the impact between his ski and the victim's head fractured the thickest part of the victim's skull — created a substantial and unjustifiable risk of death to another person. A reasonable person could infer that the defendant, a former ski racer trained in skier safety, consciously disregarded that risk. For the limited purposes of a preliminary hearing, the prosecution provided sufficient evidence to show probable cause that the defendant recklessly caused the victim's death. . . .

Like other activities that generally do not involve a substantial risk of death, such as driving a car or installing a heater, "skiing too fast for the conditions" is not widely considered behavior that constitutes a high degree of risk. However, we hold that the specific facts in this case support a reasonable inference that Hall created a substantial and unjustifiable risk that he would cause another's death. . . .

QUESTIONS

1. When, if ever, is it appropriate to criminally prosecute for player conduct that occurs during competitive or recreational sporting events? What factors should be considered?
2. Will the possibility of criminal liability have the detrimental effect of chilling vigorous participation and competition in athletic activities? *Hall* illustrates the possibility of criminal liability for engaging in dangerous conduct during recreational sports. In *People v. Hall*, 59 P.3d 298 (Colo. Ct. App. 2002), the court upheld a jury verdict finding the defendant guilty of criminally negligent homicide. See Davis & Duru, *supra* at 318-23 (providing an overview of criminal prosecutions in sports).

   After finding Marty McSorley guilty of assaulting Donald Brashear with a weapon (a hockey stick), Judge Kitchen provided the following explanation for the sentence he imposed:

   The finding of guilt is the real consequence here; the further step of entering a conviction is not necessary. I have concluded that specific deterrence and rehabilitation are served by this. I have concluded that protection of the public is a lesser consideration here. The real concern is that such a sentence may not send the correct message to the community. It must be kept in mind that the consequences to Mr. McSorley are already considerable. He has been without income since the incident, and he has had significant expense in preparing his defence. He has had to endure embarrassing publicity, much more than would be the situation in other assault matters. He will carry the stigma of this with him for the rest of his career; even the rest of his life. If that is not enough to convince anyone that such an offence is to be avoided, there is nothing more a court can do to persuade such a person otherwise. . . .

I grant you a conditional discharge for 18 months. You must keep the peace and be of good behaviour. You are bound by a condition that you will not engage in any sporting event where Donald Brashear is on the opposition.

Regina v. McSorley, 2000 B.C. Prov. Ct., 0117 (Oct. 6, 2000).

3. By comparison, consider the following sentences for criminal convictions resulting from on-field conduct (i.e., does the punishment fit the crime?):

   a. In 1988 Minnesota North Star player Dino Ciccarelli was sentenced to one day in jail and fined $1,000 for striking an opposing player several times in the head with his stick during an NHL game.
   b. In February 2001, after being convicted of criminally negligent homicide, Nathan Hall was sentenced to 90 days in jail, was ordered to perform 240 hours of community service, and was barred from drinking alcohol and recreational skiing during a probationary term.
   c. In February 2000, Tony Limon, a Texas high school basketball player, was sentenced to five years in the state penitentiary for deliberately elbowing an opponent in the face (who suffered a concussion and fractured nose) during a game. This conduct was unrelated to any ongoing play, but no foul was called. Limon had previously pled guilty to burglary and was given four years' probation, but he had no prior history of violent behavior.
   d. In September 2000, a 16-year-old Illinois high school hockey player was sentenced to two years' probation, ordered not to participate in any contact sports during that time, and required to perform 120 hours of community service after entering an Alford plea (no admission of guilt, but acknowledgment that sufficient evidence to convict exists) to a misdemeanor battery charge. As a high school hockey game was ending, he cross-checked an opponent from behind, causing him to crash headfirst into the boards and permanently paralyzing him from the chest down.
   e. In 2009, a Canadian high school rugby player was found guilty of manslaughter for an opponent's death, which was caused by fatal injuries resulting from the player's lifting his opponent into the air with his feet facing upward and driving him headfirst into the ground. The trial judge found that the "defendant intentionally applied force that was outside the rules of the game or any standard by which the game is played." See *Canadian Player Guilty of Manslaughter Over Spear Tackle*, New Zealand Herald (May 29, 2009).

NOTE

Similar to tort law, physical contact resulting in even severe injury is not criminal if it is "part of the game." Consent is a defense to alleged criminal assault, and it is necessary to determine "whether the conduct of defendant constituted foreseeable behavior in the play of the game" and whether a plaintiff's injury "occurred as a by-product of the game itself." *State v. Shelley*, 929 P.2d 489, 493 (Wash. Ct. App. 1997). Courts have, however, affirmed criminal convictions for injuries caused by intentionally thrown punches during basketball and football games. See, e.g., *Shelley*, 929 P.2d at 493 (stating "[t]here is nothing in the game of basketball, or even rugby or hockey, that would permit consent as a defense to such conduct"). See generally Jeffrey Standen, *The Manly Sports: The Problematic Use of Criminal Law to Regulate Sports Violence*, 99 J. Crim. L. & Criminology 619 (2009) (discussing *Schacker* and the principles on which courts rely in determining whether to apply criminal sanctions in the athletics context).

Problem 7-2

During warm-up between innings, a college pitcher deliberately threw at an opposing team batter standing in the on-deck circle 24 feet away from the batter's box. A high-speed fastball hit the batter in the face, causing a broken cheekbone and orbital fracture. The batter, who had been attempting to gauge the speed and time of pitches, did not see the thrown ball in time to avoid it. The batter now has two permanent blind spots in his left eye. The pitcher's coach had told pitchers to "brush back" any opponents attempting to time their pitches. Although admitting an effort to intimidate the batter, the pitcher denied trying to intentionally hit the batter with the thrown ball. Should the pitcher be criminally prosecuted?

LIABILITY OF EDUCATIONAL INSTITUTIONS (AND ORGANIZATIONS)

A high school, college, or university acts through the conduct of its employees and is responsible under limited circumstances for injuries to student-athletes. The applicable standard of care, however, often absolves institutions of tort liability along with defenses including tort immunity and contractual waivers. Nevertheless, courts have imposed liability on educational institutions based on the tortious conduct of employees such as coaches, athletic trainers, and administrative personnel.

A. High School

KEY TERMS
- Assumption of risk
- Duty of care
- Proper supervision

A high school is not an insurer of a student-athlete's safety and is not strictly liable for his or her injuries. To recover for an injury, a high school athlete is required to prove tortious conduct on the part of a school district or its employees. Historically, negligence was the theory athletes relied upon when suing their high schools for sports-related injuries. For example, in *Beckett v. Clinton Prairie Sch. Corp.*, 504 N.E.2d 552, 553 (Ind. 1987), the court recognized that high school personnel have a duty to exercise ordinary and reasonable care for safety of student-athletes under their authority.

Increasingly, courts limit the range of risks for which high schools will incur tort liability to their athletes. This is true, in part, because of judicial extension of the reckless and intentional conduct standard adopted in co-participant injury cases (see *supra*), which limits the liability of coaches and trainers for certain forms of conduct that result in injury to high school athletes. Similarly, some courts' increased willingness to enforce liability waivers against high school athletes has limited institutions' tort liability.

In determining the appropriate liability standard for injuries suffered while participating in interscholastic athletics, the following case illustrates that courts must strike a balance between the responsibility that arises out of the custodial relationship between schools and their athletes (most of whom are minors) and the participants' assumption of the risk of injury inherent in athletic participation. Other relevant policy considerations include the age, skill, and experience levels of those involved in the activity and the extent to which imposing liability may fundamentally alter the nature of the sport. Timothy Davis, *Avila v. Citrus Community College District: Shaping the Contours of Immunity and Primary Assumption of the Risk*, 17 Marq. Sports L. Rev. 259 (2006).

Kahn v. East Side Union High School District
75 P.3d 30 (Cal. 2003)

GEORGE, C.J.

This case presents a question concerning the proper application of the doctrine of primary assumption of risk. At the time of her injury, plaintiff was a 14-year-old novice member of defendant school district's junior varsity swim team. She was participating in a competitive swim meet when she executed a practice dive into a shallow racing pool that was located on defendant school district's property and broke her neck. She alleged that the injury was caused in part by the failure of her coach, a district employee, to provide her with any instruction in how to safely dive into a shallow racing pool. She also alleged lack of adequate supervision and further that the coach breached the duty of care owed to her by insisting that she dive at the swim meet despite her objections, her lack of expertise, her fear of diving, and the coach's previous promise to exempt her from diving.

In *Knight v. Jewett* (1992) 3 Cal.4th 296, 11 Cal.Rptr.2d 2, 834 P.2d 696 (*Knight*), we considered the proper duty of care that should govern the liability of a sports participant for an injury to a co-participant. We concluded that, in recognition of the circumstance that some risk of injury is inherent in most sports, . . . it is appropriate to hold that a participant breaches a duty of care to a co-participant only if he or she "intentionally injures another player or engages in conduct that is so reckless as to be totally outside the range of the ordinary activity involved in the sport." In the present case, we recognize that the relationship of a sports instructor or coach to a student or athlete is different from the relationship between co-participants in a sport. But because a significant part of an instructor's or coach's role is to challenge or "push" a student or athlete to advance in his or her skill level and to undertake more difficult tasks, and because the fulfillment of such a role could be improperly chilled by too stringent a standard of potential legal liability, we conclude that the same general standard should apply in cases in which an instructor's alleged liability rests primarily on a claim that he or she challenged the player to perform beyond his or her capacity or failed to provide adequate instruction or supervision before directing or permitting a student to perform a particular maneuver that has resulted in injury to the student. A sports instructor may be found to have breached a duty of care to a student or athlete only if the instructor intentionally injures the student or engages in conduct that is reckless in the sense that it is "totally outside the range of the ordinary activity" involved in teaching or coaching the sport.

The general proposition that a sports instructor or coach owes a duty of due care not to increase the risk of harm inherent in learning an active sport is consistent with a growing line of Court of Appeal opinions that have applied the *Knight* analysis to claims against such defendants. In these cases, . . . the Courts of Appeal have agreed that although the coach or athletic instructor did not have a duty to eliminate the risks presented by a sport, he or she did have a duty to the student not to increase the risk inherent in learning, practicing, or performing in the sport.

Subsequent decisions have clarified that the risks associated with *learning* a sport may themselves be inherent risks of the sport, and that an instructor or coach generally does not increase the risk of harm inherent in learning the sport simply by urging the student to strive to excel or to reach a new level of competence. . . . The cases point out that instruction in a sport frequently entails challenging or "pushing" a student to attempt new or more difficult feats, and that "liability should not be imposed simply because an instructor asked the student to take action beyond what, with hindsight, is found to have been the student's abilities." (*Bushnell v. Japanese-American Religious & Cultural Center, supra*, 43 Cal.App.4th at p. 532, 50 Cal.Rptr.2d 671). As a general matter, although the nature of the sport and the relationship of the parties to it and to each other remain relevant, a student's inability to meet an instructor's legitimate challenge is a risk that is inherent in learning a sport. To impose a duty to mitigate the inherent risks of learning a sport by refraining from challenging a student, as these cases explain, could have a chilling effect on the enterprise of teaching and learning skills that are necessary to the sport. At a competitive level, especially, this chilling effect is undesirable. . . .

We agree that the object to be served by the doctrine of primary assumption of risk in the sports setting is to avoid recognizing a duty of care when to do so would tend to alter the nature of an active sport or chill vigorous participation in the activity. This concern applies to the process of learning to become competent or competitive in such a sport. Novices and children need instruction if they are to participate and compete, and we agree with the many Court of Appeal decisions that have refused to define a duty of care in terms that would inhibit adequate instruction and learning or eventually alter the nature of the sport. Accordingly, we believe that the standard set forth in *Knight* as it applies to co-participants, generally should apply to sports instructors, keeping in mind, of course, that different facts are of significance in each setting. In order to support a cause of action in cases in which it is alleged that a sports instructor has required a student to perform beyond the student's capacity or without providing adequate instruction, it must be alleged and proved that the instructor acted with intent to cause a student's injury or that the instructor acted recklessly in the sense that the instructor's conduct was "totally outside the range of the ordinary activity" involved in teaching or coaching the sport.

[W]e believe that triable issues of material fact exist regarding the question whether coach McKay breached a duty of care owed to plaintiff, thereby causing her injury, by engaging in conduct that was reckless in that it was totally outside the range of ordinary activity involved in teaching or coaching the sport of competitive swimming. . . .

Concurring and Dissenting Opinion by KENNARD, J.

Persons participating in active sports have to expect that a co-participant may play too roughly and thus cause injury. By contrast, coaches of student athletes teach them the skills necessary to perform their sport of choice safely and effectively. Because student athletes, particularly minors, often consider their coach a mentor or role model, they trust the coach not to carelessly and needlessly expose them to injury. The majority's decision puts an end to that trust: Coaches are under no legal obligation to use reasonable care in training their students how best to perform a sport without incurring personal injury. . . .

Because participation in active sports always entails some risk of harm, the traditional negligence standard imposes liability on an athletic coach only for conduct that exposes players to an "*unreasonable* risk" of such harm. . . . Thus, contrary to the majority's view, applying the negligence standard here would leave coaches free to challenge or push their students to advance their skills level as long as they do so without exposing the student athletes to an unreasonable risk of harm. . . .

Although coaches generally have a legal duty to use reasonable care and not to increase the risks of injury inherent in a sport, some courts recently have ruled that a coach is liable only for intentionally injuring a student or engaging in reckless conduct that is "totally outside the range of the ordinary activity" involved in teaching or coaching the sport. *Kahn*, 75 P.3d at 32–33. These courts have reasoned that applying an intentional/reckless standard is appropriate because a significant aspect of a coach's job is to push students to advance their skills, which requires encouraging them to attempt more difficult tasks. Coaches may, however, be held liable under a negligence theory for not adequately informing students of the need to wear protective equipment, requiring a high school athlete to continue play notwithstanding the coach's knowledge of an existing injury, and not providing prompt medical treatment to a high school athlete.

QUESTIONS

Does *Kahn* strike an appropriate balance between enabling coaches to promote athletic performance and protecting young athletes from increased risks of injury? Considering the objectives of competitive interscholastic athletics, what policy considerations should be given paramount weight? Should injury resulting from negligent coaching be an inherent risk of playing a sport that is assumed by a young athlete?

NOTES

1. Determining inherent risks. A school is not liable for a player's injury resulting from the inherent risks of a sport. Determining inherent risks of a sport requires a fact-specific analysis of which activities are "part of the game" and which risks of injury are assumed by all participants. An inherent risk is one that is indivisible from the sport. The inherent risk inquiry focuses on whether the activity at issue constitutes a risk that is among the consequences attendant to normal competition in a sport. In *Rutherford v. Talisker Canyons Finance, Co., LLC*, 445 P.3d 474, 498 (Utah 2019), the Utah Supreme Court adopted an objective standard for determining whether a risk is inherent to a game or recreational activity. "Under a primary assumption of risk analysis, the question is not necessarily whether a skier would 'wish' to encounter a certain risk, but whether a risk is inherent or essential to the sport of skiing and therefore whether the risk is one that a skier reasonably expects to encounter when participating in the sport." *Id.* at *20–21. See *Grady v. Chenango Valley Cent. Sch. Dist.*, No. 23, *3–4 (N.Y. Ct. App. Apr. 27, 2023) (resolving two lower court cases, in *Secky v. New Paltz Cent. Sch. Dist.*, the court provides an excellent discussion of primary assumption of the risk in rejecting the claim of basketball player injured during a drill because the injury resulting from a collision between two players was an inherent risk of playing basketball; in the second case, *Grady*, the court overturns the lower court's grant of summary judgment which had been based on primary assumption of the risk because material issues of fact existed as to whether the nature of the drill leading to the injury constituted an inherent risk and if so, whether the drill unreasonably increased the inherent risk of the sport); Kelton R. Ekblad, *Inconsistent Judicial Interpretations of the Utah Inherent Risk of Skiing Statute and Economic Implications*, 10 Miss. Sports L. Rev. 227 (2021) (summarizing Utah's inherent risk statute for skiing and inconsistencies in its application).

There are some "divisible risks," however, that are not inherent to the sport, including injuries from safety equipment required to be worn or defective equipment that was not properly inspected. *Henney v. Shelby City Sch. Dist.*, 2006 WL 747475, at *3 (Ohio Ct. App. Mar. 23, 2006) (coach can be held negligent for failing to supply proper athletic equipment); *Baker v. Briarcliff Sch. Dist.*, 613 N.Y.S.2d 660, 663 (N.Y. App. Div. 1994) (coach inadequately warned players about the "risks involved in not wearing a mouthpiece . . . thereby exposing [plaintiff] to unreasonably increased risks of injury"); *Annitto v. Smithtown Cent. Sch. Dist.*, 177 N.Y. S.3d 620 (N.Y. App. Div. 2022) (adopting a primary assumption of the risk standard in holding that injury allegedly arising from coach's inadequate instruction during weight training was not an inherent risk of the football); see also *Bukowski v. Clarkson Univ.*, 19 N.Y.3d 353, 357 (N.Y. Jun. 5, 2012) (refusing to impose liability, the court draws a distinction between accidents resulting from defective equipment and those resulting from suboptimal playing conditions).

2. Athlete overuse and training. Increasingly, physicians and others warn of the dangers associated with coaches who overtrain young athletes, particularly where an athlete specializes at an early age in one sport. For discussions of this and the potential legal implications, see Phoebe Friesen, et al., *Overuse Injuries in Youth Sports: Legal and Social Responsibility*, 28 J. Legal Aspects Sport 151 (2018) (discussing the increased risk of injuries to athletes in youth sports from overuse, and repetitive and cumulative microtrauma); see also Sam C. Erlich & John T. Holden, *Throwing the Book at Irresponsible Coaches: The Need for Consistent Pitch Limit Laws in Amateur Sports*, 47 Hofstra L. Rev. 527 (2018) (discussing how overwork of pitchers in youth and high school baseball results in athlete injuries and suggesting guidelines).

Relying on the reasoning of the *Kahn* majority, a Maryland appellate court held that a 13-year-old softball player assumed the risk of her injury, a fractured ankle, while attempting to tag an opposing player who slid into her at second base. Rejecting plaintiff's inadequate instruction claim, the court stated: "Inadequate instruction and training claims have progressed to trial only when a coach provided little or no training before asking the injured athlete to engage in a significantly dangerous play and compounded that omission by failing to adequately supervise that play." *Kelly v. McCarrick*, 841 A.2d 869, 886–87 (Md. Ct. Spec. App. 2004); *Arnzen v. Temecula Valley Unified Sch. Dist.*, 2017 WL 4942896 (Cal App. Ct. Oct. 31, 2017) (stating that "instructors and coaches owe their students a duty of ordinary care not to direct their students to perform the sport or activity under unsafe conditions, or risks of injury above and beyond the risk inherent in performing the sport *under customary or normal conditions*").

A few courts have held coaches liable for negligence. In *Dennehy v. East Windsor Regional Bd. Educ.*, 284 A.3d 102 (N.J. 2022), a field hockey player was injured when she was struck by an errant soccer ball after her coach allowed the field hockey team to practice on a field adjacent to an ongoing soccer practice. The injured player sued alleging that the coach acted negligently in making the decision. In case of first impression, the court adopts a negligence rather than an intentional and reckless standard.

> Indeed, the essence of plaintiff's theory of liability—that [the coach] chose the wrong place and an unpropitious time to commence practice—is no different than the decisions that might be made by a biology teacher taking a class out to study marine life at the beach. In these and other similar settings, parents have the right to expect that teachers and coaches will exercise reasonable care when in charge of their children and that courts will not immunize a teacher's negligence by imposing a higher standard of care.

Id at 106. See *Sherry v. East Suburban Football League*, 807 N.W.2d 859, 862 (Mich. Ct. App. 2011) (applying negligence standard in a case alleging coach failed to properly train and supervise cheerleaders engaged in "privately sponsored recreational activities").

3. Failure to provide proper emergency medical care. High school coaches have a duty to promptly obtain emergency medical care for an injured athlete. *Mogabgab v. Orleans Parish Sch. Bd.*, 239 So. 2d 456, 460–61 (La. Ct. App. 1970) (noting that when coaches did not seek medical attention for an injured athlete until two hours after his symptoms appeared, they were negligent in causing his death). Although lay athletic personnel are not charged with the knowledge of medical experts, they must recognize a medical emergency and act reasonably under the circumstances. *Pirkle v. Oakdale Union Grammar Sch. Dist.*, 253 P.2d 1, 4 (Cal. 1953). Courts have found coaches liable for improperly providing first aid that worsens an injured athlete's condition. See *Gahan v. Mineola Union Free Sch. Dist.*, 660 N.Y. S.2d 144 (N.Y. App. Div. 1997).

4. Liability for aggravation of existing injury. Requiring a high school athlete to continue playing with a known injury may create tort liability for aggravation of the injury. In *Morris v. Union High Sch. Dist. A*, 294 P. 998 (Wash. 1931), the Washington Supreme Court held that a school district was liable for a coach's negligence in inducing a student to continue playing football with a back injury. The court ruled, "[If] the coach knew that a student in the school was physically unable to play football, or in the exercise of reasonable care should have known it, but nevertheless permitted, persuaded, and coerced such student to play, with the result that he sustained injuries, the district would be liable." *Id.* at 999. See *Bradley v. United States*, 619 F. Supp. 3d 141 (D. D.C. 2022) (awarding injured college field hockey player $1,037,047 in damages against physician who allowed player to return to play aggravating effects of concussion); *Clark v. Univ. of Oregon*, 512 P.3d 457 (Oregon Ct. App. 2022), *rev. denied*, 520 P.3d 883 (Or. 2022) (reversing trial court's dismissal of negligence claim of high school basketball player, who aggravated a previous knee injury while on an official recruiting visit to university, because risk of harm exceeded the risk inherent to athletic participation given that coaches instructed plaintiff to participate in basketball workouts and drills "despite their knowledge of Plaintiff's previous knee surgery and despite the fact that most of the acts, including the act of allowing or requiring Plaintiff to participate in any workout with coaches at all, violated NCAA rules").

Permitting an injured athlete to return to play without using reasonable care to determine his or her medical condition may result in institutional liability. *Jarreau v. Orleans Parish Sch. Bd.*, 600 So. 2d 1389 (La. Ct. App. 1992). However, in *Cerny v. Cedar Bluffs Junior/Senior Pub. Sch.*, 679 N.W.2d 198 (Neb. 2004), the Nebraska Supreme Court affirmed the lower court's finding that a coach exercised reasonable care by properly evaluating a high school football player for symptoms of a concussion and allowing him to re-enter a game. See *Zemke v. Arreola*, 2006 WL 1587101 (Cal. Ct. App. Jun. 12, 2006) (coaches not liable for brain injury caused by second impact syndrome, which was not foreseeable, because student did not appear to have or report symptoms of initial head injury); Sam C. Ehrlich, *Points of No Return: How the Ninth Circuit's New Voluntary Undertaking Doctrine Changes Return-to-Play in Sports*, 56 U.S.F. L. Rev. 1 (2021) (discussing development of current return-to-play doctrine in the Ninth Circuit).

5. Duty of state high school athletic association to protect athlete's health and safety. State high school athletic associations often promulgate competition and equipment rules for interscholastic sports played within their respective jurisdictions. Courts have held that these governing bodies may have a legal duty to exercise reasonable care when formulating safety rules governing high school athletic competition. See, e.g., *Mohr v. St. Paul Fire & Marine Ins. Co.*, 674 N.W.2d 576 (Wis. App. 2003). By comparison, what legal duty, if any, should be imposed on the National Federation of State High School Associations, which promulgates proposed rules for interscholastic sports but does not have rulemaking and enforcement authority? See *Mehr v. FIFA*, 115 F.Supp.3d 1035 (N.D. Cal. 2015) (dismissing negligence claims against worldwide, national, and state soccer governing bodies because "[p]laintiffs have alleged no basis for imputing to any defendant a legal duty to reduce the risks inherent in the sport of soccer, or to implement any of the 'Consensus Statement' guidelines or concussion management protocols, and have alleged no facts showing that any defendant took any action that increased the risks beyond those inherent in the sport").

Mayall ex rel. R.C. v. USA Water Polo, Inc., 909 F.3d 1055 (9th Cir. 2018), involved secondary injuries a minor suffered after returning to play following an initial hit. The court held that the first hit was an inherent risk of water polo but defendant's failure to have a return-to-play policy given knowledge of the dangers of head trauma gave rise to cognizable claims of negligence, voluntary undertaking, and gross negligence against the association. See *Doe v. United States Youth Soccer Assoc.*, 214 Cal.Rptr.3d 552, 559 (Cal. Ct. App. 2017) (in a case involving a minor allegedly abused by her soccer coach ruling that "defendants had a duty to conduct criminal background checks on all adults who would have contact with children involved in their programs.").

B. Colleges and Universities

KEY TERMS
- Foreseeability
- Special relationship

Like the body of law defining a high school's legal duty to protect its students' health and safety, the nature and scope of a university's corresponding legal duty also continues to develop. As you read the following cases, consider how the differences between intercollegiate and interscholastic athletics, as well as the nature of the relationship between a university and its student-athletes, influence judicial definitions of the parameters of this duty.

In *Kleinknecht v. Gettysburg College*, 989 F.2d 1360 (3d Cir. 1993), the Third Circuit ruled that a university has a legal duty to use reasonable care to provide prompt and adequate emergency medical care to student-athletes injured while participating in intercollegiate athletics. Drew Kleinknecht was a 20-year-old sophomore student at Gettysburg College, which had recruited him for its Division III intercollegiate lacrosse team. During practice, Drew, who had no history of heart problems, collapsed and suffered cardiac arrest. At the time Drew was stricken, there was no athletic trainer or other person qualified to perform cardiopulmonary resuscitation or provide emergency medical care present. No telephone was readily available to call for help; rather, coaches and other student-athletes had to run to an off-field site on campus to summon help. Despite resuscitation efforts, which allegedly were delayed by the college's failure to have an appropriate emergency medical plan, Drew died of cardiac arrest. No athlete at the college had experienced cardiac arrest while playing lacrosse or any other sport.

The Third Circuit held that "a special relationship existed between the College and Drew that was sufficient to impose a duty of reasonable care on the College" for the following reasons:

> Drew chose to attend Gettysburg College because he was persuaded it had a good lacrosse program, a sport in which he wanted to participate at the intercollegiate level. Head Trainer Donolli actively recruited Drew to play lacrosse at the College. At the time he was stricken, Drew was not engaged in his own private affairs as a student at Gettysburg College. Instead, he was participating in a scheduled athletic practice for an intercollegiate team sponsored by the College under the supervision of College employees. . . .
>
> Drew was not acting in his capacity as a private student when he collapsed. Indeed, the Kleinknechts concede that if he had been, they would have no recourse against the College. There is a distinction between a student injured while participating as an intercollegiate athlete in a sport for which he was recruited and a student injured at a college while pursuing his private interests, scholastic or otherwise. This distinction serves to limit the class of students to whom a college owes the duty of care that arises here. [T]he fact that Drew's cardiac arrest occurred during an athletic event involving an intercollegiate team of which he was a member does impose a duty of due care on a college that actively sought his participation in that sport. We cannot help but think that the College recruited Drew for its own benefit, probably thinking that his skill at lacrosse would bring favorable attention and so aid the College in attracting other students. . . .

Id. at 1368. The court ruled that, although no other athlete at the college had experienced cardiac arrest while playing lacrosse or any other sport, the risk of death or serious injury to an intercollegiate athlete is sufficiently foreseeable to impose a legal duty of reasonable care:

> [T]he Kleinknechts produced ample evidence that a life-threatening injury occurring during participation in an athletic event like lacrosse was reasonably foreseeable. . . . The foreseeability of a life-threatening injury to Drew was not hidden from the College's view. Therefore, the College did owe Drew a duty to take reasonable precautions against the risk of death while Drew was taking part in the College's intercollegiate lacrosse program.

Having determined that it is foreseeable that a member of the College's inter-scholastic lacrosse team could suffer a serious injury during an athletic event, it becomes evident that the College's failure to protect against such a risk is not reasonable. The magnitude of the foreseeable harm—irreparable injury or death to one of its student athletes as a result of inadequate preventive emergency measures—is indisputable.

Id. at 1370.

In the following case, another court refused to extend the duty of care that universities owe to their student-athletes beyond the context of emergency medical care.

Orr v. Brigham Young University
960 F. Supp. 1522 (D. Utah 1994), *aff'd*, 108 F.3d 1388 (10th Cir. 1997)

SAM, District Judge.

[Editors' note: Plaintiff Vernon Peter Orr attended Brigham Young University (BYU) from the fall of 1988 until April 1990 and played on the varsity football team for two football seasons. Orr denied having any lower back pain or injury prior to attending BYU. He asserted that he experienced back pain resulting from participating in football practice and intercollegiate competition. Following postseason bowl practice at the conclusion of the 1989 playing season, Orr experienced back pain and a medical examination revealed three herniated disks. Orr left BYU to play professional football in Finland. Orr did not return to BYU to complete his education.

Orr asserted a litany of conduct that represented BYU's alleged negligent breach of its duty of care owed to him, including (1) engendering a win-at-all-cost mentality, (2) using psychological pressure to increase performance at the sacrifice of his health, (3) employing unqualified persons to diagnose and treat football-related injuries, (4) misdiagnosing his injuries, (5) approving him for and encouraging him to play after being injured, (6) placing greater emphasis on winning football games than on his physical and mental health, and (7) losing interest in him and failing to assist him further in his education.]

BYU argues that "[e]xcept for those duties relating to claims of medical negligence or violations of medical standards of care, the long list of alleged duties owed to Orr and breached by BYU are ones that have never been identified or recognized as duties owed as a matter of law."

Much of Orr's claim of negligence is based upon the breach of purported duties of care created by the special relationship between a university and its student athletes. . . . Orr, in essence, urges that BYU, having recruited him to play football, assumed the responsibility for his safety and deprived him of the normal opportunity for self-protection. . . .

Arguably, Orr, as a collegiate football player, had both demands and advantages distinct from those of the average college student. However, in the court's view, any distinctions are more of a contractual nature than a custodial nature mandating special duties of care and protection beyond those traditionally recognized under a simple negligence theory of liability. BYU, in exchange for a student's promise to play football, agrees to provide the student with such benefits as special consideration in meeting entrance requirements, financial assistance, training table meals, training equipment, medical services, and academic support. Certainly when training and medical services are provided and then negligently performed, liability could result under existing theories of negligence. However, nothing in the facts supports Orr's contentions that, by playing football for BYU, he became in essence a ward of the university without any vestige of free will or independence. At the time Orr began attending BYU, he was twenty-two years old, married with one child. The court finds no facts which suggest that Orr's relationship with BYU was custodial in nature. . . .

An athlete's choice to participate in a sport is not coerced. Voluntary association with a collegiate athletic team does not make the student less of "an autonomous adult or the institution more a caretaker." *Beach [v. University of Utah]*, 726 P.2d [413], at 419. n. 5. As noted earlier, the court views any distinctions between a regular student and a student athlete as more contractual in nature than custodial. In short, the court finds no compelling reasons to impose upon colleges and universities additional duties beyond those owed to other students or those presently recognized and available to collegiate athletes under acknowledged legal theories. . . . [T]he court concludes that the supreme court of Utah would reject Orr's claim that duties are owed to him on the basis of a special relationship with the university by virtue of his football player status. . . .

[Editors' note: The court granted BYU's motion for summary judgment on all of Orr's claims except any arising out of the alleged negligent provision of medical care.]

QUESTIONS

Should a university owe a duty of care to student-athletes that is different than the duty of care it owes to all students? The courts have recognized that, under some circumstances, colleges and universities have a duty of reasonable care for the health and safety of athletics participants. In *Searles v. Trustees of St. Joseph's College*, 695 A.2d 1206 (Me. 1997), a scholarship basketball player sued his coach, alleging that, notwithstanding medical advice that he should not continue to play basketball with a knee injury, the coach required him to continue playing, thereby causing an aggravated and permanent knee injury. The Maine Supreme Court recognized previous precedent that imposes a duty on college coaches and athletic trainers to exercise reasonable care for the health and safety of student-athletes. The court concluded that whether the trainer failed to advise the coach and the player that the latter injuries warranted the athlete not playing was a question for the jury. How does the *Searles* holding differ from that of the court's holding in *Orr*? According to the *Orr* court, under what limited circumstances might a university be held liable in tort to an injured student-athlete? See Davis & Duru, *supra* at 396–99 (identifying cases in which courts have addressed the liability of coaches and trainers to athletes); see also

Mark R. Hamilton, Jr., *Pros and Kahns: The Proper Coach Liability Standard for Athlete Injuries in Collegiate Athletics*, 32 Marq. Sports L. Rev. 599 (2022). See also *Lamorie v. Warner Pacific College*, 850 P.2d 401 (Or. Ct. App. 1993) (appellate court ruled that a jury could reasonably find that the player's re-injury of his eye was a foreseeable risk of being directed to resume playing basketball, for which the university could be held liable); *Davidson v. University of North Carolina at Chapel Hill*, 543 S.E.2d 920 (N.C. App. 2001), *cert. denied*, 550 S.E.2d 771 (N.C. 2001) (holding that a university has a duty to use reasonable care to protect members of school-sponsored intercollegiate cheerleading team from injury). But see *Bukowski v. Clarkson Univ.*, 2012 WL 1986521, *3 (N.Y. Jun. 5, 2012) (ruling that a coach and university were not liable for injuries sustained by a pitcher who was hit by a line drive during indoor practice because the player, who was a knowledgeable and experienced baseball player, assumed the inherent risk of being hit by a line drive); *Sandford v. Long*, 2012 WL 874678 (Cal Ct. App. Mar. 15, 2012) (rejecting student-athlete's argument that special relationship between university and student-athlete imposed duty of coach to protect an athlete against the intentional conduct of a teammate).

NOTES

1. Medical treatment. In *Feleccia v. Lackawanna College*, 215 A.3d 3, 12–13 (Pa. 2019), the Pennsylvania Supreme Court held that the lower court erred in finding that a college owes a "duty of care to its intercollegiate student athletes requir[ing] it to have qualified medical personnel available at [athletic events, including a] football tryout, . . . and to provide adequate treatment in the event that an intercollegiate student athlete suffer[s] a medical emergency." In so ruling, the court rejected the lower court's reliance on *Kleinkneck*. The court went on to hold, however, that it was the "affirmative conduct" by the university that "created a 'special relationship' with and increased risk of harm to its student athletes such that appellants had a duty to 'exercise reasonable care to protect them against an unreasonable risk of harm arising' from that affirmative conduct." *Id.* at 14–15. According to the court, the special relationship arose from the athletes providing services by playing sports for the university. The court concluded that by virtue of this special relationship, the university "undertook a duty to provide duly licensed athletic trainers for the purpose of rendering treatment to its student athletes participating in athletic events, including the football practice. . . ." *Id.* at 15. See *Stineman v. Fontbonne College*, 664 F.2d 1082 (8th Cir. 1981) (holding that a university has a duty to refer an injured intercollegiate athlete to a physician for medical treatment).

The National Collegiate Athletic Association (NCAA) publishes a sports medicine handbook on its website that provides guidelines for protecting the health and safety of student-athletes and for minimizing the risk of significant injury for participants in intercollegiate athletics. These guidelines may be relevant in determining the nature and scope of a university's duty to use reasonable care in connection with sports medicine issues affecting its athletics program. See *Wallace v. Broyles*, 961 S.W.2d 712, 713–16 (Ark. 1998) (asserting that a university may be liable for negligently permitting student-athletes, in violation of NCAA guidelines, to have access to controlled substances in athletic department facilities without prescriptions, labels, instructions, or warnings regarding the dangers or side effects of usage).

2. University duty to protect opponents' health and safety. The law continues to develop regarding the scope of a university's legal duty to prevent one of its athletes from injuring an opposing player. Courts have refused to recognize that a special relationship exists between a university and student-athletes at another school. *Avila v. Citrus Community College Dist.*, 131 P.3d 383 (Cal. 2006) (although university has a legal duty not to increase the risks inherent in an intercollegiate sport, it has no legal duty to prevent its pitcher from intentionally throwing at an opposing team's batter because "being intentionally thrown at is a fundamental part and inherent risk" of baseball).

3. Association liability for safety rules. Like state high school athletics governing bodies, a question has arisen whether the NCAA has a legal duty to use reasonable care when promulgating rules to protect athletes' safety. In *Sanchez v. Hillerich & Bradsby Co.*, 128 Cal. Rptr. 2d 529 (Cal. App. 2002), the court held that the NCAA may be liable for approving baseball bat if its performance capabilities are proved to increase unreasonably a pitcher's inherent risk of being hit by a batted ball. An Indiana court came to a different conclusion. In *Lanni v. NCAA*, 2015 WL 5037294 (Ind. Ct. App. Aug. 26, 2005), a student-athlete who was struck in the face with a sabre while observing a fencing competition asserted a negligence claim against the NCAA. The plaintiff claimed that by virtue of its role in regulating the field of play and adopting rules and policies regarding safety issues, the NCAA possessed a general duty of care and assumed a duty of care to protect spectators from the risks that resulted in her injury.

In upholding the trial court's motion for summary judgment in favor of the NCAA, the appellate court turned to Indiana Supreme Court precedent that refused to hold national fraternities liable for the conduct of local chapters. As to a general duty of care, the court cited to *Yost v. Wabash College*, 3 N.E.3d 509 (Ind. 2014), in which the court emphasized the absence of day-to-day management by the national fraternity over a local fraternity's affairs. The *Yost* court also reasoned that imposing liability would discourage national fraternal organizations from adopting programs to promote safety. Finding that the NCAA's relationship with student-athletes mirrored that between a national fraternity and its chapters, the *Lanni* court concluded that it would not impose a general duty of care on the NCAA.

Holding also that the NCAA did not assume a duty of care, the *Lanni* court also relied on decisions involving fraternities.

> Just as in *Yost* and *Smith* [*v. Delta Tau Delta*, 9 N.E.3d 154 (Ind. 2014)], the specific duties taken by the NCAA with respect to the safety of student-athletes was simply to provide information and guidance to the NCAA's member institutions and student-athletes. . . . Actual oversight and control cannot be imputed from the fact that the NCAA has promulgated rules and regulations and required compliance

with those rules and regulations. The NCAA's conduct does not demonstrate that it undertook or assumed a duty to actually oversee or directly supervise the actions of the member institutions and the NCAA's student-athletes.

Lanni, 2015 WL 5037294, *10.

In *Bradley v. NCAA*, 249 F. Supp. 3d 149, 168 (D.D.C. 2017), the court ruled that the following allegations stated a negligence claim against the NCAA:

> [T]he plaintiff asserts that "[d]efendant NCAA undertook and assumed a duty to protect the physical and mental well-being of all student-athletes participating in intercollegiate sports, including [her,] . . . [and] a duty to protect student-athletes from brain injuries." The plaintiff then alleges that "[d]efendant NCAA failed in its duties" by, among other things, failing to ensure that the coaches, athletic trainers and graduate assistants were educated about the signs, symptoms[,] and risks of concussions, second-impact syndrome, and post-concussive syndrome; implement appropriate safety procedures and policies regarding care, treatment, and monitoring of student-athletes suffering from concussions, concussion symptoms, and post-concussive symptoms; implement appropriate oversight over its member institutions in their implementation of Concussion Management Plans; provide appropriate guidance to its member institutions on concussion management; [and] safeguard[ ] its student-athletes from preventable concussion and post-concussion injuries.

The court, however, dismissed the plaintiff's negligence claim against the Patriot League alleging it "assumed the same duties and responsibilities as the NCAA . . . because [its] Policies and Procedures provides that 'Patriot League institutions are expected to abide by all rules and procedures set forth in both the NCAA and Patriot League Materials.'" *Id.* at 175. It reasoned:

> Because considerations of fairness and public policy play a role in a court's analysis of foreseeability in determining duty, the Court agrees with the Patriot League that such public policy considerations provide support for shielding athletic conferences from litigation involving an injury to an athlete based on an athlete's participation in a sporting event sanctioned by the athletic conference, without a showing that the athletic conference took affirmative steps to establish a requisite duty of care.

Id. at 177.

Problem 7-3

Amos is a scholarship athlete who is the star wide receiver at Big U, a private university with an outstanding football program team. The week before the game with Large U, Big U's hated rival, Amos suffered a very painful neck injury that prevented him from practicing. Although Big U's team physician recommended that Amos not play, Big U's coach pressured Amos to play because the Large U game would decide the conference championship.

> Amos suffered a broken neck, causing permanent paralysis, when he was injured during the game in a vicious helmet-to-helmet tackle by Brutus, a Large U defensive back, who was penalized 15 yards for "spearing." Is Big U liable for Amos's permanent neck injury and paralysis? Is Large U liable?

C. Injury to Spectators

KEY TERMS
- Invitee
- Licensee
- Limited duty rule
- Premises liability
- Trespasser

The previous section focused on the duties of participants and sport managers for the safety and welfare of those playing the game. The focus now shifts to the safety and welfare of those who come to watch those participating. *Premises liability* is the responsibility of a landowner for injuries that happen to others on the landowner's property. The status or reason that the person is on the property is an important consideration in determining the liability of the landowner. An *invitee* is someone who comes onto the property by either an express or implied invitation. A *licensee* is a person whose presence on the property is known and tolerated by the landowner but is on the land for his or her own interest or convenience. A *trespasser* does not have the permission of the landowner to be on the property. Landowners must take reasonable care to keep the premises in safe condition for invitees, but they are required to keep licensees safe only from known dangers that may be concealed. The landowner owes no duty to keep trespassers safe unless the landowner creates an unjustified risk of injury, such as setting traps or spring guns.

Sports event spectators are generally characterized as invitees, meaning they are invited to enter a venue to view a game or event (usually as a paying customer). Thus, "the owner of a [sports] facility has a duty of reasonable care under the circumstances to invitees." *Allred v. Capital Area Soccer League, Inc.*, 669 S.E.2d 777 (N.C. App. 2008). This duty requires a facility owner or operator to maintain the premises and equipment therein in a reasonably safe condition to prevent spectator injury from normal use of the facility. If this duty is breached and causes harm to a spectator, there is potential liability for negligence. *Shear v. Trail Blazers et. al.*, 329 So.3d 819, 822 (La. 2021) (finding that seating configuration of basketball arena, which did not have a barrier between court and spectator seats, did not create an unreasonable risk of harm).

In June 2018, a California jury ordered the Los Angeles Rams to pay former NFL running back, Reggie Bush, $12.5 million in damages ($4.95 million in compensatory damages and $7.5 million in punitive damages) for injuries he suffered when he slipped on concrete after he ran out of bounds on a punt return. In his lawsuit, Bush alleged that the Rams permitted a "dangerous condition to exist at the Edward Jones Dome" in St. Louis, the stadium at which the Rams played before relocating the team to Los Angeles. A week before Bush suffered his season-ending injuries, then-Cleveland Browns quarterback, John McCown, suffered an injury on the same concrete slab. See *DeLong v. R.I. Sports Center, Inc.*, 182 A.3d 1129, 1134–35 (R.I. 2018) (articulating the following standard for determining if a plaintiff has established a prima facie case of premises liability: (1) the existence of a dangerous or defective condition on the defendants' premises; (2) defendants' notice of that condition for a sufficient period of time; and (3) a causal link between that condition and the plaintiff's injury.

In *Edward C. v. City of Albuquerque et al.*, 241 P.3d 1086 (N.M. 2010) the court rejected what was historically defined as the "baseball rule," which absolved a stadium owner or operator of liability for injuries to spectators if the stadium made protected seating available. See *Mills v. Durham Bulls Baseball Club, Inc.*, 274 N.C. App. 618 (N.C. Ct. App. 2022) (adhering to the traditional characterization of the baseball rule). Today, the majority of courts have adopted a standard (often characterized as either the limited duty rule, primary assumption of the risk, or the inherent risk standard) that examines whether the spectator's injury resulted from a risk inherent to the sport. Davis & Duru, *supra* 324–30 (discussing the confusion caused by the differing formulations of what has emerged as the majority approach). Pursuant to this rule, "there is no legal duty to protect or warn spectators about the 'common, frequent, and expected' inherent risks of observing a sporting event such as being struck by flying objects that go into the stands." *Jones v. Three Rivers Mgmt. Corp.*, 394 A.2d 546, 551 (Pa. 1978).

A rationale frequently articulated in support of the limited duty rule is that spectators assume injury-causing risks that are an inherent part of the activity in question. Another rationale rests on the protection of consumer preference. Proponents of this view argue that not imposing a duty on facility owners for risks inherent in the game promotes allowing owners to construct facilities that enhance consumer choice. Consumers may elect to sit in protected seats or find seats in unprotected areas where their view may be unobstructed and they can become more intimately involved in the particular game.

Notwithstanding their limited duty, facility operators and teams possess a legal duty not to increase the inherent risks of injury from watching a game or athletic event. This exception to the limited duty rule was addressed in *Lowe v. California League of Professional Baseball*, 65 Cal. Rptr. 2d 105 (Cal. App. 1997), where a spectator was hit in the face by a foul ball after having been distracted by a team mascot The court found that the presence of a team mascot was not an integral part of the game of baseball. It held that the mascot's antics in hitting plaintiff with his tail, while the game was being played, created a triable issue of fact as to whether the club increased the inherent risks of watching a baseball game by distracting plaintiff and preventing him from seeing and protecting himself from injury by a batted ball. In *Harting v. Dayton Dragons Prof. B'ball Club*, 870 N.E.2d 766 (Ohio App. 2007), however, the court held that a spectator assumed the risk of injury from a foul ball by watching the mascot perform rather than the game.

What if the flying object that hits a spectator is a piece of food rather than a piece of game equipment? Robert Coomer was sitting in the stands watching a Kansas City Royals baseball game when he was struck in the eye by a hot dog that the Royals' mascot, Sluggerrr, threw into the stands as part of a product promotion. Sluggerrr took no care with the throw, tossing it behind his back, and the damage to Coomer's eye required surgery. Coomer sued, and the Royals defended based on the "baseball rule," arguing that they were no more liable to Coomer than they would have been if he were hit by a foul ball. On appeal, the Missouri Supreme Court concluded as a matter of law that:

> [T]he risk of injury from Sluggerrr's hotdog toss is not one of the risks inherent in watching the Royals play baseball that Coomer assumed merely by attending a game at Kauffman Stadium. This risk can be increased, decreased or eliminated altogether with no impact on the game or the spectators' enjoyment of it. As a result, Sluggerrr (and, therefore, the Royals) owe the fans a duty to use reasonable care in conducting the Hotdog Launch and can be held liable for damages caused by a breach of that duty.

Coomer v. Kansas City Royals, 437 S.W. 3d 184, 203 (Mo. 2014).

A facility operator also may be liable for failing to use reasonable care in regulating crowd control and fan conduct during sporting events. Courts have considered whether a spectator's injury caused by fellow spectators while pursuing a ball that goes into the stands as a souvenir is an inherent risk of attending and observing a game. Ruling that a university has a legal duty to protect spectators against a foreseeable risk of such harm, the court in *Hayden v. Univ. of Notre Dame*, 716 N.E.2d 603 (Ind. App. 1999), explained:

> [W]e find that the totality of the circumstances establishes that Notre Dame should have foreseen that injury would likely result from the actions of a third party in lunging for the football after it landed in the seating area. As a result, it owed a duty to Letitia Hayden to protect her from such injury. . . . Notre Dame well understands and benefits from the enthusiasm of the fans of its football team. It is just such enthusiasm that drives some spectators to attempt to retrieve a football to keep as a souvenir. There was evidence that there were many prior incidents of people being jostled or injured by efforts of fans to retrieve the ball.

716 N.E.2d at 606.

The application of the limited duty rule owed to a spectator attending a sporting event is illustrated in the following case.

Thurmond v. Prince William Professional Baseball Club, Inc.
574 S.E.2d 246 (Va. 2003)

KEENAN, Justice.

In August 1997, Thurmond attended a night baseball game conducted by the Prince William Professional Baseball Club, Inc. . . . In the stadium, spectators were warned of the risk of being struck by objects batted or thrown from the field. Warning signs, measuring three feet by three feet, were posted at entrances to the seating areas. These signs stated: "Be Alert! Objects batted or thrown into the stands may be dangerous." All persons entering the stadium walked past one of these entrances, regardless of the location of their seats.

In addition, the back of each admission ticket contained a printed warning that stated, in relevant part:

> The holder of this ticket assumes all risk and danger incidental to the game of baseball . . . including specifically (but not exclusively) the danger of being injured by thrown bats, thrown or batted balls, . . . and agrees that the participating clubs or their officials, agents and players are not liable for injury related from such causes.

Twenty to thirty seats were reserved for each game in the screened area behind home plate for those spectators who requested to be reseated because they were not comfortable sitting in the unscreened areas of the stadium.

Thurmond sat with her family and friends "high in the bleachers" on the third base side of the stadium. This was Thurmond's first visit to the stadium, and she did not know that she could have requested a seat in the screened area behind home plate. She also did not read the warning printed on the back of the admission ticket because she never had possession of her ticket, which her friends had given to her husband. However, Thurmond remained alert at all times during the game, watching the hitters and batted baseballs.

During the eighth inning, a "line drive foul" ball was batted toward Thurmond. Although Thurmond saw the baseball approaching in her direction, the ball was moving too rapidly to allow her to take any evasive action. The ball struck Thurmond directly on the right side of her face, and she sustained various injuries, including fractures of her facial bones, damage to her right eye socket, and extensive nerve damage.

Thurmond . . . alleged that she was injured as a result of the defendants' negligence in failing to provide adequate warnings at the stadium and to operate and maintain the stadium in a safe condition to prevent injuries to invitees. In response, the defendants [argued] that Thurmond assumed the risk of injury as a matter of law when she chose to sit in an unscreened area of the stadium. . . .

In deciding this issue, we first state the general principles that govern our inquiry. In this Commonwealth, a person's voluntary assumption of the risk of injury from a known danger operates as a complete bar to recovery for a defendant's alleged negligence in causing that injury. Application of the defense of assumption of risk requires use of a subjective standard, which addresses whether a particular plaintiff fully understood the nature and extent of a known danger and voluntarily exposed herself to that danger. Thus, the defense of assumption of risk ordinarily presents a jury question, unless reasonable minds could not differ on the issue. . . .

[The assumption of the risk] doctrine requires us to consider whether a particular plaintiff fully understood the nature and extent of a known danger and voluntarily exposed herself to that danger. Thus, we hold that when a particular adult spectator of ordinary intelligence is familiar with the game of baseball, that spectator assumes the normal risks of watching a baseball game, including the danger of being hit by a ball batted into an unscreened seating area of a stadium.

We conclude that reasonable persons could not disagree that Thurmond, who conceded that she remained alert throughout the game and observed hitters and batted balls for more than seven innings before being injured, was familiar with the game of baseball, knew the risk of being injured by a batted ball, and voluntarily exposed herself to that risk by remaining seated in an unscreened area.

Accordingly, we hold that the trial court did not err in awarding summary judgment to the defendants, because Thurmond's assumption of the risk was a complete bar to her recovery in this negligence action.

The prevailing principle is that there is no legal duty to protect or warn spectators about the "common, frequent, and expected inherent risks of observing a sporting event such as being struck by flying objects that go into the stands." *Jones v. Three Rivers Mgmt. Corp.*, 394 A.2d 546, 551 (Pa. 1978). Although an owner may not owe a duty of care to spectators for inherent risks, the owner or facility operator must not enhance the risks that are inherent to a particular sport. *Edward C. v. City of Albuquerque*, 241 P.3d 1086, 1088 (N.M. 2010) ("spectator must exercise ordinary care to protect himself or herself from the inherent risk of being hit by a projectile that leaves the field of play and the owner/occupant must exercise ordinary care not to increase that inherent risk"). See generally Timothy Davis, *Avila v. Citrus Community College District: Shaping the Contours of Immunity and Primary Assumption of the Risk*, 17 Marq. Sports L. Rev. 259 (2006).

QUESTIONS

Why did the *Thurmond* court reject the plaintiff's negligence claim? Are there sound public policy reasons for doing so?

NOTES

1. The scope of the limited duty rule. In *Thurmond*, the court rejected the negligence claim of a spectator who was injured while seated as a game was being played. Courts have also rejected the negligence claims of spectators who were injured before a game had officially begun. In *Allred v. Capital Area Soccer League, Inc.*, 669 S.E.2d 777, 781 (N.C. App. 2008), the court stated, "principles of assumption of the risk apply not only to being struck during the course of a game, but also to preliminary and warm-up activities." See *Hurst v. East Coast Hockey League*, 637 S.E.2d 560, 562 (S.C. 2006) ("risk of being injured by a foul ball at a baseball game and the risk of being injured by a flying puck at a hockey game are similar risks").; *Wheeler v. Central Carolina Scholastic Sports, Inc.*, 798 S.E.2d 438 (N.C. Ct. App. 2017), *aff'd*, 370 NC 390 (2017) (unpublished) (holding that North Carolina's version of the baseball rule "shields a baseball field operator from liability, even when a patron is struck in an unusual way by a batted ball, so long as the operator provides a screened section."). Even if the facility operator or club is not liable for a spectator's initial injury ensuing from being struck by a fly ball or puck, liability may be premised on a defendant's negligent failure to ascertain the nature and extent of a spectator's symptoms after she or he is struck by a foul ball. *Fish v. Los Angeles Dodgers Baseball Club*, 128 Cal. Rptr. 807 (Cal. Ct. App. 1976).

2. Challenging baseball's limited duty rule. Should conceptions of stadium owner liability change in light of what Professor Michael McCann calls the "modern day baseball experience"? McCann writes:

> Attending an MLB game in 2017 is a very different experience from attending one 20 years ago. Now-a-days, many, if not most, fans routinely check their phones and go on the Internet while the game is taking place—especially given that some ballparks offer complimentary Wi-Fi. They also take photos of one another and post them on their social media accounts.

Michael McCann, *Yankees Incident Revives an Old Question: How Responsible Are Teams for Foul Ball Injuries?*, SI.com, Sept. 21, 2017. Like McCann, two authors argue for the abolition of the baseball rules because of a convergence of factors including: (1) trends in baseball construction that place fans in closer proximity to the field of play; (2) changes in how the game is played, such as the greater velocity at which balls are thrown by pitchers, which decrease a fan's time to react to protect him or herself; (3) ticket policies that drastically limit fans' ability to choose to sit in protected seats if they desire; (4) the increase in fan distraction from what's occurring on the field resulting from electronic scoreboards, team mascots, team encouraging fans to use smartphones during games, and other activities; and (5) law and economics policy which concludes that teams are the low-cost provider and the best risk avoider for foul-ball related spectator injuries. The authors urge adoption of a strict liability approach, which would incentivize teams to extend protective netting and enact other safety features at baseball stadia given the relatively low cost to MLB teams to add more protective netting. Nathaniel Grow & Zachary Flagel, *The Faulty Law and Economics of the "Baseball Rule"*, 60 Wm. & Mary L. Rev. 59 (2018); see also Randy Gerlach, *Out of the Rough: How the PGA Tour Can Be Held Accountable for Fan Safety*, 2021 U. Ill. L. Rev. 229 (2021) (arguing that the baseball rule should not apply to the PGA).

A California court adopted a ruling sympathetic to the views expressed above. In *Mayes v. La Sierra Univ.*, 288 Cal.Rptr.3d 693 (Cal. App. 4th 2022), a spectator, who attended a college baseball game, suffered serious injuries after being struck in the face by a foul ball. Adopting the primary assumption of the risk standard, the court rejects the most protective iteration of the baseball rule. The court holds that the "primary assumption of risk doctrine is a rule of limited duty that holds owners and operators of sports venues responsible for (1) not increasing the risks of injury inherent in the activity, and (2) taking reasonable steps to increase safety and minimize the inherent risks of injury, if such steps can be taken without altering the nature of the activity." *Id.* at 704. It concluded that triable issues of fact remained, including: "(1) whether it was reasonable for the defendant to install protective netting beyond the dugouts; (2) whether defendant had a duty to warn spectators of the absence of protective netting beyond certain areas." *Id.* at 705.

During the 2017 MLB season, injuries requiring hospitalization to a toddler girl at New York's Yankee Stadium and a man at Chicago's Wrigley Field (neither of whom was seated in areas with protective netting) shone light on the duty sports facility operators owe to spectators. MLB had previously recommended (but had not required) that all clubs expand netting to the end of teams' dugouts; only some clubs followed the recommendations. Following the girl's injury, the Yankees committed to providing greater protection before the start of the 2018 season. All 30 MLB teams have since voluntarily extended protective netting to the end of teams' dugouts. In July 2019, the Chicago White Sox extended protective netting to the foul poles of its stadium, now shielding fans from line drives. In taking this action, the White Sox joined the Washington Nationals as the only MLB teams at that time to add this extra level of protection. The expanded protection occurred after several spectator injuries from batted balls in 2019. See Teddy Greenstein, *White Sox Become One of the First MLB Teams to Extend Protective Netting to the Foul Poles: 'The Game Is Changing,'* Chi. Trib., Jul. 22, 2019. In August 2019, MLB's Toronto Blue Jays announced that the club would extend protective netting down the baselines of its ballpark before the start of the 2020 baseball season. Ian Harrison, *Blue Jays to Extend Protective Netting for 2020 Season*, ABC News, Aug. 6, 2019, https://abcnews.go.com/Sports/wireStory/blue-jays-extend-protective-netting-2020-season-64807396.

3. Application to minors. Should the limited duty rule apply to minors? As it relates to a spectator's knowledge, generally "adult spectators of ordinary intelligence" who are familiar with the sport at issue will be presumed to possess an awareness of the normal risk of watching a sport. In 2002, the parents of a 13-year-old girl, who died after being struck in the head by a deflected hockey puck while watching an NHL game between the Columbus Blue Jackets and the Calgary Flames, received a $1.2 million settlement from the NHL and arena. Phil Taylor, *Death of a Fan*, Sports Illustrated, April 1, 2002 at 58. Following a common practice in European hockey rinks, the NHL subsequently required its member clubs to install protective netting approximately 30 feet in height and 120 feet in width behind the goals in their playing facilities.

Problem 7-4

A spectator, an avid hockey fan, attended a professional ice hockey game. The spectator, who was seated in an unscreened area, was struck during pregame warm-ups when a player took a shot at the goal. The shot misfired, and the puck hit the spectator. The hockey club, which owned the arena, communicated no warnings to spectators of the risk of being struck by an errant puck.

Is the club liable in tort to the spectator? See *Hurst v. East Coast Hockey League, Inc.*, 2005 WL 6218747 (S.C. Com. Pl.).

TORT IMMUNITIES

KEY TERMS
- Charitable immunity
- Discretionary function
- Ministerial function
- Qualified immunity
- Sovereign immunity

There are times when a defendant is granted an exemption, or immunity, from a duty or penalty contrary to the general rule of law. Under the doctrine of *sovereign immunity*, a public educational institution, as a subsidiary agency of the state, may be immune from tort liability for negligent acts of its employees, such as coaches, athletic trainers, and administrative personnel, that cause injury to a high school athlete. See also *Evans v. Oaks Mission Pub. Sch.*, 945 P.2d 492 (Okla. 1997); *Grandalski v. Lyons Township High Sch. Dist.* 204, 711 N.E.2d 372 (Ill. App. Ct. 1999). The scope of sovereign immunity, which may be statutory or common law, varies on a state-by-state basis.

An exception to sovereign immunity occurs when the injury was caused by a state actor engaged in commercial activity rather than its usual governance function. Courts generally hold that the operation of an interscholastic athletics program is a governmental function that is covered by the immunity defense rather than a proprietary function, which is not. *Fowler v. Tyler Indep. Sch. Dist.*, 232 S.W.3d 335 (Tex. Ct. App. 2007). In *Lovitt v. Concord Sch. Dist.*, 228 N.W.2d 479 (Mich. Ct. App. 1975), a Michigan appellate court held that a public high school football program was a physical education activity encompassed within the governmental function of providing education. Finding that the district's athletics program had been operating at a deficit for five years, the court rejected plaintiff's claim that the football program was a proprietary function because an admission fee was charged to games. For a discussion of sovereign immunity in the athletic context, see Davis & Duru, *supra* at 339–46 (providing overview of sovereign immunity in the high school sports context).

Like a public high school system, a public university may have sovereign immunity from liability for negligence in connection with the operation of its athletic program, although this immunity may be waived to the extent that negligent conduct arising out of a public university's sports program is covered by insurance. *Shriver v. Athletic Council of Kan. State Univ.*, 564 P.2d 451, 455 (Kan. 1977). Some courts have held that sponsoring revenue-generating sports such as intercollegiate football is a proprietary function of a public university that is not protected by sovereign immunity. *Brown v. Wichita State Univ.*, 540 P.2d 66, 86–89 (Kan. 1975). Thus, sovereign immunity would not bar negligence suits by athletes injured while participating in these sports. Other courts have reached the opposite conclusion, ruling that university sponsorship of intercollegiate athletics is a governmental function of a public university that confers sovereign immunity, even if some sports generate revenue. *Harris v. Univ. of Mich. Bd. of Regents*, 558 N.W.2d 225, 228 (Mich. Ct. App. 1996)). See also *Ward v. Michigan State Univ.*, 782

N.W.2d 514 (Mich. App. 2010) (university's operation of hockey rink constituted a governmental function because it did not operate the rink primarily to generate a profit); *University of Texas at El Paso v. Moreno*, 172 S.W.3d 281 (Tex. Ct. App. 2005) (university entitled to immunity from liability for claims filed by fan who asserted he was injured by conduct of other fans after he streamed onto football field and hung from goal post following postgame celebration).

Some athletes have turned to federal constitutional law in their largely unsuccessful efforts to circumvent the application of sovereign immunity In *Burden v. Wilkes-Barre Area School District*, 16 F. Supp. 2d 569 (M.D. Pa. 1998), a federal district court rejected plaintiff's contention that an educational institution's decision not to hire a certified athletic trainer to protect the health and safety of students participating in competitive sports violated an athlete's constitutional right to life and liberty. See also *Davis v. Carter*, 555 F.3d 979 (5th Cir. 2009) (rejecting parents' constitutional claims as means of circumventing immunity defense because evidence failed to establish coaches acted willfully or maliciously in case in which minor football player died during intense voluntary workout); *Yarbrough v. Sante Fe Indep. Sch. Dist.*, 2022 WL 885093 (5th Cir. Mar. 25, 2022) (finding plaintiffs did not show deliberate indifference). *Hickey ex rel. R.B. v. Enterline*, 304 F. Supp. 3d 456 (M.D. Pa. 2018) (discussing elements of state-created danger theory); but see *Lesher v. Zimmerman*, 822 Fed. Appx. 116, 119–20 (3rd Cir. 2020) (holding that student, who suffered facial injuries after being struck by a ball hit by her softball coach, failed to establish the foreseeability and deliberate indifference elements of a state-created danger claim under the Fourteenth Amendment Due Process Clause). Private universities may be protected from negligence suits by intercollegiate athletes by the doctrine of *charitable immunity*. Charitable immunity exempts an organization from legal liability based on its charitable purpose. Application of this doctrine varies by jurisdiction. See *Gilbert v. Seton Hall Univ.*, 332 F.3d 105 (2d Cir. 2003) (applying conflict of law principles to determine applicability of charitable immunity doctrine in suit by injured club team player against private university).

The doctrine of *qualified immunity* may protect public school employees (e.g., coaches and athletic trainers) from negligence liability when they are exercising a discretionary act, but not a ministerial act. A discretionary act involves exercising personal deliberation or judgment, such as examining facts, weighing options, and reaching an independently reasoned conclusion that is not specifically directed. Conversely, the execution of a specific action given a specific situation is a ministerial act. In *Prince v. Louisville Municipal School Dist.*, 741 So. 2d 207 (Miss. 1999), the Mississippi Supreme Court distinguished between a coach's discretionary and ministerial functions. A high school football player alleged that he suffered a heat stroke during practice as a result of his coaches' negligent failure to properly monitor his health and condition, to provide necessary liquids, and to provide necessary medical care in a timely manner. The court ruled that the qualified immunity doctrine shielded the coaches from negligence liability because they were engaged in a discretionary function while conducting practice:

> In a typical practice there are strains, sprains, and complaints from a coach's players. A coach must consider the good order and discipline of the team when confronted

with situational complaints by the players. A coach must use his discretion in judging whether or not an individual player is injured and then, whether the player should report to a trainer or seek other medical aid. There was no evidence presented in the lower court to show that either Bowman or Chambliss did anything beyond exercising ordinary discretion in supervising the Nanih Waiya football practice on August 29, 1991. Prince produced no facts that evidenced any disregard for his health or any other outrageous action on the part of Bowman or Chambliss that might have warranted a departure from our previous holdings. The trial court correctly found the coaches were protected by qualified immunity. . . .

Id. at 212.

Dissenting from the majority's conclusion, another judge asserted:

[T]he coaches were acting in their ministerial capacities, not with discretion. Qualified immunity is not warranted. . . . Coaches Chambliss and Bowman maintained duties to manage their players. Randall Prince suffered harm because his coaches failed to perform their duties such that he suffered heatstroke, and because those same coaches failed to take proper actions afterwards. As coaches directly responsible for serving the general needs of Prince while he is under their power as a football player, the coaches should have more closely monitored Prince's condition. When it became possible that Prince was a candidate for heatstroke, the coaches should have given him rest out of the sun, provided him additional liquids, or simply excused him from practice. There are no means by which to grant qualified immunity. The instant case deals with an extracurricular activity internal to the school, not a promotion of government policy and public good. Accordingly, I dissent. . . .

Id. at 215–16. See also *Karalyos v. Bd. of Educ. of Lake Forest Cmty. High Sch. Dist.*, 788 F. Supp. 3d 727, 731 (N.D. Ill. 2011) (a discretionary act involves an act of discretion and a policy decision); *Clark Cty. Sch. Dist. v. Payo*, 403 P.3d 1270 (Nev. 2017) (discretionary-function immunity applies to school district's decisions to add floor hockey as a part of physical education curriculum and not to provide safety equipment because the decisions were discretionary and policy-based; discretionary-function immunity did not extend, however, to decisions related to "negligent administration, instruction, and supervision of the floor hockey class" because such decisions were discretionary but were not policy-based); *Covington Cty. Sch. Dist. v. Magee*, 29 So. 3d 1 (Miss. 2010) (school district was immunized from tort liability relating to the heat stroke death of a high school football player during practice; a coach's decision to hold practice was considered a discretionary act); but see *Elston ex rel. Elston v. Howland Local Schs.*, 865 N.E.2d 845 (Ohio 2007) (where there was no showing that a coach's position involved policy-making, planning, or enforcement powers, his position did not involve "the exercise of a high degree of official judgment or discretion"; therefore, immunity was not an available defense). For commentary regarding institutional liability for heat-related deaths, see David Feingold, *Who Takes the Heat? Criminal Liability for Heat-Related Deaths in High School Athletics*, 17 Cardozo J.L. & Gender 359, 373 (2011).

Courts also recognize exceptions, including gross negligence or reckless conduct, to the availability of qualified immunity as a defense. *Al-Jahmi v. Ohio*

Athletic Comm., 2022 WL 2373589 (Ohio. App. 10 Dist. 2022) (in a case involving a professional boxer, court discusses availability of qualified immunity defense when defendant acts recklessly). In *Smith v. Kroesen*, 9 F. Supp. 3d 439 (D. N.J. 2014), a plaintiff injured by a co-participant alleged the other player's coach was liable for negligent coaching. Attempting to avoid the coach's qualified immunity defense, the plaintiff argued that the coach's gross negligence triggered the gross negligence exception to the qualified immunity afforded volunteer coaches. Defining gross negligence as referring to "behavior which constitutes indifference to consequences," the court found that the plaintiff failed to present evidence that the coach was grossly negligent in performing his coaching duties. *Id.* at 443. See also, *Swank v. Valley Christian Sch.*, 398 P.3d 1108 (Wash. 2017) (in determining whether coach's conduct precluded him from successfully asserting volunteer immunity as a defense, the court discusses the distinction between simple negligence and gross negligence or recklessness); *Barr v. Cunningham*, 89 N.E.3d 315 (Ill. 2017) (rejecting plaintiff's claim to invoke willful and wanton exception to the qualified immunity defense because coach's discretionary act of not requiring an injured athlete to wear safety glasses did not rise to the level of willful and wanton conduct).

For informative discussions of the sovereign and qualified immunity defenses, see Davis & Duru, *supra* at 339–53; David Feingold, *Who Takes the Heat? Criminal Liability for Heat-Related Deaths in High School Athletics*, 17 Cardozo J.L. & Gender 359 (2011).

QUESTION

Is it fair that an individual who is injured as a result of the negligence of a coach at a public school would not be compensated for his or her injuries, even when compensation would have been granted if the coach were at a private athletics club?

Problem 7-5

Consider whether a coach at a public educational institution would be entitled to qualified immunity in the following scenarios.

(a) An instructor accidentally hits a college student-athlete with a baseball bat during a hitting demonstration at a baseball camp. See *Quinn v. Mississippi State Univ.*, 720 So. 2d 843, 849 (Miss. 1998) (overruled on other grounds, *City of Jackson v. Estate of Stewart ex rel. Womack*, 908 So. 2d 702. 709 (Miss. 2005)).

(b) A high school baseball player, who was not wearing a batting helmet, was injured by a ball thrown by one of his teammates during batting practice. Prior to his injury, the player's coach failed to enforce a rule requiring all student-athletes to wear batting helmets while taking batting practice. See *Yanero v. Davis*, 65 S.W.3d 510, 529 (2002).

Problem 7-6

Jordan, a high school athlete, was assaulted by another player, Lee, while the two were walking unsupervised to the locker room from the practice field. The coach stopped the assault but did not otherwise attempt to ascertain the cause of the attack. The following day, Jordan suffered injury resulting from another assault by Lee when the two were left unsupervised in the locker room. The public school district's handbook states that the school possesses a duty to supervise and maintain discipline of students at school. Jordan sued the school district alleging a negligent failure to supervise. Will the school district be successful in asserting sovereign immunity as a defense?

VALIDITY OF LIABILITY WAIVERS

KEY TERMS
- Adhesion contract
- Exculpatory agreement

The following materials explore the enforceability of pre-injury contracts pursuant to which a person agrees to release a school district or its employees from liability for negligent failure to use reasonable care to protect the health and safety of students during athletic activities. These contracts may be referred to by many names, including liability waivers, exculpatory clauses, releases, covenants not to sue, and hold harmless agreements. Although technical differences exist in specific types of such contracts, what lies at their core is an agreement by one party to accept the risk of harm resulting from another's conduct. If enforceable under applicable state law, these waivers of liability bar a plaintiff's ability to seek recovery from the defendant for harm caused by certain tortious conduct.

Some courts have refused to enforce pre-injury waivers because they violate public policy. In one group of cases, courts rely on public policy grounds to refuse to permit a high school to enforce waivers against a student-athlete or his or her parents or guardian who signed it. In what can be characterized as an intermediate approach, other jurisdictions allow high schools to enforce such waivers against a parent or guardian who signs it, but not against a minor. Another group of jurisdictions have adopted a position that permits parents to sign a release that binds both the parent and minor. The cases that follow, *Wagenblast* and *Sharon*, represent contrasting perspectives on the validity of liability waivers.

Wagenblast v. Odessa School District No. 105-157-166J
758 P.2d 968 (Wash. 1988)

ANDERSEN, Justice.

Can school districts require public school students and their parents to sign written releases which release the districts from the consequences of all future school district negligence, before the students will be allowed to engage in certain recognized school related activities, here interscholastic athletics?

We hold that the exculpatory releases from any future school district negligence are invalid because they violate public policy.

Probably the best exposition of the test to be applied in determining whether exculpatory agreements violate public policy is that stated by the California Supreme Court. In writing for a unanimous court, the late Justice Tobriner outlined the factors in *Tunkl v. Regents of Univ. of Cal.*, 60 Cal.2d 92, 383 P.2d 441, 32 Cal.Rptr. 33, 6 A.L.R.3d 693 (1963):

1. *The agreement concerns an endeavor of a type generally thought suitable for public regulation.*

Regulation of governmental entities usually means self-regulation. Thus, the Legislature has by statute granted to each school board the authority to control, supervise, and regulate the conduct of interscholastic athletics. In some situations, a school board is permitted, in turn, to delegate this authority to the Washington Interscholastic Activities Association (WIAA) or to another voluntary nonprofit entity. In the cases before us, both school boards look to the WIAA for regulation of interscholastic sports. The WIAA handbook contains an extensive constitution with rules for such athletic endeavors. . . .

Clearly then, interscholastic sports in Washington are extensively regulated, and are a fit subject for such regulation.

2. *The party seeking exculpation is engaged in performing a service of great importance to the public, which is often a matter of practical necessity for some members of the public.*

This court has held that public school students have no fundamental right to participate in interscholastic athletics. Nonetheless, the court also has observed that the justification advanced for interscholastic athletics is their educational and cultural value. As the testimony of then Seattle School Superintendent Robert Nelson and others amply demonstrate, interscholastic athletics is part and parcel of the overall educational scheme in Washington. The total expenditure of time, effort and money on these endeavors makes this clear. The importance of these programs to the public is substantive; they represent a significant tie of the public at large to our system of public education. Nor can the importance of these programs to certain students be denied; as Superintendent Nelson agreed, some students undoubtedly remain in school and maintain their academic standing only because they can participate in these programs. Given this emphasis on sports by the public and the school system, it would be unrealistic to expect students to view athletics as an activity entirely separate and apart from the remainder of their schooling. . . .

In sum, under any rational view of the subject, interscholastic sports in public schools are a matter of public importance in this jurisdiction.

3. *Such party holds itself out as willing to perform this service for any member of the public who seeks it, or at least for any member coming within certain established standards.*

Implicit in the nature of interscholastic sports is the notion that such programs are open to all students who meet certain skill and eligibility standards. This conclusion finds direct support in the testimony of former Superintendent Nelson and the WIAA eligibility and nondiscrimination policies set forth in the WIAA handbook.

4. *Because of the essential nature of the service, in the economic setting of the transaction, the party invoking exculpation possesses a decisive advantage of bargaining strength against any member of the public who seeks the services.*

Not only have interscholastic sports become of considerable importance to students and the general public alike, but in most instances there exists no alternative program of organized competition. . . . While outside alternatives exist for some activities, they possess little of the inherent allure of interscholastic competition. Many students cannot afford private programs or the private schools where such releases might not be employed. In this regard, school districts have near-monopoly power. And, because such programs have become important to student participants, school districts possess a clear and disparate bargaining strength when they insist that students and their parents sign these releases.

5. *In exercising a superior bargaining power, the party confronts the public with a standardized adhesion contract of exculpation, and makes no provision whereby a purchaser may pay additional reasonable fees and obtain protection against negligence.*

Both school districts admit to an unwavering policy regarding these releases; no student athlete will be allowed to participate in any program without first signing the release form as written by the school district. In both of these cases, students and their parents unsuccessfully attempted to modify the forms by deleting the release language. In both cases, the school district rejected the attempted modifications. Student athletes and their parents or guardians have no alternative but to sign the standard release forms provided to them or have the student barred from the program.

6. *The person or property of members of the public seeking such services must be placed under the control of the furnisher of the services, subject to the risk of carelessness on the part of the furnisher, its employees or agents.*

A school district owes a duty to its students to employ ordinary care and to anticipate reasonably foreseeable dangers so as to take precautions for protecting the children in its custody from such dangers. This duty extends to students engaged in interscholastic sports. As a natural incident to the relationship of a student athlete and his or her coach, the student athlete is usually placed under the coach's considerable degree of control. The student is thus subject to the risk that the school district or its agent will breach this duty of care.

In sum, the attempted releases in the cases before us exhibit all six of the characteristics denominated in [*Tunkl*]. Because of this, and for the aforesaid reasons, we hold that the releases in these consolidated cases are invalid as against public policy. . . .

Sharon v. City of Newton
769 N.E.2d 738 (Mass. 2002)

CORDY, Judge.

[Editors' note: A 16-year-old student was injured while participating in cheerleading practice at her high school. The injured cheerleader sued, and the defendant asserted as a defense a waiver of liability that she and her father had signed.]

2. Summary Judgment

We conclude that enforcement of the release is consistent with our law and public policy, and Newton is entitled to judgment as a matter of law. . . .

b. Public Policy

Merav . . . contends that enforcement of the release against her claims would constitute a gross violation of public policy. This argument encompasses at least three separate public policy contentions: first, that it is contrary to public policy to permit schools to require students to sign exculpatory agreements as a prerequisite to participation in extracurricular school sports; second, that public policy prohibits a parent from contracting away a minor child's right to sue for a future harm; and third, that the enforcement of this release would undermine the duty of care that public schools owe their students. . . .

(1) Releases. Massachusetts law favors the enforcement of releases. . . . "There can be no doubt . . . that under the law of Massachusetts . . . in the absence of fraud a person may make a valid contract exempting himself from any liability to another

which he may in the future incur as a result of his negligence or that of his agents or employees acting on his behalf." *Schell v. Ford*, 270 F.2d 384, 386 (1st Cir. 1959).

Although Merav has suggested that, if the release at issue here is valid, there is nothing to prevent cities or towns from requiring releases for "simply allowing a child to attend school," such a conclusion does not necessarily follow. We have not had occasion to rule on the validity of releases required in the context of a compelled activity or as a condition for the receipt of essential services (e.g., public education, medical attention, housing, public utilities), and the enforceability of mandatory releases in such circumstances might well offend public policy. . . . In this case, Merav's participation in the city's extracurricular activity of cheerleading was neither compelled nor essential, and we conclude that the public policy of the Commonwealth is not offended by requiring a release as a prerequisite to that participation.

(2) *Parent's waiver of a minor's claim.* Merav contends that a parent cannot waive, compromise, or release a minor child's cause of action, and that enforcement of such a release against the child would violate public policy.

The purpose of the policy permitting minors to void their contracts is "to afford protection to minors from their own improvidence and want of sound judgment." *Frye v. Yasi*, 327 Mass. 724, 728, 101 N.E.2d 128 (1951). . . . Moreover, our law presumes that fit parents act in furtherance of the welfare and best interests of their children, . . . and with respect to matters relating to their care, custody, and upbringing have a fundamental right to make those decisions for them.

In the instant case, Merav's father signed the release in his capacity as parent because he wanted his child to benefit from participating in cheerleading, as she had done for four previous seasons. He made an important family decision cognizant of the risk of physical injury to his child and the financial risk to the family as a whole. In the circumstance of a voluntary, nonessential activity, we will not disturb this parental judgment. This comports with the fundamental liberty interest of parents in the rearing of their children, and is not inconsistent with the purpose behind our public policy permitting minors to void their contracts.

c. The Encouragement of Athletic Activities for Minors

To hold that releases of the type in question here are unenforceable would expose public schools, who offer many of the extracurricular sports opportunities available to children, to financial costs and risks that will inevitably lead to the reduction of those programs. It would also create the anomaly of a minor who participates in a program sponsored and managed by a nonprofit organization not having a cause of action for negligence that she would have had had she participated in the same program sponsored as an extracurricular activity by the local public school. This distinction seems unwarranted, inevitably destructive to school-sponsored programs, and contrary to public interest.

Merav contends that to enforce the release would convey the message that public school programs can be run negligently, in contravention of the well-established responsibility of schools to protect their students. We disagree. There are many reasons aside from potential tort liability why public schools will continue to take steps to ensure well-run and safe extracurricular programs — not the least of which is their ownership by, and accountability to, the citizens of the cities and towns they serve. Moreover, the Legislature has already made the judgment that the elimination of liability for negligence in nonprofit sports programs is necessary to the encouragement and survival of such programs. . . . The enforcement of the release is consistent with the Commonwealth's policy of encouraging athletic programs for youth and does not contravene the responsibility that schools have to protect their students. . . .

C. Conclusion

For the reasons set forth above, we conclude that Merav's father had the authority to bind his minor child to an exculpatory release that was a proper condition of her voluntary participation in extracurricular sports activities offered by the city. Summary judgment for the city that was entered on the basis of the validity of that release is therefore affirmed. . . .

NOTES

1. The enforceability of parental liability waivers. Consistent with *Sharon*, some courts have exhibited a willingness to enforce liability waivers for negligent injury to minors participating in competitive or recreational sports. *Mohney v. USA Hockey, Inc.*, 5 Fed. Appx. 450 (6th Cir. 2001) (release signed by minor hockey player and his father was valid and applied to injuries sustained by the player); *Zivich v. Mentor Soccer Club, Inc.*, 696 N.E.2d 201 (Ohio 1998) (release signed by mother of injured child barred child's claim for negligence against volunteers and sponsors of nonprofit sport activities). In *Platzer v. Mammoth Mountain Ski Area*, 128 Cal. Rptr. 2d 885 (Cal. App. 2002), a mother who enrolled her eight-year-old son in a ski resort's sports school signed a form assuming the risk of injury associated, among other things, with use of chairlifts. Her son fell from a lift during a lesson. In upholding the validity of the exculpatory clause, the court rejected plaintiff's argument that public policy precluded enforcement of the release. The court noted that California courts have consistently refused to invalidate exculpatory agreements in the recreational sports context. See also *Pollock v. Highlands Ranch Community Assn., Inc.*, 140 P.3d 351 (Colo. App. 2006) (discussing statute superseding case that had invalidated a release waiving minor child's negligence claim).

Although the foregoing decisions represent an erosion of the rule established in *Wagenblast*, courts in other jurisdictions remain reluctant to enforce waiver clauses. See *Rutherford v. Talisker Canyons Fin., Co., LLC*, 445 P.3d 474 (Utah 2019) (court holds that: "Absent a relevant, contrary expression of intent from the legislature, . . . a parent cannot release his or her minor child's prospective claims for negligence" because such a release violates public policy); *Miller ex rel. E.M. v. House of Boom Ky.*, 575 S.W.3d 656 (Ky. 2019) (court holds that a pre-injury waiver signed by parents that released for-profit entities from negligence liability for injuries to child was void as a matter of law); *Galloway v. State*, 790 N.W.2d 252, 258 (Iowa 2010) (holding that public policy precludes the enforceability of pre-injury waiver a parent signs on behalf of child and characterizing *Sharon* as reflective of the minority rule); A helpful discussion of the validity of waivers appears in Elisa Lintemuth, *Parental Rights v. Parens Patriae: Determining the Correct Limitations on the Validity of Pre-Injury Waivers Effectuated by Parents on Behalf of Minor Children*, 2010 Mich. St. L. Rev. 169 (2010). See also Davis & Duru, *supra* at 354–64 (providing overview of judicial rulings enforcing and invalidating pre-injury liability waivers signed by parents).

2. Other grounds for invalidating waivers. In jurisdictions in which a release of liability for negligence is enforceable, a waiver that attempts to relieve a defendant of liability for its willful misconduct, gross negligence, and intentional torts is invalid. See, e.g., *Eriksson v. Nunnink*, 120 Cal. Rptr. 3d 90 (Cal. Ct. App. 2011) (a finding that an equestrian coach's gross negligence in selecting an unfit horse for the plaintiff would invalidate a liability waiver). Mary A. Connell & Frederick G. Savage, *Releases: Is There Still a Place for Their Use by Colleges and Universities?*, 29 J.C. & U.L. 579, 603 (2003). Courts will also resort to contract interpretation as a mechanism for invalidating waivers that are ambiguous and inconspicuous. Such strict interpretations of contracts ease the burden on courts to reconcile the tensions between contract and tort. *Id.* at 605–06.

QUESTIONS

1. In *Wagenblast*, the Washington Supreme Court held that requiring a student and his parent or guardian to sign a standard form releasing the school district from liability for negligence in connection with the student's participation in interscholastic athletics violated public policy. What factors did the court rely on to reach its decision? Although *Sharon* recognized the ability of a minor (i.e., person under the age of 18) to void a contract, the court upheld a waiver signed by the minor's parent. Which factors most influenced the court's decision?
2. Which court, *Wagenblast* or *Sharon*, most effectively reconciles the competing public policies regarding whether pre-injury liability waivers should be enforced?

Although the law is still developing, courts are more likely to uphold waivers executed by adult intercollegiate athletes than minor interscholastic athletes:

> In recent years, some college athletes have chosen to play a sport in spite of a known medical condition, although doing so exposes them to an enhanced risk of injury. For example, Monte Williams played basketball at Notre Dame University, and Stephen Larkin played baseball at the University of Texas—both with known heart conditions that may have increased their risk of sudden death during competition. Both athletes signed waivers releasing their universities from liability for any harm that might result from playing with their medical condition. Fortunately, neither of them experienced any adverse health effects while playing their respective intercollegiate sports.

Courts generally uphold pre-injury waivers of liability for negligent acts by sponsors of recreational athletic events executed by competent adult athletes. Relying on this authority, a court might enforce a university's pre-injury liability waiver against an intercollegiate athlete for harm arising out of that athlete's informed and voluntary decision to play a sport with a known medical condition. On the other hand, a court may find that such a waiver violates public policy and is unenforceable.

Matthew J. Mitten, *Emerging Legal Issues in Sports Medicine: A Synthesis, Summary, and Analysis*, 76 St. John's L. Rev. 5, 65 (2002); see also *Feleccia*, 156 A.3d (although liability waivers signed by college student-athletes are generally valid, language of waiver did not indicate that college was being absolved for its own negligence, and trial court improperly failed to consider whether the defendant college's recklessness or gross negligence invalidated the waiver); *Sinu v. Concordia Univ.*, 983 N.W.2d 511 (Neb. 2023) (upholding release because it was clear and unambiguous and was not unconscionable); *Bradley v. NCAA*, 464 F. Supp.3d 273 (D. D.C. 2020) (in upholding the enforceability of a liability waiver, the court grants summary judgment in favor of defendant university, head coach, athletic trainer, and team physician; the court finds exculpatory language contained in the "Acknowledgement of Risk" form signed by the athletes was "conspicuous, clear, and unambiguous," and sufficiently broad to encompass plaintiff's negligence claims. It also held that the waiver was neither adhesive nor unconscionable. *Id.* at * 11.

Problem 7-7

Jordan Abel, who played soccer for a private high school, collapsed during a game following a collision with a player on the opposing team. The opposing player was penalized for the hit, which was hard but typical of hits that frequently occur during soccer matches. Within seconds after Abel collapsed, Abel's coach and the athletic trainer ran onto the soccer field and immediately asked that an assistant coach call an ambulance, which she did. By the time the coach and trainer arrived on the field, Abel had stopped breathing and lost consciousness. The trainer unsuccessfully administered CPR and called for an automated external defibrillator (AED), which was housed in a building at Abel's school. However, it was not brought to the field until 10 minutes after Abel initially collapsed, which was approximately two minutes after Abel died.

It was subsequently determined that Abel suffered from a previously undetected underlying heart condition and that if the AED had been used in a timely manner, Abel most likely would have been revived. It was also determined that prior to the game, Abel's coach noticed during warm-ups that Abel's breathing seemed slightly labored. When Abel was questioned by the coach, Abel responded that "I feel fine" and insisted on returning to play. The coach agreed but told Abel to inform them if Abel began feeling poorly during the game. Prior to the beginning of the soccer season, as a condition to Abel's ability to play sports, both Abel and Abel's parents signed a form that conspicuously absolved the school district and its employees and agents from liability for all negligent conduct arising from Abel's participation in soccer.

Abel's parents have sought your advice regarding the likely success of a tort suit to recover for Abel's death and, if so, against whom. In providing your advice, consider which claims to assert against whom and any potential defenses such parties might assert. If Abel attended a public high school, identify and discuss any other defenses that might be applicable.

Sports Medicine, Concussions, Compensation, and Impairment in Sports

INTRODUCTION

This chapter further illustrates the wide range of health and safety issues in the sports context set forth in the previous chapter. Here, the discussion continues with a focus on sports medicine, concussions, compensation, and impairment issues. In addition to tort and criminal law principles, state and federal statutes (e.g., workers' compensation and disability antidiscrimination statutes) are increasingly being used to regulate relationships among sports industry professionals that present health and safety issues.

SPORTS MEDICINE MALPRACTICE LIABILITY

KEY TERMS
- Contributory negligence
- Informed consent
- Malpractice

A. Team Physicians

Professional teams and collegiate educational institutions generally hire a physician or group of physicians to provide medical care to their athletes. Many high schools also select a physician to provide pre-participation physical examinations and emergency medical care to athletes participating in interscholastic athletics.

A "team physician" provides medical services to athletes that are arranged for, or paid for, at least in part, by an institution or entity other than the patient or the patient's parent or guardian. See Steve P. Calandrillo, *Sports Medicine Conflicts: Team Physicians vs. Athlete-Patients*, 50 St. Louis U. L.J. 185, 190–95 (2005). The team physician's primary responsibility is to provide for the physical well-being of athletes. The team physician must provide medical treatment and advice consistent with an individual athlete's best health interests because there is a physician-patient relationship between them. Although one of the team physician's objectives is to avoid the unnecessary restriction of athletic activity, a physician's paramount responsibility should be to protect the competitive athlete's health. See generally Matthew J. Mitten, *Team Physicians and Competitive Athletes: Allocating Legal Responsibility for Athletic Injuries*, 55 U. Pitt L. Rev. 129, 140–41 (1993). Team physicians may face extreme pressure from coaches, team management, fans, or the athlete to provide medical clearance to participate or treatment enabling immediate return to play.

There are few reported cases discussing the appropriate standard of care for malpractice in the sports medicine setting. In malpractice suits involving a medical specialist, the trend is to apply a national standard of care because national specialty certification boards exist to ensure standardized training and certification procedures. Although physicians assigned to care for athletes, whether in the team or individual sport context, are generally internists, family practitioners, or orthopedic surgeons, physicians with more tangentially related specialties also serve in this role. See, e.g., *Al-Jahmi v. Ohio Athletic Comm'n*, 2022 WL 2373589 * 6, 22 (Ohio App. 2022) (finding that a state athletic commission was not negligent in appointing as a boxing ringside physician an osteopathic dermatologist with no formal neurological-related training since finishing school roughly 20 years earlier).

Historically, courts have ruled that sports medicine is not a separate medical specialty, because no national medical specialty board certification or standardized training previously existed. See, e.g., *Serge v. Reconstructive Orthopaedics & Sports Med., Inc.*, 2007 WL 1880206 (Ohio Ct. App. July 2, 2007); *Fleischmann v. Hanover Ins. Co.*, 470 So. 2d 216, 217 (La. Ct. App. 1985). This judicial view, however, is changing as sports medicine continues to become a recognized and accepted area of specialization within the medical profession. The American Osteopathic Association has a certification board for sports medicine, and the specialty boards for family practice, internal medicine, emergency medicine, and pediatrics within the American Board of Medical Specialties now recognize sports medicine as a subspecialty. See generally Matthew J. Mitten, *Emerging Legal Issues in Sports Medicine: A Synthesis, Summary, and Analysis*, 76 St. John's L. Rev. 5 (2002).

Sports medicine malpractice cases adopt an "accepted practice" standard of care in determining physician liability. Under this standard, acceptable or reasonable (rather than idiosyncratic) medical practices define the boundaries of a physician's legal duty of care in treating athletes. As the court in *Bradley v. United States*, 619 F. Supp. 3d 141, 174 (D. D.C. 2022) established:

> [e]xpert testimony "is not sufficient if it consists merely of the expert's opinion as to what he or she would do under similar circumstances. Nor is it enough for the expert simply to declare that the [defendant] violated the national standard of care. Rather, the expert must clearly articulate and reference a standard of care by which the defendant's actions can be measured. Thus, the expert must clearly relate the standard of

care to the practices in fact generally followed by other comparable . . . facilities or to some standard nationally recognized by such units." (quoting *Briggs v. Wash. Metro. Area Transit Auth.*, 481 F.3d 839, 846 (D.C. Cir. 2007).

Notably, a team physician must have an athlete's informed consent before providing any medical treatment. Informed consent occurs when a participant has a clear understanding of the facts, risks, and potential consequences of voluntarily choosing to engage in an activity. This doctrine is based on the principle of individual autonomy—namely, that a competent adult has the legal right to determine what to do with his, her, or their body, including accepting or refusing medical treatment. A competent adult athlete can provide consent to medical care, but consent for treatment of athletes who are minors generally must be obtained from a parent or guardian. Consent may be implied under the circumstances, such as when an athlete has been rendered unconscious during play and needs emergency medical treatment. In these cases, the law generally assumes that if the injured athlete had been aware of the condition and was competent mentally, then the athlete would have authorized appropriate treatment.

In addition to following accepted or reasonable sports medicine practices in providing diagnosis and treatment of athletic injuries and in making medical eligibility recommendations, the team physician must fully inform an athlete of any material risks of playing a sport in light of the athlete's physical condition. Failure to do so may expose the team physician to liability based on intentional tort or negligence principles.

Courts have held that a team physician's intentional or negligent failure to provide an athlete with full disclosure of material information about playing with a medical condition or the potential consequences of proposed treatment is actionable. In *Krueger v. San Francisco Forty Niners*, 234 Cal. Rptr. 579 (Cal. Ct. App. 1987), a California appellate court held that a professional football team's conscious failure to inform a player that he risked a permanent knee injury by continuing to play was fraudulent concealment. The court found that the plaintiff was not informed by team physicians of the true nature and extent of his knee injuries, the consequences of steroid injection treatment, or the long-term dangers associated with playing professional football with his medical condition. The court found that the purpose of this nondisclosure was to induce plaintiff to continue playing football despite his injuries, thereby constituting fraud. The jury awarded Krueger $2.36 million in damages, and he ultimately settled his claim for between $1 million and $1.5 million. In other cases, athletes have been unable to prove that a physician violated the informed consent doctrine. For instance, in *Martin v. Casagrande*, 559 N.Y.S.2d 68 (N.Y. App. Div. 1990), a New York appellate court rejected a professional hockey player's claim that a physician intentionally concealed the condition of his knee to induce him to continue playing hockey. Because x-rays and tests performed by the physician did not indicate ligament or meniscal damage to the player's knee, the court held there was no basis for finding that the physician fraudulently withheld this information. The court observed that, at most, the player might have a negligence claim against the physician for failing to properly diagnose the condition of his knee.

For years, most sports medicine professionals who performed medical services outside their states of licensure were not covered by medical malpractice insurance, which exposed physicians traveling with sports teams to financial risk when they treated players at away games. On October 5, 2018, however, the long-debated Sports Medicine Licensure Clarity Act became law, clarifying that health care services provided by a sports medicine professional in a state outside the state in which the provider is licensed can be covered by the provider's medical malpractice insurer.

B. Athletic Trainers

Athletic trainers typically provide a variety of sports medicine services to athletes, such as physical conditioning, injury prevention, emergency medical care, and injury rehabilitation, which may give rise to legal liability if rendered improperly. See, e.g., *Howard v. Mo. Bone & Joint Ctr., Inc.*, 615 F.3d 991 (8th Cir. 2010) (expert testimony establishes athletic trainer's negligence in conducting workout program that caused injury to college athlete).

An athletic trainer, like any other provider of sports medicine care, is not negligent merely because the treatment provided exacerbates an athlete's injury. In *Gillespie v. Southern Utah State College*, 669 P.2d 861 (Utah 1983), the Utah Supreme Court held that a student athletic trainer was not liable for treating a basketball player's ankle injury that ultimately would have healed by itself without medical treatment. The court ruled that the athletic trainer's liability depended on proof of negligent treatment contributing to the athlete's enhanced injury.

An athletic trainer will also avoid liability if a coach misapplies the athletic trainer's treatment plan, resulting in an athlete's injury. In *Ramsey v. Gamber*, 469 F. App'x 737 (11th Cir. 2012), the United States Court of Appeals for the Eleventh Circuit held that a football trainer, who provided a rehabilitation plan for an athlete returning from a spinal injury, was not liable for the player reinjuring his spine when the strength coach instructed the player to lift heavier weights. Although the trainer had provided the strength coach with the rehabilitation plan, the trainer was not liable for the strength coach's instructions because the strength coach independently managed the weight room and was not supervised by the trainer.

C. Athlete's Contributory Negligence

An athlete has a legal duty to use reasonable care to protect the athlete's own health and safety. The doctrine of contributory negligence prohibits a plaintiff from recovering damages if the plaintiff contributed in any way to his, her, or their own harm. See, e.g., *McGee v. Covington County Sch. Dist.*, 2012 WL 48026 (Miss. App.) (absolving from liability nurse practitioner who conducted pre-participation physical examination of high school student-athlete who later died during practice where the athlete and his mother failed to truthfully disclose the athlete's medical history).

An athlete may generally rely on the recommendations of the team physician or the physician's designated consulting specialists, without seeking a second medical opinion, regarding when it is appropriate to return to play after an injury. Both *Krueger, supra,* and *Mikkelsen v. Haslam,* 764 P.2d 1384, 1386 (Utah Ct. App. 1988), held that reliance on the team physician's recommendations ordinarily is considered reasonable because of the doctor's sports medicine expertise and because the athlete is not required to obtain a confirming medical opinion.

On the other hand, an athlete's failure to follow the physician's instructions constitutes contributory negligence that may reduce or bar any recovery. In *Gillespie v. Southern Utah State College,* 669 P.2d 861 (Utah 1983), a college basketball player was found to be solely responsible for aggravating an ankle injury by not following physician instructions concerning proper treatment and rehabilitation. See also *Holtman v. Reese,* 460 S.E.2d 338 (N.C. Ct. App. 1995) (engaging in high-impact aerobics, snow skiing, and waterskiing contrary to chiropractor's advice). But see *Howard v. Missouri Bone & Joint Center, Inc.,* 615 F.3d 991 (8th Cir. 2010) (engaging in squat lifts against an athletic trainer's recommendations did not constitute contributory negligence because the athlete was following the directions of his weight training coach).

Importantly, an athlete does not assume the risk of injury from negligent emergency medical care rendered by a physician during a sporting event. In *Classen v. Izquierdo,* 520 N.Y.S.2d 999, 1002 (N.Y. Sup. Ct. 1987), a New York court denied a summary judgment motion made by a ringside physician who allegedly was negligent in allowing a boxer to continue fighting and thereby received injuries that caused his death.

INJURY COMPENSATION FOR PROFESSIONAL ATHLETES

KEY TERMS
- Compensable event
- Injury by accident
- Intentional injury exception
- Voluntary participation
- Workers' compensation

Like other athletes, professional athletes generally assume the inherent risks of injury while participating in their respective sports. However, league collective bargaining agreements and standard player contracts generally establish a contractual right of professional athletes to receive team-provided or paid medical care and rehabilitation for injuries suffered during training and games. Major league professional athletes also have contractual injury protection guarantees and benefits for career-ending injuries and sport-related disabilities. Disputes between a player and team concerning the parties' respective rights and responsibilities under these agreements generally must be submitted to binding arbitration. *Smith v. Houston*

Oilers, Inc., 87 F.3d 717 (5th Cir. 1996); but see *Bentley v. Cleveland Browns Football Co.*, 2011 WL 2652343 (Ohio App. July 7, 2011) (club's alleged fraudulent and negligent misrepresentations regarding its postoperative rehabilitation facility for players do not require interpretation of NFL CBA and are not required to be submitted to arbitration).

As employees, professional team sport athletes also may be eligible to recover state workers' compensation benefits for injuries or diseases arising from playing a sport. See, e.g., *Norfolk Admirals v. Jones*, 2005 WL 2847392 (Va. App. 2005) (professional hockey player entitled to receive workers' compensation benefits for injuries suffered in a fight, which was ordered by his coach, with an opposing player during a game). Workers' compensation laws provide a simple and inexpensive method for employees to obtain compensation and medical expenses for work-related injuries and illnesses. These laws are premised on the idea that workplace accidents are a cost of doing business and that their burden should therefore be borne by the enterprise that engendered them. In this sense, workers' compensation is a transfer of economic losses from injured workers to industry and, ultimately, to the public.

Under workers' compensation legislation, benefits are available to injured workers without having to prove breach of an employer's common law tort or other statutory liability. Defenses available in common law tort actions, such as contributory negligence and assumption of risk, are unavailable to employers in workers' compensation actions. The removal of such requirements enables injured employees to avoid the impediments that left many workers uncompensated under the common law.

Employees obtain the security of workers' compensation benefits on a no-fault basis in exchange for relinquishing rights to pursue tort actions against their employers. A worker who accepts workers' compensation benefits or has successfully prosecuted a workers' compensation claim is barred from bringing a common law tort action. Limitations are also imposed on the amount of damages that workers can recover. For example, workers' compensation statutes generally preclude employees from recovering for pain and suffering or punitive damages. Available remedies are typically limited to compensation for disability, medical, death, and burial expenses. Thus, employees waive tort claims against their employers in exchange for a simplified but limited recovery under workers' compensation laws.

State statutes are generally the source of employee rights to workers' compensation benefits. Therefore, absent a specific exclusion under a particular state's law, injured professional athletes normally are eligible to receive workers' compensation benefits. A few states exclude professional athletes from the definition of "employee" for workers' compensation purposes or otherwise severely limit the extent to which workers' compensation benefits are available to professional athletes. See, e.g., Fla. Stat. Ann. §440.02(17)(c)(3) (West 2006); Mass. Gen. Laws Ann. Ch. 152, §1(4)(b) (West 2008); and 2003 Wyo. Sess. Laws, §27-14-102(vii)(F) (2007). The Florida and Wyoming statutes provide coverage for professional athletes when their team purchases insurance for the specific purpose of providing workers' compensation benefits for its athletes.

Typically, the right of an employee to receive benefits under workers' compensation laws is dependent on two important criteria: (1) Is the person seeking benefits as an "employee," as defined by the relevant state statute?; and (2) Is the injury for which compensation is sought work-related, or, as is commonly stated, did the injury arise "out of" and "in the course of" the claimant's employment? A helpful review and analysis of general workers' compensation principles is provided in Larson's Workers' Compensation (Matthew Bender, Rev. Ed., 2019).

To be in a position to claim benefits, an injured employee must provide timely notice to the employer and must file a claim within the time frame established by the relevant workers' compensation statute. The purpose of these requirements is two-fold: "First, to enable the employer to provide immediate medical diagnosis and treatment with a view to minimizing the seriousness of the injury; and second, to facilitate the earliest possible investigation of the facts surrounding the injury." 11 Larson's Workers' Compensation Law §126.01 (2019).

Although professional athletes most often can readily establish the existence of an employee–employer relationship, this characterization sets the stage for the introduction of a myriad of other legal issues that potentially affect injured athletes' entitlement to workers' compensation benefits. The following material provides two illustrations of contemporary issues involving workers' compensation and professional athletics: (1) what injuries are compensable under workers' compensation statutes; and (2) what exceptions exist to the exclusivity of workers' compensation benefits systems as the sole state law remedy for player injuries.

Pro-Football, Inc. v. Uhlenhake
558 S.E. 2d 571 (Va. App. 2002)

BENTON, Judge.

The Workers' Compensation Commission entered an award of permanent partial disability benefits in favor of Jeffrey A. Uhlenhake, a professional football player, for injury to his left foot and denied him an award of benefits for injury to his left knee. Pro-Football, Inc., trading as the Washington Redskins, contends that injuries to a professional football player are not covered by the Act and, alternatively, that the evidence does not support the award of benefits for injury to Uhlenhake's left foot. Uhlenhake contends the evidence proved a compensable injury to his left knee. For the reasons that follow, we affirm the commission's award.

Pro-Football contends that "injuries resulting from voluntary participation in activities where injuries are customary, foreseeable, and expected are not accidental within the meaning of the Virginia Workers' Compensation Act." It argues that "in determining whether an injury is accidental, the relevant focus is upon the predictability of the injury based upon the activity performed."

As a guiding principle, the Workers' Compensation Act provides that "'injury' means only injury by accident arising out of and in the course of employment." Code

§65.2-101. The Act does not . . . specifically define the term "injury by accident." Consequently, the phrase has been the subject of judicial interpretation. . . .

To establish an "injury by accident," a claimant must prove (1) that the injury appeared suddenly at a particular time and place and upon a particular occasion, (2) that it was caused by an identifiable incident or sudden precipitating event, and (3) that it resulted in an obvious mechanical or structural change in the human body. . . .

Pro-Football initially posits that Uhlenhake seeks to recover for "injuries resulting from *voluntary* participation in activities." (Emphasis added.) The evidence proved, however, that Uhlenhake was engaged in an activity required by his employment. He was employed by Pro-Football to train, practice, and play in football games, which is the business of Pro-Football. No evidence proved Uhlenhake undertook a voluntary task when he engaged in the activity, which he alleges caused his injury. This is not a case of an injury "resulting from an employee's voluntary participation in employer-sponsored off-duty recreational activities which are not part of the employee's duties." Code §65.2-101 (specifying an exclusion from injury by accident). Likewise, this is not a case in which the "injury was the direct result of [an employee] taking a risk of his own choosing, independent of any employment requirements, and one that was not an accepted and normal activity at the place of employment." *Mullins v. Westmoreland Coal Co.*, 10 Va. App. 304, 308, 391 S.E.2d 609, 611 (1990). Uhlenhake was at all relevant times engaged in an activity within the scope of his employment contract.

Pro-Football argues that by engaging in conduct which is physically dangerous and which has a high likelihood of injury, Uhlenhake must "automatically expect to be injured. . . . Pro-Football . . . asserts that "professional football players must accept the risk of injury if they wish to play the game" and argues that "the commission's broadened definition will extend compensability to . . . others who voluntarily participate in employment where injury is either highly probable or certain." It has long been understood, however, that the legislature abolished various common law doctrines, including assumption of the risk, when it adopted the Workers' Compensation Act. . . . In effect, Pro-Football's argument, if accepted, would introduce into the workers' compensation law the concept of assumption of the risk for a hazard that is undisputedly an incident of a worker's occupation.

"To say that football injuries are not accidental because of the probability of injury is, if one looks at it more closely, no more than to say that any activity with a high risk factor should be ruled noncompensable." 2 Larson at §22.04[1][b]. The commission properly rejected this misguided notion and ruled that "the nature of the employment and the foreseeability of a potential injury does not determine whether an injury sustained in the ordinary course of an employee's duties is an accident." The business of Pro-Football is to engage in the activity of professional football. It employs individuals to constantly perform in a strenuous activity that has risks and hazards. As with coal miners, steel workers, firefighters, and police officers, who are covered by the Act, other classes of employees are regularly exposed to known, actual risks of hazards because "the employment subjects the employee to the particular danger." *Olsten v. Leftwich*, 230 Va. 317, 319, 336 S.E.2d 893, 894 (1985). The commission correctly ruled that professional football players are not exempt from the coverage of the Act when they suffer injuries in the game they are employed to perform.

[Editors' note: Based on the foregoing standard of review, the court found that credible evidence supported the commission's finding awarding Uhlenhake permanent partial disability benefits for loss of the use of his left foot. The court next considered Uhlenhake's challenge to the sufficiency of the evidence to support the commission's finding that his left knee injury resulted from cumulative trauma and, therefore, is not compensable. Noting that the employee bears the burden of proving by a preponderance of the evidence that an injury by accident occurred, the court concluded that credible evidence supported the commission's finding "that the [knee] injury was the result of cumulative events" and consequently was not compensable.]

For these reasons, we affirm all aspects of the commission's decision.

NOTE

Off-season injuries. The time of an injury's occurrence may affect a player's right to workers' compensation benefits. See, e.g., *Robinson v. Dept. of Labor & Indus.*, 326 P.3d 744 (Wash. Ct. App. 2014) (holding that a free agent who injured his knee during an off-season minicamp tryout was not an "employee" entitled to recover workers' compensation benefits; but see *Farren v. Baltimore Ravens*, 720 N.E.2d 590 (Ohio Ct. App. 1998) (summary judgment inappropriate where player, who was injured during the off-season while between contracts, received ambiguous communications and instructions from the team concerning his employment status, thereby creating a question of fact as to that status).

While workers' compensation laws generally mandate that workers' compensation be an employee's exclusive remedy, they will not bar a tort action against an employer for harm caused by conduct that is intended to injure an employee. If the requisite intent is established, an employee may elect to either receive workers' compensation benefits or bring a tort claim. As the following case illustrates, however, courts generally are not receptive to a professional athlete's claim that the athlete's team "intended" the athlete's injury.

DePiano v. Montreal Baseball Club, Ltd.
663 F. Supp. 116 (W.D. Pa. 1987)

WEBER, District Judge.

[Editors' note: Jeffrey DePiano, a minor league baseball player, suffered a career-ending shoulder injury during a game. DePiano sued his minor league team and its major league parent, the Montreal Expos, alleging "negligence in their failure to provide timely and adequate medical care for his injury, and for requiring him to continue playing despite his injury. Plaintiff alleges that continued play aggravated his injury and ended his career."]

The intentional injury exception to the exclusivity of New York's Workers' Compensation Act is very narrow. In *Finch v. Swingly*, 42 A.D.2d 1035, 348 N.Y.S.2d 266 (1973), the New York Supreme Court recited the rule:

> Where injury is sustained to an employee due to an intentional tort perpetrated by the employer or at the employer's direction, the Workmen's Compensation Law is not a bar to a common law action for damages. A valid complaint under this theory of recovery must allege an intentional or deliberate act by the employer causing harm to the employee. In order to constitute an intentional tort, the conduct must be engaged in with the desire to bring about the consequences of the act. A mere knowledge and appreciation of a risk is not the same as the intent to cause injury. . . .

In the present case, the only evidence advanced by plaintiff in response to the summary judgment motion goes to the employers' negligence in failing to provide medical treatment and in leaving that decision to an allegedly unqualified person, the team trainer. However, there is nothing in the evidence to indicate that the defendants' intention was to injure plaintiff. Negligence alone, no matter the degree, does not satisfy the intentional injury exception to the compensation bar. Despite full opportunity to advance evidence of intentional injury, plaintiff has succeeded only in establishing a prima facie case of negligence.

Plaintiff insists that defendants knew of the risk of further injury or even that injury was "substantially certain" to occur. As we noted above, such evidence is insufficient. . . . Plaintiff also argues that defendants insisted on keeping plaintiff in the lineup despite his injury because the Jamestown team was short of outfielders. If indeed this is true, it disproves rather than supports plaintiff's case because it establishes a motive for defendants' conduct other than an intention to injure plaintiff. . . .

Summary judgment will be granted in favor of defendants. . . .

NOTE

In jurisdictions that recognize the intentional injury exception to the exclusivity effect of workers' compensation laws, courts are rather exacting with regard to the burden imposed on the employee. As *DePiano* illustrates, the employee must prove that the employer intended to injure or aggravate an injury when requiring a player to continue playing. See *Brocail v. Detroit Tigers, Inc.*, 268 S.W.3d 90, 108 (Tex. App. 2008) (discussing standard for determining when a tort is deemed intentional in the workers' compensation context).

In an effort to assert claims for sports medicine malpractice, players have attempted to characterize the team physician as an independent contractor rather than a team employee to avoid the workers' compensation bar to tort claims against co-employees. Despite earlier authority adopting such a characterization, see *Bryant v. Fox*, 515 N.E.2d 775 (Ill. App. Ct. 1987), more recent case law has rejected it. *Lotysz v. Montgomery*, 766 N.Y.S.2d 28 (N.Y. App. Div. 2003); *Daniels v. Seattle Seahawks*,

968 P.2d 883 (Wash. App. Ct. 1998). In *Hendy v. Losse*, 819 P.2d 1 (Cal. 1991), a professional football player sued team physicians for negligently diagnosing and treating a knee injury suffered during a game and for advising him to continue playing football. In dismissing these claims, the California Supreme Court held that California's workers' compensation law bars tort suits between co-employees for injuries caused within the scope of employment. The court found that the plaintiff and defendant were both employed by the San Diego Chargers and that the defendant acted within the scope of his employment in treating the plaintiff. Thus, the plaintiff's exclusive remedy for his harm was workers' compensation. See also *Stringer v. Minnesota Vikings Football Club, LLC*, 705 N.W.2d 746 (Minn. 2005) (workers' compensation co-employee doctrine bars tort claim against NFL club's athletic trainers for alleged improper treatment of player who died from heatstroke during preseason practice).

COMMENT: CONCUSSIONS

Research conducted over the past two decades has increased awareness of the medical severity of head injuries suffered during sports participation. All 50 states now have some type of concussion legislation, primarily modeled after the Zackery Lystedt Law enacted by the Washington state legislature in 2009 (2009 Wa. HB 1824). Such legislation typically requires schools to provide education about head injuries to sports participants and their parents and to develop concussion identification and treatment protocols. Additionally, if an athlete is suspected of having sustained a concussion in practice or competition, the athlete is required to be removed from participation immediately and evaluated by an appropriate health care professional, and cannot return to play until receiving written clearance from the health care professional. In many states, schools that comply with the legislation have immunity from head injury-related lawsuits. (See Chapter 2 for more information about head injury and youth sports.)

The National Collegiate Athletic Association (NCAA) and all American professional sports leagues have also developed concussion safety policies, prompted in part by a rash of litigation brought by athletes. The first and most notable of these lawsuits was filed by former NFL players alleging that the NFL knowingly exposed them to debilitating brain trauma and failed to disclose the risk. The lawsuits asserted that the NFL knew or should have known since 1928 that football caused brain damage. Instead of warning the players of these dangers and enacting rules to protect player safety and long-term welfare, the NFL allegedly engaged in a campaign to deny the risks and deliberately deceive players with faulty research that refuted the link between concussions and neurodegenerative disease. The cases were eventually consolidated, with thousands of players represented in the class. In 2013, the parties agreed to settle, requiring the NFL to pay for medical exams for retired players, make payments to former players identified as having suffered cognitive injury, and provide additional funding for head trauma research and education. The district court hearing the case initially expressed concern as to whether the settlement sufficiently compensated the players. In response, the parties adjusted the terms of the deal. The settlement was finally officially approved in 2015. *In re Nat'l Football League Players' Concussion Injury Litig.*, 2015 WL 1822254 (E.D.Pa.) (April 22, 2015). The amount of money distributed through the settlement will depend on the number of players who ultimately file claims under the settlement's provisions. As of June 2023, over 20,571 NFL players had joined the class, 3,688 claims had been filed, and 1,620 claims had been approved for payments that have totaled over $1,173,000,000. See NFL Concussion Settlement: Reports and Statistics, *https://www.nflconcussionsettlement.com/*.

The NFL's settlement has spawned additional legal disputes including players' eligibility to receive compensation from the fund, whether the comprehensive settlement precludes loss of consortium claims, and the validity of liens asserted by medical providers, lawyers, and credit card companies against settlement fund payments intended for former NFL players. The most notable such legal dispute, however, involved an allegation of racial discrimination. Two former NFL players, Najeh Davenport and Kevin Henry, sued the NFL with respect to the league's use of "race-norming" in its cognitive ability testing plan under the settlement. The race-based adjustments under the testing plan prevented hundreds of African-American former players with dementia from securing awards that averaged $500,000 or more. Lawyers for the African-American players asserted that white players were qualifying for awards at two or three times the rate of African-American players since the payouts began in 2017. After the lawsuit was filed, the NFL and the plaintiffs' lawyers entered mediation, and the NFL ultimately agreed to eliminate the race-based testing. With the removal of race-based testing, African-American retirees are able to have their tests rescored or seek a new round of cognitive testing. See NFL Agrees to End Race-Based Brain Testing in $1B Settlement on Concussions, NPR, Oct. 20, 2021, *https://www.npr.org/2021/10/20/1047793751/nfl-concussion-settlement-race-norming-cte*.

The NFL concussion lawsuit has inspired other concussion-related lawsuits against sports organizations, most notably the NCAA and the NHL. At the college level, in 2011, former Eastern Illinois University football player Adrian Arrington filed what became a class action lawsuit against the NCAA for injuries and lingering pain related to multiple concussions he had suffered while playing. See *Arrington et al. v. Nat'l Collegiate Athletic Ass'n*, No. 11-cv-06356 (N.D. Ill.). In 2019, the court approved a settlement that provided $70 million for a Medical Monitoring Fund and an additional $5 million for concussion research. See *In re NCAA Student-Athlete Concussion Injury Litigation*, 2019 WL 3776955 (N.D. Ill. 2019). Unlike the NFL and NCAA plaintiffs, the NHL plaintiffs were unable to gather their claims together in a class action lawsuit through class certification. See *In re National Hockey League Players' Concussion Injury Litigation*, 327 F.R.D. 245 (D. Minn. 2018). Consequently, NHL plaintiffs had to move forward with their suits individually, which lessened their leverage. In 2018, the players and the league settled for $18.9 million.

Increased awareness of concussion danger has begun to impact elite athletes' perspectives on their careers, prompting some at the highest level to retire prematurely for fear of brain injury. It will be interesting to see how further litigation and legislative efforts affect the manner in which professional and amateur sports organizations treat concussions, as well as how players evaluate and respond to the risks and potential long-term effects of brain trauma.

PARTICIPATION RIGHTS OF ATHLETES WITH PHYSICAL OR MENTAL IMPAIRMENTS

KEY TERMS
- Disability
- Major life activity
- Reasonable accommodation

Health and safety issues in sports are generally a matter of tort law. However, constitutional law principles have been invoked when athletes with physical or mental medical conditions seek the opportunity to play. The U.S. Supreme Court has ruled that persons with a physical disability are not a suspect or quasi-suspect class justifying a heightened level of scrutiny for alleged discrimination in violation of the equal protection clause of the U.S. Constitution. *City of Cleburne v. Cleburne Living Center, Inc.*, 473 U.S. 432 (1985). Because a professional sports league is not a state actor whose rules and conduct are subject to federal constitutional scrutiny, courts have rejected claims by physically impaired professional athletes that their exclusion from athletics violates the federal constitution. In *Grube v. Bethlehem Area School District*, 550 F. Supp. 418, 423 (E.D. Pa. 1982), the court expressed doubt that a public high school's exclusion of a student with one kidney from contact sports denies equal protection of the law. Such exclusion is constitutionally justifiable if the school's reliance on its team physician's medical recommendation that an athlete not play rationally furthers its permissible objective of ensuring students' health and safety.

However, in *Neeld v. American Hockey League*, 439 F. Supp. 459 (W.D.N.Y. 1977), the court enjoined enforcement of a professional league bylaw prohibiting athletes with one eye from playing hockey. The court ruled that this bylaw violated New York's Human Rights Law, which protected employees from discrimination based on disability unless the characteristic is a bona fide occupational qualification. There was no evidence that blindness in one eye substantially detracted from the plaintiff's ability to play hockey.

Today, disability discrimination claims by athletes against professional sports leagues or clubs, sports governing bodies, or educational institutions are most likely to be brought under the federal Rehabilitation Act of 1973 or the Americans with Disabilities Act of 1990.

A. Rehabilitation Act of 1973

The Rehabilitation Act, 29 U.S.C.A. §§701 et seq., is primarily intended to provide persons with physical or mental impairments an opportunity to participate fully in activities they have the physical capabilities and skills to perform. Qualified handicapped athletes must be given an "equal opportunity for participation" in interscholastic and intercollegiate athletics.

To prevail in a claim alleging violation of the Rehabilitation Act, an athlete with a physical impairment must establish that the athlete is: (1) an "individual with handicaps;" (2) "otherwise qualified" to participate; (3) who is excluded or discriminated against solely by reason of the handicap; and (4) is excluded from a program or activity receiving federal funds.

The athletics programs of most colleges and high schools generally do not receive direct federal funding, but they nevertheless are subject to the Rehabilitation Act if the educational institution of which they are a part receives federal financial assistance in any way, which generally is the case. Professional sports leagues and governing bodies generally are not subject to the Rehabilitation Act because they do not receive federal funding.

An athlete is an "individual with handicaps" entitled to the Act's protection if the athlete has a permanent physical impairment that substantially limits a major life activity. It is relatively easy for an athlete to establish the existence of a permanent physical impairment such as a heart condition, congenital back or spine abnormality, or loss of a paired organ (e.g., eye or kidney)—all of which are covered under the Act. It is more difficult to satisfy the requirement that the athlete's physical impairment substantially limits a major life activity. Most courts have held that exclusion of an impaired athlete from intercollegiate or interscholastic sports does not constitute a substantial limitation on a major life activity. See *Knapp v. Northwestern University*, 101 F.3d 473 (7th Cir. 1996), *cert. denied*, 520 U.S. 1274 (1997), discussed *infra*.

Even if being barred from participation in athletics were deemed to impair a major life activity, the athlete must be "otherwise qualified" (i.e., have the requisite physical ability and skills to play the sport in spite of the physical impairment) and excluded "solely by reason of handicap" (i.e., ineligibility to participate in a sport is based entirely on consideration of the physical impairment or medical condition) to have a valid disability discrimination claim under the Act. Failure to select an otherwise qualified disabled athlete for a position on a competitive sports team is not necessarily a violation of the Act. In *Doe v. Eagle-Union Community School Corp.*, 101 F. Supp. 2d 707 (S.D. Ind. 2000), *vacated on other grounds*, 248 F.3d 1157 (7th Cir. 2001), a federal district court held that a coach's decision not to select a disabled student for the varsity basketball team after a tryout did not violate the Act. The court found that the disabled student was given the same opportunity to try out for the team as students without disabilities, and was graded in a nondiscriminatory manner based on the coach's uniform subjective and objective criteria. The court explained that "the term 'otherwise qualified' did not mean that the student must be selected for the basketball team despite his handicap; it prohibited the non-selection of the student when the student had the skills to make the team but was not selected."

An educational institution must make reasonable accommodations to enable physically impaired athletes to participate in its athletic programs. An impaired athlete is "otherwise qualified" if able to meet a school's physical and medical requirements with reasonable accommodations, such as medication, monitoring, or protective padding or braces, that effectively reduce the risk of injury to the impaired athlete or others. For example, in *Grube v. Bethlehem Area School District*, 550 F. Supp. 418, 424 (E.D. Pa. 1982), the court ruled that the Act required a high school to permit a student-athlete with one kidney to play football if he wore a protective flak jacket, which it found to be a reasonable accommodation.

Courts have ruled that preventing a significant risk of harm to the health and safety of other participants, if supported by valid medical evidence, is a reasonable ground for refusing to permit an athlete covered by the Act to play a particular sport. In *Doe v. Woodford County Board of Education*, 213 F.3d 921 (6th Cir. 2000), the Sixth Circuit held that a public high school district's decision to place a member of its junior varsity basketball team, who suffered from hepatitis B, on "hold" status pending receipt of medical clearance from his physician, did not violate the Rehabilitation Act. Observing that one could be excluded from athletics if one's participation posed a direct threat to the health and safety of others, the court found that the school district was attempting to determine whether there was a significant risk of transmission of hepatitis B to other athletes. The student's membership on the team was never terminated, and the school district ultimately allowed him to participate fully on the team with no medical restrictions.

The Rehabilitation Act permits the exclusion of a physically impaired athlete from a sport if necessary to prevent a significant risk of substantial harm to the athlete. In *Pahulu v. University of Kansas*, 897 F. Supp. 1387 (D. Kan. 1995), a federal district court upheld the team physician's "conservative" medical disqualification of a college football player with an abnormally narrow cervical canal after an episode of transient quadriplegia during a scrimmage. After consulting with a neurosurgeon, the team physician concluded that the athlete was at extremely high risk for sustaining permanent, severe neurologic injury, including permanent quadriplegia, if he continued playing football. The athlete wanted to resume playing because three other medical specialists concluded that he was at no greater risk of permanent paralysis than any other player. The university agreed to honor the athlete's scholarship, although he was not allowed to play football despite his willingness to sign a waiver absolving the university of legal liability if he were injured. The court held that university officials' adherence to the team physician's recommendation against playing does not violate the Rehabilitation Act, concluding that the university's medical disqualification decision "has a rational and reasonable basis and is supported by substantial competent evidence for which the court is unwilling to substitute its judgment."

Similarly, in *Knapp v. Northwestern University*, 101 F.3d 473 (7th Cir. 1996), *cert. denied*, 520 U.S. 1274 (1997), the Seventh Circuit held that Northwestern University did not violate the Rehabilitation Act by accepting its team physician's recommendation that an athlete with idiopathic ventricular fibrillation not play intercollegiate basketball because doing so would expose him to a significant risk of cardiac arrest. The team physician's recommendation was based on Knapp's medical records and history, the 26th Bethesda Conference guidelines for athletic participation with cardiovascular abnormalities, and opinions of two consulting cardiologists.

As a high school senior, Nicholas Knapp suffered sudden cardiac arrest while playing recreational basketball, which required cardiopulmonary resuscitation and defibrillation to restart his heart. Thereafter, he had an internal cardioverter-defibrillator implanted in his abdomen. He subsequently played competitive recreational basketball without any incidents of cardiac arrest and received medical clearance to play college basketball from three cardiologists who examined him. Northwestern agreed to honor its commitment to provide Knapp with an athletic scholarship, although he was medically disqualified from playing intercollegiate basketball.

At the time, no person had ever played college or professional basketball after suffering sudden cardiac arrest or after having a defibrillator implanted. Taking into account his internal defibrillator, Knapp's experts testified that playing intercollegiate basketball would expose him to a risk of death between 1 in 34 and 1 in 100; although this risk is higher than that for the average male collegiate basketball player, they believed it to be an acceptable level of risk. Northwestern's experts agreed with the school's team doctor that, although the precise risk cannot be quantified, Knapp's participation in intercollegiate basketball significantly increased his risk of death to an unacceptable degree.

Observing that "legitimate physical qualifications may in fact be essential to participation in particular programs," the Seventh Circuit ruled that Knapp's exclusion from the Northwestern University basketball team did not violate the Rehabilitation Act:

> A significant risk of personal physical injury can disqualify a person from a position if the risk cannot be eliminated. But more than merely an elevated risk of injury is required before disqualification is appropriate. Any physical qualification based on risk of future injury must be examined with special care if the Rehabilitation Act is not to be circumvented, since almost all disabled individuals are at a greater risk of injury. . . .
>
> We do not believe that, in cases where medical experts disagree in their assessment of the extent of a real risk of serious harm or death, Congress intended that the courts—neutral arbiters but generally less skilled in medicine than the experts involved—should make the final medical decision. Instead, in the midst of conflicting expert testimony regarding the degree of serious risk of harm or death, the court's place is to ensure that the exclusion or disqualification of an individual was individualized, reasonably made, and based upon competent medical evidence. So long as these factors exist, it will be the rare case regarding participation in athletics where a court may substitute its judgment for that of the school's team physicians.
>
> In closing, we wish to make clear that we are *not* saying Northwestern's decision necessarily is the right decision. We say only that it is not an illegal one under the Rehabilitation Act. On the same facts, another team physician at another university, reviewing the same medical history, physical evaluation, and medical recommendations, might reasonably decide that Knapp met the physical qualifications for playing on an intercollegiate basketball team. Simply put, all universities need not evaluate risk the same way. What we say in this case is that if substantial evidence supports the decision-maker—here Northwestern—that decision must be respected.
>
> [The Rehabilitation Act] prohibits authorities from deciding without significant medical support that certain activities are too risky for a disabled person. Decisions

of this sort cannot rest on paternalistic concerns. Knapp, who is an adult, is not in need of paternalistic decisions regarding his health, and his parents—more entitled to be paternalistic toward him than Northwestern—approve of his decision.... But here, where Northwestern acted rationally and reasonably rather than paternalistically, no Rehabilitation Act violation has occurred. The Rehabilitation Act "is carefully structured to replace . . . reflexive actions to actual or perceived handicaps with actions based on reasoned and medically sound judgments. . . ."

101 F.3d, at 485-86.

The court in *Class v. Towson Univ.*, 806 F.3d 236 (4th Cir. 2015), took a similar approach, deferring to the university's judgment, as long as it is reasonable. *Class* involved a Towson University football player, Gavin Class, who suffered exertional heat stroke during practice. The heat stroke caused liver failure necessitating a liver transplant, forcing Class to cease his collegiate football career. Upon recovery, Class desired to return to the football team, but the university's team physician medically disqualified Class from participation. Class unsuccessfully challenged the determination. The Fourth Circuit found:

[T]he standard for assessing [the team physician's] judgment not to clear Class for return to football under Towson University's Return-to-Play Policy is not whether we share that judgment or whether she had a better judgment than some other doctor. Rather, the standard is whether her judgment was reasonable—i.e., whether it was individualized to Class, was reasonably made, and was based on competent medical evidence. When applying that standard, we conclude that [her] decision was supported by legitimate health and safety concerns, manifested by the medical records, which were not eliminated by the proposed monitoring system. Therefore, we conclude that her decision was not unreasonable.

806 F.3d, at 251.

B. Americans with Disabilities Act of 1990

The Americans with Disabilities Act (ADA), 42 U.S.C. §§12101 et seq., is patterned after the Rehabilitation Act and has similar policy objectives. The ADA's scope, however, is broader than that of the Rehabilitation Act because it covers entities that do not receive federal funding, such as professional sports leagues and their member teams. Depending on the particular sport, the ADA's provisions covering employers, public entities, and places of public accommodation may apply. The ADA applies to public entities such as public high schools, universities, and colleges; employers, such as professional leagues and clubs, with 15 or more employees; and private persons or entities that own, lease, or operate a place of public accommodation, such as the Professional Golfers' Association Tour, the NCAA, youth sports leagues, and sports instructional schools.

Courts generally construe the ADA in a manner consistent with judicial interpretations of the Rehabilitation Act. The factors governing the legality of excluding a physically disabled athlete from a sport under the ADA are essentially the same as those relevant under the Rehabilitation Act. *Bragdon v. Abbott*, 524 U.S. 624, 631–32 (1998).

Like the Rehabilitation Act, the ADA requires a valid medical basis for excluding an athlete from competition on the ground that the athlete's physical condition exposes other participants to an increased risk of serious harm. In *Anderson v. Little League Baseball, Inc.*, 794 F. Supp. 342 (D. Ariz. 1992), a federal district court held that a youth baseball league policy prohibiting coaches in wheelchairs from being on the field violated the ADA because the plaintiff's on-field coaching in a wheelchair did not pose a direct threat to the health and safety of others. It enjoined enforcement of the baseball league's policy because the policy illegally discriminated against the plaintiff.

Courts have held it is legally permissible to exclude an athlete with an infectious disease from participating in competitive sports if no reasonable accommodation will prevent a direct threat to the health and safety of other participants. In *Montalvo v. Radcliffe*, 167 F.3d 873 (4th Cir.), *cert. denied*, 528 U.S. 813 (1999), the Fourth Circuit ruled that a karate studio was permitted to exclude an HIV-positive 12-year-old boy from full-contact karate classes, which involved frequent physical contact among students and instructors that sometimes resulted in bloody injuries. Relying on medical expert testimony that HIV can be transmitted through blood-to-blood contact and evidence that this type of contact frequently occurred in these karate classes, the court concluded that the plaintiff's participation would pose a direct threat to the health and safety of others by exposing them to the risk of HIV transmission. The court further found that there were no possible modifications that could effectively reduce the significance of this risk while also maintaining the fundamental nature of the studio's "hard-style" Japanese karate. The studio's offer to give the plaintiff private karate lessons, which was rejected by him and his parents, was found to be a reasonable accommodation of the plaintiff's disability. See generally John T. Wolohan, *An Ethical and Legal Dilemma: Participation in Sports by HIV Infected Athletes*, 7 Marq. Sports L.J. 373 (1997).

Unlike the well-established judicial precedent recognizing harm to one's self as a valid justification for exclusion from athletics under the Rehabilitation Act, there is little precedent regarding whether exclusion of a disabled athlete from a sport solely because of a potentially enhanced risk of injury is a legally valid justification under the ADA. To date, there have been no ADA cases in which a professional athlete with a physical abnormality has challenged his or her medical disqualification from a sport to prevent exposure to an enhanced risk of significant harm. Although the underlying medical issues may be the same, courts may develop a different legal framework for resolving participation disputes involving professional athletes than the one for college athletes established by the *Pahulu* and *Knapp* cases, *supra*, under the Rehabilitation Act. An important distinction is that sports are a professional athlete's livelihood, rather than an extracurricular activity that is one component (although perhaps a substantial component) of a student's collegiate experience. See Matthew J. Mitten, *Enhanced Risk of Harm to One's Self as a Justification for Exclusion from Athletics*, 8 Marq. Sports L.J. 189 (1998).

In *PGA Tour, Inc. v. Martin*, 532 U.S. 661 (2001), the U.S. Supreme Court ruled that, although the essence of sports is that everyone plays by the same rules, a sports governing body (including those that regulate professional sports at the highest level of competition) must make reasonable accommodations to provide a physically impaired athlete with an opportunity to compete. The PGA Tour had refused to provide Casey Martin, a professional golfer with a circulatory disorder that inhibits his ability to walk, with an exception to its rule that all golfers must walk the course during tournament play because of its position that walking injected an element of fatigue into championship golf. This decision effectively precluded him from playing in PGA tournaments, although his demonstrated golf skills qualified him to participate.

The Court ruled that waiver of the PGA Tour's walking rule to allow Martin to use a cart was a reasonable accommodation that did not fundamentally alter the nature of professional championship golf. The "essence of the game has been shot-making," according to the Court, and the "walking rule . . . is not an essential attribute of the game itself." The Court recognized that "waiver of an essential rule of competition for anyone would fundamentally alter" the PGA's tournaments, but concluded that "the walking rule is at best peripheral to the nature of petitioner's athletic events, and thus it might be waived in individual cases without working a fundamental alteration." *Id.* at 689.

Relying on undisputed trial testimony that "Martin easily endures greater fatigue even with a cart than his able-bodied competitors do by walking," the Court held:

> Under the ADA's basic requirement that the need of a disabled person be evaluated on an individual basis, we have no doubt that allowing Martin to use a golf cart would not fundamentally alter the nature of petitioner's tournaments. As we have discussed, the purpose of the walking rule is to subject players to fatigue, which in turn may influence the outcome of tournaments. Even if the rule does serve that purpose, it is an uncontested finding of the District Court that Martin "easily endures greater fatigue even with a cart than his able-bodied competitors do by walking." The purpose of the walking rule is therefore not compromised in the slightest by allowing Martin to use a cart. A modification that provides an exception to a peripheral tournament rule without impairing its purpose cannot be said to "fundamentally alter" the tournament. What it can be said to do, on the other hand, is to allow Martin the chance to qualify for and compete in the athletic events petitioner offers to those members of the public who have the skill and desire to enter. That is exactly what the ADA requires. As a result, Martin's request for a waiver of the walking rule should have been granted.
>
> The ADA admittedly imposes some administrative burdens on the operators of places of public accommodation that could be avoided by strictly adhering to general rules and policies that are entirely fair with respect to the able-bodied but that may indiscriminately preclude access by qualified persons with disabilities. But surely, in a case of this kind, Congress intended that an entity like the PGA not only give individualized attention to the handful of requests that it might receive from talented but disabled athletes for a modification or waiver of a rule to allow them access to the competition, but also carefully weigh the purpose, as well as the letter, of the rule before determining that no accommodation would be tolerable.

Id. at 690–91. In a vigorous dissent, Justice Scalia asserted:

Nowhere is it writ that PGA TOUR golf must be classic "essential" golf. Why cannot the PGA TOUR, if it wishes, promote a new game, with distinctive rules (much as the American League promotes a game of baseball in which the pitcher's turn at the plate can be taken by a "designated hitter")? If members of the public do not like the new rules—if they feel that these rules do not truly test the individual's skill at "real golf" (or the team's skill at "real baseball") they can withdraw their patronage. But the rules are the rules. They are (as in all games) entirely arbitrary, and there is no basis on which anyone—not even the Supreme Court of the United States—can pronounce one or another of them to be "nonessential" if the rulemaker (here the PGA TOUR) deems it to be essential. . . .

Id. at 699–700.

Justice Scalia expressed concern with a legal standard establishing "one set of rules that is 'fair with respect to the able-bodied' but 'individualized' rules, mandated by the ADA, for 'talented but disabled athletes.'" *Id.* at 703. He cautioned "it should not be assumed that today's decent, tolerant, and progressive judgment will, in the long run, accrue to the benefit of sports competitors with disabilities." *Id.* at 704. In his view, because the *Martin* majority's legal standard requires courts to determine which rules of a sport are "essential," sports governing bodies that "value their autonomy have every incentive to defend vigorously the necessity of every regulation" and "to make sure the same written rules are set forth for all levels of play and to never voluntarily grant any exceptions." *Id.* at 704–05.

QUESTIONS

1. Should the federal disability discrimination laws be construed to permit judicial modification of uniform and neutral playing rules on a case-by-case basis? If not, what is an effective alternative means of ensuring that impaired persons have an equal opportunity to participate in athletics commensurate with their interests, skills, and abilities?
2. Is there a principled judicial basis for distinguishing between "an essential rule of competition" and a nonessential rule that has a peripheral impact on the game?

NOTES

1. Post-Martin cases: Reasonable accommodations versus fundamental alterations. In May 2007, the Ladies Professional Golfers Association (LPGA) allowed MacKinzie Kline, a 15-year-old golfer with a congenital heart condition that prevented her from walking long distances without becoming fatigued, to ride in a cart and use an oxygen delivery system when necessary during an LPGA Tour event. LPGA commissioner Carolyn Bivens determined that these accommodations would not provide her with an unfair competitive advantage.

Barron v. PGA Tour, Inc., 670 F. Supp. 2d 674 (W.D. Tenn. 2009), presented a different context. In that case, the court held that the PGA Tour did not violate a professional golfer's rights under the ADA by suspending him for one year for testing positive for exogenous testosterone, a banned substance under its anti-doping program, and refusing to grant him a therapeutic use exemption. Plaintiff alleged he suffers from abnormally low testosterone, which causes him to have a reduced sex drive, experience fatigue, and have a compromised immune system, and that by refusing to allow him to take medically prescribed exogenous testosterone and suspending him for using it, the PGA Tour discriminated against him in violation of the ADA. The court concluded that he had not shown a likelihood of success on his claim:

> Barron has not shown that the "reasonable accommodation" he has requested (allowing him to continue taking exogenous Testosterone) is necessary in order for him to continue playing golf in PGA Tour events. His complaint and post-hearing brief, at most, claim that he needs these Testosterone shots to address specific medical concerns relating to a reduced sex drive, fatigue, and a compromised immune system-not to play golf. While Barron's abnormally low Testosterone may in some way cause him to be a less competitive golfer than he would be if he were permitted to take the Testosterone injections, [the ADA] simply does not provide a remedy under those circumstances.

Id. at 685–86. After Barron's suspension ended, the PGA Tour granted him a therapeutic use exemption to use testosterone while attempting to qualify for the 2011 PGA Tour, which was based on new medical information he submitted. See generally Travis Tygart and Anthony R. Ten Haagen, *The Americans With Disabilities Act, The United States Anti-Doping Agency, and the Effort Toward Equal Opportunity: A Case Study of the* United States Anti-Doping Agency v. George Hartman *Matter*, 2 Harv. J. Sports & Ent. L. 199 (2011) (discussing ADA's reasonable accommodation requirement as applied to athlete's therapeutic use of synthetic testosterone).

2. Learning differences and age eligibility thresholds. Students with mental impairments or learning differences sometimes take longer to complete their schooling than students without such impairments or differences and therefore find themselves too old to participate in interscholastic athletics as juniors or seniors in high school. Consider Eric Dompierre, a Michigan high school athlete with Down syndrome. Dompierre played sports throughout his childhood in Ishpeming, Michigan. When he entered Ishpeming High School as a freshman, Dompierre joined the football and basketball teams. Because of his Down syndrome, however, Dompierre progressed through his academic career more slowly than most others of his age, and by January 2012—the second semester of his junior year—he was already 19 years old. This made him ineligible under a Michigan High School Athletic Association rule prohibiting any student who turns 19 before September 1 of senior year from participating in interscholastic athletics. See Tim Rohan, *Age Is Obstacle for Athlete with Down Syndrome*, N.Y. Times, April 12, 2012, at B13. In response to a national outcry spurred by an

Internet and social media campaign to "Let Eric Play!" the MHSAA member schools voted in May 2012 to enact a waiver provision to permit age-ineligible athletes to participate if:

(1) [The applicant's educational progress] was delayed prior to initial enrollment in the ninth grade solely because of a medically documented disability under the federal Americans with Disabilities Act or Michigan's Persons With Disabilities Civil Rights Act; and

(2) At the time of the waiver request, [the] student [has] a defined disability documented to diminish both physical and either intellectual or emotional capabilities, does not create a health or safety risk to participants, and does not create a competitive advantage for the team.

See MHSAA Regulation 1 §2(B) (2011–12). Although Dompierre's athletic eligibility status was resolved without litigation, the two cases discussed below—*Cruz v. Pennsylvania Interscholastic Athletic Assn.*, 157 F. Supp. 2d 485 (E.D. Pa. 2001) and *Baisden v. West Virginia Secondary Schools Activities Commission*, 568 S.E.2d 32 (W.Va. 2002)—provide guidance regarding the individualized assessments of size, speed, and skill that courts engage when litigation in such matters does come to pass.

In *Cruz*, a federal district court ruled that a 19-year-old public school special education student who was classified as "educable mentally retarded" could not be excluded from participation in any high school sport without an individualized evaluation of whether doing so was necessary to prevent a threat to the health and safety of other participants or to prevent competitive unfairness. The court noted that Cruz is five foot three inches tall and weighs 130 pounds and is not a "star" player in any of his interscholastic sports. Observing that there is a no "cut" policy for football and track, the court suggested he should be permitted to continue playing football because he is only "a marginal player" and participating in track because he "is not a fast runner." However, it implied that he could be excluded from wrestling because "he may have a competitive advantage based on his outstanding dual meet record."

Similarly, in *Baisden*, which involved a learning disabled student, the West Virginia Supreme Court approved of the lower court's engagement in an individual assessment:

While we decide, through this opinion, that individualized assessments are required in cases of this nature and that reasonable accommodations may be made through waiver of the age nineteen rule under certain circumstances, we do not believe that the facts of this case justify waiver as an accommodation. Mr. Baisden turned nineteen on July 27, 2001. He is six feet four inches tall and weighs 280 pounds. He runs the forty-yard-dash in 5.3 seconds. His participation in high school football would permit him to compete in this contact sport against students approximately five years younger. The safety of younger, smaller, more inexperienced students would be unreasonably compromised. In our view, this would fundamentally alter the structure of the interscholastic athletic program, a result which is not required by reasonable accommodation standards in anti-discrimination law.

3. Competition between non-disabled and disabled athletes. In *Badgett v. Alabama High School Athletic Assn.*, 2007 WL 2461928 (N.D. Ala.), an Alabama federal district court refused to order a state high school athletics association to allow the state's only track and field wheelchair division athlete, who suffered from cerebral palsy, to compete against able-bodied runners in the state track and field championship based on its conclusion that her doing so "would raise legitimate competitive, fairness and administrative concerns" and fundamentally alter the sport of track and field. It also determined that her participation "would raise legitimate safety concerns that are inherent in having able-bodied athletes and wheelchair athletes compete in mixed heats." The court concluded that the establishment of a separate wheelchair division for track and field, whose competing athletes earned equivalent recognition and medals for state championship results, was a reasonable accommodation, which satisfied the requirements of the ADA.

This use of prosthetics, rather than a wheelchair, in track and field has also provoked controversy and litigation. South African athlete Oscar Pistorius had both legs amputated below the knee when he was 11 months old because he was born without the fibula in his lower legs and had defects in his feet. Running with "Cheetah" prosthetic legs—a pair of J-shaped carbon fiber blades that touch only a few inches of ground and that attach to his knees—he easily won the 100 and 200-meter dashes at the 2007 Paralympic World Cup. In addition, he set world records for disabled athletes in the 100-, 200-, and 400-meter dashes.

In 2008, the Court of Arbitration for Sport (CAS) ruled that Pistorius was eligible to run in track events sanctioned by the International Association of Athletics Federations (IAAF) with his prosthetic legs. *Pistorius v. IAAF*, CAS 2008/A/1480, award of 16 May 2008. An IAAF rule prohibited the use of "any technical device that incorporates springs, wheels or any other element that provides the user with an advantage over another athlete not using such a device." However, the CAS panel rejected the IAAF's argument that the use of a technical device providing an athlete "with any *advantage*, however small, in any part of a competition . . . must render that athlete ineligible to compete regardless of any compensating disadvantages." It concluded that the use of a passive device such as the "Cheetah" prosthetic legs does not violate this rule "without convincing scientific proof that it provides him with *an overall net advantage* over other athletes." The panel concluded that because scientific evidence did not prove that Pistorius obtained a metabolic or biomechanical advantage from using the "Cheetah" prosthetic legs, his exclusion would not further the rule's purpose of ensuring fair competition among athletes. Pistorius was unable to qualify for the 2008 Beijing Olympics, but four years later, he qualified for the 2012 London Olympics, representing South Africa in both the 400-meter individual race and the 4×400-meter relay.

More recently, American sprinter Blake Leeper, who like Pistorius is missing both legs and uses prosthetics to compete, also dominated Paralympic events before transitioning to events involving non-disabled runners. After taking fifth place at the 2020 U.S. Championships and approaching the time threshold necessary to qualify for the 2021 Tokyo Olympics, World Athletics (formerly the IAAF) banned Leeper from competing with his prosthetics in sanctioned events. It argued that the prosthetics made Leeper far taller than a man with Leeper's torso would otherwise be and therefore gave Leeper an unfair advantage in violation of the Maximum Allowable Standing Height (MASH) rule. Leeper appealed to CAS and lost. Although he subsequently adopted shorter prostheses, World Athletics again banned him on MASH grounds, and he again lost his appeal before CAS. *The Court of Arbitration for Sport (CAS) Dismissed the 2nd Appeal of Black Leeper*, Court of Arbitration for Sport (June 11, 2021), https://qqq.tas-cas.org/fileadmin/user_upload/CAS_Media_Release_7930.pdf.

4. Disabled spectator protections. Disabled spectators have experienced mixed success in bringing ADA or Rehabilitation Act discrimination claims against professional leagues or operators of sports venues. See, e.g., *Landis v. Wash. State Major League Baseball Stadium Pub. Facilities Dist.*, 11 F.4th 1101 (9th Cir. 2021) (finding liability appropriate if spectators in wheelchairs are unable to see the field over the heads of standing spectators two rows ahead); *Miller v. California Speedway Corp.*, 536 F.3d 1020 (9th Cir. 2008) (holding race track operator responsible under the ADA to provide their handicapped spectators with a line of sight comparable to members of the general public); *Paralyzed Veterans of America v. D.C. Arena L.P.*, 117 F.3d 579 (D.C. Cir. 1997) (violation to not provide line of sight over standing spectators for those in wheelchairs); *Stoutenborough v. NFL*, 59 F.3d 580 (6th Cir. 1995) (NFL television "blackout" rule does not discriminate against hearing-impaired persons); *Feldman v. Pro Football, Inc.*, 579 F. Supp. 2d 697, 709 (D. Md. 2008) (ADA requires NFL club and stadium operator to provide equal access to aural information broadcast over FedExField public address system, including "music with lyrics, play information, advertisements, referee calls, safety/emergency information, and other announcements"); *Access Now Inc. v. S. Fla. Stadium Corp.*, 161 F. Supp. 2d 1357 (S.D. Fla. 2001) (stadium has reasonable number of wheelchair seating spaces; no evidence that plaintiff's proposed facility modifications would actually make stadium more accessible to disabled); *Cortez v. NBA*, 960 F. Supp. 113 (W.D. Tex. 1997) (rejecting hearing-impaired patron's demand for captioning and interpretative services while attending NBA games).

Problem 8-1

Able is a paraplegic and a nationally ranked player in wheelchair racquetball competitions. He wants to play in an A-level open tournament with footed players but asks that he be permitted two bounces to hit the ball. The Official Rules of Racquetball require the ball to be returned on one bounce in a game between footed players but allow for two bounces if both participants are playing in wheelchairs.

The general manager of the Metropolis Athletic Club, which is organizing the tournament, has refused to grant Able's request. However, she will allow him to play in a novice league with footed players and be given only one bounce, or, alternatively, she will set up a wheelchair league if there are a sufficient number of other wheelchair players. Some footed players have expressed concern about whether it would be safe to play against Able in tournament competition. Able rejected these proposed alternatives and insists on being placed in the A-League tournament and given two bounces.

Does Able have a valid disability discrimination claim against the Metropolis Athletic Club for refusing to allow him to participate in its A-League tournament with his requested rules modification?

Intellectual Property Issues in Sports

INTRODUCTION

Sports-related intellectual property rights such as trademarks, service marks, and copyrights generate billions of dollars in annual revenue for sports entities such as professional leagues and clubs, the U.S. Olympic and Paralympic Committee (USOPC), and the National Collegiate Athletic Association (NCAA), and university and high school athletics programs. These revenues are derived from various sources, including television, radio, and Internet broadcasting rights contracts for sports events; trademark and official team logo licensing agreements; and league, team, or event sponsorship deals with advertisers. In addition, popular athletes and coaches license various aspects of their identity, such as their names or images, to others for commercial purposes, thereby earning a substantial amount of money for endorsing various products and services. At the outset, consider how intangible intellectual property differs from personal and real property (e.g., an autographed player jersey; sports stadium or arena) as well as why intellectual property rights may be substantially more valuable.

Sports event broadcasting rights are the largest source of revenue for professional sports leagues and organizations, as well as for the NCAA and its member universities; sports events are one of the few things people watch live, which maximizes the viewing audience and attracts the substantial advertising dollars necessary for broadcasters to pay multibillion-dollar rights fees to these entities. For example, the television contracts that the National Football League (NFL) has with Fox, CBS, NBC, ESPN, and Amazon will pay the NFL an average of $10 billion a year in rights fees over the life of these 11-year deals through 2034. The Los Angeles Dodgers will receive $8.35 billion from Time Warner Cable to televise its games for 25 years beginning in 2014, and a 30-year television deal between the New York Yankees and the YES Network paid $95 million in its first year (2012) and increases 5 percent annually each year thereafter. In April 2010, the NCAA entered into an agreement with CBS and Turner Sports pursuant to which they will pay almost $11 billion for the television rights to the "Final Four" men's basketball tournament for 14 years. In 2016, CBS and Turner Sports extended their agreement with the NCAA until 2032 for an additional $8.8 billion.

The licensing and merchandising of sports brands (i.e., trademarks and logos) also generate billions of dollars in aggregate revenues for professional and amateur sports leagues and other entities. Grand View Research found that the global value of licensed sports merchandise sales in 2022 was $33.48 billion. Sports sponsorship revenues, which includes naming rights and sponsorship of professional, Olympic, and intercollegiate teams, sports events, and organizations, and professional leagues and their member clubs, were valued at $63.1 billion in 2021 and are estimated to grow to $109.1 billion by 2030.

Well-known athletes and coaches have entered into lucrative deals to promote and endorse a variety of products and services. For the most popular athletes, income earned from the licensing of their identities to sell products and services may be greater than that derived from their athletic ability or success. For example, Michael Jordan signed his first Nike endorsement contract in 1985 for $2.5 million, and he has earned more money from endorsement deals than from playing NBA basketball. Before ever playing in an NBA game, LeBron James signed a five-year, $5 million endorsement deal with Upper Deck trading cards and a seven-year shoe endorsement deal with Nike worth more than $90 million. According to Forbes, the 50 highest-paid athlete endorsers earned $1.08 billion in endorsement income in 2023. Soccer star Cristiano Ronaldo, the world's highest-paid athlete endorser, earned $136 million. Tennis player Serena Williams earned approximately $45 million as the highest-paid female athlete endorser.

This chapter initially considers how trademark and unfair competition law protects the owners of sports-related trademarks, logos, and other identifying insignia from infringement and economic harm to their rights. Next, the nature and scope of legal protection for real-time game accounts and broadcasting of sporting events under federal copyright law, as well as state misappropriation and unfair competition laws, is addressed. Finally, an athlete's protected interest in their privacy, reputation, and identity is considered.

TRADEMARKS, LOGOS, AND OTHER IDENTIFYING SPORTS INSIGNIA

KEY TERMS

- Anticybersquatting Consumer Protection Act of 1999 (ACPA)
- Inherently distinctive mark
- Lanham Act
- Likelihood of confusion
- Secondary meaning
- Ted Stevens Olympic and Amateur Sports Act (ASA)
- Trademark Counterfeiting
- Trademark Dilution Revision Act of 2006 (TDRA)

- Trademark/service mark
- Trademark/service mark infringement
- Unfair competition
- Uniform Domain Name Dispute Resolution Policy (UDRP)

A. Trademark Infringement and Unfair Competition

Common law trademark and service mark rights are acquired by first usage of a name, logo, or other symbol to identify one's products or services and to distinguish them from those of others. In *White v. Board of Regents of Univ. of Nebraska*, 614 N.W.2d 330 (Neb. 2000), the court determined that a university acquired rights in "Husker Authentics" by virtue of its first use of this mark in connection with the advertising and sale of products to season ticket holders, alumni, and boosters. Professor Thomas McCarthy observes that "the exclusive 'property' right of a trademark is defined by consumer perception." 1 J. Thomas McCarthy, McCarthy on Trademarks and Unfair Competition (5th ed.), §2:10 (West June 2023 Update). In other words, the nature and scope of one's property interest in a trademark generally is only the right to prevent consumer confusion. As the Seventh Circuit explained, "the trademark laws exist . . . to protect the consuming public from confusion, concomitantly protecting the trademark owner's right to a non-confused public." *James Burrough, Ltd. v. Sign of the Beefeater, Inc.*, 540 F.2d 266, 276 (7th Cir. 1976).

A sports team's name functions as a trademark or a service mark by virtue of public association of that name with a particular team. Sports team names generally are either inherently distinctive or have acquired "secondary meaning," therefore entitling them to trademark protection. An inherently distinctive mark is one that is coined or arbitrary in relation to the goods or services it identifies, such as "Miami Dolphins" for an NFL club, or it is suggestive of the club's desired characteristics, such as "Tennessee Titans." *In re WNBA Enterprises LLC*, 70 U.S.P.Q.2d 1153 (TTAB 2003) (finding "Orlando Miracle" to be an inherently distinctive mark for a Women's National Basketball Association (WNBA) club in Orlando). As one court explained, "Secondary meaning is the consuming public's understanding that the mark, when used in context, refers, not to what the descriptive word ordinarily describes, but to the particular business that the mark is meant to identify." *Maryland Stadium Authority v. Becker*, 806 F. Supp. 1236, 1241 (D. Md. 1992) (finding that public identifies "Camden Yards" with a Baltimore baseball stadium). Courts have recognized that the popularity of NFL football, combined with its extensive media coverage and advertising, creates a public association of its team names with its member clubs (*NFL Properties, Inc. v. N.J. Giants, Inc.*, 637 F. Supp. 507 (D. N. J. 1986)), which is also true of the other U.S. major professional leagues.

Sports team logos such as the Las Vegas Raiders' pirate and The Ohio State University's "Brutus Buckeye" function as trademarks that identify particular teams. Distinctive helmet and uniform designs and colors also can function as trademarks. See, e.g., *Board of Supervisors of the La. State Univ. v. Smack Apparel*

Co., 550 F.3d 465 (5th Cir. 2008) (finding that well-known and long-used color schemes, logos, and designs identify university's sports teams even without accompanying use of its name or nicknames); *Dallas Cowboys Cheerleaders, Inc. v. Pussycat Cinema, Ltd.*, 604 F.2d 200, 204 n.5 (2d Cir. 1979) (finding trademark rights in uniform "universally recognized as the symbol of the Dallas Cowboys Cheerleaders"). In addition, a term or phrase may become associated with a sports team (e.g., "Evil Empire" for the New York Yankees baseball club) through public usage or fan recognition, thereby conferring trademark rights on the team. *New York Yankees Partnership v. Evil Enterprises, Inc.*, 2013 WL 1305332 (T.T.A.B.).

Trademark rights exist indefinitely as long as the mark continues to be used and serves as an indication of the source of the seller's goods or services. *Boston Prof'l Hockey Assn. v. Dallas Cap & Emblem Mfg., Inc.*, 510 F.2d 1004, 1011 (5th Cir. 1975) ("[T]here is no reason why trademarks should ever pass into the public domain by the mere passage of time."). However, trademark rights are lost if usage of the mark to identify, advertise, or promote the seller's goods or services is discontinued.

The Lanham Act, 15 U.S.C. §1051, et seq., provides nationwide legal protection for federally registered trademarks. Federal registration provides *prima facie* evidence (i.e., rebuttable presumption) of the registrant's ownership and exclusive right to use the mark for the subject goods or services as well as the validity of the registration. For example, Augusta National Inc., which hosts the well-known Masters golf tournament, owns federal trademark registrations for both the word mark "Green Jacket" and logo for a green sports jacket with gold buttons awarded to the tournament's winning player. Legal proceedings to prevent and remedy infringement of federally registered marks may be brought in federal courts.

1. Name of Sports Team or Event

Courts have held that a professional sports club retains the right to continue using its name with a different geographical identifier if it relocates to another city. In *Johnny Blastoff, Inc. v. L.A. Rams Football, Co.*, 188 F.3d 427 (7th Cir. 1999), the Seventh Circuit held that the NFL's Los Angeles Rams club retained its rights to continue using "Rams" to identify the team name when it relocated to St. Louis). Observing that the franchise was founded in 1937 as the Cleveland Rams, it moved to become the Los Angeles Rams in 1946 and moved again to become the St. Louis Rams in 1995, the court concluded, "[T]he Rams organization and the NFL had a long-established priority over the use of the 'Rams' name in connection with the same professional football team, regardless of urban affiliation." (The Rams moved back to Los Angeles in 2016.) See also *Indianapolis Colts, Inc. v. Metropolitan Baltimore Football Club Ltd. P'ship*, 34 F.3d 410 (7th Cir. 1994) ("A professional sports team is like Heraclitus's river: always changing, yet always the same. . . . [T]he record discloses there is as much institutional continuity between the Baltimore Colts of 1984 and the Indianapolis Colts of 1994 as there was between the Baltimore Colts of 1974 and the Baltimore Colts of 1984.").

Legal considerations aside, business reasons may justify treating the favorable goodwill with fans developed by a popular local sports franchise over the years as "a non-transportable cultural institution." For example, the NFL decided to leave the "Browns" identity in Cleveland when the franchise relocated to Baltimore in 1996. The franchise formerly named the "Cleveland Browns" established a new identity as the "Baltimore Ravens." The NFL expansion club that began playing in Cleveland in 1999 is named the "Cleveland Browns."

Infringement of the prior user's trademark rights occurs if another's use of the same or similar mark creates a likelihood of consumer confusion regarding the source, affiliation, endorsement, or sponsorship of sports-related products or services. For example, in *Champions Golf Club, Inc. v. Champions Golf Club, Inc.*, 78 F.3d 1111 (6th Cir. 1996), the court found a likelihood of consumer confusion regarding the (nonexistent) affiliation between two independently owned and operated golf courses located in Nicholasville, Kentucky, and Houston, Texas, which were concurrently using the "Champions" mark.

On the other hand, the use of the same mark by different teams, even if playing the same sport, does not inevitably create a likelihood of consumer confusion. Rather, a fact-specific inquiry must be made on a case-by-case basis. In *Harlem Wizards Entertainment Basketball, Inc. v. NBA Properties, Inc.*, 952 F. Supp. 1084 (D. N.J. 1997), the court held that an NBA club's proposed name change to the "Washington Wizards" would not infringe a "show basketball" team's prior use of "Harlem Wizards." Unlike the Washington NBA club, the Harlem club was not a competitive sports team that played in a professional league. The Harlem Wizards combined trick basketball and comedic basketball in a form of entertainment similar to that of the world-famous Harlem Globetrotters. Although the Harlem club had the right to use "Wizards" for its entertainment services, the court concluded that the NBA club's concurrent use of the same mark would not create a likelihood of confusion among basketball fans. The teams did not compete with each other for fan patronage. The Harlem club marketed its games to event organizers at high schools, colleges, and charitable organizations through direct mail, trade shows, and trade magazines; the NBA club advertised its games directly to fans. According to the court, survey results evidenced that consumer familiarity with the Harlem Wizards team "is almost nonexistent." There was a significant disparity between the parties' respective ticket prices, and the court found it "unlikely that consumers will attend a Harlem Wizards' game expecting to see NBA basketball or purchase NBA tickets expecting to see the Harlem Wizards perform show basketball."

2. Unauthorized Affixation of Sports Team Mark to Merchandise

Sports fans annually purchase billions of dollars' worth of merchandise bearing the names and logos of their favorite teams. Do they do so to identify with the team, because of a belief that the team produced or licensed such merchandise, or for other reasons?

In *National Football League Properties, Inc. v. Consumer Enterprises, Inc.*, 327 N.E.2d 242, 246 (Ill. App. 1975), the court observed that the NFL's "trademarks are associated with highly successful football teams that enjoy tremendous notoriety. Through the extensive licensing arrangements developed and perpetuated by [the NFL] and its licensees, the buying public has come to associate the trademark with the sponsorship of the NFL or the particular member team involved." It concluded "that the trademarks of the teams copied by defendant indicate sponsorship or origin in addition to their ornamental value." See also *University Bookstore v. Board of Regents of the Univ. of Wis. Sys.*, 33 U.S.P.Q.2d 1385, 1405 (TTAB 1994) ("[T]he mark of a university on clothing can signify that the university endorses and licenses the sale of such wearing apparel by the manufacturer. . . . It is a question of fact as to whether consumers view such indicia as 'merely ornamental' or as symbols that identify a secondary source of sponsorship.").

Major professional sports leagues such as the NFL, NBA, MLB, and the National Hockey League (NHL) currently market, license, and enforce their clubs' trademark rights collectively through a central league-operated entity.[1] The NCAA and many of its member universities utilize Collegiate Licensing Company, an Atlanta company, to individually market and license their respective marks for use by third parties. To avoid weakening valuable trademark rights, a trademark owner (or an entity authorized to act on the owner's behalf) must carefully monitor the marketplace, protest unauthorized third-party usage of his or her trademarks, and, when necessary, bring litigation to stop infringement of their marks.

Under the Lanham Act or similar state trademark infringement laws, a "likelihood of confusion" must be shown to prove infringement. The existence of actual confusion of consumers is a factor to be considered, but it is not a required element of trademark infringement. In *Board of Governors of the Univ. of North Carolina v. Helpingstine*, 714 F. Supp. 167, 172 (M.D. N.C. 1989), the court observed:

> While cases have indicated at one extreme that an alleged infringer's use of a mark with the knowledge that the public will be aware of the mark's origin is enough to establish likelihood of confusion, . . . and at the other that likelihood of confusion occurs only where there would be confusion as to the origin of the goods themselves, . . . the majority of courts have taken the middle ground on this issue. This middle position, which both parties recognize in this case, is that the requisite likelihood of confusion will exist where there is likelihood of confusion as to source, sponsorship or endorsement of the goods.

The following case illustrates how courts apply a multifactor test to determine whether the unauthorized usage of a sports team mark creates a likelihood of consumer confusion.

---

[1]To maximize the revenues from its national sponsorship agreements, which generally are distributed pro rata to its member clubs, a sports league may have exclusive agreements with its official sponsors and corresponding limits on its member clubs' individual sponsorships with other companies. A club that violates league restrictions on its local sponsorship agreements may be liable for breach of contract and fiduciary duty, tortious interference with contractual relationships, and trademark infringement. See *NFL Properties, Inc. v. Dallas Cowboys Football Club, Ltd.*, 922 F. Supp. 849 (S.D. N.Y. 1996). See Chapter 11, Internal League Governance and Commissioner Authority, section C.5, for a discussion of antitrust law challenges to a professional league's exclusive control and licensing of its member clubs' trademarks.

National Football League Properties, Inc. v. New Jersey Giants, Inc.
637 F. Supp. 507 (D. N.J. 1986)

BARRY, District Judge.

[Editors' note: Plaintiff, the New York Football Giants, Inc., owned and operated the New York Giants, an NFL team that had played all of its home games at Giants' Stadium in East Rutherford, New Jersey, since 1976. In what was then the New York Football Giants' 60-year history, the team's home games had been played at several locations in the New York metropolitan area, including Connecticut and New Jersey. To maintain continuity of tradition, the club always had used the name "New York Giants," which along with "Giants" is a federally registered trademark under the Lanham Act and under New Jersey and New York state law.

Plaintiff National Football League Properties, Inc. (NFLP), is the marketing arm of the NFL's member clubs and is licensed by the clubs to use their trademarks and is authorized to protect them from infringement. NFLP had licensed selected companies to use the "Giants" and "New York Giants" marks on a wide variety of merchandise, including T-shirts, sweatshirts, caps, jackets, and other wearing apparel. NFLP had a quality control program in which it supervised and approved the conception, design, color combinations, production, and distribution of all merchandise licensed to bear the marks of the Giants and other NFL clubs.

Defendant, the New Jersey Giants, Inc., in an effort to exploit the anomaly of a team bearing the name of one state while playing in another, began to sell various items of inferior-quality sports-related apparel bearing the words "New Jersey GIANTS" without authorization from NFLP or the New York Giants club.]

Defendant's "New Jersey GIANTS" merchandise competes directly with licensed NFL merchandise bearing the New York Football Giants' marks, because NFLP has licensed the same types of merchandise sold by defendant. Moreover, defendant's "New Jersey GIANTS" merchandise is likely to confuse consumers into believing that it is part of the wide array of licensed merchandise sponsored and approved by the New York Football Giants and available to the public through NFLP's licensing program.

The Giants and NFLP have no control over defendant's business activities or over the nature and clearly inferior quality of the merchandise sold by defendant and, indeed, the quality of that merchandise does not satisfy the quality control standards imposed by NFLP on its licensees. The sale of inferior quality merchandise bearing the NFL marks, or colorable imitations thereof, will adversely affect NFLP's business including the poor impression of the NFL and its Member Clubs that will be held by the consumer. . . .

Defendant's use of its trade name and the solicitation and sale of "New Jersey GIANTS" merchandise is also likely to confuse the public into believing that the New York Football Giants has changed the team's name to the New Jersey Giants or does not object to being referred to by that name. Neither is true, of course, and while one may wonder why the New York Giants resist a new name and may wish, perhaps, that it were otherwise, the fact remains that the Giants have the right to retain the long-standing goodwill and reputation they have developed in the name "New York Giants" and efforts in that regard will be undermined were defendant's conduct permitted to continue. . . .

In a case for service mark or trademark infringement and unfair competition, a plaintiff is entitled to a permanent injunction against a defendant by showing that that defendant's activities are likely to confuse consumers as to the source or sponsorship of the goods. In order to be confused, a consumer need not believe that a plaintiff actually produced a defendant's merchandise and placed it on the market. Rather, a consumer's belief that a plaintiff sponsored or otherwise approved the use of the mark satisfies the confusion requirement.

In a suit, as here, involving competing goods, the relevant factors to be considered in a determination as to whether a likelihood of confusion exists are:

(1) The degree of similarity between the owner's mark and the alleged infringing mark;
(2) The strength of the owner's mark;
(3) The price of the goods and other factors indicative of the care and attention expected of consumers when making a purchase;
(4) The length of time the defendant has used the mark without evidence of actual confusion;
(5) The intent of the defendant in adopting the mark;
(6) The evidence of actual confusion.

Defendant's mark "New Jersey GIANTS" is similar to the Giants' registered marks "New York Giants" and "Giants" and the dominant element of the mark — "Giants" — is identical, rendering those marks particularly confusing . . .

The second . . . factor is similarly satisfied. Through extensive media coverage and commercial use, the NFL marks, including those of the Giants, are extremely strong, and, accordingly, are entitled to a wide range of protection.

With reference to the third . . . factor, the likelihood of confusion in this case is enhanced because both NFLP's licensed apparel bearing the Giants' marks and defendant's apparel, which is the same type of apparel, are low to moderately priced and purchasers will not exercise a high degree of care in determining whether the merchandise has been sponsored or approved by the NFL and the Giants.

Defendant, which only began selling its merchandise in 1982 and had total sales of less than $5000.00 at the time its activities were halted by the restraining order, used the mark without evidence of actual confusion. In establishing the existence of a likelihood of confusion in actions such as this, however, there is no requirement that incidents of actual confusion be shown and such evidence is unnecessary where other factors so strongly suggest the likelihood of confusion.

[T]he consumer survey conducted by Dr. Jacoby and Guideline Research demonstrated substantial actual confusion and a substantial potential for further actual confusion. The results of the survey, which found that over 57% of respondents were actually and likely confused and that football fans were confused in even higher percentages (67%), is extremely strong evidence of likely confusion, and far in excess of the evidence relied upon by courts for this purpose. . . .

Defendant's intentional, willful, and admitted adoption of a mark closely similar to the existing marks "Giants" and "New York Giants" manifested . . . an intent to confuse. . . .

Defendant's use of the Giants' marks is likely to cause confusion or mistake or deceive purchasers of such merchandise as to the source, sponsorship or approval by the NFL and the Giants. . . .

QUESTION

Why was the defendant's unauthorized use of "New Jersey Giants" on apparel found to infringe the New York Giants' marks for "entertainment services in the form of professional football games and exhibitions"?

NOTES

1. Application of likelihood of confusion standard. Whether the requisite likelihood of confusion exists is a question of fact decided on a case-by-case basis. Examples of infringement cases include *Johnny Blastoff, Inc. v. L.A. Rams Football Co.*, 188 F.3d 427 (7th Cir. 1999) (use of "St. Louis Rams" for a fictional, cartoon sports team); *NFL v. Coors Brewing Co.*, 205 F.3d 1324 (2d Cir. 1999) (advertising Coors beer as "Official Beer of the NFL Players" without NFL's permission); *Boston Athletic Assn. v. Sullivan*, 867 F.2d 22 (1st Cir. 1989) (unauthorized use of "Boston Marathon" to sell T-shirts); *University of Ga. Athletic Assn. v. Laite*, 756 F.2d 1535 (11th Cir. 1985) (unauthorized use of University of Georgia bulldog mark and logo portraying an English bulldog for "Battlin' Bulldog Beer"); *Auburn Univ. v. Moody*, 2008 WL 4877542 (M.D. Ala.) (enjoining unauthorized use of Auburn's trademarks on six-finger foam hands).

The intentional and unauthorized use of a mark on a product that is known to be "identical with, or substantially indistinguishable from" a federally registered mark (15 U.S.C. §1127) and creates a likelihood of confusion also constitutes trademark counterfeiting (15 U.S.C. §1114), which may enable the mark owner to recover statutory damages and attorneys' fees under the Lanham Act. See, e.g., *Ohio State University v. Skreened, Ltd.*, 16 F. Supp. 3d 905 (S.D. Ohio 2014) (defendant's unauthorized sale of shirts bearing marks identical to or substantially indistinguishable from a university's federally registered marks on shirts sold by its licensees constitutes counterfeiting, as well as trademark infringement and unfair competition).

2. Non-infringing fair use or parody of a trademark. In *WCVB-TV v. Boston Athletic Association*, 926 F.2d 42, 46 (1st Cir. 1991), the First Circuit explained, "In technical trademark jargon, the use of words for descriptive purposes is called a 'fair use,' and the law usually permits it even if the words themselves also constitute a trademark." The court held that a television station's use of "Boston Marathon" to describe its unlicensed broadcast of the event is not trademark infringement, although another local television station was exclusively authorized to broadcast this event. This was judicially characterized as fair use of the Boston Marathon mark merely to describe the event the defendant was broadcasting that did not create any viewer confusion.

For the same reason that underlies the fair use defense, the parody of a trademark is not infringing. In *Cardtoons, L.C. v. Major League Baseball Players Assn.*, 95 F.3d 959 (10th Cir. 1996), the Tenth Circuit held that trading cards with caricatures of baseball players and critical commentary do not create public confusion regarding the source of the cards. The court explained that "as with all successful parodies, the effect of the cards is to amuse rather than confuse." *Id.* at 967.

B. Trademark Dilution

The Trademark Dilution Revision Act of 2006 (TDRA), which is part of the Lanham Act, protects the owner of a "famous mark" from unauthorized use of its mark or similar mark that is likely to cause dilution of the mark's distinctiveness. 15 U.S.C. §1125(c). Proof that the defendant's unauthorized usage creates an actual or likelihood of confusion is not required. The statute provides a remedy for tarnishing the goodwill associated with a famous mark by using it in a disparaging manner outside the context of permissible parody, or a blurring of the mark's distinctiveness because it is used to identify a wide range of unrelated goods and services.

To be "famous," the mark must be "widely recognized by the general consuming public of the United States as a designation of source of the goods or services of the mark's owner." 15 U.S.C. §1125(c)(2)(A). The trademarks and logos of major U.S. sports events, such as the Indianapolis 500 auto race, Kentucky Derby horse race, and Masters golf tournament, as well as those of major league professional teams; sports governing bodies such as the USOPC, the NCAA, and the National Association of Stock Car Auto Racing (NASCAR); and many universities with successful football and basketball teams are well known among sports fans and may be considered "famous" marks. In *New York City Triathlon LLC v. NYC Triathlon Club Inc.*, 95 U.S.P.Q.2d 1451 (S.D. N.Y. 2010), the court ruled that the "New York City Triathlon," "NYC Triathlon," and "NYC Tri" marks are famous because of their extensive national and international promotion and recognition. See also *Dallas Cowboys Football Club, Ltd. v. America's Team Properties*, 616 F. Supp. 2d 622 (N.D. Tex. 2009) (the Dallas Cowboys' "long duration and geographic reach" of the "America's Team" mark in connection with various products advertised and sold to the public, combined with survey evidence showing recognition of the mark among a relevant consumer base, establishes that the mark is "famous" under federal dilution statute).

In *Dallas Cowboys Football Club*, the court ruled that the unauthorized use of "America's Team" on apparel "blurs the uniqueness" of the mark and tarnishes it because it is used in connection with the defendant's inferior goods. Similarly, in *New York City Triathlon*, another court held that defendant's unauthorized usage of the "New York City Triathlon" marks as the name of its athletic club blurred and tarnished their distinctiveness in violation of the dilution statute by creating a negative association because of defendant's reputation for poor customer service.

The following cases, which were decided prior to the 2006 enactment of the TDRA, provide examples of usages that tarnish sports marks. In *NBA Properties v. Untertainment Records LLC*, 1999 WL 335147 (S.D. N.Y. 1999), a New York federal district court held that the unauthorized use of an altered NBA logo showing a silhouetted basketball player dribbling a basketball with a handgun in his other hand to advertise a rap album violates the federal dilution statute. Because "linking the NBA Logo with violence and drugs will adversely color the public's impressions of the NBA," the court concluded that "[a]ny suggestion that the NBAP or the NBA endorses violence, gunplay, or drug use, or that they have chosen to associate themselves with those who do, will likely tarnish their reputation with their corporate customers and partners, as well as the public at large." Similarly, in *Dallas Cowboys Cheerleaders, Inc. v. Pussycat Cinema, Ltd.*, 604 F.2d 200, 205 (2d Cir. 1979), the Second Circuit ruled that the unauthorized use of female actors wearing well-known Dallas Cowboys Cheerleaders uniforms in a "sexually depraved film . . . has 'tendency to impugn (plaintiff's services) and injure plaintiff's business reputation.'"

C. Anticybersquatting Consumer Protection Act of 1999

The significant expansion and use of the Internet has given rise to "cybersquatting," which is the registration of well-known trademarks (including those of sports teams and events) as domain names (i.e., website addresses) by non–trademark holders. Their objective is to try to sell rights to the domain names back to the trademark owners at a profit or to attract Internet users to their websites, which may offer services such as online sports gambling. Cybersquatting that creates a likelihood of consumer confusion constitutes trademark infringement and unfair competition. See, e.g., *March Madness Athletic Assn. v. Netfire, Inc.*, 2003 WL 22047375 (N.D. Tex. 2003) (www.marchmadness.com infringes NCAA's federally registered "March Madness" mark for basketball tournament); *Quokka Sports, Inc. v. Cup Int'l Internet Ventures*, 99 F. Supp. 2d 1105 (N.D. Cal. 1999) (defendants' website, www.americascup.com, "masquerad[es] as an official site associated with the America's Cup event," located at *www.americascup.org*, and infringes registered mark "America's Cup"). It also may constitute trademark dilution and violate the Anticybersquatting Consumer Protection Act (ACPA) of 1999, 15 U.S.C. §1129.

The ACPA provides a trademark owner with a cause of action against a defendant for bad-faith registration or use of a domain name that is (1) identical to or confusingly similar to a distinctive mark; or (2) identical to or confusingly similar to, or dilutes, a famous mark. 15 U.S.C. §1125 (d)(1). *March Madness Athletic Assn. v. Netfire, Inc.*, 2003 WL 22047375 (N.D. Tex.) (finding that defendants' registration and use of www.march-madness.com violates ACPA, entitling NCAA to injunctive relief). In addition to available remedies under the Lanham Act, the

ACPA provides for statutory damages for bad-faith registration of domain names after the November 29, 1999, effective date of the statute. 15 U.S.C. §1117(d). The ACPA also authorizes an action against the domain name itself for forfeiture or transfer to the trademark owner if the domain name registrant cannot be located or is not subject to a U.S. court's personal jurisdiction. 15 U.S.C. §1125(d)(2)(A).

D. Olympic Marks

The USOPC owns the exclusive right to use and license the Olympic marks within the United States. *United States Olympic Comm. v. Intelicense Corp., S.A.*, 737 F.2d 263 (2d Cir. 1984), *cert. denied*, 469 U.S. 982 (1984). The Ted Stevens Olympic and Amateur Sports Act (ASA) prohibits the unauthorized usage of the Olympic name and marks, including the five-ring Olympic symbol, "for the purpose of trade, to induce the sale of any goods or services, or to promote any theatrical exhibition, athletic performance, or competition." 36 U.S.C. §220506(c). Pursuant to the ASA, the USOPC's exclusive property rights also include the "Pan-American" and "Paralympic" marks, which are protected from infringement to the same extent as the Olympic marks. *United States Olympic Comm. v. Toy Truck Lines, Inc.*, 237 F.3d 1331 (Fed. Cir. 2001).

The Olympic marks have a broader scope of protection under federal law beyond that generally provided to other trademarks and service marks under the Lanham Act. In *San Francisco Arts & Athletics, Inc. v. United States Olympic Committee*, 483 U.S. 522 (1987), the Supreme Court held that the ASA's language and legislative intent evidenced Congress' intent to grant the USOPC exclusive rights to control use of the Olympic marks regardless of whether their unauthorized usage creates a likelihood of confusion. The Court explained:

> One reason for Congress to grant the USOC exclusive control of the word "Olympic," as with other trademarks, is to ensure that the USOC receives the benefit of its own efforts so that the USOC will have an incentive to continue to produce a "quality product," that, in turn, benefits the public. See 1 J. McCarthy, Trademarks and Unfair Competition §2:1, pp. 44–47 (1984). But in the special circumstance of the USOC, Congress has a broader public interest in promoting, through the activities of the USOC, the participation of amateur athletes from the United States in "the great four-yearly sport festival, the Olympic Games." . . . The USOC's goal under the Olympic Charter, Rule 24(B), is to further the Olympic movement, that has as its aims: "to promote the development of those physical and moral qualities which are the basis of sport"; "to educate young people through sport in a spirit of better understanding between each other and of friendship, thereby helping to build a better and more peaceful world"; and "to spread the Olympic principles throughout the world, thereby creating international goodwill." Congress' interests in promoting the USOC's activities include these purposes as well as those specifically enumerated in the USOC's charter. Section 110 directly advances these governmental interests by supplying the USOC with the means to raise money to support the Olympics and encourages the USOC's activities by ensuring that it will receive the benefits of its efforts.

Id. at 537–38. Defendant's unauthorized use of "Gay Olympic Games" for an athletics competition in San Francisco was found to be infringing even if it is not likely to cause any likelihood of confusion regarding whether it is affiliated with or approved or sponsored by the USOPC. See also *USOC v. Xclusive Leisure & Hospitality Ltd.*, 2008 WL 3971120 (N.D. Cal.) (enjoining unauthorized usage of Olympic marks in United States to advertise and sell tickets and hospitality packages to the 2008 Beijing Olympic Games).

The ASA "grandfathers" the rights of those who lawfully used the Olympic marks prior to 1950 (the date that the ASA's predecessor statute was enacted) to advertise and sell their goods or services. But preexisting users may not expand the scope of their goods or services sold under the Olympic mark or adopt new marks with the word "Olympic" therein. In *O-M Bread, Inc. v. United States Olympic Comm.*, 65 F.3d 933 (Fed. Cir. 1995), the Federal Circuit held that the proposed use of "Olympic Kids" for bakery products is not a permitted extension of a prior user's grandfathered right to use the Olympic mark for bakery products. The court found these "different marks present a different commercial impression and are not legal equivalents" and concluded that "commercial growth into new 'Olympic'-based marks is outside the letter of the statute, as well as outside its spirit." *Id.* at 938.

The ASA does not prohibit all unauthorized uses of the Olympic marks. As one court observed, "[B]ecause the [ASA] grants the USOC rights over and above both the common law and [the Lanham Act], the language and scope of the Act must be strictly construed." *United States Olympic Comm. v. American Media, Inc.*, 156 F. Supp. 2d 1200, 1209 (D. Colo. 2001). For example, the media may report about Olympic sports competitions, which would include use of the word "Olympic" and photographs showing the Olympic marks in news reporting. In *American Media*, the court ruled that publication of an Olympic preview magazine titled "Olympics USA" does not infringe the USOPC's rights under the ASA, although the publisher's usage of the Olympic marks in a manner falsely suggesting that the USOPC officially endorses or authorizes its magazine would violate the Lanham Act.

Problem 9-1

(a) Can the NFL prevent a women's professional football league from identifying itself as the "National Women's Football League" and calling its championship game the SupHer Bowl?

(b) Consider whether any of the following unauthorized usages violates the USOPC's rights in the Olympic marks:

   (i) An Iowa farmer prunes his cornfield into the shape of the five interlocking Olympic rings during the summer before the Olympic Games. What if he charges a fee to enter his cornfield and view the Olympic rings?

   (ii) A group holds the "Redneck Olympics," featuring the cigarette flip, bobbing for pigs' feet, mud pit belly flop, toilet seat throwing, big hair contest, and seed spitting.

AMBUSH MARKETING

Ambush marketing is a creative advertising practice by a business other than an official sponsor that seeks to create an association with a sports event without using the event's name, trademarks, or logos. It encompasses "intentional efforts to weaken [a] competitor's official association with a sport organization, which has been acquired through the payment of sponsorship fees," as well as seeking "to capitalize on the goodwill, reputation, and popularity of a particular sport or event by creating an association without the authorization or consent of the necessary parties." Steve McKelvey and John Grady, *Ambush Marketing: The Legal Battleground for Sports Marketers*, 21 Ent. & Sports L. 8, 9 (2004).

Official event sponsors claim that ambush marketing dilutes the value of their sponsorships. Ambush marketing may harm event organizers, which need sponsorship money to fund production of a sporting event. When ambush marketers receive commercial benefits by free-riding on an event's popularity or goodwill, the value of an official sponsorship may be significantly reduced. This creates an economic disincentive to be an official event sponsor, with a corresponding incentive to engage in ambush marketing instead. This in turn reduces the value of official sponsorships and causes sports event organizers to lose sponsorship revenues. See *United States Olympic Comm. v. American Media, Inc.*, 156 F. Supp. 2d 1200, 1204 (D. Colo. 2001) (alleging that defendant's ambush marketing will encourage other companies to do so, which will adversely affect the USOPC's ability to fund U.S. participation in the Olympic Games). Successful ambush marketing campaigns also may harm consumers of sporting events. A decrease in sponsorship revenues potentially could force event organizers to find new revenue sources (e.g., cable or pay-per-view television broadcasts rather than free-to-air telecasts), or possibly result in the discontinuance of sports events that lack adequate commercial sponsorship support.

Currently, ambush marketing is illegal under U.S. law only if it creates a likelihood of consumer confusion. In *Federation Internationale de Football v. Nike, Inc.*, 285 F. Supp. 2d 64 (D. D.C. 2003), the court refused to preliminarily enjoin Nike's use of "USA 03" to advertise and sell various products in connection with its sponsorship of the U.S. Women's National Soccer Team. Plaintiff Fédération Internationale de Football (FIFA) used "USA 2003" in connection with its 2003 women's soccer World Cup held in the United States. Nike was not a World Cup sponsor and was not authorized to use FIFA's marks. Although Nike did not use FIFA's name or refer to the World Cup, FIFA alleged that Nike's usage of "USA 03" was infringing and illegally interfered with its official sponsorship contracts.

Holding that FIFA has not shown a substantial likelihood of success on the merits of its claims, the court observed:

> Nike argues that its use of "USA 03" (or "United States 2003") is innocent, given the company's sponsorship of the Women's National Team. After all, the team that Nike is backing is the United States team for the year 2003, and therefore, "USA 03" is

an appropriate and understandable way for Nike to associate itself with that group of players. The Court agrees that Nike's preexisting and entirely legitimate relationship with the Women's World Cup provides an important context for its use of the disputed marks. For there can be little doubt, in light of the success that the U.S. women enjoyed in the 1999 World Cup, that the team and the event are already linked in the public mind. As such, Nike's careful use of a mark that might be affiliated with both is not necessarily an indication of bad faith, but instead of savvy marketing. Whenever that team plays in this country, it is to be expected that the sponsors of both the team and the event would want to use trademarks that reflect the United States and that emphasize this year's date. Nike's doing so here thus may not indicate a deliberate attempt to deceive the buying public.

Id. at 73–74.

Even if there currently are only limited legal remedies for combating ambush marketing, a sports event organizer can minimize its successful use and resulting detrimental effects by developing a comprehensive anti–ambush marketing plan. For example, it can contractually prohibit broadcasters from selling commercial time to the competitors of official sponsors. Nonsponsor advertisements and signage in connection with a sporting event should be carefully monitored to ensure that the event's name, marks, and logos are not included therein. See generally Anne M. Wall, *The Game Behind the Games*, 12 Marq. Sports L. Rev. 557 (2002) (describing Olympic sports governing bodies' defensive strategies to deter ambush marketing and to protect official sponsors' exclusive contractual rights).

Courts will enforce contract rights to prevent unfair competition that causes a likelihood of consumer confusion. In *Mastercard International, Inc. v. Sprint Communications Co.*, 1994 WL 97097 (S.D. N.Y.), *aff'd*, 23 F.2d 397 (2d Cir. 1994), an international soccer federation granted exclusive rights to Mastercard to use the 1994 World Cup Soccer Tournament trademarks on "all card-based payment and account access devices." The court held that Mastercard's contract rights precluded the U.S. Local Organizing Committee from authorizing Sprint Communications to use and imprint those marks on phone cards. Finding that Sprint's conduct violated the Lanham Act, the court concluded: "Sprint wishes to use the World Cup marks to convey to the world the false impression that its use of the marks on calling cards is officially sanctioned by the World Cup organization. Clearly, that is not the case, and Mastercard, which has the exclusive right to use the mark for such purposes, is entitled to enjoin this deceptive use."

Problem 9-2

Koors Brewing Company provides free NCAA men's basketball "Final Four" tickets as grand prizes to winners of its "Koors Light Tourney Time Sweepstakes" beer promotion held during the month of March. The back of each ticket states, "Unless specifically authorized in advance by the NCAA,

> this ticket may not be offered in a commercial promotion or as a prize in a sweepstakes or contest." The NCAA permits only official sponsors of its "Final Four" men's basketball tournament to do so, and it refuses to allow any manufacturers of alcoholic beverages to become official sponsors. Is Koors's conduct legal?

REAL-TIME GAME ACCOUNTS AND BROADCASTING RIGHTS

KEY TERMS
- Athletic events not copyrightable
- Copyright Act of 1976
- Copyright infringement
- Misappropriation
- Patent law
- Unauthorized public performance of copyrighted work

A. Historical Background

Historically, in the early 20th century, producers of sporting events sought to protect live game broadcasts and play-by-play descriptions from unauthorized viewer usage under state misappropriation, unfair competition, and contract laws. The then-current federal copyright laws did not provide any legal protection for sports events or their broadcasts. Relying primarily on the misappropriation doctrine established by the Supreme Court in *International News Service v. Associated Press*, 248 U.S. 215 (1918), courts broadly held that the creator of a game or athletic event has an exclusive property right in its real-time commercial value under state law. Recognizing that the production of athletic events requires the expenditure of substantial time, effort, and money, these courts prohibited observers and listeners—whether inside or outside the facility in which the event occurred—from unauthorized transmission of live game broadcasts and descriptions to the public for commercial benefit.

For example, in *Pittsburgh Athletic Co. v. KQV Broadcasting Co.*, 24 F. Supp. 490 (W.D. Pa. 1938), the court held: "the Pittsburgh Athletic Company [owner of the Pittsburgh Pirates professional baseball club], by reason of its creation of the game, its control of the park, and its restriction of the dissemination of news therefrom, has a property right in such news, and the right to control the use thereof for a reasonable time following the games." The Pittsburgh Athletic Company sold the exclusive rights to broadcast Pirates games played at Forbes Field to General Mills, Inc. The defendant broadcast play-by-play accounts of Pirates games as described by observers stationed outside Forbes Field who were able to see them being played. Finding that the defendant's conduct violated the baseball club's property rights, the court ruled that its unauthorized broadcast of Pirates games constitutes misappropriation, unfair competition, and unlawful interference with the parties' contract rights.

B. Nature and Scope of Copyright Law Protection

To encourage creative expression such as books, movies, music, and other products, the federal Copyright Act of 1976 protects only "original works of authorship fixed in any tangible medium of expression." 17 U.S.C. §102(a). It does not protect ideas, procedures, systems, or methods of operation "regardless of the form in which it is described, explained, illustrated, or embodied." 17 U.S.C. §102(b). Therefore, neither the underlying idea for a type of athletic event nor a system or method of playing a sport is copyrightable.

In *Hoopla Sports and Entertainment, Inc. v. Nike, Inc.*, 947 F. Supp. 347 (N.D. Ill. 1996), the court held that the concept of an international high school all-star basketball game is not copyrightable and plaintiff cannot prevent defendant from using its idea to conduct a similar event. The court observed that "the methods or rules of playing basketball games are not generally copyrightable."

Similarly, in *Seltzer v. Sunbrock*, 22 F. Supp. 621, 639 (S.D. Cal. 1938), the court rejected the plaintiff's claim that his idea of staging a transcontinental roller-skating race is protected by copyright law. It held: "What [plaintiff] really composed was a description of a system for conducting races on roller skates. A system, as such, can never be copyrighted. If it finds any protection, it must come from the patent laws."[2]

In *NBA v. Motorola, Inc.*, 105 F.3d 841 (2d Cir. 1997), the Second Circuit ruled that athletic events are not copyrightable and explained:

> In our view, the underlying basketball games do not fall within the subject matter of federal copyright protection because they do not constitute "original works of authorship" under 17 U.S.C. §102(a). Section 102(a) lists eight categories of "works of authorship" covered by the act, including such categories as "literary works," "musical works," and "dramatic works." The list does not include athletic events, and, although the list is concededly non-exclusive, such events are neither similar nor analogous to any of the listed categories.
>
> Sports events are not "authored" in any common sense of the word. There is, of course, at least at the professional level, considerable preparation for a game. However, the preparation is as much an expression of hope or faith as a determination of what will actually happen. Unlike movies, plays, television programs, or operas, athletic events are competitive and have no underlying script. Preparation may even

---

[2] To be patentable under federal law, a sport or game must be useful, nonobvious, and novel and satisfy other requirements established by the Patent Act. For example, the Patent Office issued U.S. Patent No. 4,911,433 to the Arena Football League (AFL) for its unique system for playing indoor professional football. See generally Carl A. Kukkonen, III, *Be a Good Sport and Refrain from Using My Patented Putt: Intellectual Property Protection for Sports Related Movements*, 80 J. Pat. & Trademark Off. Soc'y 808 (Nov. 1998). See also *ProBatter Sports, LLC v. Sports Tutor, Inc.*, 680 Fed. Appx. 972 (Fed. Cir. 2017) (affirming validity of patented designs for pitching machine that simulates pitches by analyzing a video projection of an actual pitcher).

cause mistakes to succeed, like the broken play in football that gains yardage because the opposition could not expect it. Athletic events may also result in wholly unanticipated occurrences, the most notable recent event being in a championship baseball game in which interference with a fly ball caused an umpire to signal erroneously a home run.

What "authorship" there is in a sports event, moreover, must be open to copying by competitors if fans are to be attracted. If the inventor of the T-formation in football had been able to copyright it, the sport might have come to an end instead of prospering. Even where athletic preparation most resembles authorship—figure skating, gymnastics, and, some would uncharitably say, professional wrestling—a performer who conceives and executes a particularly graceful and difficult—or, in the case of wrestling, seemingly painful—acrobatic feat cannot copyright it without impairing the underlying competition in the future. A claim of being the only athlete to perform a feat doesn't mean much if no one else is allowed to try.

Id. at 846.

Although the underlying sports event is not copyrightable, the broadcast of a sports event is subject to copyright protection under the Copyright Act of 1976. The *Motorola* court explained:

[R]ecorded broadcasts of NBA games—as opposed to the games themselves—are now entitled to copyright protection. The Copyright Act was amended in 1976 specifically to insure that simultaneously-recorded transmissions of live performances and sporting events would meet the Act's requirement that the original work of authorship be "fixed in any tangible medium of expression." 17 U.S.C. §102(a). . . . Congress specifically had sporting events in mind: "[T]he bill seeks to resolve, through the definition of 'fixation' in section 101, the status of live broadcasts—sports, news coverage, live performances of music, etc.—that are reaching the public in unfixed form but that are simultaneously being recorded." H.R. No. 94-1476 at 52, *reprinted in* 1976 U.S.C.C.A.N. at 5665. The House Report also makes clear that it is the broadcast, not the underlying game, that is the subject of copyright protection. . . .

Id. at 847.

The Copyright Act of 1976 grants a copyright owner several exclusive rights, including, as most relevant for purposes of this discussion, the right to copy or duplicate a copyrighted broadcast of a sports event and to "publicly perform" it. 17 U.S.C. §106. The act provides that anyone who violates any of these exclusive rights engages in copyright infringement. 17 U.S.C. §501(a). The owner of a copyright has a variety of available remedies for infringement, including injunctive relief and the recovery of actual or statutory damages, the infringer's profits, and attorney fees. 17 U.S.C. §§502-505.

An important threshold issue is who owns the copyright to the broadcast of a sporting event—the clubs playing the particular game, the league, the broadcaster of the game, or the players participating in the game? In general, the author of the work owns its copyright. 17 U.S.C. §201(a). *In re National Football League Sunday Ticket Antitrust Litigation*, 933 F.3d 1136, 1154 (9th Cir. 2019), *cert. denied*, 141 S. Ct. 56 (2020) ("[I]n the absence of an agreement otherwise, the person or company that creates the telecast is the 'author' of the telecast for the purposes of copyright law.... Assuming that this rule applies in the league sports setting, the team or network that creates the telecasts would be the sole owner of the copyright in the telecasts, absent some agreement to the contrary."). A broadcaster's camera angles, types of shots, use of instant replays, split screens, special effects, and commentary supplies the creativity necessary for "authorship" of a broadcast sports event for purposes of copyright law. *Baltimore Orioles, Inc. v. Major League Baseball Players Assn.*, 805 F.2d 663, 668–69 (7th Cir. 1986); *National Assn. of Broadcasters v. Copyright Royalty Tribunal*, 675 F.2d 367, 377–79 (D.C. Cir. 1982). Ownership of the copyright for a sports broadcast vis-à-vis the league/clubs and the broadcaster generally is also contractually determined. See, e.g., *NFL v. Insight Telecomm. Corp.*, 158 F. Supp. 2d 124, 128 (D. Mass. 2001) ("The NFL owns the copyright in all regular season and post-season NFL game telecasts, as confirmed by the League's contracts with the networks").

Team sport players (or individual sport athletes) generally do not own the copyright to a sports broadcast. In *Baltimore Orioles, Inc. v. Major League Baseball Players Assn.*, 805 F.2d 663, 670 (7th Cir. 1986), the Seventh Circuit held:

> Because the Players are employees and their performances before broadcast audiences are within the scope of their employment, the telecasts of major league baseball games, which consist of the Players' performances, are works made for hire within the meaning of §201(b).... Thus, in the absence of an agreement to the contrary, the Clubs are presumed to own all of the rights encompassed in the telecasts of the games. The district court found that there was no written agreement that the Clubs would not own the copyright to the telecasts, and, therefore, that the copyright was owned by the Clubs.

See also *Big Fights Inc. v. Ficara*, 40 U.S.P.Q.2d 1377, 1378 (S.D.N.Y. 1996) (the promoter of a professional boxing match, not the participating boxers, owns copyright in the film of the match).

C. Copyright Infringement of a Sports Broadcast

In *NFL v. McBee & Bruno's, Inc.*, 792 F.2d 726 (8th Cir. 1986), the court ruled that the unauthorized interception of the broadcast of a sports event through the use of satellite dish antennae by a commercial establishment, which occurred in the mid-1980s, constitutes copyright infringement. It explained, "The Copyright Act protects 'original works of authorship fixed in any tangible medium,' 17 U.S.C. §102(a), including 'motion pictures and other audiovisual works,' 17 U.S.C. §102(a)(6). As for live broadcasts, such as the football games at issue here, the Act states that '[a] work consisting of sounds, images, or both, that are being transmitted, is "fixed" ... if a fixation of the work is being made simultaneously with its transmission,' 17 U.S.C. §101; '[t]o "transmit" is defined as "to communicate ... by any device or process whereby images or sounds are received beyond the place from which they are sent." *Id.* at 731–32. This was an unauthorized public performance of a copyrighted sports broadcast, which violates federal copyright law.

The following case illustrates that the Internet provides a modern means for infringing copyrighted sports event broadcasts, including by transmissions originating outside the United States, and enables unauthorized webcasts to occur throughout the world—conduct that violates U.S. law, but possibly not foreign laws.

NFL v. TVRadioNow Corp.
53 U.S.P.Q.2d 1831 (W.D. Pa. 2000)

ZIEGLER, J.

This is a civil action for money damages and equitable relief, filed by the National Football League ("NFL"), National Basketball Association ("NBA"), and NBA Properties, Inc. ("NBA Properties") (collectively "the Sports Leagues") . . . contending that defendants violated the Copyright Act, 17 U.S.C. Section 106. . . .

The gravamen of this dispute concerns the public performance of plaintiffs' copyrighted programming from Toronto, Canada, to computer users in the United States since November 30, 1999, over the Internet. Specifically, defendants have streamed copyrighted professional football and basketball games as well as copyrighted programs such as "60 Minutes," "Ally McBeal," and "Star Trek Voyager," framed with advertisements obtained by defendants. Plaintiffs allege that defendants have captured United States programming from television stations in Buffalo, New York and elsewhere, converted these television signals into computerized data and streamed them over the Internet from a website called iCraveTV.com. According to plaintiffs, any Internet user may access iCraveTV.com by simply entering three digits of any Canadian area code, one of which is provided to the user on the site itself, and by clicking two other buttons. Further, Internet users from the United States and elsewhere easily may revisit the site because iCraveTV causes a small file, or cookie, to be deposited in a user's computer during his or her initial visit so that the user can automatically bypass defendants' screening process. . . . [T]he Court is mindful of the long-standing precept that the United States copyright laws do not have extraterritorial operation. *See Allarcom Pay Television, Ltd. v. General Instrument Corp.*, 69 F.3d 381 [36 USPQ2d 1654] (9th Cir. 1995).

Defendants argue that their website is for Canadian viewers only and it is not intended for citizens of the United States and elsewhere. Thus, the argument continues, the alleged improper acts are limited to Canada.

Plaintiffs have presented testimony, sworn affidavits and declarations establishing that Pennsylvania residents have accessed defendants' website and viewed the programs which were streamed thereon. Further, defendants posted an article on the Website by a United States citizen noting that access to defendants' website could be obtained by any United States citizen with little or no difficulty.

Accordingly, when an allegedly infringing act occurring without the United States is publicly performed within the United States, the Copyright Act is implicated and a district court possesses jurisdiction. Subject matter jurisdiction exists because, although the streaming of the plaintiffs' programming originated in Canada, acts of infringement were committed within the United States when United States citizens received and viewed defendants' streaming of the copyrighted materials. These constitute, at a minimum, public performances in the United States. . . .

The plaintiffs have established without rejoinder from the defendants that they have copyright . . . ownership of several items, including, among others, the Super Bowl, the NBA Finals, and the NFL playoff games and regular League games. . . .

Defendants do not deny that they have copied these items, represented themselves as the authors and that they have publicly performed them over the Internet. Rather, defendants argue that there is no desire on the part of defendants for any United States residents to access iCraveTV. Notwithstanding defendants' intentions, the Court finds that plaintiffs have presented sufficient facts to establish their claims of copyright . . . infringement. . . .

A January 25, 2000 breakdown of "impressions" and "clicks" onto the iCraveTV website, generated by a private ad serving system (DART) utilized by Cox, reported 1.6 million impressions (page views) from United States visitors on the iCraveTV website. This figure was second only to the figure for Canada, which was 2.0 million.

Defendants also use a "Real Video" server to stream video programming through their website. This server maintains "logs" of the Internet Protocol addresses of computers that contact defendants' server to obtain access to video programming. An analysis of the Real Video server logs shows that substantial numbers of persons in the United States received the streaming of programming, including programming in which plaintiffs own copyrights. . . . [E]vidence in the record shows that plaintiffs are likely to succeed in showing that defendants are unlawfully publicly performing plaintiffs' copyrighted works in the United States. Defendants do so by transmitting (through use of "streaming" technology) performances of the works to the public by means of the telephone lines and computers that make up the Internet. 17 U.S.C. Section 101. This activity violates plaintiffs' rights to perform their works publicly and to authorize others to do so. 17 U.S.C. Sections 106, 501(a). . . .

Defendants have submitted a declaration of a Canadian law professor, Michael Geist, which argues that defendants' activities are permissible under Canadian law. However, because plaintiffs seek relief under U.S. law for infringements of the U.S. Copyright Act, there is no need for this Court to address any issue of Canadian law. . . .

[Editors' note: The court preliminarily and permanently enjoined defendants from infringing plaintiffs' copyrighted works through streaming or other means into the United States via the iCraveTV.com site or any other Internet site or online facility without plaintiffs' prior consent.]

QUESTION

Why does the defendants' conduct constitute copyright infringement?

> **NOTE**

What is and is not infringing conduct? Tape-recording televised sports broadcasts for solely in-home, personal use is not copyright infringement. *Sony Corp. of Am. v. Universal City Studios, Inc.*, 464 U.S. 417, 449 (1984) (characterizing this activity as "time-shifting for private home use" that is non-infringing fair use of copyrighted broadcast pursuant to §107 of Copyright Act).

By comparison, the unauthorized public performance of taped broadcasts of sports events (which includes posting on YouTube) constitutes copyright infringement. In *New Boston Television, Inc. v. Entertainment Sports Programming Network, Inc.*, 215 U.S.P.Q. 755 (D. Mass. 1981), ESPN contended that its rebroadcast of taped sports event highlights is permissible fair use. Rejecting this alleged defense and finding copyright infringement, the court stated:

> While protection of the public right of access to [newsworthy] information is a primary justification for the fair use defense, this right is sufficiently protected merely by enabling defendants to report the underlying facts which the plaintiff's videotapes record. It does not however permit defendants to appropriate the plaintiff's expression of that information by copying the plaintiff's films themselves.

Id. at 756.

In *NBA v. Motorola, Inc.*, 105 F.3d 841 (2d Cir. 1997), the Second Circuit held that the defendants' reproduction of real-time NBA basketball game statistics (e.g., teams playing, score, time in possession of the ball, time remaining in game) which information was obtained from games broadcast on television and radio does not constitute copyright infringement. Defendants hired persons to gather this real-time game information from NBA games broadcast on television, which was keyed into a computer and then compiled and formatted for retransmission via satellite and FN radio networks to purchasers of its SportTrax paging devices that displayed this information. The court explained:

> Although the broadcasts are protected under copyright law, the district court correctly held that Motorola and STATS did not infringe NBA's copyright because they reproduced only facts from the broadcasts, not the expression or description of the game that constitutes the broadcast. The "fact/expression dichotomy" is a bedrock principle of copyright law that "limits severely the scope of protection in fact-based works." *Feist Publications, Inc. v. Rural Tel. Service Co.*, 499 U.S. 340, 350, 111 S. Ct. 1282, 1290, 113 L. Ed. 2d 358 (1991). "'No author may copyright facts or ideas. The copyright is limited to those aspects of the work—termed 'expression'—that display the stamp of the author's originality.'" *Id.* (quoting *Harper & Row, Publishers, Inc. v. Nation Enter.*, 471 U.S. 539, 547, 105 S. Ct. 2218, 2224, 85 L. Ed. 2d 588 (1985)).
>
> We agree with the district court that the "[d]efendants provide purely factual information which any patron of an NBA game could acquire from the arena without any involvement from the director, cameramen, or others who contribute to the originality of a broadcast."

Id. at 847.

D. Misappropriation of Real-Time Game Accounts and Scores

In *Motorola*, the Second Circuit ruled that federal copyright law preempted (i.e., barred or precluded) the NBA's state law commercial misappropriation claim because the defendants' collection and dissemination of "strictly factual information about the games," which was obtained from NBA games broadcast on television and radio at their own expense and already in the public domain, did not have an adverse economic effect on the production or broadcasting of NBA games.

Consistent with *Motorola*, even if there is no preemption of state because the data is obtained from sources other than a copyrighted broadcast of an athletic event, courts have held that unauthorized commercial use of sports statistics in the public domain does not violate state misappropriation law. In *National Football League v. Governor of the State of Delaware*, 435 F. Supp. 1372 (D. Del. 1977), the court refused to enjoin the unauthorized use of NFL game schedules and scores as the basis for a Delaware state football lottery. Although defendants profited from public popularity generated by NFL games, the court found no misappropriation of the league's property because this information was "obtained from public sources and are utilized only after plaintiffs have disseminated them at large and no longer have any expectation of generating revenue from further dissemination." But it cautioned that defendants could not use NFL game scores in a manner that creates a likelihood of consumer confusion regarding the NFL's authorization or sponsorship of its lottery. This case became more important after *Murphy v. NCAA*, 138 S. Ct. 1461 (2018), in which the U.S. Supreme Court ruled that the Professional and Amateur Sports Act of 1992, 28 U.S.C. §3701 et seq., which generally prohibited states from permitting sports betting, is unconstitutional. Soon thereafter, most states enacted laws permitting regulated sports betting.

In *Morris Communications Corp. v. PGA Tour, Inc.*, 235 F. Supp. 2d 1269 (M.D. Fla. 2002), *aff'd*, 364 F.3d 1288 (11th Cir. 2004), *cert. denied*, 543 U.S. 919 (2004), a federal district court held that the producer of a sports event may prohibit commercial usage of real-time scores and game information by contract (for example, by allowing admission only if ticket holders or members of the media agree to comply with certain conditions), which would constitute illegal misappropriation under state law if violated. The court stated:

> The PGA Tour's property right does not come from copyright law, as copyright law does not protect factual information, like golf scores. *See Feist Publications v. Rural Tel. Serv. Co.*, 499 U.S. 340, 348, 111 S. Ct. 1282, 113 L. Ed. 2d 358 (1991). However, the PGA Tour controls the right of access to that information and can place restrictions on those attending the private event, giving the PGA Tour a property right that the Court will protect.... [T]he instant case deals with facts that are not subject to copyright protection. The compiler of the information ... collects information, which it created, at a cost. Also the events occur on private property to which the general public does not have unfettered access, and the creator of the event can place restrictions upon those who enter the private property. The vastly increased speed

that the Internet makes available does not change the calculus or the underlying property right. Accordingly, the PGA Tour . . . has a property right in the compilation of scores, but that property right disappears when the underlying information is in the public domain.

Id. at 1281-82.

In *Wisconsin Interscholastic Athletic Assn. v. Gannett Co., Inc.*, 658 F.3d 614 (7th Cir. 2011), the Seventh Circuit held that a high school athletic association (which the parties stipulated is a state actor subject to the requirements of the U.S. constitution) has a property right in its tournament games and that its exclusive contract with a third party to stream games over the Internet does not violate the media's First Amendment right to report newsworthy facts and information. The court ruled that the "WIAA has the right to package and distribute its performance; nothing in the First Amendment confers on the media an affirmative right to broadcast entire performances" without its authorization. *Id.* at 622.

Problem 9-3

MLB Advanced Media (MLBAM), MLB's Internet subsidiary, claims ownership of all real-time data used by sports websites to provide live graphic simulations of MLB games over the Internet. Some webcasters operate sites providing very detailed game accounts, including the location of each pitch, that are updated every 30 to 90 seconds. Some webcasters obtain this information from employees who are present at MLB games; whereas, others get their data from employees who are watching televised games or listening to radio broadcasts. One webcaster is licensed by MLBAM to use real-time data from MLB games, but no others are willing to pay the substantial fee for obtaining licensing rights. Does the unauthorized detailed description of a baseball game over the Internet infringe MLB's intellectual property rights?

ATHLETES' LANHAM ACT AND STATE LAW PRIVACY, REPUTATION, AND PUBLICITY RIGHTS

Today's professional athlete is a celebrity and probably attains that status, at least locally, much earlier than the onset of his or her professional career. The best-known athletes have entered into lucrative deals to promote and endorse a wide variety of products and services. Income earned from the licensing of a player's identity to sell products and services may be greater than that derived from his or her athletic earnings. For example, the most elite and widely recognized male and female athletes, such as LeBron James, Lionel Messi, and Serena Williams, earn millions annually, far surpassing their income from purely athletic accomplishments. All of them have multiple endorsement deals that are carefully negotiated by their business representatives. The evolution of the various laws protecting an athlete's personality rights requires consideration of trademark and unfair competition under the Lanham Act, which was previously considered in this chapter, as well as state defamation, privacy, and publicity laws.

A. Lanham Act

The unauthorized misappropriation of an athlete's name, likeness, or other aspects of his or her identity violates §43(a) of the Lanham Act, 15 U.S.C. §1125(a), if it causes consumer confusion regarding whether he or she has endorsed or sponsored particular products and services. This federal statutory claim provides a consumer protection–based cause of action. Various state laws establish a similar standard as well. As the Ninth Circuit has observed: "Many people may assume that when a celebrity's name is used in a television commercial, the celebrity endorses the product advertised." *Abdul-Jabbar v. General Motors Corp.*, 85 F.3d 407, 413 (9th Cir. 1996).

In *Hillerich & Bradsby v. Christian Brothers*, 943 F. Supp. 1136 (D. Minn. 1996), the defendant was selling its Pro-Rite hockey blades with the name "Messier" clearly affixed on the blade and product label, without the permission of Mark Messier, one of professional hockey's most recognized players, who led the Edmonton Oilers and the New York Rangers to a total of six Stanley Cup championships and was twice voted the most valuable player in the NHL. The court ruled that this unauthorized commercial use of Messier's name created the false impression that he endorsed the defendant's hockey blades and enjoined the defendant from using Messier's name on its products or in connection with their advertising and sale without his express permission.

An athlete may use their name as a trademark or service mark, and it may be federally registered under the Lanham Act after acquiring secondary meaning as the source or origin of goods or services (i.e., it is a brand name the public associates with an identifiable athlete). For example, the name "Tiger Woods" has been federally registered as a trademark for art prints, calendars, mounted photographs, notebooks, pencils, pens, posters, trading cards, and unmounted photographs. Unauthorized usage of an athlete's federally registered name that creates a likelihood of consumer confusion regarding the source or sponsorship of goods or services constitutes trademark infringement and unfair competition in violation of the Lanham Act and various state laws.

B. State Laws

KEY TERMS
- Defamation
- First Amendment
- Right of publicity

In the United States, state laws, which vary by jurisdiction, protect the reputation, privacy, and publicity rights of athletes. The First Amendment of the U.S. Constitution, which protects freedom of speech and expression, significantly limits state laws' recognition and protection of individuals' reputation, privacy, and publicity rights and must always be considered.

1. Defamation

The tort of defamation includes both oral (slander) and written (libel) statements. The scope of its legal protection is not limited to celebrities, such as well-known athletes, but defamation assumes special significance in this context. Athletes are a constant source of media and other commentary. Their lives, both professionally and personally, are scrutinized, at times to excruciating degrees, and statements made may be false and harm an athlete's reputation.

Although state law definitions vary, a general definition of defamation is set forth in the Restatement (Second) Torts, §558, which provides, "To create liability for defamation, there must be: (a) a false and defamatory statement concerning another; (b) an unprivileged communication to a third party; (c) fault amounting at least to negligence on the part of the publisher; and (d) either actionability of the statement irrespective of special harm or the existence of special harm caused by the publication."

Statements must be both false and defamatory, meaning that they tend to damage the reputation of the person identified by the statement in the minds of others. Not expressly included in the above definition but generally accepted as a part thereof is that the false statement must be one of fact, not merely opinion. Most of what is written about the performance of athletes as well as coaches and game officials is opinion, which is not legally actionable even if it harms one's reputation. For example, a statement in a newspaper article that a coach "usually finds a way to screw things up" and "[t]his season will be no different" is nonactionable opinion regarding a team's potential for the upcoming season and the coach's ability. *Washington v. Smith*, 893 F. Supp. 60 (D. D.C. 1995), 80 F.3d 555 (D.C. Cir. 1996). On the other hand, asserting that an athlete "fixed" a boxing match and used cocaine with his opponent thereafter, *Cobb v. Time, Inc.*, 278 F.3d 629 (6th Cir. 2002), or knowingly used "loaded" boxing gloves, *Dempsey v. Time, Inc.*, 252 N.Y.S.2d 186 (N.Y. Sup. Ct. 1964), are statements of fact that harm one's professional reputation and may cause resulting economic loss. Making false factual statements about an athlete's personal life, such as criminal conduct, also is defamatory.

Beginning with the seminal *New York Times v. Sullivan*, 376 U.S. 254 (1964) Supreme Court ruling, the traditional state law elements of defamation have been modified by federal constitutional law; therefore, First Amendment free speech issues must also be considered. A prominent athlete generally is characterized as a "public figure" who must prove by clear and convincing evidence that a defamatory statement was made with "actual malice," meaning the defendant had knowledge of its falsity or a reckless disregard regarding whether or not it was true. For example, in *Higgins v. Kentucky Sports Radio, LLC*, 951 F.3d 728 (6th Cir. 2020), the Sixth Circuit ruled that the First Amendment barred a referee's defamation and other claims against a radio station and its commentators for vociferously criticizing his officiating during a 2017 NCAA basketball tournament game that the University of Kentucky lost, which allegedly caused angry Kentucky fans to negatively review his roofing business on its Facebook page as well as to make unwanted phone calls to and physical threats against him. It observed: "Kentucky Sports Radio could fairly discuss the game—and could freely criticize those who participated in it, including the referees, the coaches, the players, the fans, and for that matter the commentators." *Id.* at 735–36. Although this commentary "did more to fan the flames of discontent than to extinguish them," the court rejected plaintiff's assertation that it incited fans to act illegally and is not protected by the First Amendment because he failed to identify "any statement made by the defendants, explicitly or implicitly, that fans should attack his business." *Id.* at 737–39. The court ruled that he is a "public figure" and criticism of his refereeing is a matter of public concern; therefore, he must prove the commentary was made with "actual malice," which he failed to do: "Merely repeating potentially false reviews generated by other users may be in bad taste. But it cannot by itself constitute defamation." *Id.* at 739.

2. Right of Privacy

The right of privacy, as a distinct concept of legal protection, was first enunciated in a famous law review article by Samuel Warren and Louis Brandeis that was published in the *Harvard Law Review* in 1890, in which they argued that a distinct tort protecting a person's right to privacy existed at common law and should be recognized. Samuel D. Warren and Louis D. Brandeis, *The Right to Privacy*, 4 Harv. L. Rev. 193 (1890). A further impetus to the development of the right of privacy occurred some years later through the various writings of Professor William Prosser. His last formulations set forth four separate categories that he advocated should be subsumed under a general concept of privacy: (1) protection against intrusion into one's private affairs; (2) avoidance of disclosure of one's embarrassing private fact; (3) protection against publicity placing one in a false light in the public eye; and (4) remedies for appropriation, usually for commercial advantage, of one's name or likeness. William Prosser, *Privacy*, 49 Cal. L. Rev. 383 (1960). All or some of these four categories of torts have largely been adopted in all states by either common law or statute.

The first three torts concern intrusions into one's private life and affairs, and athletes have relied on one or more of these legal theories in asserting various invasion of privacy claims. See, e.g., *Spahn v. Julian Messner, Inc.*, 286 N.Y.S.2d 832 (N.Y. 1967) (publication of unauthorized fictionalized biography of well-known baseball player violates statutory privacy law); *Erin Andrews v. Marriott International Inc.* (Tenn. Cir. Ct. 2016) (Nashville jury awards sports broadcaster Erin Andrews $55 million in damages arising out of a 2008 peeping Tom incident and posting of a video of her naked on the Internet); *Jason Pierre-Paul v. ESPN Inc.* 2016 WL 4530884 at *1 (S.D. Fla.) (refusing to dismiss NFL player's invasion of privacy claim because improperly obtained medical records concerning amputation of his right index finger after hand injury in a fireworks accident are "not publicly available" and "generally considered private").

3. Right of Publicity

The unauthorized commercial appropriation of an individual's identity is distinguishable from the other three privacy torts because of its recognition of the commercial value in one's name or likeness. Today, most states recognize a separate right of publicity (also referred to as name, image, and likeness (NIL) rights), either as a common law or statutory right. Unlike an individual's rights of reputation and privacy, the right of publicity is a property right that may be transferred and is descendible to the celebrity's surviving heirs in many states (if the jurisdiction recognized such right at the time of the person's death).

Courts initially refused to characterize celebrity names and likenesses as protectable property rights. In *Hanna Mfg. Co. v. Hillerich & Bradsby Co.*, 78 F.2d 763, 766 (5th Cir. 1935), the Fifth Circuit held that "fame is not merchandise." It concluded that an athlete has a valid claim for unauthorized commercial use of his name only if such usage falsely suggests that he uses or endorses the product, thereby constituting unfair competition under federal and state laws.

In 1953, a U.S. court recognized the right of publicity for the first time. *Haelan Laboratories, Inc. v. Topps Chewing Gum, Inc.*, 202 F.2d 866 (2d Cir. 1953), *cert. denied*, 346 U.S. 816 (1953). The case involved a dispute over the rights to use baseball players' images on bubble gum trading cards. One company had been assigned these rights by the players; however, the defendant produced its own cards without the players' permission. One of the central issues was whether the players' rights, if any, were assignable, or were they strictly personal to the player. The Second Circuit held that New York law recognized a common law right of publicity, which is a freely transferable property right, not just a personal right. The court explained "in addition to and independent of the right of privacy . . . a man has a right in the publicity value of his photograph, i.e., the right to grant the exclusive privilege of publishing his picture." *Id.* at 868.

Since *Haelan Laboratories*, a majority of states (but not all) now recognize a right of publicity property-based claim for unauthorized commercial use of an athlete's identity by common law or statute. See generally 1 J. Thomas McCarthy, *Rights of Publicity and Privacy* §§6:2–6:6 (2d ed. 2023). As one court observed, "a celebrity has a legitimate proprietary interest in his public personality. A celebrity must be considered to have invested his years of practice and competition in a public personality which eventually may reach marketable status. . . . A name is commercially valuable as an endorsement of a product or for use for financial gain only because the public recognizes it and attributes good will and feats of skill or accomplishments of one sort or another to that personality." *Uhlaender v. Henricksen*, 316 F. Supp. 1277, 1282–83 (D. Minn. 1970).

A well-known sports journalist has observed:

> As sports passed from Jackie Robinson to Curt Flood to free agency, athletes were branded less by team than by their own personhood. They had become, in the parlance of marketers and agencies, their own brands. Social media—Twitter in particular—allowed them to bypass magazines and television entirely and speak directly to their "followers," while "monetizing" their various "platforms."

Steve Rushin, *There and Back*, Sports Illustrated, Aug. 11, 2014, *http://www.si.com/vault/2014/08/11/106623799/there-and-back*.

a. Nature and Scope of the Right of Publicity

In *Newcombe v. Adolph Coors Co.*, 157 F.3d 686 (9th Cir. 1998), the Ninth Circuit held that Don Newcombe, a well-known former MLB pitcher, had California common law and statutory right of publicity claims against a brewery for using an identifiable likeness of his distinctive pitching style without his permission in a magazine advertisement for one of its products. The court observed:

> Having viewed the advertisement, we hold that a triable issue of fact has been raised as to whether Newcombe is readily identifiable as the pitcher in the advertisement. Initially, we note that the drawing in the advertisement and the newspaper photograph of Newcombe upon which the drawing was based are virtually identical. The pitcher's stance, proportions, and shape are identical to the newspaper photograph of Newcombe; even the styling of the uniform is identical, right down to the wrinkles in the pants. . . . It may be the case that Newcombe's stance is essentially generic, but based on the record before us, Newcombe is the only one who has such a stance. The record contains pictures of other pitchers in the windup position but none of these pitchers has a stance similar to Newcombe's, thus giving us no basis to reach the conclusion proposed by the defendants that the pitcher in the advertisement is 'generic.' . . . [T]here is a genuine issue of material fact as to whether Newcombe's stance was so distinctive that the defendants used his likeness by using a picture of Newcombe's stance.

Id. at 692–93.

Consistent with *Newcombe*, courts have broadly defined the protected aspects of an athlete's identity to encompass more than merely his or her name or photo, including an athlete's birth name (even after it was changed, such as after conversion to Islam or as a personal choice), nickname, or voice, a robotic caricature of an athlete, a distinctive car driven by a professional racer, an athlete's facial features, and athletes' monikers such as "The Greatest" and "Crazy Legs." In a case involving the famous entertainer Johnny Carson, a court even extended publicity rights to the phrase "Here's Johnny!" *Carson v. Here's Johnny Portable Toilets, Inc.*, 698 F.2d 831 (6th Cir. 1983). A state statutory or common law right of publicity may even protect an athletic performance—for example, a human cannonball act. Athletes earn royalties for licensing the use of their individual publicity rights in commercials, print ads, and in-person appearances, as well as by exploiting their fame online via Twitter (e.g., by including @SPONSOR/COMPANY in a tweet) or Instagram (e.g., showing their use of a product or including it in photos of them).

Infringement of an athlete's right of publicity or NIL rights occurs if an aspect of his or her identity was used without permission to advertise and sell a product or service. Other examples of infringing commercial usage include incorporating an athlete's photo into a product such as sports trading cards, drinking glasses, or clothing. Courts generally refuse to characterize the use of a famous athlete's name or identity in connection with the sale of a product as legally permissible incidental or informational use. Rather, such usage is unauthorized commercial appropriation of the athlete's persona that violates one's right of publicity. In *Abdul-Jabbar v. General Motors Corp.*, 85 F.3d 407 (9th Cir. 1996), the Ninth Circuit held that, although such information is newsworthy, an auto manufacturer's use of the name and college basketball records of Kareem Abdul-Jabbar (formerly Lew Alcindor) in a television advertisement is commercial usage. The auto manufacturer gained an economic benefit from the advertisement, which attracted the attention of television viewers of the 1993 NCAA men's basketball tournament.

Unauthorized usage of an athlete's identity is a necessary element of a claim for misappropriation or infringement of publicity rights. An athlete's consent to the use of his or her identity for commercial purposes may be either express or implied under the circumstances. The nature and scope of such consent is necessarily determined on a case-by-case basis and requires careful review of a contract to determine which rights are licensed either exclusively or nonexclusively.

Although intercollegiate and interscholastic athletes have legally protected publicity rights in the respective states in which they are domiciled, college and state high school sports governing body amateurism rules historically prohibited them from earning any income from their individual or group licensing. On June 30, 2021, NCAA Divisions I, II, and III member schools and conferences adopted a uniform interim policy suspending the current NCAA amateurism rules prohibiting their respective student-athletes from doing so. Effective July 1, 2021, all incoming and current NCAA student-athletes in all sports are permitted to earn fair market value–based NIL income from third parties other than their respective universities. This policy requires student-athletes to comply with the NIL law of the state in which their university or college is located or the specific rules of their individual schools if there is no applicable state law, while prohibiting "pay for play" and improper recruiting inducements by NCAA member schools. Currently, there is no federal NIL rights legislation, and more than 30 states have enacted statutes permitting intercollegiate athletes to earn income from NIL rights agreements. In several states, including California and New York, state laws or state high school athletic associations permit high school athletes to receive NIL rights income.

The available remedies for violation of one's NIL or publicity rights are damages and injunctive relief. In 2015, a Chicago jury awarded Michael Jordan $8.9 million in damages for violation of his right of publicity by Dominick's, a Chicago grocery store chain that included a coupon for discounts on steaks in its congratulatory ad in a Sports Illustrated commemorative issue recognizing his induction into the Naismith Hall of Fame. In 2016, current and former Division

I college football and former men's basketball players began receiving checks ranging from less than $100 to $9,300 from a $60 million fund settling their NIL rights infringement litigation against Electronic Arts, Inc. and the NCAA arising out of the unauthorized use of their images in college video games, which is discussed in Chapter 3.

b. First Amendment Limitations

The First Amendment of the U.S. Constitution limits the protection of publicity rights under state law. In *Titan Sports, Inc. v. Comics World Corp.*, 870 F.2d 85, 88 (1989), the Second Circuit explained there is an "inherent tension between the protection of an individual's right to control the use of his likeness and the constitutional guarantee of free dissemination of ideas, images, and newsworthy matter in whatever form it takes."

In *Zacchini v. Scripps-Howard Broadcasting, Inc.*, 433 U.S. 562 (1977), the U.S. Supreme Court held that the media's right to report newsworthy events does not permit the unauthorized broadcast of a performer's entire act, which threatens harm to its economic value. A local Ohio television station sent a news crew to film the act of Hugo Zacchini, the "human cannonball," who was performing at a county fair. This was done despite Zacchini's request that his performance not be filmed. His entire 15-second performance was shown on the evening news. Rejecting Zacchini's misappropriation claim, the Ohio Supreme Court held in favor of the television station, citing its right to report newsworthy events under the First Amendment. In a 5–4 decision, the Supreme Court reversed and ruled that showing his entire act is not permitted by the First Amendment's protection of news reporting because it reduces the commercial value of Zacchini's entertainment product and corresponding economic incentive to produce his performance.

Since *Zacchini*, lower courts have struggled to draw the line between unauthorized commercial use of one's identity that may be prohibited by state law and communicative or expressive use protected by the First Amendment. At this point of the law's development, when the usage of an athlete's identity moves from the purely commercial (e.g., in connection with the advertising or sale of a product) to a more mixed medium—such as in films, television, radio, newspapers, and other literary and artistic works—the more likely that First Amendment issues will arise.

The First Amendment broadly immunizes the media from state law liability for infringement of NIL or publicity rights, even though media publications and broadcasts usually are for-profit commercial activities. The media may use an athlete's name, photograph, and other aspects of one's identity in connection with truthful news reporting. Courts have broadly extended constitutional protection to media republications of news coverage of sporting events and athletic accomplishments, even if used for advertising purposes. For example, in *Montana v. San Jose Mercury News, Inc.*, 34 Cal. App. 4th 790 (Cal. Ct. App. 1995), the court held that a newspaper may contemporaneously reproduce a full-page account of the San Francisco 49ers' four Super Bowl victories in the 1990s in poster form for public sale without violating the publicity rights of Joe Montana, the team's quarterback. Even though his name and likeness appeared on the posters, they were depictions of newsworthy events in which Montana had played a prominent role. See also *Namath v. Sports Illustrated*, 371 N.Y.S.2d 10 (App. Div. 1975), *aff'd*, 352 N.E.2d 584 (N.Y. 1976) (dismissing athlete's right of publicity claim against magazine for using his photograph in advertisements to promote subscriptions).

On the other hand, the use of news coverage of an athletic event incorporating an athlete's name or likeness to advertise or sell unrelated products is not constitutionally protected. In *Pooley v. National Hole-in-One Association*, 89 F. Supp.2d 1108 (D. Ariz. 2000), the defendant made a videotape of a professional golfer's hole-in-one and used his name to promote its hole-in-one fund-raising competitions. Denying the defendant's motion to dismiss the plaintiff's right of publicity claim, the court ruled:

> [W]hile Plaintiff's hole-in-one at the Bay Hill Classic was open to national observation and public videotaping, its *subsequent* unauthorized reproduction was not automatically privileged simply because the hole-in-one continued to be a "newsworthy" event. Defendant did not create the videotape in connection with a news account. Defendant did not include Plaintiff's name and videotape footage simply to communicate an idea. It capitalized on Plaintiff's name, reputation, and prestige in the context of an advertisement. The promotional videotape went one step further and implied a false connection between the Plaintiff and its business. The Court finds that the use of Plaintiff's identity was strictly commercial and not protected by the First Amendment.

Id. at 1114.

The First Amendment has been judicially construed to permit the usage of historical accounts of player records and accomplishments as well as video depictions of their athletic performances. In *Gionfriddo v. Major League Baseball*, 94 Cal. App. 4th 400 (Cal. Ct. App. 2001), a group of retired professional baseball players claimed that MLB's unauthorized use of their names and likenesses in for-profit print and video publications providing historical information violated their right of publicity. The court found that "[t]he public has an enduring fascination in the records set by former players and in memorable moments from previous games[which] are the standards by which the public measures the performance of today's players." Affirming summary judgment for defendants, it concluded: "Balancing plaintiffs' negligible economic interests against the public's enduring fascination with baseball's past, we conclude that the public interest favoring the free dissemination of information regarding baseball's history far outweighs any proprietary interests at stake." *Id.* at 415.

Similarly, in *C.B.C. Distribution and Marketing, Inc. v. Major League Baseball Advanced Media*, 505 F.3d 818 (8th Cir. 2007), *cert. denied*, 553 U.S. 1090 (2008), the Eighth Circuit ruled that the unauthorized use of MLB players' names and statistics in online fantasy baseball games is protected by the First Amendment. The court explained that "the information used in CBC's fantasy baseball games is all readily available in the public domain, and it would be strange law that a person would not have a first amendment right to use information that is available to everyone." The court found the *Gionfriddo* court's views "persuasive": "recitation and discussion of factual data concerning the athletic performance of [players on MLB's website] command a substantial public interest, and, therefore, is a form of public expression due substantial constitutional protection." *Id.* at 823–24. See also *CBS Interactive Inc. v. National Football League Players Assn., Inc.*, 259 F.R.D. 398 (D. Minn. 2009) (fantasy football game's unauthorized use of NFL players' names, player profiles, up-to-date statistics, injury reports, participant blogs, pictures, images, and biographical information does not violate their publicity rights); *Daniels v. FanDuel, Inc.*, 109 N.E.3d 390, 396–97 (Ind. 2018) (unauthorized commercial use of former college football players' names and likenesses in online fantasy sports contests, which "bears resemblance to the publication of the same information in newspapers and websites," is within Indiana's right of publicity statute's "newsworthiness" or "public interest" exceptions, while observing "it would be difficult to draw the conclusion that the athletes are endorsing any particular product such that there has been a violation of the right of publicity").

In *Cardtoons, L.C. v. Major League Baseball Players Assn.*, 95 F.3d 915, 969 (10th Cir. 1996), the Tenth Circuit recognized a First Amendment parody defense to a right of publicity claim challenging Cardtoons' production of a series of baseball cards lampooning readily identifiable individual MLB players and explained:

> Cardtoons' parody trading cards receive full protection under the First Amendment. The cards provide social commentary on public figures, major league baseball players, who are involved in a significant commercial enterprise, major league baseball. While not core political speech (the cards do not, for example, adopt a position on the Ken Griffey, Jr., for President campaign), this type of commentary on an important social institution constitutes protected expression.

In *ETW v. Jireh Publishing, Inc.*, 332 F.3d 915 (6th Cir. 2003), the Sixth Circuit held that the First Amendment protects a sports artist's freedom of expression to include the likenesses of famous professional athletes (e.g., Tiger Woods and other legendary professional golfers) in a painting commemorating Woods's historic victory in the 1997 Masters tournament, reprints of which were sold to the public. The court explained that the First Amendment protects expressive materials "including music, pictures, films, photographs, paintings, drawings, engravings, prints, and sculptures," which is not limited even if it is sold. Observing that famous athletes, "through their pervasive presence in the media . . . have come to symbolize certain ideas and values in our society and have become a valuable means of expression in our culture," the court concluded, "While the right of publicity allows celebrities like Woods to enjoy the fruits of their labors, here Rush has added a significant creative component of his own to Woods's identity. Permitting Woods's right of publicity to trump Rush's right of freedom of expression would extinguish Rush's right to profit from his creative enterprise." *Id.* at 938.

Courts have ruled that the unauthorized use of identifiable traits and characteristics of college athletes in videogames is not protected by the First Amendment. In *In re NCAA Student-Athlete Name and Licensing Litigation*, 724 F.3d 1268

(9th Cir. 2013), the Ninth Circuit held that an NCAA college football video game produced by Electronic Arts (EA) violated former Arizona State and Nebraska quarterback Sam Keller's right of publicity. It ruled that EA's depiction of him in its NCAA Football videogame is not sufficiently transformative for the First Amendment to bar his California right of publicity claims. In the game, the virtual quarterback for Arizona State and Nebraska shares many of his characteristics. For example, the virtual player wears his same jersey number, is the same height and weight, and is from the same home state. Although Keller's name is omitted from the virtual player's jersey, a videogame user can upload rosters of college football team names obtained from third parties so that their names appear on the virtual players' jerseys.

The Ninth Circuit concluded EA's use of Keller's likeness does not have sufficient transformative elements that add "significant creative elements so as to be transformed into something more than a mere celebrity likeness or imitation." *Id.* at 1273. Rather, EA replicated his physical characteristics, and users of its game manipulated the virtual player incorporating these traits while performing his same real-life activity—namely, college football. In other words, "Keller is represented as 'what he was: the starting quarterback for Arizona State and Nebraska,' and 'the game's setting is identical to where the public found [Keller] during his intercollegiate career: on the football field.'" *Id.* at 1275. The court rejected EA's contention that "focusing primarily on Keller's likeness and ignoring the transformative elements of the game as a whole" improperly applies the transformative use defense, explaining "[the fact] that the avatars appear in the context of a videogame that contains many other creative elements does not transform the avatars into anything other than exact depictions of [college football players] doing exactly what they do as celebrities." *Id.* at 1276. See also *Electronic Arts, Inc. v. Davis*, 775 F.3d 1172 (9th Cir. 2013), *cert. denied*, 136 S. Ct. 1448 (2016) ("historic teams" featured in Madden NFL games, which allows gamers to control avatars resembling retired NFL players, is not an "incidental use" protected by the First Amendment because their likenesses are "central to the creation of an accurate virtual simulation of an NFL game").

By comparison, in *Hamilton v. Speight*, 827 Fed. Appx. 238, 241 (3d Cir. 2020), the Third Circuit affirmed the district court's rejection of former pro football player and wrestler "Hard Rock Hamilton's" claim that the developer of video game character "Augustus Cole" infringed his right of publicity because "[i]f Hamilton was the inspiration for Cole, the likeness has been 'so transformed that it has become primarily the defendant's own expression.'"

Although *In re NCAA Student–Athlete Name & Likeness Licensing Litigation*, 990 F. Supp. 2d 996 (N.D. Cal. 2013) held that neither the First Amendment nor the Copyright Act preempts a claim by college football and basketball players that the unauthorized use of their images in televised games violates their state law right of publicity, most courts have ruled that the Copyright Act preempts athletes' claims that unauthorized broadcast of games or athletic competitions in which they participated violates their publicity rights. See, e.g., *Dryer v. NFL*, 814 F.3d 938 (8th Cir. 2016); *Baltimore Orioles, Inc. v. Major League Baseball Players Assn.*, 805 F.2d 663 (7th Cir. 1986); *Somerson v. McMahon*, 956 F. Supp. 2d 1345

(N.D. Ga. 2012). Moreover, the Sixth Circuit rejected the claim that "college players have a 'right of publicity' in their names and images as they might appear in television broadcasts of football or basketball games in which the plaintiffs participate," characterizing it as "a legal fantasy" under Tennessee law. *Marshall v. ESPN, Inc.*, 111 F. Supp. 3d 815 (M.D. Tenn. 2015), *aff'd*, 668 Fed. Appx. 155, 157 (6th Cir. 2016).

Problem 9-4

Consider whether the following use of player names or identities without authorization from the player or players union violates any legally protected rights.

(a) A minor professional baseball league affixes the names and photos of players selected for its All-Star team to merchandise such as T-shirts, mugs, and other souvenirs that are sold in the venue hosting its All-Star Game (assume there is nothing in the players' contracts with their respective clubs that permits the league to do so).

(b) A company makes and sells bobblehead dolls depicting famous professional athletes and identifies them by name on the product's packaging.

Coaches' Contracts and Related Issues

INTRODUCTION

It was once common for coaches to negotiate contracts with professional teams or educational institutions without the assistance of lawyers or agents. In fact, more than a few coaching contracts were sealed with a handshake. Written contracts between coaches and their colleges and professional teams, however, are now the norm. The past several years also have been marked by escalating salaries paid to college football and men's basketball coaches. Increased compensation has been accompanied, however, by expanded duties and increased pressure on these coaches to win. This pressure is also a product of the breadth of a coach's duties, which not only include coaching in games and practices but "recruiting prospective athletes, fundraising, coordinating their athletes' academics, serving as public figures and media personalities, and performing administrative tasks such as budgeting." Josh Lens, *Terminating College Head Coaches' Employment with Cause for NCAA Rules Infractions*, 67 Vill. L. Rev. 35, 44–45 (2022). The end result is a profession notable for high visibility and job stress, but low job security. Consequently, the terms that regulate the rights and duties of parties to coaching contracts have taken on more significance than perhaps in the past. Given the foregoing and other dynamics, coaches require the assistance of agents or lawyers in drafting and negotiating contracts that adequately protect the interests of both parties.

Those who represent coaches in contract negotiations must be prepared to address many issues, including the scope of a coach's responsibilities, the duration of a contract, reassignment to noncoaching positions, termination of the relationship for cause and without cause, entitlement to perquisites and fringe benefits, and buyout provisions. The materials that follow offer a glimpse of clauses that increasingly find their way into coaching contracts, provide the source of disputes, and raise other issues that confront those who enter into the coaching profession. (Issues involving coaches are also discussed in other chapters, including Chapters 5, 6, 7, and 8, which examine gender equity, racial equity, health and safety issues, and impairment and concussion issues, respectively.)

The relationships between coaches and their colleges or professional teams are governed largely by the general principles of contract law to which you are introduced in Chapter 4. As discussed in this chapter, however, specific contract law principles (e.g., employment at will) take on particular significance in the coaching context. In addition, constitutional law (e.g., property and liberty interests and due process), to which you are introduced in Chapters 2 and 3, plays a limited role in determining the nature of the relationships between coaches and their employers.

IS THERE A PROPERTY INTEREST IN ATHLETIC EMPLOYMENT?

KEY TERMS
- Employment at will/at-will employment
- Implied-in-fact promise
- Indefinite duration
- Just cause termination
- Liberty interest
- Property interest

A frequently litigated issue is what procedures, if any, an employer must follow before terminating a coach. Because professional coaches are typically hired for a specified number of years, most of the litigation regarding this issue involves high school and college coaches hired under contracts of indefinite duration (i.e., contracts without a set time period). These contracts are often referred to as establishing *at-will employment*, which generally permits a high school or college to terminate a coach without the institution having to establish just cause (i.e., conduct by an employee that gives an employer a legally justifiable reason to fire the employee). Another important aspect of the at-will concept is the right of a college or high school to terminate a coach without allowing the coach, absent special circumstances, to present evidence at a hearing challenging the termination.

Kish v. Iowa Central Community College, 142 F. Supp. 2d 1084 (N.D. Iowa 2001), provides a good illustration of the factual circumstances in which these issues arise. There, a coach who was fired alleged that the mere existence of a contract between him and his employer gave rise to a property interest that required that he be afforded due process (a hearing) before being relieved from his coaching responsibilities. Rejecting the coach's claim, the court stated, "Kish had no cognizable property interest in his coaching contract." *Id.* at 1097. The court further stated that "Kish has not demonstrated any contractual or statutory limitations on Iowa Central's ability to terminate his coaching contract, nor has he demonstrated that a protectable property interest arose from any implied contract arising out of customs, practices, or de facto policies. . . . Instead, Kish's coaching contract expressly provided to the contrary, by stating, 'This contract is not continuing in nature and may be terminated at the pleasure of the Board [of Iowa Central].'"

Id. at 1098. See *Sneed v. Connell*, 2022 WL 4454337 (M.D. Ga. Sept. 23, 2022) (holding that a teacher had no property interest in a coaching position after the contract term ended); *Price v. Univ. of Alabama*, 318 F. Supp. 2d 1084 (N.D. Ala. 2003) (holding that a university was entitled to fire a coach without allowing him to permit evidence at a hearing contesting his termination because the coach had not signed and finalized his employment contract). Note that a coach terminated before a contract term (e.g., terminated in the first year of a two-year contract) has a constitutionally protected property interest in continued employment. *Smith v. Highland Cmty. College*, 2023 WL 372016 (D. Kan. Jan. 23, 2023).

There are exceptions to the general rule articulated in *Kish*, including where a terminated coach proves the existence of an implied-in-fact promise that the coach would not be terminated absent cause. *Kingsford v. Salt Lake City School District*, 247 F.3d 1123, 1132 (10th Cir. 2001). The *Kingsford* court noted, "An implied-in-fact promise to terminate only for cause can be demonstrated by 'conduct of the parties, announced personnel policies, practices of that particular trade or industry, or other circumstances which show the existence of such a promise.'" *Id.*

QUESTIONS

1. In *Kish*, why was the coach not entitled to a hearing that would have permitted him to challenge the college's decision to terminate his employment? Do you think all coaches should receive a hearing when terminated?
2. What responsibilities do you feel should be covered in a head coach's contract? List them. After completing your list, rank the responsibilities in order of importance.

Problem 10-1

William Barr was the head coach of the Richfield football team. His current contract term was from 2023 to 2026. During a football game, a local sports reporter informed Jordan Reynolds, Richfield's principal, that Barr had shouted a racial epithet at a player on the opposing team. Thereafter, the principal met with the school district's superintendent and discussed the renewal of Barr's coaching contract. In January 2024, at the conclusion of the football season, Reynolds informed Barr that he would be fully compensated for the entire term of his contract, but all of his duties as coach would cease immediately. Reynolds did not provide any reasons for terminating Barr and did not afford Barr a hearing to contest his termination. The school denied Barr's request to present evidence at a hearing to address why his contract should be renewed. Reynolds announced to the local media that "Coach Barr's contract will not be renewed." Reynolds did not offer any explanation. Following his termination, Barr applied for several head football coaching positions but received no job offers.

> Barr has filed suit alleging breach of contract and that he has been deprived of his fundamental rights to continued employment and to his reputation. Is Barr likely to prevail? Consider the preceding materials. Also see *Puchalski v. School Dist. of Springfield*, 161 F. Supp. 2d 395 (E.D. Penn. 2001); *Ridpath v. Board of Governors Marshall Univ.*, 447 F.3d 292 (4th Cir. 2006) (university's labeling as "corrective action" its reassignment of athletic director to a position outside of athletic department created a charge of a serious character defect, which in turn gave rise to a liberty interest and entitled plaintiff to a hearing that allowed him to contest the reassignment).

A. Termination

The following materials initially discuss conduct (e.g., violations of NCAA bylaws and engaging in personal indiscretions) that may constitute grounds for an educational institution or a professional team to justifiably terminate a coach. The discussion then addresses the compensation issues that may arise when an institution's termination of a coach is unjustified and therefore constitutes a breach of contract. The materials conclude with a discussion of payment issues that emerge when a coach leaves one institution, prior to the expiration of his or her contract term, to coach a team at another institution.

1. What Constitutes Termination for "Cause"?

An array of events may give an institution or team a right to terminate a coach's employment for cause. At the collegiate level, contracts typically contain provisions granting an institution the right to terminate a coach if the coach has committed serious violations of NCAA bylaws, particularly if the NCAA penalizes the college as a result of the violations. Similarly, a contract may include a provision that grants the institution the discretion to terminate a coach if a member of his or her coaching staff committed an NCAA rules violation if such violation was under the control or direction of the head coach. In addition, contracts include so-called "morals clauses" on which institutions base decisions to terminate a coach's employment for off-the-field conduct. Other common provisions in coaching contracts at both the collegiate and professional levels are those that permit termination for cause if a coach: (1) refuses or is unable (e.g., because of death or incapacity) to perform duties either stipulated in the contract or reasonably associated with the position of coach; (2) is convicted of a serious criminal offense; (3) engages in fraud or dishonesty in the performance of his or her duties; (4) participates or encourages participation in gambling or betting involving sports; or (5) engages in conduct that is detrimental to the best interests of the institution or club. Finally, an institution may include a contractual provision that permits it to terminate a coach without cause, while recognizing the institution's obligation to compensate the coach in such an instance.

An issue that may arise at both the collegiate and professional levels is whether a team's poor winning percentage provides grounds to terminate a coach for cause. At the professional level, this issue arose when Larry Brown was terminated from his position as head coach of the National Basketball Association's (NBA's) New York Knicks. Brown was fired in the first year of a five-year contract after posting a then franchise low record of 23–59. The Knicks withheld payment of the remaining amount due under the contract, $41 million, claiming that Brown was fired for cause. Brown sued to recover the contract amount, as well as $12 million in damages. In a settlement, the Knicks agreed to pay Brown $18.5 million. See ESPN, *Knicks, Brown Reach Undisclosed Contract Settlement*, Oct. 30, 2006, *http://sports.espn.go.com/espn/print?id=2644227&type=HeadlineNews&imagesPrint=off*; and Phil Sheridan, *Leave Larry Brown Behind Forever*, Philadelphia Inquirer, April 29, 2010, at D01.

This issue was also addressed by the Montana Supreme Court in *Cole v. Valley Ice Garden, L.L.C.*, 113 P.3d 275 (Mont. 2005). A five-year employment contract between a coach and a professional hockey team provided the coach could be terminated for cause. The agreement failed to define cause. After the team terminated the coach because of his team's poor performance, he filed suit for breach of contract alleging that he was wrongfully terminated. The coach argued that because the contract failed to expressly require that he maintain a specific win-loss ratio, the court could not imply such a term into the agreement. He did not contest the right of the team to terminate him. Rather, he argued that termination would not end the team's obligation to pay off the remainder of the compensation due to him under the contract. Relying on definitions from other contexts to lend meaning to the term "cause," the court ruled in favor of the team, finding that "[d]ischarging the coach of a professional sports team which is performing poorly, despite management's good faith efforts, is a discretionary decision related to the legitimate needs of the business and constitutes 'cause.'" *Id.* at 280. See *Chang v. Univ. of R.I.*, 606 F. Supp. 1161, 1256 (D. R.I. 1985) (identifying a win-loss record as an objective measure for evaluating a coach); *but see Bd. of Directors of the Jessup Cmty. Sch. Dist. v. Wall*, 801 N.W.3d 33, *6 (Iowa App. 2011) (holding that a football team's poor win-loss record was one of many factors relevant to determining whether a coach's employment can be terminated for cause).

QUESTIONS

If a professional coach leads a team to a poor record, should the organization be able to terminate his or her contract for cause? What about a collegiate coach? What about a high school coach? At the high school and collegiate levels, should factors other than a winning record impact an educational institution's decision to terminate a coach?

2. Termination for Rules Violations and Non-Sports-Related Indiscretions

a. Non-Sports-Related Indiscretions

Institutions and teams have terminated coaches for exercising poor judgment that ranges from violations of NCAA rules to off-the-field indiscretions. In 2003, the number and severity of incidents involving alleged and established improper conduct by coaches in intercollegiate basketball reached such a level that, in a move characterized as unprecedented, the National Association of Basketball Coaches convened a mandatory ethics summit for all NCAA Division I (D-I) men's head coaches. One of the more notorious incidents, which also provided a major catalyst for the coaching summit, involved Dave Bliss, former head men's basketball coach at Baylor University. Bliss was forced to resign following an investigation that revealed that Bliss lied to school officials who were investigating the death of Baylor basketball player Patrick Dennehy, that Bliss instructed coaches and players to lie to those investigators and to portray Dennehy as a drug dealer, and that Bliss improperly paid the tuition for players on the basketball team. See Jeff Caplan, *Baylor's Situation Catalyst for Summit*, Star-Telegram (Sept. 5, 2003).

Other 2003 incidents involving poor judgment and indiscretions by coaches include: Mike Price's termination as the University of Alabama's head coach for conduct that included a visit to a topless bar and reports that a young woman charged $1,000 for room service at a hotel at which Price stayed; University of Washington fired head football coach Rick Neuheisel after he admitted that he bet more than $6,000 on the NCAA D-I men's basketball tournament; Larry Eustachy's resignation as Iowa State University's head men's basketball coach after the release of a photograph showing him surrounded by and kissing younger women and drinking a beer at a college party following a basketball game. Craig Bennett et al., *One Year Later: A Look Back at College Scandals, the People Involved and Where They Stand*, USA Today, June 15, 2004, at C3; Welch Suggs, *A Hard Year in College Sports*, Chron. Higher Educ., Dec. 19, 2003, at A37; John L. Pulley and Welch Suggs, *Coaches Will Be Coaches?*, Chron. Higher Educ., May 16, 2003, at A40. See also Martin J. Greenberg, *Termination of College Coaching Contracts: When Does Adequate Cause to Terminate Exist and Who Determines Its Existence?*, 17 Marq. Sports L. Rev. 197 (2006).

Notwithstanding the negative attention such indiscretions attract, coaches in high-profile collegiate athletics continue to find themselves embroiled in scandal. In a highly publicized 2012 incident, Bobby Petrino, the successful former head football coach at the University of Arkansas, was terminated following revelations of an affair with a female staff employee and misleading statements he made to university officials. See Tom Weir, *Petrino Dumped by Arkansas*, USA Today, April 11, 2012. Petrino would subsequently secure football coaching positions at Western Kentucky University, Missouri State University, and Texas A&M. In October 2015, the University of Southern California (USC) fired its head football coach Steve Sarkisian. The termination occurred in the aftermath of incidents in which Sarkisian slurred his words during a speech and showed signs of intoxication during a game and a team meeting. Sarkisian went into an alcohol treatment program after he was fired. In 2023, controversy surrounded West Virginia University's head men's basketball coach following his arrest for DUI.

On September 18, 2023, Michigan State University notified its suspended head football coach, Mel Tucker, that it planned to terminate his employment for cause. The notice stated that Tucker had seven days within which to present reasons why he should not be terminated. The notice of termination was based on allegations that Tucker "'made unwelcome sexual advances towards' an activist contracted by the university to provide sexual misconduct education to the school's football team," without her consent. Tucker stated that the allegations are "completely false," the investigation has "not been fair or unbiased," and the sexual phone call with the activist was consensual. Wayne Sterling & Zoe Sottile, *Michigan State University Announces Plans to Fire Mel Tucker Amid Sexual Harassment Allegations*, CNN.com, Sept. 19, 2023, https://www.cnn.com/2023/09/19/football/mel-tucker-michigan-state-fired/index.html.

b. Rules Violations

The following scenario illustrates the issues involved when a court determines whether NCAA rules violations constitute grounds for a good-cause termination. In *O'Brien v. Ohio State University*, 2007 WL 2729077 (Ohio Ct. App. Sept. 20, 2007), the former head coach of Ohio State's men's basketball team was terminated for violating NCAA rules prohibiting institutional representatives from providing extra benefits to players (giving a loan to a student-athlete). Plaintiff filed a breach of contract action alleging wrongful termination. The dispositive issue was whether O'Brien's violations of NCAA rules constituted a material breach of contract so as to discharge the university's obligations and allow it to terminate him without pay. In concluding that O'Brien's failure to comply with NCAA rules did not constitute a material breach, the court found that compliance with NCAA rules represented only one of the coach's duties stipulated in the contract. The court also identified contract language providing that the contracting party's failure to perform in each instance would not necessarily justify termination for cause. Since O'Brien's violation of NCAA rules and his failure to promptly report his violations were not so fundamental that they defeated "the essential purpose of the contract" and "thus rendered performance by defendant impossible," the court held that O'Brien's breach was not material and defendant did not have cause to terminate his employment. The court upheld the trial court's damages award of approximately $2.49 million. See Lens, *supra* at 65–88 (providing a detailed discussion of the termination of O'Brien and other coaches for NCAA rules violations).

c. Compensation Issues Following Termination

The termination of a coach for cause will not necessarily result in a denial of compensation. In 2017–18, several terminated coaches received sizable payments following their terminations. For example, Baylor University paid its former head football coach $15 million after it terminated him as a consequence of sexual assault allegations brought by female students against Baylor football players. A 2021 ESPN report found that between January 1, 2010, and January 31, 2021, "public universities in FBS conferences paid out more than $533.6 million in dead money to head coaches and assistant coaches in football and men's and women's basketball." Paula Lavigne & Mark Schlabach, *FBS schools spent over $533 million in dead money over 10+ years*, Nov. 5, 2021, https://www.espn.com/college-football/story/_/id/32552130/schools-spent-5336-million-dead-money. See Lens, *supra* at 42–43 (finding that in 2020, two-thirds of Power Five institutions made severance payments to coaches whose employment had been terminated).

d. College Basketball and College Admissions Scandals

The college basketball and college admissions scandals reveal additional grounds pursuant to which a college or university may terminate a coach's contract. In September 2017, federal prosecutors issued a criminal complaint against four assistant men's basketball coaches: Chuck Person (Auburn University), Tony Bland (University of Southern California), Emanuel "Book" Richardson (University of Arizona), and Lamont Evans (Oklahoma State University). The complaint alleged solicitation of bribes and wire services fraud arising from coaches funneling money from Adidas to the families of high school basketball recruits to influence the recruits to attend and play basketball at certain universities. Michael McCann, *Unpacking Louisville's Countersuit Against Rick Pitino*, SI.com, Dec. 14, 2017; see also Sealed Complaint, *United States v. Person* (S.D. N.Y. Sept. 25, 2017), https://www.justice.gov/usao-sdny/press-release/file/999001/download. The complaint followed a two-year FBI investigation of college basketball coaches, Adidas executives, and agents. Mitch Sherman, *Everything You Need to Know About the College Basketball Scandal*, ESPN.com, Feb. 23, 2018; Aaron Moody, *Here's a Master Guide to College Basketball Corruption Scandal and FBI Investigation*, The News & Observer, Oct. 4, 2018. See Lens, *supra* at 92 (providing a detailed discussion of the coaches involved in the scandal and their criminal sentences).

There were numerous ramifications of the scandal. For example, shortly after the investigation was made public, the University of Louisville terminated its head men's basketball coach Rick Pitino. Because Louisville terminated Pitino for cause, the university asserted it was not obligated to pay Pitino compensation based on a liquidated damages provision in the parties' contract. In November 2017, Pitino sued Louisville for breach of contract seeking "payments of $4,307,000 per year, through 2026," which is allegedly consistent with the liquidated damages provision of the parties' contract. In December 2017, Louisville asserted a counterclaim against Pitino asserting that "Pitino was liable for breach of contract, negligence, and unlawful interference with business relationships between the university and the NCAA, Atlantic Coast Conference, media companies, TV networks, and sponsors. Louisville also demanded that Pitino indemnify the school for any penalties it must pay to the NCAA for wrongdoing connected to his acts." McCann, *supra*. In August 2018, Pitino's lawsuit was dismissed pursuant to a clause in the parties' contract requiring arbitration. Rick Pitino and the University of Louisville Athletics Association eventually reached a settlement in which each party dropped their respective claims against the other. Under the terms of the settlement, Pitino received no money, but Louisville agreed to have his personnel file reflect that Pitino resigned from his position as head basketball coach. Danielle Lerner, *Rick Pitino reaches settlement with University of Louisville Athletics Association*, Courier Journal.com, https://www.courier-journal.com/story/sports/college/louisville/2019/09/18/rick-pitino-university-louisville-athletics-association-reach-settlement/2354450001/. See Lens, *supra* at 80–84 (providing detailed discussion of the Pitino matter). The NCAA infraction implications of the basketball scandal are discussed in Chapter 3.

In March 2019, prosecutors revealed a wide-ranging illicit college admission scheme tied to NCAA athletics. The mastermind, Rick Singer, "admitted to funneling portions of $25 million in bribes from rich parents to coaches, test-cheaters and others to get their children into some of the nation's top universities." Joey Garrison, *Felicity Huffman Is Just the Beginning: Who's Guilty in the College Admissions Scandal—and Who's Still Fighting*, USA Today, June 4, 2019. One aspect of the scheme, dubbed "Varsity Blues," allegedly involved coaches helping "undeserving students" gain admissions to elite universities by portraying the students as top athletes when they were not. *College Admissions Scandal: Your Questions Answered*, NY Times, Mar. 14, 2019.

Coaches who faced federal charges include: Jovan Vavic (USC Men's Water Polo Coach), Gordon Ernst (Georgetown Women's Tennis Coach), William Ferguson (Wake Forest Women's Volleyball Coach), Jorge Salcedo (UCLA Men's Soccer Coach), Ali Krosroshahin (USC Women's Soccer Coach), Laura Janke (USC Assistant Women's Soccer Coach), Rudy Meredith (Yale Women's Soccer Coach), John Vandemoer (Stanford Sailing Coach), and Michael Center (Texas Men's Tennis Coach). Andrew Das, Marc Tracy & Naila-Jean Meyers, *The Coaches Connected to the College Admission Fraud Case*, NY Times, Mar. 12, 2019. The actions taken by universities against the coaches range from termination to administrative leave. *Id*; see Joshua Lens, *Operation Varsity Blues and the NCAA's Special Admission Exception*, 31 J. Legal Aspects Sport 147 (2021) (providing a detailed discussion of the scandal).

QUESTIONS

1. The termination or forced resignations of coaches for conduct, such as that noted above, raises several questions. Are coaches held to standards that are too high, particularly if their indiscretions do not involve rules violations or matters related to the athletics program? What signal does a school send when it hires a coach so quickly after the coach was terminated for such behavior elsewhere? Do schools signal that such behavior is irrelevant to a coach's effectiveness and that terminations for such behavior have more to do with saving face in the media and among some supporters than with running a successful athletic program? What interest does a university have in regulating the personal behavior of coaches? Which clause or clauses within a coach's contract is an institution likely to contend justify its termination of a coach for cause for nonathletic-related behavior? See generally Greenberg, *Termination of College Coaching Contracts, supra*; Patricia Sanchez Abril & Nicholas Green, *Contracting Correctness: A Rubric for Analyzing Morality Clauses*, 74 Wash. & Lee L. Rev. 3, 69–70 (2017).

2. How could Ohio State have avoided the result reached in its dispute with former basketball coach O'Brien?

> **Problem 10-2**
>
> You are a coach of a D-I men's basketball team. You violate an NCAA rule by sending a prospective student-athlete two more text messages than NCAA rules permit. Should such a violation give your school grounds for just cause termination? Should the school have grounds to terminate you if the violation was committed by one of your assistants? What factors will determine if the school can terminate you under either scenario?

3. Termination for Abusive Conduct

When a coach crosses the line that separates appropriate tough discipline from abuse, institutions are justified in terminating a coach for cause. In *Campanelli v. Bockrath*, 100 F.3d 1476 (9th Cir. 1996), Louis Campanelli was fired as head coach of the men's basketball team at the University of California at Berkeley. Newspaper accounts attributed Campanelli's firing to his conduct toward players. A *Washington Post* article described Campanelli as "an abusive bully" who "perpetuate[d] a cycle of abuse" and psychologically attacked his players. Tony Kornheiser, *When the Boot Fits*, Washington Post, Feb. 17, 1993, at C1. In another matter, Winston Bennett was suspended and later fired from his position as head men's basketball coach at Kentucky State University after he struck a player in the face. The player later filed assault charges that ended in a plea bargain. Bennett was ordered to complete 200 hours of community service and to obtain anger management counseling or serve 90 days in jail. *Finish Line*, Rocky Mountain News, Feb. 27, 2004, at 22C. See *Board of Directors of Ames Cmty. Sch. Dist. v. Cullinan*, 745 N.W. 2d 487 (2008 Iowa) (evidence establishing that a coach engaged in threatening and intimidating treatment of student-athletes is sufficient to support a good-cause termination); see also Adam Epstein & Barbara Osborne, *Teaching Ethics with Sports: Recent Developments*, 28 Marq. Sports L. Rev. 301 (2018) (discussing abusive, criminal, and other improper conduct by high school and college coaches and the ethical dimensions of coaching).

Allegations of coach abuse of players have led to other high-profile terminations. Mike Leach, the highly successful football coach at Texas Tech University, who compiled a ten-season record of 84–43, was fired for cause on December 30, 2009, based on allegations that the coach had improperly treated a player who had suffered a concussion. On January 10, 2010, Leach, who had signed a five-year contract extension on January 1, 2009, filed a lawsuit against Texas Tech alleging wrongful termination and defamation. Leach alleged that the university fired him to avoid making an $800,000 bonus payment due to Leach on December 31, 2009. In 2010, a judge rejected Texas Tech's sovereign immunity defense and allowed Leach's breach of contract claim to move forward. The university appealed the ruling. On January 20, 2011, a state appellate court reversed the trial court ruling and found that Texas Tech was immune from Leach's breach of contract claim. *Leach v. Texas Tech*, 335 S.W.3d 386 (Tex. Ct. App. 2011). Leach asked the Texas Supreme Court to review his case. Without explanation, the Texas Supreme Court issued an order denying Leach's request for review on February 17, 2012. See *Leach v. Texas Tech*, 335 S.W.3d 386 (Tex. Ct. App. 2011), review denied, Feb. 17, 2012. In 2020, Leach was hired to become the head football coach at Mississippi State University.

In April of 2013, video footage emerged of former Rutgers University head men's basketball coach, Mike Rice, physically assaulting his players. Brittany Brady, *Rutgers coach fired after abusive video broadcast*, CNN.com, Apr. 4, 2013, http://www.cnn.com/2013/04/03/sport/rutgers-video-attack/. The video showed Rice throwing basketballs at his players and forcefully pushing them while verbally insulting them. *Id.* Although such coaching tactics are certainly not novel and are viewed by some as appropriate hard-nose coaching, others find them appalling. Rutgers initially punished Rice with a three-game suspension and a $75,000 fine, but the University terminated him after it was pressured by state officials. *Id.* Still, Rice received $475,000 in severance pay. Angela Delli Santi, *Rutgers, Mike Rice Settlement: Fired Basketball Coach to Receive $475,000 Under Agreement*, Huffington Post, Apr. 18, 2013.

In 2023, Northwestern University terminated the contract of its head baseball coach, Jim Foster, after allegations surfaced of a toxic baseball culture involving bullying and verbal abuse. Jonathan Franklin, *Northwestern Baseball Coach Jim Foster Is Fired Days after Football Hazing Scandal*, NPR, July 14, 2023, https://www.npr.org/2023/07/14/1187748113/northwestern-baseball-coach-jim-foster-fired. Foster was terminated a few days after Northwestern suspended and then fired its head football coach, Pat Fitzgerald, "after an investigation found that his players had participated in widespread hazing including forced nudity and sexualized acts." In response to the termination of his contract for cause, Fitzgerald stated his "agent and lawyer would 'take all necessary steps to protect his rights in accordance with the law.'" Eduardo Medina, *Northwestern Fires Pat Fitzgerald, Football Coach, Amid Hazing Allegations*, NY Times, Jul. 10, 2023, https://www.nytimes.com/2023/07/10/sports/pat-fitzgerald-northwestern-fired-hazing.html. In July 2023, several former football players sued Northwestern for the alleged harm arising from the hazing.

Allegations of coaches mistreating athletes have led to the termination of women coaches as well. Georgia Tech fired its head women's basketball coach, MaChelle Joseph, for her alleged emotional and mental mistreatment of her players. Joseph subsequently sued Georgia Tech alleging gender-based discrimination. Longtime UNC head women's basketball coach, Sylvia Hatchell, resigned after a university-commissioned report allegedly concluded Hatchell had made racially insensitive comments to players and had exerted pressure on medical staff to clear injured players to return to play. Hatchell denied the allegations. Madeline Holcombe, *UNC's women's basketball coach resigns after review finds she made "racially insensitive" comments*, CNN, Apr. 19, 2019, *https://www.cnn.com/2019/04/19/us/unc-womens-basketball-sylvia-hatchell-resigns/index.html*. For a case involving alleged abuse by a coach of athletes, see *Taylor-Travis v. Jackson State Univ.*, 984 F.3d 1107 (5th Cir. 2021). In upholding a jury verdict in favor of a dismissed women's basketball coach, the court found that there was sufficient evidence to support a jury's verdict that the coach did not mistreat her players.

QUESTIONS

1. In the absence of contract language specifying behavior that is cause for termination, what types of conduct should always be unacceptable? Are colleges too willing to hire coaches who were fired in the past for abusive conduct toward athletes?
2. Assuming the former Northwestern football players can prove they suffered harm resulting from the hazing, should Northwestern be held liable for the hazing-related conduct of players? Which additional facts, if any, would influence your opinion?

Problem 10-3

Coach entered into a five-year contract with University at an annual base salary of $250,000, not including perquisites, which contained the following provision:

> NOTICE OF APPOINTMENT AND CONTRACT: During the term of Coach's contract, Coach shall hold the appointment, title, and duties of Head Coach in the University's women's basketball program, except that at any time during the Appointment Term with 30 days' notice, the appointment, title, and duties of Head Coach may be terminated and another title and duties assigned. The University's termination of Coach's appointment, title, and duties as Head Coach of the women's basketball program, and its reassignment of Coach to other appointment, title, and duties within the University shall be within the discretion of University and may be exercised with or without cause.

During the first two years of her contract, the basketball team had a losing record of 8–45. University, which previously had a highly regarded women's basketball program, lost money on its women's basketball program and

> attendance was down during these two years. In a letter to Coach dated March 15 of her third year, University's athletic director stated:
>
>> University hereby notifies you that your appointment as Head Coach of University's women's basketball team, and all duties associated with your title as Head Coach, will terminate as of April 16. University hereby offers to reassign you to the position of compliance coordinator for NCAA rules and regulations. A change in leadership of the basketball team is required and this reassignment is for the good of the athletic department. If you accept University's offer of reassignment, it will take effect April 16, 2024. You will continue to receive your annual base salary of $250,000 for each of the remaining three years of your contract, except you will not be entitled to receive perquisites that are normally associated with the position of head basketball coach.
>
> Coach is very upset and believes University's reassignment of her constitutes an effort to get her to resign. She is also concerned that accepting a noncoaching position will detrimentally affect her ability to secure another coaching position. Coach would like nothing better than to sue University and comes to you for advice. What advice would you offer to Coach? What are the legal and professional consequences of Coach accepting the reassignment, and of Coach rejecting the reassignment? What type of compromise might Coach consider? In advising Coach, consider the following materials: *Monson v. Oregon*, 901 P.2d 904 (Or. Ct. App. 1995); and Martin J. Greenberg & James T. Gray, Sports Law Practice, vol. 1, pp. 585–87 (2d ed. 1998). See also *Dennison v. Murray State Univ.*, 465 F. Supp. 2d 733 (W.D. Ky. 2006) (holding that even though athletic director's contract stated that the university could only reassign him to a job with responsibilities consistent with the duties of an athletic director, university acted properly in reassigning plaintiff to position of director of corporate giving since contract also included a provision provided that it was subject to all university policies, which included its transfer/reassignment policy).

4. Free Speech and Retaliation Issues

In *Ridpath v. Board of Governors Marshall University*, 447 F.3d 291 (4th Cir. 2006), a compliance officer at Marshall University became aware of a number of violations of NCAA rules, including the school's practice of providing student-athletes with jobs at "above-market" wages. After bringing this information to the attention of university officials, the compliance officer alleged he was prevented from assisting in the investigation, blamed for the violations, and subjected to "corrective action" and transferred to another position on campus that significantly diminished his ability to obtain future employment in his chosen occupation of athletic compliance. The court denied the university's immunity defense and found that the compliance officer had a liberty interest in his reputation or choice of occupation for due process purposes. The court held, in this regard, that the transfer was in fact a demotion and was only labeled as a transfer as a way of avoiding potential liability for demoting the compliance officer.

The court next examined the First Amendment issue and confirmed that a public employer "contravenes a public employee's First Amendment rights when it discharges or refuses to rehire the employee or when it makes decisions relating to the promotion, transfer, recall, and hiring in the exercise of that employee's free speech rights." The court held that the plaintiff had sufficiently alleged that he was speaking as a private citizen and not as a public employee, and that his interest in exercising his First Amendment rights was not outweighed by the university's interest in his speech because the school was unable to show how the plaintiff's remarks had interfered with its legitimate operations. On the other hand, in *Richardson v. Sugg*, 448 F.3d 1046 (8th Cir. 2006) (discussed in Chapter 6), the court held that the firing of an African-American head basketball coach was not an abridgment of his First Amendment rights and was not racially motivated. As to the First Amendment claim, the court held that the detrimental impact of Richardson's comments regarding the university outweighed any free speech right he may have asserted. The *Richardson* and *Ridpath* cases illustrate the nature of proof that must be proffered to prevail on free speech and retaliation grounds and how public universities must respond to such allegations.

B. Compensation and Other Financial Matters

KEY TERMS
- Performance incentive
- Perquisites

In the event that a coach is justifiably terminated pursuant to one of the circumstances set forth in a contract, the institution is not liable to the coach for compensation other than that which was stipulated in the parties' contract. Coaches are often, however, terminated prior to the lapse of the contract term because of the poor performance of the team or other matters, such as conflicts with players, team owners, or university administrators. When a coach is relieved of coaching responsibilities, whether justified or unjustified, conflicts may arise regarding the compensation to which a coach is entitled.

These issues are addressed in *Rodgers v. Georgia Tech Athletic Assn.*, 303 S.E.2d 467 (Ga. App. 1983). Franklin C. "Pepper" Rodgers was relieved from his duties as head football coach at Georgia Tech approximately two years before his contract term was to end. He remained employed by the university. The court held that the "disassociation of Rodgers from his position and duties was not 'for cause' pursuant to the terms of the contract. Therefore, the Association was obligated to pay Rodgers that part of the amount set forth in the contract 'which he himself was entitled to receive as compensation for his services.'" *Id.* at 470–71. In addition to his salary, Rodgers's contract provided that he was entitled "'to various insurance and pension benefits and perquisites' as he became eligible therefore."

Id. at 471. Rodgers brought a breach of contract lawsuit against the Georgia Tech Athletic Association to recover the value of certain perquisites to which he was entitled under his employment contract.

The court stated that Rodgers was entitled to recover his base salary for the remainder of his contract term. In addition to a salary, health insurance, and pension benefits, the contract provided that Rodgers, as an employee of the association, was entitled to "perquisites" as he became eligible therefore. The dispute between Rodgers and Georgia Tech involved his entitlement to "recover the value of certain perquisites or 'fringe benefits' of his position as head coach of football under the terms of his contract of employment with the Association." *Id.* at 469.

The court defined "perquisites" as "'[e]moluments or incidental profits attaching to an office or official position, beyond the salary or regular fees.' Black's Law Dictionary 1299 (4th ed. 1968)." *Id.* Alternatively, the court defined perquisites as "'a privilege, gain, or profit incidental to an employment in addition to regular salary or wages; *esp*: one expected or promised [e.g.,] the [perquisites] of the college president include a home and car. . . .' Webster's Third New International Dictionary 1685 (1981)." *Id.* It stated as a general guideline that Rodgers was entitled to the perquisites (or their value) for which he was eligible during the duration of his contract.

Rodgers listed 29 separate items as perquisites for which he claimed he should be compensated. They were divided into two categories. One category consisted of items provided directly to him by the association but discontinued when Rodgers was relieved of his duties. Items in this category included season tickets to Georgia Tech home football and basketball games, automobile expenses, parking privileges at Georgia Tech sporting events, meals available at the Georgia Tech training table, and expenses related to joining certain country clubs.

The other grouping consisted of items provided by sources other than the Association by virtue of Rodgers's position as head coach of football and included profits from Rodgers's radio and television football shows, use of an automobile, and profits from Rodgers's summer football camps.

In resolving the dispute, the court first found that Rodgers's entitlement to receive perquisites must turn on whether the parties intended that Rodgers would receive perquisites, as he became eligible for them, based on his position as head coach of football and not merely as an employee of the Association.

Examining the items in the first grouping, Georgia Tech argued that "Rodgers was not entitled to any of the items . . . because they were expense account items—'tools' to enable him to execute his duties more effectively as head coach of football. Rodgers counter[ed] that those items were an integral part of the total compensation package that he received as head coach of football and constituted consideration for his contract of employment." *Id.* at 471–72. The court concluded that "with three exceptions, we cannot say as a matter of law either that Rodgers was entitled to the items listed in Section A as perquisites of his employment, or that he was not." *Id.* at 472. The three items disallowed "the services of a secretary, the services of an administrative assistant, and the cost of trips to football conventions [and] clinics" related to aiding Rodgers in fulfilling his duties as a head coach. *Id.*

With respect to perquisites Rodgers received from sources other than the Association by virtue of his position as head coach of football, the court adopted the following principles to guide its analysis: "[T]he consideration of a contract need not flow directly from the promise [or] [here, the Association], but may be the promise or undertaking of one or more third persons. *Bing v. Bank of Kingston*, 5 Ga. App. 578, 580, 63 S.E. 652 (1908)." *Id.* at 473. "'Damages growing out of a breach of contract, in order to form the basis of a recovery, must be such as can be traced solely to the breach, must be capable of exact computation, must have arisen naturally and according to the usual course of things from such breach, and must be such as the parties contemplated as a probable result of the breach.' *Sanford-Brown Co. v. Patent Scaffolding Co.*, 199 Ga. 41, 33 S.E.2d 422 (1945)." *Id.*

Applying these principles, the court disallowed recovery for items relating to housing and the cost of premiums on a life insurance policy because they were discontinued several years prior to the Association's breach of contract and were, in fact, not related to the breach. It also disallowed voluntary gifts which Rodgers had occasionally received from third parties in the past because "such voluntary contributions to his financial well-being are totally incapable of exact computation, for a gift made in one year is no assurance of a similar gift in the next. In fact, Rodgers concedes that he did not receive these gifts each year. Thus, the item which listed various financial gifts was properly excluded from recovery." *Id.* Finally, the court concluded that Rodgers was not entitled to compensation for several items, including free lodging at certain hotels and certain club membership, because there was no evidence "showing that the Association had any knowledge" of them. *Id.* Therefore, the "loss of these items could not be such as was contemplated as a probable result of a breach of the contract." *Id.* Items identified as commonly falling within perquisites coaches received included "profits from his television and radio shows and from his summer football camp plus the loss of use of a new automobile and tickets to professional sporting events." *Id.* at 473–74. These items would be recoverable if Rodgers established that "such items were contemplated by the parties at the time the contract was executed as perquisites or fringe benefits to which Rodgers would be entitled as the result of his position as head coach of football at Georgia Tech." *Id.* at 474. If the evidence so established, Rodgers's "removal from that position would result in the loss of these benefits." *Id.*

QUESTION

In the *Rodgers* case, the court identified three perquisites in category 1 that Rodgers was not entitled to: (1) the services of a secretary, (2) the services of an administrative assistant, and (3) the cost of trips to football conventions and clinics. Why did the court deem these perquisites nonrecoverable?

• • • • • • • • •

A major component of what has been characterized as the athletics arms race in big-time intercollegiate athletics is escalating salaries paid to coaches. In 2012 when 66 major-college football coaches had annual salaries in excess of $1 million, 42 had compensation in excess of $2 million, 13 had compensation in excess of

$3 million, 4 had compensation in excess of $4 million, and 2 had compensation in excess of $5 million. Erik Brady, Steve Berkowitz & Jodi Upton, *College Football Coaches Continue to See Salary Explosion*, USA Today, Nov. 20, 2012, http://www.usatoday.com/story/sports/ncaaf/2012/11/19/college-football-coaches-contracts-analysis-pay-increase/1715435/. By the 2018 football season, the average salary for an FBS head coach had increased to $2.6 million. Steve Berkowitz, *Analysis: After Dabo Swinney's deal, how high can college football salaries go? Keep Watching*, USA Today, Apr. 26, 2019.

Factors fueling the dramatic rise in the salaries of college football coaches include the proliferation of money from football bowl games and television contracts. Another factor has been the substantial rise since the mid-1990s in agents representing coaches in their contract negotiations. Increased competition for coaches, fueled by the willingness of NFL teams to hire college coaches and colleges to hire NFL coaches, has also contributed to rising salaries. Other variables include promotion by coaches and their agents and the illegality of efforts to cap coaches' salaries. For an insightful article discussing the economics of college coaching contracts, see Richard T. Karcher, *The Coaching Carousel in Big-Time Intercollegiate Athletics: Economic Implications and Legal Considerations*, 20 Fordham Intell. Prop. Media & Ent. L.J. 1 (2009). Acknowledging the foregoing factors, Professor Karcher identifies several additional factors that have contributed to the dramatic increase in coaches' salaries, including: "the desire to win and the prospects of generating more revenue, the granting of contract extensions to keep winning coaches from being poached . . . , the payment of huge buyouts when coaches do not win, and the tremendous leverage that coaches have over schools in the hiring and contract negotiation process." *Id.* at 4. He also attributes the increase to the refusal of colleges to pay student-athletes a portion of the income generated in football and men's basketball. *Id.* at 44–45. See Richard Johnson, *A history of skyrocketing college football coach salaries from Walter Camp to Nick Saban*, SBNation, Oct. 4, 2019 (providing a historical overview of the increase in football coach salaries); Jasmine Harris, *How Bonuses for Winning Coaches Became a Tradition in College Football*, HigherEdJobs, Dec. 24, 2018 (discussing the historical emergence of bonus provisions in football coaching contracts).

Examples of the approximate annual compensation (which details university- and non-university-based compensation, excluding bonuses) earned by FBS head football coaches in 2022 include:

- Nick Saban (University of Alabama): $11 million
- Dabo Swinney (Clemson University): $10.5 million
- Kirby Smart (University of Georgia): $10.3 million

College Football Head Coach Salaries, USA Today, Oct. 12, 2022, https://sports.usatoday.com/ncaa/salaries/football/coach.

Examples of the approximate annual compensation for head basketball coaches in 2023 include:

- John Calipari (University of Kentucky): $8.5 million
- Bill Self (University of Kansas): $5.96 million
- Tom Izzo (Michigan State University): $5.7 million

Men's Basketball Head Coach Salaries, USA Today, Mar. 7, 2023, https://sports.usatoday.com/ncaa/salaries/mens-basketball/coach. As a part of its oversight responsibility regarding the tax-exempt status of organizations, the Ways and Means Committee sent inquiries to nine universities asking whether "spending on lucrative football and basketball program aligns with their federal tax-exempt status." U.S. House of Representatives, *Report on Universities' Responses to Compensation of Athletic Coaches Inquiry*, Subcommittee on Oversight, Committee on Ways and Means, Dec. 1, 2022, https://pascrell.house.gov/uploadedfiles/v.3_university_coaches_report-pascrell.pdf. The report also stated that "reports about compensation that UNIVERSITY pays its current and former football [and/or basketball] coaches have raised significant concerns about whether the university is operating consistent with its tax-exempt status."

Perquisites and various performance incentives continue to represent significant components of college coaches' salaries. In 2013, 57 percent of the income of Division I FBS head coaches was derived from "radio, television, Internet, speeches, alumni club appearances, and similar engagements," summer camps, and endorsements. Randall Thomas & Lawrence Van Horn, *College Football Coaches' Pay and Contracts: Are They Overpaid and Unfairly Treated?*, 91 Indiana L. J. 189, 217–18 (2016). Is the compensation paid to Division I-A coaches justified? See *Id.* at 203 (arguing that college football coaches "create value for their universities far in excess of the value they capture").

Increasingly, colleges and coaches will enter into a memorandum of understanding ("MOU") before executing a formal contract. The MOU will typically outline the elements of the terms that will eventually appear in the formal contract. These terms include salary, contract duration, perquisites, "incentive pay, guaranteed pay from television, radio and shoe contracts, termination benefits," and buyout clauses. Thomas & Van Horn, *supra* at 207; James K. Gentry, *Deals Within the Deal*, NY Times, Jan. 1, 2012; see also Randal S. Thomas & R. Lawrence Van Horn, *Are College Presidents Like Football Coaches? Evidence from Their Employment Contracts*, 58 Ariz. L. Rev. 901 (2016) (discussing MOUs in coaching contracts); Chris Low, *Greg Schiano's Agreement with Tennessee Wasn't Signed by Chancellor*, ESPN, Nov. 17, 2017 (discussing the dispute involving the University of Tennessee and a coach, Greg Schiano, who signed a memorandum of understanding to become the university's head football coach before the university backed out of the deal).

QUESTIONS

1. Is the compensation paid to D-I coaches justified? See Karcher, *supra*; and Martin J. Greenberg & Jay S. Smith, *A Study of Division I Assistant Football and Men's Basketball Coaches' Contracts*, 18 Marq. Sports L. Rev. 25 (2007).
2. Should the contracts of college coaches include financial incentives and disincentives related to the academic performance and off-campus conduct of

student-athletes? Professor Linda Greene's analysis of the contracts of head football coaches revealed a trend in which a coach's responsibility for student-athlete academic performance was explicitly articulated in contractual provisions. In contrast, fewer coaches' contracts included provisions penalizing coaches for student-athlete misbehavior. According to Professor Greene, "The . . . trend of contracts without explicit coach responsibility for athlete misconduct seems counterintuitive." Linda S. Greene, *Football Coach Contracts: What Does the Student-Athlete Have to Do with It?*, 76 UMKC L. Rev. 665, 688–89 (2008).

3. In 2010, it was reported that institutions are beginning to insert clauses into contracts with coaches that are tied to teams' Academic Progress Rates (APR). For example, the Connecticut head men's basketball coach reportedly will lose $100,000 of annual salary if his team loses scholarships based on APR penalties. Do you agree with the approach adopted by the University of Connecticut?

TERMINATION, BREACH, AND LIQUIDATED DAMAGES

KEY TERMS
- Buyout
- Liquidated damages provision
- Negative injunctive relief

It is common for coaches to attempt to move up to a more prestigious college or university. For this reason, institutions increasingly seek some form of compensation when a coach leaves an institution prior to the expiration of the contract term. When the coach quits before the contract has expired, that coach has committed a breach of contract. The options theoretically available to an institution are to seek negative injunctive relief (i.e., a court order that would prevent the coach from coaching for another institution), to sue for damages, or simply to cancel the contract and allow the coach to leave. Institutions will most likely resort to an additional option: seek compensation under a buyout or liquidated damages provision. Liquidated damages are the amount specified in a contract that the parties have agreed is a reasonable estimation of the losses incurred by the non-breaching party in the event of a breach. This amount must be a good faith estimate of actual damages and not merely a deterrence for breach or a penalty for the party that breaches. The amounts due to institutions under such provisions are often paid by the breaching coaches' new institutions.

The *DiNardo* case discusses the standards that courts apply in determining the validity of these contractual provisions, which are commonly referred to a liquidated damages clauses or provisions in coaching contracts.

Vanderbilt University v. DiNardo
174 F.3d 751 (6th Cir. 1999)

GIBSON, Circuit Judge.

[Editors' note: In November 1994, Louisiana State University (LSU) contacted Vanderbilt in hopes of speaking with Gerry DiNardo about becoming the head football coach for LSU. Paul Hoolahan, Vanderbilt's athletic director, gave DiNardo permission to speak to LSU about the position. On December 12, 1994, DiNardo announced that he was accepting the LSU position. Vanderbilt demanded that DiNardo pay liquidated damages under section 8 of the contract. Vanderbilt believed that DiNardo was liable for three years of his net salary: one year under the original contract and two years under the addendum. DiNardo did not respond to Vanderbilt's demand for payment.

The contract contained reciprocal liquidated damage provisions. Vanderbilt agreed to pay DiNardo his remaining salary should Vanderbilt replace him as football coach, and DiNardo agreed to reimburse Vanderbilt should he leave before his contract expired. Section 8 of the contract stated:]

> Mr. DiNardo recognizes that his promise to work for the University for the entire term of this 5-year Contract is of the essence of this Contract to the University. Mr. DiNardo also recognizes that the University is making a highly valuable investment in his continued employment by entering into this Contract and its investment would be lost were he to resign or otherwise terminate his employment as Head Football Coach with the University prior to the expiration of this Contract. Accordingly, Mr. DiNardo agrees that in the event he resigns or otherwise terminates his employment as Head Football Coach (as opposed to his resignation or termination from another position at the University to which he may have been reassigned), prior to the expiration of this Contract, and is employed or performing services for a person or institution other than the University, he will pay to the University as liquidated damages an amount equal to his Base Salary, less amounts that would otherwise be deducted or withheld from his Base Salary for income and social security tax purposes, multiplied by the number of years (or portion(s) thereof) remaining on the Contract.

[Vanderbilt sued DiNardo for breach of contract. The district court entered summary judgment for Vanderbilt, awarding $281,886.43 pursuant to section 8 of the employment contract. On appeal, DiNardo argued that the district court erred in concluding "that the contract provision was an enforceable liquidated damage provision and not an unlawful penalty under Tennessee law."]

We affirm the district court's ruling that the employment contract contained an enforceable liquidated damage provision and the award of liquidated damages under the original contract. . . .

I

DiNardo first claims that section eight of the contract is an unenforceable penalty under Tennessee law. DiNardo argues that the provision is not a liquidated damage provision but a "thinly disguised, overly broad non-compete provision," unenforceable under Tennessee law. . . .

Contracting parties may agree to the payment of liquidated damages in the event of a breach. . . . The term "liquidated damages" refers to an amount determined by the parties to be just compensation for damages should a breach occur. . . . Courts will not enforce such a provision, however, if the stipulated amount constitutes a penalty. . . . A penalty is designed to coerce performance by punishing default. . . . In Tennessee, a provision will be considered one for liquidated damages, rather than a penalty, if it is reasonable in relation to the anticipated damages for breach, measured prospectively at the time the contract was entered into, and not grossly disproportionate to the actual damages. . . . When these conditions are met, particularly the first, the parties probably intended the provision to be for liquidated damages. However, any doubt as to the character of the contract provision will be resolved in favor of finding it a penalty. . . .

The district court held that the use of a formula based on DiNardo's salary to calculate liquidated damages was reasonable "given the nature of the unquantifiable damages in the case." The court explained:

> The potential damage to [Vanderbilt] extends far beyond the cost of merely hiring a new head football coach. It is this uncertain potentiality that the parties sought to address by providing for a sum certain to apply towards anticipated expenses and losses. It is impossible to estimate how the loss of a head football coach will affect alumni relations, public support, football ticket sales, contributions, etc. . . . As such, to require a precise formula for calculating damages resulting from the breach of contract by a college head football coach would be tantamount to barring the parties from stipulating to liquidated damages evidence in advance.

Id. at 642.

DiNardo contends that there is no evidence that the parties contemplated that the potential damage from DiNardo's resignation would go beyond the cost of hiring a replacement coach. He argues that his salary has no relationship to Vanderbilt's damages and that the liquidated damage amount is unreasonable and shows that the parties did not intend the provision to be for liquidated damages.

DiNardo's theory of the parties' intent, however, does not square with the record. The contract language establishes that Vanderbilt wanted the five-year contract because "a long-term commitment" by DiNardo was "important to the University's desire for a stable intercollegiate football program," and that this commitment was of "essence" to the contract. Vanderbilt offered the two-year contract extension to DiNardo well over a year before his original contract expired. Both parties understood that the extension was to provide stability to the program, which helped in recruiting players and retaining assistant coaches. Thus, undisputed evidence, and reasonable inferences therefrom, establish that both parties understood and agreed that DiNardo's resignation would result in Vanderbilt suffering damage beyond the cost of hiring a replacement coach.

This evidence also refutes DiNardo's argument that the district court erred in presuming that DiNardo's resignation would necessarily cause damage to the University. That the University may actually benefit from a coaching change (as DiNardo suggests) matters little, as we measure the reasonableness of the liquidated damage provision at the time the parties entered the contract, not when the breach occurred, *Kimbrough & Co.*, 939 S.W.2d at 108, and we hardly think the parties entered the contract anticipating that DiNardo's resignation would benefit Vanderbilt.

The stipulated damage amount is reasonable in relation to the amount of damages that could be expected to result from the breach. As we stated, the parties understood that Vanderbilt would suffer damage should DiNardo prematurely terminate his contract, and that these actual damages would be difficult to measure. *See Kimbrough & Co.*, 939 S.W.2d at 108. . . .

Vanderbilt hired DiNardo for a unique and specialized position, and the parties understood that the amount of damages could not be easily ascertained should a breach occur. Contrary to DiNardo's suggestion, Vanderbilt did not need to undertake an analysis to determine actual damages, and using the number of years left on the contract multiplied by the salary per year was a reasonable way to calculate damages considering the difficulty of ascertaining damages with certainty. *See Kimbrough & Co.*, 939 S.W.2d at 108. The fact that liquidated damages declined each year DiNardo remained under contract, is directly tied to the parties' express understanding of the importance of a long-term commitment from DiNardo. Furthermore, the liquidated damages provision was reciprocal and the result of negotiations between two parties, each of whom was represented by counsel.

We also reject DiNardo's argument that a question of fact remains as to whether the parties intended section eight to be a "reasonable estimate" of damages. The liquidated damages are in line with Vanderbilt's estimate of its actual damages. . . . Vanderbilt presented evidence that it incurred expenses associated with recruiting a new head coach of $27,000.00; moving expenses for the new coaching staff of $86,840; and a compensation difference between the coaching staffs of $184,311. The stipulated damages clause is reasonable under the circumstances, and we affirm the district court's conclusion that the liquidated damages clause is enforceable under Tennessee law.

Accordingly, we affirm the district court's judgment that the contract contained an enforceable liquidated damage provision, and we affirm the portion of the judgment reflecting damages calculated under the original five-year contract. . . .

DAVID A. NELSON, Circuit Judge, concurring in part and dissenting in part.

It seems to me that [section 8 of the contract] was designed to function as a penalty, not as a liquidation of the university's damages.

My principal reasons for viewing section eight as a penalty are these: (1) although the damages flowing from a premature resignation would normally be the same whether or not Coach DiNardo took a job elsewhere, section eight does not purport to impose liability for liquidated damages unless the coach accepts another job; (2) the section eight formula incorporates other variables that bear little or no relation to any reasonable approximation of anticipated damages; and (3) there is no evidence that the parties were attempting, in section eight, to come up with a reasonable estimate of the university's probable loss if the coach left. . . .

QUESTIONS

Do you agree with the majority or the dissent? What is the likely practical effect of buyout clauses such as that in *DiNardo*? Are liquidated damages clauses such as in *DiNardo* intended primarily to deter a coach from leaving an institution or to compensate an institution for the damages attributable to the loss of a coach's services? Shortly after the trial began, DiNardo settled the dispute by agreeing to pay Vanderbilt an undisclosed sum. As an attorney representing DiNardo, what would be your strategy during settlement negotiations?

NOTE

A state appellate court cited *DiNardo* in upholding a $1.2 million damages award to a university based on a liquidated damages provision in a head men's basketball coach's contract. *Kent State Univ. v. Ford*, 26 N.E.3d 868 (Ohio Ct. App. 2015) (also discussing the factors courts consider in determining the validity of a liquidated damages provision). In a related action, an appellate court found that issues of material fact precluded summary judgment on claims that Bradley University wrongly interfered with Ford's contract with Kent State and that Kent State was entitled to recover attorneys' fees. *Kent State Univ. v. Bradley Univ.*, 2019 WL 2269154 (Ohio. Ct. App. May 28, 2019). See Richard T. Karcher, *Redress for a No-Win Situation: Using Liquidated Damages in Comparable Coaches' Contracts to Assess a School's Economic Damages from the Loss of a Successful Coach*, 64 S.C. L. Rev. 429 (2012) (discussing the reasons that support validating liquidated-damages provisions in coaching contracts).

EXPLORING OTHER CONTRACTUAL RELATIONSHIPS

As alluded to in Chapter 1's discussion of the role of contract law in sports, and as demonstrated in the foregoing discussion, contract is the predominant body of law in regulating many relationships in sports. The following discussion provides two illustrations of how contract law defines the rights and obligations of parties in two relationships: sport sponsorships and venue agreements.

A. Sponsorship Agreements

A *sponsorship agreement* is a contractual relationship whereby a company or organization sponsors (i.e., compensates) a sports league, team, athlete, or event in exchange for brand recognition. For example, in the National Association of Stock Car Auto Racing (NASCAR), a corporation may be a sponsor of NASCAR, an event, a team, or a driver. To enhance its brand recognition, a corporation may purchase the naming rights to a stadium at which a college or professional sports team plays its games. Similarly, a beer manufacturer will pay hundreds of millions of dollars to become the official beer sponsor of a sports league. A shoe manufacturer will enter into a sponsorship agreement with an athlete to wear and promote the manufacturer's athletic shoes, or a headphone company will enter into such an agreement with an athlete to advertise the company's headphones.

The increase in sports sponsorships and the evolution of sports sponsorship from traditional forms of advertising have increased the range of relevant legal and business issues that implicate substantive legal doctrine, including the law of agency, intellectual property, tax, and torts, which ultimately affect whether parties involved in sponsorship relationships achieve their business objectives.

Contract law, however, lies at the core of determining the contours of sports sponsorship relationships. Contract determines the scope of the sponsorship relationship, including whether it is an exclusive relationship; the outlines of the product categories to which the sponsorship relates; its duration, renewal, and termination of the relationship; and the parties' rights upon breach by one party or the other. In its endorsement contract with a coach or player, a company will include a "morals clause" in an effort to allow it to terminate the agreement if an athlete engages in behaviors that the company believes may damage its brand. See *Mendenhall v. HanesBrand, Inc.*, 856 F. Supp. 2d 717 (M.D. N.C. 2012); see *Bernsen v. Innovative Legal Marketing, LLC*, 2012 WL 3525612 (June 20, 2012, E.D. Va.) (discussing actor's alleged breach of moral clause). Contract law will also serve as the source of law if a conflict should arise between a team and league regarding whether a team can enter into a sponsorship arrangement with a beer or apparel company other than the company with which the league has entered into an exclusive sponsorship arrangement. See *NFL Properties v. Dallas Cowboys*, 922 F. Supp. 849 (S.D. N.Y. 1996). Finally, a party's right to renew a sponsorship agreement will be largely governed by the law of contract. For a detailed discussion of sports sponsorship, see John A. Fortunato, Sports Sponsorship: Principles and Practices (2013).

B. Venue Agreements

Another type of agreement in which contract law plays a prominent role is the *venue agreements* which typically means the lease agreement that a team enters into so that their team can have a stadium at which to play. These agreements are complicated for many reasons, including that the team leases the stadium or facility from a city or other governmental entity. Contract law principles are critically relevant to matters relating to venue agreements, including the duration of the lease agreement; the purposes for which a team can use a stadium; a team's rental payment for use of the stadium; the allocation of responsibility for maintaining the stadium; the division of revenue generated by the facility; and the manner in which the lease agreement can be terminated. The venue agreement also intersects with other types of agreements, such as sponsorships and insurance, which also implicate contract law. For a detailed discussion of venue agreements, see Peter A. Carfagna, Negotiating and Drafting Sports Venue Agreements (2d ed. 2011).

Professional Sports League Governance and Legal Regulation

INTRODUCTION

This chapter focuses primarily on the internal governance and legal regulation of professional sports leagues, although it is important to recognize that other types of professional sports associations have similar characteristics and encounter similar legal problems. The greatest emphasis is on major league sports, particularly the National Football League (NFL), the National Basketball Association (NBA), Major League Baseball (MLB), and the National Hockey League (NHL). Other leagues (e.g., Major League Soccer (MLS), Women's National Basketball Association (WNBA)) and individual-performer sports (e.g., golf, tennis, auto racing, and mixed martial arts) also are briefly considered. Professional sports enterprises are for-profit entertainment businesses that are overwhelmingly driven by economics, which significantly influences most of the league or governing body's decision-making and creates most of the legal issues. Like other for-profit industries, where money is to be made, legal issues surge in the wake.

We begin by describing the development of the North American professional sports industries (particularly team sports), their unique features, and their primary components. Next, internal league governance and a league commissioner's "best interests" of the sport authority are discussed. An introduction to federal antitrust law (specifically §1 of the Sherman Act), baseball's broad antitrust exemption, and antitrust law limits on other professional sports league rules and internal governance are considered. Finally, the historical responses of established leagues to the formation of rival leagues and resulting antitrust litigation under §2 of the Sherman Act is briefly reviewed.

ORIGIN AND EVOLUTION OF MODERN NORTH AMERICAN PROFESSIONAL SPORTS INDUSTRIES

The origins of today's most popular North American individual and team professional sports are at least somewhat shrouded in mystery. The great American pastime of baseball actually may not be American in origin. The well-known American claim for decades was that baseball started with Abner Doubleday in Cooperstown, New York in 1839. But a more accurate view is that baseball was first played on the Elysian Fields in New Jersey in 1845, perhaps as a derivative of the English game of rounders.

Football, the American version, has equally obscure beginnings. Most would attribute its modern origin to soccer-like games at Harvard, in 1871, when the rules were altered to allow players to scoop up the round ball and run with it. From that point forward, football would be played by participating athletes with more than their feet.

The origin of the word *hockey* is uncertain. Some of the theories are certainly amusing. It may have come from the French word *hoquet*, meaning "shepherd's crook." A more fanciful theory is that French explorers in North America observed Iroquois Indians playing a version of the game, striking a hard ball with sticks, and yelling, "Hogee!" ("It hurts!"). What is known is that something resembling the modern version was played in Canada as early as the 1830s.

One sport whose origins are uncontroversial is basketball. In 1891, Dr. James Naismith nailed a peach basket to a wall in the YMCA gymnasium in Springfield, Massachusetts to provide youths with an indoor sport to play when snow and wind prevented outdoor activity. Dr. Naismith first instructed them to play soccer (undisputedly of British origin), but their lack of ball control resulted in broken windows, leading him to develop a game in which players used their hands rather than their feet to control the ball.

As popular as these sports are today, none can equal the origin of golf and its journey to the modern day. Golf was so popular that in 1457, King James II of Scotland had his parliament ban it, lest it detract from more serious pursuits such as archery. But this ban was largely ignored and was overturned when King James IV of Scotland took up the game in the early sixteenth century. His granddaughter Mary, Queen of Scots, was a great devotee of the sport and took the game with her to France. She attracted many young male admirers, known as *cadets*, who followed her over the meadows. They eventually were called *caddies*. Most caddies today probably are unaware of their noble lineage.

This brief history highlights the unique appeal that sports have always had throughout the history of the United States. It is not surprising that professional team and individual performer sports have evolved into one of the twenty-first century's most popular forms of entertainment, and that they generate billions of dollars in revenue from a variety of sources, including gate receipts, media contracts, trademark licensing, and sponsorships.

A. Evolution of Sports into a Business and Profession

Sports as activities, diversions, and cohesive societal events have been with us for centuries, but sports as professions, businesses, and industries are of more recent vintage. Contemporaneously with the Industrial Revolution in the 1800s, a sports revolution occurred as well. This was no coincidence. Recreational activity became a business, and business evolved into industry. For sports, the roots were perhaps not as obvious as the invention of steam locomotion or electricity harnessed into light, but sports took advantage of emerging industrial technologies just as surely as the wings of birds inspired the flight of man.

Each new step in the advancement of technology led to increased opportunities for sports exposure and thus expansion. Transportation was the first crucial ingredient. Communications was the second. The two have been powerful concomitants—necessary elements to allow sports to transcend the confines of the ballpark or arena and to enter the homes of millions of sports fans, initially through radio, then via television, and more recently the Internet and handheld mobile devices. Although the movers and shakers in early professional sports ventures could not have recognized fully the enormous commercial potential within their grasp, this is not true today. The preeminent modern sports business entrepreneurs are those with the greatest vision and ability to exploit this vast revenue-generating potential. Sports as commercial successes owe much to technological advances and to greater understanding of business and marketing techniques. There is still the game itself, with its drama and winners and losers, but there is a driving force—off-field economic success—that is equally influential in just how, when, and where a game is played and who ultimately plays it.

In the United States, the sport of baseball was the pioneer for modern-day professional team sport leagues, clubs, and players. The Cincinnati Red Stockings are generally acknowledged as the first truly professional team, touring the country in 1869 and taking on all challengers. The National League, which still exists today, was founded in 1876. Although it is now part of Major League Baseball, and some may take issue with it being designated as the first professional sports league, the National League was a significant start on the road to professionalization.

Decades later than baseball, other professional sports leagues began to form. The NFL was founded in 1920 in Canton, Ohio, where the NFL Hall of Fame is located. The NFL's astounding popularity and commercial success are beyond dispute. The NHL actually predated the NFL by two years, starting in 1918 in the aftermath of a one-year wonder, the National Hockey Association. The "national" designation signified Canada, not the United States. The first U.S. team, the Boston Bruins, did not join the league until 1924. Today, the number of American clubs significantly exceeds that of Canadian clubs.

The history of professional basketball has been circuitous. Players used to be *cagers*, which referred to the wire netting originally surrounding the court to keep the players from hurtling into the stands near the sidelines. This makeshift, precarious nature of the court was a fitting description for the business of basketball as well. Through the 1920s and 1930s, the sport gained popularity but headed in directions both unknown and uncharted. The end of World War II provided the American public with more leisure time to seek new diversions, which generally resulted in the increased popularity of professional sports, including basketball. The National Basketball Association (NBA)'s genesis was the Basketball Association of America (BAA) in 1946. In 1996, the NBA founded the Women's National Basketball Association (WNBA), which now operates as an independent professional league.

Soccer, known to the rest of the world as "football," is truly global in its nature and fan appeal, more so than any other American team sport. Its men's World Cup is the premier worldwide team sports event (with apologies to the NFL's Super Bowl). Although Major League Soccer—the top division men's league in the United States—lags behind the other American sports leagues economically, its fan base is large and growing as is the National Women's Soccer League (NWSL)'s popularity.

Men's and women's tennis and golf are very popular individual-performer sports, both in the United States and globally. Professional tennis tournaments began in the 1920s, but amateur tournaments initially were more popular. The professional players were reduced to barnstorming, with the prevailing champion taking on the latest challenger from the amateur ranks. The big tournaments were closed to professionals. Only with the arrival of the open tennis era in 1968 did professional tennis truly emerge. Golf also had its share of early professional tournaments, with the U.S. Open dating from 1895 and later with Walter Hagen's winning of the first Professional Golfers' Association Championship in 1921. However, it was not until after World War II that professional players began dominating the sport of golf. Tennis and golf are more global than virtually all team sports except soccer because the top players in both sports come from all parts of the world.

Auto racing is one of the country's most popular professional spectator sports. The first Indianapolis 500-Mile Race was held in 1911. The National Association for Stock Car Auto Racing (NASCAR) has been in existence since 1951. NASCAR and IndyCar each sponsor an annual series of auto races at tracks throughout the United States.

The Ultimate Fighting Championship (UFC), a promoter of professional mixed martial arts (MMA) competitions involving martial arts, wrestling, and other combat sports that was created in 1993, has developed a huge following worldwide. As MMA's popularity has grown, other MMA promotors, such as Bellator MMA, have begun to challenge UFC for dominance in the market. MMA competition has a long history, which can be traced to the Ancient Olympic Games in Athens. Vale Tudo, a Brazilian form of MMA that means "anything goes," reinvigorated public interest in MMA about 80 years ago. The New York legislature's March 2016 vote to legalize MMA competitions in the Empire state is viewed by many as removing the final obstacle to the acceptance of MMA sports (which now are legal nationwide) as a legitimate mainstream sport.

B. Unique Features of Professional Team Sports

Professional team sports have several unique features that significantly influence how they are operated, structured, and internally governed, which give rise to complex legal issues. It is important to keep these features in mind when analyzing and developing an understanding of how general areas of law, particularly contract, fiduciary duty, private association, and antitrust law, have been judicially applied to regulate professional team sports.

A professional sports team must have other teams to play against on a regular basis for individual game and seasonal championship competition to exist, which is why multiple teams join together to form national or continental sports leagues such as the MLB, MLS, NBA, NFL, NHL, NWSL, and WNBA. To sustain fans' interest and to generate the very substantial revenues necessary for a North American major professional sports league to produce a financially viable entertainment product, on-field competition among league teams cannot be too one-sided in favor of any single team from year to year. Team owners, players, and ultimately consumers tire of being perennial losers (although a few teams in each league have an unfortunate knack for annually doing so).

Without any agreed-on limitations, there is nothing to prevent teams from being off-field economic competitors for fans, broadcasters, and sponsors as well as players and coaches. Although on-field competition in the form of close, exciting games economically benefits the league and its member clubs by increasing fan support and total revenues, too much off-field economic competition among teams can be harmful, not only to individual teams but also to the league as a whole. Thus, a sports league's financial viability and the economic health of all teams necessitate some limits on economic competition among member clubs, so that a league and its clubs can collectively compete against other professional leagues and other forms of entertainment.

Economic competition for fan patronage (which may be national, regional, and/or local) exists among the various North American sports leagues, either those that offer games in the same sport (e.g., MLB Cubs and White Sox teams in Chicago) or those that offer different sports (e.g., in addition to the two MLB clubs, MLS Fire, NBA Bulls, NFL Bears, NHL Blackhawks, NWSL Red Stars, and WNBA Sky in Chicago). Each team needs a large local fan base and must appeal to consumers with limited discretionary income and recreational time who may transfer their allegiance as the on-field success of the various local teams ebb and flow. For example, NBA and NHL clubs in the same city, whose playing seasons largely overlap, often experience the whims of fair-weather fans.

There are no analogous business models in other industries comparable to the unique features of a professional sports league. The strong desire to compete successfully on the playing field with the simultaneous need to limit economic competition among league clubs to some degree presents significant challenges to businesspeople accustomed to ruthless competition in other industries. To work both competitively and cooperatively as part of a professional sports league can be very difficult and frequently leads to business and legal disputes.

When players (along with their unions and agents) are added to this mix, business and legal issues multiply in their complexity. Highly skilled players are essential to the game's attractiveness to consumers and economic success. Sports leagues, as commercial enterprises, thrive on the special talents of players, their celebrity status, and their resulting marketability. Major league professional athletes have unique talents and playing abilities, but their necessarily symbiotic relationship with the league and teams for their respective sport often gives rise to contentious economic and legal issues, which are analyzed in Chapter 12.

The following section explores in greater depth how the respective roles of clubs, leagues, players, and other important components of sports industries interact and often conflict. This interplay illustrates the need for legal regulation of this complex web of relationships.

C. The Principal "Players" in the Professional Sports Industries

The old cliché "you can't tell the players without a scorecard" aptly describes why we cannot appreciate the broad dimensions of professional sports business and legal problems unless we identify the various parties' differing interests and how they both intersect and conflict. The following discussion concerning the principal professional sports industry players (i.e., components) uses the team-sports model, which has some common elements with the individual-performer sports industry.

In general, the league, its commissioner, and the clubs are aligned on one side; the players, their union, and player agents are on the other side. A host of related entities play integral roles in a professional sports league's operations. For example, television and Internet media, advertisers and corporate sponsors, and financial institutions significantly influence the business aspects of the professional team sports and individual-performer sports industries. Each of these components adds a layer of complexity and raises corresponding legal issues.

1. Leagues

North American professional sports leagues, which generally are "closed" (i.e., new clubs are added only by majority vote of existing clubs) and governed by an "independent" commissioner, have existed since baseball's National League was founded in 1876. In essence, a sports league is a group of clubs that join together in a formal association defined by a series of contracts to produce, market, and sell its product: organized athletic competition among its member teams. The formation of a league raises complex questions as to its legal relationship with and between its member clubs. Consider the multitude of important issues that must be considered and resolved: for example, number, ownership, and location of league clubs; league internal governance; and business relationships with others such as league clubs' host cities, broadcasters, and sponsors, etc.

2. Clubs or Teams

The terms *club* and *team* are used interchangeably in the professional sports context. Each major professional league (e.g., NFL, MLB, NBA, NHL, MLS, NWSL, and WNBA) has several member clubs located in cities throughout the United States or Canada, which may be expanded from time to time. The growth in the popularity of professional sports is often tracked by the expansion in the dominant league's number of teams. With few exceptions (e.g., the Green Bay Packers, which is publicly owned), league clubs generally are separately owned and operated by private parties (usually very wealthy individuals) that have an exclusive geographical territory (shared in the largest markets such as New York, Los Angeles, Chicago, and others), which share revenues but not profits or losses. Within a particular league, all clubs generally are not on equal footing. There frequently is substantial variation in their on-field competitive success, business approach, and profitability. A club's geographical location is a significant factor that determines its potential consumer (fan) and economic base. Another important factor is the club's ownership, which in turn determines who operates and manages the club, thereby undoubtedly influencing who plays for the team and its performance level as well as its generally corresponding economic performance.

The legal nature and character of the interrelationships between a league and its member clubs, as well as among clubs, are very important, particularly for the purposes of federal antitrust law, which constrains a league's internal governance autonomy.

3. Commissioners

The concept of a league commissioner with broad governing authority came to fruition when American League and National League baseball club owners appointed their first commissioner, Judge Kenesaw Mountain Landis in 1920. This unprecedented step was taken to ensure that baseball would not experience another scandal such as befell the Chicago White Sox in 1919 when several of its players allegedly accepted money to purposefully lose the World Series. Commissioner Landis was given sweeping power to act "in the best interests of baseball," which he and his successors have used when necessary. The other North American major professional sports leagues generally have followed baseball's example by adopting a league commissioner model of governance. The existence of a commissioner with broad powers invites legal conflict; there have been several disputes regarding a league commissioner's exercise of "best interests" authority in a wide variety of situations, as explored later in this chapter.

4. Players

Although many professional athletes playing for MLB, NBA, NFL, and NHL clubs earn multimillion-dollar salaries, not all of them do, and very few (if any) MLS, NWSL, or WNBA players do so. Most professional team sport athletes have relatively short playing careers (especially at the sport's highest level), and they must be cognizant of the cold realities of this frequently harsh business, which may implicate their legal rights. The multitude of legal issues involving players and the league or its respective clubs (primarily contract, labor, and antitrust law matters) are explored in Chapter 12.

5. Players Associations

For each major league team sport, there is a players association that exists for the purpose of advancing the players' interests. It generally is a labor union chosen by the players that represents them in labor and employment matters with the league and clubs. Professional sports give rise to unique labor relations issues not typically found in other industries, which are considered in-depth in Chapter 12.

6. Player Agents

Player agents (also referred to as sports agents) generally are lawyers and trained professionals who represent professional team sport athletes in contract negotiations with their respective clubs. They also represent individual-performer sport athletes. Player agents frequently handle or participate in the management of most aspects of their players' business affairs. As discussed in Chapter 13, agents who represent athletes in major league team sports are regulated by the players' union for the particular sport, and they also are subject to various federal and state laws.

7. Other Industries Integral to Modern Professional Sports

Several industries have both contributed to and benefited from the operation of professional sports leagues and associations. A prime example is the media, which extensively broadcasts, comments on, and reports about major league professional sports. Society today is pervasively connected to North American professional sports, which can be accessed domestically and throughout many parts of the world through television, radio, print media, the Internet, and mobile devices. Pervasive media coverage has stimulated enormous consumer interest in professional sports as well as in collateral products such as trademarked merchandise and activities such as fantasy sports and gambling. Media broadcasting rights fees have injected billions of dollars into the professional sports industries. Corporations that sell a variety of goods and services provide huge sums to professional sports leagues and associations, clubs, and athletes for advertising and sponsorships. This produces a complex set of often conflicting economic interests and objectives with corresponding intellectual property legal issues, as discussed in Chapter 9.

INTERNAL LEAGUE GOVERNANCE AND COMMISSIONER AUTHORITY

A professional sports league or association generally has a constitution and bylaws that establish its internal system of governance pursuant to a contract among its member clubs. One particular individual, usually designated as the commissioner, often is given substantial authority to oversee the league's general operations and business affairs. The following material primarily focuses on relations and disputes between leagues and their member clubs. To a limited extent, it also considers the nature and scope of the regulatory authority of associations formed to govern individual-performer sports.

A. Legal Limits on Internal League Governance

KEY TERMS
- Contract law
- *De novo* judicial review
- Fiduciary duty
- Law of private associations

American professional sports leagues and associations are private entities that are not required to respect the federal constitutional rights of their member clubs and players, including First Amendment rights of free speech and freedom of association or due process or equal protection. *Long v. National Football League*, 870 F. Supp. 101 (W.D. Pa. 1994), *aff'd*, 66 F.3d 311 (3d Cir. 1994). The league or association constitution, bylaws, and rules create binding contractual rights and responsibilities if they are reasonable and do not violate applicable laws. The legal relationships among member clubs or individuals of professional sports leagues are primarily governed by contract law and the law of private associations. The federal antitrust laws also play a significant role in regulating the governing activities of professional leagues and associations.

A sport's governing body has a legal obligation to follow its own rules and bylaws; its failure to do so may give rise to a breach of contract claim by an aggrieved member whose interests are harmed. Courts will intervene and grant appropriate legal relief "(1) where the rules, regulations or judgments of the association are in contravention to the laws of the land or in disregard of the charter or bylaws of the association and (2) where the association has failed to follow the basic rudiments of due process of law." *Charles O. Finley & Co. v. Kuhn*, 569 F.2d 527, 544 (7th Cir. 1978). In addition, courts will intervene if an association's decision-making process is arbitrary or capricious or is tainted by malice or bad faith.

Courts recognize that professional sports leagues and associations must be given considerable latitude in rule making and enforcement to accomplish their legitimate objectives. They generally are permitted to freely establish their respective systems of self-governance, and courts are reluctant to interfere with or second-guess their internal decision making. See, e.g., *Mayfield v. NASCAR*, 674 F.3d 369 (4th Cir. 2012) (enforcing the disciplinary suspension imposed on a professional race car driver for breaching contractual obligation to comply with NASCAR's Substance Abuse Policy as well as a release of liability and covenant not to sue NASCAR for any claims arising out of the implementation of its policy). Courts generally provide broad discretion to a professional sports league or association to interpret and apply its own internal rules without judicial intervention, as illustrated by the following cases.

In *Koszela v. National Association of Stock Car Auto Racing, Inc.*, 646 F.2d 749 (2d Cir. 1981), the Second Circuit rejected the claims of a stock car owner and driver that NASCAR misapplied its rules in determining that another car and driver were the winners of two races. The court found that the plaintiffs' membership contract with NASCAR did not provide for an administrative appeal or judicial review of official decisions regarding race procedures or determination of car positions. The court concluded that the plaintiffs had been given an opportunity to be heard by NASCAR officials and had exhausted all available rights. The court affirmed the dismissal of the plaintiffs' claims and held that NASCAR was not in violation of any contractual duties owed to the plaintiffs. See also *Crouch v. National Association for Stock Car Auto Racing, Inc.*, 845 F.2d 397 (2d Cir. 1988) (rejecting allegations that NASCAR violated its own rules or acted in bad faith in reviewing the plaintiffs' challenge to their determination of the official race results and the lower court erred by delving into NASCAR's rulebook and conducting a *de novo* inquiry regarding winner of the race).

Despite a general judicial reluctance to oversee a professional sports organization's affairs to avoid becoming mired down in areas outside their expertise, courts will nevertheless provide a forum for resolution of internal governance disputes. At least at the major league level, a professional sports league is often without direct competition from another league in the same sport. Because of the for-profit and monopolistic nature of major professional sports leagues and associations, there is a recognized need for some limited judicial oversight to prevent exploitation and blatant unfairness toward any of the organization's members or participants. As the *Koszela* court observed, when a sports organization has such a "'strangle-hold'" that all teams or individuals desiring to participate in a sport must join it, "rigid adherence to a 'hands off' policy is inappropriate." 646 F.2d at 754.

Courts have also imposed an implied covenant of good faith and fair dealing in contracts governing the internal affairs of professional sports leagues; an example is a case arising out of the Oakland (now Las Vegas) Raiders' initial move to Los Angeles in the early 1980s. The Ninth Circuit applied California law in ruling that league teams owed each other a reciprocal duty "to refrain from doing anything to injure the right of the other to receive the benefits of the agreement . . . [and] the duty to do everything that the contract presupposes that he will do to accomplish the purpose." *Los Angeles Memorial Coliseum Commission v. National Football League*, 791 F.2d 1356, 1361 (9th Cir. 1986). Concerning franchise relocation, the court held that each league club must exercise its contractual right of discretionary approval or disapproval over the interests of others in good faith (i.e., reasonably).

Depending on how a sports league is legally structured, its member clubs may have a fiduciary duty to act and vote on matters of internal governance consistent with the league's best interests, which imposes a more stringent obligation than the implied covenant of good faith and fair dealing. In *Professional Hockey Corp. v. World Hockey Assn.*, 191 Cal. Rptr. 773, 777 (Cal. Ct. App. 1983), the court ruled that each club's representative on the board of directors of a professional sports league structured as a corporation "owes the league as a whole the traditional fiduciary duties in this commonly shared corporate purpose." It explained: "The law requires, irrespective of the competitive personal feelings the various owners of teams may have towards each other, when they or their representatives sit on the board of directors of [the league] to the extent they have common corporate goals, they have a duty to make decisions for the benefit of the corporation, the hockey league as a whole." *Id.*

In summary, these cases illustrate that courts generally are reluctant to interfere with the internal affairs of a professional sports league or association unless there are specific breaches of its rules or contracts with its member clubs or others, failure to provide procedural due process (i.e., fair notice of required or prohibited conduct and a fair opportunity to be heard), bad faith conduct, or violations of state (e.g., implied duty of good faith and fair dealing; fiduciary duty) or federal law (e.g., antitrust law).

B. League Commissioner's "Best Interests of the Game" Authority and Legal Limits

KEY TERMS
- Commissioner "best interests of the game" authority
- Procedural due process

The major professional sports leagues have adopted a model of organization and governance that places an independent commissioner, who is selected by and answerable to the league club owners, in control of internal affairs. The commissioner generally is more powerful than a chairperson of the board of a corporation and probably wields more power than a typical president of a company. The first league commissioner in any sport was Judge Kenesaw Mountain Landis, who assumed that position for professional baseball in 1920 to ensure that the infamous Black Sox scandal arising out of the 1919 World Series would not recur. Reportedly, at his insistence, Judge Landis was accorded the authority to do whatever was necessary to protect the "best interests" of baseball. Today, all commissioners of the North American major professional sports leagues have broad authority to act in the best interests of the sport through their respective decision-making, disciplinary, and dispute resolution powers.

Regarding Major League Baseball, former commissioner Bud Selig described this role as follows:

> Along with inherent administrative authority to further baseball's best interests (analogous to the United States president's executive order authority), the MLB commissioner historically and currently has enjoyed broad investigative, remedial, preventative, and disciplinary power to ensure that baseball players, coaches, and other personnel engage in honest athletic competition and to refrain from activities that harm the sport's integrity such as gambling on or improperly influencing the results of baseball games. In addition, the commissioner's "best interests" power encompasses plenary authority to take appropriate steps to preserve league-wide competitive balance as well as fair play (both on-field and off-field) among MLB league clubs. This authority enables the MLB commissioner to maintain the integrity of and public confidence in the game of baseball.

Allan H. "Bud" Selig & Matthew J. Mitten, *Baseball Jurisprudence: Its Effects on America's Pastime and Other Professional Sports Leagues*, 50 Ariz. St. L. J. 1171, 1174 (2018).

A league's commissioner is an integral part of the league's governance structure, whose role often consists of the following functions:

1. To create a fair and impartial internal authority to resolve disputes within the league and to enforce independently a disciplinary process—these being essential to maintain the game's integrity and provide rudimentary due process protections necessary to avoid judicial oversight of league affairs.
2. To take action when needed to restrain the unwarranted exercise of power by the league's owners to the detriment of fans and others, again to avoid judicial intervention.
3. To serve as a centralized administrative authority to facilitate efficient decision making and league governance.
4. To be a skillful mediator when owners cannot agree.
5. To be the lead negotiator for leaguewide contracts, such as the all-important television deals.
6. At times, to become involved in labor disputes between the owners and the players—in fact, in some leagues, the commissioner is the lead negotiator on behalf of the owners. (Such is the case today in the NBA and the NHL.)

A sports league commissioner's authority is contractual in nature and derived from the league's constitution, bylaws, and operating rules. The broadest authority that a league commissioner is typically granted is the ability to take action deemed necessary to further the best interests of the sport. In January 2020, MLB Commissioner Rob Manfred fined the Houston Astros $5 million and required the club to forfeit its first- and second-round draft selections for the 2020 and 2021 draft for using a television camera during home games in violation of MLB rules to steal signs from catchers to pitchers, which were relayed to Astros batters by banging on trash cans in its dugout, during the club's 2017 World Series championship season. He also suspended Astros' General Manager Jeff Luhnow, Assistant General Manager Brandon Taubman, and Manager AJ Hinch for one season. All of them were subsequently fired by Astros' owner Jim Crane, whom Manfred found had no knowledge of any of the team's conduct. In his ruling, Commissioner Manfred stated: "I find that the conduct of the Astros, and its senior baseball operations executives, merits significant discipline. [This] conduct . . . has caused fans, players, executives at other MLB clubs, and members of the media to raise questions about the integrity of games in which the Astros participated. And while it is impossible to determine whether the conduct actually impacted the results on the field, the perception of some that it did causes significant harm to the game."

As illustrated by the following case, interpretation of the nature and scope of the commissioner's contractual authority ultimately is a question for judicial resolution, but courts usually provide substantial deference to the commissioner's judgment.

Charles O. Finley & Co., Inc. v. Kuhn
569 F.2d 527 (7th Cir. 1978), cert. denied, 439 U.S. 876 (1978)

SPRECHER, Circuit Judge.

The defendant Bowie K. Kuhn is the Commissioner of baseball (Commissioner), having held that position since 1969. On June 18, 1976, the Commissioner disapproved the assignments of the contracts of [Joe] Rudi, [Rollie] Fingers and [Vida] Blue [by the Oakland Athletics MLB club] to the Red Sox and Yankees "as inconsistent with the best interests of baseball, the integrity of the game and the maintenance of public confidence in it." The Commissioner expressed his concern for (1) the debilitation of the Oakland club, (2) the lessening of the competitive balance of professional baseball through the buying of success by the more affluent clubs, and (3) "the present unsettled circumstances of baseball's reserve system." . . .

II

Basic to the underlying suit brought by Oakland and to this appeal is whether the Commissioner of baseball is vested by contract with the authority to disapprove player assignments which he finds to be "not in the best interests of baseball." In assessing the measure and extent of the Commissioner's power and authority, consideration must be given to the circumstances attending the creation of the office of Commissioner, the language employed by the parties in drafting their contractual understanding, changes and amendments adopted from time to time, and the interpretation given by the parties to their contractual language throughout the period of its existence. . . .

In November, 1920, the major league club owners unanimously elected federal Judge Kenesaw Mountain Landis as the sole Commissioner of baseball and appointed a committee of owners to draft a charter setting forth the Commissioner's authority. In one of the drafting sessions an attempt was made to place limitations on the Commissioner's authority. Judge Landis responded by refusing to accept the office of Commissioner.

On January 12, 1921, Landis told a meeting of club owners that he had agreed to accept the position upon the clear understanding that the owners had sought "an authority . . . outside of your own business, and that a part of that authority would be a control over whatever and whoever had to do with baseball." Thereupon, the owners voted unanimously to reject the proposed limitation upon the Commissioner's authority, they all signed what they called the Major League Agreement, and Judge Landis assumed the position of Commissioner. Oakland has been a signatory to the Major League Agreement continuously since 1960. The agreement, a contract between the constituent clubs of the National and American Leagues, is the basic charter under which major league baseball operates.

The Major League Agreement provides that "[t]he functions of the Commissioner shall be . . . to investigate . . . any act, transaction or practice . . . not in the best interests of the national game of Baseball" and "to determine . . . what preventive, remedial or punitive action is appropriate in the premises, and to take such action. . . ." Art. I, Sec. 2(a) and (b).

The Major League Rules, which govern many aspects of the game of baseball, are promulgated by vote of major league club owners. Major League Rule 12(a) provides that "no . . . (assignment of players) shall be recognized as valid unless . . . approved by the Commissioner."

The Major Leagues and their constituent clubs severally agreed to be bound by the decisions of the Commissioner and by the discipline imposed by him. They further agreed to "waive such right of recourse to the courts as would otherwise have existed in their favor." Major League Agreement, Art. VII, Sec. 2. . . .

The Commissioner has been given broad power in unambiguous language to investigate any act, transaction or practice not in the best interests of baseball, to determine what preventive, remedial or punitive action is appropriate in the premises, and to take that action. He has also been given the express power to approve or disapprove the assignments of players. In regard to nonparties to the agreement, he may take such other steps as he deems necessary and proper in the interests of the morale of the players and the honor of the game. Further, indicative of the nature of the Commissioner's authority is the provision whereby the parties agree to be bound by his decisions and discipline imposed and to waive recourse to the courts. . . .

In view of the broad authority expressly given by the Major League Agreement to the Commissioner, particularly in Section 2 of Article I, we agree with the district court that Section 3 does not purport to limit that authority.

III

Despite the Commissioner's broad authority to prevent any act, transaction or practice not in the best interests of baseball, Oakland has attacked the Commissioner's disapproval of the Rudi-Fingers-Blue transactions on a variety of theories which seem to express a similar thrust in differing language.

The complaint alleged that the "action of Kuhn was arbitrary, capricious, unreasonable, discriminatory, directly contrary to historical precedent, baseball tradition, and prior rulings and actions of the Commissioner." In pre-trial answers to interrogatories, Oakland acknowledged that the Commissioner could set aside a proposed assignment of a player's contract "in an appropriate case of violation of (Major League) Rules or immoral or unethical conduct." . . .

The plaintiff has argued that it is a fundamental rule of law that the decisions of the head of a private association must be procedurally fair. Plaintiff then argued that it was "procedurally unfair" for the Commissioner to fail to warn the plaintiff that he would "disapprove large cash assignments of star players even if they complied with the Major League Rules."

It must be recalled that prior to the assignments involved here drastic changes had commenced to occur in the reserve system and in the creation of free agents. In his opinion disapproving the Rudi, Fingers, and Blue assignments, the Commissioner said that "while I am of course aware that there have been cash sales of player contracts in the past, there has been no instance in my judgment which had the potential for harm to our game as do these assignments, particularly in the present unsettled circumstances of baseball's reserve system and in the highly competitive circumstances we find in today's sports and entertainment world."

Absent the radical changes in the reserve system, the Commissioner's action would have postponed Oakland's realization of value for these players. Given those changes, the relative fortunes of all major league clubs became subject to a host of intangible speculations. No one could predict then or now with certainty that Oakland would fare better or worse relative to other clubs through the vagaries of the revised reserve system occurring entirely apart from any action by the Commissioner. . . .

[T]he Commissioner was vested with broad authority and that authority was not to be limited in its exercise to situations where Major League Rules or moral turpitude was involved. When professional baseball intended to place limitations upon the Commissioner's powers, it knew how to do so. In fact, it did so during the 20-year period from 1944 to 1964.

The district court found and concluded that the Rudi-Fingers-Blue transactions were not, as Oakland had alleged in its complaint, "directly contrary to historical precedent, baseball tradition, and prior rulings." During his almost 25 years as Commissioner, Judge Landis found many acts, transactions, and practices to be detrimental to the best interests of baseball in situations where neither moral turpitude nor a Major League Rule violation was involved, and he disapproved several player assignments.

On numerous occasions since he became Commissioner of baseball in February 1969, Kuhn has exercised broad authority under the best interests clause of the Major League Agreement. Many of the actions taken by him have been in response to acts, transactions or practices that involved neither the violation of a Major League Rule nor any gambling, game-throwing or other conduct associated with moral turpitude. Moreover, on several occasions Commissioner Kuhn has taken broad preventive or remedial action with respect to assignments of player contracts. . . .

We conclude that the evidence fully supports, and we agree with, the district court's finding and conclusion that the Commissioner "acted in good faith, after investigation, consultation and deliberation, in a manner which he determined to be in the best interests of baseball" and that "(w)hether he was right or wrong is beyond the competence and the jurisdiction of this court to decide." . . .

We affirm the district court's judgment. . . .

NOTE

Judicial interpretation of "best interests of the game" power. As in *Finley*, in *Oakland Raiders v. National Football League*, 131 Cal. App. 4th 621, 32 Cal. Rptr. 3d 266 (Cal. App. 2005), a California state appellate court rejected the Oakland Raiders club's claim that NFL Commissioner Paul Tagliabue took various actions that were discriminatory toward the Raiders and placed it at a competitive disadvantage vis-à-vis other member clubs. Finding that "the Raiders had not shown any evidence of a violation of a clear and unambiguous provision of the NFL constitution," the court explained, "We observe that the rationale of [judicial] abstention from intra-association disputes applies with particular force in this instance. Given the unique and specialized nature of this association's business—the operation of a professional football league—there is significant danger that judicial intervention in such disputes will have the undesired and unintended effect of interfering with the League's autonomy in matters where the NFL and its commissioner have much greater competence and understanding than the courts." *Id.* at 284.

Although a court generally will not second-guess a league commissioner's exercise of discretionary judgment, it will require that the commissioner have valid authority to take the challenged action. In *Chicago National League Ball Club, Inc. v. Vincent*, 1992 WL 179208 (N.D. Ill. 1992), a federal district court held that the MLB commissioner could not order involuntary realignment of the teams in the National League pursuant to his "best interests of the game" authority. The Chicago Cubs successfully challenged Commissioner Vincent's authority to transfer the club to the Western Division of the National League. In 1992, ten National League clubs voted to realign their two divisions so that the Cubs and St. Louis Cardinals would move to the Western Division, and the Atlanta Braves and Cincinnati Reds would move to the Eastern Division. The Cubs and New York Mets voted against the proposed realignment. The National League Constitution required approval by three-fourths of the league's clubs for divisional realignment but provided that no club could be transferred to a different division without its consent. Nevertheless, acting on the request of several National League clubs to intervene, Commissioner Vincent ordered the proposed realignment in accordance with his "best interests" power. The court preliminarily enjoined the commissioner's order from taking effect based on its finding that he exceeded his authority and impaired the Cubs' contract rights under the National League Constitution. Although the Major League Agreement empowered the commissioner to resolve disputes among member clubs and conferred broad "best interests of the game" power, this authority did not extend to disputes whose resolution is otherwise expressly provided for in the constitution of either Major League.

When exercising disciplinary authority, courts require a league commissioner to provide due process to the party subject to sanctions. A party is entitled to notice of the alleged misconduct and a fair opportunity to be heard before any discipline is imposed or its rights are adversely affected. The league's constitution generally establishes contractual procedural safeguards or enables the commissioner to formulate rules necessary to satisfy the minimum requirements of due process in connection with a disciplinary proceeding. A league commissioner must act in an impartial and fair manner without prejudging the merits of the matter before him. In *Rose v. Giamatti*, No. A8905178, 1989 WL 111447 (Ct. Com. Pl. Ohio, Hamilton Co., June 26, 1989), a state trial judge temporarily enjoined MLB commissioner Bart Giamatti from holding a disciplinary hearing to determine whether Pete Rose placed bets on MLB games. The court relied on affidavit testimony alleging that Rose was being denied his right to a fair hearing before the commissioner. After reviewing a report prepared by his special investigator, the commissioner wrote a letter to a federal judge on behalf of Ron Peters, a convicted drug dealer who was awaiting sentencing. The letter stated that Peters had provided sworn testimony concerning allegations that Rose had bet on MLB, and that the commissioner was satisfied that Peters had told the truth to his special investigator. Commissioner Giamatti and Rose ultimately entered into a settlement agreement pursuant to which Rose accepted a lifetime suspension from baseball, which has prevented Rose from being eligible for induction into baseball's Hall of Fame.

> **Problem 11-1**
>
> Soon after 2014 an audio recording became public in which Los Angeles Clippers owner Donald Sterling made racist comments indicating that he did not welcome African Americans at Clippers games, NBA Commissioner Adam Silver fined him $2.5 million and indefinitely banned him from having any involvement in the management or operation of the club. Sterling's comments promptly attracted substantial outrage: Clippers team members protested by tossing their warm-up jackets on the floor at midcourt and wearing their team jerseys inside out before a game, several companies terminated their sponsorship agreements with the Clippers, and a number of NBA players publicly condemned his remarks and suggested the possibility of boycotting Clippers games. Consider whether this disciplinary action against Sterling was a valid exercise of Commissioner's Silver's "best interests" authority, and whether a court would uphold it if challenged by Sterling.

FEDERAL ANTITRUST LAW LIMITS ON LEAGUE RULES AND GOVERNANCE

A. Overview

The federal antitrust laws, specifically §1 of the Sherman Act (15 U.S.C. §1), prohibit agreements and collective action that unreasonably restrain "interstate trade or commerce" in order to preserve a competitive marketplace that provides consumers with a variety of desired and affordable products and services. In other words, businesses that produce the same product should compete with each other on price, product quality, and other characteristics rather than agree to eliminate economic competition among themselves. Because of the unique nature of professional sports (particularly team sports), it is very difficult for courts to apply the antitrust laws in a principled and consistent fashion. In order to produce professional team sports competition in a form attractive to consumers (e.g., close and exciting games), numerous agreements (including rules) between and among a league, its member clubs, and its players are necessarily required—all of which are potentially subject to antitrust challenge under §1. Traditional antitrust law jurisprudence does not provide a simple means of accurately measuring whether a professional sports league's governing rules, agreements, and conduct enhance or harm consumer welfare (i.e., the interests of sports fans).

Like any other business enterprise, the member clubs of a professional sports league collectively seek to maximize their profits. However, unlike members of other industries that sell the same product and compete among themselves for consumer support (for example, McDonald's, Wendy's, and Burger King franchised fast-food systems), a professional sports league's member clubs do not have an economic self-interest in driving each other out of business. To the contrary, league clubs have an inherent economic interdependence. As one court explained:

> Professional teams in a league . . . must not compete too well with each other, in a business way. On the playing field, of course, they must compete as hard as they can all the time. But it is not necessary and indeed it is unwise for all the teams to compete as hard as they can against each other in a business way. . . . [If this happened,] not only would the weaker teams fail, but eventually the whole league, both the weaker and the stronger teams, would fail, because without a league no team can operate profitably.

United States v. NFL, 116 F. Supp. 319, 323 (E.D. Pa. 1953).

To further league clubs' collective economic interests, it is essential that on-field competitive balance among teams exists within the league and that the outcome of games be relatively uncertain to maintain fan interest in the league's product:

> For maximum customer receptivity and profit it is in the best interest of any club that its opponents not generally be viewed by the public as totally incompetent and utterly unable to compete effectively. For if the latter occurs, thousands of customers will not spend their dollars for tickets to view hundreds of games when the contest seems to present no more of a challenge than an ant confronting an elephant.

Philadelphia World Hockey Club, Inc. v. Philadelphia Hockey Club, Inc., 351 F. Supp. 462, 504 (E.D. Pa. 1972).

League clubs do not share profits like the members of a typical business joint venture or partnership, and they do not subsidize an individual team's economic losses. On the other hand, to maintain the financial integrity of all member clubs, to protect economically weaker teams from stronger ones, and to further all clubs' collective interest in producing competitive games, professional sports leagues share certain revenues (e.g., broadcasting, trademark licensing, sponsorship rights, etc.) as well as limit the permissible degree of economic competition among their teams. Substantial economic disparities may have the undesirable effect of adversely impacting competition among league clubs on the playing field. Therefore, league rules limiting off-field economic competition among clubs may be necessary to preserve and enhance the on-field competition between clubs that is attractive to the sport's fans.

B. Baseball's Antitrust Exemption

In 1922, the Supreme Court decided its first antitrust case involving professional sports, deciding specifically the issue of whether organized professional baseball is subject to the Sherman Act while demonstrating its reluctance to apply the federal antitrust laws to professional sports. In *Federal Baseball Club of Baltimore, Inc. v. National League of Professional Baseball Clubs*, 259 U.S. 200 (1922), the Court ruled that professional baseball is a business, but that it is not interstate "trade or commerce," as required to be regulated by the Sherman Act (which Congress enacted pursuant to its authority to regulate interstate commerce):

> The business is giving exhibitions of baseball, which are purely state affairs. It is true that, in order to attain for these exhibitions the great popularity that they have achieved, competitions must be arranged between clubs from different cities and States. But the fact that in order to give the exhibitions the Leagues must induce free persons to cross state lines and must arrange and pay for their doing so is not enough to change the character of the business. . . . [T]he transport is a mere incident, not the essential thing. That to which it is incident, the exhibition, although made for money would not be called trade or commerce in the commonly accepted use of those words. As it is put by the defendants, personal effort, not related to production, is not a subject of commerce. . . . To repeat the illustrations given by the Court below, a firm of lawyers sending out a member to argue a case . . . does not engage in such commerce because the lawyer . . . goes to another State.

In a 1953 case, *Toolson v. New York Yankees*, 346 U.S. 356 (1953), the Supreme Court reaffirmed *Federal Baseball Club*, observing that baseball had been allowed to develop for more than 30 years without being subject to the antitrust laws. The Court also observed that Congress did not eliminate baseball's antitrust exemption, thereby evidencing its intention that organized baseball is not covered by the antitrust laws. Two dissenting justices vigorously argued that professional baseball is interstate in nature and that Congress had not expressly exempted baseball from the Sherman Act.

On the other hand, after *Toolson*, the Supreme Court held that other professional sports such as football (*Radovich v. National Football League*, 352 U.S. 445 (1957)), basketball (*Haywood v. NBA*, 401 U.S. 1204 (1971)), and boxing (*United States v. Int'l Boxing Club of N.Y., Inc.*, 348 U.S. 236 (1955)) are subject to antitrust laws because their respective business activities occur in interstate commerce. Regarding baseball, however, federal appellate court decisions continued to follow *Toolson*, holding that professional baseball retained its immunity from federal antitrust laws. See, e.g., *Salerno v. American League of Prof'l Baseball Clubs*, 429 F.2d 1003 (2d Cir. 1970); *Portland Baseball Club, Inc. v. Baltimore Baseball Club, Inc.*, 282 F.2d 680 (9th Cir. 1960).

This background set the stage for the Supreme Court's 1972 reconsideration of whether professional baseball is subject to federal antitrust law.

Flood v. Kuhn
407 U.S. 258 (1972)

Mr. Justice BLACKMUN delivered the opinion of the Court.

For the third time in 50 years the Court is asked specifically to rule that professional baseball's reserve system is within the reach of the federal antitrust laws. . . .

[Editors' note: Curt Flood rose to fame as a center fielder with the St. Louis Cardinals during the years 1958–1969 and distinguished himself as a star player. But at the age of 31, in October 1969, Flood was traded to the Philadelphia Phillies of the National League in a multiplayer transaction. He was not consulted about the trade. He was informed by telephone and received formal notice only after the deal had been consummated. In December, he complained to the baseball commissioner and asked that he be made a free agent and be placed at liberty to strike his own bargain with any other major league team. His request was denied. Thereafter, he filed an antitrust challenge to baseball's reserve system, which effectively precluded him from contracting with the major league baseball club of his choice. Flood declined to play for Philadelphia in 1970, despite a $100,000 salary offer, and he sat out the year. After the season was concluded, Philadelphia sold its rights to Flood to the Washington Senators. Washington and the petitioner were able to come to terms for 1971 at a salary of $110,000. Flood started the season, but apparently because he was dissatisfied with his performance, he left the Washington club on April 27, early in the campaign. From this time until he filed suit, Flood had not played baseball. Relying on *Federal Baseball Club* and *Toolson*, the U.S. Court of Appeals for the Second Circuit affirmed the district court's dismissal of Flood's suit.]

It seems appropriate now to say that:

1. Professional baseball is a business and it is engaged in interstate commerce.
2. With its reserve system enjoying exemption from the federal antitrust laws, baseball is, in a very distinct sense, an exception and an anomaly. *Federal Baseball* and *Toolson* have become an aberration confined to baseball.
3. Even though others might regard this as "unrealistic, inconsistent, or illogical," the aberration is an established one, and one that has been recognized not only in Federal Baseball and *Toolson*, but in *Shubert, International Boxing*, and *Radovich*, as well, a total of five consecutive cases in this Court. . . . It is an aberration that has been with us now for half a century, one heretofore deemed fully entitled to the benefit of stare decisis, and one that has survived the Court's expanding concept of interstate commerce. It rests on a recognition and an acceptance of baseball's unique characteristics and needs.
4. Other professional sports operating interstate — football, boxing, basketball, and, presumably, hockey and golf — are not so exempt.
5. The advent of radio and television, with their consequent increased coverage and additional revenues, has not occasioned an overruling of *Federal Baseball* and *Toolson*.

6. The Court has emphasized that since 1922, baseball, with full and continuing congressional awareness, has been allowed to develop and to expand unhindered by federal legislative action. Remedial legislation has been introduced repeatedly in Congress but none has ever been enacted. The Court, accordingly, has concluded that Congress as yet has had no intention to subject baseball's reserve system to the reach of the antitrust statutes. This, obviously, has been deemed to be something other than mere congressional silence and passivity.
7. The Court has expressed concern about the confusion and the retroactivity problems that inevitably would result with a judicial overturning of *Federal Baseball*. It has voiced a preference that if any change is to be made, it come by legislative action that, by its nature, is only prospective in operation.
8. The Court noted in *Radovich*, 352 U.S., at 452, 77 S.Ct., at 394, that the slate with respect to baseball is not clean. Indeed, it has not been clean for half a century.

This emphasis and this concern are still with us. We continue to be loath, 50 years after *Federal Baseball* and almost two decades after *Toolson*, to overturn those cases judicially when Congress, by its positive inaction, has allowed those decisions to stand for so long and, far beyond mere inference and implication, has clearly evinced a desire not to disapprove them legislatively.

Accordingly, we adhere once again to *Federal Baseball* and *Toolson* and to their application to professional baseball. We adhere also to *International Boxing* and *Radovich* and to their respective applications to professional boxing and professional football. If there is any inconsistency or illogic in all this, it is an inconsistency and illogic of long standing that is to be remedied by the Congress and not by this Court. If we were to act otherwise, we would be withdrawing from the conclusion as to congressional intent made in *Toolson* and from the concerns as to retrospectivity therein expressed. Under these circumstances, there is merit in consistency even though some might claim that beneath that consistency is a layer of inconsistency. . . .

The judgment of the Court of Appeals is affirmed. . . .

QUESTION

If all other professional sports leagues, organizations, and governing bodies are subject to the federal antitrust laws, why should baseball continue to have a broad common law antitrust immunity?

Former MLB Commissioner Bud Selig has explained the importance of baseball's antitrust immunity:

> Baseball's antitrust exemption provides the MLB commissioner and league clubs with substantial internal governing autonomy regarding their economically interdependent business affairs. It enables MLB to prevent unilateral relocation by a club into another club's home territory, or to reject the geographical movement of a club that would be inconsistent with MLB's league-wide interests, either of which

generally also implicates consumer welfare considerations (i.e., the interests of baseball fans in the team's current location). It also protects their collective right to approve or disapprove the purchase and sale of clubs without fear of potential antitrust liability.

In addition, this antitrust exemption has enabled development of baseball's national minor league system, which provides a popular, relatively inexpensive form of entertainment in small and medium communities throughout the U.S. and has facilitated a very successful system of player development that creates thousands of employment opportunities for aspiring MLB players. Development of future MLB players through the minor league system is a proven means of building a competitive MLB team as illustrated by the recent postseason success of clubs such as the Kansas City Royals (2015 World Series champions and 2014 World Series American League representative), the Chicago Cubs (2016 World Series champions, its first championship since 1908), and the Houston Astros (2017 World Series champions, the first championship in its history).

Allan H. "Bud" Selig & Matthew J. Mitten, *Baseball Jurisprudence: Its Effects on America's Pastime and Other Professional Sports Leagues*, 50 Ariz. St. L. J. 1171, 1187–88 (2018).

NOTE

Lower courts' interpretation of *Flood*. Federal appellate courts have broadly construed *Flood* to exempt all aspects of the "business of baseball" from the federal antitrust laws, not only player-management labor relations. See, e.g., *City of San Jose v. MLB*, 776 F.3d 686, 690 (9th Cir.), *cert. denied*, 136 S. Ct. 36 (2015) ("*Flood*'s congressional acquiescence rationale applies with special force to franchise relocation. In 1998, Congress passed the Curt Flood Act, which withdrew baseball's antitrust exemption with respect to the reserve clause and other labor issues, but explicitly maintained it for franchise relocation"). Some federal district courts have distinguished *Flood* and narrowly limited the scope of its antitrust immunity to the reserve clause and matters integral to baseball's structure. See, e.g., *Laumann v. NHL*, 56 F. Supp. 3d 280, 297 (S.D. N.Y. 2014) (declining "to apply the exemption to a subject that is not central to the business of baseball . . . namely baseball's contracts for television broadcast rights," which Congress did not intend to exempt in enacting the Curt Flood Act of 1998).

In December 2020, Major League Baseball restructured its Minor League Baseball (MiLB) system, which resulted in the elimination of 40 of the 160 previously existing clubs. Based on existing Supreme Court precedent, the Second Circuit affirmed the dismissal of a 2022 antitrust suit alleging that MLB's restructuring of the MiLB system is illegal conduct "to cement MLB's dominance over all professional baseball and to reduce output and boycott the 40 Ousted Teams from MLB affiliation" and that "[t]he time is at hand to cast the baseball exemption into the dust bin of history." *Nostalgic Partners LLC v. Office of the Commissioner of Major League Baseball*, 2023 WL 4072836 (2d Cir.) at *1 ("[W]e must continue to apply Supreme Court precedent unless and until it is overruled by the Supreme Court.").

C. Application of Sherman Act §1

1. Concerted Action Requirement

KEY TERM • Single economic entity defense

The express language of Sherman Act §1 broadly prohibits "[e]very contract, combination in the form of trust or otherwise, or conspiracy" that restrains trade, which literally encompasses virtually all professional sports league rules (which are the product of an agreement among league clubs) and decisions. Nevertheless, as a defense to Sherman Act §1 claims, professional sports leagues (particularly the NFL) have historically argued that the league and its member clubs jointly produce a single product (e.g., NFL football) that no individual club is capable of producing; therefore, league rules and member clubs' collective governance should not be subject to §1 because they are not economic competitors who produce separate products. Thus, it is necessary to resolve an important threshold issue: Is a professional sports league a single economic entity whose agreements and rules are not subject to §1 scrutiny, or is it a joint venture of separate economic entities (i.e., its clubs) whose collective conduct is subject to §1?

Most federal appellate courts historically rejected the "single economic entity" defense. For example, in *Los Angeles Memorial Coliseum Comm'n v. NFL*, 726 F.2d 1381 (9th Cir.), *cert. denied*, 469 U.S. 990 (1984), the Ninth Circuit rejected the NFL's claim that the league is in essence a single economic entity, like a partnership that shares profits and losses, precluding application of §1, which prohibits only agreements among business entities with economically separate interests that restrain trade:

> Our inquiry discloses an association of teams sufficiently independent and competitive with one another to warrant rule of reason scrutiny under §1 of the Sherman Act. The NFL clubs are, in the words of the district court, "separate business entities whose products have an independent value." The member clubs are all independently owned. Most are corporations, some are partnerships, and apparently a few are sole proprietorships. Although a large portion of League revenue, approximately 90%, is divided equally among the teams, profits and losses are not shared, a feature common to partnerships or other "single entities." In fact, profits vary widely despite the sharing of revenue. The disparity in profits can be attributed to independent management policies regarding coaches, players, management personnel, ticket prices, concessions, luxury box seats, as well as franchise location, all of which contribute to fan support and other income sources.
>
> In addition to being independent business entities, the NFL clubs do compete with one another off the field as well as on to acquire players, coaches, and management personnel. In certain areas of the country where two teams operate in close proximity, there is also competition for fan support, local television and local radio revenues, and media space.

Subsequently, in *American Needle, Inc. v. NFL*, 560 U.S. 183 (2010), the Supreme Court unanimously ruled that a professional sports league comprising separate, independently owned and operated, and for-profit member clubs is not a single economic entity immune from §1 as a matter of law when engaged in joint marketing and licensing of its member clubs' trademarks (e.g., Chicago Bears). The Court explained that the key inquiry is whether there is an agreement "among 'separate economic actors pursuing separate economic interests.'" *Id.* at 195. In other words, "[t]he key is whether the agreement joins together 'independent centers of decisionmaking.'" *Id.* at 195. It concluded that "[a]lthough NFL teams have common interests such as promoting the NFL brand, they are still separate, profit-maximizing entities, and their interests in licensing team trademarks are not necessarily aligned. Common interests in the NFL brand '*partially* unit[e] the economic interests of the parent firms,' but the teams still have distinct, potentially competing interests." *Id.* at 198. The Court's ruling suggests that other aspects of a professional sports league's cooperative operations and internal governance decisions also are subject to §1. See, e.g., *Laumann v. NHL*, 907 F. Supp. 2d 465 (S.D. N.Y. 2012) (alleged agreements among MLB and NHL clubs to create exclusive local television territories and broadcasting rights for each club and to grant their respective leagues the exclusive right to sell television and Internet broadcasting rights to those games outside these local territories are subject to §1 scrutiny).

On the other hand, if a professional sports league or association is governed by an entity that wholly owns and controls all of its member clubs, or by an independent company with separate ownership and control from its clubs (similar to NASCAR's business model), it appears that there would be the requisite complete unity of economic interest under *American Needle* to justify characterizing it as a single economic entity whose rules and decisions are not subject to §1 antitrust law scrutiny. For example, MLS operates as "Major League Soccer, L.L.C.," which owns the league, clubs, and player contracts. MLS is governed by a Management Committee of league investors/shareholders who each have the right to operate one or more of its member clubs. Major League Rugby also operates as a single entity.

2. Unreasonable Restraint of Trade

KEY TERMS
- Anticompetitive effects
- Intrabrand economic competition
- Procompetitive effects
- Rule of reason
- Substantially less restrictive alternative

If §1 applies, it is necessary to then consider whether the challenged league rule or agreement among its clubs unreasonably restrains trade. The production of professional sports athletic competition requires many aspects of cooperation and some limits on intrabrand economic competition among league teams for exciting and appealing games and events with vigorous on-field competition to exist. Thus, league rules and internal agreements precluding or limiting off-field economic competition among league clubs for fans' support or revenues are not irrefutably presumed to be anticompetitive (i.e., per se illegal). It is well-settled law that the 3-step rule of reason, which involves a complicated case-by-case analysis, is the applicable standard for evaluating the competitive effects of collective action by professional sports league clubs or organizations under §1 of the Sherman Act. *American Needle, Inc. v. NFL*, 560 U.S. 183 (2010); *National Collegiate Athletic Association v. Board of Regents of the Univ. of Oklahoma*, 468 U.S. 85 (1984). Virtually all professional sports industry restraints that allegedly violate §1 require detailed consideration of (1) its anticompetitive effects; (2) procompetitive benefits that the challenged restraint achieves or furthers; and (3) any substantially less restrictive means to achieve these benefits. See generally *NCAA v. Alston*, which is discussed in Chapter 3. If the restraint has predominately anticompetitive effects, it is unreasonable and illegal. Conversely, if it has predominately procompetitive effects, it is reasonable and legal.

a. Acquisition, Ownership, and Sale of a Franchise

The following case considers an antitrust suit by a prospective club owner denied entry into a league. As you read this case, consider why the court rejected his claim that the league's refusal to approve the proposed sale of the club is an antitrust violation.

Levin v. NBA
385 F. Supp. 149 (S.D. N.Y. 1974)

Owen, District Judge.

The plaintiffs, two businessmen, in 1972 had an agreement to buy the Boston Celtics basketball team, one of the 17-member National Basketball Association.

The N.B.A., as its constitution recites, is a joint venture "organized to operate a league consisting of professional basketball teams, each of which shall be operated by a member of the Association." It has been in existence since 1946. Each of its joint venturers holds a franchise to operate a team. While the teams compete vigorously on the basketball court, the joint venturers are dependent upon one another as partners in the league format to make it possible. N.B.A. operates through its Board of Governors which consists of one governor designated by each member. Action by the Board on a transfer of membership requires the affirmative vote of three-quarters of the members of the Board. [Editors' note: When the plaintiffs applied to become owners of the Celtics franchise, only 2 votes were cast favorable to their application, 13 were opposed, and 1 club owner was not present.]

Plaintiffs immediately demanded and were granted a personal hearing before the Board. Following the presentation of their case a second vote was taken. It was, however, to identical effect.

There is a sharp dispute on the reason for the rejection. Plaintiffs contend that they were rejected because of their friendship and business associations with one

Sam Schulman, owner of the Seattle SuperSonics, who was an anathema to the other members of the league. . . .

On the other hand, the reason given by the N.B.A. for the rejection was that the business association between the plaintiffs and Schulman violated the "conflict of interest" provision of the N.B.A. constitution. That provision reads: A member shall not exercise control, directly or indirectly, over any other member of the Association. . . . This provision is necessary, N.B.A. claims, in order that the league may enjoy public support because there is in fact, and the public believes there is, intense competition in the league framework between the teams operated by the N.B.A. members. . . .

In order to survive defendants' motion for summary judgment, plaintiffs must demonstrate that the conduct complained of is a violation of the antitrust laws. While it is true that the antitrust laws apply to a professional athletic league, and that joint action by members of a league can have antitrust implications, this is not such a case. Here the plaintiffs wanted to join with those unwilling to accept them, not to compete with them, but to be partners in the operation of a sports league for plaintiffs' profit. Further, no matter which reason one credits for the rejection, it was not an anti-competitive reason. Finally, regardless of the financial impact of this rejection upon the plaintiffs, if any, the exclusion of the plaintiffs from membership in the league did not have an anticompetitive effect nor an effect upon the public interest. The Celtics continue as an operating club, and indeed are this year's champion. . . .

Since there was no exclusion of plaintiffs from competition with the alleged excluders, nor anti-competitive acts by them and no public injury occasioned thereby, the defendants' acts did not constitute a violation of the antitrust laws and defendants' motion for summary judgment is granted.

NOTE

Judicial reluctance to invalidate league rules and votes regarding sale of clubs. As illustrated by *Levin*, it is difficult for a prospective purchaser of a professional sports club (even one who has reached an agreement with the current owner to buy the team) to prove that the league's refusal to approve the sale has anticompetitive effects, which is the plaintiff's burden of proof under the first prong of the 3-step rule of reason. This rejection does not reduce the number of NBA clubs, which remains the same as before the denial of the proposed transfer of club ownership, or reduce any economic competition among NBA clubs. As the *Levin* court observed, all it does is preclude a particular party from owning a league franchise. Even if the requisite anticompetitive effects could be proven, rejection of a prospective owner based on proof that the purchaser lacks the minimally necessary financial capital, character and fitness, or business skills to successfully operate a league club may have the procompetitive effect of preventing the league from being weakened with a corresponding reduction in its ability to compete successfully against other forms of entertainment for consumer patronage. See *Nat'l Basketball Assn. v. Minnesota Professional Basketball Limited Partnership*, 56 F.3d 866 (8th Cir. 1995).

b. Franchise Relocation

Pursuant to its franchise agreement with the league, a club owner generally has the exclusive right to operate its team in a particular city, although large markets such as New York City, Los Angeles, and Chicago may have two league clubs. For economic reasons, a club may want to relocate the team to another city to increase its local revenues and/or to play in a new facility. For example, in 2016, the St. Louis Rams relocated back to the Los Angeles metropolitan area (specifically, Inglewood), where its club owner built a $1.86 billion stadium. The Chargers, which moved from San Diego, shares the stadium with the Rams.

In the 1990s, local communities, including mid-major cities such as Nashville, Memphis, Charlotte, Oklahoma City, and Seattle, have provided multimillion-dollar public subsidies for playing facilities to attract major league professional sports franchises. Many other communities have made similar investments of public funds to keep their local sports franchises and prevent them from relocating. Courts generally rule that these arrangements are a legitimate use of state and local tax dollars to promote the public good, although these significant public expenditures combined with favorable lease terms provide substantial economic benefits to privately owned professional sports clubs. See, e.g., *Libertarian Party of Wis. v. State*, 546 N.W.2d 424, 438 (Wis. 1996) (bonds issued by a local professional baseball park district are "obligations of . . . a revenue-producing enterprise that serves a public purpose").

Depending on the specific circumstances, a professional sports league's refusal to permit one of its clubs to relocate to another city may violate the antitrust laws. Former Oakland Raiders owner Al Davis's antitrust litigation against the NFL provides an example of a successful case arising out of the league's initial rejection of his 1980 request to move the Raiders from Oakland to Los Angeles.

In 1978, the owner of the Los Angeles Rams, Carroll Rosenbloom, decided to locate his team in a new stadium, the "Big A," in Anaheim, California, which left the Los Angeles Coliseum without a major tenant. Coliseum officials then began searching for a new NFL team occupant. After NFL Commissioner Pete Rozelle informed them it was not possible to place an expansion franchise there at the time, they negotiated with existing NFL teams in the hope that one might leave its home and move to Los Angeles.

The L.A. Coliseum ran into a major obstacle in its attempts to convince a team to move because it was located in the home territory of the Rams franchise. Rule 4.3 of Article IV of the NFL Constitution stated: "The League shall have exclusive control of the exhibition of football games by member clubs within the home territory of each member. No member club shall have the right to transfer its franchise or playing site to a different city, either within or outside its home territory, without prior approval by the affirmative vote of three-fourths of the existing member clubs of the League."

After the Oakland Raiders' lease with the Oakland Coliseum expired in 1978, Davis, the club's majority owner, and L.A. Coliseum officials signed a March 1, 1980, "memorandum of agreement" outlining the terms of the Raiders' proposed relocation to Los Angeles. However, on March 10, 1980, the NFL clubs voted 22–0 against the Raiders' proposed move (with five teams abstaining), which did not meet Rule 4.3's three-quarters approval requirement.

In response, the Raiders brought a §1claim in Los Angeles federal court alleging that the refusal of the NFL and its member clubs to permit the club to relocate to Los Angeles was an unreasonable restraint of trade. This lawsuit resulted in a jury verdict in favor of the Raiders awarding $11.55 million in damages, which was automatically trebled (i.e., tripled) as a prevailing party in an antitrust suit. The trial court enjoined the NFL from preventing the Raiders from moving to Los Angeles.

In *Los Angeles Memorial Coliseum Comm'n v. NFL*, 726 F.2d 1381 (9th Cir. 1984), *cert. denied*, 469 U.S. 990 (1984), the Ninth Circuit affirmed the jury's finding that the NFL's refusal to approve the Raiders club's relocation to Los Angeles violated the rule of reason. It concluded that Rule 4.3 has the anticompetitive effect of dividing geographical markets among the NFL clubs, precluding the Raiders from engaging in economic competition with the Rams in the Los Angeles NFL market. These exclusive territories insulated each NFL team from economic competition with other clubs, enabling them to set monopoly prices for tickets to the detriment of consumers.

Regarding the NFL's claim that Rule 4.3 has procompetitive effects because it helps the league maintain its overall geographical scope, regional balance, and coverage of both major and minor markets, the court acknowledged:

> Exclusive territories aid new franchises in achieving financial stability, which protects the large initial investment an owner must make to start up a football team. Stability arguably helps ensure no one team has an undue advantage on the field. Territories foster fan loyalty, which in turn promotes traditional rivalries between teams, each contributing to attendance at games and television viewing.

But the court determined that the NFL's denial of the Raiders' proposed move did not actually further any of these objectives:

> [T]he NFL made no showing that the transfer of the Raiders to Los Angeles would have any harmful effect on the League. Los Angeles is a market large enough for the successful operation of two teams, there would be no scheduling difficulties, facilities at the L.A. Coliseum are more than adequate, and no loss of future television revenue was foreseen. Also, the NFL offered no evidence that its interest in maintaining regional balance would be adversely affected by a move of a northern California team to southern California.

Subsequently, in *Nat'l Basketball Assn. v. SDC Basketball Club, Inc.*, 815 F.2d 562, 567 (9th Cir. 1987), the Ninth Circuit reiterated that league rules regarding franchise relocation, including requiring a club to seek league approval before moving, are not per se illegal; rather, "rule of reason analysis governed a professional sports league's efforts to restrict franchise movement." Thus, a professional sports league can avoid antitrust liability if its franchise relocation rules are carefully tailored and properly applied to achieve legitimate procompetitive objectives, such as franchise financial stability, competitive balance among its member clubs, and an appropriate geographical distribution of its teams. Alternatively, rather than prohibiting a club from moving, a league may permit it to do so upon payment of a relocation fee that is divided pro rata (i.e., equally) among its clubs.

The relocation of professional sports franchises causes great upset among the local populace and has spawned both breach of contract and antitrust litigation against club owners by their respective host cities, states, or local governing bodies. Such litigation is motivated by the potential loss of economic benefits to a city and its local businesses, outstanding bond indebtedness to finance the departing club's playing facility, and wounded community pride resulting from the loss of a major league professional sports franchise. These lawsuits seek to prevent loss of the franchise, to keep the local team from moving before its stadium lease expires and without an opportunity to retain the franchise, or to require the league to provide a replacement franchise.

A well-drafted stadium lease is the most effective means of protecting a host community's (generally) multimillion dollars of public investment in the playing facility that houses a local team and ensuring that the local populace receives the full benefit of its contractual bargain. For example, expressly authorizing a court to enjoin a club from relocating prior to the expiration of its lease or requiring a relocating club to pay liquidated damages (i.e., an agreed-upon predetermined amount) of several million dollars for breach of a playing facility lease may be an effective contractual means of protecting a host community's interests. In *Metropolitan Sports Facilities Comm'n v. Minnesota Twins Partnership*, 638 N.W.2d 214, 225 (Minn. Ct. App. 2002), the court rejected the contention that money damages are adequate to compensate a public stadium authority for the breach of a playing facility lease if MLB contracted its number of clubs by eliminating the Minnesota Twins franchise prior to the 2002 season. Finding that the Twins club does not pay rent for using the Metrodome to play its home games, the court observed "that the use agreement at issue here is not a typical commercial lease." The court explained, "[T]he benefit of the bargain that the commission received was the Twins' promise to play their home games at the Metrodome for the duration of their lease. Indeed, the stated purpose for building and operating the stadium was to attract major league sport franchises to play at the stadium for the enjoyment of fans." The trial court's injunction requiring the Twins club to play its 2002 home games in the Metrodome and prohibiting MLB from interfering with this contractual obligation was affirmed.

c. Restrictions on Intellectual Property Rights Licensing

North American major professional sports leagues are geographically dispersed throughout the United States and Canada. Their respective clubs are located in cities with vastly different populations and economic bases — for example, large-market metropolitan areas such as New York City, Los Angeles, and Chicago, as well as much smaller markets like Kansas City, Milwaukee, and Pittsburgh. Thus, league clubs' respective revenue-generating potential from ticket sales (including personal seat licenses), concessions, parking fees, sponsorships, merchandising rights, and game broadcasts within differing local markets varies considerably.

As a means of preventing significant disparities in local revenue streams from inhibiting or destroying on-field competitive balance and fan interest in league games, the NFL, MLB, NBA, and NHL have implemented varying degrees of revenue sharing among their member clubs. In each league, national television and broadcasting rights revenues are shared equally among league clubs. Individual clubs' trademarks (i.e., team names and logos) are collectively licensed by a central league entity, with net revenues equally distributed to all league clubs. For example, professional leagues have required their clubs' Internet rights to be consolidated and centrally licensed (while prohibiting or limiting each club's ability to do so), with revenues shared equally among league clubs. Gate receipts from individual ticket sales frequently are also shared between the home and visiting teams in an agreed percentage.

The NFL currently has the most significant degree of revenue sharing among its member clubs, which provides the Green Bay Packers, located in a metropolitan area of approximately 100,000 people, with the financial resources to compete effectively on the field with large market clubs such as the Chicago Bears. Except for designated local advertising and facility-related revenues, NFL clubs share virtually all other revenues in an effort to jointly produce exciting games between closely matched teams that attract fan interest. In his 1983 testimony before Congress, former NFL commissioner Pete Rozelle stated that "revenue sharing is the key to maintaining geographic and competitive balance in professional football . . . and ensure[s] that each club, irrespective of the size of its community, stadium, or television market, has a comparable opportunity to field a championship team." See William J. Hoffman, Comment, *Dallas' Head Cowboy Emerges Victorious in a Licensing Showdown with the NFL*: National Football League Properties v. Dallas Cowboys Football Club, 7 Seton Hall J. Sport L. 255, 262 (1997).

The exclusive licensing of pooled intellectual property rights by a central league marketing arm (e.g., NFL Properties), along with corresponding restrictions on individual clubs, is designed to (and often does) maximize their aggregate economic value and total revenues generated by the league. Because the pro rata revenue shares received by the most popular individual league clubs or those in the largest markets may be significantly less than the percentage of total revenues generated by the intellectual property associated with those clubs, league-imposed restrictions on a club's individual licensing of intellectual property rights have been challenged on antitrust grounds by league clubs and third parties.

In *Major League Baseball Properties, Inc. v. Salvino, Inc.*, 542 F.3d 290 (2d. Cir. 2008), the Second Circuit rejected a §1 antitrust claim challenging Major League Baseball Properties (MLBP)'s centralized trademark licensing program. The court ruled that MLBP's refusal to grant a trademark license to plaintiff, a manufacturer of plush filled bears called "Bammers," was not clearly anticompetitive. The agreement among MLB clubs establishing MLBP as the exclusive licensor of their trademark rights did not expressly limit or necessarily reduce the number of licenses issued to third parties. In fact, the total number of trademark licensees increased substantially after the formation of MLBP by facilitating "one stop shopping" for the right to use MLB clubs' trademarks, thereby having the pro-competitive effect of increasing the quantity of trademarked MLB merchandise available to consumers.

Consistent with *Salvino*, in *Madison Square Garden, L.P. v. NHL*, 270 Fed. Appx. 56, 2008 WL 746524 (2d Cir.), the Second Circuit ruled that requiring the New York Rangers to migrate its website to a common technology platform managed by the NHL, rather than allowing its independent operation by the club, is not clearly anticompetitive conduct that violates §1. It affirmed the lower court's finding that the NHL's challenged conduct has several plausible procompetitive effects, including a standardized website layout to attract national sponsors and advertisers interested in uniform exposure across the NHL.com network, which is a key element of the NHL's strategy to enhance its national brand to better compete against other sports and entertainment products.

In *American Needle, Inc. v. NFL*, 560 U.S. 183 (2010), a hat manufacturer alleged that the NFL's exclusive trademark licensing program, which resulted in the termination of its nonexclusive trademark license, and corresponding restrictions on its member clubs' ability to license their respective trademarks violate §1 of the Sherman Act. Although the Supreme Court rejected the NFL's argument that NFL Properties' trademark licensing decisions are unilateral conduct not subject to §1, the Court recognized that a professional sports league has a "legitimate and important interest" in maintaining competitive balance among its clubs and that it is "unquestionably an interest that may well justify a variety of collective decisions made by the teams." *Id.* at 204. See also *American Needle, Inc. v. New Orleans Louisiana Saints*, 2014 WL 1364022 (N.D. Ill.) (observing that "exclusive license arrangement encouraged additional licensee commitment and had numerous procompetitive effects, including improvements in product design, quality, distribution, and coordination of styles with other apparel items," which justified application of the rule of reason to determine its legality). The parties subsequently reached a settlement, pursuant to which the NFL paid an undisclosed sum to American Needle, and NFL Properties' exclusive product licensing regime remained intact.

Regarding media rights restrictions, in *Laumann v. NHL*, 56 F. Supp. 3d 280 (S.D. N.Y. 2014), the court held that full rule of reason analysis applies to NHL and MLB rules prohibiting their member clubs from televising their home games outside of their respective exclusive broadcast territories, which each league sold exclusively in television and Internet packages of all clubs' out-of-market games not nationally televised). See also *Laumann v. NHL*, 2015 WL 2330107 (S.D. N.Y.) at *11 (challenged NHL and MLB territorial restraints injured every consumer of broadcast out-of-market baseball and hockey games because they are "deprived of an option—a la carte channels—that would have been available absent the territorial restraints."). The NHL and MLB both ultimately settled the *Laumann* case by agreeing to offer a full-season Internet subscription for all their respective clubs' games for a lower price than previously offered as well as a full-season Internet subscription for a single league team.

In *In re National Football League Sunday Ticket Antitrust Litigation*, 933 F.3d 1136 (9th Cir. 2019), cert. denied, 141 S. Ct. 56 (2020), a group of individuals and commercial establishments alleged that an exclusive agreement between the NFL and DirecTV, pursuant to which DirecTV created its "Sunday Ticket" satellite television package of NFL game broadcasts and received the exclusive rights to broadcast all NFL games not shown on over-the-air local television within any given geographical area, is anticompetitive and violates federal antitrust law.

Pursuant to the "Teams-NFL Agreement," the 32 NFL clubs pool their game telecasting rights and give the NFL exclusive authority to exercise those rights, which precludes a club from individually entering into telecasting rights agreements with networks, satellite TV providers, or Internet streaming services. Under the "NFL-Network Agreement," CBS and Fox coordinate to create a single telecast for every Sunday-afternoon NFL game, which is shown in some but not all television markets in the United States. Under the "NFL-DirecTV Agreement," the NFL allows DirecTV to obtain all live game telecasts produced by CBS and Fox, package those telecasts, and deliver the bundled telecasts to NFL Sunday Ticket subscribers, which enables them to view local and all out-of-market NFL games. Fans are required to buy the entire "Sunday Ticket" package of NFL games (which requires purchase of a basic television package from DirecTV) and cannot purchase out-of-market NFL games individually or a particular team's games.

Reversing the district court's dismissal of plaintiffs' claims, the Ninth Circuit ruled:

> [*NCAA v. Bd. of Regents*] controls our analysis. In that case, the Supreme Court held that an agreement among college football teams and the NCAA violated Section 1 of the Sherman Act because the agreement eliminated competition in the market for college football telecasts. Here, the interlocking agreements impose similar restrictions. [T]he Supreme Court noted in *NCAA* that the agreement at issue "limits the total amount of televised intercollegiate football and the number of games that any one team may televise." The complaint here alleges that the interlocking agreements in this case impose analogous limitations: plaintiffs assert that the Teams-NFL and NFL-DirecTV Agreements limit the "amount of televised [professional] football" that one team may televise because they restrict the number of telecasts made to a single telecast for each game. . . .
>
> Because the complaint alleges that the interlocking agreements in this case involve the same sorts of restrictions that *NCAA* concluded constituted an injury to competition, we likewise conclude that the complaint plausibly alleges an injury to competition. Further, because the alleged restrictions on the production and sale of telecasts constitute "a naked restriction" on the number of telecasts available for broadcasters and consumers . . .

Id. at 1151-1152.

Does *Sunday Ticket Antitrust Litigation* suggest that antitrust law requires a sports league to license multiple broadcasters to market and sell a package of all its member clubs' game broadcasts to consumers rather than providing a single broadcaster with the exclusive right to do so? If so, how does doing so benefit sports fans?

D. Application of Sherman Act §2

KEY TERMS
- Attempted monopolization
- Illegal exclusionary conduct with anticompetitive effects
- Interbrand economic competition
- Legal, fair competition on the merits
- Monopolization
- Monopoly power
- Sherman Act §2

This section considers antitrust issues arising out of the formation of a new league that challenges an established league's dominance of a major league professional sport. Our focus here is on challenged restraints affecting interbrand competition between professional sports leagues (or clubs) that sell competing products within the U.S. sports industry. Similar issues have arisen in connection with competition between producers of individual performer sports such as tennis, auto racing, rodeo competitions, mixed martial arts, and golf. See, e.g., *Deutscher Tennis Bund v. ATP Tour, Inc.*, 610 F.3d 820 (3d Cir. 2010); *Kentucky Speedway, LLC v. National Assn. for Stock Car Auto Racing, Inc.*, 588 F.3d 908 (6th Cir. 2009); *Volvo N. Am. Corp. v. Men's Int'l Prof'l Tennis Council*, 857 F.2d 55 (2d Cir. 1988); *Elite Rodeo Ass'n v. Prof'l Rodeo Cowboys Ass'n*, 2016 WL 429886 (N.D. Tex.); *Le v. Zuffa*, 216 F.Supp.3d 1154 (D. Nev. 2016); *Mickelson v. PGA Tour, Inc.*, 2022 WL 3229341 (N.D. Cal.). Interbrand competition exists among sellers of different brands of products that are reasonable substitutes from the perspective of consumers (e.g., sports fans). For example, this encompasses competition between professional leagues or in the same sports (e.g., PGA Tour and LIV golf) or other sports with overlapping seasons (e.g., NBA and NHL), as well as competition between clubs in a different sport within the same geographical area (e.g., the Chicago Bulls NBA team and the Chicago Blackhawks NHL team).

There has been a historical tendency toward a single major professional league for the most popular North American team sports of baseball, football, basketball, and hockey. Competition among rival leagues in the same sport has never continued for any appreciable period of time. As a recent example, two competing women's professional basketball leagues, the American Basketball League (ABL) and the Women's National Basketball Association (WNBA), began play in the late 1990s. The ABL, despite having some of the best women's basketball players on its clubs' rosters, ceased operations after only a few years of existence because of its inability to market its product and finance its operations as well as did the WNBA, many of whose clubs are owned and operated by the NBA teams in their respective locations. Unlike most industries in which there are multiple producers of similar products, there is currently only one North American professional league that produces baseball (MLB), basketball (the NBA), football (the NFL), hockey (the NHL), and soccer (MLS) as well as women's basketball (WNBA) and soccer (NWSL) at the major league level.

North American major professional leagues are "closed," which means the requisite majority of its existing clubs (usually three-fourths) must agree to the entry of new clubs, thereby providing each league with a monopoly over its particular sport at the major league level of play. By comparison, professional sports leagues in other parts of the world, particularly Europe, generally are "open": "[M]embership in the league is contingent on success. Professional sports leagues in soccer, rugby, basketball, and cricket are organized in ascending tiers (generally called divisions), and every year the teams with the worst record are relegated to a lower division and replaced by the most successful teams from that lower division." Stephen F. Ross & Stephan Szymanski, *Open Competition in League Sports*, 2002 Wis. L. Rev. 625, 626. Courts have not been receptive to claims that a closed league structure violates antitrust law. *Warnock v. NFL*, 356 F. Supp. 2d 535 (W.D. Pa. 2005), *aff'd*, 154 Fed. Appx. 291 (3d Cir. 2005), *cert. denied*, 547 U.S. 1021 (2006) (holding that a Pittsburgh municipal taxpayer lacks standing to sue the NFL and its member clubs for allegedly violating antitrust law by acting in concert to force the league's cities, including Pittsburgh, to build new football stadiums). *Hamilton County Bd. of County Comm'rs v. NFL*, 491 F.3d 310 (6th Cir. 2007) (dismissing a county's antitrust claim against the NFL after it agreed to highly favorable lease terms to prevent the Bengals club from relocating because its officials knew or should have known the NFL was a monopoly during lease negotiations).

To be economically viable, a major professional sports league needs several resources, including (1) franchise owners with the financing and business acumen to successfully operate its member clubs, (2) teams in several large cities throughout the country with the population and economic base to support them, (3) access to adequate playing facilities, (4) major league–quality players, and (5) a national media broadcasting contract. Even if a new league is able to satisfy these minimum requirements, its long-term survival as a profitable independent entity is not ensured. Upstart leagues often fold after a relatively short period of existence because of financial problems or improper management and bad business decisions, or fans may choose to continue supporting an established league rather than a new league.

The formation of a new league challenges an established league's dominance of a major professional league sport and threatens its popularity and profitability. Whether the threat is actual or simply potential, the established league may be tempted to react in ways that are anticompetitive and raise antitrust concerns. On several occasions during the twentieth century and with mixed results, a new league has brought antitrust litigation against the preexisting dominant league for allegedly restricting access to one or more of the essential inputs necessary to produce competing professional team sports in a national or local market in the United States.

Most antitrust challenges have been brought under §2 of the Sherman Act, 15 U.S.C. §2, which prohibits monopolization or attempted monopolization. Unlike §1 that governs only concerted action, §2 applies to unilateral conduct such as a professional sports league's conduct in response to the formation of a rival league. Monopolization requires proof that (1) the defendant possesses monopoly power in the relevant market; and (2) the defendant has wilfully acquired or maintained that power rather than having grown or developed power as a consequence of a superior product, business acumen, or historic accident. *United States v. Grinnell Corp.*, 384 U.S. 563, 570-71 (1966). Attempted monopolization requires proof "(1) that the defendant has engaged in predatory or anticompetitive conduct with (2) a specific intent to monopolize and (3) a dangerous probability of achieving monopoly power." *Spectrum Sports, Inc. v. McQuillan*, 506 U.S. 447, 456 (1993). Although the elements of monopolization and attempted monopolization are different, both require analysis of the defendant league's degree of control over the relevant market and a determination of whether its conduct is legal, fair competition on the merits, or is illegal exclusionary conduct with anticompetitive market effects.

The mere fact that there is only a single major league for a particular sport does not violate §2 of the Sherman Act because there may be certain inherent conditions in the professional sports industries that predispose each sport to dominance by one league at the major league level. One potential reason for this phenomenon is that fans may prefer a single champion for the highest level of competition within the sport. If so, over time, fans will prefer the product of one league over that of another, thereby leading to the demise of the disfavored league. There is no §2 violation if a league's market dominance results from winning the off-field competitive economic struggle by providing a superior on-field entertainment product that is more desirable to sports fans. On the other hand, this phenomenon may be the result of an established league's efforts to illegally prevent a rival league from competing with it in violation of §2.

Determining whether a professional sports league has monopoly power for Sherman Act §2 purposes requires definition of both the relevant product and geographical markets, as well as calculation of the defendants' market share, in order to evaluate the actual or potential anticompetitive effects of the challenged league rules or conduct. Although courts generally require at least a 70 percent market share to justify a finding of monopoly power, no rigid mathematical approach has been used in §2 sports antitrust cases. Rather, the dispositive issue is whether the relevant market is appropriately defined, which usually necessarily determines whether the league has monopoly power and the corresponding ability to exclude rivals and prevent economic competition.

For example, in *American Football League v. National Football League*, 323 F.2d 124, 130 (4th Cir. 1963), the Fourth Circuit ruled that the NFL did not have sufficient control of the market to prevent a newly formed rival from competing with it:

> The relevant market is nationwide, though the fact that there are a limited number of desirable sites for team locations bears upon the question of [the NFL]'s power to monopolize the national market. The District Court's finding that [the NFL] did not have the power to monopolize the relevant market appears plainly correct. In 1959, it occupied eleven of the thirty-one apparently desirable sites for team locations, but its occupancy of some of them as New York and San Francisco-Oakland was not exclusive, for those metropolitan areas were capable of supporting more than one team. Twenty of the thirty-one potentially desirable sites were entirely open to American. Indeed, the fact that the American League was successfully launched, could stage a

full schedule of games in 1960, has competed very successfully for outstanding players, and has obtained advantageous contracts for national television coverage strongly supports the District Court's finding that [the NFL] did not have the power to prevent, or impede, the formation of the new league. Indeed, at the close of the 1960 season, representatives of the American League declared that the League's success was unprecedented.

A large market share or monopoly power does not violate §2 by itself. Even a monopolist is not prohibited from fairly competing on the merits for fan support. The antitrust laws do not prohibit the dominant professional sports league from winning a competitive marketplace struggle by producing a product that is highly desirable to consumers (e.g., NFL football). In *American Football League*, the court held that the NFL could expand its business operations by adding expansion teams in response to increasing consumer demand for its product and to compete with the AFL for the best available remaining geographical areas in which to place a professional football franchise, which is legal, fair competition on the merits.

The essence of illegal monopolization is conduct that excludes actual or potential rivals from the market by unfair or predatory means. To draw the line between lawful competition on the merits and unlawful exclusion or predation, it is important to consider the effects of a monopolist's challenged conduct on consumers. For example, a dominant league's clubs are permitted to compete with an upstart rival league's clubs for the services of the best available players and to enforce valid, existing player contracts, thereby preventing their players from switching leagues before their respective contracts expire. As one court explained, "[n]obody has ever thought, so far as we can find, that in the absence of some monopolistic purpose everyone had not the right to offer better terms to another's employee so long as the latter is free to leave." *Washington Capitols Basketball Club, Inc. v. Barry*, 419 F.2d 472, 478 (9th Cir. 1969). On the other hand, in *Philadelphia World Hockey Club, Inc. v. Philadelphia Hockey Club, Inc.*, 351 F. Supp. 462 (E.D. Pa. 1972), the court ruled that the NHL's efforts to control the supply of major league professional hockey players through a series of agreements with Canadian and U.S. amateur and minor professional leagues was illegal monopolistic conduct designed to prevent the WHA from competing in the North American major league professional hockey market.

If a new league successfully proves the dominant league has engaged in monopolization or attempted monopolization in violation of §2 of the Sherman Act, the typical remedies are an injunction against the illegal practices and damages. In *Philadelphia World Hockey Club*, the court enjoined the NHL from attempting to prevent players from signing new contracts with WHA clubs after their NHL contracts expired. In *United States Football League v. NFL*, 842 F.2d 1335 (2d Cir. 1988), the Second Circuit affirmed the jury's award of only nominal damages (i.e., $1.00, which is automatically trebled under the antitrust laws) to the United States Football League (USFL). Although the jury found that the NFL had illegally monopolized the U.S. major professional football market, it determined that the USFL's poor, self-destructive business decisions were the primary cause of its inability to compete successfully against the NFL.

In *United States Football League*, 842 F.2d at 1380, the court rejected the USFL's proposed judicial restructuring of major league professional football as a remedy for the NFL's antitrust violation, which included its request that all USFL clubs be granted membership in the NFL; separation of the NFL into two leagues, with each league being limited to one network television contract; or a prohibition on the NFL from broadcasting its games in more than one afternoon time slot on Sunday. The court explained:

> Absent a showing of an unlawful barrier to entry, however, new sports leagues must be prepared to make the investment of time, effort, and money that develops interest and fan loyalty and results in an attractive product for the media. The jury in the present case obviously found that patient development of a loyal following among fans and an adherence to an original plan that offered long-run gains were lacking in the USFL.

Problem 11-2

After the ABL ceased operations in 1998, the WNBA has been the only women's professional basketball league in the United States. It currently has 12 teams, primarily in cities in which NBA teams play, including Atlanta, Chicago, Connecticut (Hartford), Dallas, Indiana (Indianapolis), Las Vegas, Los Angeles, Minnesota (Minneapolis), New York, Phoenix, Seattle, and Washington. It is a summer league that plays its games from mid-May through early October (when the NBA is not playing) to avoid any significant overlap with the NBA season. Each WNBA team has a roster of 11–12 players and plays 40 regular-season games. Assume that CBS nationally televises several regular-season games and all of the league's playoff games, and that the WNBA currently is negotiating with both ESPN and ESPN2 to televise more games in the future.

Because of the increasing popularity of women's professional basketball, a group of wealthy investors is seeking to resurrect the ABL as an 8-team league with franchises in different American cities than the WNBA's current clubs. The ABL plans to play a 24-game regular season, with each club having a roster of 10 players. The ABL's season will run from November through January.

The WNBA is considering whether the league should increase its regular season to 45 games and to have all 12 teams (rather than the current 8 teams with the best regular-season records) participate in the WNBA playoffs. This would extend the WNBA's season into November. It also is pondering whether to recommend that the league go forward with its recent plan to expand into Boston and Denver, two cities without current WNBA representation and in which ABL clubs will be located.

Would any of the WNBA's proposed actions violate §2 of the Sherman Act?

Professional Sports Labor Law and Labor Relations

INTRODUCTION

Contract, labor, and antitrust fields of law historically have been the most important areas of law regulating labor relations between professional athletes and either professional sports clubs and leagues or the organizers of individual performer sports events. From the 1970s to the present, the combination of these three areas of law has significantly influenced the development of professional sports in the United States. It is important to understand the basics and interrelated nature of contract, labor, and antitrust law as applied to labor relations.

CONTRACT LAW

KEY TERM • Negative injunction

Owners of the first professional sports teams encountered player contract problems almost from the outset of their business operations. When an outstanding player was contractually bound to play for a particular club, but another club desired his services, legal problems ensued.

A leading early case, *Philadelphia Ball Club, Ltd. v. Lajoie*, 51 A. 973 (Pa. 1902), emanated from conflicts associated with the formation of the American League in 1900. National League star Napoleon Lajoie attempted to leave the league's Philadelphia club before his player contract expired and join its crosstown rival in the new American League. Lajoie's club sought a court order preventing him from playing for another club during the period covered by his contract. Although it could not compel Lajoie to play for his current club, the court granted this request and explained:

> Where one person agrees to render personal services to another, which require and presuppose a special knowledge, skill, and ability in the employee, so that in case

of a default the same service could not easily be obtained from others, although the affirmative specific performance of the contract is beyond the power of the court, its performance will be negatively enforced by enjoining its breach. . . . The damages for breach of such contract cannot be estimated with any certainty, and the employer cannot, by means of any damages, purchase the same service in the labor market.

Id. at 973. Finding that Lajoie was an outstanding baseball player, the court concluded:

He has been for several years in the service of the plaintiff club, and has been re-engaged from season to season at a constantly increasing salary. He has become thoroughly familiar with the action and methods of the other players in the club, and his own work is peculiarly meritorious as an integral part of the team work which is so essential. In addition to these features which render his services of peculiar and special value to the plaintiff, and not easily replaced, Lajoie is well known, and has great reputation among the patrons of the sport, for ability in the position which he filled, and was thus a most attractive drawing card for the public. He may not be the sun in the baseball firmament, but he is certainly a bright particular star. We feel, therefore, that the evidence in this case justifies the conclusion that the services of the defendant are of such a unique character, and display such a special knowledge, skill, and ability, as renders them of peculiar value to the plaintiff, and so difficult of substitution that their loss will produce "irreparable injury," in the legal significance of that term, to the plaintiff. . . .

Id. at 974.

For more than a century, *Lajoie* has represented the prevailing judicial view regarding the availability of equitable relief to remedy a professional athlete's breach of contract. Pursuant to a "negative injunction," a player is not ordered to perform for a particular club but is instead ordered to not perform for any other club. A negative injunction may be granted if the court concludes that damages alone (which may be uncertain and very difficult to ascertain) are not an adequate legal remedy for the loss of a player's services. The *Lajoie* court concluded that a professional player of Lajoie's status was sufficiently special to merit injunctive relief to prevent the player's breach of contract. The court focused on the irreparable harm to Lajoie's club if it lost a player of his ability prior to the expiration of his contract, observing that "[h]e may not be the sun in the baseball firmament, but he is certainly a bright particular star."

In evaluating whether a professional athlete has "unique" skills, courts have reached different conclusions using various measures. In *Winnipeg Rugby Football Club v. Freeman*, 140 F. Supp. 365 (N.D. Ohio 1955), a federal court opined that even if the player was not unique by simply being a "good" National Football League (NFL) player, he might be unique in the Canadian Football League, where the quality of play might be lower. Thus, the player, who was in breach, was enjoined from playing for an NFL club. In *Dallas Cowboys Football Club, Inc. v. Harris*, 348 S.W.2d 37 (Tex. Civ. App. 1961), the court ruled that a player who played only for one year, with minimal success, could be found not "unique," but the subject player had not proved his "nonunique" status. Based on these cases and others, even if a court considers evidence that a player is not unique, the player has a substantial burden to prove this factually. Today, it is probably a safe assumption that those who make the major leagues in any sport are almost certain to be characterized as "unique."

The uniform player contracts in North American major leagues typically have a provision stating that the player acknowledges being unique and that a negative injunction can be obtained against the player if the player refuses to perform. Although this is not necessarily conclusive and a court might refuse to enforce this provision, it is highly unlikely. The greatest hurdle to obtaining a negative injunction relates to the injunction's scope and duration. If a court finds the requested injunction will create an unreasonable hardship to the party sought to be restrained, the injunction will be denied or its scope may be limited. What constitutes unreasonableness, or undue harshness, varies with the particular circumstances. Factors considered by a court may include the length of the requested injunction, its geographical reach, the types of employment or activities prohibited under the injunction, and its potential effects in preventing employment or other opportunities for the restrained party. However, these factors are balanced against the resulting damage to the plaintiff if an injunction is not granted.

In the absence of an express agreement, an injunction normally will not be imposed beyond the time period specified in the contract. For example, when basketball star Rick Barry decided to abandon the National Basketball Association (NBA) for the American Basketball Association (ABA) in the late 1960s, he had an option year (with the club holding the option) remaining on his NBA contract. Faced with an injunction barring his immediate move to the ABA, Barry simply sat out his option year and did not play for anyone. After that year, when Barry joined the ABA, his old NBA club sought a further injunction preventing him from playing in the ABA until he fulfilled his option year obligation. However, the court ruled that the duration of his contract had lapsed and that an injunction would not be granted for any additional length of time. See *Lemat Corporation v. Barry*, 275 Cal. App. 2d 671 (1969).

Today, there are professional leagues for many sports (e.g., soccer, basketball, baseball, and hockey) in several countries throughout the world. If a player breaches a contract with a club in one country by choosing to play with a club in another country, breach of contract litigation may have global implications. In *Boston Celtics v. Shaw*, 908 F.2d 1041 (1st Cir. 1990), a U.S. court ordered Brian Shaw to honor a valid contract with the Boston Celtics and not to breach this contract by playing basketball for an Italian professional team. Although the court could not require Shaw to play for the Celtics, it had the power to hold Shaw in contempt of court if he failed to honor his Celtics contract. Shaw ultimately complied with the court's negative injunction by playing for the Celtics rather than risking contempt sanctions by playing for the Italian club.

The duration and scope of an injunction may present complex issues when the activity contemplated in the contract is a single event, such as a tennis or golf tournament or a boxing match. For example, in *Lewis v. Rahman*, 147 F. Supp. 2d 225 (S.D. N.Y. 2001), Lennox Lewis, the former heavyweight champion of the world in boxing, claimed a contractual right to fight a rematch against Hasim Rahman, the heavyweight champion of the world at the time, within 150 days of an April 21, 2001, match in which Rahman had defeated Lewis. Lewis sought to enjoin Rahman from fighting another opponent before the rematch occurred. Granting the requested injunctive relief, the court stated:

> I find that Lewis would suffer irreparable harm were he denied the opportunity to regain his championship title. It is undisputed that the heavyweight championship is the most prestigious title in professional boxing. The opportunity to fight for the heavyweight championship, and especially the opportunity to regain the championship, cannot be measured in money. Because of his age, Lewis has only a limited time to regain his title and restore his reputation. Rahman, in contrast, is only 28 years old. Even if he chose not to box for 18 months, he would still have several productive years left in his career. Rahman concedes that he has a contractual obligation to fight Lewis in a rematch eventually, although he prefers to fight an interim bout. When asked if he wished to fight Lewis immediately, he said, "I don't have a problem with it." . . .
>
> A preponderance of the credible evidence shows that Lewis will not be able to fight for more than the next two years. Even during the next two years, his boxing abilities may diminish. An injunction for 18 months provides an effective remedy for Lewis' irreparable harm and does not unfairly impede Rahman. Cf. *Machen*, 174 F. Supp. at 529–531 (denying injunctive relief based on the finding that a limited injunction would be ineffective and an indefinite injunction would unduly burden the defendant). If I were to limit the injunction to 150 days, as Rahman urges, I would be permitting Rahman to escape his obligation by letting a short period of time elapse. As soon as Rahman complies with his obligation, he will be free to fight other bouts. The power to end the restriction is in his hands.

Id. at 232–37.

QUESTIONS

1. Why won't a court order a player under contract to play for his, her, or their current club?
2. How would a club's damages for a player's breach of contract be calculated? (Hint: The standard measure of damages for breach of contract is to award the nonbreaching party the "benefit of the bargain" expected to be gained if the contract had been fully performed by the breaching party.)

Problem 12-1

Driver Johnny Joe Milton has compiled an enviable record on the National Association of Stock Car Auto Racing (NASCAR) circuit since joining the Il Penseroso racing team two years ago. In fact, he has been so successful that he has attracted the attention of other race team owners, including Claude Forsooth. Despite the fact that Johnny has a year remaining on his three-year contract with Il Penseroso, not to mention two one-year options exercisable by Il Penseroso, Johnny agrees to leave that team and join Forsooth and his Formula One racing team. Though Johnny regrets leaving the NASCAR circuit, he looks forward to the new challenges of Formula One. He will race mainly in Europe in Grand Prix events but will also be in the United States for such races as the Indianapolis 500 (and two or three other similar events).

Il Penseroso's owner, Alfonse Allegro, is not about to allow Johnny to leave his team that easily. He points to wording in his written contract with Johnny whereby Johnny promises to render "his race driving services *exclusively*" to Il Penseroso for the term of the contract. Allegro files suit against Johnny for breach of contract and seeks a worldwide injunction to restrain him from racing for Forsooth for the three-year remaining duration of his contract.

Considering the governing law and practical realities, what would be the best-case resolution of this matter from the perspective of each of the parties?

LABOR LAW

KEY TERMS
- Mandatory subjects of bargaining
- National Labor Relations Act (NLRA)
- National Labor Relations Board (NLRB)
- Fair Labor Standards Act (FLSA)

The federal labor laws have had a profound impact on the development of professional sports leagues in the United States. If sports leagues engage in interstate commerce, which almost all do, they come under the aegis of these labor laws. Players are employees of teams; when players organize into groups to voice and advance their interests collectively, they become labor unions. To understand the effects of labor on professional sport more fully, we need to first consider the general role of the National Labor Relations Act (NLRA) and then analyze its application to the professional sports industries.

The NLRA, 29 U.S.C. §§151 et seq. was enacted by Congress in 1935. This statute, also known as the Wagner Act, and its numerous amendments (in particular, the Taft-Hartley Act of 1947 and the Landrum-Griffin Act of 1959) provide the basic legal structure governing management-workers relations in the United States. Section 7 of the NLRA provides three basic rights for workers: (1) the right to form, join, and assist labor organizations; (2) the right to bargain collectively through representatives chosen by the workers; and (3) the right to engage in "concerted activities" such as picketing and strikes to advance and protect their interests. 29 U.S.C. §157.

Section 8(a) of the NLRA sets forth prohibited employer conduct, including interference with employees' rights to organize and bargain collectively, interference with the formation or administration of a labor union, discrimination against employees to discourage union membership, retaliation against employees for exercising their rights, and refusing to bargain in good faith. 29 U.S.C. §158(a). All these prohibited employer actions may constitute unfair labor practices. The NLRA also prohibits unfair labor practices by a labor union; for example, a refusal to bargain collectively in good faith. 29 U.S.C. §158(b).

The oversight and enforcement of these rights comes under the jurisdiction of the National Labor Relations Board (NLRB) and the federal courts. The NLRB enforces the federal labor laws by adjudicating claims of "unfair labor practices" allegedly committed by either management or the union. The NLRB also administers the process that determines appropriate units or groups of employees qualified to vote in a union representation election. In addition, it conducts such elections to determine which, if any, union will represent all employees who are part of that unit.

The NLRB also determines which issues are subject to negotiation under the labor laws, delving into questions concerning the required scope of bargaining. Under the NLRA, scope of bargaining includes all issues relating to wages, hours, and terms and conditions of employment. 29 U.S.C. §158(d). Wages include pay, fringe benefits, and bonus payments; hours encompass time spent on the job; and working conditions cover factors influencing the work environment, such as work rules, seniority, and safety. Most importantly, these three areas—wages, hours, and working conditions—are considered mandatory subjects of bargaining. If either labor or management requests bargaining on issues that are mandatory under the labor laws, the other side must bargain over these issues in good faith. A failure to do so is an unfair labor practice that violates §8 of the NLRA. However, what actually constitutes wages, hours, or conditions of employment is not always crystal clear. In particular, it is not uncommon for labor and management to disagree regarding what is a condition of employment. Such disputes must be resolved by the NLRB.

If an issue is not a mandatory subject of bargaining, it is either an illegal or permissive subject. See *NLRB v. Wooster Div. of Borg-Warner Corp.*, 356 U.S. 342 (1958). It is an illegal subject of bargaining if one or more federal or state laws prohibit it from being implemented, even if it was successfully negotiated (for example, if the union and league agreed to pay some players less than the legally required minimum wage). If the subject is illegal, neither side has the freedom to bargain about such issues. If, however, a subject of bargaining is permissive, management may choose to negotiate with the union on that issue, but it is not required to do so and may choose instead to unilaterally include or impose terms and conditions regarding such issues.

For purposes of the NLRA, there are two additional important factors to consider. First, a union that is duly certified by the NLRB pursuant to the prescribed procedures becomes the exclusive bargaining agent for all employees within the unit. As a practical matter, all active players in a professional sports league with clubs in the United States come under the aegis of the union that has been chosen to represent them. Although a player is not required to become a member of the union that the NLRB recognizes, the player is bound by (and benefits from) the union's actions and the terms of any collective bargaining agreement (CBA) it negotiates with the league and its member clubs.

Second, those who are not currently active players for clubs in the league (as defined by the bargaining unit) are *not* members of the union and, as such, have no vote and little voice in union affairs. Even so, to a large extent, the actions of the union may determine or otherwise affect their rights. For example, college players who want to play professionally usually find that their eligibility to do so is determined by the CBA between the league and the players' union. (See the discussion of Maurice Clarett's unsuccessful litigation challenging the rule that three years must have elapsed since a player graduated from high school before being eligible for the NFL draft, *infra*.) The same may be true for foreign players and others, such as high school graduates seeking the opportunity to play in a unionized professional league. It is important to understand that the union does not represent former or retired players in collective bargaining negotiations or disputes with the league or its clubs because they are not members of the bargaining unit.

Until 1969, the NLRB was reluctant to assert jurisdiction over labor relations in the context of professional sports. However, in *American League of Professional Baseball Clubs and Association of National Baseball League Umpires*, 180 N.L.R.B. 190 (1969), the NLRB ruled that professional baseball is an industry affecting interstate commerce and, as such, is within the board's jurisdiction. This case, which involved the efforts of umpires to unionize, enabled professional athletes to form unions and avail themselves of the protections of the NLRA. Thus, the stage was set for the federal labor laws to govern labor relations in the professional sports industries.

Shortly thereafter, the first CBAs were entered in the major professional sports leagues. Labor and management reached rudimentary (by today's standards), but significant, agreements. Within months of each other, the National Basketball Association (NBA), National Football League (NFL), and Major League Baseball (MLB) all reached formal agreements with the players' unions in their respective sports. The National Hockey League (NHL) also reached a series of less formal agreements with the National Hockey League Players' Association.

The benefits to athletes of unionization and collective bargaining are perhaps most clearly seen when examining baseball's minor leagues. Since MLB players formed the Major League Baseball Players Association (MLBPA), MLB minimum salaries have increased by roughly 5,000 percent. Over the same time period, until minor league players unionized as a part of the MLBPA in 2022 and entered into a CBA with MLB, minor league salaries had increased by less than 100 percent. A Fair Labor Standards Act (FLSA) suit, *Senne v. Kansas City Royals Baseball*, 105 F. Supp. 3d 981 (N.D. Cal. 2015), brought in 2014 by a group of minor league players and settled in 2022 for $185 million, sparked the unionization effort. Under the CBA, which lasts until 2027, minor league pay is roughly twice what it was previously and minor league players are, for the first time, guaranteed housing. See Evan Drellich, *MLBPA, MLB Agree to First Minor-League CBA*,

Athletic, Mar. 29, 2023, *https://theathletic.com/4360686/2023/03/29/minor-league-bargaining-cba-mlbpa/?source=emp_shared_article*.

One group of athletes who have not yet unionized, but may soon do so, are esports athletes. Traditionally, these athletes have not unionized because competition has largely taken the form of tournament play without clear employee-employer relationships. As esports have grown more popular, however, leagues resembling traditional sports organizations have formed. As such, legal scholars argue that esports unions mirroring organizations such as the NFLPA or MLBPA are necessary and likely to emerge in the near future. See Laura C.S. Newberry, *The ABCs of Gaming: Activision, Biden, and Covid-19 Set the Stage for Labor Unionization in the Video Game Industry*, 2022 Wis. L. Rev. 1027 (2022); Kelsey F. Ridenhour, *Traditional Sports and Esports: The Path to Collective Bargaining*, 105 Iowa L. Rev. 1857 (2020).

The national labor laws, discussed above, are intended to guide relations between management and labor, but it is questionable whether they have effectively achieved this objective. Even so, the impact of national labor policy and regulation has been crucial in shaping and defining much of professional sports in the United States.

The rest of this section explores how labor law has influenced the development of North American major professional sports leagues and examines its application to the professional sports industries. Five important, interrelated areas are explored and analyzed: (1) the collective bargaining process; (2) drug testing in professional sports; (3) the activities of either a league and its clubs or of the players' union that constitute unfair labor practices under the NLRA; (4) the duty of a players' union to represent all of its members fairly; and (5) the labor arbitration process, which is established pursuant to the CBA to resolve disputes between players and the league or a club. Careful consideration of these topics provides a sense of the pivotal role that labor law and relations have played in the context of professional sports over the past approximately 50 years and also forecasts their future effects.

A. Collective Bargaining in the Professional Sports Industries

KEY TERMS
- Collective bargaining agreement (CBA)
- Competitive balance or luxury tax
- Free agency restrictions
- Reserve clause
- Salary cap
- Uniform player contract (UPC)

Prior to the dawn of CBAs, athletes were largely powerless vis-à-vis the clubs for which they played. Beginning in the 1890s with the National League in baseball, major professional leagues and their clubs have unilaterally established rules tying players to a particular team. Chief among these was the "reserve clause," a clause in a player's employment contract that purportedly gave a club perpetual rights to the player even after the player's contract expired. In some instances, as discussed *infra*, NFL, NBA, and NHL players have successfully challenged such free agency restrictions on antitrust grounds, a means of legal recourse not available to MLB players because of baseball's broad common law antitrust immunity. The CBA, however, has become the players' primary tool with which to assert power in their relationships with their clubs. This subsection of the chapter further explores the CBA concept and how it has taken hold in the professional sports industry.

A CBA is an agreement reached between the players' union and the owners' multiemployer bargaining unit, which prevails over a league's rules and any individual player-club agreements. The focus of collective bargaining between players and owners has shifted since the first CBAs in the late 1960s, which largely concentrated on player job security issues such as minimum salaries, fringe benefits such as health and life insurance, and pension plans. These are still important considerations, but three main issues driven by the changing economics of sports have dictated a shifting focus in collective bargaining negotiations. The first issue is the assignment of a player to a particular club through a draft of new or rookie players initially eligible to play in the league. The second issue involves free agency restrictions (i.e., limitations on a player's ability to play for another league club after contract expiration). Leagues contend that both a player draft and free agency restrictions are necessary to maintain competitive balance among their member clubs. Third, leagues have sought restrictions on aggregate player salaries by clubs through constraints such as team salary caps, competitive balance or luxury taxes, and other devices aimed at discouraging excessive spending. All of the foregoing restrictions directly affect players' wages and conditions of employment and are thus mandatory subjects of bargaining, which raise contentious issues in CBA negotiations and have triggered strikes or lockouts in all of the major professional leagues at one time or another. A fourth issue, which has become increasingly important in recent years, is the nature and scope of a league commissioner's authority to discipline players for off-field misconduct.

The NBA was the first league to institute a salary cap on the maximum amount that each club could annually pay in player salaries. This occurred in 1983, at a time when the NBA was clearly struggling financially. In an unprecedented move, the league opened its books for inspection. The picture was bleak. The players association (NBPA), through a CBA with the NBA, reluctantly acquiesced to a cap on player salaries, but it was fraught with vagueness. No one had contemplated the many ways in which its provisions could be circumvented. The chief exception, often used, was to pay salaries to a team's veteran players that sent the overall team salary far beyond the official league team limit. This became known as the "Larry Bird Exception," because the famous Celtics Hall of Famer was completing the final year of his first contract when the new CBA was to take effect. When the league and the union fashioned a method by which veterans were not penalized by the cap if their original team was willing to pay their asking price on the market, Bird was the prime example of the largesse accorded to the league's superstars. Since its inception, the NBA cap has gone through several revisions, including more explicit limits on both veteran and rookie salaries, but it still remains rather malleable in many respects, and is thus known as a "soft" cap.

Ten years after the NBA instituted its salary cap, the NFL instituted one of its own. The NFL, however, was able to get its players to agree to a "hard cap." Under this approach, a team maximum salary is determined each year based on prior and projected league revenues. Every team has to fit its total salaries into that maximum figure, with no give at the top. This sounds fairly simple, but it is not. The agreement has led to multiple schemes to restructure player contracts to free up room under the salary cap in a particular year. By this device, players enter into a new contract wherein their immediate salary is low, but a signing bonus gives them most of the money that would have been received under previous contracts. The signing bonus, however, is then allocated equally over the years of the new contract, thus reducing the club's immediate cap obligation. Another device to change a club's cap obligation is to have the player sacrifice the immediate income provided in their previous contract for even greater future rewards in a new agreement struck between the parties.

The economics of Major League Baseball breed local revenue disparities among large and small market clubs. In an effort to remedy this disparity, national broadcast, trademark licensing, and Internet (i.e., Major League Baseball Advanced Media (MLBAM)) revenues are equally shared among MLB clubs, and Commissioner Rob Manfred has broad authority to redistribute MLB central fund revenues created by each club's payment of a fixed percentage of its locally generated revenues. In addition, because MLB has never had a salary cap, it has collectively bargained attempts to curtail some clubs' profligate spending on player salaries by requiring them to pay some type of tax if their annual aggregate spending exceeds a certain amount. The first attempt was a so-called "luxury tax," which expired under the terms of the collective bargaining agreement provision that created it. The 2002 CBA created a "competitive balance tax," which is similar to the earlier tax and requires teams above a certain aggregate player salary level to pay a tax into MLB coffers for distribution to lower-income clubs. The "competitive balance tax" is also used to help finance an Industry Growth Fund, established in 1997, to "promote the growth of baseball in the United States and Canada, as well as throughout the world." With some negotiated modifications, this tax has continued to be a key feature of subsequent MLB CBAs.

The NHL had no salary cap or competitive balance tax through 2004, and the players had long staunchly opposed the imposition of any such salary controls. When the NHL CBA expired at the end of the 2004 season, however, the owners refused to enter a new CBA without a salary cap, which triggered a collective bargaining stalemate and led to the cancellation of the 2004–05 season. Only after a ten-month lockout did the NHL and NHLPA agree to a salary cap. The cap remains in place in the current NHL CBA, which has been extended to continue through the 2025–26 season.

Each league has a uniform player contract (UPC; also called a *standard player contract*) incorporated into its CBA. Although each league's UPC is distinct, they are all quite similar. As a collectively bargained agreement, the terms of the UPC (which frequently incorporate specific CBA terms) take precedence over the league's constitution, bylaws, and rules, as well as the provisions of individually negotiated contracts between clubs and players.

Unless prohibited or otherwise limited by the CBA or UPC, the following terms in individual player contracts generally are negotiable: (1) basic salary above the collectively bargained league minimum amount; (2) individual and team signing, roster, and performance bonuses; (3) guaranteed income clauses; (4) limitations on the assignment of a player's contract rights to other clubs; (5) additional economic protections in case of injury; and (6) length of contract.

Because player disciplinary sanctions for misconduct are mandatory subjects of collective bargaining, the players' union is empowered to protect the players' interests by negotiating with a sports league the conduct subject to discipline, sanctions for violations, and grievance or appeal mechanisms. In most instances, the union is able to limit the otherwise broad authority of a club or league commissioner to discipline players through effective use of the collective bargaining process. There generally is a collectively bargained range of disciplinary sanctions for on-field or off-field player misconduct that violates league or club rules promulgated to: (1) maintain competitive balance (e.g., doping, use of impermissible equipment, etc.); (2) preserve the sport's integrity (e.g., gambling, doping); (3) maintain the sport's public image (e.g., criminal conduct, domestic violence, doping); (4) protect player health and safety (e.g., violence injuring opposing player, doping); and (5) maintain team unity and appropriate decorum. Absent limits imposed by the CBA, courts generally provide a professional sports league and its clubs with substantial discretion to impose player discipline and are very deferential to their decisions. See, e.g., *Molinas v. NBA*, 190 F. Supp. 241 (S.D. N.Y. 1961) (upholding league commissioner's indefinite suspension of player for admittedly gambling on his team's games in violation of his contract and league rules). On the other hand, as discussed *infra*, an arbitrator may be more willing to reduce the severity of discipline imposed on a player by the league commissioner.

B. Drug Use in Professional Sports

Two categories of drugs have plagued professional sports in recent years: performance-enhancing drugs and "recreational" drugs. Some athletes use performance-enhancing drugs, such as anabolic steroids, despite associated health risks, to improve performance. The use of these banned drugs constitutes a form of cheating that provides an unfair competitive advantage over athletes not using these substances. Some athletes also, at times, use "recreational" drugs such as cocaine and ecstasy. Various questions arise when a professional sports league regulates either type of drug. One is whether, in that these drugs are generally illegal in United States' jurisdictions, detection and enforcement should be left to the criminal legal system. Another is whether sports club owners and leagues have any legitimate reason to interfere with the private decisions made by individual athletes, at least in instances when their on-field athletic performances are not impaired and no threat is posed to the safety of others. Marijuana, which is legal for recreational use in many states but illegal in others, presents a special case.

Three major issues differentiate the legal framework governing drug testing in professional sports as contrasted with those governing drug testing in interscholastic, intercollegiate, and Olympic sports (which are discussed in other chapters of this book). First, professional sports leagues are private entities. There are no public professional sports leagues, in contrast to the thousands of public universities and public high school systems. Thus, the U.S. Constitution does not provide the basis for any legal challenge to drug-testing programs in the professional ranks because no governmental or "state" action, which is required to assert federal constitutional law claims, is involved. Thus, players such as Terry Long of the Pittsburgh Steelers, who tested positive for anabolic steroids, have been unable to show a sufficient nexus between a professional sports league's drug policies and the actions of government officials or state actors to assert any federal constitutional claims such as violation of their privacy rights. *Long v. National Football League*, 66 F.3d 311 (3d Cir. 1994).

Second, despite the lack of federal constitutional law oversight, professional sports leagues are in many respects more constrained in their ability to implement drug testing programs than are universities or other educational institutions. Professional team sport athletes are usually employees either of a club, the league, or both. When athletes agree to have a union represent them, they gain the protections of the NLRA, pursuant to which drug testing programs are mandatory subjects of collective bargaining. Consequently, in unionized professional team sports, leagues and teams cannot unilaterally institute drug programs. Instead, they must be implemented through collective bargaining with the agreement of the players' union. Although one would expect a players' union to consent to a drug-testing program because drug usage has adverse health effects on players, a program's nature and scope, as well as sanctions for violations, often are the subject of considerable debate and negotiation. Individual athlete privacy concerns, the validity of testing measures for specific substances, and the consequences of proven drug usage have caused players' unions to have significant trepidation about wide-ranging testing procedures and the penalties for impermissible drug use. As new drugs enter the scene, and new pressures arise, problems multiply.

Third, a strong reason for union hesitancy to agree to stringent drug-testing programs is pressure from athletes and their agents. A great deal is at stake for professional athletes, arguably more so than for amateur athletes at the interscholastic and intercollegiate levels or even Olympic athletes. Professional careers may end prematurely through noncompliance with league drug-testing and treatment programs. Salaries, bonuses, and endorsement opportunities may be lost, often costing a professional athlete hundreds of thousands, even millions, of dollars. Economically, the stakes are high. Consequently, both the players' union and the clubs' multiemployer bargaining unit must scramble to reach reasonable solutions, with common ground and compromise frequently difficult to achieve.

In general, two overriding concerns need to be addressed and resolved if adequate drug-testing programs are implemented. One is the protection of the privacy of the individual athlete, to the greatest extent possible. In addition, there must be a clear and definite articulation of the program's purposes, procedures, and sanctions.

In 2005, several members of the U.S. Congress raised questions about performance-enhancing drug use by professional athletes, and various congressional committees held hearings. Subsequently, without any legislative action by Congress, the major professional sports leagues and their respective unions agreed to more extensive drug-testing measures and stricter penalties for violations. Current collectively bargained suspensions for a first drug-testing violation include 80 games for MLB players, 4 games for NFL players, 25 games for NBA players, 10 games for WNBA players, and 20 games for NHL players. These numbers increase significantly for subsequent offenses. For example, MLB players face a 162-game suspension for a second positive drug test and a lifetime ban (which can be lifted after two years by the MLB commissioner) for a third positive drug test.

League-imposed penalties for drug use, of course, do not preempt criminal penalties, and professional athletes' use of performance-enhancing drugs have on some occasions given rise to criminal prosecutions. Perhaps most notably, in 2011, MLB star Barry Bonds was tried for perjury and obstruction of justice in relation to a governmental investigation of steroid use in MLB. Several years earlier, federal authorities had seized drug-testing information for approximately 100 MLB players who tested positive for performance-enhancing drugs, reportedly including Bonds, David Ortiz, Manny Ramirez, Alex Rodriguez, and Sammy Sosa. The Ninth Circuit held that the seizure violated the players' federal constitutional rights, see *U.S. v. Comprehensive Drug Testing, Inc.*, 621 F.3d 1162 (9th Cir. 2010), and as a result, federal authorities were ordered to return the seized information to the MLBPA for destruction. The government was permitted to retain Bonds' positive test results and used them in securing his criminal conviction, but the conviction was ultimately overturned on appeal. MLB star Roger Clemens was federally prosecuted twice for perjury and obstruction of justice with respect to a steroid investigation, but unsuccessfully both times.

The outcomes of the Bonds and Clemens trials convinced some observers that high-profile MLB players accused of performance-enhancing drug use are — whether because of technicalities or expensive lawyers — more likely than not to "get off," and that criminal prosecutions are a waste of scarce government resources. Other observers argue that performance-enhancing drug development tends to outpace performance-enhancing drug detection technology, resulting in the continuous creation of undetectable performance-enhancing drugs. Although the decade-long inquiry that prompted the United States Anti-Doping Agency's August 2012 lifetime ban of renowned cyclist Lance Armstrong was widely hailed as a victory for the fight against doping, it starkly revealed (1) the myriad means by which athletes can manipulate drug-testing procedures (Armstrong passed over 500 drug tests during his career, never failed one, and was ultimately sanctioned only on the strength of circumstantial evidence and extensive testimony from fellow cyclists before finally admitting his doping history in a televised interview with Oprah Winfrey), and (2) the exorbitant costs involved in such investigations. See Alexander Wolff & David Epstein, *A Massive Fraud Now More Fully Exposed*, Sports Illustrated, Oct. 22, 2012, at 40.

QUESTIONS

1. Why should professional athletes be prohibited from using certain performance-enhancing substances (e.g., anabolic steroids) if they are willing to subject themselves to the associated health risks?
2. Do you believe the current professional sports league drug-testing programs adequately deter the use of banned substances by professional athletes? If not, what changes would you propose?
3. Considering both the challenges involved in administering performance-enhancing drug-testing programs and athletes' continued attempts to circumvent them (as illustrated by the Lance Armstrong discussion, above), should professional sports leagues abandon attempts to prohibit performance-enhancing drugs and instead permit and regulate them? One commentator writes:

> Imagine a world where performance enhancement was open and regulated. Instead of forcing athletes to sneak through back alleys to stay competitive, sports authorities should admit that drugs are essential—then help athletes cope with the side effects. Once legalized, drug use would still have limits, but they would be established by physicians and athletes—based on their ability to handle performance enhancers. Bad outcomes would be far less frequent if players were not forced to rely on quacks. . . . Innovation in performance enhancers would accelerate in the light of day.

Drea Knufken, *Could Doping Be Effectively Legalized, Regulated?*, Bus. Pundit, May 20, 2010, http://www.businesspundit.com/?s=Could+Doping+Be+Effectively+Legalized.

Do you agree with this argument?

Problem 12-2

You are the commissioner of the indoor professional lacrosse league for which the current CBA expires at the end of this year. Recently, several high-profile lacrosse players have been arrested for possession or use of illegal recreational drugs. Consistent with the World Anti-Doping Code, the international lacrosse federation has banned several athletes for two years for using performance-enhancing substances. What recommendations would you make to club owners regarding a drug-testing program for the league?

To address adequately the concerns of the players and their union regarding mandatory drug testing, note that a wide range of issues will have to be agreed on through collective bargaining with the lacrosse players' union, including the following:

1. Which players would be subject to testing? Would random testing be instituted, or would players be tested only if there was reasonable cause that they were using performance-enhancing substances?

2. How would the tests be conducted, and how often? Who would conduct tests, and with what safeguards? Would there be an opportunity to appeal a positive test result?
3. Which drugs are prohibited? How is this determined? What is the basis for initial selection? Can the list of prohibited drugs be expanded (or reduced), and by what procedure?
4. What are the sanctions for a positive test result? Mandatory treatment? Suspension? Loss of salary and other benefits?
5. What appeal procedures are available?

C. Unfair Labor Practices

KEY TERMS
- Exclusive bargaining representative
- Failure to bargain in good faith
- Impasse
- Lockout
- Multiemployer collective bargaining unit
- Strike
- Unfair labor practice

Section 8(d) of the NLRA imposes a mutual obligation on representatives of both management and labor "to meet at reasonable times and confer in good faith with respect to wages, hours, and other terms and conditions of employment," so-called mandatory subjects of collective bargaining. 29 U.S.C. §158(d). Either side's failure to bargain in good faith constitutes an unfair labor practice. However, this obligation "does not compel either party to agree to a proposal or require the making of a concession." *Id*. Labor disputes are to be resolved by collective bargaining or resort to economic coercion in the form of a strike by players or a lockout by league clubs.

The NLRB enforces the requirements of the NLRA and polices the unionization and collective bargaining processes. After issuance of an administrative complaint alleging that a party has committed an unfair labor practice, the NLRB may petition a federal district court for an injunction prohibiting a party from engaging in the alleged unfair labor practice pending its final resolution. 29 U.S.C. §160(j). After an administrative hearing, the NLRB is empowered to order either labor or management to cease and desist from engaging in any unfair labor practice. 29 U.S.C. §160(a). The NLRB may petition the appropriate federal circuit court for judicial enforcement of its order if either side refuses to comply with it. 29 U.S.C. §160(e).

In the context of professional sports, allegations of unfair labor practices have arisen in a variety of circumstances. A refusal by the league's multiemployer bargaining unit to bargain in good faith over a mandatory subject of collective bargaining is a relatively common allegation. Other illustrative examples of alleged unfair labor practices arising in the professional sports industries follow.

1. League Interference with Players' Rights to Unionize

Section 8(a) prohibits an employer from attempting to interfere with the rights of employees to choose freely which union represents them, or from discriminating against any employee to encourage or discourage union membership. 29 U.S.C. §158(a)(1) and (2). In September 2000, the NLRB filed unfair labor practice charges against the Arena Football League (AFL), alleging that its club owners both threatened players and illegally promised them benefits to coerce them to accept the Arena Football League Players Organizing Committee (AFLPOC) as their union. Two AFL players alleged that players had been illegally pressured to select AFLPOC—which was unduly sympathetic to league management and had been formed primarily at the club owners' behest to immunize them from antitrust liability—as their union. The NLRB found evidence that an uncoerced majority of players did not support AFLPOC. After the NLRB's complaint was filed, the AFL reached a settlement that resolved both the unfair labor practice claims and the pending antitrust litigation. Through the settlement, the players received a $5 million payment and regained the right to choose which union would represent them.

2. League Refusal to Recognize Union as Exclusive Bargaining Representative

Player associations in professional sports date as far back as the 1880s, but effective associations were not formed until the 1950s and 1960s. It was several years before these associations, functioning as unions, were able to obtain the first CBAs with the various major professional sports leagues. A difficult threshold task was obtaining full recognition as the players' exclusive bargaining representative, especially by a newly formed league. This was particularly true in the case of the now-defunct North American Soccer League (NASL). Two cases underscore the difficulties that a nascent union faced in its initial efforts to collectively bargain with NASL club owners. The legal principles developed in these cases have general application to labor relations involving professional team sports.

In *North American Soccer League v. National Labor Relations Bd.*, 613 F.2d 1379 (5th Cir. 1980), the NASL disputed the NLRB's certification of "all NASL players of clubs based in the United States" as the appropriate collective bargaining unit, which was requested by the players' union. The Fifth Circuit upheld the NLRB's determination that there is a "joint employer relationship" among the NASL and its member clubs:

> [T]he League exercises a significant degree of control over essential aspects of the clubs' labor relations, including but not limited to the selection, retention, and termination of the players, the terms of individual player contracts, dispute resolution,

and player discipline. Furthermore, each club granted the NASL authority over not only its own labor relations but also, on its behalf, authority over the labor relations of the other member clubs.

Id. at 1382.

The court concluded that a "leaguewide unit of players" for purposes of collective bargaining is appropriate:

> Notwithstanding the substantial financial autonomy of the clubs, the Board found they form, through the League, an integrated group with common labor problems and a high degree of centralized control over labor relations. In these circumstances the Board's designation of a leaguewide bargaining unit as appropriate is reasonable, not arbitrary or capricious.

Id. at 1383. This effectively required the NASL's member clubs to function as a multiemployer collective bargaining unit in labor relations issues with the players, which means that all clubs are represented by the same negotiator and are bound by the terms of the CBA.

Once certified, the union is the exclusive bargaining representative of the league's players. 29 U.S.C. §159(a). In *Morio v. North American Soccer League*, 501 F. Supp. 633 (S.D. N.Y. 1980), the court enjoined the NASL from refusing to collectively bargain with the players' union and continuing to negotiate contracts with individual players. To avoid undermining the union's authority, the league's "duty to bargain with the exclusive representative carries with it the negative duty not to bargain with individual employees." *Id.* at 639.

While there continue to exist disputes as to what constitutes the proper bargaining unit in a particular circumstance, leaguewide bargaining remains the norm in North American professional sports, even in cases in which a league includes clubs based in different nations (e.g., MLB, MLS, the NHL, and the NBA).

3. Retaliation Against Union Activists

Section 8(a)(3) prohibits an employer from discriminating against any employee to encourage or discourage union membership. 29 U.S.C. §158(a)(3). A club's release of a player or termination of the player's contract because of the player's union activities, if proved, is an unfair labor practice. The following case illustrates the difficulty of determining why a player involved in union activities was cut by a team and raises the question of whether federal labor law potentially interferes with a club's efforts to field its best possible team.

In *Nordstrom d/b/a Seattle Seahawks*, 292 NLRB 899 (1989), Sam McCullum asserted that the Seattle Seahawks NFL club cut him from the team's final roster in violation of §8(a)(3). McCullum started as a wide receiver for the Seahawks from 1976 through 1981. In 1981, his teammates selected him to be their union player representative. McCullum's union activities incurred head coach Jack Patera's ire, particularly for his orchestration of a "solidarity handshake" between his teammates and players on the opposing team prior to the first 1982 preseason game. Despite starting all of the Seahawks' 1982 preseason games, McCullum was cut shortly after the club acquired Roger Carr, another wide receiver.

McCullum and the National Football League Players Association claimed that his union activities were a "motivating factor" in the termination of his employment with the Seahawks. The club asserted that he would have been cut even without his participation in union activities based on his relative skills in comparison to the team's other wide receivers. The Seahawks claimed a stronger need for Carr's services and the inability to keep McCullum as a fifth wide receiver considering the need for players at other positions.

In a divided opinion, the NLRB affirmed the administrative law judge's ruling that McCullum's termination was illegal discrimination based on his role "as a fairly aggressive union spokesman." The board found that Patera's attempted heavy fines for team players' participation in the solidarity handshake evidenced his animus toward union activity, for which McCullum was the focal point. Patera also had the final authority regarding player cuts, and there was some evidence that Carr was acquired to enable McCullum's release because of his union activities. A dissenting NLRB member concluded that McCullum's release was a valid exercise of team management's business judgment regarding its personnel needs, which decision would have been made absent any antiunion motivation.

Section 8(a)(3) retaliation claims are, predictably, even more complex when athletes' right to unionize is unclear. Unlike NFL players, Ultimate Fighting Championship (UFC) fighters are not unionized. In February 2018, UFC fighter Leslie Smith launched an effort, dubbed Project Spearhead, to organize fighters into a union. Two months later, when Smith's contract with UFC expired, UFC declined to renew it. Smith attributed UFC's declination to its distaste for her organizing efforts, and, in May 2018, she filed an NLRB retaliation charge against UFC. In addition to the challenge that McCullum faced of establishing the adverse action at issue was related to his union activities, Smith had to establish the threshold requirement that UFC fighters are "employees" eligible under the NLRA to unionize and that the statute's anti-retaliation provisions protect her.

UFC classifies its fighters as independent contractors (who are not capable of unionizing under the NLRA) rather than employees (who are), but Smith alleged this is a misclassification. She argued that UFC exerts substantial control over the fighters (e.g., they must wear a required uniform, are restricted in how they may display their sponsors' names and logos, and may not participate in bouts organized by other combat organizations), and, therefore, the fighters should be considered employees.

In September 2018, the NLRB dismissed the matter but did not reach the issue of UFC's classification of its fighters. The Board found that although Smith provided sufficient evidence to establish that she tried to organize UFC fighters, she provided insufficient evidence to establish the UFC's nonrenewal of her contract was based on her union-organizing efforts. Finding as such, the NLRB determined it was "unnecessary to decide whether Smith is a statutory employee." *ZUFFA, LLC, d/b/a Ultimate Fighting Championship ("UFC") Case 04-CA-219498.*

4. Breach of Duty to Bargain in Good Faith or Provide Relevant Information Concerning Mandatory Subjects of Collective Bargaining

Both the league's multiemployer bargaining unit and the players' union have a duty to collectively bargain over wages, hours, and other terms and conditions of employment. The players' union generally wants to bargain over a wide range of issues, but league clubs may be reluctant to do so. The following material considers what constitutes mandatory subjects of collective bargaining in the context of professional sports labor relations as well as the parties' mutual obligation to provide the other side relevant information concerning these subjects.

Silverman v. Major League Baseball Player Relations Committee, Inc. (Silverman I)
516 F. Supp. 588 (S.D. N.Y. 1981)

Believing that [the] bargaining position [of Major League Baseball's Players Relations Committee (PRC)] on the issue of player "compensation" was based at least in part on the financial difficulties of certain member clubs, on May 7, 1981, the Players Association filed an unfair labor practice charge with the Board alleging respondents' failure to bargain in good faith by refusing to comply with the Players Association's request for financial disclosure in violation of Sections 8(a)(1) and (5) of the Act, 29 U.S.C. §§158(a)(1) and (5).

Following investigation and pursuant to Section 10(b) of the Act, 29 U.S.C. §160(b), the Board filed a complaint charging respondents with violating Sections 8(a)(1) and (5) of the Act [and sought a court order requiring the PRC to provide the requested financial information]. . . .

The Board alleges in its petition that the public statements by club owners regarding claims of financial difficulties created a reasonable belief on the part of the Players Association that respondents' bargaining position during this second round of negotiations was based, "at least in part, on the present or prospective financial difficulties of certain of Respondents' member clubs." Although Marvin Miller has expressed some doubt as to club owners' inability to pay rising player salaries, he nevertheless takes the position that the Players Association must have the financial information it requests if it is to fulfill its duty of fair representation. If deprived of that information, the Association claims that it must blindly decide whether to press its demands and risk the loss of jobs for its members if the clubs cannot survive under the "compensation" terms proposed by the Association, or to recede from its position and accept the PRC's proposal without verifying owners' claims of financial distress caused by "free agency." Thus, the Association brought an unfair labor practice charge against the PRC for its failure to disclose the requested financial data after the clubs allegedly put into issue their inability to pay. . . .

Petitioner admits that at no time during bargaining sessions have respondents made a claim of inability to pay. Nevertheless, petitioner urges the Court to find that public statements made by several club owners as well as the Commissioner of Baseball about the financial condition of the industry are sufficient to support a finding of reasonable cause to believe that respondents have injected the inability to pay into the negotiations.

The cases cited by petitioner in support of its position are simply inapposite. In each case, inability to pay was put in issue at the bargaining table. . . .

Thus, Petitioner concedes, as it must, that the Board and courts have never found that an employer has injected financial condition into negotiations, absent statements or conduct by the employer at the bargaining table. Nevertheless, it urges this Court to find, on the basis of statements by Commissioner Kuhn and various owners, that the financial issue has become relevant to the negotiations regarding "compensation" because of the unique nature of collective bargaining in baseball. . . .

It is the PRC Board of Directors which is charged with the exclusive authority to formulate the collective bargaining position of the clubs and to negotiate agreements with the Players Association. Indeed, Grebey, the official spokesman for the PRC in collective bargaining matters, has consistently denied that the clubs' financial status is at issue in the current negotiations. . . .

In a multi-employer bargaining unit as large and publicly visible as the Major League Baseball Clubs, it is inevitable that extraneous statements will be made by individuals affiliated in some way with the group which are inconsistent with the official position of the unit. This only underscores the necessity, recognized by the PRC, for centralized bargaining responsibility and authority. Clearly, individual expressions of opinion cannot serve to bind the entire bargaining unit in the absence of authority to speak for the group. . . .

The Act has provided for collective bargaining between the parties through their authorized representatives. If this Court were to find that the several public statements by club officials and the Commissioner were sufficient to support a finding that the PRC and its negotiating team view the respondents' "compensation" proposal as related to the financial condition of the clubs, it would do violence to the intent and purpose of the Act which limits the jurisdiction of this Court. . . .

NOTE

Labor dispute legal requirements and options. The *Silverman I* judge was following well-established legal precedent in finding that the PRC's refusal to provide the MLB Player Association with the requested financial information does not constitute an unfair labor practice. It generally takes more than a few outsider comments, even by owners, about potential economic hardship to require the clubs to open their books. In general, league clubs prefer not to disclose information about their finances. However, there have been some instances in which disclosure of league financial information has occurred. In 1982, the NFLPA filed a successful unfair labor practices claim, pursuant to which the NFL was required to divulge the terms of its television contracts to allow the players association to evaluate its fair share of such proceeds. In 1982–1983, the NBA voluntarily opened its books to demonstrate to players the tenuous state of its finances, thus leading to the first professional sports CBA with an aggregate player salary cap.

In *Silverman v. Major League Baseball Player Relations Committee, Inc.*, 880 F. Supp. 246 (S.D. N.Y. 1995) (*Silverman II*), the court distinguished between mandatory and permissive subjects of collective bargaining. The case provides guidance on the role that labor law plays in regulating unilateral action by a league's multiemployer bargaining unit in a labor dispute. It ruled:

> Having freely entered into the free agency and reserve systems in their Basic Agreement, the Owners are bound to that system until they bargain in good faith to an impasse.
>
> In view of the abundant case law in the professional sports context that has found that constituent parts of the reserve/free agency system are mandatory subjects of collective bargaining, I find that the Board had substantial reasonable cause to conclude, and a substantial likelihood of success ultimately in establishing, that the unilateral changes made by the Owners to the free agency system before impasse violated the rule against changes to mandatory subjects of bargaining. In summary, the Board has clearly met its injunctive remedy standard in demonstrating that the Owners committed an unfair labor practice by their unilateral abrogation of Article XX(F) and the free agency system. . . .

Id. at 257.

In an effort to ensure stable, peaceful labor relations, the federal labor laws require the league and its member clubs to maintain the status quo when the CBA expires. The expired CBA's terms must remain in effect until the parties reach a new agreement, bargaining negotiations reach an impasse, or the collective bargaining process ends by the players' decertification of their union or an extremely long impasse accompanied by the defunctness of the league's multiemployer bargaining unit. An "impasse" is "a recurring feature in the bargaining process, . . . a temporary deadlock or hiatus in negotiations which in almost all cases is eventually broken, through either a change of mind or the application of economic force." *Charles D. Bonanno Linen Service, Inc. v. NLRB*, 454 U.S. 404, 412 (1982). If there is an impasse in collective bargaining negotiations, which is frequently a recurring part of this process, the league may (but is not required to) unilaterally implement new terms and conditions of player employment "'reasonably comprehended' within [its] preimpasse proposals (typically the last rejected proposals)" if it has bargained in good faith and has not otherwise committed any unfair labor practices. *Brown v. Pro Football, Inc.*, 518 U.S. 231, 238 (1996). However, if a league does so, it invites a strike by the union or the union's filing of unfair practice charges with the NLRB alleging that there is no impasse or that the league failed to bargain in good faith. Alternatively, the players may terminate the union's status as their collective bargaining representative and bring an antitrust suit claiming that the unilaterally imposed new terms and conditions of employment are an unreasonable restraint of trade.

5. Discrimination Against Striking Players

Players have a statutory right to strike, which is an important aspect of U.S. labor law and is designed to facilitate peaceful and productive collective bargaining relations. If the players strike, league clubs may choose to hire replacement players for the duration of the strike, as the NFL did during the 1987 three-week strike by its players. In the alternative, a professional sports league may cease operations and lock out its players, as the NHL did in 2004 and 2012, as both the NFL and NBA did in 2011, and as MLB did in 2021. In the case of a strike, as set forth in *NFL Management Council and NFLPA*, 309 N.L.R.B. 78 (1992), leagues and their member clubs are prohibited from retaliating against striking players. In that matter, the NFL sought to punish striking players, and the NLRB ruled it illegal:

> In sum, the Respondents' Wednesday deadline prohibited employees who returned from the strike on October 15 from playing in the following weekend's games and prohibited their Club from paying them for that game on the basis of their absence from the Club during the strike. The only players subject to such restrictions were those who chose to participate in the strike, a concerted activity protected by the Act. Players absent from their Club for other reasons were not subject to any similar restriction on their eligibility to participate in games; players ineligible to play for other reasons were nevertheless still entitled to be paid. Accordingly, for the reasons stated above, we find that the Respondents' maintenance and enforcement of its Wednesday deadline rule violated Section 8(a)(1) and (3) of the Act. . . .
>
> To remedy the unfair labor practices which we have found, we shall order the Respondents to cease and desist, and to take certain affirmative action necessary to effectuate the purposes of the Act. Specifically, we shall order the Respondents to make whole all employees who were denied wages and declared ineligible for the games played on October 18 and 19, 1987, on the basis of the Respondents' Wednesday eligibility rule for strikers, with interest computed in the manner set forth in the judge's decision. The Respondents shall also make whole those injured players denied compensation on account of their participation in the strike in the manner set forth in the judge's decision. . . .

Id. at 83–87.

QUESTIONS

1. In each of the major professional sports leagues (e.g., NFL, NBA, WNBA, MLB, NHL, NWSL, MLS), do club owners or players have greater economic leverage to exercise in a labor dispute?
2. Section 8(d) of the NLRA defines mandatory subjects of bargaining as "wages, hours, and other terms and conditions of employment." Consider which of the following examples are mandatory subjects of bargaining:
   a. Whether players can be fined for leaving the bench and going onto the field when there is an altercation among other players
   b. The dimensions of a hockey rink or soccer field

c. The establishment of the universal designated hitter rule in baseball
   d. The expansion or contraction of the number of teams in a league, including which teams and locations will be affected

D. Union's Duty of Fair Representation

The NLRB has determined that a union's breach of its duty of fair representation is an unfair labor practice. *Miranda Fuel Co.*, 140 N.L.R.B. 181 (1962). In the sports industry, however, it can be difficult to determine when such a breach comes to pass. This is because labor unions representing professional athletes face unique challenges. They must represent the diverse interests of hundreds or thousands of extremely talented athletes who have overcome difficult odds to rise to the top of a very elite profession. The small number of athletes who ever get the chance to play their sport at a major league level for even a brief period is far outnumbered by those who seek and fail to do so. Even within the membership ranks of players, there are significant divisions, with a spectrum that includes relatively few superstars, several very good players, numerous marginal players, and some perennial benchwarmers.

The career of a major league professional athlete is, on average, very short in relation to most other careers; for example, the average NFL player's career is approximately 3.25 years. Thus, the substantial economic rewards that may be gained in the brief time allotted to a professional athlete must be maximized. That is why professional athletes have turned to agents, attorneys, accountants, marketing specialists, and others in an effort to maximize their earning potential. It is also why the task of the labor union representing them is difficult.

The NLRA grants a union exclusive negotiating and other rights to act on behalf of all members of the collective bargaining unit. As a result, the union has the ability and authority to sacrifice or compromise particular players' rights to further the collective good of all players. In 1944, the U.S. Supreme Court held that the NLRA implicitly requires a union to fairly represent all members of the collective bargaining unit, *Steele v. Louisville & Nashville Railroads*, 323 U.S. 192 (1944), which has been interpreted to include incoming rookie players and those currently ineligible to play in the league (e.g., Maurice Clarett, discussed *infra*).

Because the nonstatutory labor exemption, discussed *infra*, precludes any antitrust challenge to the terms of the CBA, the union's duty to fairly represent all current and prospective players' interests is particularly important. But, breach of this duty has seldom been proved in the sports context. In *Peterson v. Kennedy*, 771 F.2d 1244, 1253 (9th Cir. 1985), the Ninth Circuit explained:

> A union breaches its duty of fair representation only when its conduct toward a member of the collective bargaining unit is "arbitrary, discriminatory, or in bad faith." The duty is designed to ensure that unions represent fairly the interests of all of their members without exercising hostility or bad faith toward any. It stands "as a bulwark to prevent arbitrary union conduct against individuals stripped of traditional forms of redress by the provisions of federal labor law." . . .
>
> The Supreme Court has long recognized that unions must retain wide discretion to act in what they perceive to be their members' best interests. . . . To that end, we

have "stressed the importance of preserving union discretion by narrowly construing the unfair representation doctrine." . . . We have emphasized that, because a union balances many collective and individual interests in deciding whether and to what extent it will pursue a particular grievance, courts should "accord substantial deference" to a union's decisions regarding such matters.

A union's representation of its members "need not be error free." . . . We have concluded repeatedly that mere negligent conduct on the part of a union does not constitute a breach of the union's duty of fair representation. . . .

E. Labor Arbitration

KEY TERM • Law of the shop

Most disputes between a league and the players' union (or a player and his or her club) regarding the meaning of terms in the CBA, UPC, or individual player contract are resolved by an independent arbitrator mutually selected by the league and players' union for each sport. Although arbitration decisions do not have the same precedential effect as court decisions, arbitrators generally consider previous arbitration awards when resolving similar issues, particularly those in the same league.

In contract dispute arbitration, the arbitrator usually is given broad authority to construe the meaning of the parties' contract(s) and to grant appropriate relief to the nonbreaching party, including damages and ordering an action that is necessary to remedy a breach of contract. For example, an arbitrator ordered basketball player Brian Shaw, discussed *supra*, to comply with the terms of his new contract with the Boston Celtics, which meant: (1) rescinding the second year of Shaw's contract with an Italian club; and (2) requiring that he not play for any other club for the duration of his Celtics' contract. *Boston Celtics Ltd. Partnership v. Shaw*, 908 F.2d 1041 (1st Cir. 1990) (judicially confirming labor arbitration award).

Arbitration by an independent arbitrator also is generally used to resolve player legal challenges to discipline imposed by the club or league for on- and off-field misconduct. The union typically files a grievance on the player's behalf and represents the player in the arbitration proceeding. The arbitrator determines whether the league or club had "just cause" to impose the challenged disciplinary sanction, which is upheld if this standard has been met, or nullified or reduced if it has not. See, e.g., *NBA Players Association on Behalf of Player Latrell Sprewell and Warriors Basketball Club and NBA* (Feerick, Arbitrator; May 4, 1998) (reducing NBA's one-year suspension of Latrell Sprewell to 68 games with $6.4 million loss of salary for attacking Golden State Warriors head coach P.J. Carlesimo twice during a team practice). The NFL CBA, interestingly, provides for an arbitration system in which the commissioner may serve as arbitrator in some matters (e.g., alleged "conduct detrimental" to the league) but not in others (e.g., alleged violations of the "personal conduct policy"). Predictably, this scheme has spawned confusion and raised questions about partiality.

Both MLB and the NHL use a collectively bargained arbitration process to resolve salary disputes between teams and individual players, which is available only in limited situations but has far-reaching effects on player salaries within the league. The MLB CBA's salary arbitration provisions generally apply only to players who have between three and six years of credited major league service. One of the most notable aspects of baseball salary arbitration is that it utilizes "final offer arbitration." This means that, without knowing what the other side will submit as a salary figure, the team and the player each submit an amount for a one-year contract. This requires substantial thought by both parties, because the arbitration panel must select one figure or the other. There can be no compromise. Thus, if the matter is decided by arbitration, the end result will be a one-year, nonguaranteed contract (with no bonuses) at a salary submitted by the club or the player.

Unlike MLB's final offer arbitration, the NHL's salary arbitration system is premised on a conventional arbitration model. Like MLB's system, the NHL's salary arbitration system contains eligibility requirements that must be met in order for players to seek salary arbitration. Procedures are in place for selecting arbitrators, and limitations are imposed on the factors the arbitrator can consider in determining a player's compensation. Because it is based on a conventional arbitration model, the salary determined by the arbitrator can be the offer of either the player or the club, or any amount ranging between the two offers. Another notable difference is the binding effect of the arbitrator's award. Generally, the arbitrator's decision is final and binding on both the player and club. However, clubs have a limited right to reject a salary award (a walk-away right), which may be exercised no more than three times in two continuous years and not more than twice in the same year. If this right is exercised, the player becomes a free agent. If the player does not receive a better offer from another team, the player may accept the last offer the player received before becoming a free agent.

Although an arbitration award generally binds only the parties thereto, some awards have broader implications and have significantly altered the way in which a league conducts its business with players. For example, the following 1976 arbitration involving baseball players Dave McNally and Andy Messersmith invalidated MLB's nearly 100-year-old reserve clause, which had been unilaterally imposed by the clubs and unsuccessfully challenged in the *Flood v. Kuhn* antitrust litigation. This arbitration award effectively laid the groundwork for a collectively bargained system of free agency for MLB players.

National & American League Professional Baseball Clubs v. Major League Baseball Players Association

66 Labor Arbitration 101 (1976)

SEITZ, Arbitrator.

The Chairman understands the dispute in arbitration to be as follows: The Association claims that the terms of the Uniform Player Contracts of [Andy] Messersmith and [Dave] McNally, respectively, having expired, the two players are at liberty to negotiate contract relationships with any of the other clubs in the leagues and that they are not to be regarded as having been "reserved" by the Los Angeles and Montreal clubs, respectively, in such manner as to inhibit clubs from dealing with them.

The leagues and the clubs assert that the terms of the contracts of these players have not expired; that they are still under contract; and that, in any event, the grievants have been duly "reserved" by their respective clubs; and, accordingly, they are not free to deal with other clubs for the performance of services for the 1976 season; nor are such other clubs free to deal with them for that season excepting under circumstances and conditions not here obtaining. . . .

The league's argument is based on the language in §10(a) of the Player's Contract that the Club "may renew this contract for the period of one year *on the same terms*" (emphasis supplied); and that among those "terms" is the right to further contract renewal.

In the law of contract construction, as I know it, there is nothing to prevent parties from agreeing to successive renewals of the terms of their bargain (even to what has been described as "perpetuity"), provided the contract expresses that intention with explicit clarity and the right of subsequent renewals does not have to be implied. . . .

There is nothing in Section 10(a) which, explicitly, expresses agreement that the Players Contract can be renewed for any period beyond the first renewal year. The point the leagues present must be based upon the implication or assumption, that if the renewed contract is "on the same terms" as the contract for the preceding year (with the exception of the amount of compensation) the right to additional renewals must have been an integral part of the renewed contract. I find great difficulties, in so implying or assuming, in respect of a contract providing for the rendition of personal services in which one would expect a more explicit expression of intention. . . .

Traditionally, the leagues have regarded the existence of a contract as a basis for the reservation of players. In Club's Exhibit No. 15 there is set forth the Cincinnati Peace Compact of the National and American Leagues, signed January 10, 1903 — probably the most important step in the evolution and development of the present Reserve System. In that document it provided:

Second — A *reserve rule* shall be recognized, by which each and every club may reserve *players under contract*, and that a uniform contract for the use of each league shall be adopted. (Emphasis supplied.)

This emphasis on the existence of a contract for reservation of a player to be effective was perpetuated in the Major League Rules. . . .

Thus, I reach the conclusion that, absent a contractual connection between Messersmith and the Los Angeles Club after September 28, 1975, the Club's action in reserving his services for the ensuing year by placing him on its reserve list was unavailing and ineffectual in prohibiting him from dealing with other clubs in the league and to prohibit such clubs from dealing with him.

In the case of McNally whom the Montreal Club had placed on its disqualified list, a similar conclusion has been reached. . . .

I am not unmindful of the testimony of the Commissioner of Baseball and the Presidents of the National and American League given at the hearings as to the importance of maintaining the integrity of the Reserve System. It was represented to me that any decision of the Arbitration Panel sustaining the Messersmith and McNally grievances would have dire results, wreak great harm to the Reserve System and do serious damage to the sport of baseball.

Thus, for example, it was stated that a decision favoring these grievants would encourage many other players to elect to become free agents at the end of the renewal years; that this would encourage clubs with the largest monetary resources to engage free agents, thus unsettling the competitive balance between clubs, so essential to the sport; that it would increase enormously the already high costs of training and seasoning young players to achieve the level of skills required in professional baseball and such investments would be sacrificed if they became free agents at the end of a renewal year; that driven by the compulsion to win, owners of franchises would over-extend themselves financially and improvident bidding for players in an economic climate in which, today, some clubs are strained, financially; that investors will be discouraged from putting money in franchises in which several of the star players on the club team will become free agents at the end of a renewal year and no continuing control over the players' services can be exercised; and that even the integrity of the sport may be placed in hazard under certain circumstances.

I do not purport to appraise these apprehensions. They are all based on speculations as to what may ensue. Some of the fears may be imaginary or exaggerated; but some may be reasonable, realistic, and sound. After all, they were voiced by distinguished baseball officials with long experience in the sport and a background for judgment in such matters much superior to my own. However, as stated above, at length, it is not for the Panel (and especially the writer) to determine what, if anything, is good or bad about the reserve system. The Panel's sole duty is to interpret and apply the agreements and undertakings of the parties. If any of the expressed apprehensions and fears are soundly based, I am confident that the dislocations and damage to the reserve system can be avoided or minimized through good faith collective bargaining between the parties. There are numerous expedients available and arrangements that can be made that will soften the blow — if this decision, indeed, should be regarded as a blow. This decision is not the end of the line by any means. The parties, jointly, are free to agree to disregard it and compose their differences as to the reserve system in any way they see fit. . . .

However strong my conviction that the basic dispute should be determined by the parties, in collective bargaining rather than by an Arbitration Panel, that Panel could not justify any further delay, and the accompanying Award, accordingly, is being rendered. The parties are still in negotiation, however, and continue to have an opportunity to reach agreement on measures that will give assurance of a reserve system that will meet the needs of the clubs and protect them from the damage they fear this decision will cause, and, at the same time, meet the needs of the players. . . .

Grievance upheld.

NOTES

1. Aftermath. The MLB club owners were given advance notice of the arbitrator's probable resolution of the Messersmith and McNally grievances. Rather than attempting to reach a new agreement with the players regarding free agency restrictions, the club owners appealed the arbitrator's decision to the federal courts. In *Kansas City Royals v. Major League Baseball Players Association*, 532 F.2d 615, 632 (8th Cir. 1976), the Eighth Circuit upheld the *Messersmith-McNally* arbitration decision:

> The arbitration panel had jurisdiction to hear and decide the Messersmith-McNally grievances, that the panel's award drew its essence from the collective bargaining agreement, and that the relief fashioned by the District Court was appropriate. Accordingly, the award of the arbitration panel must be sustained, and the District Court's judgment affirmed. In so holding, we intimate no views on the merits of the reserve system. We note, however, that Club Owners and the Players Association's representatives agree that some form of a reserve system is needed if the integrity of the game is to be preserved and if public confidence in baseball is to be maintained. The disagreement lies over the degree of control necessary if these goals are to be achieved. Certainly, the parties are in a better position to negotiate their differences than to have them decided in a series of arbitrations and court decisions. We commend them to that process and suggest that the time for obfuscation has passed and that the time for plain talk and clear language has arrived. Baseball fans everywhere expect nothing less.

After going through an initial period of readjustment, in which every MLB player then in the American League or National League was given one opportunity to be a free agent and to sign a contract with the club of his choosing, the owners and players entered into a new CBA providing that a player can earn free agent status after six years of credited major league service, which remains the standard today.

2. Judicial review of arbitration awards. An arbitration award is final and binding on the parties, but it is subject to judicial review by a federal court under the Labor Management Relations Act. Although an arbitrator's "evident partiality" is a ground for vacating an arbitration award, the party challenging the award has the "heavy burden" of proving that the parties' agreed arbitrator had "improper motives." See, e.g., *Williams v. NFL*, 582 F.3d 863, 885-886 (8th Cir. 2009) (rejecting NFLPA's claim that an arbitration award by Jeff Pash, the NFL's general counsel, is inherently partial because the NFL CBA provided that "the Commissioner or his designee will preside as Hearing Officer" and resolve the dispute). A court's review of the merits of an arbitration award is very limited, and the award will be vacated only on very narrow grounds. In *Major League Baseball Players Association v. Garvey*, 532 U.S. 504, 509 (2001), the U.S. Supreme Court explained:

> Courts are not authorized to review the arbitrator's decision on the merits despite allegations that the decision rests on factual errors or misinterprets the parties' agreement.

We recently reiterated that if an "arbitrator is even arguably construing or applying the contract and acting within the scope of his authority," the fact that "a court is convinced he committed serious error does not suffice to overturn his decision." It is only when the arbitrator strays from interpretation and application of the agreement and effectively "dispenses his own brand of industrial justice" that his decision may be unenforceable. When an arbitrator resolves disputes regarding the application of a contract, and no dishonesty is alleged, the arbitrator's "improvident, even silly, factfinding" does not provide a basis for a reviewing court to refuse to enforce the award.

One of the most closely followed and contentious sagas in American sports history involved judicial review of arbitration awards. When the Indianapolis Colts played the New England Patriots in the NFL's 2015 AFC Championship game, the Colts suspected that the Patriots under-inflated their footballs (each NFL club is responsible for providing the balls its team will use on offense) to satisfy quarterback Tom Brady's preference for softer, easier-to-grip balls. The Colts believed that, in light of the cold and rainy conditions, the under-inflation may have been providing Brady and the Patriots a particular unfair advantage. At halftime, league officials tested all of the game balls, and while all of the Colts' balls were within the NFL's permissible 12.5–13.5 pounds per square inch range, all of the Patriots' balls fell below it. Thus began a two-year legal battle, which came to be known as "Deflategate."

Within the week, the league retained a law firm to conduct an independent investigation, which ultimately concluded that it was "more probable than not" that two Patriots equipment managers purposely deflated the balls and that Tom Brady had been "at least generally aware" of their actions. The law firm also reported that Brady had impaired the investigation by refusing "to make available any documents or electronic information (including text messages and emails)." It was later determined that during the investigation, Brady ordered his assistant to destroy Brady's cell phone. NFL Commissioner Roger Goodell suspended Brady for four games and then, pursuant to an unorthodox CBA provision that permits the NFL Commissioner or his designee arbitral power, Goodell affirmed the suspension he handed down. The league then brought an action in federal court to confirm the arbitration award, and the NFLPA countered with an action to vacate the award. The two cases were consolidated, and in *National Football League Management Council v. National Football League Players Association*, 125 F. Supp. 3d 449 (S.D. N.Y. 2015), the court vacated Commissioner Goodell's arbitration award. The court determined that Goodell "failed to draw [his] award from the essence of the collective bargaining agreement" because Brady had no notice that a player's involvement in deflating footballs during a game and his failure to cooperate in an ensuing league investigation would result in the same discipline (i.e., a four-game suspension) that applied to a player who violated the NFL Policy on Anabolic Steroids and Related Substances for the first time. *Id.* at 465. The court reasoned: "It is the '*law of the shop*' to provide professional football players with (advance) notice of prohibited conduct and of potential discipline (italics added.). . . . Because there was no notice of a four-game suspension in the circumstances presented here, Commissioner Goodell may be said to have 'dispense[d] his own brand of industrial justice.'" *Id.* at 466.

On appeal, however, the United States Court of Appeals for the Second Circuit reversed the lower court's decision. The Second Circuit found that Commissioner Goodell properly exercised his broad discretion under the CBA, which "empowers the Commissioner to take disciplinary action against a player whom he 'reasonably judge[s]' to have engaged in 'conduct detrimental to the integrity of, or public confidence in, the game of professional football.'" *Id.* at 537. The NFLPA claimed that the commissioner improperly suspended Brady because Brady did not have adequate notice that his conduct could lead to a suspension, but the court concluded the provision of the CBA relied on by the NFLPA only listed minimum disciplinary actions that "do not foreclose suspensions." *Id.* at 539. The Second Circuit also rejected the NFLPA's claim of impartiality in the commissioner "adjudicat[ing] the propriety of his own conduct." *Id.* at 548. The court noted that "the parties contracted in the CBA to specifically allow the Commissioner to sit as the arbitrator. . . . They did so knowing full well that the Commissioner had the sole power of determining what constitutes 'conduct detrimental,' and thus knowing that the Commissioner would have a stake both in the underlying discipline and in [the] arbitration." *Id.* As such, it held, "the parties to an arbitration can ask for no more impartiality than inheres in the method they have chosen." *Id.*

THE INTERSECTION OF ANTITRUST AND LABOR LAW

KEY TERMS
- Anticompetitive effect
- Curt Flood Act of 1998
- Decertification
- Nonstatutory labor exemption
- Procompetitive effect
- Rule of reason
- Statutory labor exemption

One of the more perplexing aspects of labor relations in professional team sports is the inherent tension between, and intersection of, federal antitrust and labor law.

The objective of federal antitrust law is to promote competition among buyers and sellers of goods and services, including labor. Section 1 of the Sherman Antitrust Act prohibits agreements that unreasonably restrain interstate trade or commerce. 15 U.S.C. §1. Applied literally, §1 prohibits both employees and employers from engaging in joint activity or making agreements that unreasonably restrain the labor market. Section 1 requires employers in an industry (e.g., league clubs) to compete independently for employee (e.g., player) services. Similarly, employees must individually compete for employment. Theoretically, consumers will benefit because the operation of free market forces in the labor market will result in the most efficient allocation of human resources.

In the 1970s, players sought to use antitrust law to advance their economic interests by challenging leagues' unilaterally imposed labor market restraints such as player drafts and free agency restrictions. NFL players successfully challenged the then-existing 16-round draft and certain free agency restrictions on antitrust grounds. See, e.g., *Smith v. Pro Football, Inc.*, 593 F.2d 1173 (D.C. Cir. 1978); *Kapp v. National Football League*, 586 F.2d 644 (9th Cir. 1978); *Mackey v. Nat'l Football League*, 543 F.2d 606 (8th Cir. 1976). Antitrust litigation challenging similar restraints that had been unilaterally implemented by the NBA and NHL also was successful. *Robertson v. Nat'l Basketball Assn.*, 389 F. Supp. 867 (S.D. N.Y. 1975); *Philadelphia World Hockey Club, Inc. v. Philadelphia Hockey Club, Inc.*, 351 F. Supp. 462 (E.D. Pa. 1972). From the players' perspective, the antitrust laws became powerful weapons for effectuating changes in how sports leagues conduct business vis-à-vis the players. (Notably, MLB's unique antitrust exemption barred professional baseball players' antitrust claims. *Flood v. Kuhn*, 407 U.S. 258 (1972).)

On the other hand, federal labor law permits employees of private employers, including professional athletes, to unionize and collectively bargain, which is an allowable form of anticompetitive behavior that reduces economic competition among them regarding employment opportunities. Multiemployer bargaining within an industry pursuant to which one entity represents all employers, which is similarly anticompetitive, is also legal under labor law. Such concerted action among otherwise competing groups of employees (e.g., players) and employers (e.g., league clubs) squarely conflicts with §1 of the Sherman Act.

To resolve this conflict, Congress enacted two statutes (§6 of the Clayton Act and the Norris-LaGuardia Act), the combined effect of which is to create a *statutory labor exemption*, which provides a labor union with immunity from antitrust liability for its unilateral efforts to further its members' economic interests. Thus, in general, union collective bargaining activities over issues of wages, hours, and conditions of employment, as well as strikes, picketing, and boycotts of employers, do not violate the antitrust laws. *United States v. Hutcheson*, 312 U.S. 219 (1941). To facilitate the collective bargaining process, courts have held that the activities of multiemployer bargaining units to further their members' common interests, such as collective strike insurance and lockouts, also are protected by the statutory labor exemption. *Kennedy v. Long Island Rail Road Co.*, 319 F.2d 366 (2d Cir. 1963), *cert. denied*, 375 U.S. 830 (1963).

The statutory labor exemption, which applies only to unilateral union conduct such as collective bargaining and strikes, does not immunize the terms of CBAs with employers from antitrust challenge on the ground that they are anticompetitive terms and conditions of employment. In *Connell Construction Co. v. Plumbers, Local 100*, 421 U.S. 616, 622 (1975), the Supreme Court recognized the need for a nonstatutory labor exemption to further "the strong labor policy favoring the association of employees to eliminate competition over wages and working conditions" through collective bargaining.

Courts have created a broad nonstatutory labor exemption, which not only precludes the parties from challenging the terms of an existing CBA on antitrust grounds, but also precludes any antitrust litigation even after the CBA expires, so long as there is an ongoing collective bargaining relationship between the league and its players. This furthers the strong U.S. labor policy that permits employees, including professional athletes, to unionize and engage in collective bargaining concerning their wages and working conditions.

In a series of cases, federal appellate courts held that the nonstatutory labor exemption immunized the terms of existing CBAs from antitrust attack by any of the parties subject to those terms (i.e., league players and clubs), thereby permitting league clubs and the players' union to agree to contract terms such as a player draft, salary cap, and free agency restrictions that otherwise may violate antitrust laws. *Wood v. Nat'l Basketball Assn.*, 809 F.2d 954 (2d Cir. 1987); *McCourt v. California Sports, Inc.*, 600 F.2d 1193 (6th Cir. 1979); *Reynolds v. National Football League*, 584 F.2d 280 (8th Cir. 1978). In *Clarett v. Nat'l Football League*, 369 F.3d 124 (2d Cir. 2004), *cert. denied*, 544 U.S. 961 (2005), the Second Circuit held that the nonstatutory labor exemption precludes a prospective player from bringing an antitrust challenge to eligibility requirements in a CBA that prevented him from playing NFL football for a particular period of time, specifically until three NFL seasons have elapsed since the date of his actual or expected high school graduation. The court ruled that the union has the exclusive authority to negotiate the terms and conditions of prospective NFL players' employment (e.g., requiring that at least three full college seasons have elapsed since their high school graduation before they are eligible to be drafted or signed as free agents). Eligibility rules are a mandatory subject of collective bargaining between the league and the players' union because they pertain to players' wages, hours, and other terms and conditions of employment. As part of its efforts to obtain a CBA providing the best overall deal for all NFL players, federal labor law gives the union the ability to disadvantage one category of players (e.g., prospective players) vis-à-vis other players (e.g., those who meet the eligibility requirement) if doing so does not breach its federal labor law duty of fair representation or violate federal laws prohibiting unfair labor practices or employment discrimination.

In *Powell v. Nat'l Football League*, 930 F.2d 1293 (8th Cir. 1989), *cert. denied*, 498 U.S. 1040 (1991), the Eighth Circuit extended the scope of the nonstatutory labor exemption by ruling that the terms of an expired CBA (which labor law generally requires the league to maintain in effect until a new CBA is reached) do not lose their antitrust immunity even if the players' union and the league multiemployer collective bargaining unit reach an impasse (i.e., a temporary deadlock) in their efforts to negotiate a new agreement.

In 1996, in *Brown v. Pro Football, Inc.*, 518 U.S. 231 (1996), the U.S. Supreme Court expanded the scope of the nonstatutory labor exemption even further by holding that it bars antitrust litigation challenging new terms and conditions of employment unilaterally imposed by the league so long as there is an ongoing collective bargaining relationship with the players. In that case, the Court held that the exemption shielded all restraints on the labor market for players' services (e.g., player drafts, team salary caps, and player free agency restrictions) from antitrust challenge because that ongoing relationship existed. Specifically, the NFL clubs had unilaterally established a maximum weekly salary of $1,000 for all developmental squad players (i.e., nonroster players) after collectively bargaining to impasse. The players argued that this conduct was illegal wage-fixing in violation of §1 of the Sherman Act, but the Court ruled that they could not bring their antitrust claim:

> [T]he [nonstatutory] antitrust exemption applies to the employer conduct at issue here. That conduct took place during and immediately after a collective-bargaining negotiation. It grew out of, and was directly related to, the lawful operation of the bargaining process. It involved a matter that the parties were required to negotiate collectively. And it concerned only the parties to the collective-bargaining relationship.

518 U.S. at 250.

The Court, however, explained that its holding "is not intended to insulate from antitrust review every joint imposition of terms by employers, for an agreement among employers could be sufficiently distant in time and in circumstances from the collective bargaining process that a rule permitting antitrust intervention would not significantly interfere with that process." *Id.* It suggested that the nonstatutory labor exemption would end if the players terminated the collective bargaining process with the league by decertification of their union, which would then permit the players to bring an antitrust suit challenging any expired CBA terms or agreements among league clubs that restrained the market for their services. *Decertification* is a formal process requiring that at least 50 percent of the players vote to decertify the union in an NLRB-supervised election. If this occurs, they cannot vote to reunionize (and thereby engage in collective bargaining with the league) before the lapse of a 12-month period.

Because of the broad scope of the nonstatutory labor exemption, it generally precludes professional athletes from using antitrust law to resolve labor relations disputes. However, there are three general situations in which it is inapplicable, and courts will consider the merits of antitrust challenges to anticompetitive restraints on the terms and conditions of professional athletes' employment.

First, players in team sports can choose not to unionize (in the case of a newly formed professional league) or they (including MLB players) may decertify their union, thereby preventing or discontinuing the collective bargaining process and negating the applicability of the nonstatutory labor exemption. A federal statute, the *Curt Flood Act of 1998*, 15 U.S.C. §26b, limits the otherwise broad scope of baseball's common law antitrust immunity (see Chapter 11). Because the *Curt Flood Act* is not intended to affect judicial construction and application of the nonstatutory labor exemption, *unionized* MLB players do not have any antitrust remedies. 15 U.S.C. §26b(d)(4). Like players in other professional sports leagues, MLB players could decertify their union to challenge any unilaterally imposed terms and conditions of their employment on antitrust grounds. If they do so, the Act expressly permits antitrust challenges only to conduct or agreements "directly relating to or affecting employment of MLB players to play baseball at the major league level." 15 U.S.C. §26b(a). It does not provide a basis for challenging conduct or agreements relating to employment as a minor league baseball player, the amateur or first-year player draft, or any reserve clause applied to minor league players. 15 U.S.C. §26b(b)(1).

Second, courts generally hold that the nonstatutory labor exemption does not bar an antitrust challenge by nonparties to CBA terms that have anticompetitive effects outside the internal league labor market for players' services. In *Philadelphia World Hockey Club, Inc. v. Philadelphia Hockey Club, Inc.*, 351 F. Supp. 462 (E.D. Pa. 1972), the court ruled that this exemption does not preclude a rival league's claim that the NHL's reserve clause violates the antitrust laws. The World Hockey Association (WHA) prevailed on its antitrust claim by proving that the reserve clause in the NHL's CBA, which provided an NHL club with rights to a player's services for three years after his contract expired, deprived the WHA from competing for the services of players with the ability to play major league professional hockey. The WHA needed access to such players in order to produce major league professional hockey in competition with the NHL.

Third, the nonstatutory labor exemption does not apply to individual-performer sports, such as tennis, golf, and boxing. See, e.g., *Blalock v. Ladies Prof'l Golfers Assn.*, 359 F. Supp. 1260 (N.D. Ga. 1973) (finding that golfer's one-year suspension imposed by the LPGA with "completely unfettered, subjective discretion" by a group of her competitors violates the antitrust laws). Professional athletes in individual-performer sports are generally independent contractors rather than employees who have the right to unionize and engage in collective bargaining activities. Even if athletes in the sport form a players' association and enter into agreements with event promoters or organizers, this generally does not constitute unionized collective bargaining under the federal labor laws or make the nonstatutory labor exemption applicable.

Because there are several circumstances in which antitrust litigation is not barred by the nonstatutory labor exemption, we must examine briefly the developing framework of antitrust analysis applicable to challenged labor market restraints. Most litigation seeking to invalidate player labor market restraints involves claimed violations of §1 of the Sherman Act, which requires concerted conduct that unreasonably restrains trade. In *McNeil v. NFL*, 790 F. Supp. 871 (D. Minn. 1992), the court held that agreements among league clubs to reduce competition for player services are subject to §1. However, courts recognize that some agreement among league clubs regarding the permissible scope of competition for player services is necessary to jointly produce competitive games attractive to fans; therefore, a league's need for competitive balance among its clubs is an important factor to be considered when assessing the reasonableness of the particular challenged player restraints. *McNeil v. Nat'l Football League*, 1992 WL 315292 at *4 (D. Minn. 1992).

Because the unique features of the sports industry require some uniform rules and agreements among competing teams in order to produce on-field competition that is appealing to consumers, *National Collegiate Athletic Association v. Board of Regents of the University of Oklahoma*, 468 U.S. 85, 101 (1984), courts generally apply the flexible *rule of reason* on a case-by-case basis to determine whether particular restraints affecting the market for player services violate the antitrust laws rather than automatically invalidating them. See, e.g., *Nat'l Hockey League Players' Assn. v. Plymouth Whalers Hockey Club*, 325 F.3d 712 (6th Cir. 2003); *McNeil v. Nat'l Football League*, 790 F. Supp. 871 (D. Minn. 1992).

Applying the rule of reason to player restraints requires complicated analysis and balancing of several different factors and their economic effects. Considering the validity of the NBA's then-current draft eligibility rules, one court observed:

> The primary disadvantages of the "rule of reason" are that it requires difficult and lengthy factual inquiries and very subjective policy decisions which are in many ways essentially legislative and ill-suited to the judicial process. For instance, in the present case, a complex economic inquiry would be required to determine the economic necessity of action of this type. In addition, the court would be required to determine a standard which could be used to weigh the various public policy goals which might be alleged as justification by the NBA. The court would further be forced to determine whether the [player restraint] was genuinely motivated by the purposes given or by other reasons. Frequently, these motives are closely intertwined.

See *Denver Rockets v. All-Pro Mgmt.*, 325 F. Supp. 1049, 1063 (C.D. Cal. 1971).

Under the rule of reason, a player must prove that the challenged restraint has the anticompetitive effect of reducing economic competition among league clubs for player services. For example, agreements among league clubs to fix players' wages, which thereby eliminate individual salary negotiations, have clear anticompetitive effects. *McNeil v. Nat'l Football League*, 790 F. Supp. 871 (D. Minn. 1992). Because their adverse economic effects are not as direct and less clear, other labor market restraints such as player drafts, free agency restrictions, and related forms of allocating players among league clubs may require detailed market analysis to determine their effects on economic competition. In such cases, the plaintiff must prove the relevant market for the services of players and that the defendant league and its clubs have a sufficiently large market share to adversely affect competition. The relevant market has both a product and a geographical component. The product market includes all prospective purchasers of player services that are reasonable substitutes from the players' perspective in terms of earning potential, prestige, and other economic factors. *Smith v. Pro Football, Inc.*, 593 F.2d 1173, 1185 n.48 (D.C. Cir. 1979) (finding that employment in the Canadian Football League is not reasonable substitute for employment with an NFL team). The geographical market is the geographical area "to which players can turn, as a practical matter, for alternate opportunities for employment" as professional athletes. *Fraser v. Major League Soccer, LLC*, 284 F.3d 47, 63 (1st Cir. 2002), *cert. denied*, 537 U.S. 885 (2002) (upholding jury finding of an international market for the services of professional soccer players).

If the player proves the requisite anticompetitive effects, the league (and its clubs) must prove the challenged restraint is necessary to achieve the procompetitive effect of enhancing a professional sports league's ability to more effectively compete with other forms of entertainment. *Sullivan v. NFL*, 34 F.3d 1091, 1111–13 (1st Cir. 1994). In *American Needle, Inc., v. NFL*, 560 U.S. 183 (2010), the Supreme Court recognized that a professional sports league's interest in maintaining on-field competitive balance among its member clubs is "legitimate and important," which is "unquestionably [a procompetitive] interest that may well justify a variety of collective decisions made by teams." Even if it furthers this objective, a labor market restraint may be invalidated if there is a less restrictive means of achieving this objective. *Smith v. Pro Football, Inc.*, 593 F.2d 1173, 118 (D.C. Cir. 1979) (holding that the NFL's 16-round draft violated §1 of the Sherman Act because "significantly less anticompetitive alternatives," such as a draft of fewer rounds, exist as a means of maintaining competitive balance among NFL teams).

As an illustration of how courts have applied the rule of reason to labor market restraints, see *Mackey v. NFL*, 543 F.2d 606, 620–22 (8th Cir. 1976):

> The focus of an inquiry under the Rule of Reason is whether the restraint imposed is justified by legitimate business purposes, and is no more restrictive than necessary. . . .
>
> In defining the restraint on competition for players' services, the district court found that the Rozelle Rule [which required NFL Commissioner Pete Rozelle to award compensation in the form of players, draft choices, or both from the club that contracted with a free agent player to his former club if they could not agree on compensation for the player] significantly deters clubs from negotiating with and signing free agents; that it acts as a substantial deterrent to players playing out their options and becoming free agents; that it significantly decreases players' bargaining power in contract negotiations; that players are thus denied the right to sell their services in a free and open market; that as a result, the salaries paid by each club are lower than if competitive bidding were allowed to prevail; and that absent the Rozelle Rule, there would be increased movement in interstate commerce of players from one club to another.
>
> We find substantial evidence in the record to support these findings. Witnesses for both sides testified that there would be increased player movement absent the Rozelle Rule. . . .
>
> In support of their contention that the restraints effected by the Rozelle Rule are not unreasonable, the defendants asserted a number of justifications. First, they argued that without the Rozelle Rule, star players would flock to cities having natural advantages such as larger economic bases, winning teams, warmer climates, and greater media opportunities; that competitive balance throughout the League would thus be destroyed; and that the destruction of competitive balance would ultimately lead to diminished spectator interest, franchise failures, and perhaps the demise of the NFL, at least as it operates today. Second, the defendants contended that the Rozelle Rule is necessary to protect the clubs' investment in scouting expenses and player development costs. Third, they asserted that players must work together for a substantial period of time in order to function effectively as a team; that elimination of the Rozelle Rule would lead to increased player movement and a concomitant reduction in player continuity; and that the quality of play in the NFL would thus suffer, leading to reduced spectator interest, and financial detriment both to the clubs and the players. Conflicting evidence was adduced at trial by both sides with respect to the validity of these asserted justifications.
>
> The district court held the defendants' asserted justifications unavailing. . . . The court further concluded that elimination of the Rozelle Rule would have no significant disruptive effects, either immediate or long term, on professional football. In conclusion the court held that the Rozelle Rule was unreasonable in that it was overly broad, unlimited in duration, unaccompanied by procedural safeguards,

and employed in conjunction with other anticompetitive practices such as the draft, Standard Player Contract, option clause, and the no-tampering rules.

We agree that the asserted need to recoup player development costs cannot justify the restraints of the Rozelle Rule. That expense is an ordinary cost of doing business and is not peculiar to professional football. Moreover, because of its unlimited duration, the Rozelle Rule is far more restrictive than necessary to fulfill that need.

We agree, in view of the evidence adduced at trial with respect to existing players' turnover by way of trades, retirements and new players entering the League, that the club owners' arguments respecting player continuity cannot justify the Rozelle Rule. . . .

In sum, we hold that the Rozelle Rule, as enforced, unreasonably restrains trade in violation of §1 of the Sherman Act. . . .

QUESTIONS

1. What is the statutory labor exemption, and what conduct does it preclude from being challenged on antitrust law grounds?
2. What is the nonstatutory labor exemption, and according to *Brown*, why does it bar any antitrust claims as long as there is an ongoing collective bargaining process between a league's clubs and players?
3. What are MLB players' options under federal labor law if MLB and its clubs unilaterally impose a team salary cap after the current CBA expires?
4. Consider whether a team salary cap unilaterally imposed by MLB clubs would violate §1 of the Sherman Act.

Representing Players and Teams: The Athlete-Agent Industry

The use of agents by professional athletes can be traced back to the mid-1920s, when Charles Pyle negotiated a football contract and endorsement and movie deals for National Football League (NFL) player Harold "Red" Grange. The proliferation in the number and use of agents by athletes occurred in the 1960s and 1970s as a result of the demise of reserve and option clauses in standard-form contracts between players and clubs; competition for players between rival leagues (e.g., the NFL and the American Football League (AFL)); the growing strength of labor unions and their positive impact on players' salaries; players' increased need for advice on matters ranging from taxes to estates; and the increase in players' opportunities to generate outside income through endorsement contracts.

The proliferation in the use of agents has also been accompanied by an expansion in the range of services that they perform. The role of agents extends beyond the commonly held belief that their job is to negotiate a player's contract with his or her club. The functions performed by agents include contract negotiation; endorsement advice and solicitation; tax, estate, and financial planning; and career, personal development, legal, insurance, and sports medicine consultation. Walter T. Champion, Jr., *Attorneys Qua Sports Agents: An Ethical Conundrum*, 7 Marq. Sports L.J. 349, 351–52 (1997). Agents also assist athletes in brand building by leveraging endorsements, digital content, and philanthropy.

The range of services that athlete agents perform is indicative of the breadth of substantive expertise required for agents to effectively represent athletes. Few people, however, have the ability or expertise to perform all the tasks identified above. Perhaps out of ignorance or greed, some agents take on more than they can competently handle. Unless they are affiliated with an agency that employs individuals with diverse professional expertise, agents may well overreach and perform at levels approaching negligence. Despite the useful services provided by agents, inappropriate agent conduct that is detrimental to athletes is a reality of the athlete-agent industry. This chapter examines various legal mechanisms that regulate the athlete-agent relationship and seek to enhance the likelihood that agents and athletes fulfill their respective obligations. This matrix consists of a web of common law rules, state and federal legislation, and regulations promulgated by players' associations.

THE NATURE OF THE ATHLETE-AGENT RELATIONSHIP

A. The Agent's Basic Duties

KEY TERMS
- Agent
- Fiduciary
- Principal

This section examines the legal duties that agents owe to their athlete clients and the standard of care adopted by courts to determine if those duties are competently performed. The agent's relationship with athletes is governed by many of the basic contract principles introduced in Chapter 3. Agency law principles also play a major role in governing the agent-client relationship. The following excerpt[1] introduces basic agency law principles and provides the legal framework within which to consider the materials in this chapter:

> The agency relationship is defined as "the fiduciary relationship which results from the manifestation of consent by one person to another that the other shall act in his behalf and subject to his contract, and consent by the other so to act." The principal is "the one for whom action is to be taken." In the sports context, the athlete is the principal. The agent is "the one who is to act" for the principal. The essential nature and character of the agency relationship is that the principal authorizes his agent to contract on his behalf with one or more third parties." [Restatement (Second) of Agency, §1(1) (1958).]
>
> These definitions tell us that the agency relationship is consensual—typically expressed in a contract. This is certainly the case in the sports context in which the major sports leagues have developed model contracts for the agent/principal relationship. For example, the National Football League Players Association (NFLPA) has developed a "Standard Representation Agreement" for mandatory use by agents and their football-player clients. [T]he NFLPA agreement sets forth general principles including the concept that the "Contract Advisor" acts "in a fiduciary capacity." . . .
>
> The above definitions relating to agency also inform us that the most basic obligations that agents owe to their principals are defined not only by contract, but by the fiduciary characteristics of the relationship. A fiduciary is defined as "one who acts primarily for the benefit of another." [Restatement (Third) of Agency §1.01 (2006).] Consequently, the essence of the principal/agent relationship spawns a fundamental obligation that the "agent owes his principal the fiduciary duty of undivided loyalty and the duty to act in good faith at all times. This fiduciary relationship is imposed by law upon the agent because the very nature of the agency relationship involves the principal entrusting his fortune, reputation, and legal rights and responsibilities to his

---

[1] Originally published in Kenneth L. Shropshire, Timothy Davis & N. Jeremi Duru, The Business of Sports Agents (3d ed. 2015). Reprinted with permission of the University of Pennsylvania Press.

agent whose actions, for better or worse, vitally affect the economic well-being and reputation of the principal." Leonard Lakin and Martin Schiff, The Law of Agency 2 (Kendall/Hunt 2d ed. 1996), at 97.

[I]t is an agent's duty to carry out the desires of its principal. This certainly makes sense, as the agent acts not to carry on its own business affairs, but those of the principal. Thus it is the agent's duty to act in accordance with his or her principal's instructions even if the agent believes they are unwise. As stated by two commentators, "[a]n agent has the duty to obey all of his principal's lawful instructions no matter how arbitrary or capricious any of those instructions seem to the agent or anyone else. . . . By contrast, if the principal's instructions are illegal, immoral, unethical, or opposed to public policy, as where the principal instructs his agent to bribe another to obtain business for his principal, the agent has no duty to obey." *Id.* at 97–98. Moreover, by acting on its principal's behalf, the agent assumes a duty that it "possesses a degree of skill commensurate with the job to be done and that he will use such skill with diligence." *Id.* at 124. In exercising this duty of reasonable care and skill, it is important to emphasize that the agent does not guarantee or ensure that he or she will achieve the result desired by the client unless the agent has expressly agreed to do so. Rather the agent has fulfilled his or her duty by acting with the care and skill employed by a reasonable person under the same circumstances. . . .

Another basic duty of the agent to the principal seems particularly relevant in the sports context. The agent must account to its principal for all of the principal's funds that come into the agent's possession as a part of the agency relationship. *Id.* at 100. Other basic duties that the agent owes to the principal include the duty to comply with the law, the duty to notify the principal of all matters that may affect the principal's interests, and the duty not to delegate their performance to another without the consent of the principal. *Id.*

Finally, the agent owes a duty of loyalty and good faith to its principal. This duty precludes an agent from acting on behalf of parties adverse to his or her principal. Courts have attempted to incorporate these core concepts into rulings addressing matters ranging from agent malpractice to conflict of interest. . . .

In summary, the agent-athlete relationship is governed primarily by contract law principles. In addition, the agent is viewed as having a fiduciary relationship with the athlete. A fiduciary is defined as "one who acts primarily for the benefit of another." Duties that flow from the fiduciary character of the relationship between athletes and agents include the duties of loyalty and good faith.

B. The Agent's Standard of Care

As noted above, agents agree to perform certain services and athletes agree to pay for those services. Athletes sometimes assert that they have been relieved of their payment obligation because an agent failed to provide competent services. In addition to arguing that agents have provided substandard service, athletes assert that agents breached other obligations or engaged in illegal conduct. The *Zinn* case, which follows, examines the legal principles that courts use in assessing whether agents performed their services competently, which imposes obligations on athletes to pay for those services.

Zinn v. Parrish
644 F.2d 360 (7th Cir. 1981)

BARTELS, Judge.

[Editors' note: Leo Zinn, an experienced agent, negotiated Lamar Parrish's first NFL contract with the Cincinnati Bengals. Zinn received a commission of 10 percent of Parrish's $16,500 salary. Thereafter, on April 10, 1971, Zinn and Parrish signed a one-year renewable representation agreement, under which Zinn agreed to "use 'reasonable efforts' to procure pro-football employment for Parrish." Under the agreement, Zinn also agreed, at Parrish's request, to (1) negotiate job contracts, (2) furnish advice on business investments, (3) secure professional tax advice, (4) obtain endorsement contracts, and (5) attempt to secure for Parrish "gainful off-season employment."

Between 1971 and 1973, Zinn negotiated base salaries and bonuses for Parrish. In 1974, Zinn negotiated a three-year contract for Parrish that saw Parrish's yearly base salary increase from $35,000 to $250,000 (the salary increase was a result of competition between the NFL and the rival World Football League (WFL) for players' services). Zinn performed a number of other services at Parrish's request, including assisting Parrish in purchasing a residence and an apartment building to be used for rental income, assisting in managing the apartment building, forwarding to Parrish the stock purchase recommendations of other individuals, negotiating an endorsement contract, unsuccessfully attempting to obtain off-season employment for Parrish, and arranging for Parrish's taxes to be prepared each year by H&R Block.

Shortly after he signed the 1974 series of contracts with the Bengals, Parrish informed Zinn (orally, and later in writing) that he "no longer needed his services." He also stated he would not pay Zinn a 10 percent commission on those contracts. Zinn sued Parrish for breach of contract, alleging he was entitled to receive commissions totaling $304,500 plus interest.]

We consider next the district court's judgment that Zinn failed to perform the terms and conditions of his contract. . . . [T]he court concluded that Zinn "was unable to and did not provide the services which he was obligated to provide by the contract under which he sues."

Employment Procurement

Zinn's obligation under the 1971 Management Contract to procure employment for Parrish as a pro football player was limited to the use of "reasonable efforts."

Parrish had no objection to Zinn's performance under the professional management contract for the first three years up to 1973, during which time Zinn negotiated football contracts for Parrish. A drastic change, however, took place in 1974 when a four-season contract was negotiated with the Bengals for a total of $250,000 plus a substantial signing bonus. At that time, the new World Football League came into existence and its teams, as well as the teams of the Canadian Football League, were offering good terms to professional football players as an inducement to jump over to their leagues from the NFL. In order to persuade Parrish to remain with the team, the Bengals club itself first initiated the renegotiation of Parrish's contract with an offer of substantially increased compensation. This was not surprising.

Parrish claims, however, that Zinn should have obtained offers from the World Football League that would have placed him in a stronger negotiating position with the Bengals. . . . Given what Zinn accurately perceived as the unreliability of any offers he might have obtained from the WFL, his representation of Parrish during this period was more than reasonable. . . . We conclude that up to that point, it is impossible to fault Zinn in the performance of his contract, nor can we find any basis for Parrish to complain of Zinn's efforts in 1974 with respect to procuring employment for him as a pro-football player.

Other Obligations

Zinn was further obligated to act in Parrish's professional interest by providing [other services]. Each of these obligations was subject to an implied promise to make "good faith" efforts to obtain what he sought. . . . Under Illinois law, such efforts constitute full performance of the obligations. . . . Until Parrish terminated the contract, the evidence was clear that Zinn made consistent, good faith efforts to obtain off-season employment and endorsement contracts. Indeed the district court found that Zinn at all times acted in good faith, with a willingness "to provide assistance within his ability." The district court confused success with good faith efforts in concluding that Zinn's failure to obtain in many cases jobs or contracts for Parrish was a failure to perform. Moreover, Zinn did give business advice to Parrish on his real estate purchases, and he did secure tax advice for him.

[Editors' note: The court ruled that Zinn had the right to recover a 10 percent commission on all amounts earned by Parrish under the 1974, 1975, 1976, and 1977 Bengals contracts.]

QUESTIONS

1. The athlete-agency relationship is defined as a "fiduciary relationship." What are the special characteristics of a fiduciary, and how do they differ from those present in other types of contractual relationships, such as an athlete-team relationship?
2. In *Zinn*, the court adopted two standards in rejecting Parrish's defense. What was the first standard adopted by the court and its source? The court also adopted a standard of good faith as a basis for determining whether an agent has competently performed his or her duties.

C. Agent Financial Improprieties

A serious issue confronting the athlete-agent industry is agent conduct that has a negative impact on an athlete's financial well-being. Inappropriate conduct ranges from agents and financial advisors misappropriating for their own use funds that athletes have entrusted with them, to their persuading athletes to enter into poor investment schemes. One of the more notorious cases of financial mismanagement and illegal conduct involved William "Tank" Black, who rose to fame as a successful agent of clients including Sterling Sharpe, Vince Carter, Fred Taylor, and Ike Hilliard. An investigation resulted in allegations that Black not only made under-the-table payments to players; he also fraudulently involved athletes in a pyramid scheme and laundered money. Black and his company's general counsel eventually pled guilty to federal charges that they laundered the money of drug traffickers. In June 2001, Black received a federal sentence of six years and ten months, followed by three years of supervised probation. In a separate lawsuit, a Florida jury convicted Black of conspiring to commit mail and wire fraud.

In asserting claims against agents and financial advisors for alleged mismanagement of their financial affairs, athletes have resorted to several legal theories. Legal theories on which athletes seek to recover include breach of contract, fraud, breach of fiduciary duty, and negligence. Athletes include tort-based claims such as fraud to increase the possibility of recovering punitive damages, which cannot be recovered in a breach of contract claim.

An illustrative case is *Williams v. CWI, Inc.*, 777 F. Supp. 1006 (D. D.C. 1991). Reginald Williams, a young basketball player, signed a contract worth $1 million per year to play for the NBA's Los Angeles Clippers. Looking for investment opportunities, Williams and his wife met with a financial advisor who agreed to provide financial and tax advice for the couple. Claiming a high investment return and tax benefits, the advisor persuaded the couple to invest in a venture involving the purchase of a device known as an atmospheric reverse refrigeration heating unit. The Williamses agreed to purchase $1 million worth of the devices at $10,000 each. They forwarded $50,000 to the advisor, who appropriated the money for his own use. The Williamses sued the advisor alleging breach of contract and fraud. The court entered a judgment for the Williamses on both their breach of contract and fraud theories in the amount of $137,300, which included $50,000 in punitive damages.

The court made the following observations concerning the predicament of many young athletes such as Williams:

> Like many young professional athletes, Mr. Williams was earning a considerable salary but had no experience in making investments or managing his money. He needed reliable expert advice and did not find any readily available. Because Mr. Williams' predicament appears to be a recurring problem for basketball players and other athletes who suddenly receive large disposable incomes, it seems that it would be appropriate for either the NBA, or the players' team, or the players' organization to develop a three-pronged program to assist these young people. First, they could offer at least some rudimentary education in business and finance. Second, they could assemble a package of low-risk blue chip investments for young players that will provide for their futures, as well as a system for referring them to wise and ethical professionals who can advise them on managing money. Third, they might offer a financial incentive for players to place a portion of their funds in a deferred investment program.

Id. at 1007. A Securities and Exchange Commission (SEC) lawyer involved in the Tank Black matter offered similar observations: "Professional athletes are prime candidates for financial fraud. Many are unsophisticated in financial matters and suddenly find themselves with a six- or seven-figure salary. They're young, they're trusting, and they've been taken care of most of their lives." L. Jon Wertheim, *Web of Deceit*, Sports Illustrated, May 29, 2000, at 80.

A major problem confronting the agent-athlete industry is agent and financial advisor misappropriation of athletes' money. Agents and financial advisors will often place athletes' monies in risky investments or simply use it to cover agents' and advisors' personal and business expenses. Several legal theories, including breach of contract, negligence, and fraud, have been employed by athletes in their efforts to recover misappropriated money. In March 2018, investment advisor Jeremy Joseph Drake entered a consent decree relating to an SEC complaint alleging he had fraudulently siphoned approximately $1.2 million from the account of an NFL player and his wife. *SEC v. Drake*, 2017 WL 6507766 (C.D. Cal. Dec. 18, 2017). The complaint alleged that the defendant engaged in mail and bank fraud and identity theft in obtaining money and property from the athlete and his wife. In early 2019, Drake was sentenced to over two years in prison. *Prison Sentence for L.A. Money Adviser Who Conned Athlete Out of $1.2 Million*, LA.com, Mar. 22, 2019, https://mynewsla.com/crime/2019/03/22/prison-sentence-for-l-a-money-adviser-who-conned-athlete-out-of-1-2-million/.

Former NBA star Tim Duncan fared better than many athletes who are victims of financial improprieties. Duncan entered a settlement under which he recovered $7.5 million of the $20 million he allegedly lost as a result of the fraudulent conduct of his financial advisor, Charles Banks IV. As a result of his interactions with Duncan, Banks was sentenced to four years in federal prison after having been found guilty of wire fraud. Guillermo Contreras, *Duncan gets back $7.5 million in settlement with ex-advisor*, MySanAntonio.com, Jan. 25, 2018, https://www.mysanantonio.com/news/local/article/Tim-Duncan-gets-back-7-5-million-in-settlement-12526295.php. Banks figured prominently in a lawsuit filed by another former NBA player, Kevin Garnett, who alleged his former accountant worked with Banks in misappropriating $77 million of Garnett's money. Janet Levaux, *Kevin Garnett Sues for Fraud Involving Tim Duncan's Ex-Advisor*, Think Advisor, Sept. 7, 2018; see also *Groves v. Morgan Stanley Smith Barney*, Award: FINRA Office of Dispute Resolution, Case Number 16-02052 (Dec. 19, 2018) (awarding $4.2 million to former NFL player Assante Samuel relating to defendant's negligent supervision of an investment advisor who solicited millions from the athlete for investment in nightclubs). Peggy Ann Fulford, who falsely advertised herself as a Harvard-educated lawyer and financial advisor when soliciting athlete clients, was held accountable for her actions. She was sentenced to 120 months in prison and ordered to make restitution of over $5.5 million for defrauding professional athletes. *Self-styled "Financial Advisor" Ordered to Prison after Defrauding Professional Athlete Out of Millions*, Dept. of Justice, U.S. Attorney's Office, S.D. Tex. (Nov. 7, 2018).

Today, disputes between agents and athletes are generally subject to arbitration because the standard player-agent contracts promulgated by players associations include mandatory arbitration provisions. See *Wichard v. Suggs*, 95 F. Supp. 3d 935 (E.D. Va. 2015) (applying mandatory arbitration provision of standard representation agreement between football player and agent); but see *Dogra v. Griffin*, 2020 WL 5411187 at ★3–4 (E.D. Mo. Sept. 9, 2020) (in an agent's action for alleged unpaid fees, ruling athlete waived mandatory arbitration arising from NBPA regulations governing agents by participating in legal proceedings).

An illustrative case is the dispute between NBA player, Nerlens Noel, and his agent, Rich Paul of Klutch Sports Group. In 2021, Noel sued Paul alleging that he signed a representation agreement with Paul and Klutch because of representations by Paul that he could assist Noel in obtaining a max-level NBA contract. Based on Paul's alleged representation, Noel alleged he declined a $70 million four-year contract extension tendered by the Dallas Mavericks. Noel did not obtain a max deal and bounced around the league on different teams and earned only $12.7 million over the four-year period. Noel filed a lawsuit against Paul seeking $58 million, the difference between what Noel actually earned over the four-year period and what Paul allegedly promised. In late 2022, the presiding judge dismissed Noel's lawsuit and ordered that the dispute be resolved in arbitration because the parties signed the NBA standard player-agent contract, which mandates that player-agent disputes be resolved in arbitration. Paul had countersued to recover a $200,000 commission on a $5 million contract he negotiated for Noel with the New York Knicks prior to the 2020–21 season. In early 2023, the parties reportedly settled their lawsuit with Noel agreeing to pay Paul the $200,000 commission. As the forgoing matter illustrates, players will not always prevail in lawsuits against their agents. Agents have argued successfully that they properly performed the services rendered. Moreover, an agent will argue that an athlete's financial plight is the result of athletes' poor handling of their financial resources rather than the agent's mishandling. In one case, an agent successfully argued that the athlete's assets had been depleted because the athlete "wasted his assets by making exorbitant purchases, transferring large sums of money to his family members and friends, and refusing to save for the future or consider the consequences if he were injured or unable to continue playing football. . . ." *Clark v. Weisberg*, 1999 WL 543191, at ★2 (N.D. Ill., Jul. 23, 1999).

A similar occurrence came to a head on July 16, 2009, when Nevada deputies arrested former National Basketball Association (NBA) star Antoine Walker after Walker wrote a series of ten bad checks totaling $1 million in Las Vegas. After the arrest, it was revealed that Walker owed over $4 million to various creditors and was broke despite earning over $110 million as an NBA player. The squandering of Walker's fortune was based on several factors. Walker traveled with a massive entourage. Walker's mother estimates that during his playing days, Walker was supporting 70 different friends and family members in one way or another. Walker also had a mansion built for his mother, which included an indoor pool, ten bathrooms, and a full-size basketball court. Walker was also a top-line watch collector and had a fleet of cars, including two Bentleys, two Mercedes, a Range Rover, a Cadillac Escalade, and a bright red Hummer. Those close to Walker also described him as a notoriously large gambler. Shira Springer, *For Walker, Financial Fouls Mount*, Boston Globe, Oct. 25, 2009.

Other factors that contribute to players' financial problems are their dealings with financial advisers and family issues such as divorce and child support. Because many professional athletes have large bank accounts but minimum knowledge in managing financial matters, they are often targets for con artists and shady financial advisers. An NFLPA report stated that from 1999 to 2002, at least 78 players lost more than $42 million combined to their financial advisers.

Unofficial estimates by sports agents and athletes put the divorce rate for professional athletes between 60 and 80 percent. What often makes divorces particularly damaging for professional athletes is that many of them occur in retirement, when a player's peak earning period is over and making a comparable living is virtually impossible. Further exacerbating the problem is that, according to celebrity divorce lawyer Raoul Felder, "[t]he percentage of prenups amongst athletes is appreciably lower compared with nonathletes at the same economic level." Another frequent issue is that of child support. For example, former NFL running back Travis Henry was ordered to pay $170,000 each year to support his nine kids. Pablo S. Torre, *How (and Why) Athletes Go Broke*, Sports Illustrated, Mar. 23, 2009.

In 2002, the NFLPA became the first professional sports union to attempt to curb the abuse of financial advisors with its promulgation of the NFLPA Regulations and Code of Conduct Governing Registered Player Financial Advisors. The regulations represented the NFLPA's response to incidents involving mismanagement of players' financial affairs. Financial advisors, who agreed to participate, applied to become registered in the voluntary program. They were given "unique information on NFL players, their benefits, and compensation structure." *Introduction*, NFLPA Regulations and Code of Conduct Governing Registered Player Financial Advisors 1 (as amended March 2017. For a discussion of the NFLPA's Financial Advisor Regulations, see Shropshire, Davis & Duru, *supra* note 1, at 140–43).

In *Atwater v. National Football League Players Assn.*, 626 F.3d 1170 (11th Cir. 2010), former NFL players sued the NFLPA alleging that it had negligently performed background checks on Kirk Wright, a financial advisor, who defrauded the athletes and other investors out of more than $100 million. Although the NFLPA prevailed in the lawsuit, it suspended its financial advisor program, only to reinstate it in 2012 after making changes (e.g., requiring applicants to have eight rather than the previously required five years of licensed experience). See NFLPA Regulations and Code of Conduct Governing Registered Player Financial Advisors (as amended March 2017 and edited May 2023), Final-Financial-Advisors-Regs-Edited-May-2023.pdf (windows.net).

QUESTIONS

1. The *Williams* court identified several factors that render athletes particularly vulnerable to unscrupulous agents and financial managers. Do you agree with the court? The court also suggested the development of a three-pronged program to assist young athletes with money management. What were the three parts of the proposed system, and what practical approaches would you

recommend be included in such a program? Who do you think should be responsible for the creation of such a system?
2. As an agent, what is your duty if one of your clients asks you to procure a deal that you are sure is financially irresponsible? What is your duty if one of your clients asks you to procure a deal that your professional judgment informs you is unethical?

> ### Problem 13-1
>
> William Wills, a professional football player, hired Jordan Smith as his sports agent. Smith, an attorney, is registered as a player representative with the NFLPA. Wills and Smith entered into the NFLPA's standard representation agreement between a player and contract advisor. From 2019 to 2023, with Wills's authorization, Smith received most of Wills's income. He gave Wills an allowance for living expenses and occasionally gave Wills advances against his salary when Wills asked for them. In addition to his salary, Wills was paid $50,000 a year to be invested in an annuity on his behalf. Smith was supposed to invest these amounts each year in an annuity for Wills but did not do so. Between 2019 and 2023, Smith used much of Wills's income to cover Smith's business and personal expenses. In 2022, Wills began to suspect that Smith was misappropriating his income and requested an accounting, which Smith said was forthcoming but never provided. Wills became certain that something was wrong when in 2023, he was informed by the Internal Revenue Service (IRS) that he had not paid his tax deficiencies for the years 2020 to 2022. Smith had told Wills that Smith had paid Wills's taxes at the time he filed Wills's tax returns. The tax returns, which were signed by Wills, were filed by Smith, who had not paid the tax deficiencies. Wills has a tax liability of over $240,000 as a result of the actions taken by Smith. What causes of action may Wills assert in a lawsuit against Smith? See *Willoughby v. Commissioner of Internal Revenue*, 1994 WL 444427 (Tax Ct., Aug. 18, 1994).

D. Agent Conflicts of Interest with Athletes

KEY TERMS
- Conflict of interest
- Nondisclosure

One of an agent's fundamental obligations is not to compromise the interests of his or her principal. The requirement that an agent avoid conflicts of interest is derived from the duties of undivided loyalty and good faith that agents owe to their principals. In the sports context, numerous factual scenarios present real or potential conflicts of interest. Historically, the classic conflict of interest scenario has involved "nondisclosure by an agent of a financial interest that conflicts with that of the athlete client." Shropshire, Davis & Duru, *supra*, at 86. See also Joshua Lens, *When a College Coach's Agent Recruits the Coach's Players: Potential Legal and NCAA Ramifications*, 26 Jeffrey S. Moorad Sports L.J. 1 (2019) (discussing conflicts of interest by sports agents); Jamie E. Brown, *The Battle the Fans Never See: Conflicts of Interest for Sports Lawyers*, 7 Geo. J. Legal Ethics 813, 816 (1994); MLBPA Regulations Governing Player Agents, Section 5(B)(12) (2010, as amended 2019); NFLPA Regulations Governing Contract Advisors, Section 3 (2011, as amended May 2017), *infra*; NBPA Regulations Governing Player Agents, Section 3 (1998, as amended 2019), *infra*.

As the following discussion reveals, however, nondisclosure represents only one of the factual scenarios where conflicts arise in the sports representation business. Nevertheless, we begin our discussion with a case that presents the paradigmatic conflict of interest.

The Detroit Lions, Inc. v. Argovitz
580 F. Supp. 542 (D. Mich. 1984)

DeMascio, District Judge.

[Editors' note: On July 1, 1983, Billy Sims, a former college football Heisman Trophy winner, signed a contract with the Houston Gamblers of the fledgling United States Football League (USFL). Later that year, Sims and the team for which he had been under contract, the NFL's Detroit Lions, requested that a court invalidate the contract between Sims and the Gamblers because Sims's agent breached fiduciary duties when he negotiated Sims's contract with the Gamblers. Sims and the Lions also alleged the Sims-Gamblers contract was otherwise tainted by fraud and misrepresentation.

In February or March 1983, Sims's agent, Jerry Argovitz, told Sims that he had applied for a Houston franchise in the newly formed USFL, but Argovitz failed to disclose to Sims the extent of the agent's interest in the Gamblers. Argovitz was obligated for 29 percent of a $1.5 million letter of credit and, if his application was approved, would receive from the Gamblers an annual salary of $275,000 and 5 percent of the yearly cash flow. While his application for the franchise was pending, Argovitz continued his negotiations with the Lions on behalf of Sims.

Following the approval of his application, Argovitz sought an offer for Sims from the Gamblers. Later, one of Argovitz's partners in the Gamblers, Bernard Lerner, agreed to negotiate a contract with Sims. At a point in negotiations where the Lions were very close to reaching an agreement on the value of Sims's services, at Lerner's behest, Sims and his wife went to Houston to negotiate with the Gamblers, with Sims believing that the Lions organization was not negotiating in good faith based on information supplied by Argovitz. On June 30, 1983, the Gamblers offered Sims a

"$3.5 million five-year contract, which included three years of skill and injury guarantees. The offer included a $500,000 loan at an interest rate of 1 percent over prime. It was from this loan that Argovitz planned to receive the $100,000 balance of his fee for acting as an agent in negotiating a contract with his own team. The offer received the guarantee that Sims wanted from the Lions, guarantees that Argovitz dropped without too much quarrel." Argovitz failed to inform Sims that he thought the Lions would match the Gamblers' financial package or ask Sims whether he (Argovitz) should telephone the Lions. During the negotiations at the Gamblers' office, Argovitz declined to accept a telephone call from the Lions' representative, even though Argovitz was at his office. Sims agreed to become a Gambler on the terms offered.]

Conclusions of Law . . .

3. An agent's duty of loyalty requires that he not have a personal stake that conflicts with the principal's interest in a transaction in which he represents his principal. . . .
4. A fiduciary violates the prohibition against self-dealing not only by dealing with himself on his principal's behalf, but also by dealing on his principal's behalf with a third party in which he has an interest, such as a partnership in which he is a member . . .
5. Where an agent has an interest adverse to that of his principal in a transaction in which he purports to act on behalf of his principal, the transaction is voidable by the principal unless the agent disclosed all material facts within the agent's knowledge that might affect the principal's judgment.
6. The mere fact that the contract is fair to the principal does not deny the principal the right to rescind the contract when it was negotiated by an agent in violation of the prohibition against self-dealing. . . .
7. Once it has been shown that an agent had an interest in a transaction involving his principal antagonistic to the principal's interest, fraud on the part of the agent is presumed. The burden of proof then rests upon the agent to show that: his principal had full knowledge, not only of the fact that the agent was interested, but also of every material fact known to the agent that might affect the principal and that, having such knowledge, the principal freely consented to the transaction.
8. It is not sufficient for the agent merely to inform the principal that he has an interest that conflicts with the principal's interest. Rather, he must inform the principal "of all facts that come to his knowledge that are or may be material or which might affect his principal's rights or interests or influence the action he takes." *Anderson v. Griffith*, 501 S.W.2d 695, 700 (Tex. Civ. App. 1973).
9. Argovitz clearly had a personal interest in signing Sims with the Gamblers that was adverse to Sims' interest — he had an ownership interest in the Gamblers and thus would profit if the Gamblers were profitable, and would incur substantial personal liabilities should the Gamblers not be financially successful. Since this showing has been made, fraud on Argovitz's part is presumed, and the Gamblers' contract must be rescinded unless Argovitz has shown by a preponderance

of the evidence that he informed Sims of every material fact that might have influenced Sims' decision whether or not to sign the Gamblers' contract.

10. We conclude that Argovitz has failed to show by a preponderance of the evidence either: (1) that he informed Sims of the following facts, or (2) that these facts would not have influenced Sims' decision whether to sign the Gamblers' contract.
    a. The relative values of the Gamblers' contract and the Lions' offer that Argovitz knew could be obtained.
    b. That there was significant financial differences between the USFL and the NFL not only in terms of the relative financial stability of the Leagues, but also in terms of the fringe benefits available to Sims.
    c. Argovitz's 29 percent ownership in the Gamblers; Argovitz's $275,000 annual salary with the Gamblers; Argovitz's five percent interest in the cash flow of the Gamblers.
    d. That both Argovitz and Burrough failed to even attempt to obtain for Sims valuable contract clauses which they had given to [another player Jim] Kelly on behalf of the Gamblers.
    e. That Sims had great leverage, and Argovitz was not encouraging a bidding war that could have advantageous results for Sims. . . .
11. The careless fashion in which Argovitz went about ascertaining the highest price for Sims' service convinces us of the wisdom of the maxim: no man can faithfully serve two masters whose interests are in conflict.

Judgment will be entered for the plaintiffs rescinding the Gamblers' contract with Sims.

QUESTIONS

Describe how Argovitz violated his duties of undivided loyalty, good faith, and fair dealing. Will an athlete's knowledge of a conflict or a potential conflict necessarily absolve an agent of liability for a conflict of interest? Why did the *Argovitz* court conclude that knowledge by Sims of Argovitz's ownership of the Gamblers franchise or approval of the application failed to absolve the agent of responsibility?

NOTE

In *Sports Management Network v. Busch*, NASCAR driver Kurt Busch alleged, *inter alia*, a conflict of interest resulting in a breach of fiduciary duties by his agent, John Caponigro. Both the sports management agency and the law firm that employed Caponigro also represented entities that employed or had formerly employed Busch. *Sports Management Network v. Busch*, 2019 WL 1057314 (E.D. Mich. Mar. 6, 2019). Concluding that Caponigro's conduct and his firm's conduct gave rise to a conflict of interest that breached Caponigro's duty of loyalty, the court stated:

> The conflict between SMN and Busch was exacerbated by SMN's representation of several of the driving teams that employed Busch. SMN provided sponsorship representation for Penske Racing, for whom Busch drove from 2005 to 2011. . . . SMN also represented Busch in several negotiations adverse to Penske, including a buyout from Busch's previous racing team, the terms of his 2010 extension, and the terms of his 2011 separation, which included a waiver of all of his rights under his driver agreement. . . . Caponigro considered Penske and Busch not to be clients but to be "benefactors to this effort that I was putting forth. . . ." He saw himself as one "facilitating a meeting of the minds. . . ." Indeed, Penske Racing paid Caponigro, in the capacity of FCWS [the law firm for which Caponigro worked], a substantial sum for his "coordination" between Busch and Penske in 2005. . . .
>
> This underscores the unfairness at the heart of Caponigro's conflict of interest. He billed himself as Busch's agent and attorney, but when Busch's interests were adverse to his other clients, the best he could provide was facilitation. . . . The conflict ran even deeper with Andretti Autosport, with whom SMN negotiated several contracts on Busch's behalf. Andretti Autosport was a client of both FCWS and SMN, and Michael Andretti has been a client of John Caponigro and FCWS since 1990. . . . Regardless of whether Busch can prove injury from these conflicts, they are sufficiently egregious to infect the entire [representation agreement].

Sports Mgmt. Network, 2019 WL 1057314, at *4-5. See Lise Vitter, *The Ethical Sports Lawyer: Does Avoiding Conflicts of Interest Mean Avoiding Competition?*, 35 Geo. J. Legal Ethics 1169 (2022) (discussing conflicts of interest in sports).

Problem 13-2

Agent represents basketball players Williams and Smith, who play for different teams in the same NBA conference. Williams, who is considered by many to be the greatest basketball player of all time, is also the highest-paid athlete (salary and endorsements) in the world. One of Williams's teammates complains about the aggressive play of Smith, who is a solid player but not a superstar. Williams takes these complaints to Agent, who is currently in the midst of negotiating Smith's contract with his current team, Team A. Team B has also expressed an interest in Smith. Agent rejects Team A's offer of $8.1 million for three years and secures for Smith a $9.6 million deal with Team B, which plays in another NBA conference. Under his contract with Team B, Smith will receive only $6.4 million in his first three years. Agent says that the deal with Team B is better because it will pay Smith $3.2 million ($1.5 million of which is guaranteed) in his fourth year and has less deferred money. Team A's president says that Team A was willing to compromise on the issue of deferred money. What, if any, conflicts or potential conflicts are present here?

COMPETITION FOR CLIENTS: CONFLICTS BETWEEN AGENTS

A. Introduction

The underlying source of conflicts between agents is the fierce competition for clients. Factors that contribute to the intense competition that breeds conflict among agents include the significant fees that are potentially available if an agent signs an athlete; the substantial increase in the number of agents between the 1960s and the present; the relatively small pool of potential athlete clients; industry consolidation; and the ease with which provisions in standard agent representation agreements allow athletes to terminate their contracts with agents.

B. Consolidation

The wave of consolidations that proliferated during the 1990s and continue today increased the competition for clients among smaller firms and individual agents who often lack the resources to compete effectively against larger firms. In addition, agents within larger sports representation firms often employ aggressive tactics in recruiting athletes; some of these tactics are products of resources that give larger athlete representation firms a competitive edge.

One byproduct of consolidation may be the domination of a small group of agencies of the athlete-agent market. *Forbes'* list of the most powerful sports agents in 2022 includes agents affiliated with the most powerful agent representation firms including: Boras Corporation; Excel Sports Management; Wasserman; Klutch Sports Group; MVP Sports Group; WME Sports; Rosenhaus Sports Representation; and Athletes First. For a list of the agents, their commissions, and the monetary value of the deals they negotiated, see Brett Knight, *Forbes: The Most Powerful Sports Agents*, 2022, Forbes.com, Nov. 17, 2022, *https://www.forbes.com/lists/sports-agents/?sh=1985bc5a4d35*; see also NBA Agents, HoopsHype, *https://hoopshype.com/reps/* (listing NBA-certified agents and players they represent).

It is not uncommon for agencies to consolidate or for agents to join larger sports representation agencies. After a few years of working at the new agency, the agent may be terminated or voluntarily depart to establish a competing agency. Similarly, agents, who begin their careers at an agency, will gain experience and later depart to join another agency or establish a new agency. Litigation is often a consequence of these shifting relationships.

An example is the dispute between David Dunn and Leigh Steinberg. Dunn, a partner in what was then Steinberg, Moorad & Dunn (a division of Assante), departed to start his own firm. His new firm represented several clients of his previous firm. This led to a lawsuit in which the Steinberg firm alleged that Dunn's new firm conspired to lure clients away from it and that Dunn violated a noncompete covenant. A Los Angeles jury awarded Steinberg $44.66 million in damages after it decided that Dunn had breached his contract, engaged in unfair competition, and had acted with fraud and malice. In 2005, a California appellate court vacated the $44.66 million jury award. *Steinberg Moorad & Dunn Inc. v. Dunn*, 136 Fed. Appx. 6 (9th Cir. 2005).

For additional illustrations of the range of issues that arise in disputes between agents, see the following: *Núñez Guadalupe v. Lagardere Unlimited*, 2019 WL 2212134 (Tribunal De Apelaciones, Feb. 27, 2019) (in a case decided by a Mexican appellate court, the court rejects an agent's claims that he was entitled to a commission for assisting another agent in negotiating an NBA player/team contract; the court finds the commission payment was not mentioned in the contract and an alleged consulting contract was not signed by defendant agent); *Hendrickson v. Octagon, Inc.*, 225 F. Supp. 3d 1013 (N.D. Cal. 2016) (discussing validity of fee-sharing and non-solicitation provisions in employment contracts of sports agency's former agents); *Indep. Sports & Entm't LLC v. Fegan*, 2017 WL 2598550 (C.D. Cal. May 30, 2017) (state-based claims alleging breach of non-competition provisions asserted by a sports agency against a former agent were not preempted by Section 301 under the Labor Management Relations Act; the claims neither arose from nor were substantially dependent on an analysis of the collective bargaining agreement); *Rosenhaus v. Jackson*, 2016 WL 4592180 (C.D. Cal. Feb. 26, 2016) (vacating arbitration award in favor of agent against athlete who alleged evident partiality by the arbitrator; a new arbitrator ruled in favor of the agent awarding him approximately $950,000 including compensatory damages, attorneys' fees, and court costs); *Dogra v. CAA Sports, LLC.*, AAA Case No. 01-15-0002-7781 (2016) (Vaughn, Arb.) (an arbitrator relied on contract law principles and the terms of the parties' contract in ruling that CAA's termination of an agent was improper and that the agent was entitled to commissions).

As is true of disputes between agents and players, disputes between agents are subject to mandatory arbitration. See, e.g., *Dye v. Sexton*, 2017 WL 7615571 (N.D. Ga. Dec. 13, 2017) (relying on the NFL CBA, and NFLPA agent regulations, finding that a dispute between agents is subject to arbitration); *Branion v. Wallace*, 2:16-cv-07992-SVW-JC (C.D. Cal. Jan. 18, 2017) (agent's action alleging that another agent and agency intentionally interfered with his contractual relationship with an athlete was subject to NFLPA's mandatory arbitration process, but noting that not all disputes between agents are subject to arbitration).

C. Termination

Competition in the athlete-agent industry is also intensified by the ease at which agent representation agreements can be terminated. A representative example of a termination provision in a standard player-agent contract follows.

NFLPA STANDARD REPRESENTATION AGREEMENT

(as amended through March 2016)[2]

12. Term

The term of this Agreement shall begin on the date hereof and shall remain in effect until such time that it is terminated by either party in which case termination of this Agreement shall be effective five (5) days after written notice of termination is given to the other party. Notice shall be effective for purposes of this paragraph if sent by confirmed facsimile or overnight delivery to the appropriate address contained in this Agreement. . . .

If the Contract Advisor's Certification is suspended or revoked by the NFLPA or the Contract Advisor is otherwise prohibited by the NFLPA from performing the services he/she has agreed to perform herein, this Agreement shall automatically terminate, effective as of the date of such suspension or termination.

D. Disparagement

In the fierce competition for clients, agents try to convince athletes to sign with them by expressing both the virtues of their organization and by disparaging the competition. A trend that may contribute to the increase in tampering allegations was described as follows: "In the past, while agents competed against each other as aggressively as anyone could imagine, once the client came to an agreement with an agent, everybody in essence backed off. . . . That was the end of the game. What is going on now is once an agent signs a client, the second game begins." Liz Mullen, *Sleaze Factor off the Charts, Agents Allege*, Sports Bus. J., June 24–30, 2002, at 1, 30.

Bauer v. The Interpublic Group of Companies, Inc., 255 F. Supp. 2d 1086 (N.D. Cal. 2003) represents a fairly realistic depiction of the recruiting techniques employed by agents. Sports agent Frank Bauer contended that David Carr's decision to terminate their contractual relationship was based on negative information concerning Bauer that was disseminated by the defendant's agents. The court rejected Bauer's claim for lack of evidence to support the allegations. In the aftermath of *Bauer*, the NFLPA changed the termination provisions of its Standard Representation Agreement. Generally, either the agent or athlete may terminate the relationship effective five days after written notice is given to the other party. However, an agreement between an agent and a rookie (a player who has never signed an NFL player contract) cannot be terminated by the rookie until 30 days after the player signed the representation agreement. Another case involving issues of disparagement is *Champion Pro Consulting Group, Inc. v. Impact Sports Football, LLC*, 2013 WL 5461829, *17–18 (M.D. N.C., Sept. 30, 2013).

---

[2] The complete NFLPA Standard Representation Agreement can be found in Appendix D of NFLPA Regulations Governing Contract Advisors (2016), available at *https://nflpaweb.blob.core.windows.net/media/Default/PDFs/Agents/RegulationsAmendedAugust2016.pdf*.

E. What Is Permissible Competition?

KEY TERMS • Competitor's privilege

Agents are permitted considerable leeway in attempting to recruit the business of athletes from rival agents. However, their competitive activities are not unlimited. This was illustrated in *Speakers of Sport, Inc. v. ProServe, Inc.*, 178 F.3d 862 (7th Cir. 1999). Speakers of Sport, a sports representation agency, filed a lawsuit asserting that another athlete-agent firm, ProServ, had wrongfully interfered in Speaker's contractual relationship with baseball player Ivan Rodriguez. In 1991, Rodriguez signed the first of several one-year contracts making Speakers his agent. ProServ promised Rodriguez that it would get him between $2 million and $4 million in endorsements if he signed with it. Thereafter, Rodriguez terminated his contract with Speakers and signed a representation agreement with ProServ. ProServ's failure to obtain significant endorsements for Rodriguez subsequently led to his decision to switch to another firm.

After ruling that Rodriguez had not breached its contract with Speakers because their relationship was terminable at will, the court considered whether ProServ had exceeded the bounds of permissible competition. The court articulated the principle that there is nothing wrong with one sports agent trying to take a client from another, so long as it can be done without precipitating a breach of contract. According to the court, competition, "which though painful, fierce, frequently ruthless, sometimes Darwinian in its pitilessness, is the cornerstone of our highly successful economic system." *Id.* at 865. Characterizing this as the "competitor's privilege," the court concluded that although competition that induces a breach of contract is improper, the competitor's privilege permits conduct that induces the lawful termination of a contractual relationship.

The court stated that the competitor's privilege does not permit an agent to engage in unlawful means such as fraud in attempting to get business from a competitor. The court concluded that under Illinois law, however, ProServ had not committed fraud in stating that it could get a certain amount of endorsement income for Rodriguez:

> The promise of endorsements was puffing not in the most common sense of a cascade of extravagant adjectives but in the equally valid sense of a sales pitch that is intended, and that a reasonable person in the position of the "promisee" would understand, to be aspirational rather than enforceable—an expression of hope rather than a commitment. It is not as if ProServ proposed to employ Rodriguez and pay him $2 million a year. That would be the kind of promise that could found an enforceable obligation. ProServ proposed merely to get him endorsements of at least that amount. They would of course be paid by the companies whose products Rodriguez endorsed, rather than by ProServ.

Id. at 866. See also *Wright v. Bonds*, 117 F.3d 1427 (9th Cir. 1999) (adopting a similar approach in finding agent had not improperly interfered with an athlete's former agent).

> **QUESTIONS**

The *Speakers* court adopted the concept of the competitor's privilege, which validates a broad range of activities in which an agent can engage in attempting to lure clients away from a competitor. What limitation did the court impose on an agent's permissible conduct in attempting to recruit clients in an established relationship with an agent?

In *Lee v. Brothers*, 2021 WL 4652336 (S.D. N.Y. Oct. 6, 2021), an NBPA-certified agent alleged tortious interference by a rival agent who allegedly used an improper inducement, a new pickup truck, to poach the plaintiff's client. The court held that plaintiff failed to establish the elements of a tortious interference claim. The court also found that plaintiff could not bolster its claim by relying on the NBPA's regulations governing agents, which "strongly suggests that the players, as the members of the union promulgating the regulations, are the intended beneficiaries of the player union's rules, including its rule banning improper inducements," and that the NBPA possesses the sole right to enforce its regulations. *Id.* at *4.

One critic of the *Speakers* case argues that although it and other cases "appear legally accurate, they provide a broad spectrum of competition that borders on interference thereby tolerating unfair and corrupt dealing." Bryan Couch, Comment, *How Agent Competition and Corruption Affects Sports and the Athlete-Agent Relationship and What Can Be Done to Control It*, 10 Seton Hall J. Sport L. 111, 119 (2000). Is the range of permissible competitive behavior validated in *Speakers* too broad? For discussions of competition and its implications for the athlete-agent industry, see Joshua Lens, *Loans and Marketing Guarantees in Athlete Agent Recruiting, Why They Are Ill Advised Under Agency Law and Attorney Ethics Regulation Principles*, 7 Tex. A&M L. Rev. 543, 572 (2020); Timothy Davis, *Regulating the Athlete-Agent Industry: Intended and Unintended Consequences*, 42 Willamette L. Rev. 781 (2006); Zach Schreiber, Note, *Leveling the Playing Field for Sports Agents: How the Two-Hat Theory and the Model Rules of Professional Conduct Collide*, 19 Tex. Rev. Ent. & Sports L. 13 (2018).

F. Race and Gender Issues

Agents of color have risen to prominence in the athlete-agent industry. These include David Mulugheta, the son of Eritrean immigrants who rose from an internship at the sports agency Athletes First to become an equity partner in the firm. In 2023, the NFLPA's website stated that Mulugheta has negotiated 49 contracts. NFLPA, Agent David Mulugheta, *https://nflpa.com/profile/agent/45657*. This number includes first-round draft picks. Mulugheta is known for his talent in negotiating contracts but in 2019 he acknowledged that some people still raise questions about "whether that 'young black kid' actually negotiates his players' contracts." Jori Epstein, *NFL Agent 'Changing the Trajectory,'* USA Today, Jun. 26, 2019. In the NBA, Rich Paul, friend of and agent for NBA player LeBron James and creator of the sports agency firm Klutch Sports Group, has gained prominence for his representation of athletes. In 2018, Klutch earned $24.9 million in commissions and landed on *Forbes'* list of the world's top sports agencies. In July 2019, Paul garnered attention when he agreed for Klutch to become the new sports division within United Talent Agency, a leading representation firm that represents Angelina Jolie, Tiffany Haddish, Chris Pratt, and other high-profile actors. The alliance permits Klutch to retain its branding. The alliance better positions United Talent to compete against representation firms, such as CAA, which have sports divisions. Marc Stein, *LeBron James's Agent, Rich Paul, Starts a Sports Division at a Hollywood Firm*, NY Times, Jul. 17, 2019.

Paul, however, has generated controversy for what some allege is his too-close relationship with James and what is perceived as Paul's conflicts of interest in handling his roster of players as well as his inappropriate meddling in the internal affairs of NBA teams. Paul forcefully rejects these claims, pointing out that other prominent agents influence team affairs and have close relationships with players. James also has been vocal in attributing some of the criticism to Paul's race as well as to Paul's difference in style and approach to being an agent, particularly as it relates to Paul's relationship with players and the relationships that Paul encourages players to have with each other. S.L. Price, *Against the Rich Paul Machine*, Sports Illus., Jul. 17, 2019. For discussions of race and sports agents, see Shropshire, Davis & Duru, *supra*, at 60–63; James G. Sammataro, *Business and Brotherhood, Can They Coincide? A Search into Why Black Athletes Do Not Hire Black Agents*, 42 Howard L.J. 535 (1999).

As of 2022, 67 of an estimated 910, or 7.3 percent of certified NFL agents were women. A.P., *Kelli Masters overcomes critics, among few female NFL agents*, USA Today, Nov. 11, 2022. The low percentage of female agents is due to factors that include coaches steering players away from women and discriminatory treatment emanating from male agents. One female agent, Kristian Kuliga, states she was approached at an NFL scouting combine by a male agent who explained, "how she wouldn't be taken seriously." During a meeting at her former agency, during a search for a new agent, staff members allegedly told Kuliga they "would never [expletive] hire a woman" because "a woman can't be an agent." Nikki Baim, *NFL Agency Is Changing, and It's Because of Women*, Yahoo Sports, May 10, 2019, https://sports.yahoo.com/nfl-agency-is-changing-and-its-because-of-women-183049880.html. Nicole Lynn became the first black woman to represent a top-five NFL draft pick (Quinnen Williams) and explained that race and gender are hurdles to increasing her client base. Lynn, who works with Klutch Sports Group, made further history in 2023 when she negotiated the largest contract ("five-year, $255 million, $170 million guaranteed) in NFL history on behalf of Philadelphia Eagles quarterback Jalen Hurts. Jason Jones, *Nicole Lynn's Legacy as a Sports Agent Has Reached New Level with Jalen Hurts Deal*, The Athletic, Apr. 19, 2023, https://theathletic.com/4425647/2023/04/19/nicole-lynn-jalen-hurts-nfl-philadelphia-eagles/.

Notwithstanding barriers, the number of successful women agents has increased over the last decade as players have begun to focus more on the quality of representation than on what the representation looks like. Liz Mullen, *Women Make Gains in NFL Agent Business*, Sports Business Journal, Oct. 2, 2017. In 2010, Kelli Masters was the first woman to represent a first-round NFL draft pick in the third overall pick, Gerald McCoy. Baim, *supra*. Kim Miale of Roc Nation has represented former first-round picks, including Saquon Barkley, Ronnie Stanley, Todd Gurley, and Leonard Fournette. Morgan Moriarty, *How Kim Miale Became a Trailblazing NFL Agent with a Star-Studded Client List*, SBNation, Apr. 10, 2019, https://www.sbnation.com/nfl/2019/4/10/18292317/kim-miale-woman-agent-nfl-draft-saquon-barkley-juju-smith-schuster-brycelove. In 2018, a record 33 women took the NFLPA agent certification exam. Baim, *supra*. In 2020, Emilie Castonguay became the first female agent to represent the overall number 1 pick in the NHL player draft. In 2022, Jessica Holtz negotiated $224 million supermax extensions for NBA stars Devon Booker and Karl-Anthony Towns.

QUESTIONS

Do you believe that race shapes the views of Rich Paul? Do other factors also contribute to the criticism of Paul? Identify impediments to increasing the number of female, Latino, and African-American athlete agents.

AN INTERNATIONAL PERSPECTIVE

Similar to the conceptualization of agents in the United States, from an international perspective, the term *agent* refers to a person who acts as "an intermediary between a sports man or woman and other parties, for example between a football player (employee or potential employee) and a club (employer or potential employer)." Robert Parrish, *Regulating Players' Agents: A Global Perspective*, in Players' Agents Worldwide: Legal Aspects (Robert C.R. Siekmann et al., eds., 2007).

> Not surprisingly, the problems that have beset the athlete agent industry in the United States arise internationally. Noting the high number of licensed agents in countries such as Spain, Italy and England, one commentator articulates that regulation of agents is necessary "'to introduce professionalism and morality to the occupation of players' agent in order to protect players whose careers are short.' Rephrased, the absence of player agent regulation will result in a lack of professionalism, immorality and a lack of protection for players."

Id. at 4. This author goes on to describe *bungs*, *tapping-up*, and dual representation as examples of improper agent conduct that demonstrate the need for agent regulation.

> Bungs refer to illegal payments by and to agents (and others) in order to facilitate the transfer of a player.
> Another [Fédération Internationale de Football (FIFA)] and association rule . . . was the common practice of "tapping-up," which refers to a process, often

facilitated by agents, whereby players are offered for sale to other clubs without the knowledge and consent of the club with whom the player is registered. . . . FIFA Players' Agents Regulations state that a licensed players' agent must never "approach a player who is under contract with a club with the aim of persuading him to terminate his contract prematurely or to flout the rights and duties stipulated in the contract. . . ."

The third issue reaching prominence in the UK in the summer of 2006, . . . was the issue of dual representation. This refers to an agent who represents both a club and a player in negotiations. This is prohibited by . . . FIFA Players' Agents Regulations which state that a licensed players' agent is required "to represent only one party when negotiating a transfer."

Id. at 6. For a discussion of the legal issues involved in the representation industry, see Shropshire, Davis & Duru, *supra* note 1, at 19–21.

As to the representation of a U.S. athlete wishing to play abroad, the agent faces a series of challenges. In all likelihood, the client is not at a skill level to play in the major league of that sport in the United States. The options are narrow concerning where the athlete can play abroad. For one, many nations' sports leagues limit the number of foreign (including U.S.) players per team, so roster spots are often scarce. Although agents are not bound by union regulations, such as those in the United States, they may find other strictures in effect that vary among foreign leagues. Thus, obtaining the basic knowledge of business practices in other countries can be much more difficult than in the United States. Even whether there is something approaching a standard-form player contract may not be clear. The drafting and negotiation of contract provisions to protect the athlete if things go awry in a foreign country are no simple matter. For example, does an agent really want to have to seek enforcement of contractual obligations in the courts of a foreign country? If not, what are the alternatives? Added to this mix is the need to understand the complexities of the U.S. tax laws and foreign immigration laws. As to immigration, the foreign club may be of assistance. As to tax, agents advising the athlete are probably on their own. See Shropshire, Davis & Duru, *supra* at 177–92 (discussing the role of the agent who advises clients internationally and the challenges such agents face).

EXTERNAL REGULATION AND LEGISLATION

The problems residing within the agent industry have hastened the call for solutions. Several past incidents not only underscore the need to regulate the industry but also reveal that athlete litigation against agents will not completely solve problems within the industry.

On June 10, 2010, a National Collegiate Athletic Association (NCAA) investigation and subsequent report revealed that former University of Southern California (USC) running back, Reggie Bush, had received impermissible benefits from two men attempting to form a sports agency in conjunction with Bush and his family. The NCAA investigative report also revealed that former USC basketball player O. J. Mayo had also received impermissible benefits from a representative of a sports agency. The violations caused both Bush and Mayo to be permanently disassociated with USC and resulted in Bush voluntarily relinquishing his Heisman Trophy. (See *https://www.washingtonpost.com/blogs/early-lead/post/reggie-bush-finally-returns-heisman-trophy/2012/08/16/3a8a0aee-e7b3-11e1-a3d2-2a05679928ef_blog.html*.)

On October 11, 2010, the NCAA determined that two University of North Carolina (UNC) football players were permanently ineligible for taking improper benefits from agents. The two players were found to have accepted benefits totaling $4,952 and $5,642, respectively. The gifts provided by the agents included travel accommodations to various locations, diamond earrings, and black diamond watches. See *Agent Scandal Costs UNC Three Players*, Associated Press, Oct. 11, 2010, *http://sports.espn.go.com/ncf/news/story?id=5673405*. A third UNC football player was dismissed from the team after it was revealed that he had accepted over $10,000 in improper benefits. The fallout from the UNC scandal led to longtime NFL agent Gary Wichard receiving a nine-month suspension from the NFLPA for having impermissible contact with a player. See *Gary Wichard Suspended 9 Months*, ESPN, Dec. 3, 2010, *http://sports.espn.go.com/nfl/news/story?id=5880708*. See also Timothy G. Nelson, *Flag on the Play: The Ineffectiveness of Athlete-Agent Laws—and How North Carolina Can Take Advantage of a Scandal to Be a Model for Reform*, 90 N.C. L. Rev. 800 (2012) (discussing the evolution of the sports agent's role in American athletics, agent regulations, and how the UNC case presents an opportunity to affect change on a national scale).

The NCAA possesses no authority to regulate sports agents. The NCAA attempts, however, to prevent what it considers inappropriate agent conduct through a set of rules intended to regulate the interaction between student-athletes and agents. For example, other than instances in which an exception might apply, a student-athlete who receives money or other benefits from an agent risks losing his or her amateur status and being deemed by the NCAA to be ineligible to participate in intercollegiate competition. See 2022–23 NCAA Division I Manual, bylaw 12.3; see also discussion *infra*. The materials in this section explore the various efforts that have been and are being undertaken to sanction inappropriate conduct by sports agents.

A. Federal Legislation

1. SPARTA

In September 2004, President George W. Bush signed into law the Sports Agent Responsibility Trust Act (SPARTA), the first federal legislation that specifically regulates sports agents. Sports Agent Responsibility and Trust Act, 15 U.S.C. §§7801–7807 (2004). SPARTA is modeled after key provisions of the Uniform Athlete Agents Act (UAAA), which more than 40 states have adopted. SPARTA does not preempt but rather supplements state requirements imposed by the UAAA. Indeed, SPARTA states that it is the "sense of Congress that States should enact the

Uniform Athletes Agents Act . . . to protect student athletes and the integrity of amateur sports from unscrupulous sports agents. . . ." *Id.*

Like the UAAA, SPARTA prohibits agents from using improper inducements (e.g., cash payments and gifts) and misleading information to recruit student-athletes, predating or postdating agency contracts, and not providing certain disclosures. *Id.* at 2. The disclosure document must conspicuously notify student-athletes, as well as parents or guardians of athletes under the age of 18, of the potential loss of eligibility to compete as an amateur if he or she signs an agency agreement. Within 72 hours of signing an agency contract, or before the next athletic event in which the athlete is eligible to participate, both the student-athlete and agent must inform the athletic director of the educational institution at which the athlete is enrolled of the agency agreement. *Id.* at §7802. Violations of SPARTA can result in fines and civil actions seeking damages.

2. General Federal Laws

Prior to the enactment of SPARTA, no federal legislation existed that specifically regulated sports agents. Nevertheless, federal criminal laws have been used to address improper conduct by agents. For example, prosecutors employed the Racketeer Influenced and Corrupt Organizations Act (RICO) and mail fraud statutes in *United States v. Walters*, 997 F.2d 1219 (7th Cir. 1993); 913 F.2d 388 (7th Cir. 1990). Norby Walters along with Lloyd Bloom, who served as his "runner," enticed 58 student-athletes, with remaining collegiate eligibility, to sign exclusive representation agreements with them. The secret agreements were postdated to be effective after the expiration of the athletes' collegiate athletic eligibility. The athletes submitted false information to their universities regarding any restrictions on their eligibility. Facts providing the predicate for the alleged RICO violation included alleged extortion, mail fraud, and wire fraud. The mail fraud allegedly was committed against the NCAA and occurred when the athletes had their institutions send written documents to the NCAA indicating that the athletes were eligible for intercollegiate competition. The matter became a mail fraud case after prosecutors agreed to dismiss the RICO violations as a part of a plea bargain. The failure of the prosecutors to prove the elements of mail fraud resulted in the Seventh Circuit's dismissal of the claim against Walters. *Walters* was recently distinguished in *United States v. Gatto*, 986 F.3d 104 (2d. Cir. 2021). In upholding the wire fraud conviction of defendant involved in the Adidas basketball scandal (see discussion in Chapters 3 and 10, *supra*), the court holds that unlike in *Walters*, the critical "element in a wire fraud statute is the use of wires, which Defendants do not—and cannot—dispute." *Id.* at 126.

The use of non-agent-specific statutes and the implications of improper payments to student-athletes are demonstrated in *United States v. Piggie*, 303 F.3d 923 (8th Cir. 2002). Myron Piggie developed a scheme whereby he paid elite high school players to compete for his Amateur Athletic Union (AAU) summer basketball team. Between 1995 and 1998, Piggie realized at least $677,760 in income from his scheme and anticipated receiving a percentage of the compensation that his players would earn after they signed contracts with NBA teams. Piggie pled guilty to conspiracy to commit mail and wire fraud in violation of 18 U.S.C. §371 and failure to file an income tax return in violation of 26 U.S.C. §7203. He received a 37-month prison term and was ordered to pay $324,279.87 in restitution. The court described the consequences of Piggie's scheme as follows:

> NCAA regulations permit universities to award only thirteen basketball scholarships per year. When Piggie's payments to these players were discovered, the Universities became subject to NCAA penalties. Each school lost the use of one of the thirteen scholarships and lost the value of each player's participation due to the player's NCAA-required suspension. The scholarships were forfeited, and the Universities lost the opportunity to award the scholarships to other top amateur athletes, who had actual eligibility to play intercollegiate basketball. In 1999 and 2000, UCLA lost the benefit of playing Jaron Rush, the $44,862.88 scholarship awarded to him, and also forfeited $42,339 in tournament revenue; Missouri lost the benefit of playing Kareem Rush, and the $9,388.92 scholarship awarded to him; and OSU lost the benefit of playing Williams and the $12,180 scholarship awarded to him. Duke provided Maggette with a $32,696 scholarship for the 1998–1999 season based upon the false assertion that he was an eligible amateur. As a result of an ineligible athlete's participation, the validity of Duke's entire 1998–1999 season was called into question.[4]
>
> NCAA regulations also required each of the four Universities involved to conduct costly internal investigations after Piggie's scheme was discovered. UCLA spent $59,225.36 on the NCAA-mandated investigation of Jaron Rush, Duke spent $12,704.39 on the NCAA-mandated investigation of Maggette, Missouri spent $10,609 on the NCAA-mandated investigation of Kareem Rush, and OSU spent $21,877.24 on the NCAA-mandated investigation of Williams. The total monetary loss to the Universities was $245,882.79. The scandal following the disclosure of Piggie's scheme caused further intangible harms to the Universities including adverse publicity, diminished alumni support, merchandise sales losses, and other revenue losses.

Id. at 925–26.

The college basketball scandal discussed in Chapter 3, *supra*, spawned federal indictments against individuals including coaches, boosters, an Adidas executive, and a runner/aspiring sports agent, Christian Dawkins. Similar to *Piggie*, charges filed against Dawkins included conspiracy to commit wire fraud and wire fraud. *U.S. v. Gatto*, 986 F.3d 104 (2d Cir. 2021). Dawkins received a six-year prison sentence. *Id.* at 112. The Second Circuit denied his appeal. *Id.* at 130. Former Adidas executive James Gatto was sentenced to a nine-month prison term after being convicted on wire fraud and conspiracy to commit wire fraud charges. *Id.* Gatto agreed to pay a total of $342,437.75 to the University of Kansas and North Carolina State University. *Gatto to Pay Back $342K to NC State, Kansas*, ESPN, Apr. 8, 2019, *https://www.espn.com/mens-college-basketball/story/_/id/26473901/gatto-pay-back-342k-nc-state-kansas*.

---

[4]Maggette played the full 1998–99 season for Duke before Piggie's scheme was uncovered.

> **QUESTIONS**

In *United States v. Piggie*, the court identified several direct damages caused by Piggie's scheme. Can you think of other specific intangible harms? In light of this, do you believe the award of $324,279.87 in restitution was warranted, or did Piggie's actions call for a greater or lesser fine?

B. State Regulation: The UAAA

Two bodies of state law may be available to regulate the agent profession. One level consists of non-agent-specific civil and criminal laws that might be invoked to penalize agents for improprieties. The other level consists of agent-specific legislation. Prior to the year 2000, agent-specific legislation was in effect in 28 states (the state of Washington had adopted such legislation but repealed it in 1999). States achieved a modicum of success in prosecuting agents under these statutes. For example, in 1994, agent Nate Cebrun received 30 days in jail and was fined $2,255 for conduct related to making improper payments to a Florida State football player and for failing to register in the state as a sports agent. See Shropshire, Davis & Duru, *supra* note 1, at 142–43 (discussing the Cebrun matter and other instances in which states have sanctioned athletes pursuant to agent-specific statutes).

In 2000, the National Conference of Commissioners on Uniform State Laws (now known as the Uniform Law Commission (ULC)) finished drafting the UAAA and presented it to the states for adoption. From a regulatory perspective, the primary goal of the UAAA was to protect the interests of student-athletes and academic institutions by regulating the activities of sports agents. The UAAA's other critical goal was to achieve uniformity. In 2015, the UAAA was revised. Prior to its 2015 revision, the UAAA had been adopted in 43 states, territories, and Washington, D.C. As of June 2019, the Revised Uniform Athlete Agents Act (RUAAA), excerpts from which appear below, had been enacted in ten states and introduced in five states.

Following the college basketball scandal (see discussion *supra* and in Chapter 3, *supra*), the NCAA revised its regulations to allow basketball student-athletes greater flexibility in deciding whether to become professionals without jeopardizing their collegiate eligibility. The amended NCAA bylaws, adopted on August 8, 2018, permit sports agents to contract with and to pay student-athletes and their parents for meals and hotel and travel expenses related to agents recruiting student-athletes as clients to the extent permitted under NCAA bylaws. Consequently, the RUAAA was amended in 2019 to align with the NCAA's changes to its bylaws.

Uniform Law Commission, Revised Uniform Athlete Agents Act *3 (2015) (last amended 2019), https://higherlogicdownload.s3-external-1.amazonaws.com/UNI FORMLAWS/3e456e84-982f-076a-2a60-9a1bee9cff85_file.pdf?AWSAccessKey- Id=AKIAVRDO7IEREB57R7MT&Expires=1685837266&Signature=mw4wDUy-

qCROx3e%2BkfNxQYDDiW2o%3D. See John Sahl, *The Changing Landscape of Intercollegiate Athletics—The Need to Revisit the NCAAs "No Agent" Rule,* 61 Santa Clara L. Rev. 1, 57+ (2020).

REVISED UNIFORM ATHLETE AGENTS ACT (2015)

PREFATORY NOTE. . . .

Some 43 states have enacted the UAAA. However, several states have amended the act to, among other things, deal with a perceived lack of enforcement, broaden the coverage of the act to individuals who do not necessarily recruit or solicit a student athlete to enter into an agency contract, and require notice to educational institutions prior to contact. It became evident that the variations from state to state put uniformity at risk and may have discouraged reputable agents from complying with the act. To deal with these issues, the Uniform Law Commission adopted the Revised Uniform Athlete Agents Act (RUAAA) in July of 2015.

The purposes of the RUAAA include providing enhanced protection for student athletes and educational institutions, creating a uniform body of agent registration information for use by the state agencies registering agents, and simplifying the registration process for agents.

Specifically, the RUAAA:

- Revises the definition of "athlete agent" to include an individual who, for compensation or the anticipation of compensation, serves the athlete in an advisory capacity on a matter related to finances, business pursuits, or career management decisions or manages the business affairs of the athlete by providing assistance with bills, payments, contracts, or taxes, and an individual who gives something of value to a student athlete or another person in anticipation of representing the athlete for a purpose related to the athlete's participation in athletics. . . .
- Requires an agent to notify the educational institution at which a student athlete is enrolled before contacting a student athlete and requires an athlete agent with a preexisting relationship with a student athlete who enrolls at an educational institution and receives an athletic scholarship to notify the institution of the relationship if the agent knows or should have known of the enrollment and the relationship was motivated by the intention of the agent to recruit or solicit the athlete to enter an agency contract or the agent actually recruited or solicited the student athlete to enter a contract.
- Adds criminal penalties for athlete agents who encourage another individual to take on behalf of the agent an action the agent is prohibited from taking and gives student athletes a right of action against an athlete agent in violation of the act.

SECTION 2. DEFINITIONS. In this [Act]:

(1) "Agency contract" means an agreement in which a student athlete authorizes a person to negotiate or solicit on behalf of the athlete a professional-sports-services contract or endorsement contract.

(2) "Athlete agent":
   (A) means an individual, whether or not registered under this [act], who:
      (i) directly or indirectly recruits or solicits a student athlete to enter into an agency contract or, for compensation, procures employment or offers, promises, attempts, or negotiates to obtain employment for a student athlete as a professional athlete or member of a professional sports team or organization;
      (ii) for compensation or in anticipation of compensation related to a student athlete's participation in athletics:
         (I) serves the athlete in an advisory capacity on a matter related to finances, business pursuits, or career management decisions, unless the individual is an employee of an educational institution acting exclusively as an employee of the institution for the benefit of the institution; or
         (II) manages the business affairs of the athlete by providing assistance with bills, payments, contracts, or taxes; or
      (iii) in anticipation of representing a student athlete for a purpose related to the athlete's participation in athletics:
         (I) gives consideration to the student athlete or another person;
         (II) serves the athlete in an advisory capacity on a matter related to finances, business pursuits, or career management decisions; or
         (III) manages the business affairs of the athlete by providing assistance with bills, payments, contracts, or taxes; but
   (B) does not include an individual who:
      (i) acts solely on behalf of a professional sports team or organization; or
      (ii) is a licensed, registered, or certified professional and offers or provides services to a student athlete customarily provided by members of the profession, unless the individual:
         (I) also recruits or solicits the athlete to enter into an agency contract;
         (II) also, for compensation, procures employment or offers, promises, attempts, or negotiates to obtain employment for the athlete as a professional athlete or member of a professional sports team or organization; or
         (III) receives consideration for providing the services calculated using a different method than for an individual who is not a student athlete. . . .

(7) "Endorsement contract" means an agreement under which a student athlete is employed or receives consideration to use on behalf of the other party any value that the athlete may have because of publicity, reputation, following, or fame obtained because of athletic ability or performance. . . .

(11) "Licensed, registered, or certified professional: means an individual licensed, registered, or certified as an attorney, dealer in securities, financial planner, insurance agent, real estate broker or sales agent, tax consultant, accountant, or member of a profession, other than that of athlete agent, who is licensed, registered, or certified by the state or a nationally recognized organization that licenses, registers, or certifies members of the profession on the basis of experience, education, or testing. . . .

(13) "Professional-sports-services-contract" means an agreement under which an individual is employed as a professional athlete or agrees to render services as a player on a professional sports team or with a professional sports organization. . . .

(15) "Recruit or solicit" means attempt to influence the choice of an athlete agent by a student athlete or, if the athlete is a minor, a parent or guardian of the athlete. The term does not include giving advice on the selection of a particular agent in a family, coaching, or social situation unless the individual giving the advice does so because of the receipt or anticipated receipt of an economic benefit, directly or indirectly, from the agent. . . .

(19) "Student athlete" means an individual who is eligible to attend an educational institution and engages in, is eligible to engage in, or may be eligible in the future to engage in, any interscholastic or intercollegiate sport. The term does not include an individual permanently ineligible to participate in a particular interscholastic or intercollegiate sport for that sport. . . .

SECTION 4. ATHLETE AGENT: REGISTRATION REQUIRED; VOID CONTRACT.

(a) Except as otherwise provided in subsection (b), an individual may not act as an athlete agent in this state without holding a certificate of registration under this [act].

(b) Before being issued a certificate of registration under this [act] an individual may act as an athlete agent in this state for all purposes except signing an agency contract, if:

(1) a student athlete or another person acting on behalf of the athlete initiates communication with the individual; and

(2) not later than seven days after an initial act that requires the individual to register as an athlete agent, the individual submits an application for registration as an athlete agent in this state.

(c) An agency contract resulting from conduct in violation of this section is void, and the athlete agent shall return any consideration received under the contract. . . .

SECTION 6. CERTIFICATE OF REGISTRATION; ISSUANCE OR DENIAL; RENEWAL. . . .

(b) The [Secretary of State] may refuse to issue a certificate of registration to an applicant for registration under Section 5(a) if the [Secretary of State] determines that the applicant has engaged in conduct that significantly adversely reflects on the applicant's fitness to act as an athlete agent. In making the determination, the [Secretary of State] may consider whether the applicant has:

(1) pleaded guilty or no contest to, has been convicted of, or has charges pending for, a crime that would involve moral turpitude or be a felony if committed in this state;

(2) made a materially false, misleading, deceptive, or fraudulent representation in the application or as an athlete agent;
(3) engaged in conduct that would disqualify the applicant from serving in a fiduciary capacity;
(4) engaged in conduct prohibited by Section 14;
(5) had a registration as an athlete agent suspended, revoked, or denied in any state;
(6) been refused renewal of registration as an athlete agent in any state;
(7) engaged in conduct resulting in imposition of a sanction, suspension, or declaration of ineligibility to participate in an interscholastic, intercollegiate, or professional athletic event on a student athlete or a sanction on an educational institution; or
(8) engaged in conduct that adversely reflects on the applicant's credibility, honesty, or integrity.

SECTION 7. SUSPENSION, REVOCATION, OR REFUSAL TO RENEW REGISTRATION.

(a) The [Secretary of State] may limit, suspend, revoke, or refuse to renew a registration of an individual registered under Section 6(a) for conduct that would have justified refusal to issue a certificate of registration under Section 6(b) . . .

SECTION 10. REQUIRED FORM OF AGENCY CONTRACT.

(a) An agency contract must be in a record signed by the parties. . . .
(c) Subject to subsection (g), an agency contract must contain a conspicuous notice in boldface type and in substantially the following form:

WARNING TO STUDENT ATHLETE

IF YOU SIGN THIS CONTRACT:
(1) YOU MAY LOSE YOUR ELIGIBILITY TO COMPETE AS A STUDENT ATHLETE IN YOUR SPORT;
(2) IF YOU HAVE AN ATHLETIC DIRECTOR, WITHIN 72 HOURS AFTER SIGNING THIS CONTRACT OR BEFORE THE NEXT SCHEDULED ATHLETIC EVENT IN WHICH YOU PARTICIPATE, WHICHEVER OCCURS FIRST, BOTH YOU AND YOUR ATHLETE AGENT MUST NOTIFY YOUR ATHLETIC DIRECTOR THAT YOU HAVE ENTERED INTO THIS CONTRACT AND PROVIDE THE NAME AND CONTACT INFORMATION OF THE ATHLETE AGENT; AND
(3) YOU MAY CANCEL THIS CONTRACT WITHIN 14 DAYS AFTER SIGNING IT. CANCELLATION OF THIS CONTRACT MAY NOT REINSTATE YOUR ELIGIBILITY AS A STUDENT ATHLETE IN YOUR SPORT.

(d) An agency contract must be accompanied by a separate record signed by the student athlete or, if the athlete is a minor, the parent or guardian of the athlete acknowledging that signing the contract may result in the loss of the athlete's eligibility to participate in the athlete's sport. . . .

SECTION 11. NOTICE TO EDUCATIONAL INSTITUTION.

(a) In this section, "communicating or attempting to communicate" means contacting or attempting to contact by an in-person meeting, a record, or any other method that conveys or attempts to convey a message.

(b) [Editors' note: A student-athlete is required to provide the same notice as that described in (a) above.]

SECTION 12. STUDENT ATHLETE'S RIGHT TO CANCEL.

(a) A student athlete or, if the athlete is a minor, the parent or guardian of the athlete may cancel an agency contract by giving notice in a record of cancellation to the athlete agent not later than 14 days after the contract is signed. . . .

(c) If a student athlete, parent, or guardian cancels an agency contract, the athlete, parent, or guardian is not required to pay any consideration under the contract or return any consideration received from the athlete agent to influence the athlete to enter into the contract . . .

SECTION 14. PROHIBITED CONDUCT.

(a) An athlete agent, with the intent to influence a student athlete or, if the athlete is a minor, a parent or guardian of the athlete to enter into an agency contract, may not take any of the following actions or encourage any other individual to take or assist any other individual in taking any of the following actions on behalf of the agent:
  (1) give materially false or misleading information or make a materially false promise or representation;
  (2) furnish anything of value to the athlete before the athlete enters into the contract; or
  (3) furnish anything of value to an individual other than the athlete or another registered athlete agent.

(b) An athlete agent may not intentionally do any of the following or encourage any other individual to do any of the following on behalf of the agent:
  (1) initiate contact, directly or indirectly, with a student athlete or, if the athlete is a minor, a parent or guardian of the athlete, to recruit or solicit the athlete, parent, or guardian to enter an agency contract unless registered under this [act] . . .

SECTION 15. CRIMINAL PENALTY.

An athlete agent who violates Section 14 is guilty of a [misdemeanor] [felony] and, on conviction, is punishable by [ ].

[Editors' note: The RUAAA directs each state to determine the criminal sanctions that will result from its violation.]

SECTION 16. CIVIL REMEDY.

(a) An educational institution or student athlete may bring an action for damages against an athlete agent if the institution or athlete is adversely affected by an act or omission of the agent in violation of this [act]. An educational institution or student athlete is adversely affected by an act or omission of the agent only if, because of the act or omission, the institution or an individual who was a student athlete at the time of the act or omission and enrolled in the institution:
   (1) is suspended or disqualified from participation in an interscholastic or intercollegiate [sports] event by or under the rules of a state or national federation or association that promotes or regulates interscholastic or intercollegiate sports; or
   (2) suffers financial damage.
(b) A plaintiff that prevails in an action under this section may recover [actual damages] [treble damages] [,] [punitive damages,] [and] costs [, and reasonable attorney's fees]. An athlete agent found liable under this section forfeits any right of payment for anything of benefit or value provided to the student athlete and shall refund any consideration paid to the agent by or on behalf of the athlete. . . .

SECTION 17. CIVIL PENALTY.

The [Secretary of State] [commission] may assess a civil penalty against an athlete agent not to exceed $[50,000] for a violation of this [act]. . . .

NOTES

UAAA Prosecutions. In one of the first indictments brought pursuant to the UAAA, on October 13, 2006, a grand jury in Baton Rouge, Louisiana, charged Charles Taplin with two counts of violating Louisiana's version of the UAAA. Taplin allegedly violated the UAAA's registration and notification provisions when he sent text messages to two Louisiana State University football players on behalf of an agent. Taplin was not a registered agent and allegedly failed to notify LSU within seven days of contacting the players. Adrian Angelette, *"Runner" Indicted in Sports Agent Case*, Baton Rouge Advocate, Aug. 15, 2007. While investigating Taplin, information was allegedly uncovered that led to the arrest of Travelle Gaines, a former assistant strength coach at LSU. Gaines was booked on a felony count of engaging in activities prohibited by Louisiana's UAAA—allegedly inviting players to his home where they met a California-based agent, C.J. Laboy. Adrian Angelette, *La. Law Allows Agent-Athlete Contact Within Rules*, Baton Rouge Advocate, Oct. 26, 2006, at A1. Gaines's attorney denied that his client had done anything illegal.

In October 2008, a Virginia-based and NFLPA-certified contract advisor, Raymond L. Savage, Jr., was indicted for allegedly violating the UAAA. Savage was charged with failing to register under Alabama's UAAA and for initiating contact with a student-athlete. One of Savage's former employees, Jason Goggins, allegedly contacted Tyrone Prothro, a University of Alabama wide receiver. The indictment of Savage alleged that the agent instructed Goggins to visit the player and paid for Goggins's plane fare to Alabama. Goggins's alleged conduct led to his indictment in 2006 for the same alleged violations of Alabama's UAAA. Savage agreed to plead guilty to a misdemeanor, the payment of a $2,000 fine, and restrictions on contact with athletes. In Alabama, failure to register under the UAAA is a felony and carries a maximum sentence of ten years in prison and a fine of up to $5,000. Liz Mullen, *State of Alabama Say Agent Ran Afoul of Tough Recruiting Laws*, Sports Bus. J., Nov. 10, 2008, at 13; Peter Dujardin, *Sports Agent Denies He Violated Alabama Law, Will Fight Charges*, Daily Press (Newport News, VA), Oct. 15, 2008, at A11.

The North Carolina Secretary of State's office indicted several individuals who allegedly engaged in conduct that resulted in the imposition of NCAA sanctions against the University of North Carolina at Chapel Hill. (For background information discussing the conduct that violated NCAA rules, see NCAA, *University of North Carolina at Chapel Hill, NCAA Public Infractions Report*, March 12, 2012, and discussion in Chapter 3, *supra*). An agent, Terry Watson, was indicted for allegedly providing impermissible benefits to induce athletes to sign an agency contract. Brooke Pryor, *Sports Agent Terry Watson Indicted Related to UNC Athlete-Agent Case*, DailyTarHeel.com, Oct. 10, 2013. Watson pled guilty to 13 counts of athlete-agent inducement and was sentenced to 30 months of probation along with a $5,000 fine and a suspended 6-to-8-month jail sentence. *Ex-NFL Agent Watson Pleads Guilty to Giving Cash to 3 Former UNC Players*, ESPN.com, Apr. 17, 2017. Patrick Mitchell Jones, 43, was charged with violating the UAAA by providing an improper inducement of $725 to a former UNC football player. Aaron Beard, *Ex-agent Pleads Guilty in Multi-Year UNC Sports Agent Probe*, AP News, Apr. 17, 2017, https://apnews.com/66a89e60415e440791d1fa7bbe0ee72c. Another individual, Michael Wayne Johnson Jr., was indicted on three felony counts of improper inducements. In 2017, he entered into a plea deal under which the felony charges were reduced to misdemeanors and were to be dismissed if Johnson complied with terms of a 12-month probation. *Ex-NC Central QB Receives Probation in UNC Agents Probe*, USA Today, Apr. 18, 2017.

Notwithstanding the foregoing prosecutions, a 2010 study conducted by the Associated Press revealed that over half of the then 42 states that enacted the UAAA had "yet to revoke or suspend a single license, or invoke penalties of any sort." Zagler, *supra*. According to the Associated Press review, "[t]wenty-four states reported taking no disciplinary or criminal actions against sports agents, and were unable to determine if state or local prosecutors had pursued such cases. Others described the laws as being enforced a few times, or rarely, an indication of what a low priority they are." *Id*. Texas was reportedly one of the few states that consistently enforced the UAAA. The review found that between 2008 and 2010, Texas had disciplined 31 agents and levied fines totaling $17,500. *Id*. There is no indication that the number of UAAA prosecutions has increased significantly over the last ten years.

What reasons may underlie the under-enforcement of the UAAA?

The case that follows is unique in that it represents the only instance, to date, in which an appellate court has addressed the intersection of the UAAA and the contract relationship between athletes and their agents.

Williamson v. Prime Sports Mktg., LLC.
2021 WL 201255 (M.D. N.C. Jan. 20, 2021)

Loretta C. Biggs, District Judge.

[Editors' note: The lawsuit arose out of a marketing agreement (Agreement) between Zion Williamson, an NBA player who played college basketball at Duke University, and a Florida-based sports marketing agency and one of its agents (Gina Ford). Williamson, who was a student at Duke when the parties entered into the Agreement, requested that the court declare the contract void because Ford was not a registered agent in North Carolina as required by the UAAA. The agent argued that she was not required to be registered because Williamson had relinquished his student-athlete status by signing the Agreement. Williamson argued, in the alternative, that the Agreement was voidable by him because it failed to include language warning (required by the UAAA) the athlete that by signing the Agreement, the athlete could lose his intercollegiate eligibility.]

• • • • • • • • • •

B. The North Carolina Uniform Athlete Agent Act ("UAAA")

The UAAA provides requirements for the conduct of individuals acting as athlete agents in North Carolina and for contracts entered into between athlete agents and student-athletes. Under the statute, an individual is required to register with the North Carolina Secretary of State before acting as an athlete agent in the state, unless the individual is a North Carolina licensed and resident attorney. N.C. Gen. Stat. §78C-88(a)-(c).

The UAAA defines "athlete agent" as a person who (1) "enters into an agency contract with a student-athlete;" (2) "directly or indirectly . . . recruits or solicits a student-athlete to enter into an agency contract;" or (3) "represents to the public that" he or she "is an athlete agent." Id. §78C-86(2). Those seeking certification as an athlete agent must submit an application that provides, among other things, a description of their formal training, practical experience, and educational background relating to agent activities. Id. §78C-89. The UAAA provides that an agency contract resulting from conduct that violates Section 78C-88 of the act is void. Id. §78C-88(d).

The UAAA also provides requirements for contracts between athlete agents and student-athletes, and its definition of an "agency contract" incorporates any agreement which grants an individual the authority to negotiate or solicit "a professional-sports-services contract or an endorsement contract" on behalf of a student-athlete. Id. §78C-86(1). These requirements include, among other things, that the contract include[s] a "conspicuous" warning to the potential client that his signature will result in a loss of intercollegiate eligibility as well as the date of execution of the contract. Id. §78C-94(a)-(c). An agency contract that does not meet the express terms of the statute is voidable by the student-athlete. Id. §78C-94(d).

C. Discussion

Defendants' primary argument against the appropriateness of judgment on the pleadings is that they have made sufficient allegations to call into question Plaintiff's status as a student-athlete, which would mean that the UAAA did not apply to Plaintiff and Defendants' relationship, or the resulting Agreement. According to Defendants, "[a]t the time Plaintiff [entered] Duke University as a Freshman in 2018, the Plaintiff was not a 'student athlete' as define[d] by the [National Collegiate Athletic Association ("NCAA")] and/or as defined by [the] UAAA." This is because, allegedly, "the Plaintiff and/or third parties acting on the Plaintiff's behalf had violated one or more of the NCAA and/or UAAA rules that . . . rendered him ineligible to be a student athlete."

1. Plaintiff Was a Student Athlete Under the UAAA

Turning to the statute, the UAAA defines "student-athlete" broadly as "[a]n individual who engages in, is eligible to engage in, *or* may be eligible in the future to engage in any intercollegiate sport," but not an individual who is "permanently ineligible to participate" in the sport. N.C. Gen. Stat. §78C-86(11) (emphasis added). Defendants argue that Plaintiff alleged a conclusory assertion that he was a student-athlete just because he was playing basketball at Duke and that allegation cannot defeat Defendants' allegations that Plaintiff was ineligible/permanently ineligible to participate in collegiate sports while playing for Duke. The Court disagrees. Plaintiff's allegation that he was a student-athlete is more than merely a conclusory allegation. Plaintiff has affirmatively and specifically alleged that he enrolled as a student at Duke University in 2018 and played basketball for Duke as a true freshman during the 2018–2019 collegiate basketball season.

Though Defendants deny Plaintiff's eligibility to be a student-athlete, they nevertheless acknowledge that Plaintiff did "engage in" intercollegiate sports at Duke during the relevant period. They have additionally attached exhibits to their pleadings that refer to Plaintiff's engagement in collegiate athletics. For instance, one attachment dated May 13, 2019, states that, at one time, "the whole world was telling [Plaintiff] that there was no reason for him to even finish off the basketball season with the team." The attachment goes on to state that after a game "on February 20, when [his] left foot famously blew through his sneaker while spraining his right knee in the process, current and former NBA players encouraged [Plaintiff] to shut it down for the season." Despite this, according to the document, Plaintiff had "every intention of playing with his team 'til the very last whistle, he also had every bit of intention to remain a regular student on campus 'til the very last final exam/presentation." Given that the UAAA merely requires that an individual "engages in" an intercollegiate sport in order to be considered a student-athlete, it appears uncontested that Plaintiff meets this bar.

Even so, Defendants argue that, even if Plaintiff did engage in the intercollegiate sports, he was permanently ineligible to do so and thus would be precluded from any protections offered by the UAAA. More specifically, in their affirmative defenses and Counterclaims, Defendants allege that, prior to April 20, 2019, Plaintiff: engaged in conduct/acts that rendered and renders him ineligible to be or remain a "student-athlete" including, but not limited to:

(a) He agrees orally or in writing to be represented by any individual other than a NCAA-certified agent;
(b) He accepts any benefits from an individual other than a NCAA-certified agent; and
(c) He entered the NBA Draft AND did not intend to and did not take the appropriate steps to withdraw and declare any intention of resuming intercollegiate participation and, in fact, repeatedly and publicly declared and made it abundantly clear that he was not ever returning to intercollegiate basketball.

Yet this list is merely a recitation of purported offenses that could have led to ineligibility, permanent or otherwise, of any student player and does not serve as allegations specific to Plaintiff. Defendants have not alleged that Plaintiff had, in fact engaged in any of those activities or had been deemed permanently ineligible by the NCAA or under the UAAA at the time of the Agreement or even subsequently.

Defendants' affirmative defenses and counter claims that Plaintiff was not a student-athlete do not rely on material allegations of fact, rather a conclusion of law that flies in the face of their own pleadings as well as attachments to their pleadings. Although Defendants assert that their pleadings make clear that they contest Plaintiff's status as a student-athlete at the time that the Agreement was entered, this assertion is in direct conflict with their admission that Plaintiff was actively engaging in an intercollegiate sport — namely, men's basketball — which is one of the ways the UAAA provides that an individual can be deemed a student-athlete . . . Defendants' general allegations, denials, and affirmative defenses are insufficient to raise a genuine issue of material fact as to whether Plaintiff was a student-athlete during the time in which he was a member of Duke men's basketball team.

Further, Defendants have not alleged or provided any facts to plausibly support their conclusory claims that Plaintiff was permanently ineligible to compete in intercollegiate athletics at the time the parties entered into the Agreement. Defendants' listing of purported offenses are insufficient to raise a genuine issue of material fact as to whether Plaintiff had been deemed permanently ineligible during the time period in question and thus no longer a student-athlete under the UAAA. Defendants have provided no authority, case law or otherwise, that suggests that it is for a court to adjudicate the details of a student-athlete's eligibility under NCAA rules. Rather, in applying the statute, it would appear that the Court's role is to determine whether the student-athlete has been either determined to be or declared "permanently ineligible" by the governing body authorized to do so. Defendants have not alleged that this has occurred.

The Court finds that there is no genuine dispute that Plaintiff engaged in intercollegiate sports while a student at Duke University during the relevant time period. Further, there is no genuine dispute that he had not been declared permanently ineligible to do so at the time of the Agreement. Therefore, there is no genuine issue of material fact as to whether Plaintiff was a student-athlete under the UAAA during the time he entered into the Agreement with Defendants.

2. Neither Defendant Ford Nor the Agreement Complied with the UAAA

[T]he Court now turns to the analysis under Section 78C-88 of the UAAA. To begin, it is undisputed that Defendant Ford holds herself out as an athlete agent yet neither she nor her agency are licensed as athlete agents in North Carolina, nor have they applied for such a designation. When an individual acts as an athlete agent without holding a certificate of registration, the UAAA expressly provides that any agency contract the individual entered with a student-athlete "is void, and the athlete agent shall return any consideration received under the contract." N.C. Gen. Stat. §78C-88(d).

As stated above, a contract that authorizes a person to negotiate a professional-sports-services contract or an endorsement contract on behalf of a student-athlete, as the Agreement does, is included in the definition of an agency contract under the UAAA. Id. §78C-86(1). For such contracts, the UAAA expressly sets forth precise requirements for a warning that must be included. Specifically, it "must contain, in close proximity to the signature of the student-athlete, a conspicuous notice in boldface type in capital letters" the following language:

WARNING TO STUDENT-ATHLETE
IF YOU SIGN THIS CONTRACT:
[Editors' note: The court quotes the remaining language of the warning.]

When a contract does not contain this required disclosure, it is voidable by the student-athlete. Id. §78C-94(d).

[T]he Court concludes that Plaintiff is entitled to judgment as a matter of law on the issue of whether the Agreement is void. Specifically, there is no dispute that: (1) Plaintiff was a student at Duke University and playing on Duke University's men's basketball team at the time that the parties engaged one another; (2) he had not been determined to be permanently ineligible by any governing body at the time of the agreement; (3) Defendant Ford did not hold the requisite athlete agent certification as required by North Carolina's UAAA; (4) the parties entered into the Agreement; (5) the Agreement permits Defendants to negotiate or solicit professional-sports-services or endorsement contracts on Plaintiff's behalf; (6) the Agreement at issue did not have the statutorily required warning; and (7) Plaintiff's family communicated to Defendants that they were terminating and voiding the agreement. . . .

IT IS ORDERED that Plaintiff's Motion for Partial Judgment on the Pleadings is GRANTED. The Court hereby declares that the Agreement entered into by the parties is void as a matter of law under N.C. Gen. Stat. §78C-88 (the "UAAA").

QUESTIONS

1. **Student-Athlete Defined.** The defendants argued that Zion Williamson was not a student-athlete at the time of contracting, thus the contract was valid. What was the basis of this argument? Based on the UAAA's definition of student-athlete, why did the court reject defendants' argument? Would the outcome have changed if the court agreed with their argument?
2. **Valid Contract.** What was the court's reasoning for invalidating the contract? The UAAA requires the inclusion of specific language in contracts between student-athletes and athlete-agents. Why?
3. **NIL Agent Contracts.** As a result of state legislation, governor executive orders, and the NCAA's modification of its bylaws, college athletes may (without risking their collegiate eligibility) receive compensation from third parties for the athletes' NIL rights. This has resulted in an accompanying change in college athletes' ability to hire agents without violating the NCAA's agent regulations. Today, a college athlete may retain an agent for the limited purpose of assisting college athletes in securing and negotiating NIL deals. Any such representation agreement must specify that the agent's representation is limited to NIL-related matters.

Problem 13-3

Bruce Reynolds, a football player, met Mr. Fritz of Complete Sports Management, Inc., when Reynolds played at Allstate University. Fritz is an NFLPA-certified contract advisor. On January 3, 2023, Reynolds met Fritz at Fritz's car dealership. To enable Reynolds to purchase a car without paying anything, Fritz advanced Reynolds credit. On January 18, 2023, Reynolds signed an undated, standard-form NFLPA representation agreement with Complete Sports Management, Inc. Fritz told Reynolds not to send the agreement to the NFLPA as provided for in the union's regulations. Sometime thereafter, a coach advised Reynolds to sign with another agent, which the athlete did. Reynolds informed Fritz that he had signed with another agent and that he would return the automobile to Fritz. Reynolds also informed Fritz that he would reimburse him for the more than $2,900 in cash and goods that Fritz had extended to Reynolds since January 18. Reynolds was ultimately drafted by an NFL team and signed a three-year contract that provided a total compensation of $4.1 million and other incentive bonuses.

Did Fritz violate any rules, regulations, or laws? If so, what are the consequences of such a violation? Consider the UAAA, Section 1 of NFLPA Regulations Governing Contract Advisors, *infra*, and Article 12 of the 2019-20 NCAA Manual, *infra*. See *Walters v. Fullwood*, 675 F. Supp. 155 (S.D. N.Y. 1987) (dismissing agent's claims against athlete where agent paid athlete $4,000 to enter into postdated agency contract in violation of NCAA and

NFLPA rules); *Chiappeparelli v. Henderson*, 2005 WL 1847221 (Cal. Ct. App.) (finding that a plaintiff agent, who failed to obtain a license as required by the applicable state agent regulations, could not collect a percentage of the compensation that the defendant had earned from martial arts contests since the representation contract between the agent and defendant was illegal and unenforceable).

C. Players' Associations

1. Authority to Regulate

As noted in Chapters 11 and 12, in team sports, players' associations are unions. These unions represent a principal component of the web of regulation that affects the athlete-agent relationship. In *Collins v. National Basketball Players Association*, the court described the abuses that prompted players' unions to legislate the athlete-agent relationship as follows:

> Specifically, players complained that the agents imposed high and non-uniform fees for negotiation services, insisted on execution of open-ended powers of attorney giving the agents broad powers over players' professional and financial decisions, failed to keep players apprised of the status of negotiations with NBA teams, failed to submit itemized bills for fees and services, and, in some cases had conflicts of interest arising out of representing coaches and/or general managers of NBA teams as well as players. Many players believed that they were bound by contract not to dismiss their agents regardless of dissatisfaction with their services and fees, because the agents had insisted on the execution of long-term agreements. Some agents offered money and other inducements to players, their families, and coaches to obtain player clients.

Collins v. National Basketball Players Association, 850 F. Supp. 1468, 1471 (D. Colo. 1991).

The following excerpt describes how players' associations fit into the larger scheme of labor relations law that regulates the representation of employees once they have entered into a collective bargaining agreement with employers:

> In most industries, unions (pursuant to collective bargaining agreements with employers) negotiate terms and conditions of employment as well as all union member salaries. Professional sports unions, also pursuant to collective bargaining agreements, possess the exclusive authority to negotiate individual player salaries and other terms and conditions of employment such as minimum salaries, pension benefits, health insurance, playing conditions, travel accommodations, the ability of a player to move from one team to another, medical treatment, and grievance and arbitration procedures. However, unlike other unions, sports unions have delegated their exclusive authority to negotiate individual player salaries within the framework established by the collective bargaining agreements.

Shropshire, Davis & Duru, *supra*, at 140.

Players' associations assert similar rationales in articulating their authority to regulate player agents. The NFLPA asserts that it possesses the inherent authority to regulate agents. Pursuant to this authority, the NFLPA, in 1983, "mandated that those agents who desired to represent its members be certified by the union." *Id.* at 139. Another example is the MLBPA, which bases its authority on the NLRA and its right to be "the exclusive representative for all the employees in such unit." *Id.* at 141.

In *Collins v. National Basketball Players Association*, 976 F.2d 740 (10th Cir. 1992), a federal appellate court upheld the authority of a players' union to refuse to recertify an agent. Former NBA basketball player Kareem Abdul-Jabbar filed a lawsuit accusing his agent of financial improprieties. Prior to a settlement of Abdul-Jabbar's lawsuit against Collins, the agent had been decertified by the National Basketball Players Association (NBPA). After his application for recertification was denied, Collins sued the NBPA.

The court rejected Collins's claim, stating as follows:

> [Collins] maintains his attack on the Committee's decision to deny his certification because it was based in part on its finding that he had breached his fiduciary duty as an investment agent and money manager. He argues that his conduct outside of negotiations between players and their teams is not a legitimate interest of the union because it has no bearing on the union's interest in the wage scale and working conditions of its members. . . . The NBPA established the Regulations to deal with agent abuses, including agents' violations of their fiduciary duties as labor negotiators. It was entirely fair for the Committee to conclude that a man who had neglected his fiduciary duties as an investment agent and money manager could not be trusted to fulfill his fiduciary duties as a negotiator. The integrity of a prospective negotiating agent is well within the NBPA's legitimate interest in maintaining the wage scale and working conditions of its members.

Collins, 976 F.2d at 740. The court affirmed the district court's grant of summary judgment in favor of the NBPA. See also *Gurley v. Nat'l Basketball Players Ass'n*, 2022 WL17998878 (Dec. 30, 2022) (relying on statutory and non-statutory labor exemptions in rejecting agent applicant's antitrust claims against NFLPA and NFL).

QUESTION

U.S. professional sports unions have the unique power to regulate and certify agents in the world of employee unions. What is the rationale behind granting such authority?

2. Regulating the Athlete-Agent Relationship

a. Sanctions: Suspensions and Decertification

The most severe sanctions that a players' association can impose on an agent are suspension and decertification. Section 6 of the *NFLPA Regulations Governing Contract*

Advisors provides that discipline for violation of its regulations may include suspension, revocation of an advisor's certification (decertification), and the imposition of a fine not to exceed $25,000.

Agents representing athletes in various sports leagues have engaged in conduct that has resulted in suspension or decertification. In 2008, the NBPA suspended agent Calvin Andrews for one year for conduct involving the recruitment of then University of Southern California and later NBA player O.J. Mayo. The NBPA's disciplinary committee found that Andrews, a vice president at Bill Duffy Associates Sports Management, was an intermediary in funneling $30,000 to Mayo. In 2008, the NBPA decertified agent Josh Nochimson for, among other things, stealing approximately $500,000 from clients including Richard Hamilton of the Detroit Pistons.

In 2010, the NFLPA's revocation of Josh Luchs's certification was followed by the 2011 nine-month suspension of the late Gary Wichard, and the 2013 six-month suspension of Martin Magid. An earlier NFLPA disciplinary action against an agent includes the 2006 suspension of Carl Poston for "allegedly signing an important contract for a client without fully reading it first." Liz Mullen, *Source: NFLPA Files Complaint Against Arrington's Agent*, Sports Bus. J., Jan. 23, 2006, at 14. See Shropshire, Davis & Duru, *supra*, at 142-43. See Richard T. Karcher, *Fundamental Fairness in Union Regulation of Sports Agents*, 640 Conn. L. Rev. 355 (2007) (discussing the fairness of player association disciplinary processes).

b. Fees/Agent Compensation

Players' associations regulate varying aspects of the payment by athletes of fees for agent services. For example, the NFLPA agent regulations restrict the maximum amount of fees that an agent can charge for negotiating a player contract with a team. An agent can receive a maximum fee of 3 percent of the compensation that a player receives during the playing season covered by the contract that the agent negotiates. Note that agents are allowed to charge less than the maximum. The NBPA allows fees of up to 4 percent. MLB allows the market to control and sets no maximum on the size of fee an agent can earn for negotiating a player/team contract. Larger representation firms will often waive the fee the NBPA regulations allow in negotiating the first contract between an NBA team and draft picks. Such a firm is willing to forgo the fee as an incentive for the player to sign a representation agreement with it, and with the hope that it will collect a larger fee when the player signs a more lucrative contract three or four years later.

c. NFLPA Amendments

In attempting to confront problems aggressively in the agent industry, the NFLPA enacted several amendments to its agent regulations. In 2002, the NFLPA adopted the one-in-three rule. NFLPA-certified agents are required to negotiate at least one contract during a three-year period in order to retain their certification. See *Dickey v. National Football League*, 2018 WL 4623061 (D. Mass. Sept. 26, 2018) (agent's claim that NFLPA's implementation and enforcement of the one-in-three rule violated antitrust laws by erecting unreasonable barriers to entry to the disadvantage of less-established agent was subject to dismissal pursuant to the statutory labor exemption; the court also held that the plaintiff's antitrust violations premised on the CBA fell within the parameters of the non-statutory labor exemption).

In 2004, the NFLPA amended its regulations to require agents to disclose, in writing, payments they make to runners. In May 2005, the NFLPA amended its regulations to impose a heightened educational requirement. In order to be eligible for certification, prospective agents must have received a postgraduate degree from a college or university or demonstrate sufficient negotiation experience. Also in 2005, the NLFPA amended its regulations to require agents to obtain malpractice insurance. As with the NFLPA's one-in-three rule, a consequence of this amendment is likely to be a decrease in the number of certified NFL agents. In 2007, the NFLPA adopted a new regulation that prohibits suspended agents from directly or indirectly recruiting players during the period of his or her suspension. In 2007, the NFLPA adopted a regulation requiring an agent to disclose to player clients the identity of the coaches, including college coaches, that the agent represents. *Id.*

Amendments to the NFLPA's regulations, adopted in 2012 through 2014, include a provision requiring mandatory arbitration for disputes between NFLPA-certified agents; language clarifying the meaning of the "sufficient negotiating experience" exception to the educational requirement for certification, to specify that an applicant must have "at least seven years of sufficient negotiating experience"; language clarifying what constitutes an accredited college or university; and the requirement of additional disclosures as a part of the application process (i.e., applicants must list unsatisfied liens) NFLPA Legal Dept., *Memorandum from Legal Dep't, Nat'l Football League Players Ass'n, to Contract Advisors* (Apr. 10, 2012 and May 8, 2013).

d. MLBPA Amendments

In 2010, the Major League Baseball Players Association (MLBPA) adopted the first major substantive overall of its agent regulations since they were initially adopted in 1988. The 2010 regulations include provisions relating to client poaching, solicitation and inducements, runners, and arbitration. See MLBPA Regulations Governing Player Agents, available at *http://reg.mlbpaagent.org/Documents/AgentForms/Agent%20Regulations.pdf*. For a descriptive overview and a critical analysis of the MLBPA's new agent regulations, see Darren A. Heitner & Jason B. Wolf, *In Baseball's Best Interest? A Discussion of the October 10, 2010 MLBPA Regulations Governing Player Agents*, 10 Va. Sports & Ent. L.J. 249 (2011). In 2013, MLBPA amended its agent regulations to prohibit agents from lending money to players without first obtaining written approval from the MLBPA. MLBPA, 2013 Amendments to the MLBPA Regulations Governing Player Agents, May 3, 2013, *http://reg.mlbpaagent.org/Documents/AgentForms/Amendments%20to%20the%20MLBPA%20Regulations%20Governing%20Player%20Agents.pdf*. Its regulations were further amended in 2015 to require that agent applicants take a written exam and submit to a background check. MLBPA. Liz Mullen, *MLBPA Announces Agent Certification Now*

Includes Background Check, Written Exam, Sports Bus. J., Jan. 13, 2015, *http://www.sportsbusinessdaily.com/Daily/Issues/2015/01/13/Labor-and-Agents/MLBPA.aspx*.

e. NBPA Amendments

The NBPA made substantial revisions, effective February 15, 2016, to its agent regulations. In articulating the reasons for its first substantial revisions to its regulations since 1991, the NBPA stated:

> Given that nearly thirty (30) years have elapsed since the initial promulgation of these Regulations, the NBPA Executive Committee concluded that the time was ripe to review and analyze the experiences that both they and the Players they represent had in connection with the services provided by their Player Agents. Those experiences demonstrate that amendments to these Regulations were warranted to better reflect the reality of the business between Players and Player Agents. . . .

NBPA, *NBPA Regulations Governing Player Agents* (as amended June 2019), *https://cosmic-s3.imgix.net/e3bb4d60-7b1a-11e9-9bf5-8bad98088629-NBPAAgentRegulations.pdf*.

Among the changes to the 2016 NBPA's agent regulations are provisions emphasizing the fiduciary character of the athlete-agent relationship; articulating the NPBA's authority to adopt and enforce its agent regulations; enhancing the requirements for persons applying for certification (e.g., applicants must pass a written exam administered by the NBPA and agree to arbitrate any disputes with the NBPA relating to the applicant's certification); stating that an agent's certification will automatically expire if he or she, for a five-year period, has no player under contract with an NBA club; making the conduct of individuals who work with an agent in providing representation services chargeable against the agent if the conduct violates NBPA agent regulations; requiring that agents disclose if players are referred to financial advisors; and imposing disclosure requirements on agents who pay third parties to assist the agent in recruiting a player. The NBPA also expanded the range of possible penalties for violations of its agent regulations to include fines of up to $100,000, public reprimand, suspension, and decertification. By including fines as a possible penalty, the NBPA joins the NFLPA, MLBPA, and NHLPA, each of which includes fines as a possible penalty for violations of their respective regulations. The NBPA executive committee also announced that it will strictly enforce its prohibition against agents simultaneously representing both players and coaches and management.

In 2018, the NBPA made revisions to its regulations similar to those made by the ULC to the RUAAA, see discussion *infra*, so that the NBPA agent regulations are consistent with changes adopted by the NCAA, which permit sports agents to pay certain student-athletes and their parents for meals, lodging, and travel expenses related to agent recruitment of student-athletes. These elite basketball student-athletes may also sign representation agreements with agents. In August of 2019, the NCAA released new requirements for agents seeking to represent college basketball underclassmen who are unsure if they want to enter the NBA draft or remain in college.

The rules initially stated that, in order for an underclassman to retain his college eligibility if he chooses not to enter the NBA draft, he must sign with an NCAA-approved agent. In order to be NCAA approved, the agent must: (1) possess a bachelor's degree; (2) be certified by the NBPA for at least three years; and (3) pass an in-person exam administered at the NCAA's headquarters in Indianapolis. Jeff Borzello, *NCAA Issues Rules for Agents, Lebron Responds*, ESPN.com, Aug. 7, 2019. Critics referred to the new requirements as the "Rich Paul Rule," because the requirements would have excluded Rich Paul, the agent for several NBA players including Lebron James, Anthony Davis, and Ben Simmons. Paul has achieved success as an NBPA-certified agent, but he does not have a bachelor's degree. *Id.* The criticism led the NCAA to promptly modify its rules by dropping the college degree requirement. Mark Schlabach, *NCAA Amends "Rich Paul Rule" Amid Blowback*, ESPN.com, Aug. 12, 2019. The NCAA will continue to require these agents to "have NBPA certification for a minimum of three consecutive years, maintain professional liability insurance, complete the NCAA qualification exam and pay the required fees." *Id.*

f. Excerpts of Players' Association and NCAA Regulations

NFLPA REGULATIONS GOVERNING CONTRACT ADVISORS[3]

(as amended through Aug. 2016)

Section 1—Scope of Regulations

A. Persons Subject to Regulations No person (other than a player representing himself) shall be permitted to conduct individual contract negotiations on behalf of a player and/or assist in or advise with respect to such negotiations with NFL Clubs after the effective date of these Regulations unless he/she is (1) currently certified as a Contract Advisor pursuant to these Regulations; (2) signs a Standard Representation Agreement with the player (See Section 4; Appendix D); and (3) files a fully executed copy of the Standard Representation Agreement with the NFLPA, along with any contract(s) between the player and the Contract Advisor for other services to be provided.

B. Activities Covered The activities of Contract Advisors which are governed by these Regulations include: the providing of advice, counsel, information or assistance to players with respect to negotiating their individual contracts with Clubs and/or thereafter in enforcing those contracts; the conduct of individual compensation negotiations with the Clubs on behalf of players; and any other activity or conduct which directly bears upon the Contract Advisor's integrity, competence or ability to properly represent individual NFL players and the NFLPA in individual contract negotiations, including the handling of

---

[3] The complete NFLPA Regulations Governing Contract Advisors (as amended through August 2016) can be found at: *https://nflpaweb.blob.core.windows.net/media/Default/PDFs/Agents/RegulationsAmendedAugust2016.pdf*.

player funds, providing tax counseling and preparation services, and providing financial advice and investment services to individual players. . . .

Section 2 — Certification

After the effective date of these Regulations, any person who wishes to perform the functions of a Contract Advisor as described in Section 1 above must be certified by the NFLPA. . . .

C. Grounds for Denial for Certification Grounds for denial of Certification shall include, but not be limited to, the following:

- The applicant has made false or misleading statements of a material nature in his/her application;
- The applicant has misappropriated funds, or engaged in other specific acts such as embezzlement, theft or fraud, which would render him/her unfit to serve in a fiduciary capacity on behalf of players;
- The applicant has engaged in any other conduct that significantly impacts adversely on his/her credibility, integrity or competence to serve in a fiduciary capacity on behalf of players . . . ;
- The applicant has been denied certification by another professional sports players association;
- The applicant directly or indirectly solicited a player for representation as a Contract Advisor during the period of time between the filing of his/her Application for Certification and Certification by the NFLPA;
- The applicant has not received a degree from an accredited four-year college/university and a postgraduate degree from an accredited college/university, unless excepted from this requirement pursuant to Section 2(A). . . .

Section 3 — Standard of Conduct For Contract Advisors . . .
A. General Requirements
[A] Contract Advisor shall be required to:

(1) Disclose on his/her Application and thereafter upon request of the NFLPA all information relevant to his/her qualifications to serve as a Contract Advisor . . . ;

(5) Comply with the maximum fee schedule and all other provisions of these Regulations and any amendments thereto;

(6) Execute and abide by the printed Standard Representation Agreement with all players represented . . . ;

(9) Provide on or before May 1 each year, to every player who he/she represents, with a copy to the NFLPA, an itemized statement covering the period beginning March 1 of the prior year through February 28 or 29 of that year, which separately sets forth both the fee charged to the player for, and any expenses incurred in connection with, the performance of the following services: [(a) individual player salary negotiations; (b) management of the player's assets; (c) financial, investment, legal, tax and/or other advice to the player; and, (d) any other miscellaneous services].

(17) Act at all times in a fiduciary capacity on behalf of players. . . .

B. Prohibited Conduct

Contract Advisors are prohibited from:

(1) Representing any player in individual contract negotiations with any Club unless he/she (i) is an NFLPA Certified Contract Advisor; (ii) has signed the Standard Representation Agreement with such player; and (iii) has filed a copy of the Standard Representation Agreement with the NFLPA along with any other contract(s) or agreement(s) between the player and the Contract Advisor;

(2) Providing or offering money or any other thing of value to any player or prospective player to induce or encourage that player to utilize his/her services;

(3) Providing or offering money or any other thing of value to a member of the player's or prospective player's family or any other person for the purpose of inducing or encouraging that person to recommend the services of the Contract Advisor;

(4) Providing materially false or misleading information to any player or prospective player in the context of recruiting the player as a client or in the course of representing that player as his Contract Advisor . . . ;

(7) Holding or seeking to hold, either directly or indirectly, a financial interest in any professional football club or in any other business entity when such investment could create an actual conflict of interest or the appearance of a conflict of interest in the representation of NFL players . . . ;

(14) Engaging in unlawful conduct and/or conduct involving dishonesty, fraud, deceit, misrepresentation, or other activity which reflects adversely on his/her fitness as a Contract Advisor or jeopardizes his/her effective representation of NFL players;

(15) Failure to comply with the maximum fee provisions contained in Section 4 of these Regulations . . . ;

(21) (a) Initiating any communication, directly or indirectly, with a player who has entered into a Standard Representation Agreement with another Contract Advisor and such Standard Representation Agreement is on file with the NFLPA if the communication concerns a matter relating to [(1) Player's current Contract Advisor; (2) Player's current Standard Representation Agreement; (3) Player's contract status with any NFL Club(s); or (4) Services to be provided by prospective Contract Advisor either through a Standard Representation Agreement or otherwise].

(b) If a player, already a party to a Standard Representation Agreement, initiates communication with a Contract Advisor relating to any of the subject matters listed in Section 3(B)(21)(a) the Contract Advisor may continue communications with the Player regarding any of those matters.

(26) Directly or indirectly soliciting a prospective rookie player for representation as a Contract Advisor . . . if that player has signed a Standard Representation Agreement prior to a date which is thirty (30) days before the NFL Draft and if thirty (30) days have not elapsed since the Agreement was signed and filed with the NFLPA. . . .

A Contract Advisor who engages in any prohibited conduct as defined above shall be subject to discipline in accordance with the procedures of Section 6 of these Regulations. . . .

[Editors' note: The sanctions listed in Section 6 include the payment of fines, suspension of certification, and decertification.]

Section 4 — Agreements Between Contract Advisors and Players; Maximum Fees . . .

B. Contract Advisor's Compensation

(1) The maximum fee which may be charged or collected by a Contract Advisor shall be three percent (3%) of the "compensation" (as defined within this Section) received by the player in each playing season covered by the contract negotiated by the Contract Advisor, except as follows: [Editors' note: The Regulations stipulate lower maximum fees for certain players such as franchise and transition players.]

(2) The Contract Advisor and player may agree to any fee which is less than the maximum fee set forth in (1) above.

(3) As used in this Section 4(B), the term "compensation" shall be deemed to include only salaries, signing bonuses, reporting bonuses, roster bonuses, Practice Squad salary in excess of the minimum Practice Squad salary specified in Article 33 of the Collective Bargaining Agreement, and any performance incentives earned by the player during the term of the contract (including any option year) negotiated by the Contract Advisor. . . .

Section 6 — Oversight and Compliance Procedure. . . .

PROPOSED DISCIPLINARY ACTION

Except in cases where discipline has been imposed prior to the receipt of the answer, CARD [Editors' note: Committee on Agent Regulation and Discipline] shall, as soon as possible but no later than ninety (90) days after receipt of the answer, inform the Contract Advisor in writing . . . of the nature of the discipline, if any, CARD proposes to impose, which discipline may include one or more of the following:

(1) Issuance by CARD of an informal order of reprimand to be retained in the Contract Advisor's file at the NFLPA's office;

(2) Issuance by CARD of a formal letter of reprimand which may be made public in NFLPA publications and other media;

(3) Suspension of a Contract Advisor's Certification for a specified period of time during which Contract Advisor shall be prohibited from representing any NFL player in individual contract negotiations with an NFL club or assisting in or advising with respect to such negotiations. During such suspension Contract Advisor shall also be prohibited from engaging either directly or indirectly in any "recruiting activities." The term "recruiting activities" shall be deemed to include recruiting of any NFL players or prospective NFL players on behalf of himself/herself or any representation firm with which the suspended Contract Advisor is associated, and/or recruiting on behalf of any other Contract Advisor or representation firm. During such suspension Contract Advisor may, at the discretion of CARD, be prohibited from collecting any fees that he/she would otherwise have been entitled to receive pursuant to any Standard Representation Agreement;

(4) Revocation of the Contract Advisor's Certification hereunder;

(5) Prohibition of a Contract Advisor from soliciting or representing any new player-clients for a specified period of time. However, Contract Advisor shall retain the right to represent any player-clients signed to a Standard Representation Agreement with Contract Advisor at the time of the suspension; and/or

(6) Imposition of a fine payable within thirty (30) days of the imposition of such fine, with one-half (1/2) of such fine payable to the Players Assistance Trust (PAT).

QUESTIONS

1. May a player's parent, who is not certified by the NFLPA, represent the player in the player's contract negotiations with a team?
2. Do NFLPA regulations prohibit an agent from representing both an athlete and an NFL coach?
3. Are endorsement deals that an agent negotiates for an NFL player subject to the 3 percent maximum?
4. May an agent initiate contact with a player who is engaged in an agency agreement with another agent?
5. What types of earnings constitute compensation for purposes of an agent determining the amount of his or her fee?

NCAA BYLAW ARTICLE 12[4]

August 1, 2022

12.3 USE OF AGENTS

 12.3.1 General Rule. An individual shall be ineligible for participation in an intercollegiate sport if he or she ever has agreed (orally or in writing) to

---

[4]The 2022–23 NCAA Division I Manual is available at https://www.ncaapublications.com/p-4657-2022-2023-ncaa-division-i-manual.aspx.

be represented by an agent for the purpose of marketing his or her athletics ability or reputation in that sport. Further, an agency contract not specifically limited in writing to a sport or particular sports shall be deemed applicable to all sports, and the individual shall be ineligible to participate in any sport. . . .

12.3.1.2 Exception—NCAA-Certified Agents—Men's Basketball. [A] (*Adopted: 8/8/18.*)

12.3.1.2.1 Elite Senior Prospective Student-Athletes. In men's basketball, on or after July 1 immediately before his senior year in high school, a prospective student-athlete identified as an elite senior in accordance with established policies and procedures may be represented by an NCAA-certified agent (see Bylaw 12.02.1.2). (*Adopted: 8/8/18. Applicability to be determined after NBA and NBPA evaluation of, and determination permitting, the eligibility for high school students to enter the NBA draft. Revised: 6/12/19.*)

12.3.1.2.2 Enrolled Student-Athletes and Two-Year College Prospective Student-Athletes—After Request for Evaluation From NBA Undergraduate Advisory Committee. [A] In men's basketball, after the conclusion of the playing season, a student-athlete or a two-year college prospective student-athlete who has requested an evaluation from the NBA Undergraduate Advisory Committee may be represented by an NCAA-certified agent (see Bylaw 12.02.1.2). (*Adopted: 8/8/18.*)

12.3.1.2.3 Expenses From an NCAA-Certified Agent. [A] (*Adopted: 8/8/18.*)

12.3.1.2.3.1 Expenses Before Agreement. [A] Before signing a written agreement with an NCAA-certified agent, a prospective or enrolled student-athlete (and his family members) who is eligible to be represented by an NCAA-certified agent may receive transportation and meals from an NCAA-certified agent in the locale where the prospective or enrolled student-athlete is located (e.g., locale of home or institution) in conjunction with the process to select an agent. (*Adopted: 8/8/18. . . . Expenses permissible after appropriate changes to the Uniform Athlete Agent Act, Revised Uniform Athlete Agent Act and relevant state laws.*)

12.3.1.2.3.2 Expenses After Agreement. [A] After signing a written agreement with an NCAA-certified agent, the agent may provide the prospective or enrolled student-athlete (and his family members) with transportation, lodging and meals associated with meeting with the agent or a professional team. (*Adopted: 8/8/18. For an elite senior high school prospective student-athlete, effective date to be determined after NBA and NBPA evaluation of, and determination permitting, the eligibility for high school students to enter the NBA draft. For an enrolled student-athlete or two- year college prospective student-athlete, effective immediately.*). . . .

12.3.1.4 Benefits from Prospective Agents. An individual shall be ineligible per Bylaw 12.3.1 if he or she (or his or her family members or friends) accepts transportation or other benefits from: (*Revised: 1/14/97, 1/16/19.*)

(a) Any person who represents any individual in the marketing of his or her athletics ability. The receipt of such expenses constitutes compensation based on athletics skill and is an extra benefit not available to the student body in general; or

(b) An agent, even if the agent has indicated that he or she has no interest in representing the student-athlete in the marketing of his or her athletics ability or reputation and does not represent individuals in the student-athlete's sport. . . .

Problem 13-4

For purposes of this question, assume that Wisconsin has adopted the RUAAA in its entirety without any modifications, and that it was in effect during Jordan Cheatham's dealings with Bill Jammer.

Jordan Cheatham, an NBPA-certified agent, was licensed to practice law in both Wisconsin and Illinois and maintained a business office in Chicago. Cheatham was not registered as an athlete agent with the Wisconsin Secretary of State's office. Through a mutual acquaintance, Cheatham induced Bill Jammer, University of Wisconsin-Madison's (UW) star basketball player, to secretly sign an agent representation agreement on December 1 of Jammer's senior year. This agreement was postdated to April 15 of the following year, which was after the college basketball season ended.

The day after UW was selected for the NCAA basketball tournament, the NCAA declared Jammer ineligible for NCAA tournament competition after discovering that Jammer had entered into the agent representation agreement with Cheatham that previous December. The NCAA required UW to forfeit 20 games that Jammer played in after signing this agreement, and the university's resulting losing record caused it to be dropped from the NCAA tournament. UW lost $100,000 in revenues it would have received for participating in a first-round NCAA tournament game and potentially more revenue it could have earned by advancing to subsequent rounds of the tournament.

Although he was a projected second-round pick in this year's NBA draft if he performed well in the NCAA tournament, Jammer was not drafted by any NBA team. Jammer signed as a free agent with an NBA club but did not receive a signing bonus. The last player selected in this year's draft received a $350,000 signing bonus. Jammer signed a contract for the upcoming NBA season, but only received the minimum annual player salary for rookie players of $543,471. Cheatham negotiated Jammer's contract but did not request that the club pay Jammer a bonus or a higher salary than the NBA minimum. Cheatham was concerned that the club's payment of more money to Jammer would leave it with less available money under the NBA salary cap to pay Michael Swisher, Cheatham's prized client who was seeking a lucrative free agent deal with the same NBA club.

> **a.** Discuss Jammer's potential claims against Cheatham.
> **b.** Discuss UW's potential claims against Cheatham.
> **c.** Discuss whether Cheatham has violated the RUAAA, and if so, any potential consequences.

ETHICAL ISSUES

Given that attorneys must comply with state-imposed professional codes of conduct, the violation of which may result in disciplinary action, it is not surprising that some attorney agents have claimed that the representation of athlete clients does not involve legal work. Thus, they argue that they should not be subject to professional codes with respect to such services. Attorney agents, attempting to disavow their attorney status in this context, find justification in the fact that non-attorney agents who provide competent services on behalf of their athlete clients are not subject to the same requirements. Most fundamentally, these attorney agents argue that it is unfair to impose standards on them to which non-attorney agents are not bound. As noted by one analyst:

> "Some sports lawyers argue that based on the nature of the representation industry . . . if they enter the industry and hold out themselves as a sports agent, they avoid application of the ethical rules of the legal profession." (citing Robert E. Fraley & F. Russell Harwell, *Ethics and the Sports Lawyer: A Comprehensive Approach*, 13 J. Legal Prof. 9, 19 n.239 (1989).
>
> According to commentators:
>
> One problem with this argument lies in the nature of the services provided by agents. A principal service provided by the athlete agent is the negotiation of the athlete's contract with his or her team, and "the general service of negotiation is an area of traditional legal representation." (citing John C. Weistart & Cym H. Lowell, *The Law of Sports* 53 (1985 Supplement)). On the other hand, athlete agents provide services that do not fall within the scope of what is typically considered legal representation. Many of these services relate to the athlete's business affairs for which legal training is not required, such as advice on personal and financial matters.

Shropshire, Davis & Duru, *supra*, at 97. For discussions of the ethical dimensions of the athlete representation industry, see *id.* at 95–103; Joshua Lens, *Loans and Marketing Guarantees in Athlete Agent Recruiting: Why They Are Ill-Advised Under Agency Law and Attorney Ethics Regulations Principles*, 7 Tex. A&M L. Rev. 5, 572 (2020); Jeffrey Meehan, *Harvard or Hardball? An Examination of Ethical Issues Faced by Lawyer-Agents*, 21 Sports Law J. 45 (2014).

Sports Management Network v. Busch
2019 WL 1057314 (E.D. Mich. Mar. 6, 2019)

[Editors' note: We revisit the dispute between NASCAR driver Kyle Busch and his attorney-agent, discussed *supra*. In the following excerpt, the court states why it rejected the attorney-agent's argument that the state's rules of professional ethics governing attorneys did not apply to him.]

SMN objects to the argument that it provides legal services. John Caponigro denies that SMN practiced law. . . . There is no doubt, however, that John Caponigro practiced law while acting as Busch's agent. Though Caponigro drafted and reviewed contracts in his SMN capacity, he also "exercised [his] legal knowledge for and on Kurt's behalf. . . ." [G]iven the close intermingling of the law firm and the non-law business, and Caponigro's insouciance over the distinction between the two, delineating between legal and non-legal services is impossible. As Caponigro reflected, noting the parties' discussions of attorney "hats" and agents "hats," "I wasn't worried about what hat I was wearing at the time." When asked if he represented Busch as an agent or lawyer in his separation from Penske, Caponigro answered, "I was — I was — I brought every element of my experience, background, and knowledge, legal and otherwise, to him in that instance."

Attorneys serving as sports agents typically have dual functions. Though non-attorneys can of course serve as sports agents, representing an athlete entails many duties that would be considered traditional legal work. See Walter T. Champion, Jr., *Attorneys Qua Sports Agents: An Ethical Conundrum*, 7 Marq. Sports L.J. 349 (Spring 1997). . . . As Caponigro acknowledges, his legal skills have increased his marketability as a sports agent. . . .

Caponigro cannot profit from his law license in good times, but then claim he was only acting as a sports agent when problems arise. Whether or not SMN was engaged in the practice of law is irrelevant; Caponigro held himself out as both an attorney and as an agent of SMN. . . .

QUESTIONS

Does an attorney who negotiated a player's contract with a team engage in the practice of law? Does a non-lawyer who negotiates such a contract engage in the practice of law?

Olympic and International Sports Issues

14

INTRODUCTION

The Olympic Games, Paralympic Games, and international sports competitions such as the Fédération Internationale de Football Association (FIFA) men's and women's World Cup demonstrate that sport is a universal cultural phenomenon, which is tremendously popular and a significant part of the world's twenty-first-century global economy. It also gives rise to several important current and future potential legal issues. Professional sports also generate legal issues with global implications. For example, the labor market for players' services in many sports (e.g., soccer, basketball, baseball, and hockey) extends beyond national borders. Some North American major professional sports leagues (e.g., the National Basketball Association (NBA)) have expressed an interest in expanding to or placing clubs in European countries.

Because of the increasing globalization of sports and the historical European domination of the governance of Olympic and international sports competition, it is important to have a basic understanding of the European model of sport. Traditionally, European sport has been based on a sociocultural model, with the objective of promoting athletic participation opportunities for all through club sports. In Europe, a hierarchical or pyramid system of governance applies for both "amateur" and "professional" competition in a sport, with a worldwide regulatory authority at its apex. For example, within each country, regional federations govern soccer in their respective local areas; these regional federations are members of a national federation, which in turn is part of the Union of European Football Associations (UEFA), a confederation of 55 national federations recognized by soccer's international governing body, FIFA. Pursuant to a vertical solidarity system, the grassroots amateur clubs traditionally have received some financial support from the country's national federation and top-tier professional clubs, as well as some government subsidies. See generally James A. R. Nafziger, *EU and North American Models of Organization*, in Research Handbook on International Sports Law (2d ed.) 88–111 (James A. R. Nafziger & Ryan Gauthier, eds.) (Edward Elgar Publishing 2022).

This chapter initially provides an overview of the Olympic Games and describes how Olympic sports are structured and governed pursuant to an international hierarchy based on the European model of sport. It then discusses how Olympic sports are internally governed within the United States and regulated by a federal statute, the Ted Stevens Olympic and Amateur Sports Act (ASA). After considering the general reluctance of courts to use U.S. law to regulate Olympic and international sports competitions, this chapter describes the jurisdiction and role of the Court of Arbitration for Sport (CAS) in resolving Olympic and international sports disputes (e.g., challenged competition results; anti-doping rule violations and sanctions). It concludes by identifying and briefly discussing some developing non-Olympic international sports legal issues.

A. Origin, History, and Objectives of the Olympic and Paralympic Games

The Olympic Games have been held during two distinct historical time periods. The ancient Olympics began in 776 B.C. in Elis, Greece, in the valley of Olympia, to honor the mythical Greek god Zeus. The Olympics likely were not the first athletic competitions in Greece, but they represented the dawn of organized athletic activity for the Western world.

The first Olympic Games consisted of one event—a 200-meter footrace—and were subsequently expanded to include boxing, wrestling, chariot racing, and the pentathlon. Competitors included local residents in addition to those who lived outside the Greek city-states. Because of the highly competitive nature of the ancient Greeks, a victory at the Olympic Games was considered one of the greatest athletic accomplishments. As the Olympic Games grew in importance, athletes evolved from amateurs to professionals, began to train for their sports year-round, and received substantial gifts and money from their home cities and others.

The purpose of the ancient Olympic Games, which is the same for today's modern Olympic Movement (if not as easily recognizable today), was to promote goodwill and unity among competing nations. To facilitate this objective, a peace agreement, called *ekecheiria*, or "sacred truce," was established, providing for a three-month truce on fighting surrounding the time of the Games, which were held every four years. From their inception, the ancient Olympic Games continued for almost 1,200 years without interruption, embodying the Greek ideal of transforming violent urges into playful athletic competition and providing a forum for Greeks from all city-states to gather for attempted unification through athletic competition and religious ceremonies. In A.D. 393, the Olympic Games were abolished by the Christian Byzantine emperor Theodosius I because they were perceived to be a pagan festival. Nostos Hellenic Information Society (UK), *Brief History of the Olympic Games*, available at *http:// www.nostos.com/olympics*.

In 1892, Baron Pierre de Courbetin, a French nobleman, initiated an effort to reestablish the Olympic Games. At the Congress of Paris in 1894, representatives of 13 nations, including the United States, met to create the modern Olympic Games. The International Olympic Committee (IOC) was created, and the Olympic Games (initially consisting of only traditional summer Olympic events) were scheduled to be held every fourth year. Returning to their country of origin, in 1896 the first modern Olympic Games were held in Athens, Greece, in which 300 athletes from 13 countries participated in various events in ten sports.

Courbetin chose the Latin words "Citius, altius, fortius" as the original motto of the modern Olympic Movement. It connotes not only athletic achievement, but also moral and educational development—"Citius: fast not only in the race, but with a quick and vibrant mind as well. Altius: higher, not only toward a coveted goal, but also toward the uplifting of an individual. Fortius: not only more courageous in the struggles on the field of play, but in life, also." Pierre de Courbetin, *Olympism—Selected Writings* at 585 (International Olympic Committee 2000). He emphasized that "[t]he most important thing in the Olympic Games is not winning but taking part; the essential thing in life is not conquering but fighting well." *Id.* On July 20, 2021, the IOC adopted a new motto, "Faster, Higher, Stronger—Together" because, as IOC president Thomas Bach explained, "We can only go faster, we can only aim higher, we can only become stronger by standing together—in solidarity."

In 1914, Courbetin designed the now widely recognized Olympic rings, consisting of five interlocking rings of blue, yellow, black, green, and red with a white background. He explained that they "represent the five parts of the world now won over to Olympism, ready to accept its fruitful rivalries. In addition, the six colors combined in this way reproduce the colors of every country without exception." *Olympism—Selected Writings* at 594.

The Olympic Winter Games began in 1924 and were held in the same years as the Olympic Games until 1986, when the IOC decided to schedule the summer and winter Olympic sport competitions in different years two years apart. The Olympic Games were canceled in 1916, 1940, and 1944 because of World Wars I and II. In modern times, the ancient Olympic truce has been renewed by the IOC with the "view to protecting, as far as possible, the interests of the athletes and sport in general, and to encourage searching for peaceful and diplomatic solutions to the conflicts around the world." International Olympic Committee, *Olympic Truce*, available at *https://www.olympic.org/olympic-truce*.

The Paralympic Games, which were first held in Rome, Italy, in 1960 with 400 participating athletes from 23 countries, arose out of the Stoke Mandeville Games, a 1948 competition in Great Britain for wheelchair athletes in which 16 injured World War II servicemen and women participated in archery. On September 22, 1989, the International Paralympic Committee (IPC) was founded in Dusseldorf, Germany, to act as the global governing body of the Paralympic Movement. "Paralympic" is derived from the Greek preposition "para" (beside or alongside) and "Olympic" to signify that the Paralympics are the parallel to the Olympic Games as well as that the Olympic and Paralympic movements exist side-by-side. International Paralympic Committee, *History of the Paralympic Movement*, *https://www.paralympic.org/the-ipc/history-of-the-movement*.

B. Organization, Governance, and Structure of the Olympic Movement

KEY TERMS
- International Federation (IF)
- International Olympic Committee (IOC)
- National Governing Body (NGB) or National Federation (NF)
- National Olympic Committee (NOC)
- Olympic Charter
- Organizing Committee for the Olympic Games (OCOG)

The modern Olympic Movement "is the concerted, organised, universal and permanent action, carried out under the supreme authority of the IOC, of all individuals and entities who are inspired by the values of Olympism." International Olympic Committee, *Olympic Charter*, Fundamental Principles of Olympism (in force as from August 8, 2021). "Olympism is a philosophy of life, exalting and combining in a balanced whole the qualities of body, will and mind. Blending sport with culture and education, Olympism seeks to create a way of life based on the joy of effort, the educational value of good example, social responsibility and respect for universal fundamental ethical principles." *Id.* Numerous organizations and persons are part of the Olympic Movement, including the IOC; international sports federations (IFs); the international governing bodies for each Olympic sport; National Olympic Committees (NOCs), such as the United States Olympic and Paralympic Committee (USOPC); national governing bodies (NGBs) or national federations (NFs) for each Olympic sport that are members of their respective NOCs; the World Anti-Doping Agency (WADA); Court of Arbitration for Sport (CAS); and the Olympic Museum, as well as thousands of individual athletes, judges, and coaches throughout the world.

The Olympic Charter governs the Olympic Movement, which codifies the fundamental principles, rules, and bylaws adopted by the IOC, and establishes rules for the production and operation of the Olympic Games. The IOC is a private international not-for-profit organization based in Lausanne, Switzerland with approximately 100 elected individuals who serve as its representatives in their respective home countries (but none of these individuals are representatives of their respective countries of residence or their country's delegates to the IOC). These persons are chosen and elected by the IOC's Nominations Committee, and they serve for renewable eight-year terms.

The IOC is governed by its individual members and an executive board comprised of the IOC president, four vice-presidents, and ten other members. The current IOC president, Thomas Bach of Germany, who began his term in September 2013, has stated: "Sport is one of the few things with the power to unite all people in an increasingly fragile world [and] is an anchor of stability for so many people, regardless of background, nationality or belief." Thomas Bach, *Sport: An Anchor of Society in a Fragile World*, available at https://www.olympic.org/news/sport-an-anchor-of-stability-in-a-fragile-world (December 30, 2016).

Like the IOC, the IFs are private, nongovernmental organizations (NGOs). Each IF is recognized by the IOC as the worldwide governing body for a particular sport or group of sports; its members are the NGBs or NFs that serve as affiliates for the particular sport(s) in each country. An IF's statutes, practices, and activities must conform to the Olympic Charter and be approved by the IOC Executive Board. The IFs establish and enforce the rules for their respective sports; establish eligibility criteria for Olympic sports competition (subject to IOC approval); select referees, judges, and umpires for competitions; establish and provide an internal dispute resolution process; and are responsible for the technical control and direction of their sports during the Olympic Games or Olympic Winter Games. There are approximately 70 summer, winter, and IOC-recognized IFs that have formed the following associations to discuss their common issues and to establish their events calendars: Association of Summer Olympic International Federations (ASOIF), the Association of International Olympic Winter Sports Federations (AIOWF), the Association of the IOC Recognised International Sports Federations (ARISF), and the General Association of International Sports Federations (GAISF).

There are more than 200 NOCs, which develop and protect the Olympic Movement within their respective countries. Most of them represent a single nation, although the IOC does recognize independent territories, commonwealths, protectorates, and geographical areas as NGBs for Olympic sports. The NOCs are responsible for encouraging the development of high-performance sport and sports opportunities for all their citizens; recognizing NGBs or NFs for Olympic sports; preventing discrimination and violence in sports; and adopting and implementing the World Anti-Doping Code (WADC). Each NOC has exclusive authority regarding the representation of its country at the Olympic Games and selects its Olympic teams and athletes, usually based on the recommendations of the NGB for the particular sport. The NOCs also have the authority to designate which cities may apply to host the Olympics within their respective countries.

In carrying out their responsibilities, NOCs frequently cooperate with government agencies and other nongovernmental bodies to promote sports. Each NOC must preserve its autonomy and resist all pressures, including those of a political, religious, or economic nature, to do anything contrary to the Olympic Charter. The NOCs are subject to the laws of their respective nations as well as the provisions of the Olympic Charter and the governing authority of the IOC. For example, the USOPC must comply with the Ted Stevens Olympic and Amateur Sports Act, 36 U.S.C. §§220501 et seq., and other applicable federal and state laws.

An NGB or NF is the national governing authority for a particular sport that is affiliated with the appropriate IF and is recognized by the country's NOC. Athletes are members of their respective NGBs, which must comply with the Olympic Charter and IF rules. The NGBs serve a function at the national level similar to that of the IFs at the international level of athletic competition. Each NGB recognized by the USOPC (e.g., USA Track & Field) serves as the

United States' member representative in the IF for its particular sport (e.g., World Athletics) and must comply with its rules as well as the Olympic Charter. Like NOCs, NGBs also are subject to applicable domestic laws within their respective countries.

The following diagram illustrates that a series of hierarchical contractual relationships define the Olympic Movement's governing structure:

```
              IOC
           ↗       ↘
     IF              NOC
  World            USOPC
  Athletics
           ↘       ↗
              NGB
          USA Track
           & Field
              ↕
           ATHLETE
```

The IOC is responsible for ensuring the regular celebration of the Olympic Games and Olympic Winter Games and exclusively owns all related rights. It selects a host city for each Olympic Games, which is entrusted with the responsibility of organizing the Games along with the country's NOC, which forms an Organizing Committee for the Olympic Games (OCOG) to fulfill all responsibilities connected with the organization and hosting of the Olympic Games. An OCOG must treat every sport equally; abide by the IFs' rules of competition; ensure that no political demonstrations disrupt the Games; construct the necessary venues, stadiums, and other facilities; provide food and lodging for all athletes and officials; provide medical services; and accommodate the media. In addition, in light of recent world events, OCOGs now face the daunting task of ensuring the security of those competing in and attending the Games.

The Olympic Charter states that "The Olympic Games are competitions between athletes in individual or team events, and not between countries." *Olympic Charter, supra*, Chap. 1, Rule 6(1). (In reality, is this an accurate characterization? Is this objective furthered when sports media list medal counts by country and promote a strong spirit of nationalism?) To participate in the Olympic Games, a competing athlete must satisfy several conditions, including being a national of the country of the IOC-recognized NOC that is entering them as well as complying with the Olympic Charter, applicable IF rules for the subject sport, and the WADC. The Olympic Charter prohibits any "kind of demonstration or political, religious or racial propaganda" in any Olympic venues by athletes and others. *Olympic Charter, supra*, Chap. 5, Rule 50.

The IOC is the "authority of last resort on any question concerning the Olympic Games" (Olympic Charter, *supra*, Chap. 5, Rule 58), although those adversely affected by its decisions may submit the dispute to final and binding arbitration before the CAS. Despite its plenary governing authority, the IOC must rely on the agreement of the IFs and NOCs—and the willingness of national governments—to enforce its decisions and those of the CAS.

REGULATION OF OLYMPIC SPORTS WITHIN THE UNITED STATES

Participation in the Olympics, the Paralympic Games, and other international athletic competitions is an important part of U.S. culture. Since the modern Olympic Games began in 1896, the United States has hosted the Olympic Games in 1904 (St. Louis), 1932 (Los Angeles), 1984 (Los Angeles), and 1996 (Atlanta); and the Olympic Winter Games in 1932 (Lake Placid), 1960 (Squaw Valley), 1980 (Lake Placid), and 2002 (Salt Lake City). Los Angeles will host the 2028 Olympic Games. The United States has entered teams each year that the Olympic Games have been held with the exception of 1980 when it boycotted the Moscow Games to protest the Soviet Union's military invasion of Afghanistan.

KEY TERMS
- *De novo* arbitral review
- Ted Stevens Olympic and Amateur Sports Act (ASA)
- United States Olympic and Paralympic Committee (USOPC)
- State action

The USOPC is authorized by the IOC to represent the United States in all matters relating to its participation in the Olympic Games. It is a federally chartered corporation created by Congress that must comply with the Ted Stevens Olympic and Amateur Sports Act (ASA), 36 U.S.C. §§220501 et seq., a federal law that provides a framework for governing Olympic sports in the U.S. It has a statutory obligation to ensure "the most competent representation possible" for the U.S. in each event of the Olympic, Paralympic, and Pan-American Games. 36 U.S.C. §220503(4). Its mission is "to empower Team USA athletes to achieve sustained competitive excellence and well-being." United States Olympic Committee, *Bylaws of the United States Olympic Committee*, §2.1 (effective April 1, 2023), available at http://www.teamusa.org/Footer/Legal/Governance-Documents.

Athletes have no federal constitutional right to participate in the Olympic Games (or any other international sports competitions). In *DeFrantz v. United States Olympic Committee*, 492 F. Supp. 1181 (D. D.C. 1980), a group of athletes selected to be members of the U.S. Olympic team sought injunctive relief enabling them to compete in the 1980 Moscow Olympic Games. The President Jimmy Carter administration urged a boycott of the Moscow Games to protest the Soviet

Union's 1979 invasion of Afghanistan. Faced with political pressure from the federal government, threatened legal action by President Carter, and the possible loss of its federal funding and federal tax exemption, the USOC decided not to enter a U.S. team in the Moscow Games. The court found that under IOC rules, the USOC has the exclusive and discretionary authority to decide whether to enter a U.S. team in Olympic competition. The court held that, despite being federally chartered, the USOC is a private organization; therefore, its conduct is not "state action" subject to the constraints of the U.S. Constitution. Even if the USOC's decision constitutes state action, the court ruled that athletes have no federal constitutional right to participate in the Olympic Games. The court also held that the USOC's decision does not violate the ASA, which gave it the exclusive authority to determine whether the United States would participate in the Olympic Games.

The ASA authorizes the USOPC to select the NGB for each Olympic sport within the United States. The USOPC typically grants the recognized NGB for each sport the exclusive right to select athletes to participate in the Olympic Games and other international athletic competitions, and the NGB's eligibility and participation criteria for U.S. athletes must be consistent with those of the IF for its sport. The USOPC effectively functions as the NGB for most Paralympic sports. An NGB must provide all athletes with an equal opportunity to participate in competitions "without discrimination on the basis of race, color, religion, sex, age, or national origin" (36 U.S.C. §220522(a)(8)). Each NGB has an affirmative duty to encourage and support athletic participation opportunities for women and those with disabilities. 36 U.S.C. §220524(6)-(7). An NGB has plenary domestic authority to regulate Olympic and other international athletic competition in a sport, but it has no authority to regulate high school or college athletic competition (36 U.S.C. §220526(a)) or professional sports in the United States.

The ASA requires all NGBs to ensure that the selection criteria for U.S. athletes and teams are "fair"; "clearly articulated in writing and properly communicated to athletes in a timely manner"; and "consistently applied, using objective and subjective criteria appropriate to the applicable sport." The NGBs have wide latitude to select athletes for their teams and to discipline athletes for misconduct, but they must follow and apply their respective rules consistently and provide athletes with appropriate notice of prohibited and required conduct as well as a fair opportunity to be heard if disputes arise. *Harding v. U.S. Figure Skating Assn.*, 851 F. Supp. 1476 (D. Or. 1994), *vacated on other grounds*, 879 F. Supp. 1053 (D. Or. 1995). As a condition of being recognized as an NGB, it must agree to submit to final and binding arbitration to resolve athlete eligibility disputes as required by the ASA.

The ASA does not create any substantive rights to participate in the Olympic Games or other international sports events that athletes can enforce in a private litigation against the USOPC or an NGB. 36 U.S.C. §220505(b)(9). As Judge Richard Posner remarked, "there can be few less suitable bodies than the federal courts for determining the eligibility, or the procedures for determining the eligibility, of athletes to participate in the Olympic Games." *Michels v. USOC*, 741 F.2d 155, 159 (7th Cir. 1984).

Consistent with this view, federal courts have held that the ASA immunizes an NGB from antitrust liability for rules and decisions that adversely affect an athlete's eligibility to participate in a protected competition. In *Behagen v. Amateur Basketball Ass'n of United States*, 884 F.2d 524, 529 (10th Cir. 1989), the Tenth Circuit noted that the statute expressly authorizes only one NGB to represent the United States within each IF and to recommend to the USOC individual athletes and teams in the sports that it governs. It ruled that implied antitrust immunity is necessary because "[t]he [ASA] makes clear that Congress intended an NGB to exercise monolithic control over its particular amateur sport, including coordinating with the appropriate international sports federation and controlling amateur eligibility for Americans that participate in sport."

The USOPC and all NGBs must comply with the ASA's legal framework for protecting the participation opportunities of Olympic sport athletes. The ASA mandates that the USOPC establish a procedure for "swift and equitable resolution" of disputes "relating to the opportunity of an amateur athlete . . . to participate" in the Olympics, Paralympics, Pan-American Games, and world championship competitions." 36 U.S.C. §220509(a). These disputes generally arise out of an athlete's disappointment for not being selected by an NGB for Team USA, dissatisfaction with an NGB's resolution of a team selection issue, or its imposition of a disciplinary sanction that prevents participation in a protected competition. The USOPC has a Team USA Ombuds to provide independent advice to athletes at no cost in connection with disputes regarding their eligibility to participate in Olympic and international athletic competitions.

Section 9 of the USOPC's Bylaws creates both procedural and limited substantive rights for Olympic sport athletes. An athlete who has been denied the opportunity to participate in one of the above athletic competitions by an NGB has the right to file a complaint with the USOPC against the NGB that allegedly did so. An athlete dissatisfied with the resolution of the complaint may submit the dispute with the NGB to final and binding Section 9 arbitration. The claim must provide a list of other athletes that may be adversely affected by the arbitration, who are notified and may participate in the arbitration (with or without representation by counsel). An athlete who receives notice is bound by the arbitration award even if they choose not to participate in the arbitration proceeding. The USOPC has a right to participate in the arbitration proceeding, but Section 9.7 states it cannot be involuntarily joined by a party.

A Section 9 arbitration hearing generally is held online before a single arbitrator selected by the parties from a closed list of arbitrators. The arbitrator generally exercises *de novo* review of the NGB's decision allegedly denying the athlete's opportunity to participate in a protected competition and ensures the athlete has a fair and full opportunity to be heard. The athlete and the NBG generally are represented by legal counsel. The arbitrator must render a timely written and reasoned award resolving the dispute, which is final and binding on the parties as well as all affected athletes who received notice of the arbitration proceeding. All Section 9 arbitration awards are published on the USOPC's website at Section 9: 2010-Present *(teamusa.org)*.

For example, *Hyatt v. United States Judo, Inc.*, AAA Case Number: 01-14-0000-7635 (2014), involved a dispute arising out of United States Judo (USJ)'s rules and process for selecting athletes to compete in the 2014 International Judo

Federation (IJF) Junior World Championships, a protected competition. Claimant Alex Hyatt, who placed second in the girls' Junior 48 kg. weight division at USJ's 2014 Scholastic Nationals, contended that the winner of this event, Gabriela Prado, should not have been permitted to compete because she did not make weight by the time established by USJ's written rules for this competition. Therefore, as the second-place finisher, she was entitled to represent the United States in the girls' 48 kg. weight division at the IJF Junior World Championships pursuant to USJ's rules. The Arbitrator initially observed that:

> Section 9 jurisprudence requires [Ms. Hyatt] to prove [USJ] breached its approved and published Athlete Selection Procedures for the [2014 IJF Junior World Championships], applied them inconsistently to athletes similarly situated, acted in bad faith towards or with bias against [her], and/or violated applicable federal or state laws (e.g., Ted Stevens Olympic and Amateur Sports Act) [by a preponderance of evidence].

Id. at 10. Applying *de novo* review, the Arbitrator determined that USJ breached its published athlete selection rules for the 2014 U.S. Junior World Team by granting Ms. Prado a 30-minute extension of time to make weight and ordered it to name Ms. Hyatt as the U.S. entrant in the girls' 48 kg. weight division for the 2014 IJF Junior World Championships Team.

On the other hand, *Tibbs and United States Paralympics and 8 Affected Athletes*, Case No. 71 190 E 00406 12 (AAA 2012), illustrates that arbitrators generally are deferential regarding the discretionary selection decisions of sport-governing bodies concerning which athletes are chosen to compete on U.S. teams in protected competitions. Casey Tibbs, an outstanding, world-class Paralympic track and field athlete who won the F44 long jump competition during the Paralympic Trials, claimed that United States Paralympics (USP) abused its discretion by not selecting him for the U.S. team to compete in the combined F42/44 long jump competition at the 2012 Paralympic Games. The arbitrator initially noted: "Unlike the selection of members of the U.S. Olympic team, selection of U.S. Paralympic team members from a large group of diverse athletes with different disabilities and severities of impairment, especially those who would compete in combined events, is not based solely or even primarily on the results of head to head competition among U.S. Paralympic athletes in the same classification for a particular sport or one's world ranking in a single classification event." He determined: "Tibbs has not satisfied his burden of proving that USO[P]C abused its discretion in determining the best means of complying with its legal obligations under the ASA and the USO[P]C Bylaws. USO[P]C's selection criteria and procedures for selecting track and field athletes for the 2012 Paralympics team are reasonable, and USO[P]C has rationally and consistently applied them to all men's Paralympic track and field athletes, including Mr. Tibbs."

In Section 9 arbitration, the arbitrator has no authority to review "the final decision of a referee during a competition regarding a field of play decision," which may determine or materially influence whether an athlete is selected to participate in a protected competition, unless it was outside the referee's authority to make or was "the product of fraud, corruption, partiality, or other misconduct." USOPC Bylaw §9.12.

In February 2018, Congress created the United States Center for Safe Sport ("Center") to exercise exclusive jurisdiction over the USOPC and NGBs with the objective of protecting Olympic sport athletes from "abuse, including emotional, physical, and sexual abuse, in sports." 36 U.S.C. §220541(a) (2). The Center is responsible for developing training, oversight practices, policies, and procedures to prevent such abuse. 36 U.S.C. §220541(a) (3). It has established an arbitration procedure "to resolve allegations of sexual abuse . . . to determine the opportunity of [any Olympic sport] athlete, coach, trainer, manager, administrator, or official, who is the subject of such an allegation, to participate in [Olympic sport athletic competitions]" by JAMS arbitration. 36 U.S.C. §220541(b)(1). *Sanderson v. U.S. Center for SafeSport Inc.*, 2021 WL 3206322 (D. Colo.) at *5 ("Participants in Olympic and Paralympic sports agree to follow the SafeSport Code and its resolution procedures, including arbitration as the sole and exclusive method of resolving any challenge to SafeSport's eligibility decisions."). Chapter 5, *supra*, also discusses SafeSport issues.

Arbitral resolution of a Section 9 athlete eligibility dispute bars the merits of the arbitrator's decision from being relitigated in a subsequent judicial proceeding. *Pliuskaitis v. USA Swimming, Inc.*, 243 F.Supp.3d 1217 (D. Utah 2017), *aff'd*, 720 Fed.Appx. 481 (10th Cir. 2018). A court will provide only limited scrutiny of an AAA arbitration award determining an athlete's eligibility to participate in a sport, which is subject to review and enforcement under state law or the Federal Arbitration Act, 9 U.S.C. §§1 *et seq*. In *Gault v. United States Bobsled and Skeleton Federation*, 578 N.Y.S.2d 683, 685 (N.Y. App. Div. 1992), a New York appellate court explained: "[a]lthough we also may disagree with the arbitrator's award and find most unfortunate the increasing frequency with which sporting events are resolved in the courtroom, we have no authority to upset it when the arbitrator did not exceed his authority." However, a court will vacate or refuse to confirm an arbitration award that is "the result of 'corruption,' 'fraud,' 'evident partiality,' or any similar bar to confirmation." *Lindland v. U.S. Wrestling Ass'n, Inc.*, 227 F.3d 1000, 1003 (7th Cir. 2000).

U.S. Section 9 Arbitration Process

Athlete Complaint Against NGB → USOPC Review and Attempted Resolution → Section 9 Arbitration: • De Novo Review • Final & Binding Arbitration Award → Very Limited Judicial Review by U.S. Court

QUESTION

Why does the ASA require that athlete eligibility disputes be resolved by arbitration rather than litigation in a court?

LIMITS ON THE USE OF NATIONAL LAW TO REGULATE OLYMPIC AND INTERNATIONAL ATHLETIC COMPETITION

KEY TERM
- United Nations Convention on the Recognition and Enforcement of Foreign Arbitral Awards (New York Convention), 9 U.S.C. §201

A U.S. court has no personal jurisdiction (i.e., valid authority to render a legally binding judgment against the defendant) over a nonresident international athletics-governing body such as the IOC or an IF (which generally are based in Switzerland) unless the claims against it arise out of its activities within both the United States and the forum state. For example, in *Reynolds v. Int'l Amateur Athletic Federation*, 23 F.3d 1110 (6th Cir. 1994), the Sixth Circuit held that an Ohio court had no jurisdiction to hear U.S. world-class sprinter Butch Reynolds's state law claims against the IAAF (then based in London; now World Athletics and based in Monaco), which alleged his positive drug test was erroneous (his urine sample was collected at an event in Monaco and tested in Paris). The merits of Reynolds's legal claims were resolved adversely to him in an IAAF arbitration proceeding that was held in London, which was only subject to a British Court's judicial review.

Even if there is personal jurisdiction over an international athletics-governing body, American courts are very reluctant to apply the constraints of federal or state law to IOC or IF rules, which are private international agreements intended to provide for uniform, worldwide governance of sports.

For example, in *Martin v. IOC*, 740 F.2d 670 (9th Cir. 1984), the Ninth Circuit affirmed the denial of a preliminary injunction to require the organizers of the 1984 Los Angeles Summer Olympic Games to include 5,000- and 10,000-meter track events for women as already existed for men. The court rejected plaintiffs' claims that the failure to include these events constituted illegal gender discrimination, even though "the women runners made a strong showing that the early history of the modern Olympic Games was marred by blatant discrimination against women." *Id.* at 673. The majority explained, "[W]e find persuasive the argument that a court should be wary of applying a state statute to alter the content of the Olympic Games. The Olympic Games are organized and conducted under the terms of an international agreement—the Olympic Charter. We are extremely hesitant to undertake the application of one state's statute to alter an event that is staged with competitors from the entire world under the terms of that agreement." *Id.* at 677.

The dissenting judge argued:

> The IOC made concessions to the widespread popularity of women's track and field by adding two distance races this year. The IOC refused, however, to grant women athletes equal status by including all events in which women compete internationally. In so doing, the IOC postpones indefinitely the equality of athletic opportunity that

it could easily achieve this year in Los Angeles. When the Olympics move to other countries, some without America's commitment to human rights, the opportunity to tip the scales of justice in favor of equality may slip away. Meanwhile, the Olympic flame — which should be a symbol of harmony, equality, and justice — will burn less brightly over the Los Angeles Olympic Games.

Id. at 683.

American courts also have rejected state discrimination law claims by foreign athletes seeking to march in opening ceremonies in Olympic Games held in the United States under flags of countries not recognized by the IOC. See, e.g., *Spindulys v. Los Angeles Olympic Organizing Comm.*, 175 Cal. App. 3d 206, 220 Cal. Rptr. 565 (Cal. App. 1985).

QUESTION

Is it appropriate for courts to refuse to apply laws prohibiting discrimination to Olympic and other international sports events held in the United States?

As previously discussed, the USOPC and its NGBs are required to adopt, apply, and enforce IOC and IF rules that determine or affect American athletes' eligibility to qualify for, or participate in, Olympic or other international sports competitions. For example, the USOPC and NGBs must comply with the Olympic Charter's athlete eligibility requirements and antidiscrimination provisions protecting athlete participation opportunities. They also must comply with CAS awards resolving issues concerning the eligibility of American athletes that arise in connection with the Olympic Games or in disputes with an IF or WADA. Arbitration before the CAS generally is now the required exclusive forum for resolving eligibility disputes between a U.S. athlete and the IOC or an IF.

The New York Convention on the Enforcement of Foreign Arbitration Awards (New York Convention), 9 U.S.C. §201 *et seq.*, a treaty to which the United States is a party, requires U.S. courts to recognize and enforce valid foreign arbitration awards, including CAS awards that the USOPC, an NGB, or U.S. athletes are parties thereto. In *Slaney v. IAAF*, 244 F.3d 580 (7th Cir. 2001), the Seventh Circuit held that a valid foreign arbitration award precludes an American athlete from relitigating the merits of an eligibility dispute in a U.S. court. The court concluded that "[o]ur judicial system is not meant to provide a second bite at the apple for those who have sought adjudication of their disputes in other forums and are not content with the resolution they received." *Id.* at 592. Moreover, a U.S. court may be unable to provide effective relief to an American athlete whose eligibility to participate in sports competition is adversely affected by an IOC or IF rule or decision because its judicial authority is not binding on foreign sports-governing bodies outside its jurisdiction. See, e.g., *Michels v. USOC*, 741 F.2d 155, 159 (7th Cir. 1984) (noting that an IF "can thumb its collective nose" at the USOPC and ask the IOC to disqualify the entire U.S. Olympic weightlifting team if the USOPC placed an athlete suspended by the IF on the team).

Chapter 14: Olympic and International Sports Issues

> ### Problem 14-1
>
> Andy is the National Collegiate Athletic Association (NCAA) champion in the 100-meter butterfly swimming event. In the recently completed Olympic Trials in Indianapolis conducted by United States Swimming, Inc. (USS), he finished fourth in this event, only 0.01 seconds behind the third-place finisher. He was not selected for the Team USA swimming team because only the top three finishers qualify for this event. Andy believes that the winner of this event used an "illegal kick" during the race and should have been disqualified. He timely filed a complaint with the USS race officials overseeing this event, which was rejected on its merits within one hour after the race ended. The USS's Executive Committee, its highest internal authority, also denied his appeal. Is Andy likely to be successful in a Section 9 arbitration proceeding against USS? If he sues the USOPC and the IOC in a U.S. court, seeking a court order enabling him to participate as a member of Team USA in the 100-meter butterfly swimming event in the upcoming Olympic Games (the 2028 Los Angeles Olympic Games), is he likely to be successful?

COURT OF ARBITRATION FOR SPORT

A. Overview

KEY TERMS
- CAS Ad Hoc Division
- CAS Anti-Doping Division (ADD)
- CAS appeals arbitration
- CAS ordinary arbitration
- Code of Sports-Related Arbitration
- Court of Arbitration for Sport (CAS)
- *De novo* arbitral review
- International Council of Arbitration and Sport (ICAS)
- Lex sportiva
- Swiss Federal Tribunal

The materials in the previous section illustrate the inherent problems of national court adjudication of Olympic and international sports disputes. There are potential jurisdictional and conflicts-of-law problems as well as inherent difficulties in attempting to apply a specific country's laws to the rules and decisions of international sports organizations such as the IOC and IFs (whose governing authority is exercised worldwide) and extraterritorial enforcement of court judgments. The increasing commercialization of Olympic and international sports competitions and the corresponding rising tide of legal disputes generated the need for an independent international tribunal with final and binding authority, whose decisions would be respected and enforced, if necessary, by national courts throughout the world.

In 1983, the IOC established the CAS, which is based in Lausanne, Switzerland, and subject to Swiss law. The CAS was formed to resolve legal disputes in sports quickly and inexpensively. Its creation recognizes the need for international sport's governance to be uniform and protective of the integrity of athletics competition, while also safeguarding all athletes' legitimate rights and adhering to fundamental principles of natural justice. The CAS "provides a forum for the world's athletes and sports federations to resolve their disputes through a single, independent and accomplished sports adjudication body that is capable of consistently applying the rules of different sports organizations. . . ." Richard H. McLaren, *The Court of Arbitration for Sport: An Independent Arena for the World's Sports Disputes*, 35 Val. U. L. Rev. 379, 381 (2001). It is "a unifying institution that can help deliver sport back to its origins . . . [and] ensures fairness and integrity in sport through sound legal control and the administration of diverse laws and philosophies." *Id.*

Despite its designation as a "court," CAS is an international arbitral tribunal jurisdiction based on the parties' written agreement to submit their dispute to CAS for final adjudication. Courts will enforce a written agreement to arbitrate before the CAS, which bars litigation arising out of the subject dispute in a judicial forum. The IOC and all Olympic-sport IFs have agreed to CAS jurisdiction. In their rules and regulations, the IFs require their respective member NGBs and athletes to submit all disputes with the IF to CAS arbitration. All parties in a CAS arbitration proceeding have the right to be represented by legal counsel. CAS arbitrators have legal training and recognized competence in the field of sport and/or international arbitration, and they must be fluent in English, French, or Spanish, the working languages of the CAS.

In 1994, the Lausanne-based International Council of Arbitration for Sport (ICAS), currently a group of 22 distinguished jurists and lawyers with a sports and/or arbitration background (some of whom are Olympians), was created to oversee the CAS and to ensure its independence from the IOC. ICAS appoints the CAS's approximately 400 arbitrators, manages its budget, and promulgates the Code of Sports-Related Arbitration (Code), which governs CAS arbitration proceedings.

The CAS *ordinary arbitration procedure* is used to resolve sports-related commercial disputes such as sponsorship contracts, sports event broadcast rights contracts, and contracts between athletes and their agents. These proceedings usually are confidential and private and do not result in the publication of an award by the CAS.

The CAS *appeals arbitration procedure* is used to resolve appeals from final decisions of sports federations (requiring the exhaustion of all available internal administrative remedies) involving matters such as doping, discipline for misconduct, athlete eligibility issues, or competition results. Each party selects one arbitrator, and the president of the Appeals Arbitration Procedure (who is an ICAS member) appoints the third arbitrator who serves as the president of the panel. The applicable substantive law generally is the particular sport-governing body's rules (e.g., IOC or IF rules) and the law of the country in which it is domiciled (generally Swiss law because the IOC and most IFs are based in Switzerland). The CAS Code generally requires the case to be decided and a written operative award (i.e., ultimate adjudication of the material issues) to be provided to the parties within three months after the case file is transferred to the CAS panel, with a written final reasoned award.

The CAS *Ad Hoc Division* operates at the site of each Olympic Games to provide for expedited resolution of all disputes arising during the Games or during a period of ten days preceding the Games Opening Ceremony (e.g., nationality requirements; disputed competition results). Generally applying the Olympic Charter and general principles of Swiss law, disputes are resolved by a panel of three arbitrators from a pool of CAS arbitrators specifically chosen by the ICAS for the Olympic Games. Their decision, which must be written and provide reasons, generally must be rendered within 24 hours after the filing of a request for CAS adjudication. See generally Richard H. McLaren, *Introducing the Court of Arbitration for Sport: The Ad Hoc Division at the Olympic Games*, 12 Marq. Sports L. Rev. 517 (2001).

The CAS *Anti-Doping Division (ADD)* also operates during the Olympic Games and Olympic Winter Games and has jurisdiction to determine whether an athlete accused of an anti-doping rule violation (ADRV) (e.g., a positive A sample for a substance prohibited by the WADC) should be precluded from participating in Olympic competition. CAS *ADD* awards rendered during the Olympic Games and Olympic Winter Games may be appealed to the CAS *Ad Hoc Division* or *Appeals Division*. In 2019, the CAS *ADD's* jurisdiction was expanded to act as a first-instance authority on behalf of any sports entity (e.g., an IF) that delegates its ADRV adjudication and sanctioning powers to it. A three-arbitrator CAS *ADD* award is final and binding on the parties, and a sole arbitrator CAS *ADD* may be appealed to the CAS *Appeals Division* for final and binding adjudication.

A CAS arbitration award resolves the subject dispute, orders appropriate relief (including damages and allocation of costs), and is final and binding on the parties. CAS panels frequently cite and rely on prior CAS arbitration awards, which are creating a body of Olympic and international sports law, a so-called *lex sportiva*. See generally James A.R. Nafziger, International Sports Law at 48–61 (2d ed., Transnational 2004). Matthieu Reeb, the CAS director general, publishes digests of CAS *Ad Hoc Division* and nonconfidential *Appeals Division* awards on the CAS website at *http://www.tas-cas.org*.

Regardless of its physical location, the "seat" of all CAS arbitration proceedings is always considered to be Lausanne, Switzerland. This ensures uniform procedural rules for all CAS arbitrations, which provides a stable legal framework and facilitates efficient dispute resolution in locations convenient for the parties. A CAS award may be challenged before the Swiss Federal Tribunal, Switzerland's highest court, under the Swiss Federal Code on Private International Law of December 18, 1987 (PILA). Article 190(2) of the Code provides only very limited grounds for vacating a CAS arbitration award such as if the arbitration panel was not independent and impartial; if the award is outside the CAS's jurisdiction or did not decide a claim; if the parties' rights to be heard and treated equally were violated; or if the award is incompatible with Swiss public policy. See *Matuzalem v. FIFA*, 4A_558/2011 (1st Civil Court, Mar. 27, 2012) at 6 (CAS "substantive adjudication of a dispute violates public policy only when it disregards some fundamental legal principles and consequently becomes completely inconsistent with the important, generally recognized values, which according to dominant opinions in Switzerland should be the basis of any legal order"). Because a CAS award is a foreign arbitration award outside of Switzerland (i.e., it is always a Swiss award, regardless of where the CAS arbitration occurred), it may be judicially confirmed and enforced by a U.S. court pursuant to the New York Convention treaty.

General CAS Arbitration Process

Dispute Involving IOC, IF, or WADA → CAS Appeals Division:
- *De Novo* Review
- Final & Binding Arbitration Award

CAS Ad Hoc Division (During Olympic Games):
- *De Novo* Review
- Final & Binding Arbitration Award

→ Very Limited Judicial Review by Swiss Federal Tribunal or National Court under NY Convention

B. Disputed Competition Results

During the 2004 Athens Olympics, American Paul Hamm came from twelfth place to win the gold medal in men's all-around gymnastics when he earned scores of 9.837 in both the parallel bars and the high bar, the competition's final two events. However, judges incorrectly deducted one-tenth of a point from the start value of South Korean gymnast Yang Tae-Young's parallel bars routine. Because of this error, Yang received a lower score for his routine. Yang's final overall score was 0.049 point behind Hamm, which resulted in his winning the bronze medal rather than the gold medal.

The Korean Olympic Committee (KOC) protested the start value attributed to Yang's parallel bars routine because it was lower than he had previously received for the same routine in the gymnastics team and qualifying competitions. Acknowledging this error, the International Gymnastics Federation (FIG) suspended the three judges responsible for incorrectly determining the start value of Yang's routine.

The IOC refused to issue duplicate gold medals to both Hamm and Yang, as proposed by KOC and the USOC. But IOC president Jacques Rogge stated that the IOC would respect a request by FIG to correct the error in Yang's score and to reallocate the medals for the men's all-around gymnastics competition. FIG, however, refused to change the competition results or award a duplicate gold medal to

Yang because a timely protest on his behalf had not been made to the appropriate official in charge of the competition's judging.

FIG subsequently attempted to send a letter to Hamm stating that Yang was the "true winner" of this event because of the judges' scoring error. Its letter suggested that Hamm's voluntary decision to return his gold medal would be regarded "as the ultimate demonstration of fair play by the whole world." The USOPC rejected FIG's proposal and refused to forward the letter to Hamm.

In the following case, Yang and the KOC petitioned the CAS to correct the judging error and to rule that Yang was entitled to receive the gold medal in the men's all-around gymnastics competition.

Yang Tae Young v. International Gymnastics Federation
Arbitration CAS 2004/A/704, Award of October 21, 2004

Panel: The Hon. Michael Beloff (England); Mr. Dirk-Reiner Martens (Germany); Mr. Sharad Rao (Kenya).

[Editors' note: In gymnastics, an individual competitor's score is awarded by a combination of start values based on the degree of difficulty in a particular routine and on execution as determined by FIG's Code of Points. The primary purpose of this Code is to provide an objective means of evaluating gymnastics exercises, and each gymnast "has the right [t]o have his performance judged correctly, fairly, and in accordance with the stipulations of the Code of Points."

Unlike sports such as diving, an evaluation of the start value of a gymnastics routine is not made before its performance because gymnasts will frequently modify a planned routine in response to competitive circumstances or will fail to execute a planned element. The judges' assessment of start values is in part subjective and in part objective. Elements that make up start values, such as a *belle* or a *morisue*, are objectively identified. Whether any element has been fully performed is a matter of subjective judgment. In this case, the three judges responsible for determining the start value of Yang's parallel bars routine (the fifth of the six rotations in men's all-around competition) erroneously characterized a belle as a morisue, giving him a start value of 9.9 rather than 10. Video analysis confirmed that Yang's start value should have been 10.]

The extent to which, if at all, a Court including CAS can interfere with an official's decision is not wholly clear. An absolute refusal to recognize such a decision as justiciable and to designate the field of play as "*a domain into which the King's writ does not seek to run*" in Lord Atkin's famous phrase would have a defensible purpose and philosophy. It would recognize that there are areas of human activity which elude the grasp of the law, and where the solution to disputes is better found, if at all, by agreement. It would contribute to finality. It would uphold, critically, the authority of the umpire, judge or referee, whose power to control competition, already eroded by the growing use of technology such as video replays, would be fatally undermined if every decision taken could be judicially reviewed. And, to the extent that the matter is capable of analysis in conventional legal terms, it could rest on the premise that any contract that the player has made in entering into a competition is that he or she should have the benefit of honest "field of play" decisions, not necessarily correct ones.

Sports law does not, however, have a policy of complete abstention. In *Mendy v. AIBA*, where the challenge was to a referee's decision to disqualify a boxer for a low blow (CAS OG 96/06), the CAS ad hoc Panel accepted jurisdiction, even over a game rule, but considered it inappropriate to exercise it. It said:

> [T]he referee's decision, is a purely technical one pertaining to the rules which are the responsibility of the federation concerned. It is not for the ad hoc Panel to review the application of these rules. This restraint is all the more necessary since, far from where the action took place, the ad hoc Panel is less well-placed to decide than the referee in the ring or the ring judges. The above-mentioned restraint must be limited to technical decisions or standards; it does not apply when such decisions are taken in violation of the law, social rules, or general principles of law, which is not the case in this particular instance. . . .

In short, courts may interfere only if an official's field of play decision is tainted by fraud or arbitrariness or corruption; otherwise although a Court may have jurisdiction, it will abstain as a matter of policy from exercising it. . . .

While in this instance we are being asked, not to second guess an official but rather to consider the consequences of an admitted error by an official so that the "field of play" jurisprudence is not directly engaged, we consider that we should nonetheless abstain from correcting the results by reliance of an admitted error. An error identified with the benefit of hindsight, whether admitted or not, cannot be a ground for reversing a result of a competition. We can all recall occasions where a video replay of a football match, studied at leisure, can show that a goal was given, when it should have been disallowed (the Germans may still hold that view about England's critical third goal in the World Cup Final in 1966), or vice versa, or where in a tennis match a critical line call was mistaken. However, quite apart from the consideration, which we develop below, that no one can be certain how the competition in question would have turned out had the official's decision been different, for a Court to change the result would on this basis still involve interfering with a field of play decision. Each sport may have within it a mechanism for utilising modern technology to ensure a correct decision is made in the first place (e.g., cricket with run-outs) or for immediately subjecting a controversial decision to a process of review (e.g., gymnastics) but the solution for error, either way, lies within the framework of the sport's own rules; it does not licence judicial or arbitral interference thereafter. If this represents an extension of the field of play doctrine, we tolerate it with equanimity. Finality is in this area all important: rough justice may be all that sport can tolerate. . . .

There is another and powerful consideration, well articulated on behalf of Hamm. Had the competition been on one apparatus only, i.e., the parallel bars, then the conclusion that the judging error led to a disarray in the medal positions would follow as night follows day. (We put on one side the contention . . . that Yang had the benefit of the error — a failure by AB Judges to deduct points for a gymnastic fault exceeding the stipulated number of pauses during his exercise. . . .) But the event was not a single apparatus event, but an all around one.

After the parallel bars, there was one more apparatus on which the competitors had to perform, i.e., the high bar. We have no means of knowing how Yang would have reacted had he concluded the competition in this apparatus as the points leader rather than in third position. He might have risen to the occasion; he might have frozen (his marks on the high bar were in fact below expectation and speculation is inappropriate.) So it needs to be clearly stated that while the error *may* have cost Yang a gold medal, it did not necessarily do so. . . .

There are two victims of this unusual sequence of events, Hamm and Yang. Hamm because, as he eloquently explained, a shadow of doubt has been cast over his achievement in winning the sport's most prestigious prize. Yang because he may have been deprived of an opportunity of winning it. Both Hamm and Yang are superb athletes at the pinnacle of their sport: neither was in any way responsible for the Judge's error: each has comported himself with dignity which this controversy has subsisted. Nonetheless the Court of Arbitration is not Solomon: nor can it mediate a solution acceptable to both gymnasts or their respective NOCs. CAS must give a verdict based on its findings of fact viewed in the context of the relevant law.

For the reasons set out above, we dismiss this appeal.

NOTE

Governing body's legal duty to follow competition rules. Even if the applicable rules provide that athletics-governing body's final determination of competition results is not appealable, "CAS will always have jurisdiction to overrule the Rules of any sport federation if its decision making bodies conduct themselves with a lack of good faith or not in accordance with due process." Arbitration CAS Ad Hoc Division (O.G. Athens 2004) 009, *Hellenic Olympic Committee and Nikolaos Kaklamanakis v. International Sailing Federation*, award of August 24, 2004. The CAS has ruled that a sports-governing body must comply with and consistently apply objective criteria established by its own rules such as time or points earned by competition results when selecting athletes for a team or event.

Problem 14-2

During the 2002 Olympics, by a 5-4 judges' decision, a Russian pairs figure-skating team won the gold medal despite making a few technical errors, while the silver medalist Canadian team skated flawlessly. Shortly

> thereafter, the French competition judge claimed that the French skating federation president had pressured her to vote for the Russians. Based on a recommendation from the ISU, the IOC's executive board voted to also award gold medals to the Canadian team. Because there was no evidence of any Russian involvement in the matter, the Russian team members were permitted to keep their gold medals. (Note: Although the French judge later recanted her accusation, the ISU suspended her and the French federation president for three years plus the 2006 Olympics. This scandal also led the ISU to change its methods of judging skaters' performances.) If the IOC had allowed the initial competition results to stand, should the Canadian team have prevailed in an appeal to the CAS?

C. Doping Violations and Sanctions

KEY TERMS
- Anti-doping rule violation (ADRV)
- Principle of proportionality
- Strict liability
- Therapeutic use exemption (TUE)

1. Strict Liability Standard, Clear Notice Requirements, and Proportionate Sanctions

As a policy matter, CAS has upheld a sport's-governing body's adoption and use of a strict liability standard (i.e., liability without any personal fault) for anti-doping rule violations (ADRVs). In *USA Shooting and Q. v. Int'l Shooting Union* (*Quigley*), Arbitration CAS 94/129, Award of May 23, 1995, in Matthieu Reeb, *Digest of CAS Awards 1986–1998* (1998) at 187, the CAS stated:

> It is true that a strict liability test is likely in some sense to be unfair in an individual case, such as that of Q., where the athlete may have taken medication as the result of mislabelling or faulty advice for which he or she is not responsible—particularly in the circumstances of sudden illness in a foreign country. But it is also in some sense "unfair" for an athlete to get food poisoning on the eve of an important competition. Yet in neither case will the rules of the competition be altered to undo the unfairness. Just as the competition will not be postponed to await the athlete's recovery, so the prohibition of banned substances will not be lifted in recognition of its accidental absorption. The vicissitudes of competition, like those of life generally, may create many types of unfairness, whether by accident or the negligence of unaccountable persons, which the law cannot repair.
>
> Furthermore, it appears to be a laudable policy objective not to repair an accidental unfairness to an individual by creating an intentional unfairness to the whole body of other competitors. This is what would happen if banned performance-enhancing substances were tolerated when absorbed inadvertently. Moreover, it is

likely that even intentional abuse would in many cases escape sanction for lack of proof of guilty intent. And it is certain that a requirement of intent would invite costly litigation that may well cripple federations—particularly those run on modest budgets—in their fight against doping.

Id. at 193.

In *Quigley*, the CAS held that doping rules must provide clear notice to protect athletes' legitimate expectations. It explained that if a strict liability test is adopted, "it becomes even more important that the rules for the testing procedure are crystal clear, that they are designed for reliability, and that it may be shown that they have been followed." Moreover, "as a general matter, if breaches of specific requirements laid down by a federation for the testing procedure are sufficiently material as to call into question the validity and correctness of the positive result, any athlete would be entitled to have that federation's decision overturned." The CAS panel ruled that the athlete, who tested positive for a banned stimulant in medication prescribed by a physician for bronchitis while competing in a skeet shooting competition in Egypt, did not commit a doping violation because the IF rule defined doping as the use of a banned substance "with the aim of attaining an increase in performance." The language of this rule did not clearly articulate a strict liability standard for doping offenses.

The CAS *Ad Hoc Division* for the 2000 Summer Olympics in Sydney, Australia, upheld clearly defined IOC strict liability doping rules requiring Romanian gymnast Andreea Raducan to forfeit her gold medal in the women's individual all-around competition in artistic gymnastics. She tested positive for pseudoephedrine, a banned substance, after taking a cold and flu tablet prescribed by the Romanian gymnastics team doctor on the day she competed in this event. The CAS panel ruled that this doping violation justified the stripping of her gold medal "as a matter of fairness to all other athletes." Raducan did not challenge the identity or integrity of her urine sample or the validity of its analysis for this banned substance. The CAS also rejected her claimed defenses that pseudoephedrine impaired (rather than enhanced) her athletic performance, that heavier athletes would not produce positive test results if taking the same dosage of the drug as she did, and that she is a 16-year-old minor who should not be found guilty of doping under these circumstances. Arbitration CAS *Ad Hoc Division* (O.S. Sydney 2000) 011, *Andreea Raducan v. International Olympic Committee (IOC)*, award of September 28, 2000, in CAS Awards-Sydney: The Decisions Delivered by the Ad Hoc Division of the Court of Arbitration for Sport During the 2000 Olympic Games in Sydney (2000), at 111.

In *Chagnaud v. FINA*, Arbitration CAS 95/141, Award of April 22, 1996, the CAS panel stated that sports-governing bodies "should make allowance for an appreciation of the subjective elements in each case" in order to determine "a just and equitable sanction." Rather than a fixed minimum sanction for all doping offenses (e.g., a two-year suspension), the CAS panel expressed its preference for "a sliding scale of suspension periods depending on the degree of fault of the athlete." Applying this principle of proportionality, it reduced a swimmer's suspension from the two-year period provided by FINA's rules to approximately 13½ months because her coach mistakenly gave her a tablet, which she did not know contained a banned substance, shortly before an event.

QUESTION

Do you agree with the CAS panel's *Andreea Raducan* decision? (Note that Olympic athletes have the ability to seek prior approval from a sport-governing body to take a needed medication, a therapeutic use exemption (TUE) process not utilized by Raducan.)

2. Interpretation and Application of the World Anti-Doping Code

KEY TERMS
- International Convention Against Doping in Sport
- No fault or negligence
- No significant fault or negligence
- U.S. Anti-Doping Agency (USADA)
- World Anti-Doping Agency (WADA)
- World Anti-Doping Code (WADC)

On November 10, 1999, the World Anti-Doping Agency (WADA), an international collaborative effort between governments and sports organizations to combat doping in sport, was established in Lausanne, Switzerland. Its purpose is to promote harmonization and equity for athlete drug testing as well as to establish common and effective minimum standards for doping controls, especially for out-of-competition tests, and uniform ADRV sanctions.

On March 5, 2003, at the World Conference on Doping in Sport held in Copenhagen, Denmark, almost 80 national governments (including the United States) and all of the major international sports federations approved the first World Anti-Doping Code (WADC), which seeks to harmonize ADRV regulations across all sports and all countries of the world. The IOC, IPC, NOCs, and virtually all IFs as well as WADA and all national anti-doping organizations have adopted the WADC, which applies to their respective NGBs and athletes.

The WADC, which became effective on January 1, 2004 and subsequently has been revised three times, establishes a uniform system of drug-testing procedures and fixes sanctions for violations, which may be reduced in "exceptional circumstances" if the athlete bears "no fault or no negligence" or "no significant fault or no significant negligence." The current version of the WADC became effective on January 1, 2021 and is available at *https://www.wada-ama.org/en/resources/the-code /world-anti-doping-code*.

In July 2008, the U.S. Senate ratified the International Convention Against Doping in Sport adopted by the United Nations Educational, Scientific, and Cultural Organization on October 19, 2005, which is based on the WADC. On August 4, 2008, shortly before the 2008 Beijing Olympic Games, President George

W. Bush signed the treaty's instrument of ratification. Countries must ratify this treaty to be permitted to host future Olympic Games. It is important to understand that the NCAA and U.S. professional sports leagues and their respective athletes, which are not members of an IF or currently directly regulated by the federal government, are not automatically subject to the WADC. In accordance with federal labor law, doping regimes for unionized professional sports leagues are established by collective bargaining. See Chapter 12. All U.S. athletes must agree to comply with the WADC as a condition of competing in the Olympic Games or other international sports competitions governed by it.

The WADC seeks to protect all athletes' "fundamental right to participate in doping-free sport and thus promote health, fairness and equality." Purpose, Scope and Organization of the World Anti-doping Program and the *Code*, 2021 WADC at 9. The WADC Introduction states: "Anti-doping rules, like *competition* rules, are sport rules governing the conditions under which sport is played. *Athletes* . . . accept these rules as a condition of participation and shall be bound by these rules." *Id.* at 17. It provides that "[t]hese sport-specific rules and procedures . . . are distinct in nature from criminal and civil proceedings" and "are not intended to be subject to or limited by any national requirements and legal standards applicable to such proceedings, although they are intended to be applied in a manner which respects the principles of proportionality and human rights." *Id.* at 17–18. "When reviewing the facts and law of a given case, all courts, arbitral hearing panels and other adjudicating bodies should be aware of and respect the distinct nature of the anti-doping rules in the *Code* and the fact that those rules represent the consensus of a broad spectrum of stakeholders around the world with an interest in fair sport." *Id.* at 18.

Article 4.2.1 of the WADC states that the prohibited list shall identify the substances and methods whose usage are prohibited both in-competition and out-of-competition because of their potential to enhance performance in future competitions or their masking potential, as well as those substances and methods that are prohibited only in-competition. Article 4.3 states that WADA will consider putting a substance or method on its prohibited list if it meets any two of three criteria: (1) "[m]edical or scientific evidence, or pharmacological effect or experience demonstrates that [it], alone or in combination, has the potential to enhance or enhances sport performance"; (2) "medical or scientific evidence, or pharmacological effect or experience that [its usage] represents an actual or potential health risk" to an athlete; or (3) WADA has determined that its usage "violates the spirit of sport." Pursuant to Article 2.1, the presence of a prohibited substance (or its metabolites or markers) in an athlete's urine or blood sample (e.g., by positive laboratory analysis of both A and B samples) is an ADRV, and "it is not necessary that intent, [f]ault, [n]egligence or knowing [u]se [by the athlete] be demonstrated."

Article 3.1 of the 2021 WADC provides that an anti-doping organization "shall have the burden of establishing that an [ADRV] has occurred . . . to the comfortable satisfaction [i.e., "greater than a mere balance of probability but less than proof beyond a reasonable doubt"] of the hearing panel, bearing in mind the seriousness of the allegation which is made." Section 3.2 permits an ADRV to be "established by any reliable means, including admissions." For example, in *USADA v. Montgomery*, CAS 2004/O/645, the CAS panel found a violation of the IAAF's anti-doping rules based on sprinter Tim Montgomery's admitted usage of prohibited substances, including "the Clear" in a conversation with fellow sprinter Kelli White (who had previously admitted to doping and accepted a two-year suspension from competition) and refusal to testify in his defense. It concluded: "[B]ecause he has not offered any evidence of his own concerning his admission to Ms. White of his use of the Clear [THG], the Panel can only rely on the testimony of Ms. White. That testimony is more than merely adverse to Mr. Montgomery; it is fatal to his case."

An athlete's ability to prove "exceptional circumstances" under the WADC establishing "no fault or negligence" or "no significant fault or negligence" for an anti-doping violation is necessarily a fact-specific inquiry to determine the reasonableness of an athlete's action (or inaction) to ensure that he or she does not ingest or otherwise use a banned substance.

It is very difficult (but not impossible) for an athlete to be able to prove "no fault or negligence" for a doping offense. In *ITF and WADA v. Richard Gasquet*, Arbitration CAS 2009/A/1926 and 1930, award of December 17, 2009, the CAS determined that a professional tennis player's positive urine test for a small amount of cocaine more likely than not resulted from kissing a previously unknown woman in a nightclub multiple times. The panel concluded, "[U]nder the given circumstances, even if the Player exercised the utmost caution, he could not have been aware of the consequences of kissing a girl who he had met in a totally unsuspicious environment. It was simply impossible for the Player, even when exercising the utmost caution, to know that in kissing Pamela, he could be contaminated with cocaine. The Player therefore acted without fault or negligence." It observed that "the [ITF Anti-doping] Programme cannot impose an obligation on an athlete never to go out to any restaurant or nightclub where he might meet an attractive stranger whom he might later be tempted to kiss. This would be an unrealistic and impractical expectation that should not be imposed on athletes by sanctioning bodies in their endeavors to defeat doping."

If an athlete proves "no significant fault or negligence" for an unintentional ADRV, the general sanction of a two-year period of ineligibility may be reduced. For example, in *Sharapova v. ITF*, CAS 2016/A/4643, a CAS panel ruled that professional tennis player Maria Sharapova's fault or negligence for the presence of meldonium in her system was "not significant" and reduced the 24-month suspension imposed on her by the ITF to 15 months. Her January 26, 2016 sample collection tested positive for meldonium. For approximately ten years, she had been taking Mildronate, a heart medication containing meldonium prescribed by her doctor, a usage that was permissible and did not constitute an anti-doping rule violation until January 1, 2016, when it was added to WADA's list of prohibited substances. No specific warning had been issued by WADA, the ITF, or the Women's Tennis Association regarding meldonium's changed listing as a prohibited substance, and there was no significantly publicized case of an Olympic sport athlete or any prior case of a tennis player testing positive for meldonium. The CAS panel found that she continued taking meldonium "with the good faith belief that it was appropriate and compliant with the relevant rules and her anti-doping obligations, as it was over a long period of her career, and that she was not clearly informed by the relevant anti-doping authorities of the change in the rules."

The CAS panel explained:

> A period of ineligibility can be reduced based on [no significant fault] NSF only in cases where the circumstances justifying a deviation from the duty of exercising the "utmost caution" are truly exceptional, and not in the vast majority of cases. However, in the Panel's opinion, the "bar" should not be set too high for a finding of NSF. In other words, a claim of NSF is (by definition) consistent with the existence of some degree of fault and cannot be excluded simply because the athlete left some "stones unturned." As a result, a deviation from the duty of exercising the "utmost caution" does not imply per se that the athlete's negligence was "significant" . . . [A]n athlete can always read the label of the product used or make Internet searches to ascertain its ingredients, cross-check the ingredients so identified against the Prohibited List or consult with the relevant sporting or anti-doping organizations, consult appropriate experts in anti-doping matters and, eventually, not take the product. However, an athlete cannot reasonably be expected to follow all such steps in each and every circumstance. To find otherwise would render the NSF provision in the WADC meaningless.

It determined she bore some fault for her positive drug test, which precluded more than a 9-month reduction from the standard 24-month suspension for the presence of meldonium in her system. Although "athletes are permitted to delegate elements of their anti-doping obligations," an athlete who does so "is at fault if he/she chooses an unqualified person as her delegate, if he/she fails to instruct him properly or set out clear procedures he/she must follow in carrying out his task, and/or if he/she fails to exercise supervision and control over him/her in the carrying out of the task." It determined that Sharapova's selection of her agent and his company to ensure compliance with her anti-doping obligations was reasonable, but that she negligently failed to provide instructions regarding how to perform this task or to supervise such actions.

3. United States Anti-Doping Agency

The U.S. Anti-Doping Agency (USADA) was formed in 2000 and is an independent anti-doping agency for Olympic sports in the United States. Its operations are funded primarily by the federal government and USOPC. Pursuant to authorization from the USOPC and U.S. NGBs, USADA provides drug education, conducts drug testing of U.S. athletes and foreign nationals residing in the U.S. or participating in Olympic sport athletic events in the U.S., investigates ADRVs (e.g., positive test results and evidence of non-analytical positive anti-doping rule violations), and prosecutes anti-doping rule violations. See generally Travis T. Tygart, *Winners Never Dope and Finally, Dopers Never Win: USADA Takes Over Drug Testing of United States Olympic Athletes*, 1 DePaul J. Sports L. & Contemp. Probs. 124

(2003). Externalizing this process through USADA and using arbitration to resolve doping disputes (in contrast to the former system of internal adjudication by the particular U.S. NGB for the subject sport) has enhanced the credibility of the U.S. anti-doping efforts within the international community and has resulted in the disposition of doping cases in a manner more acceptable to all concerned parties. See generally Anne Benedetti & Jim Bunting, *There's a New Sheriff in Town: A Review of the United States Anti-Doping Agency*, [2003] I.S.L.R. 19 (concluding that "USADA has laid a strong foundation to combat doping at the national level" and "is achieving international and national respect for its commitment to eradicate doping among U.S. athletes").

If USADA determines that an ADRV has occurred (e.g., a U.S. sprinter tests positive for a banned substance), it issues a charging letter alleging the specific ADRV charges as well as the relief (e.g., disqualification of competition results) and sanctions it is seeking pursuant to the IF's (e.g., World Athletics's) anti-doping code (which is necessarily based on the WADC). The athlete has the right to request an arbitration hearing to contest USADA's allegations and proposed sanctions. The parties to the arbitration proceeding are USADA (which prosecutes the ADRV) and the athlete (who may be represented by counsel), with the IF and WADA invited to participate either as a party or observer. USADA's Procedures for the Arbitration of Olympic & Paralympic Sport Doping Disputes generally provide for a hearing by telephone or video conference before a single arbitrator selected on a rotating basis from a list of eight persons (agreed upon by the USOPC, Athletes Advisory Counsel, and USADA) within two months of the arbitrator's appointment. The arbitrator is required to issue a written arbitration award with reasons resolving the parties' dispute within 30 days after the date the hearing is closed. USADA's Protocol for Olympic and Paralympic Movement Testing is available at *https://www.usada.org/wp-content/uploads/USADA_protocol.pdf*.

Any of the parties in the arbitration proceeding (e.g., athlete or USADA) as well as the IF or WADA may appeal the award to the CAS *Appeals Division*, which reviews the USADA doping arbitration award *de novo*. The CAS panel's arbitration award is final and binding subject to very limited judicial review by the SFT (or a U.S. court under the New York Convention). This is a unique procedure that applies only to USADA arbitration doping awards because an arbitration award generally cannot be appealed to another panel of different arbitrators that reconsiders its merits.

USADA Doping Dispute Arbitration Process

USADA v. Athlete, Coach, or Others → New Era Arbitration:
• May be Appealed → CAS Appeals Division:
• *De Novo* Review
• Final & Binding Arbitration Award → Very Limited Judicial Review by Swiss Federal Tribunal

DEVELOPING INTERNATIONAL ISSUES

Sports leagues and associations around the globe must grapple with an increasing array of issues that transcend national borders. The business and legal challenges involved relate in large part to the movement of professional athletes from one country to another. *Union Royale Belge des Sociétés de Football Association, Royal Club Liégois, and Union des Associations Européennes de Football (UEFA) v. Jean-Marc Bosman (Bosman)*, Case C-415/93 (European Court of Justice, December 15, 1995) is a seminal European Court of Justice case involving trans-national player movement. It provides an excellent illustration of the complex intersection of the competing interests of players, domestic professional sports clubs, national governing federations, and international sports-governing bodies. The facts giving rise to the *Bosman* case are as follows.

The Fédération Internationale de Football Association (FIFA) organizes and exercises plenary authority over the governance of football (i.e., soccer) at the world level. Professional and amateur football clubs belong to the national governing federation in their respective countries and must comply with its rules. National federations are members of FIFA and the confederation for their continent; the Union of European Football Associations (UEFA) is the European confederation for football.

FIFA and UEFA regulations, which are incorporated into the rules of the European national associations, govern the movement of football players between clubs. These regulations are applicable to player transfers between clubs in different European Union countries or clubs belonging to the same national association within a European Union country. Pursuant to these regulations, when a player is transferred between clubs, his new club is required to pay his former club a transfer fee to compensate for the former club's development and training of the player. If the two clubs disagree as to the amount of the transfer fee, it is to be determined by a UEFA board of experts based on a predetermined formula. A transfer fee was required to be paid even if the player's contract with his former club had expired. The former club's national association must issue an international clearance certificate before a player is eligible to play for his new club.

Jean-Marc Bosman, a professional footballer of Belgian nationality, was employed from 1988 by RC Liège, a Belgian first division club, until his contract expired on June 30, 1990. Thereafter, he entered into a one-year contract with US Dunkerque, a club in the French second division. US Dunkerque agreed to pay RC Liège a compensation fee of BFR 1.2 million for the temporary transfer of Bosman for one year payable on receipt of Bosman's transfer certificate issued by the Belgian national football federation to its French counterpart. The contract between the clubs also gave US Dunkerque the option for full transfer of Bosman for the payment of BFR 4.8 million. Both contracts between US Dunkerque and RC Liège and between US Dunkerque and Bosman were subject to the condition that the Belgian transfer certificate be sent to the Belgian national football federation in time for the first match of the season. RC Liège, which had doubts as to

US Dunkerque's solvency, did not request that the Belgian transfer certificate be issued, which precluded Bosman from playing for US Dunkerque and obtaining his contractually agreed salary.

One of the claims Bosman alleged was that the FIFA and UEFA transfer rules are illegal under European Union law and sought damages for his lost earnings caused by the result of the application of the transfer rules. Specifically, he asserted that these transfer rules violated a treaty provision guaranteeing workers the freedom of movement among European Union member countries to obtain employment.

The European Court of Justice (ECJ) ruled that the transfer rules constitute an obstacle to freedom of movement for professional football players. It rejected the contention that the transfer rules are justified by the need to maintain financial and competitive balance between European football clubs and to create an incentive for clubs to identify and train young football players. The ECJ explained:

> As regards the first of those aims, Mr Bosman has rightly pointed out that the application of the transfer rules is not an adequate means of maintaining financial and competitive balance in the world of football. Those rules neither preclude the richest clubs from securing the services of the best players nor prevent the availability of financial resources from being a decisive factor in competitive sport, thus considerably altering the balance between clubs.
>
> As regards the second aim, it must be accepted that the prospect of receiving transfer, development or training fees is indeed likely to encourage football clubs to seek new talent and train young players.
>
> However, because it is impossible to predict the sporting future of young players with any certainty and because only a limited number of such players go on to play professionally, those fees are by nature contingent and uncertain and are in any event unrelated to the actual cost borne by clubs of training both future professional players and those who will never play professionally. The prospect of receiving such fees cannot, therefore, be either a decisive factor in encouraging recruitment and training of young players or an adequate means of financing such activities, particularly in the case of smaller clubs. Furthermore, as the Advocate General has pointed out, the same aims can be achieved at least as efficiently by other means which do not impede freedom of movement for workers. . . .
>
> Finally, the argument that the rules in question are necessary to compensate clubs for the expenses which they have had to incur in paying fees on recruiting their players cannot be accepted, since it seeks to justify the maintenance of obstacles to freedom of movement for workers simply on the ground that such obstacles were able to exist in the past.

Id. at ¶¶107–113.

Fifteen years after *Bosman*, the ECJ continues to invalidate sports league rules that constitute an obstacle to freedom of movement by European professional athletes whose contracts have expired if the challenged rules do not actually further a legitimate objective or require more than is necessary to achieve such a purpose. In *Olympique Lyonnais SASP v. Olivier Bernard and Newcastle UFC*, Case C-325/08 (European Court of Justice, March 16, 2010), the court ruled that the required payment that a soccer player must make to the club that trained him before being permitted to sign his first professional contract with another club is illegal if it is not reasonable in relation to the training costs incurred by that club.

NOTES

1. North American leagues in and expansion to foreign countries. At present, U.S. professional sports leagues, such as the NHL, NBA, MLB, and Major League Soccer (MLS) have clubs in the United States and Canada. In addition to cultural differences in business practices and currency valuation, there are legal issues clubs in these leagues must consider. For example, as discussed in Chapter 12, Canadian labor law is largely provincial rather than national as in the United States. More complex legal issues will result if these leagues expand beyond North America, which is a realistic possibility. In light of the ECJ's *Bosman* ruling, it is important to consider how a U.S. professional league's labor issues would become more complicated if it established a club, division, or satellite league in Europe.

2. The risk of athlete exploitation. As sport globalizes and as the potential for athletes and their agents from all over the world to make large sums of money increases, the potential for exploitation of athletes increases as well. Consider the following description of risks that professional sport's globalization poses to young soccer and baseball players from developing nations:

> One growing concern in the international soccer community . . . is a phenomenon of unscrupulous fraudsters preying on young players from impoverished nations with dreams of international glory. This phenomenon is illustrated perhaps most clearly with West African players.
>
> As European clubs have over the past two decades expanded their recruiting scope and as West African players such as Cameroon national Samuel Eto'o and Ivory Coast national Yaya Toure have found fame and fortune playing in Europe, a seemingly unending pool of young players stand anxious to leave their homes for a chance at what their heroes have achieved. Fraudulent pseudo agents capitalize on this hope.
>
> A 2009 European Commission study lays bare the pattern that repeats itself again and again and ensnares these prospects: 1) A pseudo agent sees or otherwise learns of a player interested in playing professionally in Europe; 2) the pseudo agent convinces the player's family that his prospects in Europe are bright and extracts money from the player's family ostensibly in exchange for travel and accommodations in Europe; 3) the pseudo agent arranges for the player to enter Europe on a short-term tourist visa rather than a visa appropriate for an athlete pursuing employment; 4) if the player actually has tryouts with teams, they are with less prestigious teams than promised; 5) if the player is offered a contract, it is generally disadvantageous to the player and advantageous to the pseudo agent; 6) if no contract is offered, the pseudo agent abandons the player; and, 7) the player, unlawfully in the country with few options, turns to illegal activity.

The ever-expanding reach of social media has further exacerbated the problem, with pseudo agents contacting players through Facebook and Twitter. Because FIFA's agent database provides agents' names but not their contact information, an imposter can easily use a false name and his or her own contact information to lure in young players. . . . FIFA guidelines are, by most assessments, ill-equipped to combat this threat and its potential outcome. . . . FIFA regulations aside, due to political instability and in some cases outright corruption, in many of the players' home nations broader immigration controls are often found wanting. Unregistered agents are often able to bribe immigration officials and alter documents. . . .

Like soccer, baseball involves substantial numbers of players leaving their home nations to play abroad, but whereas the destination in soccer is more likely than not Europe, the destination in baseball is more likely than not the United States. Addressing the problem of player abuse in the soccer context, as noted above, is certainly challenging. Doing so, however, in the baseball context, in which hundreds of thousands of young players from Latin America dream of traveling to the United States to play Major League Baseball, is in many ways more complex due the unique position occupied by scouts and coaches who double as informal agents. In the Dominican Republic, which exports far more baseball talent to the United States than any other nation, these quasi agents are known as buscones. Buscon, derived from the Spanish verb buscar, meaning to find, is a broad term used to describe local talent scouts who act as scout and/or coach and/or agent for baseball prospects in the overwhelmingly poor nation. And although the term buscon is specifically used in the Dominican Republic, similar talent scouts operate in other Latin American nations that supply MLB with players, such as Venezuela, Mexico, and Panama.

Often these buscones discover players when they have barely reached adolescence and work with them for years. Some buscones are largely or entirely beneficent participants in the developmental process . . . [but others] are unabashed opportunists who demand as much as 50% "of an athlete's bonus money as 'compensation' for providing assistance and training prior to signing by a major league club."

In recent years, MLB has attempted to increase the regulation of baseball development in the Dominican Republic and, in particular, of bad-acting buscones, through a number of initiatives. It has adopted guidelines requiring that players receive Spanish-language versions of contracts so that players require no intervention by a buscon or other third-party to read the terms. In addition, to reduce the theft of bonuses or portions of bonuses, MLB provides Dominican prospects tutoring on how to access and protect their money and requires that all bonuses be wired through an established Dominican bank directly to the player. The ultimate efficacy of these reforms remains untold, but it is clear that buscones continue to operate as quasi agents in the Dominican Republic.

See Kenneth L. Shropshire, Timothy Davis & N. Jeremi Duru, The Business of Sports Agents at 187–92 (3d ed. 2016).

Consider whether the sports industry, which generates huge revenues from athletes' talents and labor, has an obligation to protect young athletes from the sorts of exploitation described above. If sports organizations are unable or unwilling to protect these young athletes through regulation, which other regulatory bodies can or should step in?

Glossary

Academic progress — a student-athlete's movement toward the timely completion of a baccalaureate or equivalent degree measured by several variables, including an evaluation of the student's cumulative grade point average (GPA), earned academic credit, and the maximum time necessary for the student-athlete to complete his or her declared major.

Academic Progress Rate (APR) — a metric created by the National Collegiate Athletic Association (NCAA) that gives a real-time snapshot of the academic progress of individual teams at member institutions, accounting for the eligibility and retention of each student-athlete for each academic term.

Adhesion contract — a contract, usually between two parties of unequal bargaining power, offered on a take-it-or-leave-it basis that limits another party's acceptance to the terms written therein, all of which must be accepted for a contract to be formed.

Agent — a party acting in the interest and under the direction of another, the principal. In sports, the athlete is the principal and the agent acts to further the athlete's interests.

Amicus curiae — someone who is not a party to the case, but who offers expertise, insight or advice to the court regarding issues to be decided in the case. This information is usually provided as an amicus brief.

Anticompetitive effects — for the purposes of antitrust law, an adverse effect on market competition (which usually affects the price, quantity, or quality of goods or services) caused by the reduction or elimination of competition among entities that otherwise would engage in economic competition absent an agreement not to do so; see definitions for Input Market and Output Market, one or both of which are adversely affected by the anticompetitive effects of the challenged restraint.

Anticybersquatting Consumer Protection Act of 1999 (ACPA) — a federal law to prevent cybersquatting, the unauthorized act of registering another's trademark (defined *infra*) as an Internet domain name; the act provides a trademark owner with the right to bring suit against a defendant for bad-faith registration or for use of an identical or confusingly similar domain name.

Anti-doping rule violation (ADRV) — conduct that violates the World Anti-Doping Code (WADC) such as testing positive for the presence of a banned substance in one's system or its possession, distribution, or use.

Arbitrary and capricious — a standard of review used by courts in determining whether the decision of a private association, such as a sports governing body or a league commissioner, should be invalidated; generally requires showing that the body or individual acted in an unreasonable or irrational manner.

Assault — a tort in which an actor intends to cause harmful or offensive contact or an imminent apprehension of such contact with the person of another and the other is actually put in such imminent apprehension.

Assumption of risk — a tort law doctrine whereby an individual who voluntarily participates in an activity assumes the risk of any injury that occurs as a result of such participation.

Athletic events not copyrightable — the Copyright Act of 1976 provides that only "original works of authorship fixed in any tangible medium of expression" within one of eight statutory categories of "works of authorship" are subject to copyright protection; athletic events are not within any of these categories, and, unlike movies, plays, or television programs, they are not "authored" because they are not predetermined or scripted events.

Attempted monopolization — a violation of §2 of the Sherman Act whereby an entity with 50 percent or more of the relevant market has engaged in unlawful predatory conduct intended to exclude a rival business entity from the market through means other than fair competition on the merits of their respective products or services.

Booster — any representative with an interest in the athletic success of a university; generally, these people have made some financial donation to the school, employed student-athletes, or volunteered time to the athletic program. The technical NCAA name for booster is "representative of the institution's athletics interests."

Breach of contract — a legal claim premised on the assertion that a party to a contract has failed to sufficiently fulfill its contractual obligations or promises such that the aggrieved party has or will suffer damages as a result of the breach.

Buyout — a provision of a coaching contract designed to dissuade a coach from prematurely terminating his or her employment at an institution by requiring the coach to pay a specified amount, determined in pre-contract negotiations, in the event that the coach breaches an existing employment contract with a team.

CAS Anti-Doping Division (ADD) — division of Court of Arbitration for Sport (CAS), defined *infra*, that resolves anti-doping rule violations as a first instance tribunal for International Federations that have agreed to its jurisdiction as well as an on-site process used to resolve anti-doping rule violations occurring during the Olympic Games.

CAS Ad Hoc Division — an on-site process used to resolve legal issues and disputes that arise within ten days prior to or during the Olympic Games and other international or transnational sports events on an expedited basis.

CAS appeals arbitration — a dispute resolution process other than litigation used to resolve appeals from the final decisions of sport federations, usually involving competition results or doping, disciplinary, or eligibility issues, and competition results.

CAS ordinary arbitration — an alternative dispute resolution process used to resolve disputes relating to legal relations between parties such as contractual disputes involving sponsorships, media rights, and agent contracts.

Catastrophic injury insurance program — an insurance compensation program developed by the National Collegiate Athletic Association (NCAA) that provides for the payment of insurance benefits to student-athletes, student coaches, student managers, student trainers, and student cheerleaders who are catastrophically injured while participating in certain activities that are defined as covered events in the program.

Charitable immunity — a tort law doctrine under which an educational facility may be absolved from liability for the negligent actions of its employees because of its charitable purpose.

Civil Rights Restoration Act — an act passed by Congress in 1987 designed to restore certain civil rights that have been violated or limited by the entities that receive federal funds.

Class action — a legal action involving a large group or class of people; a few individuals initiate a court case becoming representatives of the group.

Class certification — a requirement under federal law to maintain a class action lawsuit; the initiating party must prove that the proposed class is a type of class permitted to bring such an action and that the class is "ascertainable."

Clearly erroneous — a standard of review where an appellate court will only reverse a trial court's factual determination if the appellate court firmly and unquestionably determines the trial court mistakenly found that a particular fact was present.

Clustering — the intentional concentration of student-athletes in a specific field of study.

Code of Sports-Related Arbitration — codified rules that govern the operations and procedures of the International Council of Arbitration for Sport (ICAS) and the Court of Arbitration for Sport (CAS).

Collective bargaining agreement (CBA) — the agreement reached between the players' labor union and a professional sports league clubs' multiemployer bargaining unit concerning wages, hours, and other terms and conditions of employment; the CBA is binding on all parties to the agreement, including the league, its member clubs, and current and future players.

Commissioner "best interests of the game" authority — an often-broad contractual grant of authority from league clubs to their commissioner to make decisions and take appropriate action to further the league's best interests and integrity of the game; this power may give the commissioner sole discretion in certain aspects of league governance (e.g., investigation of game fixing, other forms of corruption, and other disciplinary matters).

Committee on Infractions (COI) — a group of individuals drawn from National Collegiate Athletic Association (NCAA) member institutions and other sources that hears cases involving a college or university's violations of NCAA rules.

Common law — case law or legal precedent developed by decisions of judges rather than by legislation.

Compensable event — a Workers' Compensation Act requirement stipulating that, for an injured employee to receive available benefits, the injury sustained by that employee must be an accidental injury that arises out of and in the course of employment.

Competition on the merits — for the purposes of federal antitrust law, the lawful ability of all business entities, including those with monopoly power (e.g., the nation's only major professional league for a sport), to compete fairly against other producers of a similar product for the patronage of consumers.

Competitive advantage — a theory under which certain athletes will be prevented from participating in interscholastic or intercollegiate athletics because their participation will give them an unfair (or competitive) advantage over other competitors.

Competitive balance or luxury tax — a tax, established by the league collective bargaining agreement (CBA), that is paid to the league by a team that exceeds a maximum amount with its annual aggregate player salaries; the tax is intended to maintain competitive balance among league clubs through creating an economic disincentive for wealthier clubs to acquire the best players by paying them salaries that lower revenue clubs cannot afford to pay.

Competitor's privilege — the allowable level of competition within the law (e.g., a sport agent is allowed and expected to compete for another agent's clients).

Complainant — a person or organization that takes legal action against another; a person that files a complaint with an administrative or enforcement agency.

Compliance — generally, the following of or conforming with legal requirements or rules; in the context of sports law, the following of rules set forth by the National Collegiate Athletic Association (NCAA), such that each member institution has a compliance department whose main purpose is to make sure each athletic program is following NCAA rules.

Confidentiality — a decree or agreement to keep discussions or rulings out of the public; any information that needs to stay private will be deemed confidential.

Conflict of interest — a situation where an individual is confronted with a scenario that may provide personal gain while causing detriment to another, to whom a duty is owed. For example, a sport agent cannot engage in activities that conflict with the interests of the agent's client (the athlete).

Consideration — something of legal value that is exchanged between the parties to a contract; an essential element of an enforceable contract.

Contract — a promise or set of promises, either made by one party that another party agrees to or where two or more parties make promises to each other, the performance of which the law in some way recognizes as a duty; the law provides a remedy for a breach of such promise or set of promises.

Contract law — a body of state law that governs the agreed terms of the legal relationship between parties (e.g., terms and conditions of employment between a club and player).

Contract of hire — a contract that binds an employer to pay compensation to an employee who performs services, sets forth the place to perform such services and work to be performed, and sets the compensation for the performance of the work.

Contract rationale — a theory advanced by scholarship college athletes in Fourteenth Amendment litigation asserting that the athlete's university scholarship constitutes a contract that gives rise to a property interest of which the athlete cannot be deprived without due process of law.

Contributory negligence — a tort law doctrine whereby a plaintiff may be barred from recovering for damages resulting from the defendant's negligence if the plaintiff has contributed in any way to his or her own harm.

Cooperation — a determining factor used by the National Collegiate Athletic Association (NCAA) when imposing sanctions; schools that cooperate with the NCAA in its investigation tend to receive lesser punishments than those schools that choose not to cooperate.

Copyright Act of 1976 — a federal law that grants the copyright owner the exclusive right to use and authorize others to use copyrighted material in one of five statutorily defined ways, including the right to publicly perform an audiovisual work such as the broadcast of a sports event.

Copyright infringement — the infringing use of another's copyrighted work without consent of the copyright owner; for example, by the unauthorized public performance of the broadcast of a sports event.

Court of Arbitration for Sport (CAS) — a Lausanne, Switzerland–based private international arbitration tribunal that adjudicates sports-related disputes, primarily those involving Olympic sports.

Curt Flood Act of 1998 — a federal statute that limits the broad scope of baseball's common law antitrust immunity by providing Major League Baseball (MLB) players with the same rights as other professional athletes such as football, basketball, hockey, and soccer players to challenge anticompetitive restraints affecting the terms and conditions of their employment on antitrust law grounds.

Decertification — a formal process requiring at least 50 percent of a professional sports league's players to vote to decertify the union in a National Labor Relations Board (NLRB)-supervised election.

Declaratory and injunctive relief — an early resolution of the rights of the parties under a contract or statute in which a judge issues an order defining the contractual or statutory rights of the parties.

Defamation — a false statement of fact about a person with the requisite level of fault (at least negligence) made to a third party that harms one's reputation; can be either an oral (slander) or a written (libel) statement.

Deference — a term often used by courts to describe their belief that professional determinations by educational institutions and sport governing bodies should be given significant weight in determining whether those acts should be found to violate the law.

De novo arbitral or judicial review — a form of review pursuant to which a court or arbitration tribunal resolves a legal dispute on its merits without providing any deference to resolution by a sports governing body, league, or commissioner; this differs from traditional judicial review, whereby a court will invalidate an action or decision by a sports governing body, league, or commissioner only if it is arbitrary, capricious, or irrational.

Dictum — a view expressed by a judge in a decision that is not necessary to decide the issue before the court.

Disassociation — an action taken by a university to end a booster's ties to a university; usually occurs after a booster is found to have committed a National Collegiate Athletic Association (NCAA) violation.

Discretionary function — a function or task that requires an individual to exercise his or her own personal deliberation or judgment (e.g., examining facts, weighing options, or reaching an independently reasoned conclusion).

Disparate impact — application of a facially neutral rule or policy that has a discriminatory impact on a group or class of people.

Disparate treatment — direct or intentional discrimination against a person, group, or class of people.

Due process — the principle that the courts must procedurally and substantively respect the legal rights of parties before them.

Duty of care — the responsibility legally assigned to one for the protection of another against some harm or injury because of the nature of the relationship that exists between them or because the actor engaged in some risk-creating conduct that brought the harm into existence.

Duty of good faith — a term implied in all contracts that requires honesty in fact and the observance of reasonable commercial standards of fair dealing.

Economic rationale — a theory advanced by college scholarship athletes in Fourteenth Amendment litigation asserting that the athlete retains a property interest, which arises from training for a lucrative career as a professional athlete, of which the athlete may not be deprived without due process of law.

Educational malpractice — professional negligence premised on an educator or institution's failure to provide the educational services that are reasonably expected of such educator or institution.

Eighth Amendment (cruel and unusual punishment) — language in the Eighth Amendment to the U.S. Constitution that has been interpreted to prohibit imposing a punishment on a condemned person that is considered to be unacceptable because of the excessive measure of pain, suffering, and humiliation inflicted on that person.

Employment at will/at-will employment — an employment contract that allows the employer to discharge the employee without cause, for any or no reason, and without a hearing allowing the employee to contest the termination; the employee may also leave his or her employment relationship for any or no reason and not be held in breach of contract.

Entwinement — a legal theory expounded by the Supreme Court to determine whether a private actor or association is sufficiently engaged in public activity or with government entities to be deemed a state actor for constitutional purposes.

Equal accommodation — under Title IX, changes made to allow equal athletic participation opportunities, treatment, and benefits for men and women.

Equal protection — the commitment to equal treatment by the states (i.e., government) of persons within their jurisdiction, as embodied in the Fourteenth Amendment to the U.S. Constitution.

Equal treatment — having the same privileges, opportunities, and burdens as others (under Title IX, the opportunity for male and female athletes to have the same quantity and quality of athletic participation opportunities, equipment, training, competition, etc.).

Exclusive bargaining representative — after the players have selected a union that is certified by the National Labor Relations Board (NLRB), the union has the exclusive authority to collectively bargain with the league's multiemployer bargaining unit on the players' behalf.

Exculpatory agreement — a contractual provision in which one party agrees to fully or partially absolve another from a legal liability that could potentially arise from the use of products or services offered by the party seeking to be absolved from liability.

Express contract — a contract where the mutual assent arises from the words exchanged between the parties to the contract.

Faculty athletics representative (FAR) — a faculty member of a National Collegiate Athletic Association (NCAA) institution who acts as the liaison between the academic and athletic departments of the university and as the university's representative for the NCAA and athletic conference; the faculty member may not serve in any capacity in the athletic department.

Failure to bargain in good faith — the breach of a statutory duty imposed by the National Labor Relations Act (NLRA) on both the league's multiemployer bargaining unit and the players' union to meet at reasonable times and to confer in good faith regarding wages, hours, and other terms and conditions of employment; it is not an unfair labor practice or an act of bad faith for either side to take a hard-line stance in collective bargaining.

Fair Labor Standards Act (FLSA) — a federal law that is administered by the U.S. Department of Labor, which requires employers to pay covered employees, who are not otherwise exempt, at least the federal minimum wage and overtime pay of one-and-one-half-times the regular rate of pay; it provides exemptions for employees of certain seasonal and recreational establishments.

Felony reckless manslaughter — a form of manslaughter where a person was aware that his or her conduct created a substantial and unjustifiable risk that another person's death would result, but consciously disregarded such risk in a manner constituting a gross deviation from the conduct of a reasonable person in the same situation.

Fiduciary — a person who is invested with rights and powers to be exercised for the benefit of another person (e.g., a sport agent is a fiduciary of the athlete-client).

Fiduciary duty — a legal duty of allegiance and loyalty that a party in a position of trust owes to another person or entity (e.g., principal-agent, member of board of directors-corporation), which requires the former to make decisions and put the interests of the other above one's own personal interests.

First Amendment — a provision of the U.S. Constitution that protects freedom of religion, speech, association, and expression; it limits the scope of federal and state law creation and protection of intellectual property rights (e.g., trademarks, copyrights, right of publicity).

Foreseeability — the likelihood that some discernible future consequence will result from present conduct, behavior, or events.

Fourteenth Amendment — a provision of the U.S. Constitution that prohibits the states from making or enforcing any law that abridges the privileges or immunities of U.S. citizens or deprives such citizen of life, liberty, or property without due process of law.

Free agency restrictions — collective bargaining agreement (CBA) terms that establish when and how a player whose contract has expired becomes a "free agent," which typically means the player may sign a contract with another league club; in most leagues, a player must have played in the league for an agreed minimum number of seasons before becoming eligible to be a free agent.

Full and effective accommodation — under Title IX, an educational institution's provision of a sufficient number and range of athletic participation opportunities that fully satisfies the interests and abilities of the disfavored gender.

Gender equity — managing an athletics program in a manner that treats male and female athletes fairly by providing similar benefits and burdens for both.

Good faith and fair dealing — a requirement that the parties, in contracting and related contexts, deal with each other in a forthright and honest manner.

Hearsay — a common objection made by a lawyer to a witness's testimony that is based on what that witness has been told by another, not based on his or her own knowledge.

Horizontal restraint — for purposes of antitrust law, an agreement among direct competitors that reduces economic competition among them (e.g., two or more companies agreeing to fix prices or to limit output of goods or services that each company purchases or produces).

Illegal exclusionary conduct with anticompetitive market effects — for the purposes of §2 of the Sherman Act, an anticompetitive action other than fair competition on the merits by a business entity intended to exclude or prevent a business rival from competing in the market for the patronage of consumers.

Illegal per se — for the purposes of antitrust law, an agreement that has clear anticompetitive effects without any offsetting procompetitive justifications, which is deemed to be an unreasonable restraint of trade as a matter of law that violates §1 of the Sherman Act.

Impasse — a deadlock in the collective bargaining process that is usually temporary; prior to impasse, the courts have determined that a league is required to adhere to the terms of the expired collective bargaining agreement (CBA), and after impasse, the league's multiemployer bargaining unit may unilaterally implement new mandatory terms of employment if the proposals have been offered to the players' union and bargained in good faith prior to impasse.

Impermissible benefits — any benefit provided to a prospective student-athlete, current student-athlete, or student-athlete's friends and relatives that is not also available to the general public or general student body.

Implied contract — a contract where the mutual assent or apparent agreement arises from the conduct of the parties to the agreement.

Implied-in-fact — terms of a contract or promise, which are gleaned from the parties' words or conduct, even though not literally expressed by them.

In loco parentis — in the place of the parent.

Indefinite duration — a contractual relationship without a specified length of time.

Informed consent — a tort law doctrine under which a physician will be held liable for an intentional or negligent failure to provide a patient with full disclosure of material information regarding the patient's medical condition or potential consequences of proposed treatments for such condition.

Infraction — any violation of a National Collegiate Athletic Association (NCAA) rule.

Infractions Appeals Committee (IAC) — a group of individuals drawn from National Collegiate Athletic Association (NCAA) member institutions and other sources that hear appeals of decisions rendered by the Committee on Infractions (COI).

Inherently distinctive mark — a mark that is coined in connection within the goods or services that it identifies (e.g., "Miami Dolphins" for a National Football League (NFL) team).

Initial eligibility standards — National Collegiate Athletic Association (NCAA) academic requirements that an entering freshman must have attained to be eligible for athletics-related financial aid, practice, and intercollegiate competition during the student's first year; pursuant to such standards, the freshman must have registered with the NCAA Initial-Eligibility Clearinghouse, completed a minimum grade point average (GPA) in a defined number of "core courses," and attained a certain minimum score on either the SAT or ACT.

Injunctive relief — a court order requiring a party to do or refrain from doing some act.

Injury by accident — a Workers' Compensation Act requirement that an injured employee provide proof that the injury that he or she sustained was caused by an identifiable yet unexpected event.

Input market — for the purposes of antitrust law, products or services (e.g., players, coaches, and playing facilities) necessary to produce a product or service sold to consumers (e.g., athletic competition such as National Collegiate Athletic Association (NCAA) football or National Basketball Association (NBA) basketball).

Intentional injury exception — when an employee suffers a work-related injury as a result of an intentional tort perpetrated by the employer or at the employer's direction; the applicable state workers' compensation law is not a bar to a common law tort action for damages.

Intentional tort — a civil wrong that results in harm to another by an act knowing, willfully, or purposefully committed by the actor.

Inter alia — legal Latin translated as "among other things."

Intermediate scrutiny — a standard of review that requires gender-based distinctions to be substantially related to and in furtherance of important government objectives.

International Convention Against Doping in Sport — an international treaty based on the World Anti-Doping Code, in which countries commit to fight against sports doping by becoming signatories to the treaty.

International Council of Arbitration for Sport (ICAS) — a Lausanne, Switzerland–based organization that consists of 20 international jurists whose role is to oversee the Court of Arbitration for Sport (CAS), including appointment of its members and promulgation of the Code of Sports-Related Arbitration (which governs the operations of the CAS).

International Federation (IF) — a nongovernmental organization (NGO) recognized by the International Olympic Committee (IOC) that functions as the worldwide governing body for a single sport or group of sports.

International Olympic Committee (IOC) — an international, not-for-profit, nongovernmental organization (NGO) based in Lausanne, Switzerland, which serves as the supreme governing body of the Olympic Movement.

Interbrand economic competition — competition between producers of different brands of sports entertainment for fan support and revenues on a national level (e.g., NBA and NHL) or local level (e.g., Chicago Bulls and Chicago Blackhawks).

Intrabrand economic competition — in contrast to on-field athletic competition (i.e., games), off-field competition among league clubs, generally in the same or nearby geographic markets (e.g., NFL's Los Angeles Chargers and Los Angeles Rams) for fan support and revenues.

Investigation — an evidentiary inquiry that occurs once the National Collegiate Athletic Association (NCAA) enforcement staff has become aware of a possible major infraction of rules at an institution; it involves conducting interviews both on and off campus to determine if there is enough evidence to move forward with a full investigation or if the investigation should be dropped because no major violation has occurred or there is a lack of information.

Invitee — an individual who enters another's premises for the purpose directly or indirectly connected with the business dealings of the possessor or an individual invited to enter or remain on the land as a member of the public for a purpose for which the land is held open to the public.

Jock majors — fields of study that allow student-athletes to more easily satisfy institutional and National Collegiate Athletic Association (NCAA) academic requirements without substantially interfering with their eligibility to compete in intercollegiate athletics.

Just cause — a reasonably legitimate reason for engaging in certain conduct such as terminating an employee.

Lack of institutional control — a finding by the Committee on Infractions (COI) that an institution engaged in a major violation that occurred in part because of a failure on the part of the member institution to exercise adequate oversight of or control over its intercollegiate athletics program.

Lanham Act — a federal law that prohibits infringement of trademarks and service marks by their unauthorized usage that creates a likelihood of consumer confusion.

Law of private associations — a body of state law governing the legal relationship among members of a private association (e.g., National Collegiate Athletic Association (NCAA) universities and professional sports league clubs), which requires the parties to comply with the terms of the association's charter and bylaws, provide procedural due process, act in a rational and consistent manner, and comply with applicable public laws; courts generally will only intervene in the affairs of a private association if it fails to comply with these requirements.

Law of the shop — in the context of a professional sports collective bargaining agreement (CBA), the requirement that a player disciplinary system provide players with advance notice of prohibited conduct and potential discipline.

Lex sportiva — the developing body of Olympic and international sports law jurisprudence created by sports arbitration awards rendered by the Court of Arbitration for Sport (CAS).

Liberty interest — an interest, such as free speech or the right to vote, that is well recognized and protected regardless of how it is defined by a state; liberty interests may also include interests created by state statutes, regulations, and ordinances.

Likelihood of confusion — the unauthorized use of a trademark or service mark in a manner that creates likely consumer confusion regarding the source, affiliation, endorsement, or sponsorship of a product or service; such conduct violates the Lanham Act and similar state laws.

Limited duty rule — a tort law doctrine that holds that if a spectator at a sporting event or a sports participant voluntarily partakes in an inherently dangerous activity, there is no legal duty to protect or warn such spectator or participant about the common, frequent, and expected inherent risks of that activity.

Liquidated damages provision — a provision of a contract that includes a good-faith estimate of the loss to a nonbreaching party in the event of the other party's breach of their contract.

Lockout — a lawful means of economic pressure that a professional sports league may use in an effort to convince the players' union to agree to its proposed collective bargaining agreement (CBA) terms; during a lockout, the league's players are precluded from playing games or participating in other club activities and are not paid their respective salaries.

Major infraction — any violation of National Collegiate Athletic Association (NCAA) rules that is not secondary in nature; these violations usually give a school a substantial advantage, either through recruiting or on the field, and can subject a school to severe punishment.

Malpractice — a tort in which a professional such as a doctor or lawyer is held civilly liable for his or her failure to render proper services as a result of negligent, reckless, or criminal conduct constituting a deviation from an established industry standard of care.

Mandatory subjects of bargaining — wages, hours, and other terms and conditions of employment; if either the players' union or the league's multiemployer bargaining unit requests bargaining on these issues, the other side must bargain in good faith, and the National Labor Relations Board (NLRB) resolves disputes regarding whether particular issues constitute a mandatory subject of collective bargaining.

Manslaughter — the unlawful killing of one person by another without malice aforethought.

Ministerial function — a function or task that becomes mandatory given the circumstances and does not allow for personal discretion or judgment (e.g., reporting an athlete's use of performance-enhancing drugs or benching a player who is no longer eligible because of poor academic performance).

Misappropriation — the unauthorized use of another's intellectual property for commercial or other gain that causes harm to its owner.

Monitoring — a National Collegiate Athletic Association (NCAA) member institution's responsibility to put into place mechanisms that increase the likelihood that it will become aware of possible violations occurring on its campus; a gross lack of monitoring can lead to a "lack of institutional control" charge and severe penalties.

Monopolization — a violation of §2 of the Sherman Act whereby an entity with 70 percent or more of the relevant market has engaged in unlawful predatory conduct intended to exclude a rival business entity from the market other than by fair competition on the merits.

Monopoly power — in economic terms, the ability to charge a supracompetitive price (i.e., pricing higher than what can be sustained in a competitive market) or to exclude competitors through predatory conduct; for practical purposes, control of 70 percent or more of the relevant market (properly defined in terms of product or service and geography) based on consumer demand constitutes monopoly power.

Multiemployer collective bargaining unit — the exclusive collective bargaining representative for the league's member clubs, which has the authority to bind all clubs to the terms of agreements reached with the players union.

Mutual assent — the objective willingness of parties to be bound by the terms of an agreement usually manifested through the process of offer and acceptance.

National Collegiate Athletic Association (NCAA) — a national association of public and private universities that promulgates and enforces rules designed to regulate intercollegiate athletic competition among its members.

National governing body (NGB) — the national governing body for a particular sport recognized by the country's national Olympic committee and that is a member of the corresponding International Federation (IF) for the sport.

National Labor Relations Act (NLRA) — also known as the Wagner Act, the NLRA was enacted by Congress in 1935 and establishes the basic legal framework that governs the relationship between labor and management; it provides workers with the ability to unionize, collectively bargain, and engage in strikes and picketing to advance and protect their interests.

National Labor Relations Board (NLRB) — a federal administrative agency that enforces the federal labor laws by policing the process of unionization and collective bargaining, including adjudication of claims of unfair labor practices.

National Letter of Intent (NLI) — an agreement between a student-athlete and an institution in which the athlete agrees, for a minimum of one year, to attend the institution named in the document.

National Olympic Committee (NOC) — the governing authority for Olympic sports within a country, which is recognized by the International Olympic Committee (IOC).

Negative injunction/negative injunctive relief — an equitable remedy that a court has the discretion to grant for breach of contract when money damages are not an adequate remedy to compensate the nonbreaching party for harm suffered; although a court generally will not order a party to render the contractually agreed services, it may order the breaching party (e.g., a player) not to provide services to another club until the existing contract expires.

Negligence — a tort law cause of action that requires the plaintiff to prove by a preponderance of the evidence that (1) the defendant owed a duty of care to the plaintiff; (2) the defendant breached that duty by failing to exercise reasonable care under the circumstances; (3) the defendant's failure to exercise reasonable care is the actual and proximate (foreseeable) cause of the plaintiff's injury; and (4) the plaintiff has suffered some compensable damage, such as a loss of wages, as the result of the defendant's negligent conduct.

No fault or negligence — a defense that justifies imposing no sanction for a doping violation it requires proof that an athlete did not know or suspect, and could not reasonably have known or suspected even with the exercise of the utmost caution, that he or she used or was administered a banned substance.

Nondisclosure — a failure to relay information that may be required because of the legal nature of some relationships.

Nonstatutory labor exemption — a broad, judicially created exemption, which immunizes the terms of a collective bargaining agreement (CBA), as well as all restraints on the labor market for players' services from antitrust challenge, so long as there is an ongoing collective bargaining process between the players' union and a professional sports league.

No significant fault or negligence — a defense that justifies a reduced sanction for a doping violation, which requires proof that an athlete's fault or negligence in connection with a doping violation, when viewed in the totality of the circumstances, was not significant in relation to the doping violation.

Offer — a promise to do or not to do something conditioned on the other party's promise to do or to refrain from doing something in return.

Olympic Charter — the codified principles, rules, and bylaws that govern the Olympic Movement and Olympic Games.

One academic year in residence — a National Collegiate Athletic Association (NCAA) regulation whereby a student-athlete is required to spend one academic year (usually one contiguous fall and spring semester) enrolled full time at a specified institution in order to participate in the institution's intercollegiate athletics.

Order to show cause — a determination by the National Collegiate Athletic Association (NCAA) that a coach or staff member should be prevented from fulfilling coaching or other responsibilities for a designated period of time.

Organizing Committee for the Olympic Games (OCOG) — the legal entity responsible for conducting and funding the Olympic Games in the host city.

Output market — for purposes of antitrust law, products or services produced and sold to consumers (e.g., athletic competition such as National Collegiate Athletic Association (NCAA) football or National Basketball Association (NBA) basketball).

Patent law — a federal law that grants exclusive intellectual property rights to inventions that satisfy the statutory requirements of novelty, nonobviousness, and utility (e.g., the Arena Football League (AFL) obtained a patent for its unique system of playing indoor professional football).

Penalties — punishments that are generally determined on a case-by-case basis to fit the violation that occurred; in the sports law context, schools will often get scholarship reductions or public reprimands but rarely bowl and television bans; the most severe penalty is the "repeat offender" punishment, also known as the "death penalty," in which the National Collegiate Athletic Association (NCAA) orders the complete shutdown of a program for a given period of time.

Performance-enhancing drug — any drug used to improve performance during a sporting event; in many cases, drugs used for the purpose of improving performance that create health risks to the user or others are deemed a violation of antidoping rules.

Performance incentive — a benefit in excess of salary or wages promised to an individual and conditioned upon the individual's achievement of an expressed goal of the institution or organization promising the benefit.

Perquisites — a privilege, gain, or profit incidental to employment (in addition to regular salary or wages); especially one expected or promised.

Prima facie — the basic elements necessary to prove a legal point or to find that a violation of the law has occurred.

Principal — the party whose interests are paramount in the principal-agent relationship (e.g., the athlete in the athlete–sports agent relationship).

Principle of proportionality — a legal principle requiring that the sanction for a doping violation be proportionate to the violation, taking account of all of the relevant circumstances, particularly an athlete's degree of culpability.

Privacy interest — under the Fourth Amendment limitation on searches and seizures, courts often seek to protect parties from having their person or belongings searched without establishing sufficient cause for doing so.

Procedural due process — a constitutional limitation on government or state power which mandates that a certain amount of process or procedure (notice and hearing) must be afforded to a party.

Procompetitive effects/justification — for purposes of antitrust law, a defense claiming that a challenged restraint's positive economic effects (e.g., the production or maintenance of a brand of athletic competition desired by consumers, or the enhancement of its quality) offsets its anticompetitive effects and is a reasonable restraint that does not violate the Sherman Act.

Promise — a commitment by a person to do or not to do something in the future.

Promisee — the person to whom a promise is made.

Promissory estoppel — a doctrine that provides for the enforceability of a promise based on the promisee's justifiable and detrimental reliance on such promise, despite the nonexistence of an otherwise enforceable contract.

Proper supervision — the use of ordinary care as a reasonable person under the circumstances by one to whom an authoritative role is assigned, especially in the management of others.

Property interest or right — a legal entitlement to ownership in tangible property such as money, personal property, and real estate, or intangible property such as intellectual property, a special skill, etc.

Qualified immunity — a tort law doctrine under which an employee may be absolved from negligence occurring in the scope of his or her employment if such negligence results from the exercise of a discretionary act rather than a ministerial act.

"Quick look" rule of reason — in comparison to the per se rule of illegality, a case-by-case, fact-specific method of antitrust analysis used to weigh the anticompetitive and procompetitive effects of a restriction to determine whether on balance it is predominately anticompetitive (unreasonable and illegal under the Sherman Act) or predominately procompetitive (reasonable and legal under the Sherman Act);

in contrast to the full rule of reason, the "quick look" rule of reason is applied when a restraint has clear anticompetitive effects (usually evidenced by adverse effects on price or output) that are not offset by procompetitive justifications that cannot be achieved by other, less restrictive means.

Reckless conduct — conduct by an actor that creates a substantial and unjustifiable risk of harm or injury to another.

Repeat offender — any school that commits a major infraction within five years of having committed another major infraction; the violations do not have to occur in the same sport at a school for that school to be deemed a repeat offender, and a repeat offender is subject to severe penalties, including the "death penalty."

Reserve clause — a contractual term that restrains the labor market for a player's services by giving his or her current club perpetual rights to a player's services, even after the expiration of his or her contract.

Restitution rule — a measure of damages, sometimes referred to as *unjust enrichment*, which requires the breaching party to restore any benefits received to the party conferring those benefits.

Retaliation — to deliberately harm a person in response to some action that person has taken (or something that person is perceived to have done).

Right of publicity — a state law right created by either statute or common law that protects an individual's name, likeness, and persona from unauthorized commercial use.

Right to control — a test employed by courts to determine the existence of an employment relationship; it examines whether the employer possessed the right to control the manner, means, and details of the worker's performance.

Rule of reason — in comparison to the per se rule of illegality, a case-by-case, fact-specific three-step method of antitrust analysis used to evaluate the anticompetitive and procompetitive effects of a restriction as well as the existence of a substantially less restrictive alternative means of achieving the procompetitive benefits to determine whether it is predominately anticompetitive (unreasonable and illegal under the Sherman Act) or predominately procompetitive (reasonable and legal under the Sherman Act); in contrast to the "quick look" rule of reason, the full rule of reason requires a jury to determine disputed issues of material fact and the plaintiff to plead and prove that the relevant market (e.g., National Collegiate Athletic Association (NCAA) football or National Basketball Association (NBA) basketball) is restrained by the challenged conduct and to consider more complex economic analysis.

Salary cap — the annual maximum amount that a club may spend for aggregate player salaries, which is determined by the league's collective bargaining agreement (CBA).

Satisfactory progress — a National Collegiate Athletic Association (NCAA) regulation that requires student-athletes to declare a major early during their college tenure and complete a substantial amount of the coursework for their major within a specified period of time.

Scholarship rationale — a theory advanced by scholarship college athletes in litigation asserting that a loss of an athletic scholarship deprives the athlete of benefits that result from being awarded a scholarship in exchange for athletic participation.

Search and seizure — a Fourth Amendment term covering an examination or search of a premises (business, residence, or vehicle) or person.

Secondary infraction — any violation of National Collegiate Athletic Association (NCAA) rules that is inadvertent or accidental and does not provide the school with a substantial recruiting or competitive advantage; while secondary violations merit less severe penalties, a culmination of several secondary violations may constitute a major violation, creating exposure to potentially more severe penalties.

Secondary meaning — acquired when the consuming public associates a descriptive trademark or service mark with a particular product or service (e.g., "Warriors" as the name of a National Basketball Association (NBA) franchise).

Self-incrimination — exposing personal liability through personal statement.

Sexual harassment — unwelcome words or actions of a sexual nature, or on the basis of gender, which bother or threaten a person or the quality of the person's experience in school or the workplace.

Sherman Act §2 — a provision of federal antitrust law prohibiting monopolization and attempted monopolization.

Single economic entity defense — a defense to an alleged violation of §1 of the Sherman Act asserted by a professional sports league, which asserts that the league and its member clubs collectively constitute a single economic entity that creates a single product that none of them could make separately; therefore, their collective decisions and conduct is not covered by §1, which encompasses only concerted action between and among economic competitors.

Sovereign immunity — a tort law doctrine that precludes a party from bringing a suit against the sovereign government without the government's consent; thus, a public educational institution acting as a subsidiary agency of the state may be absolved from tort liability for negligent acts of its employees, such as coaches, athletic trainers, and administrative personnel, who cause injury to an athlete.

Special relationship — an affiliation between two or more individuals, premised on trust and confidence, that gives rise to a legal duty of care owed to the subservient or dependent members of the affiliation (e.g., between a coach and his or her student-athletes).

Speech rights (freedom of speech) — those rights of speech and expression protected by state and federal (and international) constitutions and declarations of rights.

Standing — the requirement in constitutional law that a party demonstrate sufficient connection with or harm from the action challenged to justify that party's participation in the case.

State action/state actor — for the purposes of the Fourteenth Amendment to the U.S. Constitution, a concept that is used by courts to determine whether the rules and decisions of a private entity or organization (e.g., a sport's governing body) is sufficiently governmental in nature to be subject to federal constitutional limitations and requirements.

State constitution — state constitutions and declarations of rights limit government power within the individual states and provide specific rights to persons within those states.

Statement of Financial Assistance — an agreement between a student-athlete and a college or university in which the granting institution agrees to extend financial aid to the student in exchange for the student-athlete's agreement to participate in intercollegiate athletics on behalf of the institution; financial assistance may cover costs, including tuition, fees, room, board, and books, associated with enabling a student-athlete to participate in the educational process of the institution.

Statutory labor exemption — an antitrust exemption created by two federal labor statutes that provides a labor union with immunity from antitrust liability for its unilateral efforts to further its members' (e.g., players) economic interests by unionizing, engaging in the collective bargaining process, and striking or picketing; it also immunizes the activities of multiemployer collective bargaining units (e.g., the representative of a league's clubs) from antitrust challenge.

Strict liability — liability without any personal fault; for doping offenses, this means that an athlete is liable for a doping violation based on the mere presence of a banned substance in his or her body, regardless of whether he or she intended to take a banned substance or was negligent (i.e., failed to use reasonable care to prevent a doping violation).

Strike — a lawful means of economic pressure that a players' union may use in an effort to convince a professional sports league to agree to its proposed collective bargaining agreement (CBA) terms; during a strike, the players refuse to provide services to their respective clubs, which forces the clubs not to play games or to hire replacement players (most of whom are not major league caliber).

Subpoena — a writ issued by a court or government agency requiring a party to testify or produce certain evidentiary material.

Substantial proportionality — under Title IX, the difference between the ratio of male and female students in the undergraduate student body and the ratio of male and female student-athletes is not large enough to sustain an additional team for the underrepresented sex.

Substantially less restrictive alternative — the third step of Sherman Act §1 antitrust rule of reason analysis pursuant to which a court or jury determines whether there is a substantially less restrictive alternative means of achieving the same procompetitive benefits as the challenged restraint of trade; if so, the restraint generally is unreasonable and illegal.

Substantive due process — a constitutional limitation on government or state power to enact or enforce substantive legislation or regulation that infringes on a general or unenumerated (not specifically included constitutional) right.

Suspicionless — a term used to describe searches (drug tests) permitted by courts even when there was no individualized suspicion of wrongdoing (drug use).

Swiss Federal Tribunal (SFT) — Switzerland's highest court, which has the jurisdiction to review Court of Arbitration for Sport (CAS) arbitration awards, which is rendered on very narrow procedural and substantive grounds.

Ted Stevens Olympic and Amateur Sports Act (Amateur Sports Act, or ASA) — a federal law that provides the legal framework for regulating Olympic sports in the United States and grants the United States Olympic Committee plenary governing authority; it also provides the United States Olympic Committee with the exclusive right to use and license others to use all of the Olympic marks within the United States and prohibits their unauthorized usage "for the purpose of trade, to induce the sale of any goods or services, or to promote any theatrical exhibition, athletic performance, or competition."

Temporary restraining order — a short-term order designed to protect a party while the court is considering whether it should issue an injunction in a case.

Termination for cause — the justifiable discharge of an employee that is based on certain provisions or terms of the contract existing between the employer and the discharged employee.

Therapeutic use exemption (TUE) — an exemption granted by an antidoping organization that permits an athlete to take prescribed medication containing a banned substance for legitimate health reasons.

Third-party beneficiary — a party in contract law who may assert rights under the contract, even though she or he was not a party to the original contract, on the ground that the party was an intended beneficiary of the contract.

Trademark Counterfeiting — the intentional and unauthorized use of a mark on a product that is known to be "identical with, or substantially indistinguishable from," a federally registered mark, which creates a likelihood of consumer confusion regarding its source, affiliation, endorsement, or sponsorship.

Trademark Dilution Revision Act of 2006 (TDRA) — a provision of the Lanham Act that protects the unauthorized use of a "famous mark" (e.g., "America's Cup") from dilution by blurring or tarnishment.

Trademark/service mark — a name, logo, or other symbol that identifies a product or service.

Trademark/service mark infringement — the unauthorized use of a name, logo, or other symbol that creates a likelihood of consumer confusion regarding the source, affiliation, endorsement, or sponsorship of a product or service.

Transfer rules — regulations promulgated and enforced by athletic associations to limit the ability of a student-athlete to participate in interscholastic athletics after the student moves from one school to another.

Unauthorized public performance of copyrighted work — the violation of federal copyright law by the unauthorized display of a copyrighted work "at a place open to the public or at any place where a substantial number of persons outside of a normal circle of family and its social acquaintances are gathered" (e.g., the interception of a broadcast sports event and its unauthorized streaming over the internet).

Unethical conduct — a finding by the National Collegiate Athletic Association (NCAA) that a coach, a student-athlete, an administrator, or staff member failed to act with honesty and integrity.

Unfair competition — the unauthorized use of another's intellectual property (e.g., a trademark) that causes a likelihood of consumer confusion.

Unfair labor practice — conduct by either a league multiemployer collective bargaining unit or a players' union during the collective bargaining process or otherwise that violates the obligations or rights established by the National Labor Relations Act (NLRA).

Uniform Domain Name Dispute Resolution Policy (UDRP) — a policy that provides a trademark owner with the right to arbitration as a means of remedying the unauthorized use of its trademark as an internet domain name.

Uniform or standard player contract (UPC) — the standard form agreement between a player and his or her team, the terms of which (as well as the parties' contractual freedom to amend or modify them) are established by the league's collective bargaining agreement (CBA).

United Nations Convention on the Recognition and Enforcement of Foreign Arbitral Awards, 9 U.S.C. §201 (New York Convention) — an international treaty, to which the United States is a party, which provides a procedure for national courts to recognize and confirm valid foreign arbitration awards; a national court is empowered to vacate a foreign arbitration award only on very limited grounds.

United States Anti-Doping Agency (USADA) — an independent, nongovernmental antidoping agency for Olympic sports in the United States, which provides drug education, conducts drug testing of U.S. athletes, investigates positive results, and prosecutes doping violations.

United States Olympic and Paralympic Committee (USOC) — the organization that governs the Olympic Movement in the United States; it has exclusive authority over all Olympic sports and athletes in the United States.

Vacation of records — a punishment levied by the National Collegiate Athletic Association (NCAA) against schools for using ineligible players, whether they were deemed ineligible at the time of the game or retroactively determined to be ineligible; the institution or coach may not be credited with any victories during the time frame of using an ineligible player (though any losses are still counted), and all the player's stats and accomplishments are also no longer credited.

Voluntary participation — the willful, knowing, and purposeful involvement of an individual in an activity without the coercion or influence of another.

Waiver rule — a process by which an interscholastic or intercollegiate athlete may seek to be relieved from limitations on participation on the grounds of fairness (to the athlete).

Warrant — a judge's order acknowledging sufficient cause to permit law enforcement officers to engage in a reasonable search.

Workers' compensation law — a statutory system of administrative benefits established by state law that provide a method whereby workers are able to obtain compensation and medical expenses for work-related injuries or diseases.

World Anti-Doping Agency (WADA) — an international agency based in Lausanne, Switzerland, which is the product of a collaborative effort between governments and international sports organizations to combat sports doping, which promulgates the World Anti-Doping Code (WADA Code).

World Anti-Doping Code (WADA Code) — antidoping regulations and rules created by the World Anti-Doping Agency (WADA) that aim to create a uniform system of rules and sanctions for doping violations applicable to all competitive sports played throughout the world, particularly Olympic sports.

Table of Cases

Principal cases are denoted by italics.

A

Abdul-Jabbar v. General Motors Corp., 335, 340
Access Now Inc. v. South Fla. Stadium Corp., 308
Agnew v. NCAA, 109–110
Alexander v. Sandoval, 228
Al-Jahmi v. Ohio Athletic Comm., 274–275, 286
Allarcom Pay Television, Ltd. v. General Instrument Corp., 330
Allred v. Capital Area Soccer League, Inc., 265, 269
American Football League v. NFL, 407–408
American League of Prof'l Baseball Clubs, 417
American Needle, Inc. v. New Orleans La. Saints, 403
American Needle, Inc. v. NFL, 395, 396, 397, 403, 445
Anderson v. Griffith, 460
Anderson v. Little League Baseball, Inc., 302
Andrews v. Marriott Int'l, Inc., 337
Annitto v. Smithtown Cent. Sch. Dist., 256
Anti-Fascist Comm. v. McGrath, 145
Arnzen v. Temecula Valley Unified Sch. Dist., 256
Arrington v. NCAA, 296
Association of Intercollegiate Athletics for Women v. NCAA, 100, 106
Atwater v. National Football League Players Ass'n, 457
Auburn Univ. v. Moody, 319
Avila v. Citrus Cmty. Coll. Dist., 241, 263

B

Badgett v. Alabama High Sch. Athletic Ass'n, 307
Baisden v. West Va. Secondary Schs. Activities Comm'n, 306
Baker v. Briarcliff Sch. Dist., 255
Baltimore Orioles, Inc. v. Major League Baseball Players Ass'n, 329, 344
Barr v. Cunningham, 275
Barron v. PGA Tour, Inc., 305
Bauer v. Interpublic Group of Cos., 465
Beach v. University of Utah, 261
Beckett v. Clinton Prairie Sch. Corp., 252
Behagen v. Amateur Basketball Ass'n of U.S., 509
Behagen v. International Conf. of Faculty Representatives, 143
Benitez v. New York City Bd. of Educ., 245
Bentley v. Cleveland Browns Football Co., 290

Berger v. NCAA, 151
Bernsen v. Innovative Legal Marketing, LLC, 370
Bethel Sch. Dist. No. 403 v. Fraser, 51
Biediger v. Quinnipiac Univ., 180
Big Fights Inc. v. Ficara, 329
Bilney v. Evening Star Newspaper Co., 156, 157
Bing v. Bank of Kingston, 362
Blalock v. Ladies Prof'l Golfers Ass'n, 444
Bloom v. NCAA, 92, 95, *96*
Board of Dirs. of Ames Cmty. Sch. Dist. v. Cullinan, 356
Board of Dirs. of Jessup Cmty. Sch. Dist. v. Wall, 351
Board of Educ. of Indep. Sch. Dist. No. 92 of Pottawatomie Cnty. v. Earls, 48
Board of Governors of Univ. of N.C. v. Helpingstine, 316
Board of Regents v. Roth, 144
Board of Supervisors of La. State Univ. v. Smack Apparel Co., 313–314
Bostic v. Smyrna Sch. Dist., 189
Boston Athletic Ass'n v. Sullivan, 319
Boston Celtics LP v. Shaw, 413, 434
Boston Prof'l Hockey Ass'n v. Dallas Cap & Emblem Mfg., Inc., 314
Boucher v. Syracuse Univ., 180
B.P.J. v. West Va. State Bd. of Educ., 194
Bradley v. NCAA, 264, 283
Bradley v. United States, 257, 286
Bragdon v. Abbott, 302
Brands v. Sheldon Cmty. Sch., *38*, 40
Branion v. Wallace, 464
Brennan v. Board of Trs. for Univ. of La. Sys., 94
Brentwood v. Tennessee Secondary Sch. Athletic Ass'n, 531 U.S. 288 (2001), 18, *19*
Brentwood v. Tennessee Secondary Sch. Athletic Ass'n, 127 S. Ct. 2489 (2007), 18, 22, *23*
Briggs v. Washington Metro. Area Transit Auth., 287
Brocail v. Detroit Tigers, Inc., 294
Brown v. Coach Stores, Inc., 226
Brown v. Pro Football, Inc., 431, 442
Brown v. Wichita State Univ., 272
Bryant v. Fox, 294
Brzonkala v. Virginia Polytechnic Inst., 192
Bukal v. Illinois High Sch. Ass'n, 62
Bukowski v. Clarkson Univ., 256, 262

555

Burden v. Wilkes-Barre Area Sch. Dist., 273
Bushnell v. Japanese-American Religious & Cultural Ctr., 253

C

Campanelli v. Bockrath, 356
Cannon v. University of Chi., 164, 201
Cardtoons, LC v. Major League Baseball Players Ass'n, 320, 343
Carson v. Here's Johnny Portable Toilets, Inc., 339
Carter v. Ball, 229
C.B.C. Distribution & Mktg., Inc. v. Major League Baseball Advanced Media, 342
CBS Interactive Inc. v. National Football League Players Ass'n, Inc., 343
Cerny v. Cedar Bluffs Junior/Senior Pub. Sch., 257
Chagnaud v. FINA, 522
Chalenor v. University of N.D., 185
Champion Pro Consulting Group, Inc. v. Impact Sports Football, LLC, 465
Champions Golf Club, Inc. v. Champions Golf Club, Inc., 315
Chang v. University of R.I., 351
Charles D. Bonanno Linen Serv., Inc. v. NLRB, 431
Charles O. Finley & Co. v. Kuhn, 381, *385*, 387
Cheong v. Antablin, 241
Chiapparelli v. Henderson, 487
Chicago Nat'l League Ball Club, Inc. v. Vincent, 388
Chicago Prof'l Sports LP v. NBA, 117
City of. *See name of city*
City Press Communc'ns, LLC v. Tennessee Secondary Sch. Athletic Ass'n, 22
Clarett v. NFL, 442
Clark v. University of Or., 257
Clark v. Weisberg, 456
Clark Cnty. Sch. Dist. v. Payo, 274
Class v. Towson Univ., 301
Classen v. Izquierdo, 289
Cleburne, City of v. Cleburne Living Ctr., Inc., 297
Cobb v. Time, Inc., 336
Cohen v. Brown Univ., 173, 179, 180
Cole v. Valley Ice Garden, LLC, 351
Collins v. National Basketball Players Ass'n, 487–488
Colorado Seminary v. NCAA, 143
Communities for Equity v. Michigan High Sch. Athletic Ass'n, 185
Comprehensive Drug Testing, Inc.; United States v., 423
Conard v. University of Wash., 146
Connell Constr. Co. v. Plumbers, Local 100, 441
Coomer v. Kansas City Royals, 267
Cortez v. NBA, 308
Covington Cnty. Sch. Dist. v. Magee, 274
Crouch v. National Ass'n of Stock Car Auto Racing, Inc., 382

Cruz v. Pennsylvania Interscholastic Athletic Ass'n, Inc., 31, 306
Cureton v. NCAA, 221
Curtis Publ'g Co. v. Butts, 156

D

Dallas Cowboys Cheerleaders, Inc. v. Pussycat Cinema, Ltd., 314, 321
Dallas Cowboys Football Club, Ltd. v. America's Team Props., 320
Dallas Cowboys Football Club, Ltd. v. Harris, 412
Daniels v. FanDuel, Inc., 343
Daniels v. School Bd. of Brevard Cnty., Fla., 985 F. Supp. 1458 (M.D. Fla. 1997), 183, 185
Daniels v. School Bd. of Brevard Cnty., Fla., 995 F. Supp. 1394 (M.D. Fla. 1997), 184, 185
Daniels v. Seattle Seahawks, 294
Davenport v. Randolph Cnty. Bd. of Educ., 42
Davidson v. University of N.C. at Chapel Hill, 262
Davis v. Carter, 273
Davis v. Monroe Cnty. Bd. of Educ., 189, 190, 201
Dawson v. NCAA, 151
DeFrantz v. United States Olympic Comm., 507
Deli v. University of Minn., 197, 200
DeLong v. Rhode Island Sports Ctr., Inc., 266
Dempsey v. Time, Inc., 336
Dennehy v. East Windsor Reg'l Bd. Educ., 256
Dennison v. Murray State Univ., 359
Denver Rockets v. All-Pro Mgmt., 445
DePiano v. Montreal Baseball Club, Ltd., 293, 294
Detroit Lions, Inc. v. Argovitz, 459
Deutscher Tennis Bund v. ATP Tour, Inc., 405
Dickey v. NFL, 489
Doe v. *See name of opposing party*
Dogra v. CAA Sports, LLC., 464
Dogra v. Griffin, 456
Drake; SEC v., 455
Dryer v. NFL, 344
Dye v. Sexton, 464

E

Eagle-Union Cmty. Sch. Corp.; Doe v., 298
Edward C. v. City of Albuquerque, 266, 269
Electronic Arts, Inc. v. Davis, 344
Elite Rodeo Ass'n v. Prof'l Rodeo Cowboys Ass'n, 405
Elston ex rel. Elston v. Howland Local Schs., 274
E.M. v. House of Boom Ky. *See* Miller ex rel. E.M. v. House of Boom Ky.
Employment Div. v. Smith, 57
Eppley v. University of Del., 138
Equity in Athletics, Inc. v. Department of Educ., 137–138, 186
Ericson v. Syracuse Univ., 190
Eriksson v. Nunnink, 282
ETW Corp. v. Jireh Publ'g, Inc., 343
Evans v. Oaks Mission Pub. Sch., 272

F

Farren v. Baltimore Ravens, 293
Federal Baseball Club of Balt., Inc. v. National League of Prof'l Baseball Clubs, 8, 391, 392, 393
Federation Internationale de Football v. Nike, Inc., 324
Feist Publ'ns, Inc. v. Rural Tel. Serv. Co., 332, 333
Feldman v. Pro Football, Inc., 308
Feleccia v. Lackawanna Coll., 262
Finch v. Swingly, 294
Fish v. Los Angeles Dodgers Baseball Club, 270
Fitzsimmons; People v., 244
Fleischmann v. Hanover Ins. Co., 286
Flood v. Kuhn, 392, 394, 435, 441
Force v. Pierce City R-VI Sch. Dist., 167
Fortay v. University of Miami, 138
Fowler v. Tyler Indep. Sch. Dist., 272
Franklin v. Gwinnett Cnty. Pub. Schs., 165, 201
Fraser v. Major League Soccer, LLC, 445
Frye v. Yasi, 280
Fuhr v. School Dist. of Hazel Park, 196

G

Gahan v. Mineola Union Free Sch., 257
Galloway v. State, 281
Gatto; United States v., 472, 473
Gault v. United States Bobsled & Skeleton Fed'n, 511
Gebser v. Lago Vista Indep. Sch. Dist., 189, 190, 201
George v. George Washington Univ., 138
Gilbert v. Seton Hall Univ., 273
Gillespie v. Southern Utah State Coll., 288, 289
Gionfriddo v. Major League Baseball, 342, 343
Giuliani v. Duke Univ., 138
Gorman v. St. Raphael's Acad., 42
Grady v. Chenango Valley Cent. Sch. Dist., 255
Grandalski v. Lyons Twp. High Sch. Dist., 272
Greece, Town of v. Galloway, 58
Griggs v. Duke Power Co., 228, 229
Grinnell Corp.; United States v., 407
Grove City Coll. v. Bell, 93, 164
Groves v. Morgan Stanley Smith Barney, 455
Grube v. Bethlehem Area Sch. Dist., 297, 299
Gurley v. National Basketball Players Ass'n, 488

H

Haelan Labs., Inc. v. Topps Chewing Gum, Inc., 338
Hall; People v., 248, 249
Hall v. University of Minn., 146
Hamilton v. Speight, 344
Hamilton Cnty. Bd. of Cnty. Comm'rs v. NFL, 406
Hanna Mfg. Co. v. Hillerich & Bradsby Co., 338
Harding v. U.S. Figure Skating Ass'n, 508
Harjo v. Pro-Football, Inc., 233
Harlem Wizards Entm't Basketball, Inc. v. NBA Props., Inc., 315

Harper & Row, Publishers, Inc. v. Nation Enter., 332
Harris v. University of Mich. Bd. of Regents, 272
Hart v. NCAA, 146
Harting v. Dayton Dragons Prof'l Baseball Club, 266
Hayden v. Greensburg Cmty. Sch. Corp., 42
Hayden v. University of Notre Dame, 267
Haywood v. NBA, 391
Hazelwood Sch. Dist. v. Kuhlmeier, 51
Hecox v. Little, 194
Hellenic Olympic Comm. v. International Sailing Fed'n, 520
Hendrickson v. Octagon, Inc., 464
Hendy v. Losse, 295
Hening v. Adair, 216
Hennessey v. NCAA, 100, 106
Henney v. Shelby City Sch. Dist., 255
Hickey ex rel. R.B. v. Enterline, 273
Higgins v. Kentucky Sports Radio, LLC, 337
Hillerich & Bradsby v. Christian Bros., 335
Hodges v. NBA, 215
Holsapple v. Woods, 42
Holtman v. Reese, 289
Hoopla Sports & Entm't, Inc. v. Nike, Inc., 327
Hoover v. Meiklejohn, 171
Howard v. Missouri Bone & Joint Ctr., Inc., 288, 289
Howley v. Town of Stratford, 227
Hurst v. East Coast Hockey League, Inc., 269, 271
Hutcheson; United States v., 441
Hyatt v. United States Judo, Inc., 509
Hysaw v. Washburn Univ. of Topeka, 144, 146

I

Independent Sports & Entm't LLC v. Fegan, 464
Indiana High Sch. Athletic Ass'n v. Avant, 30
Indiana High Sch. Athletic Ass'n v. Carlberg, 26, 27, 29
Indianapolis Colts, Inc. v. Metropolitan Balt. Football Club LP, 314
In re. *See name of party*
International Boxing Club of N.Y., Inc.; United States v., 391, 392, 393
International News Serv. v. Associated Press, 326
ITF v. Gasquet, 525

J

Jackson v. Birmingham Bd. of Educ., 201
Jackson v. Drake Univ., 137
Jackson v. University of New Haven, 224
Jackson, City of v. Estate of Stewart ex rel. Womack, 275
James v. New York Racing Ass'n, 226
James Burrough, Ltd. v. Sign of Beefeater, Inc., 313
Jarreau v. Orleans Parish Sch. Bd., 257
Johnny Blastoff, Inc. v. L.A. Rams Football Co., 314, 319
Johnson v. NCAA, 151
Johnston v. University of Pittsburgh of the Commonwealth Sys. of Higher Educ., 196

558 Table of Cases

Jones v. Three Rivers Mgmt. Corp., 266, 269
Jones v. West Va. State Bd. of Educ., 36

K

Kahn v. East Side Union High Sch. Dist., 252, 255
Kansas City Royals v. Major League Baseball Players Ass'n, 438
Kapp v. NFL, 441
Karalyos v. Board of Educ. of Lake Forest Cmty. High Sch. Dist. 115, 274
Kelly v. Board of Trs., 185
Kelly v. McCarrick, 256
Kennedy v. Bremerton Sch. Dist., 58, 59
Kennedy v. Long Island R.R. Co., 441
Kent State Univ. v. Bradley Univ., 369
Kent State Univ. v. Ford, 369
Kentucky Speedway, LLC v. National Ass'n for Stock Car Auto Racing, Inc., 405
Kingsford v. Salt Lake City Sch. Dist., 349
Kish v. Iowa Cent. Cmty. Coll., 348, 350
Kleinknecht v. Gettysburg Coll., 258, 262
Knapp v. Northwestern Univ., 298, 299
Knight v. Jewett, 240–241, 252, 254
Koszela v. National Ass'n of Stock Car Auto Racing, Inc., 382
Krueger v. San Francisco Forty Niners, 287, 289

L

Lamorie v. Warner Pac. Coll., 262
Landis v. Washington State Major League Baseball Stadium Pub. Facilities Dist., 308
Landow v. School Bd. of Brevard Cnty., 185
Lanni v. NCAA, 263–264
Laumann v. NHL, 394, 396, 403
Law v. NCAA, 108–109
Lawless v. LPGA, 194
Le v. Zuffa, 405
Leach v. Texas Tech, 357
Lee v. Brothers, 467
Lemat Corp. v. Barry, 413
Lesher v. Zimmerman, 273
Lesser v. Neosho Cnty. Cmty. Coll., 138
Letendre v. Missouri State High Sch. Athletics Ass'n, 30
Levin v. NBA, 397, 398
Lewis v. Rahman, 413
Libertarian Party of Wis. v. State, 399
Limones v. School Dist., 62
Lindland v. U.S. Wrestling Ass'n, Inc., 511
Long v. NFL, 381, 422
Los Angeles Mem'l Coliseum Comm'n v. NFL, 382, 395, 400
Lotysz v. Montgomery, 294
Lovitt v. Concord Sch. Dist., 272
Lowe v. California League of Prof'l Baseball, 266

Lowe v. Commack Union Free Sch. Dist., 229
Ludman v. Davenport Assumption Sch., 243

M

Mackey v. NFL, 441, 446
Madison Square Garden, LP v. NHL, 403
Mahanoy Area Sch. Dist. v. B. L., 49, 55, 157
Major League Baseball Players Ass'n v. Garvey, 438
Major League Baseball Props., Inc. v. Salvino, Inc., 402–403
Manassa v. NCAA, 141
March Madness Athletic Ass'n v. Netfire, Inc., 321
Marshall v. ESPN, Inc., 345
Martin v. Casagrande, 287
Martin v. IOC, 512
Maryland Stadium Auth. v. Becker, 313
Mastercard Int'l, Inc. v. Sprint Commc'ns Co., 325
Matal v. Tam, 233–234
Matthews v. Kountze Indep. Sch. Dist., 59
Matuzalem v. FIFA, 517
Mayall ex rel. R.C. v. USA Water Polo, Inc., 258
Mayes v. La Sierra Univ., 270
McAdoo v. University of N.C. at Chapel Hill, 137
McCants v. NCAA, 137
McCormick v. School Dist. of Mamoroneck, 182, 185
McCourt v. California Sports, Inc., 442
McDonnell Douglas Corp. v. Green, 226, 227
McGee v. Covington Cnty. Sch. Dist., 288
McNeil v. NFL, 444, 445
McRae v. School Reform Comm'n, 214
McSorley; Regina v., 246, 250
Mehr v. FIFA, 62, 258
Mendenhall v. HanesBrand, Inc., 370
Mendy v. AIBA, 519
Menora v. Illinois High Sch. Ass'n, 56
Mercer v. Duke Univ., 172
Metropolitan Sports Facilities Comm'n v. Minnesota Twins P'ship, 401
Miami Univ. Wrestling Club v. Miami Univ., 185
Michels v. USOC, 508, 513
Mickelson v. PGA Tour, Inc., 405
Mikkelsen v. Haslam, 289
Miller v. California Speedway Corp., 308
Miller ex rel. E.M. v. House of Boom Ky., 281
Mills v. Durham Bulls Baseball Club, Inc., 266
Miranda Fuel Co., 433
Mississippi High Sch. Activities Ass'n v. R.T., 25
Mississippi Univ. For Women v. Hogan, 167–168
Mogabgab v. Orleans Parish Sch. Bd., 257
Mohney v. USA Hockey, Inc., 281
Mohr v. St. Paul Fire & Marine Ins. Co., 258
Molinas v. NBA, 421
Monson v. Oregon, 359
Montalvo v. Radcliffe, 302
Montana v. San Jose Mercury News, Inc., 341

Morio v. North Am. Soccer League, 427
Morris v. Union High Sch. Dist. A, 257
Morris Commc'ns Corp. v. PGA Tour, Inc., 333
Mullins v. Westmoreland Coal Co., 292
Murphy v. NCAA, 333

N

NAACP, Inc. v. Town of E. Haven, 228
Nabozny v. Barnhill, 12–13
Namath v. Sports Illustrated, 342
National & Am. League Prof'l Baseball Clubs v. Major League Baseball Players Ass'n, 435
National Ass'n of Broadcasters v. Copyright Royalty Tribunal, 329
National Basketball Ass'n. *See* NBA
National Collegiate Athletic Ass'n. *See* NCAA
National Hockey League Players' Ass'n v. Plymouth Whalers Hockey Club, 444
National Hockey League Players' Concussion Injury Litig., In re, 296
NBA v. Minnesota Prof'l Basketball LP, 398
NBA v. Motorola, Inc., 327, 332, 333
NBA v. SDC Basketball Club, Inc., 400
NBA Players Ass'n on Behalf of Player Latrell Sprewell & Warriors Basketball Club, 434
NBA Props. v. Untertainment Records LLC, 321
NCAA v. Alston, 116, 121, 122, 397
NCAA v. Board of Regents of Univ. of Okla., 67, 101, 107–108, 109, 111, 114, 116, 118, 397, 404, 444
NCAA v. Lasege, 99
NCAA v. Smith, 92
NCAA v. Tarkanian, 18, 19–20, 70, 92, 155, 159
NCAA v. Yeo, 146
NCAA Athletic Grant-In-Aid Cap Antitrust Litig., In re, 115
NCAA Student-Athlete Concussion Injury Litig., In re, 296
NCAA Student-Athlete Name & Likeness Licensing Litig., In re, 343–344
Neal v. Board of Trs. of Cal. State Univs., 186, 188
Neeld v. American Hockey League, 297
New Bos. Television, Inc. v. Entertainment Sports Programming Network, Inc., 332
Newcombe v. Adolph Coors Co., 339
New York City Triathlon LLC v. NYC Triathlon Club Inc., 320
New York Times v. Sullivan, 336
New York Yankees P'ship v. Evil Enters., Inc., 314
NFL. *See* NFL
NFL v. Coors Brewing Co., 319
NFL v. Governor of State of Del., 333
NFL v. Insight Telecomm. Corp., 329
NFL v. McBee & Bruno's, Inc., 329
NFL v. TVRadioNow Corp., 330
NFL; United States v., 390
NFL Mgmt. Council v. National Football League Players Ass'n, 439
NFL Mgmt. Council & National Football League Players Ass'n, 432
NFL Players' Concussion Injury Litig., In re, 296
NFL Props., Inc. v. Consumer Enters., Inc., 316
NFL Props., Inc. v. Dallas Cowboys Football Club, Ltd., 316, 370
NFL Props., Inc. v. New Jersey Giants, Inc., 313, 317
NFL Sunday Ticket Antitrust Litig., In re, 328, 404
Nixon v. Clay, 243
NLRB v. *See name of opposing party*
Nordstrom d/b/a Seattle Seahawks, 427
Norfolk Admirals v. Jones, 290
North Am. Soccer League, 153
North Am. Soccer League v. NLRB, 426
Northwestern Univ. & Coll. Athletes Players Ass'n, 152
Nostalgic Partners LLC v. Office of Comm'r of Major League Baseball, 394
Núñez Guadalupe v. Lagardere Unlimited, 464

O

Oakland Raiders v. NFL, 387
O'Bannon v. NCAA, 110, 115, 121
O'Brien v. Ohio State Univ., 353
Ohio State Univ. v. Skreened, Ltd., 319
Ollier v. Sweetwater Union High Sch. Dist., 185
Olsten v. Leftwich, 292
Olympique Lyonnais SASP v. Olivier Bernard & Newcastle UFC, 529
O-M Bread, Inc. v. United States Olympic Comm., 323
Orr v. Brigham Young Univ., 260, 261

P

Pahulu v. University of Kan., 299
Paralyzed Veterans of Am. v. D.C. Arena LP, 308
Parker v. Franklin Cnty. Cmty. Sch. Corp., 185
People v. *See name of opposing party*
Person; United States v., 354
Peterson v. Kennedy, 433
Pfenning v. Lineman, 243
PGA Tour, Inc. v. Martin, 302–304
Philadelphia Ball Club, Ltd. v. Lajoie, 411–412
Philadelphia World Hockey Club, Inc. v. Philadelphia Hockey Club, Inc., 390, 408, 441, 444
Pierre-Paul v. ESPN Inc., 338
Piggie; United States v., 472–473, 474
Pinard v. Clatskanine Sch. Dist. 6J, 157
Pirkle v. Oakdale Union Grammar Sch. Dist., 257
Pistorius v. IAAF, 307
Pitts v. Oklahoma State Univ., 197
Pittsburgh Athletic Co. v. KQV Broad. Co., 326
Platzer v. Mammoth Mountain Ski Area, 281
Pliuskaitis v. USA Swimming, Inc., 511

Table of Cases

Pollock v. Highlands Ranch Cmty. Ass'n, Inc., 281
Pooley v. National Hole-in-One Ass'n, 342
Portland Baseball Club, Inc. v. Baltimore Baseball Club, Inc., 391
Portz v. St. Cloud State Univ., 185
Powell v. NFL, 442
Price v. University of Ala., 349
Prince v. Louisville Mun. Sch. Dist., 273
ProBatter Sports, LLC v. Sports Tutor, Inc., 327
Professional Hockey Corp. v. World Hockey Ass'n, 382
Pro-Football, Inc. v. Blackhorse, 233–234
Pro-Football, Inc. v. Harjo, 233
Pro-Football, Inc. v. Uhlenhake, 291
Pryor v. NCAA, 221–222
Puchalski v. School Dist. of Springfield, 350

Q

Quinn v. Mississippi State Univ., 275
Quokka Sports, Inc. v. Cup Int'l Internet Ventures, 321

R

Radovich v. NFL, 391, 392, 393
Raducan v. International Olympic Comm., 522, 523
Radwan v. Manuel, 146, 157
Ramos v. Midland Coll., 185
Ramsey v. Gamber, 288
R.B. v. Enterline. *See* Hickey ex rel. R.B. v. Enterline
R.C. v. USA Water Polo, Inc. *See* Mayall ex rel. R.C. v. USA Water Polo, Inc.
Regents of Univ. of Cal. v. Bakke, 228
Regina v. *See name of opposing party*
Reid v. Kenowa Hills Pub. Schs., 37
Rensing v. Indiana State Univ. Bd. of Trs., 149
Reynolds v. International Amateur Athletic Fed'n, 512
Reynolds v. NFL, 442
Richards v. U.S. Tennis Ass'n, 193
Richardson v. Sugg, 215, 216, 360
Ridpath v. Board of Governors Marshall Univ., 157, 350, 359, 360
Robertson v. NBA, 441
Robinson v. Department of Labor & Indus., 293
Rodgers v. Georgia Tech Athletic Ass'n, 360, 362
Rose v. Giamatti, 388
Rosenhaus v. Jackson, 464
Ross v. Creighton Univ., 135
Rutherford v. Talisker Canyons Fin. Co., 255, 281

S

St. Mary's Honor Ctr. v. Hicks, 226
Salerno v. American League of Prof'l Baseball Clubs, 391
Sanchez v. Hillerich & Bradsby Co., 263
Sanderson v. U.S. Ctr. for SafeSport Inc., 511
Sandford v. Long, 262
Sanford-Brown Co. v. Patent Scaffolding Co., 362

San Francisco Arts & Athletics, Inc. v. United States Olympic Comm., 322
San Jose, City of v. MLB, 394
Santa Fe Indep. Sch. Dist. v. Doe, 58–59
Savino v. Robertson, 10, 14
Schacker; People v., 245
Schaffner v. Glencoe Park Dist., 227
Schell v. Ford, 280
Scott v. Oklahoma Secondary Sch. Activities Ass'n, 41
Searles v. Trustees of St. Joseph's Coll., 138, 261
Seattle Seahawks. *See* Nordstrom d/b/a Seattle Seahawks
SEC v. *See name of opposing party*
Secky v. New Paltz Cent. Sch. Dist., 255
Seltzer v. Sunbrock, 327
Senne v. Kansas City Royals Baseball, 417
Serge v. Reconstructive Orthopaedics & Sports Med., Inc., 286
Sharapova v. ITF, 525
Sharon v. City of Newton, 279, 281, 282
Shear v. Trail Blazers, 265
Shelley; State v., 251
Sherry v. East Suburban Football League, 257
Shin v. Ahn, 240
Shriver v. Athletic Council of Kan. State Univ., 272
Silverman v. Major League Baseball Player Relations Comm., Inc., 516 F. Supp. 588 (S.D.N.Y. 1981), *429*, 430
Silverman v. Major League Baseball Player Relations Comm., Inc., 880 F. Supp. 246 (S.D.N.Y. 1995), 431
Simpson v. University of Colo., 192
Sinu v. Concordia Univ., 283
Slaney v. IAAF, 513
Smith v. Delta Tau Delta, 263
Smith v. Highland Cmty. Coll., 349
Smith v. Houston Oilers, Inc., 289–290
Smith v. Kroesen, 275
Smith v. NCAA, 109, 110
Smith v. Pro Football, Inc., 441, 445, 446
Sneed v. Connell, 349
Somerson v. McMahon, 344
Sony Corp. of Am. v. Universal City Studios, Inc., 332
Soule v. Connecticut Ass'n of Sch., Inc., 195–196
Spahn v. Julian Messner, Inc., 337
Speakers of Sport, Inc. v. ProServe, Inc., 466, 467
Spectrum Sports, Inc. v. McQuillan, 407
Spindulys v. Los Angeles Olympic Org. Comm., 513
Sports Mgmt. Network v. Busch, 461–462, 500
Stanley v. University of S. Cal., 199, 200
State v. *See name of opposing party*
Steele v. Louisville & Nashville Railroads, 433
Steinberg Moorad & Dunn Inc. v. Dunn, 464
Stineman v. Fontbonne Coll., 262
Stoutenborough v. NFL, 308
Stringer v. Minnesota Vikings Football Club, LLC, 295
Sullivan v. NFL, 445
Swank v. Valley Christian Sch., 275

T

Talley v. Time, Inc., 156
Taylor v. Wake Forest Univ., *133*, 135
Taylor-Travis v. Jackson State Univ., 358
Texas Dep't of Cmty. Affairs v. Burdine, 226
Thurmond v. Prince William Prof'l Baseball Club, Inc., *267*, 269
Tibbs & United States Paralympics & 8 Affected Athletes, 510
Tinker v. Des Moines Indep. Cmty. Sch. Dist., 41, 51–52, 54, 55
Titan Sports, Inc. v. Comics World Corp., 341
Toolson v. New York Yankees, 391, 392, 393
Tunkl v. Regents of Univ. of Cal., 277, 279
Turner v. Wells, 156
Tyler v. Howard Univ., 197

U

Uhlaender v. Henricksen, 338
Ultimate Fighting Championship. *See* ZUFFA, LLC, d/b/a Ultimate Fighting Championship
Union Royale Belge des Sociétés de Football Ass'n, Royal Club Liégois, & Union des Ass'ns Européennes de Football (UEFA) v. Bosman, 528–529, 530
United States v. *See name of opposing party*
United States Football League v. NFL, 408–409
United States Olympic Committee. *See* USOC
United States Youth Soccer Ass'n; Doe v., 258
University Bookstore v. Board of Regents of Univ. of Wis. Sys., 316
University of Colo. v. Derdeyn, 150
University of Ga. Athletic Ass'n v. Laite, 319
University of Tex. at El Paso v. Moreno, 273
University of W. Va. v. Rodriguez
USADA v. Montgomery, 525
USA Shooting v. International Shooting Union, 521–522
USOC v. American Media, Inc., 323, 324
USOC v. Intelicense Corp., S.A., 322
USOC v. IOC
USOC v. Toy Truck Lines, Inc., 322
USOC v. Xclusive Leisure & Hospitality Ltd., 323

V

Vance v. Spencer Cnty. Pub. Sch. Dist., 191
Vanderbilt Univ. v. DiNardo, 365, *366*, 369
Van Horn v. Industrial Accident Comm'n, 148
Vernonia Sch. Dist. 47J v. Acton, *43*, 48, 55
Volvo N. Am. Corp. v. Men's Int'l Prof'l Tennis Council, 405

W

Wagenblast v. Odessa Sch. Dist. No. 105-157-166J, 277, 282
Waldrep v. Texas Emp'rs Ins. Ass'n, 149, 150
Wallace v. Broyles, 262
Walsh v. Louisiana High Sch. Athletic Ass'n, 56
Walters v. Fullwood, 486
Walters; United States v., 472
Ward v. Michigan State Univ., 272
Warnock v. NFL, 406
Washington v. Smith, 336
Washington Capitols Basketball Club, Inc. v. Barry, 408
WCVB-TV v. Boston Athletic Ass'n, 319
Webb v. Washington State Univ., 146
Wheeler v. Central Carolina Scholastic Sports, Inc., 269
White v. Board of Regents of Univ. of Neb., 313
Wichard v. Suggs, 456
Wildman v. Marshalltown Sch. Dist., 55
Williams v. Board of Regents of Univ. Sys. of Ga., 192
Williams v. CWI, Inc., 454, 457
Williams v. NFL, 438
Williams v. School Dist. of Bethlehem, 171
Williamson v. Prime Sports Mktg., LLC, *482*
Willoughby v. Commissioner of Internal Revenue, 458
Winnipeg Rugby Football Club v. Freeman, 412
Wisconsin Interscholastic Athletic Ass'n v. Gannett Co., 334
WNBA Enters. LLC, In re, 313
Wood v. NBA, 442
Woodford Cnty. Bd. of Educ.; Doe v., 299
Wooster Div. of Borg-Warner Corp.; NLRB v., 416
Wright v. Bonds, 466

Y

Yanero v. Davis, 275
Yang Tae Young v. International Gymnastics Fed'n, *518*
Yarbrough v. Santa Fe Indep. Sch. Dist., 273
York v. Wahkiakum, 48
Yost v. Wabash Coll., 263

Z

Zacchini v. Scripps-Howard Broad. Co., 341
Zemke v. Arreola, 257
Zinn v. Parrish, *452*, 453
Zivich v. Mentor Soccer Club, Inc., 281
ZUFFA, LLC, d/b/a Ultimate Fighting Championship, 428

Index

A

AAU (Amateur Athletic Union), 16, 61, 472
ABA (American Basketball Association), 413
Abdul-Jabbar, Kareem, 340, 488
ABL (American Basketball League), 405
Abusive conduct, termination of coaches for, 356–358
Academic misconduct, 87–89
Academic Progress Rate (APR), 139, 140–141, 365
Academic reform initiatives (NCAA), 138–142
    Academic Progress Rate, 139, 140–141, 365
    initial eligibility requirements, 139–140, 220–224
    NCAA academic reform legislation, 139–140
    satisfactory progress, 139
Acquisition of franchises, antitrust law and, 397–398
Adair, Charles, 216
Adidas basketball scandal, 69, 91, 354–355, 472, 473
Administrators
    First Amendment and, 359–360
    intercollegiate sports
        First Amendment rights *See* First Amendment rights
        racial equity and, 208
        termination as retaliation, 359–360
    professional sports, racial equity and, 210, 212
AFL (American Football League), 407–408, 449
AFL (Arena Football League), 327, 426
AFLPOC (Arena Football League Players Organizing Committee), 426
African-American athletes. *See* Racial equity
Agents. *See* Athlete-agent relationship; Representation
Age rules in interscholastic sports, 31–34
AIAW (Association for Intercollegiate Athletics for Women), 162
AIOWF (Association of International Olympic Winter Sports Federations), 505
All American Girls Professional Baseball League, 162
Alves, Dani, 219
Amateur Athletic Union (AAU), 16, 61, 472
Amateur Sports Act of 1978, 31
Ambush marketing, 324–326
American Basketball Association (ABA), 413
American Basketball League (ABL), 405
American Board of Medical Specialties, 286
American Football League (AFL), 407–408, 449
American Osteopathic Association, 286

Americans with Disabilities Act of 1990
    disabled athletes, 301–304
    Rehabilitation Act compared, 301–302
Youth Soccer Association, 16, 61
America's Cup, 321
Ancient Olympics, 502–503
Andretti Autosport (agency), 462
Andrews, Calvin, 489
Anticipatory repudiation, 126
Anticybersquatting Consumer Protection Act of 1999, 321–322
Anti-Doping Division (ADD), 516
Antitrust law
    Clayton Act, 441
    horizontal restraint, 102–103, 108, 115
    input market, 108
    intercollegiate sports, 100–122
        academic stipends, 122–123
        amateurism defense, 107, 109–110, 115–116, 121–122
        broadcasting rights, 107–108
        case law, 101–122
        compensation of coaches, 108–109
        competitive balance defense, 109, 112, 121
        education-related benefits, 101, 116–122
        eligibility requirements, 109–110
        limits on scholarships, 110–115
        litigation, 67
        monopolization, 100
        nature and scope of limits on regulatory authority, 109
        overview, 100–101
        possible congressional intervention, 123–124
        rule of reason, 107–110
        unreasonable restraint of trade, 107
    labor relations and, 440–447
        anticompetitive effects, 406–407, 441, 444, 445–447
        nonstatutory labor exemption, 433, 441–444
        procompetitive effects, 445–446
        rule of reason, 444–446
    output market, 101, 103–104, 107, 108
    per se rule, 107
    procompetitive effects, 107–109, 122
    professional sports, 389–409
        acquisition, ownership and sale of franchises, 397–398
        anticompetitive effects, 406–407, 441, 444, 445–447
        baseball antitrust exemption, 391–394

563

Antitrust law *(continued)*
  concerted action requirement, 395–396
  intellectual property rights, 401–404
  licensing restrictions, 401–404
  monopolization, 405–409
  overview, 389–390
  procompetitive effects, 400, 403
  relocation of franchises, 399–401
  rival leagues, 405–409
  rule of reason, 395, 397, 398, 400, 403
  Sherman Act, 395–409
  single economic entity defense, 395–396
  unreasonable restraint of trade, 396–404
  rule of reason
    intercollegiate sports and, 107–110
    labor relations and, 444–446
    professional sports and, 395, 397, 398, 400, 403
    "quick look" rule of reason, 108–109, 117, 122
  Sherman Act *See* Sherman Act of 1890
Appeals, 7–8
APR (Academic Progress Rate), 139, 140–141, 365
Arbitrary and capricious standard, 96, 99
Arbitration
  in Court of Arbitration for Sport, 514–527
  judicial review of awards, 438–440
  in labor relations, 434–440
  Olympic Games, athlete eligibility dispute resolution, 508, 509–511
Arena Football League (AFL), 327, 426
Arena Football League Players Organizing Committee (AFLPOC), 426
ARISF (Association of the IOC Recognised International Sports Federations), 505
Armstrong, Lance, 423
ASA. *See* Ted Stevens Olympic and Amateur Sports Act of 1998
ASOIF (Association of Summer Olympic International Federations), 505
Assante (agency), 463
Assault
  liability for injuries to athletes, 250–251
  termination of coaches for, 356–357
Associated Press, 481
Association for Intercollegiate Athletics for Women (AIAW), 162
Association of International Olympic Winter Sports Federations (AIOWF), 505
Association of Summer Olympic International Federations (ASOIF), 505
Association of the IOC Recognised International Sports Federations (ARISF), 505
Assumption of risk, 13, 252, 255–256, 266, 289
Athlete-agent relationship, 450–462
  conflicts of interest, 458–462
  duties, 450–451

fiduciary relationship, 453
financial improprieties, 453–458
NIL agent contracts, 486
players associations, regulation by, 488–499
regulation of, 488–499
standard of care, 451–453
women as agents, 468–469
Athletes First (agency), 463, 467
Athlete-university relationship, 123–159. *See also* National Collegiate Athletic Association
  academic reform initiatives, 138–142
    Academic Progress Rate, 139, 140–141, 365
    initial eligibility requirements, 139–140, 220–224
    NCAA academic reform legislation, 139–140
    satisfactory progress, 139
  antitrust law and eligibility requirements, 109–110, 115, 121–122
  clustering, 140
  contract law, 123–127
    breach of contract, 137–138
    discontinuation of sports, 137–138
    institutional obligations to, 133–138
    National Letter of Intent, 128–130
    NCAA regulations, 130–133
    promises, 123, 124, 125
    promissory estoppel, 125
    Statement of Financial Assistance, 127, 128
    transfers, 131–132
  educational malpractice, 135–137
  as employees, 147–152
  First Amendment rights *See* First Amendment rights
  in loco parentis, 155
  institutional obligations to, 133–138
  "jock majors," 140
  liberty interest in athletic participation, 142, 145, 146
  loss-in-value insurance, 152
  minimum wage, 151–152
  National Letter of Intent, 128–130
  one academic year in residence, 128
  overview, 123
  property interest, 142–147
    absence of, 146
    in athletic participation, 144–146
    contractual rationale, 143
    economic rationale, 143
    educational rationale, 143
    general principles, 142–143
    rules violations and, 146–147
    scholarship rationale, 143
  Statement of Financial Assistance, 127, 128
  transgender participation in sports, 193–196
  unionization, 152–154
  workers' compensation and, 147–152
Athletic trainers, medical malpractice liability, 288, 295
Attorney agents, ethical issues, 499–500

At-will employment, coaches, 348
Austin, Marvin, 471

B

Bach, Thomas, 503, 504
Banks, Charles, IV, 455
Bargaining in good faith, breach of duty, 429–431
Barkley, Saquon, 216, 469
Barry, Rick, 413
Baseball, historical background of, 373–374
Basketball, historical background of, 374
Basketball Association of America (BAA), 375
Bathrooms, sex-segregated, 196
Bauer, Frank, 465
Baylor University, 352, 353–354
Beard, Aaron, 481
Beckham, Odell, Jr, 216
Belichick, Bill, 211
Bench trials, 7
Bennett, Winston, 356
"Best interests of the game" authority, 383–389
Big Ten Conference, 130–131
Big Twelve Conference, 108
Bivens, Carolyn, 304
Black, William "Tank," 454, 455
Black Coaches Association, 209
Blackhorse, Amanda, 233–234
Black Lives Matter, 216
Bland, Tony, 354
Bliss, Dave, 352
Bloom, Lloyd, 472
Bonds, Barry, 423
Bonuses for coaches, 363
Booker, Devon, 469
Boosters (businessmen), rules infractions process, 77–84
Boras Corporation (agency), 463
Bosman, Jean-Marc, 528–529
Boston Marathon, 319–320
Bowen, Brian, 91
Bowl Championship Series (BCS), 67
Boxing, 413–414
Bradley University, 369
Brady, Brittany, 357
Brady, Tom, 439–440
Brake, Deborah, 213
Brandeis, Louis, 337
Brashear, Donald, 249–250
Breach of contract
  athlete-university relationship, 128–129
  coaches and, 365–369
  student-athletes and, 137–138
Bribery, 69, 91, 354–355
Briefing cases, 9–14

Broadcasting rights, 311–312, 326–334
  copyright infringement, 329–332
  copyright protection, 327–329
  governance of intercollegiate sports and, 107–108
  historical background, 326–327
  misappropriation, 326–327
    real-time game accounts and scores, 333–334
  NCAA and, 66, 67, 69, 107–108
Brown, Larry, 351
Bungs, 469
Busch, Kurt, 461–462
Busch, Kyle, 499–500
Buscones (Dominican quasi-agents), 531
Bush, George W., 165, 523–524
Bush, Reggie, 265–266, 470–471
Butts, Wally, 156
Buyouts of coaches, 363, 365–369
Byers, Walter, 67

C

California, Cooley Bill, 63
Calipari, John, 363
Campanelli, Louis, 356
Canadian Football League (CFL), 412–413, 445
Cannabis, recommended removal from banned drug list, 95
Caponigro, John, 461–462, 499–500
Carlesimo, P.J., 434
Carnegie Foundation for the Advancement of Education, 66
Carr, David, 465
Carr, Roger, 428
Carson, Johnny, 339
Carter, Burlette, 2–3
Carter, Jimmy, 507–508
Carter, Vince, 454
CAS. See Court of Arbitration for Sport
Case method, 8–10
Castonguay, Emilie, 469
Cebrun, Nate, 474
Ceferin, Aleksander, 218
Center, Michael, 355
Centers for Disease Control and Prevention (CDC), 62
CFL (Canadian Football League), 412–413, 445
Charitable immunity in tort law, 273
Cheerleading as sport, 180
Child support, financial effect on athletes, 457
CIAW (Commission on Intercollegiate Athletics for Women), 162
Ciccarelli, Dino, 250
Circuit courts, 5
Civil procedure, 6–8
Civil rights
  federal and state law, 92–94
  gender equity See Gender equity; Title IX

Civil rights *(continued)*
  race and *See* Racial equity
  sexual harassment and, 193
Civil Rights Act of 1964
  gender equity, 198
  Proposition 16 and, 221
  racial equity, 221, 222
  Title IX *See* Gender equity; Title IX
Civil Rights Amendments, 18
Civil Rights Restoration Act of 1987, 93, 165
Clarett, Maurice, 417, 433
Class, Gavin, 301
Clayton Act of 1914, 441
Clearly erroneous standard, 99
Clemens, Roger, 423
Clustering, 140
Coaches, 348–371
  at-will employment, 348
  compensation, 350–365
    academic performance, linking to, 364–365
    antitrust law and, 108–109
    bonuses, 363
    escalation in, 362–365
    fringe benefits, 360–362
    housing, 362
    incentives, 364–365
    life insurance, 362
    memorandum of understanding ("MOU"), 364
    perquisites, 360–362
    for term of contract, 360
  contract law and, 348–371
    breach of contract, 365–369
    buyouts, 363, 365–369
    changes, 129–130
    compensation, 360–465
    implied-in-fact promises, 349
    indefinite duration, 348
    liquidated damages, 365–369
    negative injunctions, 412–413
    overview, 348–349
    sponsorship agreements, 370
    termination, 350–360
    venue agreements, 370–371
  employment at will, 348
  First Amendment rights *See* First Amendment rights
  NCAA rules infractions process, 89–91
  property interest in employment, 349–351
  racial equity and, 208–213
  termination, 350–360
    for abusive conduct, 356–358
    for assault, 356–357
    for cause, 350–351
    college basketball and college admissions scandals, 354–355

compensation following, 353–354
indiscretions, 352–353
just cause, 348
morals clauses, 370
non-sports-related conduct, 352–353
for poor performance, 351
as retaliation, 359–360
rules violations, 353
Cochran, Johnnie, 210–211
Code of Sports-Related Arbitration, 515–516
Cole, Augustus, 344
Collective bargaining
  breach of duty to bargain in good faith, 429–431
  overview, 418–421
College admission scandal, 354–355
College sports. *See* Intercollegiate sports
Collegiate athletic associations, 4
Collegiate Licensing Company, 316
Collins, Thomas P., 488
Commanders, 234
Commission on Intercollegiate Athletics for Women (CIAW), 162
Commission on Opportunity in Athletics, 165
Committee on Competitive Safeguards and Medical Aspects of Sports (CSMAS), 94–95
Common law, 8–10
Compensation
  of coaches *See* Coaches
  gender equity, 196–200
Competitive balance taxes, 419, 420
Competitive cheer, 180
"Competitor's privilege," 466–467
Concerted action requirement, 395–396
Concussions, 61–63, 295–297
Conflicts of interest
  in athlete-agent relationship, 458–462
  inter-agent conflicts, 463–469
    consolidation, 463–464
    disparagement, 465
    gender and, 467–469
    overview, 463
    permissible competition, 466–467
    race and, 467–469
    termination, 464–465
Connecticut Interscholastic Athletic Conference, 195–196
Constitutional protections. *See also specific Amendments*
  due process *See* Due process
  equal protection *See* Equal protection
  legal overview, 3–4, 5
Contact sports and gender equity, 171–172
Contract law
  acceptance, 124
  anticipatory repudiation, 126
  arbitrary and capricious standard, 96, 99

breach of contract, 126, 137–138
clearly erroneous standard, 99
coaches and, 348–371. *See also* Coaches
consideration, 124, 125
counteroffer, 124–125
damages, 127
enforceability, 125
excuses for nonperformance, 127
express contracts, 126
formation of contract, 123–125
governance and
    intercollegiate sports, 95–99
    professional sports, 381–383
implied contracts, 126
implied-in-fact promises, 349
labor relations, 411–415
modification, 125–126
mutual assent, 123–125
NCAA and, 95–99
offer, 124
promises, 123, 124, 125
promissory estoppel, 125
student-athletes and, 123–127. *See also* Athlete-university relationship
Contributory negligence, medical malpractice liability, 288–289
Coomer, Robert, 266–267
Cooper, Chuck, 208
Co-participant liability for injuries to athletes, 240–251
  amateur versus professional sports, 243
  consent as defense, 250–251
  criminal liability, 244–251
  intentional/reckless standard of care, 243
  negligence, 243
  tort liability, 240–244
Copyright Act of 1976, 327–332, 344
Copyrights
  broadcasting rights, 327–332
  infringement, 329–332
  protection, 327–329
  unauthorized public performance, 329–330, 332
Coubertin, Baron Pierre de, 502–503
Counterfeiting, trademarks, 319
Court of Arbitration for Sport (CAS), 514–527
  Ad Hoc Division, 516, 517
  Anti-Doping Division (ADD), 516
  arbitration in, 515–517, 527
  Code of Sports-Related Arbitration, 515–516
  disabled athletes and, 307
  disputed competition results, 517–521
  doping violations, 521–527
    notice requirements, 522
    principle of proportionality, 522–523
    sanctions, 522–523, 525
    strict liability, 521–522
    therapeutic use exemption (TUE), 523
    United States Anti-Doping Agency, 423, 526–527
    World Anti-Doping Code, 94, 505, 516, 523–527
  lex sportiva, 516
  overview, 502, 504, 514–517
  World Anti-Doping Code, 94, 505, 516, 523–527
Covenants not to sue, 276
COVID-19 pandemic
  high school sport participation and, 15
  NCAA waiver of minimum standardized test scores, 222
  social media and video use by athletes during, 215–216
Creative Artists Agency, 464, 468
Criminal liability for injuries to athletes, 244–251
Croom, Sylvester, 209
Curt Flood Act of 1998, 394, 443
Cybersquatting, 321–322

D

Daboll, Brian, 211
Dallas Cowboys, 320, 321
Davenport, Najeh, 296
Davis, Al, 399–400
Davis, Anthony, 492
Dawkins, Christian, 473
Dawson, Lamar, 151
Decertification of players associations, 431, 443
Defamation
  actual malice, 156
  First Amendment protections, 156–157
  intellectual property rights and, 336–337
  truth as defense, 156
"Deflategate," 439–440
Dennehy, Patrick, 352
DirecTV Sunday Ticket, 404
Disabled athletes, 297–309
  Americans with Disabilities Act, 301–304
  competition with able-bodied athletes, 307–308
  disabled spectators and fans, 308
  HIV/AIDS, 302
  learning disabilities, 305–306
  major life activity, 298
  overview, 297
  reasonable accommodations vs. fundamental alterations, 304–305
  Rehabilitation Act, 297–301
Discontinuation of sports, contract law and, 137–138
Discovery, 7
Discretionary function, tort law immunities, 273–274
Discrimination. *See also* Civil rights
  against disabled athletes
    Americans with Disabilities Act, 301–304
    competition with able-bodied athletes, 307–308
    disabled spectators and fans, 308

Discrimination *(continued)*
    HIV/AIDS, 302
    learning disabilities, 305–306
    overview, 297
    reasonable accommodations versus fundamental alterations, 304–305
    Rehabilitation Act, 297–301
  employment discrimination *See* Employment discrimination
  gender *See* Gender equity; Title IX
  racial *See* Racial equity
  reverse discrimination, 185–189
  against striking players, 432
Disparagement of agents, 465
Disparate impact, racial equity, 221, 222, 224, 228–230
Disparate treatment, racial equity, 224, 226–227
District courts, 5
Divorce, financial effect on athletes, 457
Domain names, 321–322
Dominican Republic, baseball players from, 531
Dompierre, Eric, 305–306
Doping violations, 521–527
  notice requirements, 522
  principle of proportionality, 52–523
  sanctions, 522–523, 525
  strict liability, 521–522
  therapeutic use exemption (TUE), 523
  World Anti-Doping Code, 94, 505, 516, 523–527
Doubleday, Abner, 374
Drake, Jeremy Joseph, 455
Drake University, 137
Drug testing
  in intercollegiate sports, 94–95
  in interscholastic sports, 43–49, 53–59
    as discipline or sanction, 48–49
    due process, 53–59
    state constitutional issues, 48–49
    suspicionless search, 48–49
    as unreasonable search, 43, 48
  limits on NCAA regulatory authority, 94–95
  performance-enhancing drugs, 94–95
  in professional sports, 421–425
Dual representation, 470
Due process
  drug testing in interscholastic sports, 43
  governance of professional sports and, 385, 388
  liberty interest
    in athletic participation, 142, 145, 146
    in employment, 359–360
  procedural due process, 38, 39–40, 42–43, 138, 142, 146, 147
  property interest, 142–147
    in athletic participation, 144–146
    in employment, 349–351

  general principles, 142–143
  rules violations and, 146–147
  state action requirement and, 19, 22
  substantive due process, 40, 43, 138, 142
Duncan, Tim, 455
Dunn, David, 463–464
Duty of fair representation, 433–434

E

EADA (Equity in Athletics Disclosure Act of 1994), 165
Eastern Michigan University, 180
ECJ (European Court of Justice), 529–530
Education Amendments of 1972. *See* Title IX
Education Department, Title IX administration, 161, 164, 165–166
EEOC (Equal Employment Opportunity Commission), 200
Effective accommodation requirement, 173–182
Electronic Arts, 341, 344
Elliot–Larsen Act (1976 Michigan), 197
Emmert, Mark, 84–85
Employment at will, coaches, 348
Employment discrimination
  disparate impact, 224, 228–230
  disparate treatment, 224, 226–227
  gender equity, 196–202
    compensation, 196–200
    punitive actions, 200–202
    retaliation, 200–202
  racial equity, 224–231
English history of sports in 1400s, 374
English Premier League, 237
Equal benefits and treatment requirement, 182–185
Equal Employment Opportunity Commission (EEOC), 200
Equal Pay Act of 1963, 196–200
Equal protection, 154
  denial of, 43
  gender-based exclusion from sports, 171
  intermediate scrutiny, 172
  interscholastic sports, transfer rules, 26, 27
  race vs. gender, 172
  reverse discrimination, 185–189
  state action, 18
  strict scrutiny, 172
Equity in Athletics Disclosure Act of 1994 (EADA), 165
Equity issues. *See* Civil rights
Erickson, Rodney, 84
Ernst, Gordon, 355
ESPN, 311, 332
Esports athletes, 418
Establishment Clause, 58–59
European Court of Justice (ECJ), 529–530
European soccer, players subject to racist behavior, 218–219
Eustachy, Larry, 352
Evans, Lamont, 354

Excel Sports Management (agency), 463
Exclusive bargaining representative, refusal to recognize union as, 426–427
Exculpatory clauses, 276
Executive branch of government, 4
Exploitation of athletes, risk of, 530–531
Express contracts, 126

F

Fair Labor Standards Act of 1938 (FLSA), 151–152, 217, 417
Fairness in Women's Sports Act (Idaho 2020), 194
Fair representation, duty of, 433–434
Fair use, 319–320
Fan-based animus, 219, 235–238
FBS (Football Bowl Subdivision), 100
Federal courts, 4, 5
Federalism, 3
Federal Rules of Civil Procedure, 7
Felder, Raoul, 457
Females and sports. *See* Gender equity
Ferguson, William, 355
Fiduciary relationship, 450–451, 453
FIFA (Fédération Internationale de Football Association), 219, 324–325, 469–470, 528–529, 531
FIG (International Gymnastics Federation), 517–518
First Amendment rights
  administrators and, 359–360
  defamation and, 156–157
  freedom of association, 49–59
  freedom of speech, 49–55
    intercollegiate athletics, 157–158
    racial equity, 214–216
  grooming rules in interscholastic sports, 42
  intellectual property rights and, 334
  intentional infliction of emotional distress and, 156
  intercollegiate athletics, 154–159
  invasion of privacy and, 156
  matters of public concern, 55
  media and, 155–157
  national anthem protests, 55, 214, 216
  publicity rights, limitations, 341–345
  race and freedom of expression, 214–216
  racial equity and, 214–216
  religious liberty
    Establishment Clause, 58–59
    free exercise, 56–58
    intercollegiate sports, 158–159
    interscholastic sports, 56–59, 159
    prayer, 58–59
  retaliation, termination of employment as, 359–360
  state action, 18
Fitzgerald, Pat, 357
Flores, Brian, 210, 211–212
Florida High School Athletic Association, 63
Florida State University, 90
Floyd, George, racial equity and public protests over death of, 215–216, 234
Football, historical background of, 374
Football Bowl Subdivision (FBS), 100
Ford, Gene A., 369
Foreign countries, professional sports' expansion to, 530, 531
Foster, Jim, 357
Fournette, Leonard, 469
Fourteenth Amendment
  state action requirement, 18, 22
  transgender participation in sports, 193, 194
Fourth Amendment, drug testing in interscholastic sports and, 43, 48–49
Franchise ownership and sales, 397–398
Free agency, 419, 431, 435, 441, 442, 445
Freedom of association, 49–55
Freedom of speech, 49–55. *See also* First Amendment rights
Free exercise of religion, 56–58
Freeh, Louis, 85
Freeh Report, 85, 87
Fringe benefits for coaches, 360–362
Fuhr, Geraldine, 196–197
Fulford, Peggy Ann, 455
Fundamental alterations for disabled athletes, 304–305

G

Gaines, Travelle, 480
GAISF (General Association of International Sports Federations), 505
Gardiner, Simone, 2
Garnett, Kevin, 455
Gatto, James, 473
Gender equity, 161–202. *See also* Title IX
  agents, 468–469
  cheerleading as sport, 180
  contact sports, 171–172
  deference to schools, 185
  effective accommodation requirement, 173–182
  employment discrimination, 196–202
    compensation, 196–200
    punitive actions, 200–202
    retaliation, 200–202
  equal benefits and treatment requirement, 182–185
  equal protection, 26, 171
  gender-based exclusion from particular sport, 166–173
  grooming standards, 42
  historical background, 161–166
  inter-agent conflicts, 467–469
  intermediate scrutiny, 26, 172
  overview, 161
  racial equity compared, 172, 213–214
  rape, 191–192
  reverse discrimination, 185–189

Gender equity *(continued)*
  "separate but equal" teams, 171
  sexual assault, 191–192
  sexual harassment, 189–193. *See also* Sexual harassment
  substantial proportionality test, 176, 179
  three-part test, 165–166, 179, 180
  transgender participation in sports, 193–196
General Association of International Sports Federations (GAISF), 505
General Mills, Inc., 326–327
George Floyd's death, racial equity and public protests, 215–216, 234
George Washington University athletic team name, 235
Giamatti, Bart, 388–389
Globalization, racial equity and, 218–220
Godsey, Keelin, 194–195
Goggins, Jason, 481
Golf
  etiquette model, 238
  historical background of, 374, 376
Good conduct rules in interscholastic sports, 38–41
Goodell, Roger, 216, 439–440
Good faith and fair dealing, duty of
  professional sports governance, 382–383
  student-athletes, 134
Good faith bargaining, breach of duty, 429–431
Governance
  of intercollegiate sports *See* National Collegiate Athletic Association
  of interscholastic sports, 16–17
  of Olympic Games, 504–507
  of professional sports, 380–389
    "best interests of the game" authority, 383–389
    contract law and, 381–383
    due process, 383, 385, 388
    good faith and fair dealing, duty of, 382–383
    legal limits on, 381–383
    overview, 373, 380–381
    private associations, 381
Graduation Success Rates (GSR), 222
Grange, Harold "Red," 449
Green, Pumpsie, 208
Green Bay Packers
  public ownership of, 379
  revenue sharing, 402
Greene, Linda, 365
"Green Jacket," 314
Grooming rules in interscholastic sports, 41–42
Grundman, Adolph, 208
Gurley, Todd, 469

H

Hagen, Walter, 376
Hair length and interscholastic sports, 42
Hall, Nathan, 250

Hamilton, Hard Rock, 344
Hamilton, Richard, 489
Hamm, Paul, 517–518
Harjo, Susan, 233
Haskins, Clem, 91
Hatchell, Sylvia, 358
Hazing, 357
Head injuries, 61–63, 295–297
"Heads-up Football," 61–62
Health and safety issues
  head injuries, 61–63, 295–297
  institutional liability *See* Institutional liability for injuries
  interscholastic sports, 61–64
  medical malpractice *See* Medical malpractice liability
  professional players *See* Professional athletes
  torts *See* Tort law
Helms, Jesse, 163
Hening, Kiersten, 216
Henry, Kevin, 296
Henry, Travis, 457
High school sports. *See* Interscholastic sports
Hilliard, Ike, 454
Historical background
  broadcasting rights, 326–327
  gender equity, 161–166
  interscholastic sports, 15–16
  NCAA, 65–69
  Olympic Games, 502–503
  professional sports, 373–376
  racial equity, 203–208
  Title IX, 162–166
HIV/AIDS and participation in sports, 302
Hockey, historical background of, 374
Hodges, Craig, 215
Hold harmless agreements, 276
Holtz, Jessica, 469
Homeschooled students and interscholastic sports, 36–37
Horizontal restraint, 102–103, 108, 115
Horton, Ray, 211–212
Hostile environment
  racial equity and, 235–238
  sexual harassment, 191–192
Housing as compensation for coaches, 362
Houston Astros, sign stealing and, 384
Hyatt, Alex, 509–510

I

IAAF (International Association of Athletics Federations). *See* World Athletics
ICAS (International Council of Arbitration and Sport), 515–516
Idaho, Fairness in Women's Sports Act (2020), 194
Illinois High School Association, 62
Image, use of. *See* Name, image, and likeness (NIL) rights
Immunities in tort law, 272–276

charitable immunity, 273
discretionary function, 273–274
ministerial function, 273–274
negligence, 272–275
qualified immunity, 273–275
sovereign immunity, 272–273
Impaired athletes. *See* Disabled athletes
Implied contracts, 126
Implied-in-fact promises, 349
Incentives for coaches, 364–365
Indianapolis 500, 320, 376
Indiscretions, termination of coaches for, 352–353
IndyCar, 376
Informed consent to medical treatment, 287
Infringement
copyrights, 329–332
trademarks, 313–321
likelihood of confusion standard, 315–321
name of team or event, 314–315
noninfringing fair use or parody, 319–320
unauthorized affixation of mark to merchandise, 315–320
Injuries. *See* Tort law
In loco parentis, 155
Institutional liability for injuries, 251–265
colleges, 258–265
foreseeability, 259–260, 262, 264
high schools, 251–258
minors, injuries to, 271
return-to-play policy, 258
special relationship, 262, 263
spectators, injuries to, 265–271
Intellectual property rights, 311–345
ambush marketing, 324–326
broadcasting rights, 326–334
copyright infringement, 329–332
copyright protection, 327–329
governance of intercollegiate sports and, 107–108
historical background, 326–327
misappropriation of real-time game accounts and scores, 333–334
NCAA, 66, 67, 69, 107–108
cybersquatting, 321–322
First Amendment rights and defamation, 334, 336–337, 341–345
Lanham Act, 335
licensing restrictions, 401–404
likenesses or names of athletes, 335
logos, 313–314
names of teams, 314–315
Olympic marks, 322–323
overview, 311–312
privacy rights, 338–339
publicity rights, 339–341
First Amendment limitations, 341–345
nature and scope of, 339–341

state laws, 336–345
trademark infringement and dilution, 313–321
likelihood of confusion standard, 315–321
name of team or event, 314–315
noninfringing fair use or parody, 319–320
unauthorized affixation of mark to merchandise, 315–320
Intentional infliction of emotional distress, 156
Inter-agent conflicts, 463–469
consolidation, 463–464
disparagement, 465
gender and, 467–469
overview, 463
permissible competition, 466–467
race and, 467–469
termination, 464–465
Intercollegiate Athletic Association, 66
Intercollegiate sports. *See also* National Collegiate Athletic Association
administrators
First Amendment rights *See* First Amendment rights
racial equity and, 209
termination as retaliation, 359–360
antitrust law and, 100–122. *See also* Antitrust law
charitable immunity, 273
contract law and, 95–99
drug testing in, 94–95
federal tax-exempt status and, 364
gender equity in *See* Gender equity
governance of *See* National Collegiate Athletic Association
injuries, institutional liability for, 258–265
NIL rights *See* Name, image, and likeness (NIL) rights
publicity rights, 338, 340, 343–345. *See also* Name, image, and likeness (NIL) rights
qualified immunity, 273–275
gross negligence as exception to, 273–274
racial equity. *See also* Racial equity
administrative opportunities, 209
coaching opportunities, 208–210
formal rules of exclusion, 204–205
informal rules of exclusion, 205–207
reintegration, 208
segregation, 203–207
socioeconomic stratification and, 217
sovereign immunity, 272–273
student athletes, penalization for off-the-field behavior, 90
transgender participation in sports, 193–196
waivers for negligence by adult athletes, 282–283
Intermediate scrutiny, 26, 172
International Association of Athletics Federations (IAAF). *See* World Athletics
International Convention Against Doping in Sport, 523–524
International Council of Arbitration and Sport (ICAS), 515–516

International Gymnastics Federation (FIG), 517–518
International Olympic Committee (IOC), 503, 504–507, 508, 512–517, 522, 523
International sports
   athlete exploitation, risk of, 530–531
   Court of Arbitration for Sport See Court of Arbitration for Sport
   developing issues in, 528–531
   Olympic Games See Olympic Games
   overview, 501–502
   representation issues, 469–470
   trans-national player movement, 530–531
   United States leagues and foreign countries, 530–531
International Sports Federations (IFs), 505–506, 508, 513, 515–517
Interscholastic sports, 15–64
   administrative processes, 16–17
   age rules, 31–34
   athletic associations, 258
   charitable immunity, 273
   concussions, 61–63
   co-participant criminal liability, 250
   COVID-19 pandemic, effect on participation, 15
   deference to governing bodies, 340
   drug testing, 43–49, 53–59
      as discipline or sanction, 48–49
      Due Process, 43
      state constitutional issues, 48–49
      as unreasonable search, 48–49
   First Amendment rights
      Establishment Clause, 58–59
      freedom of association, 49–55
      freedom of speech, 49–55
      free exercise of religion, 56–59, 159
      religious liberty, 56–59, 159
   good conduct rules, 38–41
   governance of, 16–17
   grooming rules, 41–42
   hair length and, 42
   head injuries, 61–63
   health and safety issues, 61–64
   high school athletic associations, 4, 6
   historical background, 15–16
   homeschooled students and, 36–37
   injuries, institutional liability for, 251–258
   in loco parentis, 155
   intellectual property, 334
   judicial regulation of, 17–64
      constitutional issues, 42–59
      eligibility issues, 24–42
      overview, 17–18
      state action requirement, 18–24
   "no pass, no play" rules, 35–36
   "outside competition" rules, 30–31
   prayer, 58–59
   qualified immunity, 273–275
      gross negligence as exception to, 273–274
   race
      fan-based animus and, 237–238
      socioeconomic stratification and, 217–218
   recruiting in, 18–24
   regulatory structure, 16–17
   review of game results, 60–61
   sovereign immunity, 272–273
   transfer rules, 26–29
      arbitrary and capricious standard, 26, 29
      equal protection, 27
      state constitutional issues, 29–30
   transgender athlete participation, 193–196
   United States Center for Safe Sport, 191, 511
Invasion of privacy, 156–157
Invitees, liability to, 265–267
IOC. *See* International Olympic Committee
Iowa Girls' High School Athletic Association, 162
Izzo, Tom, 363

J

James, LeBron, 312, 335, 467–468, 492
Janke, Laura, 355
Jim Crow laws, 204–205
"Jock majors," 140
Johnson, Michael Wayne, Jr., 481
Johnson-Klein, Stacy, 200–201
Jones, Patrick Mitchell, 481
Jordan, Michael, 212, 312, 340
Joseph, MaChelle, 357–358
Judicial branch of government, 4
Judicial review, 6
Jurisdiction, 4–6

K

Kaepernick, Colin, 55, 214–215
Keisel, Shane, 237
Keller, Sam, 344
Kent State University, 369
Kentucky Derby, 320
Khosroshahin, Ali, 355
Kleinknecht, Drew, 258–260
Kline, MacKinzie, 304
Klutch Sports Group (agency), 456, 463, 467–468
Knapp, Nicholas, 299–301
Kneeling by professional players during national anthem, 55, 214–216
Knight Commission, 67
Korean Olympic Committee, 517
Kuliga, Kristian, 468

L

Labor Management Relations Act of 1947, 438, 464
Labor relations, 411–447
  antitrust law and, 440–447
    anticompetitive effects, 406–407, 441, 444, 445–447
    nonstatutory labor exemption, 433, 441–444
    procompetitive effects, 445–446
    rule of reason, 444–446
  arbitration in, 434–440
  breach of duty to bargain in good faith, 429–431
  collective bargaining, 418–421
  competitive balance taxes, 419, 420
  contract law and, 411–415
  disciplinary sanctions, 421
  discrimination against striking players, 432
  drug testing, 421–425
  duty of fair representation, 433–434
  free agency and, 419, 431, 435, 441, 442, 445
  impasse, 431
  interference with right to unionize, 426
  "law of the shop," 439
  lockouts, 425
  luxury taxes, 419, 420
  mandatory bargaining subjects, 416, 419, 421, 422, 429, 431–432
  mixed martial arts (MMA) and, 428
  multiemployer bargaining units, 419, 425–426, 427, 429, 431, 441
  negative injunctions, 412–413
  NLRA, 152, 153, 415–418, 422, 425, 432
  Norris–LaGuardia Act, 441
  overview, 411, 415–418
  refusal to recognize union as exclusive bargaining representative, 426–427
  reserve clause, 394, 418–419, 431, 435, 438, 444
  retaliation against union activists, 427–428
  salary caps, 419–420, 442–443
  strikes, 425
    discrimination against striking players, 432
  Taft–Hartley Act, 415
  unfair labor practices *See* Unfair labor practices
  uniform or standard player contracts, 420–421
Laboy, C.J., 480
Ladies Professional Golfers Association (LPGA), 193–194, 304, 444
Lajoie, Napoleon, 411–412
La Liga players subject to racist behavior, 219
Landis, Kenesaw Mountain, 207, 379, 383, 385, 387
Landrum–Griffin Act of 1959, 415
Lanham Trademark Act of 1946
  ambush marketing and, 325
  athletes' rights under, 335
  cybersquatting, 321–322
  mascots and, 233–234
  Olympic marks and, 322–323
  Redskins team name, 233–234
  trademarks and, 314, 316, 319
Lapchick, Richard, 210, 212, 213
Larkin, Stephen, 282
Lasege, Muhammad, 99
Leach, Mike, 356–357
Learning disabilities, 305–306
Leeper, Blake, 307–308
Legislative branch of government, 4
Leonsis, Ted, 236–237
Lewis, Lennox, 413–414
Lexis, 10
Lex sportiva, 516
LGBTQI+ students
  OCR resources for, 194
  Title IX, 188, 194
  transgender participation in sports, 193–196
Liberty interest
  in athletic participation, 142, 145, 146
  in employment, 359–360
Licensees, liability to, 265
Licensing restrictions, antitrust law and, 401–404
Life insurance as compensation for coaches, 362
Likelihood of confusion, trademarks, 315–321
Likenesses of athletes. *See* Name, image, and likeness (NIL) rights
Limited duty rule, 266, 267, 269–271
Limon, Tony, 250
Little League, 15–16, 17, 41
Local and regulatory decision-making bodies, 4
Locker room facilities
  access to, 72–73
  sex-segregated, 196
Lockouts, 425
Logos, 313–314
Long, Terry, 422
Los Angeles Clippers, 389
Loss-in-value insurance, student-athletes, 152
Louisiana, segregation in, 204–205
LPGA (Ladies Professional Golfers Association), 193–194, 304, 444
Luch, Josh, 489
Luxury taxes, 419, 420
Lynn, Nicole, 468

M

Madden NFL videogames, 344
Magid, Martin, 489
Mahomes, Patrick, 216
Major League Baseball (MLB)
  antitrust law and, 391–394, 401, 402–403, 441, 443

MLB *(continued)*
  arbitration in, 435–438
  collective bargaining agreements, 420–
  drug testing in, 423
  fantasy baseball games, 342–343
  foreign countries, expansion to, 530, 531
  governance of, 388–389
  historical background, 375
  integration of, 208
  intellectual property rights, 316, 342–343
  labor relations and, 417–418
  Latinos in, 218
  limited duty rule and, 270–271
  Minor League Baseball system, 394, 417–418
  segregation in, 207
Major League Baseball Player Association (MLBPA), 423, 488, 490–491
Major League Baseball Properties, 402–403
Major League Rugby, 396
Major League Soccer (MLS)
  antitrust law and, 396
  foreign countries and, 530
  historical background, 376
Malpractice liability, 285–289
  athletic trainers, 288, 295
  contributory negligence, 288–289
  team physicians, 285–288, 294–295
Manfred, Rob, 384, 420
Manslaughter, liability for injuries to athletes, 245, 250
March Madness, 321
Martin, Casey, 302–304
Mascots, 231–235, 266–267
Mastercard, 325
Masters, Kelli, 468
Masters Tournament, 314, 320, 343
Mayo, O.J., 471, 489
McCann, Michael, 270
McCarthy, Thomas, 313
McCown, John, 266
McCoy, Gerald, 468
McCullum, Sam, 427–428
McMillen, Tom, 107
McNally, Dave, 435, 438
McRae, Nadirah, 214
McSorley, Marty, 249–250
Media
  First Amendment and, 155–157
  professional sports and, 380
  social media, 49–55
  television network contracts, 311–312
Medical malpractice liability, 285–289
  athletic trainers, 288, 295
  contributory negligence, 288–289
  team physicians, 285–288, 294–295

, Dave, 213
Mehri, Cyrus, 210–211
Meredith, Rudy, 355
Messersmith, Andy, 435, 438
Messi, Lionel, 335
Messier, Mark, 335
Mexico, baseball players from, 531
Miale, Kim, 468–469
Michigan High School Athletic Association (MHSAA), 37, 305–306
Milutinovich, Diane, 201
Minimum wage for student-athletes, 151–152
Minor League Baseball (MiLB) system, 394, 417–418
Mississippi, segregation in, 205
Missouri Athletic Conference, 205–206
Missouri State High School Activities Association, 30
Mitchell, George, 85
Mixed martial arts (MMA)
  historical background, 376
  labor relations and, 428
MLB. *See* Major League Baseball
MLBPA (Major League Baseball Player Association), 423, 488, 490–491
MLS (Major League Soccer)
  antitrust law and, 396
  foreign countries and, 530
  historical background, 376
Monopolization, 100, 405–409
Montana, Joe, 341–342
Montgomery, Tim, 525
Morals clauses, 370
Motions, 7
MOU (memorandum of understanding), coaches and, 364
Mulugheta, David, 467
MVP Sports Group (agency), 463

N
Naismith, James, 374
Name, image, and likeness (NIL) rights
  intercollegiate sports, 338
    agent contracts, 486
    boosters, 77–84
    litigation, 113–114, 341
    NCAA and, 69
    rules infractions process, 77–84
  publicity rights, 338, 340, 343–345
Names of athletes, 335
Names of teams, 314–315
NASL (North American Soccer League), 426–427
National anthem protests, 55, 214–216
National Association of Intercollegiate Athletics (NAIA), 65–66
National Association of Stock Car Auto Racing (NASCAR)
  antitrust law and, 396

governance of, 381–382
historical background, 376
intellectual property rights, 320
sponsorship agreements, 370
National Basketball Association (NBA)
   antitrust law and, 401, 441, 445
   collective bargaining agreements, 419–420
   drug testing in, 423
   foreign countries, expansion to, 530
   free speech in, 215
   historical background, 375
   integration of, 208
   intellectual property rights, 315, 321, 332, 333
   labor relations and, 413, 417
   non-U.S. citizens eligibility rules, 219–220
National Basketball Players Association (NBPA), 491–492
National Christian College Athletic Association (NCCAA), 66
National Collegiate Athletic Association (NCAA), 65–122
   academic misconduct, 87–89
   academic reform initiatives, 138–142
      Academic Progress Rate, 139, 140–141, 365
      initial eligibility requirements, 139–140, 220–224
      NCAA rules reform, 139–140
      satisfactory progress, 139
   admission scandal, 354–355
   antitrust law and, 100–122. *See also* Antitrust law
   broadcasting rights and, 66, 67, 69, 107–108
   Committee on Academics, 80
   Committee on Competitive Safeguards and Medical Aspects of Sports, 94–95
   Committee on Infractions, 68, 70–71, 83, 88–90
   concussions and, 295, 296
   Constitutional Compliance Committee, 67
   contracts and, 95–99, 130–133
   divisions of, 65
   doping violations and, 524
   gender equity, 165
   governance structure, 68–69
   Graduation Success Rates (GSR), 222
   historical background, 65–69
   individual responsibility for rules violations and sanctions, 89–91
   Infractions Appeals Committee, 68, 70, 77
   intellectual property rights, 311–312, 316, 320, 341, 344
   limits on regulatory authority, 92–122
      antitrust law, 100–122
      civil rights laws, 92–94
      contract and private association laws, 95–99
      drug testing and privacy, 94–95
   Management Council, 70–71
   Manual, 71
   March Madness, 321
   mascots in, 232

   negligence, 262–264
   NIL rights *See* Name, image, and likeness (NIL) rights
   orders to show cause, 90, 91
   overview, 65
   Proposition 16, 220–224
   REC Rule, 108–109
   regulatory authority and processes, 69–91
   representation, regulations regarding, 470–471, 496–499
   Review Committee, 70
   rules infractions process, 70–91
      amateurism, 72–77
      boosters, 77–84
      coaches and, 89–91
      extra benefits, 72–77
      historical background, 70–71
      institutional violations, 71–91
      lack of institutional control, 72–77
      NIL rights, 77–84
      student athletes, penalization for off-the-field behavior, 90
   "Sanity Code," 66–67
   scholarships, regulations regarding, 130–133
   Special Committee to Review the National Collegiate Athletic Association Enforcement and Infractions Process, 70
   state action requirement and, 18
   tort liability, 262–264
   transgender student-athlete participation policy, 195
   unethical behavior, 89–91
National Conference of Commissioners on Uniform State Laws, 474
National Federation of State High School Associations, 15, 43
National Football League (NFL)
   activism of players, 214–216
   antitrust law and, 395–396, 399–400, 402, 403, 404, 407–409, 441, 442–443
   Black Lives Matter statement of, 216
   collective bargaining agreements, 420
   concussions and, 295–296
   drug testing in, 423
   fantasy football, 343
   governance of, 382, 387–388
   historical background, 375
   integration of, 208
   intellectual property rights, 233–234, 311, 314–315, 333
   labor relations and, 412–413, 417
   mascots in, 233–234
   "race-norming" in cognitive ability testing, 296
   "race-norming" in cognitive ability testing and awards, 296
   Rooney Rule, 209, 211–212
   Sunday Ticket, 404
   unfair labor practices, 432
   USA Football, 16, 61–62

National Football League Players Association (NFLPA)
  agent regulations, 467, 488, 489–490
  disclosure of league financial information, 430–431
  discrimination against striking players, 432
  judicial review of arbitration awards, 438–440
  race and freedom of expression, 216
  Regulations and Code of Conduct Governing Registered Player Financial Advisors, 457
  regulations governing contract advisers, 492–496
  retaliation against union activists, 428
  standard representation agreement, 450, 465
  women as agents, 469
National Governing Boards (NGB), 505–506, 508, 509, 511, 513, 527
National Hockey League (NHL)
  antitrust law, 403, 408, 441, 444
  arbitration in, 434–435
  collective bargaining agreements, 420
  concussions, 296
  drug testing in, 423
  foreign countries, expansion to, 530
  historical background, 375
  intellectual property rights, 316
  labor relations, 417
  unfair labor practices, 432
National Junior College Athletic Association (NJCAA), 66
National Labor Relations Act of 1935 (NLRA), 152, 153, 415–418, 422, 425, 432, 433
National Labor Relations Board (NLRB), 152–154, 415–418, 426, 432
National Letter of Intent, 128–130
National Olympic Committees (NOC), 504–408
National Women's Soccer League (NWSL), 376
Native Americans
  mascots and, 231–235
  women in college sports, 213
NBA. See National Basketball Association
NBPA (National Basketball Players Association), 491–492
NCAA. See National Collegiate Athletic Association
NCCAA (National Christian College Athletic Association), 66
Negative injunctions, 412–413
Negligence
  aggravation of existing injury, 257–258
  athlete overuse and training, 256–257
  case law, 10–14
  co-participant liability, 243
  gross negligence as exception to qualified immunity, 273–274
  high school athletic associations, 258
  immunities, 272–275
  inherent risks, 255–256
  limited duty rule and, 266, 267, 269–271
  medical malpractice liability, 288–289

NCAA and, 262–264
parental liability waivers and, 281–282
tort law, 252
Negro Leagues, 207
Neuheisel, Rick, 352
Newcombe, Don, 339
New York City Triathlon, 320–321
New York Convention on the Enforcement of Foreign Arbitration Awards, 513
New York Giants, 211
New York Human Rights Law, 297
New York Lawyers for the Public Interest, 217
New York State Human Rights Law, 193
New York Yankees, 311
Neymar, 219
NFL. See National Football League
NFLPA. See National Football League Players Association
NFL Properties, 402, 403
NHL. See National Hockey League
Nike, 312, 324–325
NIL rights. See Name, image, and likeness (NIL) rights
NJCAA (National Junior College Athletic Association), 66
NLRA. See National Labor Relations Act of 1935
NLRB. See National Labor Relations Board
Nochimson, Joe, 489
Noel, Nerlens, 456
"No pass, no play" rules in interscholastic sports, 35–36
Norris–LaGuardia Act of 1932, 441
North American Soccer League (NASL), 426–427
Northwestern University hazing and toxic culture, 357
Notre Dame University mascot, 234–235

O

O'Brien, Jim, 353
OCOG (Organizing Committees for the Olympic Games), 506
Off campus speech, 49–55
Office of Civil Rights (OCR), Title IX administration, 161, 164–165, 194
O'Hara, James, 163
Ohio State University, 87, 353
Oklahoma Secondary School Activities Association, 41, 60
Olympic Games, 502–514
  ambush marketing, 324–325
  Ancient Olympics, 502–503
  athlete eligibility dispute resolution, 508, 509–511, 513
  drug testing, 94
  governance of, 504–507
  historical background, 502–503
  International Olympic Committee (IOC), 503, 504–507, 508, 512–517, 522, 523
  International Sports Federations (IFs), 505–506, 508, 513, 515–517
  National Governing Boards (NGB), 505–506, 508, 509, 511, 513, 527

national law, limitations on, 512–514
National Olympic Committees (NOC), 504–508
Olympic Charter, 504–507, 512, 513, 516
organization of, 504–507
Organizing Committees for the Olympic Games (OCOG), 506
overview, 502
Safe Sport, United States Center for, 191, 511
structure of, 504–507
trademarks, 322–323
U.S. boycott of 1980 Moscow Games, 507–508
U.S. regulation of Olympic sports, 507–511
USOPC *See* United States Olympic and Paralympic Committee
Olympic Museum, 504
One-in-three rule, 489–490
Oregon, coach hiring procedures in, 209
Organizing Committees for the Olympic Games (OCOG), 506
Ortiz, David, 423
"Outside competition" rules in interscholastic sports, 30–31

P

PAC-12 conference, 69
Paige, Rod, 165
Panama, baseball players from, 531
Pan American Games, 507.09
Paralympics, 311, 322, 501, 503, 508–511, 527
Parody, 319–320, 343
Patera, Jack, 427–428
Paterno, Joe, 85
Paul, Rich, 456, 467–468, 492
Pennsylvania
    Institution of Higher Education Monetary Penalty Endowment Act, 86
    Safety in Youth Sports Act, 63
Pennsylvania State University, 84–87
Performance-enhancing drugs, 421–425
Per se rule in antitrust law, 107
Person, Chuck, 354
Peters, Ron, 388–389
Petrino, Bobby, 352
PGA. *See* Professional Golfers' Association
Physicians, medical malpractice liability, 285–288
Piggie, Myron, 472–473
Pistorius, Oscar, 307
Pitino, Rick, 91, 354–355
Pittsburgh Athletic Company, 326–327
Players associations, 487–499. *See also specific association*
    athlete-agent relationship, regulating, 488–499
    authority to regulate, 487–488
    decertification, 431, 443, 488–489
    fees and compensation, 489
    nonstatutory labor exemption, 433, 441–444
    sanctions, 488–489
    suspensions, 488–489
"Play Smart. Play Hard" initiative, 62
Pleadings, 7
Political activism by professional players, 214–216
Pop Warner, 16, 17, 61
Poston, Carl, 489
Prado, Gabriela, 510
Prayer in interscholastic sports, 58–59
Precedent, 8–9
Premises liability, 265
Price, Mike, 352
Principle of proportionality, 522–523
Privacy rights
    drug testing and, 421–425
    intellectual property rights, 338–339
    invasion of privacy, 156–157
Private associations, 381
Private law, 3
Private organizations, 6
Procedural due process, 38, 39–40, 42–43, 138, 142, 146, 147
Procompetitive effects of antitrust law, 107–109, 122
Professional athletes
    collective bargaining, 418–421
    compensation for injuries, 289–297
        compensable event, 291
        intentional torts, 294
        off-season injuries, 293
        workers' compensation, 290–295
    disciplinary sanctions, 421
    drug testing, 421–425
    labor relations *See* Labor relations
    representation *See* Representation
    unfair labor practices *See* Unfair labor practices
    uniform or standard player contracts, 420–421
Professional Golfers' Association (PGA), 302–304, 305, 333–334, 376
Professional sports, 373–409
    administrators, racial equity and, 210, 212
    antitrust law and, 389–409. *See also* Antitrust law
    athletes *See* Professional athletes
    coaches, racial equity and, 210–213
    competitive balance taxes, 419, 420
    evolution into business and profession, 374–376
    governance of, 380–389
        "best interests of the game" authority, 383–389
        contract law and, 381–383
        due process, 383, 385, 388
        good faith and fair dealing, duty of, 382–383
        legal limits on, 381–383
        overview, 373, 380–381
        private associations, 381
    historical background, 373–376
    labor relations *See* Labor relations

578   Index

Professional sports *(continued)*
  luxury taxes, 419, 420
  media and, 380
  parties involved in, 378–380
    agents, 380
    commissioners, 379
    leagues, 378
    other integral industries, 380
    players, 379
    players associations, 380
    teams or clubs, 378–379
  racial equity
    administrative opportunities, 210, 212
    coaching opportunities, 210–213
    reintegration, 208
    segregation, 207
    sham interview problem, 210, 211–212
  representation *See* Representation
  reserve clause, 394, 418–419, 431, 435, 438, 444
  salary caps, 419–420, 442–443
  unfair labor practices *See* Unfair labor practices
  unique features of, 376–378
Promissory estoppel, 125
Property interest, 142–147
  in athletic participation, 144–146
  contractual rationale, 143
  economic rationale, 143
  educational rationale, 143
  in employment, 349–351
  general principles, 142–143
  rules violations and, 146–147
  scholarship rationale, 143
Proposition 16, 220–224
ProServ (agency), 466
Prothro, Tyrone, 481
Publicity rights, 338–341
  First Amendment limitations, 341–345
  nature and scope of, 339–341
Public law, 3
Public School Athletics League (New York City), 217
Pyle, Charles, 449

Q

Qualified immunity in tort law, 273–275
Quarterbacks, racial equity and, 213
"Quick look" rule of reason, 108–109, 117, 122

R

Racial equity, 203–238
  activism of professional sport players, 214–216
  case law, 220–238
  disparate impact, 221, 222, 224, 228–230
  disparate treatment, 224, 226–227
  employment discrimination, 224–231

  equal protection, 26
  fan-based animus, 219, 235–238
  First Amendment rights and, 214–216
  freedom of expression, 214–216
  gender equity and, 172, 213–214
  globalization and, 218–220
  historical background, 203–208
  hostile environment and, 235–238
  initial eligibility rules, 220–224
  inter-agent conflicts and, 467–469
  in intercollegiate sports
    administrative opportunities, 209
    coaching opportunities, 208–210
    formal rules of exclusion, 204–205
    informal rules of exclusion, 205–207
    reintegration, 208
    segregation, 203–207
  Jim Crow laws, 204–205
  mascots and, 231–235
  modern sports, 208–220
  NCAA eligibility rules and, 220–224
  non-U.S. citizens eligibility rules, 219–220
  overview, 203
  players subject to racist behavior, 218–219
  political activism and, 214–216
  in professional sports
    administrative opportunities, 210, 212
    coaching opportunities, 210–213
    reintegration, 208
    segregation, 207
    sham interview problem, 210, 211–212
  Proposition 16 and, 220–224
  quarterbacks, 213
  "race-norming" in cognitive ability testing and awards, 296
  retaliation and, 215
  socioeconomic stratification and, 216–218
  strict scrutiny, 172
  suspect class, 26
Racketeer Influenced and Corrupt Organizations Act of 1970 (RICO), 472
Raducan, Andreea, 522, 523
Rahman, Hasim, 413–414
Ramirez, Manny, 423
Rape, 191–192
Rapinoe, Megan, 216
Raskin, Richard, 193
Real Madrid, 219
Reasonable accommodations for disabled athletes, 304–305
Reckless and intentional conduct, 243, 252, 256, 262, 263
Recruiting
  boosters and rules infractions, 77–84
  bribery, 69, 91, 354–355
  individual responsibility and rules infractions, 89–91

interscholastic sports, 18–24
National Letter of Intent, 128–130
NCAA allowing agents to recruit student-athletes, 474–477
"Sanity Code" and, 66–67
transfer rules in interscholastic sports, 25–30, 131–132
Rehabilitation Act of 1973
Americans with Disabilities Act compared, 301–302
disabled athletes, 297–301
limits on NCAA regulatory authority, 92
Releases, 276–284
Religious liberty
Establishment Clause, 58–59
free exercise, 56–58
intercollegiate sports, 158–159
interscholastic sports, 56–59, 159
prayer, 58–59
Relocation of franchises, 399–401
Remedies, law and equity, 5
Representation, 449–500
athlete-agent relationship, 450–462
conflicts of interest, 458–462
duties, 450–451
ethical issues, 499–500
fiduciary relationship, 453
financial improprieties, 453–458
NIL agent contracts, 486
regulation of, 488–499
standard of care, 451–453
women as agents, 468–469
duty of fair representation, 433–434
federal regulation of, 471–474
RICO Act, 471
Sports Agent Responsibility Trust Act, 471–472
fiduciary relationship, 450–451, 453
importance of agents in professional sports, 380
inter-agent conflicts, 463–469
"competitor's privilege," 466–467
consolidation, 463–464
disparagement, 465
gender and, 467–469
overview, 463
race and, 467–469
termination, 464–465
international perspective, 469–470
NCAA regulations, 470–471, 496–499
nondisclosure, 459
one-in-three rule, 489–490
overview, 449
players associations, regulation by, 487–499
authority to regulate, 487–488
decertification, 488–489
fees and compensation, 489
NFLPA regulations, 489–490
sanctions, 488–489

suspensions, 488–489
principal-agent relationship, 451
regulation of, 470–471
state regulation, 474–487
Revised Uniform Athlete Agents Act, 474–480
Uniform Athlete Agents Act, 474–487
Uniform Athlete Agents Act, 471–472
Reserve clause, 394, 418–419, 431, 435, 438, 444
Restitution rule, 99
Restraint of trade, 108, 396–404
Retaliation
gender equity, 200–202
for racial equity protests, 214–216
termination of employment as, 359–360
Title IX, 200–202
against union activists, 427–428
Return-to-play policy, 258, 301
Revenue sharing, 402
Reverse discrimination, 185–189
Revised Uniform Athlete Agents Act (RUAAA), 474–480
Reynolds, Butch, 512
Rice, Mike, 357
Richards, Renee, 193
Richardson, Emanuel "Book," 354
Richardson, Nolan, 215, 360
"Rich Paul Rule," 492
RICO (Racketeer Influenced and Corrupt Organizations) Act of 1970, 472
Risk management. *See* Tort law
Rival leagues, antitrust law and, 405–409
Robeson, Paul, 206
Robinson, Jackie, 208
Roc Nation (agency), 468–469
Rodgers, Franklin C. "Pepper," 360–362
Rodriguez, Alex, 423
Rodriguez, Ivan, 466
Rogge, Jacques, 517–518
Ronaldo, Cristiano, 312
Rooney Rule, 209, 211–212
Roosevelt, Theodore, 66
Rose, Pete, 388–389
Rosenbloom, Carroll, 399
Rosenhaus Sports Representation (agency), 463
Rozelle, Pete, 399, 402
"Rozelle Rule," 446–447
RUAAA (Revised Uniform Athlete Agents Act), 474–480
Rule of reason
intercollegiate sports and, 107–110
labor relations and, 444–446
professional sports and, 395, 397, 398, 400, 403
"quick look" rule of reason, 108–109, 117, 122
Rules infractions process (NCAA), 70–91
amateurism, 72–77
boosters and recruiting, 77–84

NCAA *(continued)*
   coaches and, 89–91, 353
   extra benefits, 72–77
   historical background, 70–71
   institutions and, 71–91
   lack of institutional control, 72–77
   name, image, and likeness (NIL) rights, 77–84
Russell, Bill, 208, 210
Russell Rule, 209–210
Ryan, Michael, 219

S

Saban, Nick, 363
SafeSport Code, 191, 511
Safety. *See* Health and safety issues; Tort law
Salary caps, 419–420, 442–443
Salcedo, Jorge, 355
Samuel, Assante, 455
Sanctions
   doping violations, 522–523, 525
   drug testing in intercollegiate sports, 48–49
   players associations, regulation of representation by, 488–489
   professional athletes, 421
   student-athletes, 38–41
"Sanity Code," 66–67
Sarkisian, Steve, 352–353
Savage, Raymond L., Jr., 481
Save Women's Sports Bill (W.Va. 2021), 194
Schiano, Greg, 364
Scholarships
   limits on, 110–115
   NCAA regulations, 130–133
School districts, 4
Search and seizure, drug testing in interscholastic sports, 43, 48–49
Selig, Bud, 393–394
"Separate but equal" teams, 171
Separation of powers, 4
Service of legal documents, 7
Sex equity. *See* Gender equity
Sex-segregated bathrooms, 196
Sexual assault, 84–87, 191–192, 511
Sexual harassment, 189–193
   civil rights and, 193
   coach/athlete, 190–191
   defenses, 190
   defined, 189
   hostile environment, 191–192
   peers, 191–193
   Title IX, 189–193
Sharapova, Maria, 525–526
Sharpe, Sterling, 454
Shaw, Brian, 413, 434

Sherman Act of 1890. *See also* Antitrust law
   baseball antitrust exemption and, 391–394
   intercollegiate sports and, 100, 106–109, 113, 118–119
   labor law and, 440–447
   NCAA and, 100, 106–109, 113, 118–119
   overview, 373, 389–390
   professional sports and, 395–409
      acquisition, ownership and sale of franchises, 397–398
      application of §2, 405–409
      concerted action requirement, 395–396
      intellectual property rights, 401–404
      relocation of franchises, 399–401
      rival leagues, 405–409
      unreasonable restraint of trade, 396–404
Shropshire, Kenneth, 2
Silver, Adam, 389
Simmons, Ben, 492
Singer, Rick, 355
Single economic entity defense, 395–396
Smith, Leslie, 428
Snapchat posts with vulgar language and gestures, 49–55
Snyder, Dan, 234
Social media, 49–55
Sosa, Sammy, 423
Southeastern Conference, 128, 209
Sovereign immunity in tort law, 272–273
SPARTA (Sports Agent Responsibility Trust Act of 2004), 471–472
Speakers of Sport (agency), 466
Specialized courts, 6
Specific performance, 5
Spectators, injuries to, 265–271
Sponsorship agreements with coaches, 370
Sport and Development Organization, 25
Sports Agent Responsibility Trust Act of 2004 (SPARTA), 471–472
Sports law
   nonexistence of (traditional view), 1
   potential development of (moderate view), 1–2
   as separate field of law, 2–3
Sports Medicine Licensure Clarity Act of 2018, 288
Sprewell, Latrell, 434
Sprint Communications, 325
Stacking, 213
Standard player contracts, 420–421
Stanley, Ronnie, 469
State action requirement
   due process and, 19, 22
   entwinement, 20–21, 22
   equal protection and, 18
   First Amendment rights and, 18
   interscholastic sports, recruiting in, 18–24
   United States Olympic and Paralympic Committee (USOPC), 508

State actors, 6
State courts, 4, 5–6
State governments, 4
Statement of Financial Assistance, 127, 128
Steinberg, Leigh, 463–464
Sterling, Donald, 389
Strict liability, doping violations, 521–522
Strict scrutiny, 172
Strikes
  discrimination against striking players, 432
  labor disputes and, 425
Student-athletes. See Athlete-university relationship
Study of law, 8–10
Substantive due process, 40, 43, 138, 142
Sunday Ticket, 404
Supreme Court, 5
Suspect class, 26
Swinney, Dabo, 363
Switzerland
  awards from, U.S. enforcement of, 517
  law of, 504, 512, 516

T

Taft–Hartley Act of 1947, 415
Tagliabue, Paul, 387
Taplin, Charles, 480
Tapping-up, 469–470
Tarkanian, Jerry, 70
Tax courts, 6
Tax-exempt status federal, intercollegiate sports and, 364
Taylor, Fred, 454
Team physicians, medical malpractice liability, 285–288, 294–295
Team USA Ombuds, 509
Ted Stevens Olympic and Amateur Sports Act of 1998 (ASA), 31, 322, 323, 502, 505, 507–510
Television network contracts, 311–312
Tennessee Secondary School Athletic Association, 18–24
Tennessee Titans, 211
Tennis, historical background of, 372
Termination
  of agents, 464–465
  of coaches See Coaches
Testosterone levels and transgender student-athletes, 195
Texas, segregation in, 204
Three-part test in Title IX, 163–164, 165–166, 179, 180
Tibbs, Casey, 510
Time Warner Cable (network), 311
"Tim Tebow" laws, 37
Title VII (Civil Rights Act of 1964)
  gender equity, 198
  racial equity, 224
Title IX. See also Gender equity
  generally, 161

  complaints under, 163, 164–165
  deference to schools, 185
  effective accommodation requirement, 173–182
  employment discrimination
    compensation, 196–200
    retaliation, 200–202
  enforcement of, 164–166
  equal benefits and treatment requirement, 182–185
  gender-based exclusion from sports, 171–172
  historical background, 162–166
  investigations under, 164, 165
  limits on NCAA regulatory authority, 92–94
  litigation under, 166
  policy interpretation, 163–164
  regulations under, 162–164
  reverse discrimination, 185–189
  sexual harassment, 189–193
  three-part test, 163–164, 165–166, 179, 180
  transgender participation in sports and, 193–196
  women of color and, 213–214
Tort law, 239–284
  aggravation of existing injury, 257–258
  assumption of risk, 252, 255–256, 266, 289
  athlete overuse and training, 256–257
  co-participant liability for injuries to athletes
    amateur versus professional sports, 243
    consent as defense, 250–251
    criminal liability, 244–251
    intentional conduct standard, 243
    reckless conduct standard, 243
    tort liability, 240–244
  covenants not to sue, 276
  duty to provide medical care, 257, 262–263
  exculpatory clauses, 276
  hold harmless agreements, 276
  immunities, 272–276
    charitable immunity, 273
    discretionary function, 273–274
    ministerial function, 273–274
    qualified immunity, 273–275
      gross negligence as exception to, 273–274
  inherent risks, 255–256
  injuries to athletes, liability for, 240–251
  institutional liability for injuries, 251–265
    colleges, 258–265
    foreseeability, 259–260, 262, 264
    high schools, 251–258
    minors, injuries to, 271
    special relationship, 258–260, 262, 263
    spectators, injuries to, 265–271
  invitees, liability to, 265–267
  licensees, liability to, 265
  limited duty rule, 266, 267, 269–271
  medical malpractice liability, 285–289

Tort law *(continued)*
    athletic trainers, 288, 295
    contributory negligence, 288–289
    team physicians, 285–288, 294–295
  NCAA and, 262–264
  negligence, 252. *See also* Negligence
  opponents' health and safety, 263
  overview, 239–240
  premises liability, 265
  professional athletes, compensation for injuries, 289–297
    compensable event, 291
    intentional torts, 294
    off-season injuries, 293
    workers' compensation, 289–297
  reckless and intentional conduct, 243, 248, 252, 256, 262, 263
  releases, 276–284
  safety rules, 263–264
  trespassers, liability to, 265
  waivers of liability, 276–284
    by adult intercollegiate athletes, 282–283
    grounds for invalidating, 282
    parental liability waivers, 281–283
    pre-injury waivers of liability, 283
Tower, John, 163
Towns, Karl-Anthony, 469
Trademark Dilution Revision Act of 2006, 320–321
Trademarks
  cybersquatting, 321–322
  dilution, 320–321
  infringement, 313–320
    counterfeiting, 319
    inherently distinctive mark, 313
    likelihood of confusion, 315–320
    name of team or event, 315–315
    noninfringing fair use or parody, 319–320
    secondary meaning, 313, 335
    unauthorized affixation of mark to merchandise, 315–320
  Lanham Act *See* Lanham Trademark Act of 1946
  logos, 313–314
Trademark Trial and Appeal Board (TTAB), 233
Trainers, medical malpractice liability, 288, 295
Transfer rules in interscholastic sports, 25–30
  arbitrary and capricious standard, 26, 29
  equal protection, 27
  state constitutional issues, 29–30
Transfers in intercollegiate sports, 131–132
Transgender Law and Policy Institute, 194
Transgender participation in sports, 193–196
Trans-national player movement, 530–531
Trespassers, liability to, 265
Trials, 7
Tucker, Mel, 352–353

U
Ultimate Fighting Championship (UFC), 376, 428
Unfair labor practices, 425–440
  breach of duty to bargain in good faith, 429–431
  discrimination against striking players, 432
  interference with right to unionize, 426
  overview, 425–426
  refusal to recognize union as exclusive bargaining representative, 426–427
  retaliation against union activists, 427–428
Uniform Athlete Agents Act (UAAA), 471–472, 474–487
Uniform Law Commission (ULC), 474
Uniform player contracts, 420–421
Union of European Football Associations (UEFA), 218–219, 501, 528–529
Unions. *See also* Labor relations; Players associations
  esports athletes, 418
  exclusive bargaining representative, refusal to recognize, 426–427
  interference with right to unionize, 426
  retaliation against union activists, 427–428
  student-athletes, unionization of, 152–154
United Nations Convention on the Recognition and Enforcement of Foreign Arbitral Awards (New York Convention), 513, 517
United States Anti-Doping Agency (USADA), 423, 526–527
United States Center for Safe Sport, 191, 511
United States Collegiate Athletic Association (USCAA), 66
United States Football League (USFL), 408–409
United States Judo (USJ), 509–510
United States Local Organizing Committee, 325
United States Olympic and Paralympic Committee (USOPC)
  arbitration, 508, 509–511
  athlete eligibility dispute resolution, 508, 509–511, 513
  authority of, 507–511
  intellectual property rights, 311
  Olympic marks, 322–323
  overview, 504
United Talent Agency, 468
University of Georgia, 90, 91
University of Kansas, 205
University of Miami (Florida), 77–84
University of North Carolina, 87–89, 137, 471, 481
University of Southern California, 72–77, 87
University of Tennessee, 89–90, 364
University sports. *See* Intercollegiate sports
  relationship with student-athletes *See* Athlete-university relationship
Unreasonable restraint of trade, 102–103, 107, 108, 396–404
Upper Deck trading cards, 312
U.S. Open, 376
U.S. Soccer Federation (USSF), 216

Index

U.S. Women's National Soccer Team, 216
USA Football, 16, 61
US Lacrosse, 231–232
USOPC. *See* United States Olympic and Paralympic Committee
Utah Jazz, 237

V

Vandemoer, John, 355
Vavic, Jovan, 355
Venezuela, baseball players from, 531
Venue agreements with coaches, 370–371
Vincent, Fay, 388
Vincent, Troy, 212
Vinicius "Vini" Jr., 219
Viva, Lindy, 201
Volunteer Protection Act of 1997, 63

W

WADA. *See* World Anti-Doping Agency
Wagner Act of 1935. *See* National Labor Relations Act of 1935
Waivers of tort liability, 276–284
Waldrep, Kent, 149–150
Walker, Antoine, 456
Walters, Norby, 472
Ward, Joel, 236–237
Warren, Samuel, 337
Washington (state), Zackery Lystedt Law (2009), 295
Washington, Kenny, 208
Washington Redskins, 233–234
Wasserman (agency), 463
Watson, Terry, 481
Westbrook, Russell, 237
West Coast Conference (WCC) and Russell Rule, 209–210
Westlaw, 10
West Virginia
  Save Women's Sports Bill (2021), 194
  Secondary School Activities Commission, 36–37
WHA. *See* World Hockey Association
White, Kelli, 525

White House Conference, 66
Wichard, Gary, 471, 489
Wilks, Steve, 211–212
Williams, Monte, 282
Williams, Phoebe, 235, 236
Williams, Reginald, 454
Williams, Serena, 312, 335
Williams, Verna, 213
Williamson, Zion, 486
Wisconsin Interscholastic Athletic Association, 15, 334
WME Sports (agency), 463
Women and sports. *See* Gender equity
Women's National Basketball Association (WNBA), 219–220, 313, 375, 405, 423
Women's Tennis Association, 525
Woods, Tiger, 334, 343
Workers' compensation
  contract of hire, 149–150
  control, 149–152
  general principles, 147–148
  professional athletes and, 290–295
  student-athletes and, 147–152
  tests for, 148
World Anti-Doping Agency (WADA), 504, 513, 517, 523–527
World Anti-Doping Code (WADC), 94, 505, 516, 523–527
World Athletics, 307–308, 506, 512, 527
World Cup Soccer Tournament, 325, 376
World Hockey Association (WHA), 382–383, 408, 444
Wright, Kirk, 457

Y

Yang Tae-Young, 517–518
YES Network, 311
YMCA, 15
Youth athletics. *See* Interscholastic sports

Z

Zacchini, Hugo, 341